The Concise Columbia
Dictionary of Quotations

THE CONCISE COLUMBIA
DICTIONARY OF QUOTATIONS

Robert Andrews

Columbia University Press   New York

To my father: A Book

Columbia University Press
New York

Copyright © 1987, 1989 Robert Andrews
All rights reserved

Library of Congress Cataloging-in-Publication Data

Andrews, Robert, 1957–
    The concise Columbia dictionary of quotations / Robert Andrews.
      p.   cm.
    Includes indexes.
    ISBN 0-231-06990-1 (alk. paper)
    1. Quotations, English. 2. Quotations. I. Title.
PN6081.A653 1987   89-593
082—dc19   CIP

c 10 9 8 7 6 5 4 3 2

Casebound editions of Columbia University Press books are Smyth-sewn
and are printed on permanent and durable acid-free paper

Printed in the United States of America

Contents

Preface and acknowledgements

Here, then, is a new and carefully selected compilation of remarks and witticisms, judgements and platitudes, 'the wisdom of the wise and the experience of the ages' as Disraeli would have it . . . and rather more besides. From Buddha to Begin, a motley collection of saints, sinners, sages and fools are gathered together in sometimes uneasy proximity, to praise or advise or criticise or otherwise comment upon the widest possible range of subjects. All the great shibboleths are touched upon, the solemn institutions of love, marriage, death and religion, as well as a host of more particular issues that have sufficiently moved the famous and notorious to make more or less jaundiced observations. Often, the loftier the subjects, the less ceremoniously they are treated, and the more hallowed the theme, the more wickedly the whip of the cynics and the iconoclasts comes down upon it, though I hope too that the reader will find a variety of moods and sentiments to fit his or her own humour. The more hackneyed or clichéd sayings have been on the whole avoided, and preference given to lesser-known and perhaps more provocative statements, though all the stalwarts of our own literary tradition are well-represented. But there are surprises in store: brilliant jewels of pithy wit, asides of originality and insight, as well as phrases chosen simply for the elegance and evocativeness of their expression, some to tease and titillate and some to grate and pique. Topicality has not been avoided, and fashions and tastes nervously collide. I have no doubt that everyone will find something here to offend them, for no allowances have been made for personal sensibility. Alongside the obvious requirement of 'quotability', the main criteria for the inclusion of quotations in these pages have been aptness and variety, for efforts have been made to present as wide and contradictory a range of quotations and sources as possible (as a glance at the two indexes will confirm), encompassing extremes of prejudice and presumption and a choice of more mildly disagreeable views in between. Needless to say the compiler takes no responsibility for any of these, nor should the reader ascribe too much to the authors themselves, given the wild disparity and inconsistencies that may be contained in the utterances of the same person, even allowing for the fact that his or her remarks will always be out of context.

Nonetheless one of the pleasures in consulting this collection, as it has been in compiling it, will be in extracting a personality from the mouths and pens of the characters quoted, for it is the presence of an individual and human factor that distinguishes a quotation from a mere aphorism or proverb. Indeed, most of the names to be found in the index are eminent and interesting enough in themselves to make one want to know what they said, and their remarks will be seen to be the reflection of particular and personal experience, more accessible and quirkier than any nameless and well-honed maxim. Where the person may not be universally known, a brief description has been given with the quotation, on the basis that a remark is liable to lose much of its impact if its author is only vaguely familiar or totally obscure. Otherwise, where dates and descriptions are lacking in some twenty or so quotations, it is because these have not been found available. The two indexes provided – listing names and subjects covered (more than twice the number of the actual headings in the text) – should be entirely sufficient for the purposes of research, while the arrangement of the text itself has been made with the aim of readability paramount. I hope that it will also serve to show, by stressing the eclecticism of the sources, from the depths of history to the present day, and from shores much further than our own, how often the same issues arise, how diverse are the responses to them, and how relevant they continue to be. With foreign quotations, the original language has been given above the translation where possible and where succinctness allows, thus avoiding the necessity of relying on an often mangled concoction of English to appreciate the grace of the original.

My devoted thanks are due to Mamen, Agata, Katia and Carolyn, who not only lent their considerable time and energy to the undertaking, but lightened the task with the comfort of their company; and also to Joyce, for her unfailing support.

Calabria
1987

Absence

Absence, hear thou my protestation
Against thy strength,
Distance and length.
> John Hoskins (1566-1638)
> English poet

*L'absence diminue les médiocres passions, et
augmente les grandes, comme le vent éteint les
bougies, et allume le feu.*
Absence diminishes minor passions and
inflames great ones, as the wind douses a
candle and fans a fire.
> François, Duc de La Rochefoucauld (1613-1680)
> French writer, moralist

Judicious absence is a weapon.
> Charles Reade (1814-1884)
> English novelist

Absence blots people out. We really have no
absent friends.
> Elizabeth Bowen (1899-1973)
> British novelist

Presents, I often say, endear absents.
> Charles Lamb (1775-1834)
> English essayist, critic

I was court-martialled in my absence, and
sentenced to death in my absence, so I said
they could shoot me in my absence.
> Brendan Behan (1923-1964)
> Irish playwright

SEE Shakespeare on GRIEF

Absurdity

Du sublime au ridicule il n'y a qu'un pas.
It is only one step from the sublime to the
ridiculous.
> Napoleon Bonaparte (1769-1821)
> of his retreat from Moscow

Only man has dignity; only man, therefore,
can be funny.
> Father Ronald Knox (1888-1957)
> British clergyman, writer

It is not funny that anything else should fall
down; only that a man should fall down . . .
Why do we laugh? Because it is a gravely
religious matter: it is the fall of man. Only
man can be absurd: for only man can be
dignified.
> G. K. Chesterton (1874-1936)

There are few moments in a man's existence
when he experiences so much ludicrous distress, or meets with so little charitable com-
miseration, as when he is in pursuit of his own
hat.
> Charles Dickens (1812-1870)

Absurdity. A statement or belief manifestly
inconsistent with one's own opinion.
> Ambrose Bierce (1842-1914)
> American author

SEE Johnson on IMITATION

Abuse

It seldom pays to be rude. It never pays to be
only half-rude.
> Norman Douglas (1868-1952)
> British author

Some guy hit my fender the other day, and I
said unto him, 'Be fruitful, and multiply'. But
not in those words.
> Woody Allen (b. 1935)

A man has no more right to say an uncivil
thing to another man than he has to knock
him down.
> Dr Samuel Johnson (1709-1784)

There is more credit in being abused by fools
than praised by rogues.
> F. E. Smith (Lord Birkenhead) (1872-1930)
> British lawyer, Conservative politician

Abuse is as great a mistake in controversy as
panegyric in biography.
> Cardinal John Newman (1801-1890)
> English churchman, theologian

I will name you the degrees. The first, the
Retort Courteous; the second, the Quip
Modest; the third, the Reply Churlish; the
fourth, the Reproof Valiant; the fifth, the Lie
with Circumstance; the sixth, the Lie
with Circumstance; the seventh, the Lie
Direct.
> Touchstone, *As You Like It*
> William Shakespeare (1564-1616)

A fly, Sir, may sting a stately horse and make

him wince; but one is but an insect, and the other is a horse still.
Dr Samuel Johnson (1709-1784)

SEE Johnson on CONTROVERSY: INSULTS; Steele on PRAISE; Cohen on SWEARING

Accounts

A good accountant is someone who told you yesterday what the economists forecast for tomorrow.
Sir Miles Thomas (b. 1897)

Budget: A mathematical confirmation of your suspicions.
A.A. Latimer

Accusation

Accuse. To affirm another's guilt or unworth; most commonly as a justification of ourselves for having wronged him.
Ambrose Bierce (1842-1914)
American author

Acquaintance

I look upon every day to be lost, in which I do not make a new acquaintance.
Dr Samuel Johnson (1709-1784)

Acquaintance. A person whom we know well enough to borrow from, but not well enough to lend to.
Ambrose Bierce (1842-1914)
American author

Acting

Acting is a question of absorbing other people's personalities and adding some of your own experience.
Paul Newman (b. 1925)

Acting is the expression of a neurotic impulse. It's a bum's life. Quitting acting, that's the sign of maturity.
Marlon Brando (b. 1924)

You spend all your life trying to do something they put people in asylums for.
Jane Fonda (b. 1937)

Left eyebrow raised, right eyebrow raised.
Roger Moore (b. 1928)
on his acting range

SEE Davis on BUSTS; Burton on DRINK

Action

It is vain to say human beings ought to be satisfied with tranquillity: they must have action; and they will make it if they cannot find it.
George Eliot (1819-1880)

The shortest answer is doing.
Lord Herbert (1583-1648)
English philosopher, diplomat

Our actions are neither so good nor so evil as our impulses.
Luc, Marquis de Vauvenargues (1715-1747)
French moralist

Je préfère la pensée à l'action, une idée à une affaire, la contemplation au mouvement.
I prefer thought to action, an idea to an event, reflection to activity.
Honoré de Balzac (1799-1850)

Nothing will ever be attempted if all possible objections must be first overcome.
Dr Samuel Johnson (1709-1784)

If it were done when 'tis done, then 'twere well
It were done quickly.
Macbeth, Macbeth
William Shakespeare (1564-1616)

If a thing is worth doing, it is worth doing badly.
G. K. Chesterton (1874-1936)

An ounce of action is worth a ton of theory.
Friedrich Engels (1820-1895)

Patience has its limits. Take it too far and it's cowardice.
George Jackson (1942-1971)
American radical

What you do speaks so loud that I cannot hear what you say.
R. W. Emerson (1803-1882)
American essayist, poet, philosopher

Talk that does not end in any kind of action is better suppressed altogether.
Thomas Carlyle (1795-1881)
Scottish writer

I want to see you shoot the way you shout.
Theodore Roosevelt (1858-1919)

Men of action intervene only when the orators have finished.
Emile Gaboriau (1835-1873)
French author

SEE Halifax on CAUTION; Lloyd George on ELOQUENCE; Levi on HOPE

Actors

A walking shadow, a poor player,
That struts and frets his hour upon the stage,
And then is heard no more.
Macbeth, Macbeth
William Shakespeare (1564-1616)

Have patience with the jealousies and petulance of actors, for their hour is their eternity.
Richard Garnett (1835-1906)
English author, bibliographer

You can pick out actors by the glazed look that comes into their eyes when the conversation wanders away from themselves.
Michael Wilding (1912-1979)
British actor

And here come tired youths and maids
That feign to love or sin
In tones like rusty razor blades
To tunes like smitten tin.
Rudyard Kipling (1865-1936)

A character actor is one who cannot act and therefore makes an elaborate study of disguise and stage tricks by which acting can be grotesquely simulated.
George Bernard Shaw (1856-1950)

To see him act is like reading Shakespeare by flashes of lightning.
S. T. Coleridge (1772-1834)
of Edmund Kean

Every actor in his heart believes everything bad that's printed about him.
Orson Welles (1915-1985)

The only reason they come to see me is that I know that life is great – and they know I know it.
Clark Gable (1901-1960)

His ears made him look like a taxicab with both doors open.
Howard Hughes (1905-1976)
of Clark Gable

He has turned almost alarmingly blond – he's gone past platinum, he must be plutonium; his hair is coordinated with his teeth.
Pauline Kael (b. 1919)
American critic
of Robert Redford

An actor is something less than a man, while an actress is something more than a woman.
Richard Burton (1925-1984)

She has a face that belongs to the sea and the wind, with large rocking-horse nostrils and teeth that you just know bite an apple every day.
Cecil Beaton (1904-1980)
British photographer
of Katherine Hepburn

Actresses will happen in the best-regulated families.
Oliver Herford (1863-1935)
American poet, illustrator

For an actress to be a success she must have the face of Venus, the brains of Minerva, the grace of Terpsichore, the memory of Macaulay, the figure of Juno, and the hide of a rhinoceros.
Ethel Barrymore (1897-1959)
American actress

A deer in the body of a woman, living resentfully in the Hollywood zoo.
Clare Boothe Luce (b. 1903)
American diplomat, writer
of Greta Garbo

An actor is never so great as when he reminds you of an animal – falling like a cat, lying like a dog, moving like a fox.
François Truffaut (1932-1984)
French film director

So much of our profession is taken up with pretending, that an actor must spend at least half his waking hours in a fantasy.
Ronald Reagan (b. 1911)

SEE Quinn on HOLLYWOOD; Rock Hudson on INTERVIEWS; MONROE; Field on SELF-DOUBT; Duse on THEATRE

Addicts
Go mad, and beat their wives;
Plunge (after shocking lives)
Razors and carving knives
Into their gizzards.
C. S. Calverley (1831-1884)
English poet

All sins tend to be addictive, and the terminal point of addiction is what is called damnation.
W. H. Auden (1907-1973)

SEE Bankhead, Neville on DRUGS

Admiration
Admiration. Our polite recognition of another's resemblance to ourselves.
Ambrose Bierce (1842-1914)
American author

Admiration is a very short-lived passion that immediately decays upon growing familiar with its object, unless it be still fed with fresh discoveries, and kept alive by a new perpetual succession of miracles rising up to its view.
Joseph Addison (1672-1719)
English essayist

Usually we praise only to be praised.
François, Duc de La Rochefoucauld (1613-1680)
French writer, moralist

No animal admires another animal.
Blaise Pascal (1623-1662)

Adolescence
The imagination of a boy is healthy, and the mature imagination of a man is healthy; but there is a space of life between, in which the soul is in a ferment, the character undecided, the way of life uncertain, the ambition thick-sighted: thence proceeds mawkishness.
John Keats (1795-1821)

The big mistake that men make is that when they turn thirteen or fourteen and all of a sudden they've reached puberty, they believe that they like women. Actually, you're just horny. It doesn't mean you like women any more at twenty-one than you did at ten.
Jules Feiffer (b. 1929)
American cartoonist

Boys will be boys. And even that wouldn't matter if only we could prevent girls from being girls.
Anthony Hope Hawkins (1863-1933)
British author

For the affection of young ladies is of as rapid

growth as Jack's beanstalk, and reaches right up to the sky in a night.
> W. M. Thackeray (1811-1863)
> English author

Remember that as a teenager you are in the last stage of your life when you will be happy to hear that the phone is for you.
> Fran Lebowitz (b. 1951)
> American journalist

SEE Rosebery on BOYS

Adultery

Adultery? Thou shalt not die: die for adultery? No!
The wren goes to't, and the small gilded fly
Does lecher in my sight. Let copulation thrive.
> Lear, *King Lear*
> William Shakespeare (1564-1616)

What men all gallantry, and gods adultery Is much more common where the climate's sultry.
> Lord Byron (1788-1824)

Adultery is in your heart not only when you look with excessive sexual zeal at a woman who is not your wife, but also if you look in the same manner at your wife.
> Pope John Paul II (b. 1920)

Having a wife, be watchful of thy friend, lest false to thee thy fame and goods he spend.
> Cato the Elder (234-149 BC)
> Roman statesman

The husband who decides to surprise his wife is often very much surprised himself.
> Voltaire (1694-1778)

He that is robb'd, not wanting what is stol'n,
Let him not know't, and he's not robbed at all.
> Othello, *Othello*
> William Shakespeare (1564-1616)

SEE Menen on CATHOLICISM; Shakespeare on JEALOUSY; Bible on SUBURBS

Adventure

Adventure is the champagne of life.
> G. K. Chesterton (1874-1936)

When you're safe at home you wish you were having an adventure; when you're having an adventure you wish you were safe at home.
> Thornton Wilder (1897-1975)
> American author

One does not discover new lands without consenting to lose sight of the shore for a very long time.
> André Gide (1869-1951)

Si nous ne trouverons pas des choses agréables, nous trouverons du moins des choses nouvelles.
If we do not find anything pleasant, at least we shall find something new.
> Voltaire (1694-1778)

The true adventurer goes forth aimless and uncalculating to meet and greet unknown fate. A fine example was the Prodigal Son – when he started back home.
> O. Henry (1862-1910)
> American short story writer

SEE Halifax and Jung on CAUTION; Voltaire on MARRIAGE; Freud on SCIENCE

Adversity

The bravest sight in the world is to see a great man struggling against adversity.
> Seneca (c. 5-65)
> Roman writer, philosopher, statesman

La lutte elle-même vers les sommets suffit à remplir un coeur d'homme. Il faut imaginer Sisyphe heureux.
The struggle to the top is in itself enough to fulfil the human heart. Sisyphus should be regarded as happy.
> Albert Camus (1913-1960)

Man needs difficulties; they are necessary for health.
> Carl Jung (1875-1961)

Not everything that is more difficult is more meritorious.
> Saint Thomas Aquinas (1225-1274)

A reasonable amount o' fleas is good fer a dog – keeps him from broodin' over *bein'* a dog.
> Edward Noyes Westcott (1847-1898)
> American author

By trying we can easily learn to endure adversity. Another man's, I mean.
> Mark Twain (1835-1910)

Struggle is the father of all things . . . It is not by the principles of humanity that man lives or is able to preserve himself above the animal world, but solely by means of the most brutal struggle.
> Adolf Hitler (1889-1945)

In prosperity our friends know us; in adversity we know our friends.
> J. Churton Collins (1848-1908)
> British author, critic, scholar

Misery acquaints a man with strange bedfellows.
> Trinculo, *The Tempest*
> William Shakespeare (1564-1616)

SEE Dietrich on FRIENDS; HARD TIMES; Carlyle on SUCCESS

Advertising

The incessant witless repetition of advertisers'

moron-fodder has become so much a part of life that if we are not careful, we forget to be insulted by it.

The Times, London, 1986

You can tell the ideals of a nation by its advertisements.

Norman Douglas (1868-1952)
British author

Advertising is the rattling of a stick inside a swill bucket.

George Orwell (1903-1950)

Publicity is the life of this culture – in so far as without publicity capitalism could not survive – and at the same time publicity is its dream.

John Berger (b. 1926)
British critic

We grew up founding our dreams on the infinite promise of American advertising.

Zelda Fitzgerald (1900-1948)
wife of F. Scott Fitzgerald

The case cannot stand if it is the process of satisfying the wants that creates the wants.

J.K. Galbraith (b. 1908)
American economist

Advertising is the greatest art form of the twentieth century.

Marshall McLuhan (1911-1981)
Canadian social scientist

Advertising agency: eighty-five per cent confusion and fifteen per cent commission.

Fred Allen (1894-1957)
American comic

SEE Sampson on ROYALTY

Advice

When a man comes to me for advice, I find out the kind of advice he wants, and I give it to him.

Josh Billings (1818-1885)
American humorist

I have lived some thirty years on this planet, and I have yet to hear the first syllable of valuable or even earnest advice from my seniors.

H. D. Thoreau (1817-1862)

The advice of their elders to young men is very apt to be as unreal as a list of the hundred best books.

Dr Oliver Wendell Holmes (1809-1894)
American writer, physician

In matters of religion and matrimony I never give any advice; because I will not have anybody's torments in this world or the next laid to my charge.

Lord Chesterfield (1694-1773)
English statesman and man of letters

The only thing one can do with good advice is to pass it on. It is never of any use to oneself.

Oscar Wilde (1854-1900)

A good scare is worth more to a man than good advice.

Ed (E. W.) Howe (1853-1937)
American journalist, novelist

To ask advice is to tout for flattery.

J. Churton Collins (1848-1908)
English author, critic, scholar

Consult. To seek another's approval of a course already decided on.

Ambrose Bierce (1842-1914)
American author

I'm not a teacher: only a fellow-traveller of whom you asked the way. I pointed ahead – ahead of myself as well as you.

Bishop of Chelsea, *Getting Married*
George Bernard Shaw (1856-1950)

Never trust the advice of a man in difficulties.

Aesop (6th century BC)

One day I sat thinking, almost in despair; a hand fell on my shoulder and a voice said reassuringly: 'Cheer up, things could get worse'. So I cheered up and, sure enough, things got worse.

James Hagerty (1909-1981)
President Eisenhower's press secretary

SEE la Rochefoucauld on AGE: Old Age;
Halifax on ROYALTY

Africa

By the end of the century, Africa will either be saved or completely destroyed.

Eden Kodjo (b. 1938)
Secretary-General, Organisation of African Unity,
1978-1984

SEE Macmillan on DECOLONISATION

The Afterlife

For the sword outwears its sheath, and the soul wears out the breast.

Lord Byron (1788-1824)

We understand living for others and dying for others. The first is easy ... it's a way out of boredom. To make the second popular we had to invent a belief in personal resurrection.

Harley Granville-Barker (1877-1946)
English actor, producer, author

The dread of something after death,
The undiscovered country, from whose bourn
No traveller returns.

Hamlet, *Hamlet*
William Shakespeare (1564-1616)

The chief problem about death, incidentally, is the fear that there may be no afterlife – a depressing thought, particularly for those who have bothered to shave. Also, there is the fear

that there is an afterlife but no one will know where it's being held.
Woody Allen (b. 1935)

I don't want to express an opinion. You see, I have friends in both places.
Mark Twain (1835-1910)
on his belief in heaven or hell

Oh, one world at a time!
H. D. Thoreau (1817-1862)

Never did Christ utter a single word attesting to a personal resurrection and a life beyond the grave.
Leo Tolstoy (1828-1910)

All argument is against it; but all belief is for it.
Dr Samuel Johnson (1709-1784)

Heaven for climate, hell for society.
Mark Twain (1835-1910)

SEE Scott, Waller on CHRISTIANITY;
Woolwich on The CHURCH;
IMMORTALITY

Age

At twenty years of age, the will reigns; at thirty, the wit; and at forty, the judgement.
Henry Grattan (1746-1820)
Irish politician

The old believe everything; the middle-aged suspect everything; the young know everything.
Oscar Wilde (1854-1900)

Si jeunesse savoit; si vieillesse pouvoit.
If youth but knew; if age but could.
Henri Estienne (1531-1598)
French scholar, publisher

What youth deemed crystal, age finds out was dew.
Robert Browning (1812-1889)

Every man over forty is a scoundrel.
George Bernard Shaw (1856-1950)

I'm 65 and I guess that puts me in with the geriatrics. But if there were fifteen months in every year, I'd only be 48. That's the trouble with us. We number everything. Take women, for example. I think they deserve to have more than twelve years between the ages of 28 and 40.
James Thurber (1894-1961)
American humorist, illustrator

What's a man's age? He must hurry more, that's all;
Cram in a day what his youth took a year to hold.
Robert Browning (1812-1889)

A man's as old as he's feeling, a woman as old as she looks.
Mortimer Collins (1827-1876)
English novelist, poet

When a woman tells you her age it's all right to look surprised, but don't scowl.
Wilson Mizner (1876-1933)
American dramatist, wit

A lady of a 'certain age', which means Certainly aged.
Lord Byron (1788-1824)

The years that a woman subtracts from her age are not lost. They are added to the ages of other women.
Diane de Poitiers (1499-1566)
mistress of Henri II of France, patron

When women pass thirty, they first forget their age; when forty, they forget that they ever remembered it.
Ninon de Lenclos (1620-1705)
French society lady and wit

You are not permitted to kill a woman who has injured you, but nothing forbids you to reflect that she is growing older every minute.
Ambrose Bierce (1842-1914)
American author

The age of a woman doesn't mean a thing. The best tunes are played on the oldest fiddles.
Sigmund Z. Engel (b. 1869-?)

Age: Old age

Have you not a moist eye? a dry hand? a yellow cheek? a white beard? a decreasing leg? an increasing belly? is not your voice broken? your wind short? your chin double? your wit single? and every part about you blasted with antiquity?
Chief Justice, *King Henry IV part 2*
William Shakespeare (1564-1616)

At seventy-seven it is time to be earnest.
Dr Samuel Johnson (1709-1784)

Forty years on, growing older and older,
Shorter in wind, as in memory long,
Feeble of foot, and rheumatic of shoulder
What will it help you that once you were strong?
E. E. Bowen (1836-1901)
English schoolmaster

All would live long, but none would be old.
Benjamin Franklin (1706-1790)

O what a thing is age! Death without death's quiet.
Walter Savage Landor (1775-1864)
English author

And we who once rang out like a bell
Have nothing now to show or to sell;
Old bones to carry, old stories to tell:
So it is to be an Old Soldier.
Padraic Colum (1881-1972)
Irish author

When a man fell into his anecdotage it was a sign for him to retire from the world.
Benjamin Disraeli (1804-1881)

Talking is the disease of age.
Ben Jonson (1572-1637)

A good old man, sir, he will be talking; as they say, 'when the age is in, the wit is out'.
Dogberry, *Much Ado About Nothing*
William Shakespeare (1564-1616)

Lord, Lord, how subject we old men are to this vice of lying!
Falstaff, *King Henry IV part 2*
William Shakespeare (1564-1616)

An old man gives good advice to console himself for no longer being able to set a bad example.
François, Duc de La Rochefoucauld (1613-1680)
French writer, moralist

Age. That period of life in which we compound for the vices that remain by reviling those we have no longer the vigor to commit.
Ambrose Bierce (1842-1914)
American author

An old man concludeth from his knowing mankind that they know him too, and that maketh him very wary.
George Savile, Lord Halifax (1633-1695)
English statesman, author

As a matter of fact, elderly people are not more contemptible than anyone else.
Evelyn Waugh (1903-1966)

One evil in old age is that, as your time is come, you think every little illness the beginning of the end. When a man expects to be arrested, every knock at the door is an alarm.
Sydney Smith (1771-1845)
English clergyman, writer

No one is so old as to think he cannot live one more year.
Cicero (106-43 BC)

To me, old age is always fifteen years older than I am.
Bernard Baruch (1870-1965)
American financier

Old age is the most unexpected of all the things that happen to a man.
Leon Trotsky (1879-1940)

I advise you to go on living solely to enrage those who are paying your annuities. It is the only pleasure I have left.
Voltaire (1694-1778)

The mere process of growing old together will make the slightest acquaintance seem a bosom friend.
Logan Pearsall Smith (1865-1946)
American essayist

The tragedy of old age is not that one is old, but that one is young.
Mark Twain (1835-1910)

Men of age object too much, consult too long, adventure too little, repent too soon.
Francis Bacon (1561-1626)

Many a man that can't direct you to a corner drugstore will get a respectful hearing when age has further impaired his mind.
Finley Peter Dunne (1867-1936)
American journalist, humorist

Young men soon give, and soon forget affronts:
Old age is slow in both.
Joseph Addison (1672-1719)
English essayist

Old men are testy, and will have their way.
P. B. Shelley (1792-1822)

Being an old maid is like death by drowning, a really delightful sensation after you cease to struggle.
Edna Ferber (1887-1968)
American writer

There are three classes of elderly women; first, that dear old soul; second, that old woman; third, that old witch.
S. T. Coleridge (1772-1834)

Growing old is more like a bad habit which a busy man has no time to form.
André Maurois (1885-1967)
French writer

I prefer old age to the alternative.
Maurice Chevalier (1888-1972)

I have lived long enough; my way of life
Is fall'n into the sear, the yellow leaf;
And that which should accompany old age,
As honour, love, obedience, troops of friends,
I must not look to have.
Macbeth, *Macbeth*
William Shakespeare (1564-1616)

What is the worst of woes that wait on age?
What stamps the wrinkle deeper on the brow?
To view each loved one blotted from life's page,
And be alone on earth, as I am now.
Lord Byron (1788-1824)

They are all gone into the world of light,
And I alone sit lingering here.
Henry Vaughan (1622-1695)
Welsh poet

SEE Holmes on ADVICE; Irving on COMPLIMENTS; Thomas on DEATH: **Dying**; Santayana on EMOTION; The GENERATION GAP; Bradbury on INNOCENCE; Goldsmith on MARRIAGE; MATURITY; MIDDLE AGE; Plato on SEX; YOUTH

Agents

Many artists have admittedly no aptitude for merchantry.

Arnold Bennett (1867-1931)
British novelist

It is well-known what a middleman is: he is a man who bamboozles one party and plunders the other.

Benjamin Disraeli (1804-1881)

The trouble with this business is that the stars keep ninety per cent of my money.

attributed to Lord Grade (b. 1906)
British film and TV entrepreneur

My agent gets ten per cent of everything I get, except my blinding headaches.

Fred Allen (1894-1957)
American comic

SEE Allen on ADVERTISING

Aggression

Attack is the reaction; I never think I have hit hard unless it rebounds.

Dr Samuel Johnson (1709-1784)

To knock a thing down, especially if it is cocked at an arrogant angle, is a deep delight to the blood.

George Santayana (1863-1952)
American philosopher, poet

Agnostics

O Lord, if there is a Lord, save my soul, if I have a soul.

Joseph Ernest Renan (1823-1892)
French writer, critic, scholar

I am an agnostic; I do not pretend to know what many ignorant men are sure of.

Clarence Darrow (1857-1938)
American lawyer, writer

I can't believe in the God of my Fathers. If there is one Mind which understands all things, it will comprehend me in my unbelief. I don't know whose hand hung Hesperus in the sky, and fixed the Dog Star, and scattered the shining dust of Heaven, and fired the sun, and froze the darkness between the lonely worlds that spin in space.

Gerald Kersh (1911-1968)
British author, journalist

Question with boldness even the existence of a God; because, if there be one, he must more approve of the homage of reason, than that of blindfolded fear.

Thomas Jefferson (1743-1826)

The sceptic does not mean him who doubts, but him who investigates or researches, as opposed to him who asserts and thinks that he has found.

Miguel de Unamuno (1864-1936)
Spanish writer, philosopher

If only God would give me some clear sign! Like making a large deposit in my name at a Swiss bank.

Woody Allen (b. 1935)

SEE Russell on HUMANISM

Agreement

It is my melancholy fate to like so many people I profoundly disagree with and often heartily dislike people who agree with me.

Mary Kingsley (1862-1900)
British traveller, writer

My idea of an agreeable person is a person who agrees with me.

Benjamin Disraeli (1804-1881)

Elinor agreed with it all, for she did not think he deserved the compliment of rational opposition.

Jane Austen (1775-1817)

When you say that you agree to a thing in principle you mean that you have not the slightest intention of carrying it out in practice.

Prince Otto von Bismarck (1815-1898)
Prussian statesman

SEE CONSENSUS; Santayana on MEN AND WOMEN

Aid

The hands that help are holier than the lips that pray.

R. G. Ingersoll (1833-1899)
American laywer

Help a man against his will and you do the same as murder him.

Horace (65-8 BC)

It was as helpful as throwing a drowning man both ends of a rope.

Bugs (Arthur) Baer (1897-1975)
American columnist, short story writer

SEE Huddleston, Rockefeller on CHARITY

AIDS

Any important disease whose causality is murky, and for which treatment is ineffectual, tends to be awash in significance.

Susan Sontag (b. 1933)
American essayist

I've spent fifteen years of my life fighting for our right to be free and make love whenever, wherever ... And you're telling me that all those years of what being gay stood for is wrong ... and I'm a murderer. We have been so oppressed! Don't you remember how it was? Can't you see how important it is for us to love openly, without hiding and without guilt?

Mickey, *The Normal Heart*
Larry Kramer (b. 1935)
American playwright, novelist

Everywhere I go I see increasing evidence of people swirling about in a human cesspit of their own making.

> James Anderton (b. 1932)
> British Chief Constable, Greater Manchester Police Force
> *of the AIDS epidemic*

We're all going to go crazy, living this epidemic every minute, while the rest of the world goes on out there, all around us, as if nothing is happening, going on with their own lives and not knowing what it's like, what we're going through. We're living through war, but where they're living it's peacetime, and we're all in the same country.

> Ned, *The Normal Heart*
> Larry Kramer (b. 1935)
> American playwright, novelist

The thing is evolving in front of one's eyes. One realises that anything one's saying is only a snapshot in time.

> London doctor, 1986

Alliances

Peace, commerce and honest friendship with all nations – entangling alliance with none.

> Thomas Jefferson (1743-1826)

When bad men combine, the good must associate; else they will fall, one by one, an unpitied sacrifice in a contemptible struggle.

> Edmund Burke (1729-1797)
> Irish philosopher, statesman

Whomsoever England allies herself with, she will see her allies stronger than she is herself at the end of this war.

> Adolf Hitler (1889-1945)
> 26 April 1942

Alliance. In international politics, the union of two thieves who have their hands so deeply inserted in each other's pockets that they cannot separately plunder a third.

> Ambrose Bierce (1842-1914)
> American author

Our desire is to be friendly to every country in the world, but we have no desire to have a friendly country choosing our enemies for us.

> Julius Nyerere (b. 1921)
> African statesman, President of Tanzania

An ally has to be watched just like an enemy.

> Leon Trotsky (1879-1940)

Altruism

As for doing good, that is one of the professions that are full.

> H. D. Thoreau (1817-1862)

He who would do good to another must do it in Minute Particulars. General good is the plea of the scoundrel, hypocrite, and flatterer; for

art and science cannot exist but in minutely organized Particulars.

> William Blake (1757-1827)

No people do so much harm as those who go about doing good.

> Mandell Creighton (1843-1901)
> English prelate, historian

Such a good friend that she will throw all her acquaintances into the water for the pleasure of fishing them out again.

> Charles, Count Talleyrand (1754-1838)
> French statesman
> *of Madame de Staël*

SEE BENEFACTORS; PHILANTHROPY

Ambition

Men would be angels, angels would be gods.

> Alexander Pope (1688-1744)

Quel vicaire de village ne voudrait pas être Pape?
What parish priest would not like to be Pope?

> Voltaire (1694-1778)

It is a strange desire to seek power and to lose liberty.

> Francis Bacon (1561-1626)

Ambition. An overmastering desire to be vilified by enemies while living and made ridiculous by friends when dead.

> Ambrose Bierce (1842-1914)
> American author

Ambition is pitiless. Any merit that it cannot use it finds despicable.

> Joseph Joubert (1754-1824)
> French essayist, moralist

As he was valiant, I honour him; but, as he was ambitious, I slew him.

> Brutus, *Julius Caesar*
> William Shakespeare (1564-1616)

Ambition can creep as well as soar.

> Edmund Burke (1729-1797)
> Irish philosopher, statesman

Ambition often puts Men upon doing the meanest offices; so climbing is performed in the same position with creeping.

> Jonathan Swift (1667-1745)

'Tis not what man does which exalts him,
But what man would do!

> Robert Browning (1812-1889)

SEE GETTING ON; Jefferson on
POLITICIANS; Juvenal on POVERTY;
Wilson on PROMOTION

America

Young man, there is America, which at this day serves for little more than to amuse you with stories of strange men and uncouth manners.

> Edmund Burke (1729-1797)
> Irish philosopher, statesman

Of course, America had often been discovered before, but it had always been hushed up.
Oscar Wilde (1854-1900)

God had a divine purpose in placing this land between two great oceans to be found by those who had a special love of freedom and courage.
Ronald Reagan (b. 1911)

America is the only nation in history which, miraculously, has gone directly from barbarism to degeneration without the usual interval of civilization.
Georges Clemenceau (1841-1929)
French statesman, premier

America is a mistake, a giant mistake!
Sigmund Freud (1856-1939)

'Keep, ancient lands, your storied
pomp!' cries she
With silent lips. 'Give me your tired,
your poor,
Your huddled masses yearning to
breathe free,
The wretched refuse of your teeming
shore.
Send these, the homeless, tempest-
tossed, to me;
I lift my lamp beside the golden door'.
Emma Lazarus (1849-1887)
American poet
'The New Colossus' – sonnet written for
inscription on the Statue of Liberty

Ours is the only country deliberately founded on a good idea.
John Gunther (1901-1970)
American journalist

I believe in America because we have great dreams – and because we have the opportunity to make those dreams come true.
Wendell L. Wilkie (1892-1944)
American lawyer, businessman, politician

Sometimes people call me an idealist. Well, that is the way I know I am an American. America is the only idealistic nation in the world.
Woodrow Wilson (1856-1924)

The American ideal is, after all, that everyone should be as much alike as possible.
James Baldwin (b. 1924)
American novelist

America is a tune. It must be sung together.
Gerard Stanley Lee (1862-1944)
American academic

There is nothing wrong with America that together we can't fix.
Ronald Reagan (b. 1911)

That impersonal insensitive friendliness that takes the place of ceremony in that land of waifs and strays.
Evelyn Waugh (1903-1966)
British novelist

America is a large, friendly dog in a very small room. Every time it wags its tail it knocks over a chair.
A. J. Toynbee (1889-1975)
British historian

America ... just a nation of two hundred million used-car salesmen with all the money we need to buy guns and no qualms about killing anybody else in the world who tries to make us uncomfortable.
Hunter S. Thompson (b. 1939)
American journalist

When great nations fear to expand, shrink from expansion, it is because their greatness is coming to an end. Are we, still in the prime of our lusty youth, still at the beginning of our glorious manhood, to sit down among the outworn people, to take our place with the weak and the craven? A thousand times no!
Theodore Roosevelt (1858-1919)

The youth of America is their oldest tradition. It has been going on now for three hundred years.
Oscar Wilde (1854-1900)

Woman governs America because America is a land of boys who refuse to grow up.
Salvador de Madariaga (1886-1978)
Spanish diplomat, writer, critic

America is not a young land: it is old and dirty and evil before the settlers, before the Indians. The evil is there waiting.
William S. Burroughs (b. 1914)
American author

The great social adventure of America is no longer the conquest of the wilderness but the absorption of fifty different peoples.
Walter Lippman (1889-1974)
American journalist

America is God's Crucible, the great Melting-Pot where all the races of Europe are melting and re-forming.
Israel Zangwill (1864-1926)
British author

America, half-brother of the world!
Philip Bailey (1816-1902)
British poet

America lives in the heart of every man everywhere who wishes to find a region where he will be free to work out his destiny as he chooses.
Woodrow Wilson (1856-1924)

The business of America is business.
Calvin Coolidge (1872-1933)
American Republican politician, President

*En Amérique l'homme n'obéit jamais à
l'homme mais à la justice ou à la loi.*
In America people never obey people, but
justice, or the law.
> Alexis de Tocqueville (1805-1859)
> French historian, politician

The United States has to move very fast to
even stand still.
> John F. Kennedy (1917-1963)

If you think the US has stood still, who built
the largest shopping-centre in the world?
> Richard Nixon (b. 1913)

In America you watch TV and think that's
totally unreal, then you step outside and it's
just the same.
> Joan Armatrading (b. 1947)
> British singer

Your women shall scream like peacocks when
they talk, and your men neigh like horses
when they laugh.
> Rudyard Kipling (1865-1936)

I have no further use for America. I wouldn't
go back there if Jesus Christ was President.
> Charlie Chaplin (1889-1977)

In Boston they ask, 'How much does he
know?' In New York, 'How much is he
worth?' In Philadelphia, 'Who were his
parents?'
> Mark Twain (1835-1910)

A Boston man is the east wind made flesh.
> Thomas Appleton (1812-1884)
> American author

Washington is a city of Southern efficiency
and Northern charm.
> John F. Kennedy (1917-1963)

The people are unreal. The flowers are unreal,
they don't smell. The fruit is unreal, it doesn't
taste of anything. The whole place is a glaring,
gaudy, nightmarish set, built upon the desert.
> Ethel Barrymore (1879-1959)
> American actress
> *of Los Angeles*

A city with all the personality of a paper cup.
> Raymond Chandler (1888-1959)
> *of Los Angeles*

California is a place where a boom mentality
and a sense of Chekhovian loss meet in uneasy
suspension; in which the mind is troubled by
some buried but ineradicable suspicion that
things had better work here, because here,
beneath that immense bleached sky, is where
we run out of continent.
> Joan Didion (b. 1934)
> American writer

Out where the handclasp's a little stronger,
Out where the smile dwells a little longer,
That's where the West begins.
> Arthur Chapman (1873-1935)
> American poet, author

If you're going to America, bring your own
food.
> Fran Lebowitz (b. 1951)
> American journalist

SEE Stevenson on CONSUMER SOCIETY;
Thurber on DISSENT; Chesterton on FAME;
Sullivan on HEROES; The NEW WORLD;
NEW YORK; James on SUCCESS; Galbraith
on TECHNOLOGY; TEXAS

Americans

I am willing to love all mankind, *except an
American.*
> Dr Samuel Johnson (1709-1784)

For other nations, utopia is a blessed past
never to be recovered; for Americans it is just
beyond the horizon.
> Henry Kissinger (b. 1923)

There is nothing the matter with Americans
except their ideals. The real American is all
right; it is the ideal American who is all
wrong.
> G. K. Chesterton (1874-1936)

People in America, of course, live in all sorts
of fashions, because they are foreigners, or
unlucky, or depraved, or without ambition;
people live like that, but *Americans* live in
white detached houses with green shutters.
Rigidly, blindly, the dream takes precedence.
> Margaret Mead (1901-1978)
> American anthropologist

American women expect to find in their
husbands a perfection that English women
only hope to find in their butlers.
> W. Somerset Maugham (1874-1965)

Only in America ... do these peasants, our
mothers, get their hair dyed platinum at the
age of sixty, and walk up and down Collins
Avenue in Florida in pedalpushers and mink
stoles – and with opinions on every subject
under the sun.
> Philip Roth (b. 1933)
> American novelist

Since the earliest days of our frontier irreverence has been one of the signs of our affection.
> Dean Rusk (b. 1909)
> American diplomat

Being American is to eat a lot of beef steak,
and boy, we've got a lot more beef steak than
any other country, and that's why you ought
to be glad you're an American. And people
have started looking at these big hunks of
bloody meat on their plates, you know, and

wondering what on earth they think they're doing.

Kurt Vonnegut (b. 1922)

When you consider how indifferent Americans are to the quality and cooking of the food they put into their insides, it cannot but strike you as peculiar that they should take such pride in the mechanical appliances they use for its excretion.

W. Somerset Maugham (1874-1965)

Americans are rather like bad Bulgarian wine: they don't travel well.

Bernard Falk (1882-1960)
British author

Americans are uneasy with their possessions, guilty about power, all of which is difficult for Europeans to perceive because they are themselves so truly materialistic, so versed in the uses of power.

Joan Didion (b. 1934)
American writer

SEE Bradbury on COURTESY; Emerson on EUROPE; Thoreau on FRIENDLINESS; Dickens on GENTLEMEN; Gallico on INSULTS; Wilde on PARIS; McCarthy on PROMISCUITY

Amorality

It is safest to be moderately base – to be flexible in shame, and to be always ready for what is generous, good and just, when anything is to be gained by virtue.

Sydney Smith (1771-1845)
English writer, clergyman

If he does really think that there is no distinction between virtue and vice, why, Sir, when he leaves our houses let us count our spoons.

Dr Samuel Johnson (1709-1784)

Anarchism

Our idea of anarchism is launched: non-government is developing as non-property did before.

Pierre-Joseph Proudhon (1809-1865)
French social theorist

Preferring personal government, with its tact and flexibility, is called royalism. Preferring impersonal government, with its dogmas and definitions, is called republicanism. Objecting broadmindedly both to kings and creeds is called Bosh – at least, I know no more philosophical word for it.

G. K. Chesterton (1874-1936)

Anarchism is the only philosophy which brings to man the consciousness of himself; which maintains that God, the State, and society are non-existent, that their promises are null and void, since they can be fulfilled only through man's subordination.

Emma Goldman (1869-1940)
American anarchist

Dame dynamite, que l'on danse vite . . .
Dansons et chansons et dynamitons!
Lady Dynamite, let's dance quickly,
Let's dance and sing and dynamite everything!

French anarchist song of the 1880s

SEE Crosland on SOCIALISM; Bakunin, Kropotkin on The STATE

Ancestry

Every man is an omnibus in which his ancestors ride.

Dr Oliver Wendell Holmes (1809-1894)
American writer, physician

Each has his own tree of ancestors, but at the top of all sits Probably Arboreal.

Robert Louis Stevenson (1850-1894)

Genealogy. An account of one's descent from an ancestor who did not particularly care to trace his own.

Ambrose Bierce (1842-1914)
American author

Englishmen hate Liberty and Equality too much to understand them. But every Englishman loves a pedigree.

George Bernard Shaw (1856-1950)

It is indeed a desirable thing to be well-descended, but the glory belongs to our ancestors.

Plutarch (46-120)

Neither give heed to fables and endless genealogies.

Saint Paul (3-67)

There is a certain class of people who prefer to say that their fathers came down in the world through their own follies than to boast that they rose in the world through their own industry and talents. It is the same shabby-genteel sentiment, the same vanity of birth which makes men prefer to believe that they are degenerate angels rather than elevated apes.

W. Winwoode Reade (1838-1875)
English traveller, author

I would rather make my name than inherit it.

W. M. Thackeray (1811-1863)
English author

I don't know who my grandfather was; I am much more concerned to know what his grandson will be.

Abraham Lincoln (1809-1865)

In church your grandsire cut his throat;
To do the job too long he tarried:
He should have had my hearty vote
To cut his throat before he married.

Jonathan Swift (1667-1745)

SEE Burton on ARISTOCRACY; Agar on
SNOBBERY; Burke, Chesterton on
TRADITION

Anecdotes

With a tale, forsooth, he cometh unto you;
with a tale which holdeth children from play,
and old men from the chimney corner.
Sir Philip Sidney (1554-1586)

The history of a soldier's wound beguiles the
pain of it.
Laurence Sterne (1713-1768)
English author

If it isn't true at least it's a happy invention.
Giordano Bruno (1548-1599)
Italian philosopher

A good storyteller is a person who has a good
memory and hopes other people haven't.
Irvin S. Cobb (1876-1944)
American writer

How is it that we remember the least triviality
that happens to us, and yet not remember how
often we have recounted it to the same
person?
François, Duc de La Rochefoucauld (1613-1680)
French writer, moralist

We may be willing to tell a story twice, never
to hear it more than once.
William Hazlitt (1778-1830)
English essayist

Faith! he must make his stories shorter
Or change his comrades once a quarter.
Jonathan Swift (1667-1745)

SEE Disraeli on AGE: Old Age

Anger

Anger is a kind of temporary madness.
Saint Basil (330-379)

Anger is one of the sinews of the soul; he that
lacks it has a maimed mind.
Thomas Fuller (1608-1661)
English cleric

Heav'n has no rage like love to hatred
turn'd,
Nor Hell a fury like a woman scorn'd.
William Congreve (1670-1729)
English dramatist

No man can think clearly when his fists are
clenched.
George Jean Nathan (1882-1958)
American critic

SEE Dryden on PATIENCE; Emerson on
SPEECHES

Angling

The charm of fishing is that it is the pursuit of
what is elusive but obtainable, a perpetual
series of occasions for hope.
John Buchan (1875-1940)
British author, statesman

We may say of angling as Dr Boteler said of
strawberries, 'Doubtless God could have made
a better berry, but doubtless God never did';
and so, if I might be judge, 'God never did
make a more calm, quiet, innocent recreation
than angling'.
Izaak Walton (1593-1683)
English author, biographer

Fly fishing may be a very pleasant amusement;
but angling or float fishing I can only compare
to a stick and a string, with a worm at one end
and a fool at the other.
Dr Samuel Johnson (1709-1784)

Animals

Nothing to be done really about animals.
Anything you do looks foolish. The answer
isn't in us. It's almost as if we're put here on
earth to show how silly they aren't.
Russell Hoban (b. 1925)
British author

They do not sweat and whine about their
condition,
They do not lie awake in the dark and weep
for their sins,
They do not make me sick discussing their
duty to God,
Not one is dissatisfied, not one is demented
with the mania of owning things,
Not one kneels to another, nor to his kind
that lived thousands of years ago.
Walt Whitman (1819-1892)

We know what animals do and what beaver
and bears and salmon and other creatures
need, because once our men were married to
them and they acquired this knowledge from
their animal wives.
Hawaiian Indians
quoted by Lévi-Strauss in *The Savage Mind*

A peasant becomes fond of his pig and is glad
to salt away its pork. What is significant, and
is so difficult for the urban stranger to
understand, is that the two statements are
connected by an *and* and not by a *but*.
John Berger (b. 1926)
British critic

Of all God's creatures there is only one that
cannot be made the slave of the lash. That one
is the cat. If man could be crossed with the cat
it would improve man, but it would deterior-
ate the cat.
Mark Twain (1835-1910)

The zoo cannot but disappoint. The public
purpose of zoos is to offer visitors the
opportunity of looking at animals. Yet
nowhere in a zoo can a stranger encounter the
look of an animal. At the most, the animal's
gaze flickers and passes on. They look side-
ways. They look blindly beyond.
John Berger (b. 1926)
British critic

SEE DOGS; HORSES

Anniversaries

Let us love nobly, and live, and add again
Years and years unto years, till we attain
To write threescore: this is the second of
our reign.
John Donne (1573-1631)

The secret anniversaries of the heart.
H. W. Longfellow (1807-1882)

Anthologies

*Quelqu'un pourrait dire de moi que j'ai
seulement fait ici un amas de fleurs étrangères,
n'y ayant fourni du mien que le filet à les lier.*
It might well be said of me that here I have
merely made up a bunch of other people's
flowers, and provided nothing of my own but
the string to bind them.
Michel de Montaigne (1533-1592)
French essayist

A well-chosen anthology is a complete dispensary of medicine for the more common mental disorders, and may be used as much for prevention as cure.
Robert Graves (1895-1985)
British poet, novelist

Lexicographer: a writer of dictionaries, a harmless drudge.
Dr Samuel Johnson (1709-1784)

Antipathy

They exchanged the quick, brilliant smile of women who dislike each other on sight.
Marshall Pugh (b. 1925)
British journalist, author

Violent antipathies are always suspicious, and betray a secret affinity.
William Hazlitt (1778-1830)
English essayist

Anxiety

But Jesus, when you don't have any money, the problem is food. When you have money, it's sex. When you have both, it's health, you worry about getting ruptured or something. If everything is simply jake then you're frightened of death.
J. P. Donleavy (b. 1926)
American author

When you suffer an attack of nerves you're being attacked by the nervous system. What chance has a man got against a system?
Russell Hoban (b. 1925)
British author

Worry is interest paid on trouble before it falls due.
W. R. Inge (1860-1954)
Dean of St Paul's, London

Women like to sit down with trouble as if it were knitting.
Ellen Glasgow (1874-1945)
American novelist

My apprehensions come in crowds;
I dread the rustling of the grass;
The very shadows of the clouds
Have power to shake me as they pass:
I question things and do not find
One that will answer to my mind;
And all the world appears unkind.
William Wordsworth (1770-1850)

Probably the only place where a man can feel really secure is in a maximum security prison, except for the imminent threat of release.
Germaine Greer (b. 1939)
Australian feminist writer

I've never met a healthy person who worried much about his health, or a good person who worried about his soul.
J. B. S. Haldane (1892-1964)
British scientist

Apathy

The difference between our decadence and the Russians' is that while theirs is brutal, ours is apathetic.
James Thurber (1894-1961)
American humorist, illustrator

Science may have found a cure for most evils; but it has found no remedy for the worst of them all – the apathy of human beings.
Helen Keller (1880-1968)

SEE INDIFFERENCE

Apocalypse

God seems to have left the receiver off the hook, and time is running out.
Arthur Koestler (1905-1983)
British author

This is the way the world ends
This is the way the world ends
This is the way the world ends
Not with a bang but a whimper.
T. S. Eliot (1888-1965)

Amen. Even so, come, Lord Jesus.
John the Divine (1st century AD)

Apologies

Never make a defence or apology before you be accused.
King Charles I of Great Britain (1600-1649)

To apologise is to lay the foundation for a future offence.
Ambrose Bierce (1842-1914)
American author

A stiff apology is a second insult.
G. K. Chesterton (1874-1936)

It is a good rule in life never to apologise. The

right sort of people do not want apologies, and the wrong sort take a mean advantage of them.

P. G. Wodehouse (1881-1975)

Appearances

To see ourselves as others see us is a most salutary gift. Hardly less important is the capacity to see others as they see themselves.

Aldous Huxley (1894-1963)

Barring that natural expression of villainy which we all have, the man looked honest enough.

Mark Twain (1835-1910)

I'm not a dictator. It's just that I have a grumpy face.

General Pinochet (b. 1915)
President of Chile

Straight trees have crooked roots.

16th century proverb

A good man often appears *gauche* simply because he does not take advantage of the myriad mean little chances of making himself look stylish. Preferring truth to form, he is not constantly at work upon the façade of his appearance.

Iris Murdoch (b. 1919)
Irish writer

He looked as inconspicuous as a tarantula on a slice of angel food.

Raymond Chandler (1888-1959)

She got her good looks from her father – he's a plastic surgeon.

Groucho Marx (1895-1977)

SEE Lincoln on The COMMONPLACE; DRESS; FACES; Umamuno on VANITY; Tertullian on WOMEN

Appeasement

And that is called paying the Dane-geld;
But we've proved it again and again,
That if once you have paid him the Dane-geld
You never get rid of the Dane.

Rudyard Kipling (1865-1936)

Thus Belial, with words clothed in reason's garb,
Counselled ignoble ease, and peaceful sloth,
Not peace.

John Milton (1608-1674)

An appeaser is one who feeds a crocodile, hoping it will eat him last.

Sir Winston Churchill (1874-1965)

Appeasers believe that if you keep on throwing steaks to a tiger, the tiger will turn vegetarian.

Heywood Broun (1888-1939)
American journalist, novelist

Applause

They named it Ovation from the Latin *ovis*, a sheep.

Plutarch (46-120)

I want to thank you for stopping the applause. It is impossible for me to look humble for any period of time.

Henry Kissinger (b. 1923)

Do not trust to the cheering, for those very persons would shout as much if you and I were going to be hanged.

Oliver Cromwell (1599-1658)

The silence that accepts merit as the most natural thing in the world is the highest applause.

R. W. Emerson (1803-1882)
American essayist, poet, philosopher

Architecture

What has happened to architecture since the second world war that the only passers-by who can contemplate it without pain are those equipped with a white stick and a dog?

Bernard Levin (b. 1928)
British journalist

A large number of us have developed a feeling that architects tend to design houses for the approval of fellow architects and critics – not for the tenants.

Prince of Wales (b. 1948)

Architecture is the art of how to waste space.

Philip Johnson (b. 1906)
American architect

Light, God's eldest daughter, is a principal beauty in a building.

Thomas Fuller (1608-1661)
English cleric

No person who is not a great sculptor or painter can be an architect. If he is not a sculptor or painter, he can only be a builder.

John Ruskin (1819-1900)
English critic

Why can't we have those curves and arches that express feeling in design? What is wrong with them? Why has everything got to be vertical, straight, unbending, only at right angles – and functional?

Prince of Wales (b. 1948)

No architecture is so haughty as that which is simple.

John Ruskin (1819-1900)
English critic

Si monumentum requiris, circumspice.
If you would see his monument, look around.

of Sir Christopher Wren, by his son

Argument

Myself when young did eagerly frequent

Doctor and Saint, and heard great
  Argument
About it and about: but evermore
Came out by the same Door wherein
I went.
from *The Rubáiyát of Omar Khayyám*
trans. Edward Fitzgerald (1809-1883)

A man never tells you anything until you
contradict him.
George Bernard Shaw (1856-1950)

One often contradicts an opinion when what
is uncongenial is really the tone in which it
was conveyed.
Friedrich Nietzsche (1844-1900)

You raise your voice when you should rein-
force your argument.
Dr Samuel Johnson (1709-1784)

You have not converted a man because you
have silenced him.
John, Lord Morley (1838-1923)
English writer, Liberal politician

Arguments are to be avoided: they are always
vulgar and often convincing.
Oscar Wilde (1854-1900)

To gain one's way is no escape from the
responsibility for an inferior solution.
Sir Winston Churchill (1874-1965)

Persons of good sense, I have since observed,
seldom fall into disputation, except lawyers,
university men, and men of all sorts that have
been bred at Edinburgh.
Benjamin Franklin (1706-1790)

The devil can cite Scripture for his purpose.
Antonio, *The Merchant of Venice*
William Shakespeare (1564-1616)

Arguments out of a pretty mouth are
unanswerable
Joseph Addison (1672-1719)
English essayist

If you wish to win a man's heart, allow him to
confute you.
Benjamin Disraeli (1804-1881)

A woman who is confuted is never convinced.
J. Churton Collins (1848-1908)
English author, critic, scholar

The only argument available with an east
wind is to put on your overcoat.
J. R. Lowell (1819-1891)
American poet, editor

Between friends differences in taste or opinion
are irritating in direct proportion to their
triviality.
W. H. Auden (1907-1973)

There are three sides to every question: your
side, his side, and to hell with it.
anonymous, 20th century

SEE Austen on AGREEMENT; Chesterton,
Gay on INTERVENTION; PERSUASION

The Aristocracy

We, my lords, may thank Heaven that we
have something better than our brains to
depend on.
Lord Chesterfield (1694-1773)
English statesman and man of letters

There are bad manners everywhere, but an
aristocracy is bad manners organised.
Henry James (1843-1916)

For what were all these country patriots
  born?
To hunt, and vote, and raise the price of
  corn?
Lord Byron (1788-1824)

We may talk what we please of lilies and lions
rampant, and spread eagles in fields *d'or* or
d'argent; but if heraldry were guided by
reason, a plough in a field arable would be the
most noble and ancient of arms.
Abraham Cowley (1618-1667)
English author

A fully equipped Duke costs as much to keep
up as two Dreadnoughts, and they are just as
great a terror – and they last longer.
David Lloyd George (1863-1945)
Welsh Liberal politician, Prime Minister

Almost in every kingdom the most ancient
families have been at first princes' bastards.
Robert Burton (1577-1640)
English clergyman, author

I have known a German Prince with more
titles than subjects, and a Spanish nobleman
with more names than shirts.
Oliver Goldsmith (1728-1774)

There is no stronger craving in the world than
that of the rich for titles, except that of the
titled for riches.
Hesketh Pearson (1887-1964)
British biographer

Lords are lordliest in their wine.
John Milton (1608-1674)

A degenerate nobleman is like a turnip. There
is nothing good of him but that which is
underground.
17th century English saying

Those comfortably padded lunatic asylums
which are known, euphemistically, as the
stately homes of England.
Virginia Woolf (1882-1941)

Stemmata quid faciunt?
What is the use of your pedigrees?
Juvenal (40-125)

SEE Arnold on The ENGLISH; Winster on
The HOUSE OF LORDS; Burton on
IDLENESS

The Arms race

Qui desiderat pacem, praeparet bellum.
Let him who desires peace prepare for war.
Vegetius (4th century AD)
Roman military strategist

The ability to get to the verge without getting into the war is the necessary art.
John Foster Dulles (1888-1959)
American Republican politician

If this phrase of the 'balance of power' is to be always an argument for war, the pretence for war will never be wanting, and peace can never be secure.
John Bright (1811-1889)
English Radical politician

Security is a game in which the final goal is never quite in reach.
Laurence Martin (b. 1928)
British author, academic

Nothing could have been more obvious to the people of the early twentieth century than the rapidity with which war was becoming impossible. And as certainly they did not see it. They did not see it until the atomic bombs burst in their fumbling hands.
H. G. Wells (1866-1946)
written in 1914

The world knows, and above all the Soviets know, that no American President will sacrifice New York or Washington to save Berlin.
Richard Nixon (b. 1913)

One cannot fashion a credible deterrent out of an incredible action.
Robert McNamara (b. 1916)
American industrialist, politician, financier

Every gun that is fired, every warship launched, every rocket fired, signifies, in the final sense, a theft from those who hunger and are not fed, those who are cold and are not clothed. The world in arms is not spending money alone. It is spending the sweat of its labourers, the genius of its scientists, the hopes of its children.
Dwight Eisenhower (1890-1969)

The emotional security and political stability in this country entitle us to be a nuclear power.
Sir Ronald Mason
retiring as Chief Scientific Adviser, *Ministry of Defence, 1983*

The superpowers often behave like two heavily-armed blind men feeling their way around a room, each believing himself in mortal peril from the other, whom he assumes to have perfect vision.
Henry Kissinger (b. 1923)

Nuclear weapons are not in my line; unfortunately I am in their line.
E. M. Forster (1879-1970)

SEE Einstein, De Gaulle, White on The
NUCLEAR AGE

The Army

The professional military mind is by necessity an inferior and unimaginative mind; no man of high intellectual quality would willingly imprison his gifts in such a calling.
H. G. Wells (1866-1946)

It has been calculated by the ablest politicians that no State, without being soon exhausted, can maintain above the hundredth part of its members in arms and idleness.
Edward Gibbon (1737-1794)

The chief attraction of military service has consisted and will consist in this compulsory and irreproachable idleness.
Leo Tolstoy (1828-1910)

Soldiers in peace are like chimneys in summer.
Lord Burghley (1520-1598)

Now, you mummy's darlings, get a rift on them boots. Definitely shine 'em, my little curly-headed lambs, for in our mob war or no war, you die with clean boots on.
Gerald Kersh (1911-1968)
British author, journalist

National Service did the country a lot of good but it darned near killed the army.
General Sir Richard Hull (b. 1907)
Chief of the Imperial General Staff
1962

He learned the arts of riding, fencing, gunnery,
And how to scale a fortress – or a nunnery.
Lord Byron (1788-1824)

The uncontrolled licentiousness of a brutal and insolent soldiery.
Baron Erskine (1750-1823)
English jurist

Drinking is the soldier's pleasure.
John Dryden (1631-1700)

The mere scum of the earth.
Duke of Wellington (1769-1852)
of his men

We aren't no thin red 'eroes, nor we aren't no blackguards too.
But single men in barracks, most remarkable like you;
And if sometimes our conduck isn't all your fancy paints,
Why, single men in barracks don't grow into plaster saints.
Rudyard Kipling (1865-1936)

I had rather have a plain, russet-coated
Captain, that knows what he fights for, and
loves what he knows, than that which you call
a Gentleman and is nothing else.
> Oliver Cromwell (1599-1658)

On becoming soldiers we have not ceased to
be citizens.
> spokesman for Cromwell's
> soldiers, 1647

Soldiers are dreamers; when the guns
begin
They think of firelit homes, clean beds,
and wives.
> Siegfried Sassoon (1886-1967)
> British poet, author

Come on you sons of bitches! Do you want to
live for ever?
> Daniel Daly (1874-1937)
> Gunnery Sergeant, US Marines

I don't know what effect these men will have
upon the enemy, but, by God, they terrify me.
> Duke of Wellington (1769-1852)

Horribly stuffed with epithets of war.
> Iago, Othello
> William Shakespeare (1564-1616)

Theirs not to make reply,
Theirs not to reason why,
Theirs but to do and die.
> Lord Tennyson (1809-1892)

Soldiers are citizens of death's grey land.
> Siegfried Sassoon (1886-1967)
> British poet, author

The third part of an army must be destroyed,
before a good one can be made out of it.
> George Savile, Lord Halifax (1633-1695)
> English statesman, author

We few, we happy few, we band of
brothers;
For he today that sheds his blood with
me
Shall be my brother; be he ne'er so vile
This day shall gentle his condition:
And gentlemen in England now a-bed
Shall think themselves accursed they
were not here,
And hold their manhoods cheap whiles
any speaks
That fought with us upon Saint
Crispin's day.
> King Henry, King Henry V
> William Shakespeare (1564-1616)

Soldiers who wish to be a hero
Are practically zero,
But those who wish to be civilians,
Jesus, they run into the millions.
> graffito
> collected by Norman Rosten

The feeling about a soldier is, when all is said
and done, he wasn't really going to do very
much with his life anyway. The example
usually is: 'he wasn't going to compose
Beethoven's Fifth'.
> Kurt Vonnegut (b. 1922)

If I should die, think only this of me,
That there's some corner of a foreign field
That is for ever England.
> Rupert Brooke (1887-1915)
> British poet

When you're wounded and left on
Afghanistan's plains,
An' the women come out to cut up
what remains,
Jest roll to your rifle an' blow out
your brains
An' go to your Gawd like a soldier.
> Rudyard Kipling (1865-1936)

SEE GENERALS; Roosevelt on
PATRIOTISM; Lawrence on UNIFORMS;
Stalin on WAR

Arrogance

How haughtily he cocks his nose,
To tell what every schoolboy knows.
> Jonathan Swift (1667-1745)

Nobody can be so amusingly arrogant as a
young man who has just discovered an old
idea and thinks it is his own.
> Sydney J. Harris (b. 1917)
> American journalist

If I cannot brag of knowing something, then I
brag of not knowing it; at any rate, brag.
> R. W. Emerson (1803-1882)
> American essayist, poet, philosopher

The arrogance of age must submit to be taught
by youth.
> Edmund Burke (1729-1797)
> Irish philosopher, statesman

Art

Art is man added to nature.
> Francis Bacon (1561-1626)

And the first rude sketch that the
world had seen
was joy to his* mighty heart
Till the Devil whispered behind the
leaves
'It's pretty, but is it art?'
*(Adam's)
> Rudyard Kipling (1865-1936)

There are painters who transform the sun into
a yellow spot, but there are others who,
thanks to their art and intelligence, transform
a yellow spot into the sun.
> Pablo Picasso (1881-1973)

What is a work of art? A word made flesh . . .
a thing seen, a thing known, the immeasurable

translated into terms of the measurable.
> Eric Gill (1882-1940)
> British sculptor

Art is the imposing of a pattern on experience, and our aesthetic enjoyment in recognition of the pattern.
> A. N. Whitehead (1861-1947)
> British philosopher

Art is I; Science is We.
> Claude Bernard (1813-1878)
> French physiologist

If only we could pull out our brain and use only our eyes.
> Pablo Picasso (1881-1973)

Great art is as irrational as great music. It is mad with its own loveliness.
> George Jean Nathan (1882-1958)
> American critic

What garlic is to salad, insanity is to art.
> Augustus Saint-Gaudens (1848-1907)
> American sculptor

Art resides in the resolution of inner and outer conflict.
> *Belfast art lecturer,*
> *explaining his appearance in*
> *the nude*

A work of art that contains theories is like an object on which the price tag has been left.
> Marcel Proust (1871-1922)

To say that a work of art is good, but incomprehensible to the majority of men, is the same as saying of some kind of food that it is very good but that most people can't eat it.
> Leo Tolstoy (1828-1910)

One reassuring thing about modern art is that things can't be as bad as they are painted.
> M. Walthall Jackson

If there were no other proof of the infinite patience of God with men, a very good one could be found in His toleration of the pictures that are painted of Him.
> Thomas Merton (1915-1968)
> American author, clergyman

I would rather see the portrait of a dog that I know, than all the allegorical paintings they can shew me in the world.
> Dr Samuel Johnson (1709-1784)

They are good furniture pictures, unworthy of praise, and undeserving of blame.
> John Ruskin (1819-1900)
> English critic

If Botticelli were alive today he'd be working for *Vogue.*
> Peter Ustinov (b. 1921)
> British actor, wit

Art is skill, that is the first meaning of the word.
> Eric Gill (1882-1940)
> British sculptor

There has never been a boy painter, nor can there be. The art requires a long apprenticeship, being *mechanical* as well as intellectual.
> John Constable (1776-1837)

Painting consumes labour not disproportionate to its effect; but a fellow will hack half a year at a block of marble to make something in stone that hardly resembles a man. The value of statuary is owing to its difficulty. You would not value the finest head cut upon a carrot.
> Dr Samuel Johnson (1709-1784)

To say of a picture, as is often said in its praise, that it shows great and earnest labour, is to say that it is incomplete and unfit for view.
> J. M. Whistler (1834-1903)
> American artist

Art consists of limitation. The most beautiful part of every picture is the frame.
> G. K. Chesterton (1874-1936)

Art is either plagiarism or revolution.
> Paul Gauguin (1838-1903)

Without tradition, art is a flock of sheep without a shepherd. Without innovation, it is a corpse.
> Sir Winston Churchill (1874-1965)

Art is dangerous. It is one of the attractions, when it ceases to be dangerous you don't want it.
> Anthony Burgess (b. 1917)
> British author

The English public takes no interest in a work of art until it is told that the work in question is immoral.
> Oscar Wilde (1854-1900)

Art does not reproduce the visible; rather, it makes visible.
> Paul Klee (1879-1940)

Art is a lie that makes us realise the truth.
> Pablo Picasso (1881-1973)

There is nothing more difficult for a truly creative painter than to paint a rose, because before he can do so he has first to forget all the roses that were ever painted.
> Henri Matisse (1869-1954)

When I am finishing a picture I hold some God-made object up to it — a rock, a flower, the branch of a tree or my hand — as a kind of final test. If the painting stands up beside a thing man cannot make, the painting is authentic. If there's a clash between the two, it is bad art.
> Marc Chagall (1889-1985)

Yes, madam, Nature is creeping up.
J. M. Whistler (1834-1903)
American artist
to a lady who said a
landscape view reminded her
of his work

I have seen, and heard, much of Cockney impudence before now; but never expected to hear a coxcomb ask two hundred guineas for flinging a pot of paint in the public's face.
John Ruskin (1819-1900)
English critic
of Whistler's 'Nocturne in
Black and Gold'

Painting can do for the illiterate what writing does for those who can read.
Pope Gregory the Great (c. 540-604)

Art for art's sake is a philosophy of the well-fed.
Cao Yu (b. 1910)
Chinese dramatist

All art is quite useless.
Oscar Wilde (1854-1900)

SEE Morris on COMPETITION; Shaw on CREEDS; PORTRAITS

Artists

You say you are incapable of expressing your thought. How then do you explain the lucidity and brilliance with which you are expressing the thought that you are incapable of thought?
letter from the surrealist
Jacques Rivière to Antonin
Artaud, 1923/24

There is only one difference between a mad-man and me. I am not mad.
Salvador Dali (b. 1904)

Before I was shot I always thought that I was more half-there than all-there.
Andy Warhol (1930?-1987)

What the public criticises in you, cultivate. It is you.
Jean Cocteau (1889-1963)
French writer, film director

Every artist writes his own autobiography.
Havelock Ellis (1859-1939)
British psychologist

The artist, like the God of creation, remains within or behind or beyond or above his handiwork, invisible, refined out of existence, indifferent, paring his fingernails.
James Joyce (1882-1941)

Artists do not prove things. They do not need to. They know them.
Kneller, *In Good King Charles's Golden Days*
George Bernard Shaw (1856-1950)

An artist must know how to convince others of the truth of his lies.
Pablo Picasso (1881-1973)

The artist's work is to shew us ourselves as we really are. Our minds are nothing but this knowledge of ourselves; and he who adds a jot to such knowledge creates new mind as surely as any woman creates new men.
Tanner, *Man and Superman*
George Bernard Shaw (1856-1950)

If they have not opened the eyes of the blind, they have at least given great encouragement to the short-sighted, and while their leaders may have all the inexperience of old age, their young men are far too wise ever to be sensible.
Oscar Wilde (1854-1900)
of the Impressionists

When he painted a road, the roadmakers were there in his imagination, when he painted the turned earth of a ploughed field, the gesture of the blade turning the earth was included in his own act. Wherever he looked he saw the labour of existence; and this labour, recognised as such, was what constituted reality for him.
John Berger (b. 1926)
British critic
of Van Gogh

The true function of art is to criticise, embellish and edit nature ... The artist is a sort of impassioned proof-reader, blue-pencilling the bad spelling of God.
H. L. Mencken (1880-1956)
American journalist

Los buenos pintores imitan la naturaleza, pero los males la vomitan.
Good painters imitate nature, but bad ones spew it up.
Miguel de Cervantes (1547-1616)

The artist ... is in the painful situation of having to choose between being despised and being despicable. If his powers are of the first order he must incur one or the other of these misfortunes – the former if he uses his powers, the latter if he does not.
Bertrand Russell (1872-1970)

The soul, too, has her virginity and must bleed a little before bearing fruit.
George Santayana (1863-1952)
American philosopher, poet

The artistic temperament is a disease that affects amateurs ... Artists of a large and wholesome vitality get rid of their art easily, as they breathe easily or perspire easily. But in artists of less force, the thing becomes a pressure, and produces a definite pain, which is called the artistic temperament.
G. K. Chesterton (1874-1936)

Many excellent cooks are spoilt by going into the arts.
> Paul Gauguin (1838-1903)

Art is a jealous mistress, and if a man have a genius for painting, poetry, music, architecture or philosophy, he makes a bad husband and an ill provider.
> R. W. Emerson (1803-1882)
> American essayist, poet, philosopher

A woman is fascinated not by art, but by the noise made by those who are in the art field.
> Anton Chekhov (1860-1904)

I should hardly think it is sensible to suffer the pains of creation just for money or the mild pleasures of praise.
> William Bolitho (1890-1930)
> British author

The notion of making money by popular work, and then retiring to do good work on the proceeds, is the most familiar of all the devil's traps for artists.
> Logan Pearsall Smith (1865-1946)
> American essayist

The artist who always paints the same scene pleases the public for the sole reason that it recognises him with ease and thinks itself a connoisseur.
> Alfred Stevens (1818-1875)
> British artist

Ruskin's counsel: For two days' work you ask two hundred guineas? Whistler: No, I ask it for the knowledge of a lifetime.
> altercation during Ruskin's
> lawsuit against Whistler

Artists, as a rule, do not live in the purple; they live mainly in the red.
> Mr Justice (later Lord) Pearce (1901-1985)
> British judge

It is very good advice to believe only what an artist does, rather than what he says about his work.
> David Hockney (b. 1937)

His work was that curious mixture of bad painting and good intentions that always entitles a man to be called a representative British artist.
> Oscar Wilde (1854-1900)

Great artists have no country.
> Alfred de Musset (1810-1857)
> French poet, novelist, playwright

SEE BOHEMIA; Hawthorne on NUDITY; Nietzsche on PARIS; Sargent on PORTRAITS

The Arts

When politicians and civil servants hear the word 'culture' they feel for their blue pencil.
> Lord Esher (b. 1913)
> British architect

All the arts in America are a gigantic racket run by unscrupulous men for unhealthy women.
> Sir Thomas Beecham (1879-1961)
> British conductor

There is a great deal to be said for the Arts. For one thing they offer the only career in which commercial failure is not necessarily discreditable.
> Evelyn Waugh (1903-1966)

[He] believes in the fine arts with all the earnestness of a man who does not understand them.
> George Bernard Shaw (1856-1950)

SEE Huxley on PATRONAGE

Asia

The mysterious East, perfumed like a flower, silent like death, dark like a grave.
> Joseph Conrad (1857-1924)

Asia is not going to be civilized after the methods of the West. There is too much Asia and she is too old.
> Rudyard Kipling (1865-1936)

Because the European does not know his own unconscious, he does not understand the East and projects into it everything he fears and despises in himself.
> Carl Jung (1875-1961)

SEE Kipling on EMPIRE

Assassination

Assassiner c'est le plus court chemin.
Assassination's the fastest way.
> Molière (1622-1673)

Assassination is the extreme form of censorship.
> George Bernard Shaw (1856-1950)

It is one of the incidents of the profession.
> King Umberto I of Italy (1844-1900)
> after an attempt on his life

Assassination is the perquisite of princes.
> European court cliché, 19th century

My family has learned a very cruel lesson of both history and fate.
> Senator Edward Kennedy (b. 1932)

The American public would forgive me anything except running off with Eddie Fisher.
> Jacqueline Kennedy Onassis (b. 1929)
> after the assassination of
> her husband

Tell my mother I died for my country. I thought I did for the best. Useless! Useless!
> John Wilkes Booth (1838-1865)
> after his assassination of
> Abraham Lincoln

A desperate disease requires a dangerous remedy.
> Guy Fawkes (1570-1606)
> Catholic conspirator
> *on the gunpowder plot to blow*
> *up the Houses of Parliament*
> *(after Hippocrates)*

Assassination has never changed the history of the world.
> Benjamin Disraeli (1804-1881)

SEE Dennis on BIOGRAPHY; Layton on POLITICIANS; Edward VII on ROYALTY; Newsweek on TELEVISION

Astrology

This is the excellent foppery of the world, that, when we are sick in fortune, often the surfeits of our own behaviour, we make guilty of our disasters the sun, the moon, and stars.
> Edmund, *King Lear*
> William Shakespeare (1564-1616)

Atheism

Here we are, we're alone in the universe, there's no God, it just seems that it all began by something as simple as sunlight striking on a piece of rock. And here we are. We've only got ourselves. Somehow, we've just got to make a go of it. *We've only ourselves.*
> Jean, *The Entertainer*
> John Osborne (b. 1929)
> British playwright

Absolute atheism starts in an act of faith in reverse gear and is a full-blown religious commitment.
> Jacques Maritain (1882-1973)
> French philosopher

Nobody talks so constantly about God as those who insist that there is no God.
> Heywood Broun (1888-1939)
> American journalist, novelist

An atheist is a man who has no invisible means of support.
> John Buchan (1875-1940)
> British author

No one can be an unbeliever nowadays. The Christian apologists have left one nothing to disbelieve.
> Saki (H. H. Munro) (1870-1916)
> Scottish author

And that inverted Bowl we call The Sky,
Whereunder crawling coop't we live and die,
    Lift not thy hands to *It* for help –
        for It
Rolls impotently on as Thou or I.
> from *The Rubáiyát of Omar Khayyám*
> *trans.* Edward Fitzgerald (1809-1883)

SEE Russell on HUMANISM

Authenticity

About as genuine as tea made from a bit of paper which once lay in a drawer beside another bit of paper which had been used to wrap up a few tea-leaves from which tea had already been made three times.
> Sören Kierkegaard (1813-1855)
> Danish philosopher

Autobiography

Autobiography is now as common as adultery and hardly less reprehensible.
> John Grigg (b. 1924)
> British author, journalist

Memoirs: The backstairs of history.
> George Meredith (1828-1909)
> English author

The man who writes about himself and his own time is the only man who writes about all people and about all time.
> George Bernard Shaw (1856-1950)

A writer is rarely so well inspired as when he talks about himself.
> Anatole France (1844-1924)
> French author

All those writers who write about their childhood! Gentle God, if I wrote about mine you wouldn't sit in the same room with me.
> Dorothy Parker (1893-1967)
> American humorous writer

I am being frank about myself in this book. I tell of my first mistake on page 850.
> Henry Kissinger (b. 1923)

Autobiography is an unrivalled vehicle for telling the truth about other people.
> Philip Guedalla (1889-1944)
> British author

When my journal appears, many statues must come down.
> Duke of Wellington (1769-1852)

I dislike modern memoirs. They are generally written by people who have either entirely lost their memories, or have never done anything worth remembering.
> Oscar Wilde (1854-1900)

Autobiographies ought to begin with Chapter Two.
> Ellery Sedgwick (1872-1960)
> American editor

If you really want to hear about it, the first thing you'll probably want to know is where I was born, and what my lousy childhood was like, and how my parents were occupied and all before they had me, and all that David Copperfield kind of crap, but I don't feel like going into it.
> J. D. Salinger (b. 1919)
> *opening words of* Catcher in the Rye

SEE Ellis on ARTISTS; BIOGRAPHY;
France on CONFESSIONS

Awards

He got the peace prize; we got the problem. If I'm following a general, and the enemy gives him rewards, I tend to get suspicious. Especially if he gets a peace award before the war is over.

Malcolm X (1925-1965)
American radical leader
of Martin Luther King

Lots of people who complained about us receiving the MBE received theirs for heroism in the war – for killing people. We received ours for entertaining other people. I'd say we deserve ours more.

John Lennon (1940-1980)

The cross of the Legion of Honour has been conferred on me. However, few escape that distinction.

Mark Twain (1835-1910)

Members rise from CMG (known sometimes in Whitehall as Call Me God) to KCMG (Kindly Call Me God) to GCMG (God Calls Me God).

Anthony Sampson (b. 1926)
British journalist, author

SEE Bennett on LITERATURE

B

Babies

A loud noise at one end and no sense of responsibility at the other.

Father Ronald Knox (1888-1957)
British clergyman, writer

Every baby born into the world is a finer one than the last.

Charles Dickens (1812-1870)

From the moment of birth, when the Stone Age baby confronts the twentieth-century mother, the baby is subjected to these forces of violence, called love, as its father and mother and their parents and their parents before them, have been. These forces are mainly concerned with destroying most of its potential.

R. D. Laing (b. 1927)
British psychiatrist

Babies are the enemies of the human race.

Isaac Asimov (b. 1920)
American author

SEE Churchill on INVESTMENT

Bachelors

It is a truth universally acknowledged that a single man in possession of a good fortune must be in want of a wife.

Jane Austen (1775-1817)

A bachelor never quite gets over the idea that he is a thing of beauty and a boy for ever.

Helen Rowland (1875-1950)
American journalist

Bachelors know more about women than married men; if they didn't, they'd be married too.

H. L. Mencken (1880-1956)
American journalist

'Come, come', said Tom's father, 'at your time of life,
There's no longer excuse for thus playing the rake –
It is time you should think, boy, of taking a wife.'
'Why, so it is father – whose wife shall I take?'

Thomas Moore (1779-1852)
Irish poet

SEE Johnson on MARRIAGE; Moore on REFORM

Baldness

Bald as the bare mountain tops are bald, with a baldness full of grandeur.

Matthew Arnold (1822-1888)
English poet, critic

There's one thing about baldness; it's neat.

Don Herold (b. 1889)
American humorous writer, artist

Banality

There is only one thing it requires real courage to say, and that is a truism.

G. K. Chesterton (1874-1936)

Men are seldom more commonplace than on supreme occasions.

Samuel Butler (1835-1902)
English author

SEE Ortega y Gasset on The COMMONPLACE

Banks

Put not your trust in money, but put your money in trust.

Dr Oliver Wendell Holmes (1809-1894)
American writer, physician

A banker is a fellow who lends his umbrella when the sun is shining and wants it back the minute it begins to rain.

Mark Twain (1835-1910)

It is easier to rob by setting up a Bank than by holding up a Bank Clerk.

Bertolt Brecht (1898-1956)

Bargaining

There are very honest people who do not think that they have had a bargain unless they have cheated a merchant.

Anatole France (1844-1924)
French author

Here's the rule for bargains: 'Do other men, for they would do you'. That's the true business precept.

Jonas Chuzzlewit, *Martin Chuzzlewit*
Charles Dickens (1812-1870)

It is naught, it is naught, saith the buyer; but when he is gone his way, then he boasteth.
Bible, Proverbs

Necessity never made a good bargain.
Benjamin Franklin (1706-1790)

SEE Leonardo on HOPE

Beards

That ornamental excrement which groweth beneath the chin.
Thomas Fuller (1608-1661)
English cleric

The hoary beard is a crown of glory if it be found in the way of righteousness.
Bible, Proverbs

A beard signifies lice, not brains.
Greek proverb

The Beatles

Christianity will go. We're more popular than Jesus now.
John Lennon (1940-1980)

SEE Lennon on AWARDS; Lennon on GETTING ON

Beauty

O Beauty, so ancient and so new!
Saint Augustine (354-430)

The ideal has many names, and Beauty is but one of them.
W. Somerset Maugham (1874-1965)

Beauty for some provides escape.
  Who gain a happiness in eying
The gorgeous buttocks of the ape
  Or Autumn sunsets exquisitely dying.
Aldous Huxley (1894-1963)

The epithet beautiful is used by surgeons to describe operations which their patients describe as ghastly, by physicists to describe methods of measurement which leave sentimentalists cold, by lawyers to describe cases which ruin all the parties to them, and by lovers to describe the objects of their infatuation, however unattractive they may appear to the unaffected spectators.
George Bernard Shaw (1856-1950)

Beauty in distress is much the most affecting beauty.
Edmund Burke (1729-1797)
Irish philosopher, statesman

It is better to be beautiful than to be good. But it is better to be good than to be ugly.
Oscar Wilde (1854-1900)

Beauty is indeed a good gift of God; but that the good may not think it a great good, God dispenses it even to the wicked.
Saint Augustine (354-430)

Beauty. The power by which a woman charms a lover and terrifies a husband.
Ambrose Bierce (1842-1914)
American author

To me, fair friend, you never can be old
For as you were when first your eye I eyed,
Such seems your beauty still.
William Shakespeare (1564-1616)

The flowers anew, returning seasons bring!
But beauty faded has no second spring.
Ambrose Philips (1674-1749)
English poet, politician

If beauty isn't genius it usually signals at least a high level of animal cunning.
Peter York (b. 1950)
British journalist

SEE Dryden on INHERITANCE; Disraeli on RELIGION; Shaw on SEX; Wollstonecraft on WOMEN

Bed

The happiest part of a man's life is what he passes lying awake in bed in the morning.
Dr Samuel Johnson (1709-1784)

The cool kindliness of sheets, that soon
Smooth away trouble; and the rough male kiss
Of blankets.
Rupert Brooke (1887-1915)
British poet

To bedward be you merry or have merry company about you, so that to bedward no anger nor heaviness, sorrow nor pensifulness do trouble or disquiet you.
Andrew Borde (1490-1549)
English traveller, physician

Whoever thinks of going to bed before twelve o'clock is a scoundrel.
Dr Samuel Johnson (1709-1784)

For I've been born and I've been wed –
All of man's peril comes of bed.
C. H. Webb (1834-1905)
American journalist

SEE Proverb on LOVERS

Belief

With most men, unbelief in one thing springs from blind belief in another.
G. C. Lichtenberg (1742-1799)
German physicist, writer

When once a man is determined to believe, the very absurdity of the doctrine does but confirm him in his faith.
Junius (18th century)
pseudonym of a writer never identified

The word 'belief' is a difficult thing for me. I don't *believe*. I must have a reason for a certain hypothesis. Either I *know* a thing, and then I know it – I don't need to believe it.

Carl Jung (1875-1961)

There are those who feel an imperative need to believe, for whom the values of a belief are proportionate, not to its truth, but to its definiteness. Incapable of either admitting the existence of contrary judgements or of suspending their own, they supply the place of knowledge by turning other men's conjectures into dogmas.

C. E. M. Joad (1891-1953)
British author, academic

'One *can't* believe impossible things'.
'I daresay you haven't had much practice', said the Queen. 'When I was your age, I always did it for half-an-hour a day. Why, sometimes I've believed as many as six impossible things before breakfast'.

Lewis Carroll (1832-1898)

The most positive men are the most credulous.

Jonathan Swift (1667-1745)

SEE CREEDS

Bella Figura

Let them cant about decorum
Who have characters to lose.

Robert Burns (1759-1796)

SEE Swift on HYPOCRISY

Benefactors

I love my fellow creatures – I do all the good I can –
Yet everybody says I'm such a disagreeable man!

W. S. Gilbert (1836-1911)
English librettist

Take Egotism out, and you would castrate the benefactors.

R. W. Emerson (1803-1882)
American essayist, poet, philosopher

We do not love people so much for the good they have done us, as for the good we have done them.

Leo Tolstoy (1828-1910)

He who wishes to secure the good of others has already secured his own.

Confucius (551-478 BC)

And learn the luxury of doing good.

Oliver Goldsmith (1728-1774)

Nobody shoots at Santa Claus.

Governor Al Smith (1873-1944)
American Democratic politician

SEE ALTRUISM; Twain on DEATH;
Gay on GOOD DEEDS; PHILANTHROPY

Bestiality

When someone behaves like a beast, he says: 'After all, one is only human'. But when he is treated like a beast, he says: 'After all, one is human'.

Karl Kraus (1874-1936)
Austrian poet, journalist

SEE Johnson on DRINK

The Bible

The Bible is for the Government of the People, by the People, and for the People.

general prologue to the
Wycliffe translation of the
Bible, 1384

The Bible is literature, not dogma.

George Santayana (1863-1952)
American philosopher, poet

No public man in these islands ever believes that the Bible means what it says; he is always convinced that it says what he means.

George Bernard Shaw (1856-1950)

Both read the Bible day and night,
But thou read'st black where I read white.

William Blake (1757-1827)

We must be on guard against giving interpretations of scripture that are far-fetched or opposed to science, and so exposing the word of God to the ridicule of unbelievers.

Saint Augustine (354-430)

The pencil of the Holy Ghost hath laboured more in describing the afflictions of Job than the felicities of Solomon.

Francis Bacon (1561-1626)

Fear is the denomination of the Old Testament; belief is the denomination of the New.

Benjamin Whichcote (1609-1683)
Provost of King's College, Cambridge

Prosperity is the Blessing of the Old Testament; adversity is the blessing of the New.

Francis Bacon (1561-1626)

It gives me a deep, comforting sense that 'things seen are temporal and things unseen are eternal'.

Helen Keller (1880-1968)

I never had any doubt about it being of divine origin ... point out to me any similar collection of writings that has lasted for as many thousands of years and is still a best-seller, world-wide. It had to be of divine origin.

Ronald Reagan (b. 1911)

SEE Paget on CENSORSHIP; Emerson on
FAITH; Russell on INTELLIGENCE

Bigotry

Bigotry tries to keep truth safe in its hand with a grip that kills it.
>   Rabindranath Tagore (1861-1941)
>   Indian author, philosopher

Defoe says that there were a hundred thousand country fellows in his time ready to fight to the death against popery, without knowing whether popery was a man or a horse.
>   William Hazlitt (1778-1830)
>   English essayist

We call a man a bigot or a slave of dogma because he is a thinker who has thought thoroughly and to a definite end.
>   G. K. Chesterton (1874-1936)

I will look at any additional evidence to confirm the opinion to which I have already come.
>   Hugh, Lord Molson (b. 1903)
>   British politician

SEE Emerson on FAITH

Bills

Alas! how deeply painful is all payment!
>   Lord Byron (1788-1824)

It is only by not paying one's bills that one can hope to live in the memory of the commercial classes.
>   Oscar Wilde (1854-1900)

Biography

One of the new terrors of death.
>   John Arbuthnot (1667-1735)
>   English writer, physician

A great American need not fear the hand of his assassin; his real demise begins only when a friend like Mr Sorensen closes the mouth of his tomb with a stone.
>   Nigel Dennis (b. 1912)
>   British author
>   reviewing Kennedy by Theodore C. Sorensen

Every great man now has his disciples, and it is always Judas who writes the biography.
>   Oscar Wilde (1854-1900)

Biography should be written by an acute enemy.
>   A. J. Balfour (1848-1930)
>   British Conservative politician, Prime Minister

The first thing to be done by a biographer in estimating character is to examine the stubs of the victim's cheque-books.
>   Silas W. Mitchell (1829-1914)
>   American physician, author

Just how difficult it is to write biography can be reckoned by anybody who sits down and considers just how many people know the real truth about his or her love affairs.
>   Rebecca West (1892-1983)
>   British author

A well-written Life is almost as rare as a well-spent one.
>   Thomas Carlyle (1795-1881)
>   Scottish author

Read no history; nothing but biography, for that is life without theory.
>   Benjamin Disraeli (1804-1881)

Biography is to give a man some kind of shape after his death.
>   Virginia Woolf (1822-1941)

Biography is a region bounded on the north by history, on the south by fiction, on the east by obituary, and on the west by tedium.
>   Philip Guedalla (1889-1944)
>   British biographer, historian

Many heroes lived before Agamemnon; but all are unknown and unwept, extinguished in everlasting night, because they have no spirited chronicler.
>   Horace (65-8 BC)

You still shall live (such virtue hath my pen)
Where breath most breathes, – even in the mouths of men.
>   William Shakespeare (1564-1616)

SEE AUTOBIOGRAPHY; Guardian on Dr JOHNSON

Birth

My mother groan'd, my father wept,
Into the dangerous world I leapt.
>   William Blake (1757-1827)

If new-borns could remember and speak, they would emerge from the womb carrying tales as wondrous as Homer's.
>   Newsweek magazine (1982)

Birth Control

No woman can call herself free who does not own and control her body. No woman can call herself free until she can choose consciously whether she will or will not be a mother.
>   Margaret Sanger (1883-1966)
>   pioneer of American birth control movement

We want far better reasons for having children than not knowing how to prevent them.
>   Dora Russell (1894-1986)
>   British author, campaigner

Contraceptives should be used on all conceivable occasions.
>   Spike Milligan (b. 1918)
>   British comedian, humorous writer

The best contraceptive is a glass of cold water: not before or after, but instead.
>   Pakistani delegate at
>   International Planned
>   Parenthood Federation
>   Conference

I want to tell you a terrific story about oral contraception. I asked this girl to sleep with me and she said 'no'.

Woody Allen (b. 1935)

If Nature had arranged that husbands and wives should have children alternately there would never be more than three in a family.

Lawrence Housman (1865-1959)
British author, artist

Blindness

O loss of sight, of thee I most complain!
Blind among enemies! O worse than chains,
Dungeon, or beggary, or decrepit age!
Light, the prime work of God, to me is extinct,
And all her various objects of delight
Annulled, which might in part my grief have eased.
Inferior to the vilest now become
Of man or worm, the vilest here excel me:
They creep, yet see; I, dark in light, exposed
To daily fraud, contempt, abuse, and wrong,
Within doors, or without, still as a fool,
In power of others, never in my own –
Scarce half I seem to live, dead more than half . . .

John Milton (1608-1674)

But who would rush at a benighted man
And give him two black eyes for being blind?

Thomas Hood (1799-1845)
English poet

If the blind lead the blind, both shall fall into the ditch.

Jesus (4 BC-29 AD)

The very limit of human blindness is to glory in being blind.

Saint Augustine (354-430)

It is not miserable to be blind; it is miserable to be incapable of enduring blindness.

John Milton (1608-1674)

Bloodsports

When a man wantonly destroys one of the works of man we call him a vandal. When he destroys one of the works of God we call him a sportsman.

Joseph Wood Krutch (1893-1970)
American essayist

Hunting was the labour of the savages of North America, but the amusement of the gentlemen of England.

Dr Samuel Johnson (1709-1784)

It is the sport of kings, the image of war without its guilt, and only five-and-twenty per cent of its danger.

R. S. Surtees (1803-1864)
English sporting novelist

There is a passion for *hunting something* deeply implanted in the human breast.

Charles Dickens (1812-1870)

It is chiefly through the instinct to kill that man achieves intimacy with the life of nature.

Lord (Sir Kenneth) Clark (1903-1973)
British critic

One knows so well the popular idea of health. The English country gentleman galloping after a fox – the unspeakable in full pursuit of the uneatable.

Oscar Wilde (1854-1900)

Women never look so well as when one comes in wet and dirty from hunting.

R. S. Surtees (1803-1864)
English sporting novelist

It is very strange, and very melancholy, that the paucity of human pleasures should persuade us ever to call hunting one of them.

Dr Samuel Johnson (1709-1784)

When a man wants to murder a tiger he calls it sport; when a tiger wants to murder him he calls it ferocity.

George Bernard Shaw (1856-1950)

The birds seem to consider the muzzle of my gun as their safest position.

Sydney Smith (1771-1845)
English writer, clergyman

A gun gives you the body, not the bird.

H. D. Thoreau (1817-1862)

Bloody-mindedness

A state of mind halfway between anger and cruelty.

Wayland Young (b. 1923)
British politician, writer

Why be disagreeable, when with a little effort you can be impossible?

Douglas Woodruff (1897-1978)
British journalist, author

Some folks are so contrary that if they fell in a river, they'd insist on floating upstream.

Josh Billings (1818-1885)
American humorist

Well, if I called the wrong number why did you answer the phone?

James Thurber (1894-1961)
American humorist, illustrator

The Blues

Sweet bird, that shunn'st the noise of folly,
Most musical, most melancholy.

John Milton (1608-1674)

I've been told that nobody sings the word 'hunger' like I do.

Billie Holiday (1915-1959)

Anybody singing the blues is in a deep pit yelling for help.

Mahalia Jackson (1911-1972)
American blues and gospel singer

It is only in his music, which Americans are able to admire because a protective sentimentality limits their understanding of it, that the Negro in America has been able to tell his story.

James Baldwin (b. 1924)
American writer

The blues was like that problem child that you may have had in the family. You was a little bit ashamed to let anybody see him, but you loved him. You just didn't know how other people would take it.

B. B. King (b. 1925)
blues guitarist

SEE JAZZ

Bohemia

I'd like to live like a poor man with lots of money.

Pablo Picasso (1881-1973)

The true artist will let his wife starve, his children go barefoot, his mother drudge for his living at seventy, sooner than work at anything but his art.

Tanner, *Man and Superman*
George Bernard Shaw (1856-1950)

Books

Immortal sons deifying their sires.

Plato (428-347 BC)

If you would not be forgotten as soon as you are dead, either write things worth reading or do things worth writing.

Benjamin Franklin (1706-1790)

O, let my books be then the eloquence
And dumb presagers of my speaking
breast.

William Shakespeare (1564-1616)

Here, my dear Lucy, hide these books. Quick, quick. Fling *Peregrine Pickle* under the toilet – throw *Roderick Random* into the closet – put *The Innocent Adultery* into *The Whole Duty of Man* . . . and leave *Fordyce's Sermons* open on the table.

R. B. Sheridan (1751-1816)

A man's library is a sort of harem.

R. W. Emerson (1803-1882)
American essayist, poet, philosopher

A room without books is as a body without a soul.

Sir John Lubbock, Lord Avebury (1834-1913)
British banker, scientist, author

No furniture is as charming as books, even if you never open them.

Sydney Smith (1771-1845)
English clergyman, writer

A book that is shut is but a block.

Thomas Fuller (1654-1734)
English physician

From the moment I picked up your book until I laid it down I was convulsed with laughter. Some day I intend reading it.

Groucho Marx (1890-1977)

Some books are to be tasted, others to be swallowed, and some few to be chewed and digested.

Francis Bacon (1561-1626)

The oldest books are only just out to those who have not read them.

Samuel Butler (1835-1902)
English author

Every condensation of a good book is a foolish mutilation.

Michel de Montaigne (1533-1592)
French essayist, moralist

It was a book to kill time for those who like it better dead.

Rose Macaulay (1889-1958)
British novelist, essayist

Books are good enough in their own way, but they are a mighty bloodless substitute for life.

Robert Louis Stevenson (1850-1894)

What is written is merely the dregs of experience.

Franz Kafka (1883-1924)

Books are fatal: they are the curse of the human race. Nine-tenths of existing books are nonsense, and the clever books are the refutation of that nonsense. The greatest misfortune that ever befell man was the invention of printing.

Benjamin Disraeli (1804-1881)

What do we, as a nation, care about books? How much do you think we spend altogether on our libraries, public or private, as compared with what we spend on our horses?

John Ruskin (1819-1900)
English critic

A good book is the best of friends, the same today and for ever.

Martin Tupper (1810-1889)
British author, poet, inventor

Everywhere I have sought rest and not found it, except sitting in a corner by myself with a little book.

Thomas à Kempis (1380-1471)

Les livres cadrent mal avec le mariage.
Books and marriage go ill together.

Molière (1622-1673)

Without books God is silent.
Thomas Bartholin (1616-1680)
Danish physician

SEE Milton on CENSORSHIP; Shenstone on
LEARNING; LITERATURE; READING;
Whitman on WRITING

Boredom

Boredom is . . . a vital consideration for the
moralist, since at least half the sins of
mankind are caused by the fear of it.
Bertrand Russell (1872-1970)

No society seems ever to have succumbed to
boredom. Man has developed an obvious
capacity for surviving the pompous reiteration
of the commonplace.
J. K. Galbraith (b. 1908)
American economist

Only the finest and most active animals are
capable of boredom. A subject for a great poet
– God's boredom on the seventh day of
creation.
Friedrich Nietzsche (1844-1900)

A yawn is a silent shout.
G. K. Chesterton (1874-1936)

SEE ENNUI

Bores

Bore. A person who talks when you wish him
to listen.
Ambrose Bierce (1842-1914)
American author

A bore is a man who, when you ask him how
he is, tells you.
Bert Leston Taylor (1866-1921)
American humorist, pioneer newspaper columnist

I have neither wit, nor words, nor worth,
Action, nor utterance, nor the power of
speech
To stir men's blood; I only speak right
on.
Mark Antony, *Julius Caesar*
William Shakespeare (1564-1616)

A bore is a man who spends so much time
talking about himself that you can't talk about
yourself.
Melville D. Landon (1839-1910)
American lecturer, wit

And 'tis remarkable that they
Talk most who have the least to say.
Matthew Prior (1664-1721)
English poet, diplomat

The age of chivalry is past. Bores have
succeeded to dragons.
Benjamin Disraeli (1804-1881)

Society is now one polished horde,
Formed of two mighty tribes, the
Bores and *Bored*.
Lord Byron (1788-1824)

A healthy male adult bore consumes each year
one and a half times his own weight in other
people's patience.
John Updike (b. 1932)

You must be careful about giving any drink
whatsoever to a bore. A lit-up bore is the
worst in the world.
Lord David Cecil (b. 1902)
British biographer, essayist

Make not thy own person, family, relations or
affairs the frequent subject of thy tattle. Say
not, My manner and custom is to do thus. I
neither eat nor drink in a morning. I am apt to
be troubled with corns. My child said such a
witty thing last night.
Thomas Fuller (1608-1661)
English cleric

If you are a bore, strive to be a rascal also so
that you may not discredit virtue.
George Bernard Shaw (1856-1950)

SEE La Rochefoucauld on ANECDOTES; La
Rochefoucauld on CONVERSATION;
DULLNESS; Churchill on FANATICS;
Emerson on HEROES

Borrowing

The human species, according to the best
theory I can form of it, is composed of two
distinct races, the men who borrow, and the
men who lend.
Charles Lamb (1775-1834)
English essayist, critic

Do not be made a beggar by banqueting upon
borrowing.
Apocrypha, Ecclesiasticus

The Bourgeoisie

And the wind shall say 'Here were decent
godless people;
Their only monument the asphalt road
And a thousand lost golf balls'.
T. S. Eliot (1888-1965)

The bourgeoisie of the whole world, which
looks complacently upon the wholesale mas-
sacre after the battle, is convulsed by horror at
the desecration of brick and mortar.
Karl Marx (1818-1883)

How beastly the bourgeois is
especially the male of the species
– presentable, eminently presentable.
D. H. Lawrence (1885-1930)

The bourgeoisie prefers comfort to pleasure,
convenience to liberty, and a pleasant temper-
ature to the deathly inner consuming fire.
Hermann Hesse (1877-1962)

The way to crush the bourgeoisie is to grind
them between the millstones of taxation and
inflation.
Vladimir Ilyich Lenin (1870-1924)

Destroy him as you will, the bourgeois always bounces up. Execute him, expropriate him, starve him out *en masse*, and he reappears in your children.
Cyril Connolly (1903-1974)
British critic

SEE Thackeray on The ENGLISH

Boys

I never see any difference in boys. I only know two sorts of boys. Mealy boys and beef-faced boys.
Mr Grimwig, *Oliver Twist*
Charles Dickens (1812-1870)

I have seen thousands of boys and young men, narrow-chested, hunched-up, miserable specimens, smoking endless cigarettes, many of them betting.
Sir Robert (Lord) Baden-Powell (1857-1941)
explaining reasons for
foundation of Boy Scouts
Association, 1907

The fact that boys are allowed to exist at all is evidence of a remarkable Christian forbearance among men.
Ambrose Bierce (1842-1914)
American author

All my life I have loved a womanly woman and admired a manly man, but I never could stand a boily boy.
Lord Rosebery (1847-1929)
British Liberal politician, Prime Minister

Boys are capital fellows in their own way, among their mates; but they are unwholesome companions for grown people.
Charles Lamb (1775-1834)
English essayist, critic

Boys will be boys, and so will a lot of middle-aged men.
Kin (F. McKinney) Hubbard (1868-1930)
American humorist, journalist

SEE Hawkins on ADOLESCENCE

The British

An Englishman is never happy unless he is miserable; a Scotsman is never at home but when he is abroad; an Irishman is never at peace but when he's fighting.
anonymous, 19th century

What annoys me about Britain is the rugged will to lose.
William Camp (b. 1926)
British author, communications consultant

We always used to be noted for understatement. The difference is that in the past we never meant it.
Sir William (later Lord) Penney (b. 1909)
British scientist

The British are a self-distrustful, diffident people, agreeing with alacrity that they are neither successful, nor clever and only modestly claiming that they have a keener sense of humour, more robust common sense, and greater staying power as a nation than all the rest of the world put together.
The Times, London, 1950

That detached and baronial air of superiority the Briton habitually affects when circumstances beyond his control bring him into the presence of creatures of a lesser breed.
Pierre Van Paassen (1895-1968)
American author, journalist, minister

The British tourist is always happy abroad as long as the natives are waiters.
Robert Morley (b. 1908)
British actor

Gorgonised me from head to foot with a stony British stare.
Lord Tennyson (1809-1892)

It is equality of monotony which makes the strength of the British Isles.
Eleanor Roosevelt (1884-1962)
wife of F. D. Roosevelt,
US delegate at UN

Very few people indeed realise how early the British go to bed.
The Times, London

The national anthem belongs to the eighteenth century. In it you find us ordering God about to do our political dirty work.
George Bernard Shaw (1856-1950)

I always enjoy appearing before a British audience. Even if they don't feel like laughing, they nod their heads to show they've understood.
Bob Hope (b. 1903)

What right have the Americans to be forecasting *our* weather?
letter to *The Times*, London

SEE Smith on DRINK; The ENGLISH; The SCOTS; Sampson on SNOBBERY; Thomas on WALES

Bureaucracy

Our greatest growth industry is the Civil Service.
Lord Lucas (1896-1967)
British public figure

This place needs a laxative.
Bob Geldof (b. 1954)
of EEC bureaucracy

The working of great institutions is mainly the result of a vast mass of routine, petty malice, self-interest, carelessness and sheer mistake. Only a residual fraction is thought.
George Santayana (1863-1952)
American philosopher, poet

Poor fellow, he suffers from files.
> Aneurin Bevan (1897-1960)
> British Labour politician
> *of Sir Walter Citrine*

Official dignity tends to increase in inverse ratio to the importance of the country in which the office is held.
> Aldous Huxley (1894-1963)

The longer the title, the less important the job.
> George McGovern (b. 1922)
> American Democratic politician

There is something about a bureaucrat that does not like a poem.
> Gore Vidal (b. 1925)

SEE Kafka on REVOLUTION; Russell on The STATE

Business

Nothing knits man to man like the frequent passage from hand to hand of cash.
> Walter Sickert (1860-1942)
> British artist

Commerce is the great civilizer. We exchange ideas when we exchange fabrics.
> R. G. Ingersoll (1833-1899)
> American lawyer

The propensity to truck, barter and exchange one thing for another . . . is common to all men, and to be found in no other race of animals.
> Adam Smith (1723-1790)
> Scottish economist

Everyone lives by selling something.
> Robert Louis Stevenson (1850-1894)

If I see something I like, I buy it; then I try to sell it.
> Lord Grade (b. 1906)
> British film and TV entrepreneur

The selfish spirit of commerce knows no country, and feels no passion or principle but that of gain.
> Thomas Jefferson (1743-1826)

No nation was ever ruined by trade.
> Benjamin Franklin (1706-1790)

What's good for the country is good for General Motors, and what's good for General Motors is good for the country.
> Charles Wilson (1890-1961)
> American industrialist, Secretary of Defence

Free enterprise ended in the United States a good many years ago. Big oil, big steel, big agriculture avoid the open marketplace. Big corporations fix prices among themselves and drive out the small entrepreneur. In their conglomerate forms, the huge corporations have begun to challenge the legitimacy of the state.
> Gore Vidal (b. 1925)

For the merchant, even honesty is a financial speculation.
> Charles Baudelaire (1821-1867)

Nothing is illegal if one hundred businessmen decide to do it.
> Andrew Young (b. 1932)
> American politician

You never expected justice from a company, did you? They have neither a soul to lose, nor a body to kick.
> Sydney Smith (1771-1845)
> English writer, clergyman

Honour sinks where commerce long prevails.
> Oliver Goldsmith (1728-1774)

When you are skinning your customers you should leave some skin on to grow again so that you can skin them again.
> Nikita Khrushchev (1894-1971)
> *advice to British businessmen*

Every crowd has a silver lining.
> Phineas T. Barnum (1810-1891)
> American showman

Half the time when men think they are talking business they are wasting time.
> Ed (E. W.) Howe (1853-1937)
> American journalist, novelist

There's no such thing as a free lunch.
> Milton Friedman (b. 1912)
> American economist

Giv'um's dead, and Lend'um's very bad. Nothink for nothink 'ere, and precious little for sixpence!
> *Punch* magazine, 19th century

I have always felt that our business men, if they had been left to themselves to make a religion, would have turned out something uncommonly like Juju.
> Mary Kingsley (1862-1900)
> British traveller, writer

SEE Coolidge on AMERICA; Dickens on BARGAINING; Stowell on DINNER PARTIES; MANAGEMENT: Carnegie, Wrigley on PARTNERSHIP; Pitt on PRIVATE INTEREST; Cassandra on PROPAGANDA; Livy on RESOLVE; Goodhart on RETIREMENT; Burke on WEALTH; Leacock on WOMEN

Busts

Uncorsetted, her friendly bust
Gives promise of pneumatic bliss.
> T. S. Eliot (1888-1965)

Dramatic art in her opinion is knowing how to fill a sweater.
> Bette Davis (b. 1908)
> *of Jayne Mansfield*

There are two good reasons why men go to see her. Those are enough.
Howard Hughes (1905-1976)
of Jane Russell

SEE Dr Gregory on DRESS; Dickens on LADIES

Lord Byron

Lord Byron is only great as a poet; as soon as he reflects, he is a child.
Johann Wolfgang von Goethe (1749-1832)

The temptation, never easily resisted by him, of displaying his wit at the expense of his character.
Thomas Moore (1779-1852)
Irish poet

Mad, bad, and dangerous to know.
Lady Caroline Lamb (1785-1828)

society figure, lover of Byron
entry in journal following their first meeting

In his endeavours to corrupt my mind he has sought to make me smile first at Vice, saying 'There is nothing to which a woman may not be reconciled by repetition or familiarity'. There is *no* Vice with which he has not endeavoured in this manner to familiarize me.
Annabella Milbanke, Lady Byron (1792-1860)

I have not loved the world, nor the
world me;
I have not flatter'd its rank breath,
nor bow'd
To its idolatries a patient knee.
Lord Byron (1788-1824)

SEE Byron on ENGLAND

Capital Punishment

It is sweet to dance to violins
   When love and life are fair:
To dance to flutes, to dance to lutes
   Is delicate and rare;
But it is not so sweet with nimble feet
   To dance upon the air.
                    Oscar Wilde (1854-1900)

I went out to Charing Cross to see Major-General Harrison hanged, drawn and quartered; which was done there, he looking as cheerful as any man could do in that condition.
                    Samuel Pepys (1633-1703)

If the Court sentences the blighter to hang, then the blighter will hang.
                    General Zia ul-Haq (b. 1924)
                    of the death sentence imposed
                    on former President of
                    Pakistan Zulfiqar Ali Bhutto,
                    1979

The highest and ultimate instrument of political power is capital punishment.
                    Philip Melanchthon (1497-1560)
                    German scholar, humanist

If we are to abolish the death penalty, I should like to see the first step taken by my friends the murderers.
                    Alphonse Karr (1808-1890)
                    French journalist, novelist

Many a good hanging prevents a bad marriage.
                    Feste, *Twelfth Night*
                    William Shakespeare (1564-1616)

SEE Pope on PUNISHMENT; TRIALS

Capitalism

We are too mealy-mouthed. We fear the word 'capitalism' is unpopular. So we talk about the 'free enterprise' system and run to cover in the folds of the flag and talk about the American way of life.
                    Eric A. Johnston (1896-1963)
                    American entrepreneur

It is a socialist idea that making profits is a vice; I consider the real vice is making losses.
                    Sir Winston Churchill (1874-1965)

The decadent international but individualistic capitalism in the hands of which we found ourselves after the war is not a success. It is not intelligent. It is not beautiful. It is not just. It is not virtuous. And it doesn't deliver the goods.
                    John Maynard Keynes (1883-1946)
                    in 1933

The forces in a capitalist society, if left unchecked, tend to make the rich richer and the poor poorer.
                    Jawaharlal Nehru (1889-1964)

Capitalists are no more capable of self-sacrifice than a man is capable of lifting himself up by his bootstraps.
                    Vladimir Ilyich Lenin (1870-1924)

Capitalism inevitably and by virtue of the very logic of its civilisation creates, educates and subsidises a vested interest in social unrest.
                    J. A. Schumpeter (1883-1950)
                    American economist,
                    sociologist

Advocates of capitalism are very apt to appeal to the sacred principles of liberty, which are embodied in one maxim: *The fortunate must not be restrained in the exercise of tyranny over the unfortunate.*
                    Bertrand Russell (1872-1970)

History suggests that capitalism is a necessary condition for political freedom. Clearly it is not a sufficient condition.
                    Milton Friedman (b. 1912)

SEE Galbraith on ECONOMICS;
Sinclair on FASCISM; Keynes on
INFLATION; Mencken on SOCIALISM

Cards

I am sorry I have not learned to play at cards. It is very useful in life: it generates kindness and consolidates society.
                    Dr Samuel Johnson (1709-1784)

It is very wonderful to see persons of the best sense passing away a dozen hours together in shuffling and dividing a pack of cards, with no other conversation but what is made up of a few game phrases, and no other ideas but those of black or red spots ranged together in different figures.

Joseph Addison (1672-1719)
English essayist

A man's idea in a card game is war – cool, devastating and pitiless. A lady's idea of it is a combination of larceny, embezzlement and burglary.

Finley Peter Dunne (1867-1936)
American journalist, humorist

SEE Birkenhead on SWINDLES

Careers

The best careers advice to give to the young is 'Find out what you like doing best and get someone to pay you for doing it'.

Katharine Whitehorn
British journalist

Be nice to people on your way up because you'll meet them on your way down.

Wilson Mizner (1876-1933)
American dramatist, wit

His was the sort of career that made the Recording Angel think seriously about taking up shorthand.

Nicolas Bentley (1908-1978)
British artist, author, publisher

I have found some of the best reasons I ever had for remaining at the bottom simply by looking at the men at the top.

F. M. Colby (1865-1925)
American editor, essayist

SEE Emerson on WORK

Caricature

Caricature is the tribute that mediocrity pays to genius.

Oscar Wilde (1854-1900)

Cars

No other man-made device since the shields and lances of the ancient knights fulfils a man's ego like an automobile.

Sir William (later Lord) Rootes (1894-1964)
British motor car manufacturer

A noisy exhaust almost amounts to a mating call.

J. A. Leavy (b. 1915)
British businessman, Conservative politician

There is no class of person more moved by hate than the motorist.

C. R. Hewitt (C. H. Rolfe) (b. 1901)
British author, journalist

I think that cars today are almost the exact equivalent of the great Gothic cathedrals: I mean the supreme creation of an era, conceived with passion by unknown artists, and consumed in image if not in usage by a whole population which appropriates them as a purely magical object.

Roland Barthes (1915-1980)
French academic

I don't even like *old* cars . . . I'd rather have a goddam horse. A horse is at least *human*, for God's sake.

J. D. Salinger (b. 1919)

SEE White on WOMEN

Catholicism

A little skill in antiquity inclines a man to Popery.

Thomas Fuller (1608-1661)
English cleric

She [the Catholic Church] thoroughly understands what no other Church has ever understood, how to deal with enthusiasts.

Lord Macaulay (1800-1859)
English historian

Good, strong, thick, stupefying incense-smoke.

Robert Browning (1812-1889)

Here is everything which can lay hold of the eye, ear and imagination – everything which can charm and bewitch the simple and ignorant. I wonder how Luther ever broke the spell.

John Adams (1735-1826)
American statesman, president

The Pope is barely Catholic enough for some converts.

John Ayscough (1858-1928)
British priest, novelist, essayist

The priest is always fascinating to an adulterous generation because they think he knows more ways of committing adultery than anybody else. It's logical. He deals in sin as much as a dustman deals in garbage.

Aubrey Menen (b. 1912)
British novelist, essayist

I don't like your way of conditioning and contracting with the saints. Do this and I'll do that! Here's one for t'other. Save me and I'll give you a taper or go on a pilgrimage.

Erasmus (1466-1536)

Outside of the Catholic church everything may be had except salvation.

Saint Augustine (354-430)

All human life is here, but the Holy Ghost seems to be somewhere else.

Anthony Burgess (b. 1917)
British author
of the Vatican

You can't run the Church on Hail Marys.

Archbishop Paul Marcinkus (b. 1922)
American ecclesiastic, Vatican financier

SEE Steele on The CHURCH OF ENGLAND; Gide on FAITH; The POPE

Caution

Set the foot down with distrust on the crust of
the world – it is thin.
Edna St Vincent Millay (1892-1950)
American poet

In skating over thin ice, our safety is in our
speed.
R. W. Emerson (1803-1882)
American essayist, poet, philosopher

Now, gentlemen, we have got our harpoon
into the monster, but we must still take
uncommon care, or else by a single flop of his
tail he will send us all to eternity.
Abraham Lincoln (1809-1865)

If we shake hands with icy fingers it is because
we have burnt them so horribly before.
Logan Pearsall Smith (1865-1946)
American essayist

An appearance of carelessness is vital in true
caution.
R. H. Benson (1871-1914)
British novelist

Put all thine eggs in one basket and – watch
that basket.
Mark Twain (1835-1910)

He that leaveth nothing to chance will do few
things ill, but he will do very few things.
George Savile, Lord Halifax (1633-1695)
English statesman, author

Caution has its place, no doubt, but we cannot
refuse our support to a serious venture which
challenges the whole of the personality. If we
oppose it, we are trying to suppress what is
best in man – his daring and his aspirations.
And should we succeed, we should only have
stood in the way of that invaluable experience
which might have given a meaning to life.
What would have happened if Paul had
allowed himself to be talked out of his journey
to Damascus?
Carl Jung (1875-1961)

Of all the thirty-six alternatives, running away
is best.
Chinese proverb

SEE Syrus on ECONOMISING

Censorship

Art made tongue-tied by authority.
William Shakespeare (1564-1616)

Those expressions are omitted which can not
with propriety be read aloud in the family.
Dr Thomas Bowdler (1754-1825)
English editor, expurgator

Fear of corrupting the mind of the younger
generation is the loftiest form of cowardice.
Holbrook Jackson (1874-1948)
British writer

I know of no book which has been a source of
brutality and sadistic conduct, both public and
private, that can compare with the Bible.
Reginald Paget (b. 1908)
British Labour politician

Who kills a man kills a reasonable creature,
God's image; but he who destroys a good
book, kills reason itself, kills the image of
God, as it were in the eye.
John Milton (1608-1674)

Censorship is like an appendix. When inert, it
is useless; when active it is extremely
dangerous.
Maurice Edelman (1911-1975)
British Labour politician

Censorship is the commonest social blasphemy
because it is mostly concealed, built into us by
indolence, self-interest, and cowardice.
John Osborne (b. 1929)
British playwright

Did you ever hear anyone say 'That work had
better be banned because I might read it and it
might be very damaging to me'?
Joseph Henry Jackson (1894-1955)
American critic, travel-writer

Every burned book enlightens the world.
R. W. Emerson (1803-1882)
American essayist, poet, philosopher

If we can't stamp out literature in the country,
we can at least stop it being brought in from
outside.
Evelyn Waugh (1903-1966)

I am confident, of course, knowing that I shall
fulfil my tasks as a writer in any circumstances, and from my grave even more success-
fully and incontestably than when I live. No
one can bar truth's course, and for its progress
I am prepared to accept even death. But
perhaps repeated lessons will teach us, at least,
not to arrest a writer's pen during his lifetime.
Alexander Solzhenitsyn (b. 1918)

They who have put out the people's eyes
reproach them of their blindness.
John Milton (1608-1674)

The artist and the censor differ in this wise:
that the first is a decent mind in an indecent
body and that the second is an indecent mind
in a decent body.
George Jean Nathan (1882-1958)
American critic

He who discommendeth others obliquely
commendeth himself.
Sir Thomas Browne (1605-1682)
English doctor, author

They can't censor the gleam in my eye.
Charles Laughton (1899-1962)
British actor

I believe in censorship. After all, I made a fortune out of it.
Mae West (1892-1980)

This film is apparently meaningless, but if it has any meaning it is doubtless objectionable.
British Board of Film Censors
banning Cocteau's The Seashell and the Clergyman, 1956

SEE Hellman on FASHION

Ceremony

Ceremony is the smoke of friendship.
Chinese proverb

Some people think that whatever is done solemnly must make sense.
G. C. Lichtenberg (1742-1799)
German physicist, writer

It is superstition to put one's hopes in formalities; but it is pride to be unwilling to submit to them.
Blaise Pascal (1623-1662)

SEE Waugh on AMERICA

Certainty

The fundamental cause of trouble in the world today is that the stupid are cocksure while the intelligent are full of doubt.
Bertrand Russell (1872-1970)

The best lack all conviction, while the worst
Are full of passionate intensity.
W. B. Yeats (1865-1939)

Ah, what a dusty answer gets the soul
When hot for certainties in this our life!
George Meredith (1828-1909)
English author

We are not certain, we are never certain. If we were we could reach some conclusions, and we could, at last, make others take us seriously.
Albert Camus (1913-1960)

If a man will begin with certainties, he shall end in doubts, but if he will be content to begin with doubts, he shall end in certainties.
Francis Bacon (1561-1626)

I am certain of nothing but the holiness of the heart's affections, and the truth of imagination.
John Keats (1795-1821)

In this world nothing is certain but death and taxes.
Benjamin Franklin (1706-1790)

The only certainty is that nothing is certain.
Pliny the Elder (c. 23-79)
Roman scholar

It is the dull man who is always sure, and the sure man who is always dull.
H. L. Mencken (1880-1956)
American journalist

SEE Junius on BELIEF; Mencken on The PUBLIC; Melbourne on SELF-CONFIDENCE

Change

Let the great world spin for ever down the ringing grooves of change.
Lord Tennyson (1809-1892)

When our first parents were driven out of Paradise, Adam is believed to have remarked to Eve: 'My dear, we live in an age of transition'.
W. R. Inge (1860-1954)
Dean of St Paul's London

Sempre una mutazione lascia addentellato per la edificazione dell'altra.
One change leaves the way open for the introduction of others.
Niccolò Machiavelli (1469-1527)

For good and evil, man is a free creative spirit. This produces the very queer world we live in, a world in continuous creation and therefore continuous change and insecurity.
Joyce Cary (1888-1957)
British author

Progress is impossible without change; and those who cannot change their minds cannot change anything.
George Bernard Shaw (1856-1950)

Change is not made without inconvenience, even from worse to better.
Richard Hooker (1554-1600)
English theologian

There is a certain relief in change, even though it be from bad to worse; as I have found in travelling in a stage-coach, that it is often a comfort to shift one's position and be bruised in a new place.
Washington Irving (1783-1859)
American author

A living thing is distinguished from a dead thing by the multiplicity of the changes at any moment taking place in it.
Herbert Spencer (1820-1903)
English philosopher

All things change, nothing is extinguished.
Ovid (43 BC-AD 17)

SEE Falkland on CONSERVATIVES

Chaos

There is nothing stable in the world; uproar's your only music.
John Keats (1795-1821)

Chaos often breeds life, when order breeds habit.
Henry B. Adams (1838-1918)
American historian

Confusion is a word we have invented for an order which is not understood.
Henry Miller (1891-1980)

In all chaos there is a cosmos, in all disorder a secret order.
Carl Jung (1875-1961)

SEE Pope on WAR

Character

Before you advise anyone 'Be yourself!' re-assess his character.
anonymous, 20th century

Character is what you are in the dark.
Dwight Moody (1837-1899)
American evangelist

Every man has three characters: that which he shows, that which he has, and that which he thinks he has.
Alphonse Karr (1808-1890)
French journalist, novelist

Men will often say that they have 'found themselves' when they have really been worn down into a groove by the brutal and compulsive force of circumstance.
Thomas Wolfe (1900-1938)
American author

Es bildet ein Talent sich in der Stille,
Sich ein Charakter in dem Strom der Welt.
Talent develops in tranquillity, character in the full current of human life.
Johann Wolfgang von Goethe (1749-1832)

The measure of a man's real character is what he would do if he knew he would never be found out.
Lord Macaulay (1800-1859)
English historian

Character – the willingness to accept responsibility for one's own life – is the source from which self-respect springs.
Joan Didion (b. 1934)
American writer

We must have a weak spot or two in a character before we can love it much.
Dr Oliver Wendell Holmes (1809-1894)
American writer, physician

In me the tiger sniffs the rose.
Siegfried Sassoon (1886-1967)
British poet

The hardest thing is writing a recommendation for someone we know.
Kin (F. McKinney) Hubbard (1868-1930)
American humorist, journalist

People always say that they are not themselves when tempted by anger into betraying what they really are.
Ed (E. W.) Howe (1853-1937)
American journalist, novelist

You can tell a lot about a fellow's character by the way he eats jelly beans.
Ronald Reagan (b. 1911)

SEE Hubbard, Paine on REPUTATION; Emerson on SOCIETY; Stendhal on SOLITUDE

Charity

In necessary things, unity; in disputed things, liberty; in all things, charity.
variously ascribed

I did give ten shillings and no more, though I believe most of the rest did give more, and did believe that I did so too.
Samuel Pepys (1633-1703)

God loveth a cheerful giver.
Saint Paul (3-67)

The most difficult part is to give. Then why not add a smile?
Jean de la Bruyère (1645-1696)
French writer, moralist

Beggars should be abolished. It annoys one to give to them, and it annoys one not to give to them.
Friedrich Nietzsche (1844-1900)

A man who sees another man on the street corner with only a stump for an arm will be so shocked the first time he'll give him sixpence. But the second time it'll only be a threepenny bit. And if he sees him a third time, he'll have him cold-bloodedly handed over to the police.
The Threepenny Opera
Bertolt Brecht (1898-1956)
trans. Desmond I. Vesey
and Eric Bentley

We do not quite forgive a giver. The hand that feeds us is in some danger of being bitten.
R. W. Emerson (1803-1882)
American essayist, poet, philosopher

In your Salvation shelter I saw poverty, misery, cold, and hunger. You gave them bread and treacle and dreams of heaven. I give from thirty shillings a week to twelve thousand a year. They find their own dreams; but I look after the drainage.
Undershaft, *Major Barbara*
George Bernard Shaw (1856-1950)

The biggest disease today is not leprosy or tuberculosis, but rather the feeling of being unwanted.
Mother Teresa (b. 1911)

The cliché 'charity begins at home' has done more damage than any other in the English tongue.

Bishop Trevor Huddleston (b. 1913)
British clergyman, campaigner

The organised charity, scrimped and iced,
In the name of a cautious, statistical
Christ.

John Boyle O'Reilly (1844-1890)
Irish author

Charity is the sterilized milk of human kindness.

Oliver Herford (1863-1935)
American poet, illustrator

Charity is injurious unless it helps the recipient to become independent of it.

John D. Rockefeller (1839-1937)
American industrialist, philanthropist

Charity creates a multitude of sins.

Oscar Wilde (1854-1900)

If begging should unfortunately be thy lot, knock at the large gates only.

Arabian proverb

He that feeds upon charity has a cold dinner and no supper.

Thomas Fuller (1608-1661)
English cleric

SEE AID; Blake on ALTRUISM; Confucius
on BENEFACTORS;
Thatcher on INTENTIONS;
Pollok on LANDLORDS

Charm

'Charm' – which means the power to effect work without employing brute force – is indispensable to women. Charm is a woman's strength just as strength is a man's charm.

Havelock Ellis (1859-1939)
British psychologist, author

It's a sort of bloom on a woman. If you have it, you don't need to have anything else; and if you don't have it, it doesn't much matter what else you have.

J. M. Barrie (1860-1937)
British playwright

Charming women can true converts
make.
We love the precepts for the
teacher's sake.

George Farquhar (1678-1707)
Irish dramatist

She lacks the indefinable charm of weakness.

Oscar Wilde (1854-1900)

Men get to be a mixture of the charming mannerisms of the women they have known.

F. Scott Fitzgerald (1896-1940)

You know what charm is: a way of getting the

answer yes without having asked any clear question.

Albert Camus (1913-1960)

I am bewitched with the rogue's company: if the rascal have not given me medicines to make me love him, I'll be hanged.

Falstaff, *King Henry IV part I*
William Shakespeare (1564-1616)

All charming people, I fancy, are spoiled. It is the secret of their attraction.

Oscar Wilde (1854-1900)

SEE Barrie on The SCOTS

Chastity

Of all sexual aberrations, perhaps the most peculiar is chastity.

Rémy de Gourmont (1858-1915)
French critic, novelist

A woman's chastity consists, like an onion, of a series of coats.

Nathaniel Hawthorne (1804-1864)
American novelist

How happy is the blameless vestal's
lot!
The world forgetting, by the world
forgot.

Alexander Pope (1688-1744)

There are few virtuous women who are not bored with their trade.

François, Duc de La Rochefoucauld (1613-1680)
French writer, moralist

These, it is true, are abstinent; but from all that they do the bitch of sensuality looks out with envious eyes.

Friedrich Nietzsche (1844-1900)

Your old virginity is like one of our French withered pears; it looks ill, it eats drily.

Parolles, *All's Well That Ends Well*
William Shakespeare (1564-1616)

An unattempted woman cannot boast of her chastity.

Michel de Montaigne (1533-1592)
French essayist

It is fatally easy for Western folk, who have discarded chastity as a value for themselves, to suppose that it can have no value for anyone else. At the same time as Californians try to re-invent 'celibacy', by which they seem to mean perverse restraint, the rest of us call societies which place a high value on chastity 'backward'.

Germaine Greer (b. 1939)
Australian feminist writer

Only the English and the Americans are improper. East of Suez everyone wants a virgin.

Barbara Cartland (b. 1901)
British author

A chaste woman ought not to dye her hair yellow.
> Menander (c. 342-c. 291 BC)
> Greek playwright

SEE Shaw on LUST

Chess

The chess-board is the world; the pieces are the phenomena of the universe; the rules of the game are what we call the laws of Nature. The player on the other side is hidden from us. We know that his play is always fair, just, and patient. But also we know, to our cost, that he never overlooks a mistake, or makes the smallest allowance for ignorance.
> T. H. Huxley (1825-1895)
> English biologist

I am still a victim of chess. It has all the beauty of art – and much more. It cannot be commercialized. Chess is much purer than art in its social position.
> Marcel Duchamp (1887-1968)
> French artist, Dadaist
> *recalling his decision in the*
> *1920s to give up art for*
> *chess*

Life's too short for chess.
> Henry J. Byron (1834-1884)
> English dramatist

Childhood

That great cathedral space which was childhood.
> Virginia Woolf (1882-1941)

What is childhood but a series of happy delusions.
> Sydney Smith (1771-1845)
> English writer, clergyman

All our adventures were by the fireside, and all our migrations from the blue bed to the brown.
> Oliver Goldsmith (1728-1774)

Heaven lies about us in our infancy!
> William Wordsworth (1770-1850)

The world begins lying about us pretty soon afterward.
> Ambrose Bierce (1842-1914)
> American author

Children

Youth is a wonderful thing; what a crime to waste it on children.
> George Bernard Shaw (1856-1950)

Alas, regardless of their doom,
The little victims play!
No sense have they of ills to come,
Nor care beyond to-day.
> Thomas Gray (1716-1771)

When childhood dies, its corpses are called adults and they enter society, one of the politer names of hell. That is why we dread children, even if we love them. They show us the state of our decay.
> Brian Aldiss (b. 1925)
> British author

If children grew up according to early indications, we should have nothing but geniuses.
> Johann Wolfgang von Goethe (1749-1832)

Don't take up a man's time talking about the smartness of your children; he wants to talk to you about the smartness of his.
> Ed (E. W.) Howe (1853-1937)
> American journalist, novelist

There is little use to talk about your child to anyone; other people either have one or haven't.
> Don Herold (b. 1889)
> American humorous writer, artist

The parent who could see his boy as he really is would shake his head and say; 'Willy is no good: I'll sell him'.
> Stephen Leacock (1869-1944)
> Canadian humorist and economist

There is no sinner like a young saint.
> Aphra Behn (1640-1689)
> English playwright, poet

We have left undone those things which we ought to have done; and we have done those things which we ought not to have done.
> Book of Common Prayer

Before I got married I had six theories about bringing up children; now I have six children, and no theories.
> John Wilmot, Earl of Rochester (1647-1680)
> English poet

To bring up a child in the way he should go, travel that way yourself once in a while.
> Josh Billings (1818-1885)
> American humorist

Telling lies and showing off to get attention are the mistakes I made that I don't want my kids to make.
> Jane Fonda (b. 1937)

Men are generally more careful of the breed of their horses and dogs than of their children.
> William Penn (1644-1718)
> religious leader, founder of Pennsylvania

Children are all foreigners. We treat them as such.
> R. W. Emerson (1803-1882)
> American essayist, poet, philosopher

Oh, grown-ups cannot understand,
And grown-ups never will,
How short the way to fairyland
Across the purple hill.
> Alfred Noyes (1880-1958)
> British author

Ignorance is a painless evil; so, I should think, is dirt, considering the merry faces that go along with it.
George Eliot (1819-1880)

Girls like to be played with, and rumpled a little, too, sometimes.
Oliver Goldsmith (1728-1774)

The child had every toy his father wanted.
Robert E. Whitten

What money is better bestowed than that of a schoolboy's tip?
W. M. Thackeray (1811-1863)
English author

There is nothing so aggravating as a fresh boy who is too old to ignore and too young to kick.
Kin (Frank McKinney) Hubbard (1868-1930)
American humorist, journalist

He followed in his father's footsteps, but his gait was somewhat erratic.
Nicolas Bentley (1907-1978)
British artist, author, publisher

Children suck the mother when they are young and the father when they are old.
English proverb

How sharper than a serpent's tooth
it is
To have a thankless child.
Lear, *King Lear*
William Shakespeare (1564-1616)

There are three degrees of filial piety. The highest is being a credit to our parents, the second is not disgracing them; the lowest is being able simply to support them.
Confucius (551-478 BC)

I am assured by a very knowing American of my acquaintance in London, that a young healthy child well nursed is at a year old a most delicious, nourishing, and wholesome food, whether stewed, roasted, baked, or boiled; and I make no doubt that it will equally serve in a fricassee, or a ragout.
Jonathan Swift (1667-1745)

SEE Coleridge on DANCING; Montessori on EDUCATION; Hemingway, Russell on FATHER; Steinem on GOD; Szasz on HAPPINESS; Saki on KNOWLEDGE; Szasz on MATURITY; Browne, Emerson, Shaw, Wilde on PARENTS

Chivalry

I thought that ten thousand swords would have leaped from their scabbards to avenge even a look that threatened her with insult. But the age of chivalry is gone. That of sophisters, economists, and calculators has succeeded.
Edmund Burke (1729-1797)
Irish philosopher, statesman
of Marie Antoinette

The age of chivalry is never past, so long as there is a wrong left unredressed on earth.
Charles Kingsley (1819-1875)
English author, clergyman

SEE Disraeli on BORES

Christianity

Who is the father of the Babe, fair maid? No, no, thou needst not answer; an Angel came to thee in a dream; it is enough, say no more. To thee and thy love child bring gifts of gold and frankincense and myrrh, to thee and thy Babe we bend the knee.
Elbert Hubbard (1856-1915)
American author

He was the Word, that spake it;
He took the bread and brake it;
And what that Word did make it,
I do believe and take it.
John Donne (c. 1571-1631)

The whole religious complexion of the modern world is due to the absence from Jerusalem of a lunatic asylum.
Havelock Ellis (1859-1939)
British psychologist

The idea of Christ is much older than Christianity.
George Santayana (1863-1952)
American philosopher, poet

What if men take to following where
He leads,
Weary of mumbling Athanasian
creeds?
Roden Noël (1834-1894)
English poet

Christianity taught men that love is worth more than intelligence.
Jacques Maritain (1882-1973)
French philosopher

The doctrine of the Kingdom of Heaven, which was the main teaching of Jesus, is certainly one of the most revolutionary doctrines that ever stirred and changed human thought.
H. G. Wells (1866-1946)

No sooner had Jesus knocked over the dragon of superstition than Paul boldly set it on its legs again in the name of Jesus.
George Bernard Shaw (1856-1950)

He who begins by loving Christianity better than Truth will proceed by loving his own sect or church better than Christianity, and end in loving himself better than all.
S. T. Coleridge (1772-1834)

Christian: One who believes that the New Testament is a divinely inspired book admirably suited to the spiritual needs of his neighbour.

Ambrose Bierce (1842-1914)
American author

To make one a complete Christian he must have the works of a Papist, the words of a Puritan, and the faith of a Protestant.

James Howell (1594-1666)
English diplomat, writer

Scratch the Christian and you find the pagan – spoiled.

Israel Zangwill (1864-1926)
British writer

The early Christian rules of life were not made to last, because the early Christians did not believe that the world itself was going to last.

Hotchkiss, *Getting Married*
George Bernard Shaw (1856-1950)

Most people believe that the Christian commandments are intentionally a little too severe – like setting a clock half an hour ahead to make sure of not being late in the morning.

Sören Kierkegaard (1813-1855)
Danish philosopher

The Eleventh Commandment: Thou shalt not be found out.

George Whyte-Melville (1821-1878)
Scottish author

The Christian ideal has not been tried and found wanting. It has been found difficult; and left untried.

G. K. Chesterton (1874-1936)

Bear the Cross cheerfully and it will bear you.

Thomas à Kempis (1380-1471)

'One loving soul', says St Augustine, 'sets another on fire'. Christianity can sometimes be caught no less than taught.

Arnold Lunn (1888-1974)
British author

I reject Christianity because it is Jewish, because it is international and because, in cowardly fashion, it preaches Peace on Earth.

Field-Marshal Erich Ludendorff (1865-1937)
German chief-of-staff

Christianity broke the heart of the world and mended it.

G. K. Chesterton (1874-1936)

Two great European narcotics, alcohol and Christianity.

Friedrich Nietzsche (1844-1900)

The fear of hell, or aiming to be blest,
Savours too much of private interest.

Edmund Waller (1606-1687)
English poet

Christianity is the world's monumental fraud if there be no future life.

Martin J. Scott (1865-1954)

The Three in One, the One in Three?
Not so!
To my own Gods I go.
It may be they shall give me greater ease
Than your cold Christ and tangled Trinities.

Rudyard Kipling (1865-1936)

People in general are equally horrified at hearing the Christian religion doubted, and at seeing it practised.

Samuel Butler (1835-1902)
English author

Kill them all, God will know his own!

Arnold of Citeaux
Papal Legate at the siege of Béziers, 1209, in the Albigensian Crusade

The world is my crucifix.

motto of the Carthusian Order

The cross has been carried forward on the hilt of the sword.

E. M. Macdonald (1865-1940)
Canadian statesman

Thou has conquered, O pale Galilean.

A. C. Swinburne (1837-1909)

SEE CATHOLICISM; The CHURCH; Ouida on DEATH; GOD; Shaw on The JEWS; Farquhar, Tertullian on SECTS

Christmas

There are some people who want to throw their arms round you simply because it is Christmas; there are other people who want to strangle you simply because it is Christmas.

Robert Lynd (1879-1949)
Anglo-Irish essayist, journalist

The Church

He cannot have God for his father who refuses to have the church for his mother.

Saint Augustine (354-430)

And of all plagues with which mankind are curst,
Ecclesiastic tyranny's the worst.

Daniel Defoe (1659-1731)

I grant you the clergy are mostly dull dogs; but with a little disguise and ritual they will pass as holy men with the ignorant.

Charles, *In Good King Charles's Golden Days*
George Bernard Shaw (1856-1950)

A Curate – there is something which excites compassion in the very name of a curate!

Sydney Smith (1771-1845)
English clergyman, writer

A congregation who can't afford to pay a clergyman enough want a missionary more than they do a clergyman.
Josh Billings (1818-1885)
American humorist

How can a bishop marry? How can he flirt? The most he can say is 'I will see you in the vestry after service'.
Sydney Smith (1771-1845)
English writer, clergyman

Archbishop: a Christian ecclesiastic of a rank superior to that attained by Christ.
H. L. Mencken (1880-1956)
American journalist

There is not in the universe a more ridiculous nor a more contemptible animal than a proud clergyman.
Henry Fielding (1707-1754)

The parson knows enough who knows a Duke.
William Cowper (1731-1800)
English poet

That clergyman soon becomes an object of contempt who being often asked out to dinner never refuses to go.
Saint Jerome (345-420)

The merriment of parsons is mighty offensive.
Dr Samuel Johnson (1709-1784)

His creed no parson ever knew,
    For this was still his 'simple plan',
To have with clergymen to do
As little as a Christian can.
Sir Francis Doyle (1810-1888)
English poet

As my poor father used to say,
When parsons came to call,
'He's not my sort, but pass the port,
– Thank God, there's room for all.'
A. P. Herbert (1890-1971)
British author, politician

Parsons always seem to be specially horrified about things like sunbathing and naked bodies. They don't mind poverty and misery and cruelty to animals nearly as much.
Susan Ertz (1894-1985)
British novelist

While I cannot be regarded as a pillar, I must be regarded as a buttress of the church, because I support it from the outside.
Lord Melbourne (1779-1848)
English statesman, Prime Minister

The Church has always been willing to swap off treasures in heaven for cash down.
R. G. Ingersoll (1833-1899)
American lawyer

Avoid like the plague a clergyman who is also a businessman.
Saint Jerome (345-420)

A little, round, fat, oily man of God.
James Thomson (1700-1748)
Scottish poet

If Jesus had wanted to make a woman an Apostle He could have done so.
Pamphlet against the
ordination of women to the
priesthood, 1985

There is neither male nor female; for ye are all one in Christ Jesus.
Saint Paul (3-67)

As the French say, there are three sexes – men, women and clergymen.
Sydney Smith (1771-1845)
English clergyman, writer

The Church has an almost pathological preoccupation with survival.
John Robinson (b. 1919)
Bishop of Woolwich

What is wrong with priests and popes is that instead of being apostles and saints, they are nothing but empirics who say 'I know' instead of 'I am learning', and pray for credulity and inertia as wise men pray for scepticism and activity.
George Bernard Shaw (1856-1950)

The Church after all is not a club of saints; it is a hospital for sinners.
George Craig Stewart (1879-1940)
Bishop of Chicago

SEE CATHOLICISM; CHRISTIANITY; The CHURCH OF ENGLAND; Chesterton on HERESY; Baudelaire on MARRIAGE; Sheen on POVERTY

Church of England

Alas the Church of England! What with Popery on one hand, and schismatics on the other, how has she been crucified between two thieves!
Daniel Defoe (1659-1731)

This is what the Church is said to want, not party men, but sensible, temperate, sober, well-judging persons, to guide it through the channel of no-meaning, between the Scylla and Charybdis of Aye and No.
Cardinal John Newman (1801-1890)
English churchman, theologian

Place before your eyes two precepts, and only two. One is Preach the Gospel; and the other is – Put down enthusiasm . . . The Church of England in a nutshell.
Mrs Humphrey Ward (1851-1920)
British novelist

The merit claimed for the Anglican Church is, that if you let it alone, it will let you alone.
R. W. Emerson (1803-1882)
American essayist, poet, philosopher

There is this difference between the Church of Rome and the Church of England: the one professes to be infallible – the other to be never in the wrong.

> Sir Richard Steele (1672-1729)
> English dramatist, essayist, editor

I have, alas, only one illusion left, and that is the Archbishop of Canterbury.

> Sydney Smith (1771-1845)
> English writer, clergyman

I must believe in the Apostolic Succession, there being no other way of accounting for the descent of the Bishop of Exeter from Judas Iscariot.

> Sydney Smith (1771-1845)
> English writer, clergyman

The Church of England seems to wish us to regard birth as the entry to sin, marriage as a means of avoiding one aspect of sin, and death to be the welcome relief whereby we can sin no more.

> Sir Steuart Wilson (1889-1966)
> British administrator, musician

A soul cannot be eternally satisfied with kindness, and a soothing murmur, and the singing of hymns.

> R. H. Benson (1871-1914)
> British novelist (and Catholic apologist)

To tolerate everything is to teach nothing.

> Dr F. J. Kinsman (1868-1944)
> American clergyman

I do hereby profess ... that Protestantism is the dreariest of possible religions; that the thought of the Anglican service makes me shiver, and the thought of the Thirty-Nine Articles makes me shudder.

> Cardinal John Newman (1801-1890)
> English churchman, theologian

Church-going

America has become so tense and nervous it has been years since I've seen anyone asleep in church – and that is a sad situation.

> Dr Norman Peale (b. 1898)
> President of the Protestant Council, New York

Light half-believers of our casual creeds.

> Matthew Arnold (1822-1888)
> English poet, critic

Too hot to go to Church? What about Hell?

> *poster in Dayton, Ohio*

She say, Celie, tell the truth, have you ever found God in church? I never did. I just found a bunch of folks hoping for him to show. Any God I ever felt in church I brought in with me. And I think all the other folks did too. They come to church to *share* God, not find God.

> Alice Walker (b. 1944)
> American author, critic

SEE Shaw on PREACHING

Churches

A church is a place in which gentlemen who have never been to heaven brag about it to persons who will never get there.

> H. L. Mencken (1880-1956)
> American journalist

I never weary of great churches. It is my favourite kind of mountain scenery. Mankind was never so happily inspired as when it made a cathedral.

> Robert Louis Stevenson (1850-1894)

Cathedrals, luxury liners laden with souls,
Holding to the east their hulls of stone.

> W. H. Auden (1907-1973)

When churchyards are consecrated I find it awfully difficult to imagine that the Holy Spirit is operating only along the dotted line on the part of the plan coloured pink.

> Canon R. L. Hussey (b. 1899)
> British clergyman

The beautiful uncut hair of graves.

> Walt Whitman (1819-1892)

Cinema

The cinema is not a slice of life but a piece of cake.

> Alfred Hitchcock (1899-1980)

The cinema, like the detective story, makes it possible to experience without danger all the excitement, passion and desirousness which must be repressed in a humanitarian ordering of life.

> Carl Jung (1875-1961)

The theatre is like a faithful wife. The film is the great adventure – the costly, exacting mistress.

> Ingmar Bergman (b. 1918)
> Swedish film and theatre director

They get excited about the sort of stuff I could get shooting through a piece of kleenex.

> Billy Wilder (b. 1906)
> American writer-director
> *on European cinema*

Film is not the art of scholars but of illiterates. Film culture is not analysis but agitation of the mind.

> Werner Herzog (b. 1942)
> German film director

Movies are so rarely great art that if we cannot appreciate the great *trash* we have very little reason to be interested in them.

> Pauline Kael (b. 1919)
> American critic

The trouble with a movie these days is that it's old before it's released. It's no accident that it comes in a can.

> Orson Welles (1915-1985)

All television ever did was shrink the demand for ordinary movies. The demand for extraordinary movies increased. If any one thing is wrong with the movie industry today, it is the unrelenting effort to astonish.

Clive James (b. 1939)
Australian writer, critic

There's only one thing that can kill the movies, and that's education.

Will Rogers (1879-1935)
American humorist

Film music should have the same relationship to the film drama that somebody's piano playing in my living room has to the book I am reading.

Igor Stravinsky (1882-1971)

A director must be a policeman, a midwife, a psychoanalyst, a sycophant and a bastard.

Billy Wilder (b. 1906)
American writer-director

Saddest movie I've ever seen – I cried all the way through. It's sad when you're eighty-two.

Groucho Marx (1890-1977)
on Last Tango in Paris

SEE HOLLYWOOD

Circumstances

It is nice to make heroic decisions and to be prevented by 'circumstances beyond your control' from ever trying to execute them.

William James (1842-1910)
American psychologist, philosopher

People are always blaming their circumstances for what they are. I don't believe in circumstances. The people who get on in this world are the people who get up and look for the circumstances they want, and, if they can't find them, make them.

Vivie, Mrs Warren's Profession
George Bernard Shaw (1856-1950)

If all our happiness is bound up entirely in our personal circumstances it is difficult not to demand of life more than it has to give.

Bertrand Russell (1872-1970)

Circumstances! I make circumstances!

Napoleon Bonaparte (1769-1821)

SEE Osler on PLANNING

City Life

City Life. Millions of people being lonesome together.

H. D. Thoreau (1817-1862)

God the first garden made, and the first city Cain.

Abraham Cowley (1618-1667)
English author

Fields and trees teach me nothing, but the people in a city do.

Socrates (469-399 BC)

If you would be known, and not know, vegetate in a village; if you would know, and not be known, live in a city.

C. C. Colton (1780-1832)
English author

A great city is the place to escape the true drama of provincial life, and find solace in fantasy.

G. K. Chesterton (1874-1936)

As a remedy to life in society I would suggest the big city. Nowadays it is the only desert within our means.

Albert Camus (1913-1960)

Crowds without company, and dissipation without pleasure.

Edward Gibbon (1737-1794)

Omnis civitas corpus est.
Every city is a living body.

Saint Augustine (354-430)

A large city cannot be experientially known; its life is too manifold for any individual to be able to participate in it.

Aldous Huxley (1894-1963)

They who have spent all their lives in cities improve their talents but impair their virtues; and strengthen their minds but weaken their morals.

C. C. Colton (1780-1832)
English author

Poiché voi, cittadine infauste mura,
Vidi e conobbi assai, là dove segue
Odio al dolor compagno.
For I have seen and known you too well, black city walls, where pain follows close behind hatred.

Giacomo Leopardi (1798-1837)
Italian poet

The city is not a concrete jungle. It is a human zoo.

Desmond Morris (b. 1928)
British anthropologist

This City now doth like a garment wear
The beauty of the morning; silent, bare,
Ships, towers, domes, theatres and temples lie
Open unto the fields and to the sky;
All bright and glittering in the smokeless air.

William Wordsworth (1770-1850)

No city should be too large for a man to walk out of it in a morning.

Cyril Connolly (1903-1974)
British critic

Cities, like cats, will reveal themselves at night.

Rupert Brooke (1887-1915)
British poet

Prepare for death if here at night you
roam,
And sign your will before you sup
from home.

> Dr Samuel Johnson (1709-1784)

SEE Byron, Shaw on COUNTRY LIFE;
LONDON; NEW YORK

Civilization

The origin of civilization is man's determination to do nothing for himself which he can get done for him.

> H. C. Bailey (1878-1961)
> British crimewriter

Civilization – by which I here mean barbarism made strong and luxurious by mechanical power.

> C. S. Lewis (1898-1963)
> British author

Civilization – a heap of rubble scavenged by scrawny English Lit vultures.

> Malcolm Muggeridge (b. 1903)
> British journalist

All civilization has from time to time become a thin crust over a volcano of revolution.

> Havelock Ellis (1859-1939)
> British psychologist

Civilization is the lamb's skin in which barbarism masquerades.

> T. B. Aldrich (1836-1907)
> American writer, editor

Our civilization is not even skin deep; it reaches no lower than our clothes. Humanity is still essentially Yahoo-manity.

> W. R. Inge (1860-1954)
> Dean of St Paul's, London

Every new generation is a fresh invasion of savages.

> Hervey Allen (1889-1949)
> American educator, poet, author

Is it progress if a cannibal uses knife and fork?

> Stanislaus J. Lec (b. 1909)
> Polish poet

Civilization is a progress from an indefinite, incoherent homogeneity toward a definite, coherent heterogeneity.

> Herbert Spencer (1820-1903)
> English philosopher

Increased means and increased leisure are the two civilizers of man.

> Benjamin Disraeli (1804-1881)

The three great elements of modern civilization, gunpowder, printing, and the Protestant religion.

> Thomas Carlyle (1795-1881)
> Scottish author

The nineteenth century regarded European civilization as mature and late, the final expression of the human spirit. We are only now beginning to realise that it is young and childish.

> C. E. M. Joad (1891-1953)
> British author, academic

Inscribe all human effort with one word,
Artistry's haunting curse, the
Incomplete!

> Robert Browning (1812-1889)

SEE Trevelyan on CURIOSITY; Knox on
The DEVIL; Russell on LEISURE;
Rogers on PROGRESS; Ellis on SUICIDE;
Menen on TOLERANCE; Meredith on
WOMEN: and Men

Class

The history of all hitherto existing society is the history of class struggles.

> Karl Marx (1818-1883) and
> Friedrich Engels (1820-1895)

A society that gives to one class all the opportunities for leisure, and to another all the burdens of work, dooms both classes to spiritual sterility.

> Lewis Mumford (b. 1895)
> American writer on environment

We educate one another; and we cannot do this if half of us consider the other half not good enough to talk to.

> George Bernard Shaw (1856-1950)

There are no persons more solicitous about the preservation of rank than those who have no rank at all.

> William Shenstone (1714-1763)
> English poet

The terrifying characteristic of British society is that many of those who are supposed to be inferior have been brainwashed into believing that they actually are.

> Tony Benn (b. 1925)
> British Labour politician

The most perfect political community is one in which the middle class is in control and outnumbers both of the other classes.

> Aristotle (384-322 BC)

The one class you do not belong to and are not proud of at all is the lower-middle class. No one ever describes himself as belonging to the lower-middle class.

> George Mikes (b. 1912)
> Czech humorist

When we say a woman is of a certain social class, we really mean her husband or father is.

> Zoë Fairbairns (b. 1948)
> British author

The classes that wash most are those that work least.

> G. K. Chesterton (1874-1936)

Ladies and gentlemen are permitted to have friends in the kennel but not in the kitchen.
George Bernard Shaw (1856-1950)

I am his Highness' dog at Kew;
Pray tell me, sir, whose dog are you?
Alexander Pope (1688-1744)

SEE The BOURGEOISIE; INEQUALITY; Herford on LADIES; Chesterfield on LAUGHTER; Chapman on SECRETS; Hammond on SLAVERY; The WORKING CLASS

Clichés
Man is a creature who lives not upon bread alone, but principally by catchwords.
Robert Louis Stevenson (1850-1894)

A good catchword can obscure analysis for fifty years.
Wendell L. Willkie (1892-1944)
American lawyer, businessman, politician

If you have to be in a soap opera try not to get the worst role.
Boy George (b. 1961)

SEE Guedalla on OXFORD

Clubs
This happy breed of men, this little world.
Gaunt, *King Richard II*
William Shakespeare (1564-1616)

Most clubs have the atmosphere of a Duke's house with the Duke lying dead upstairs.
Douglas Sutherland (b. 1919)
British author

I don't care to belong to any social organization which would accept me as a member.
Groucho Marx (1890-1977)

SEE Thoreau on INSTITUTIONS

Cocktail Parties
The cocktail party – as the name itself indicates – was originally invented by dogs. They are simply bottom-sniffings raised to the rank of formal ceremonies.
Lawrence Durrell (b. 1912)
British writer

It was one of those parties where you cough twice before you speak and then decide not to say it after all.
P. G. Wodehouse (1881-1975)
British writer

We are persons of quality, I assure you, and women of fashion, and come to see and to be seen.
Ben Jonson (1573-1637)

Consider yourselves introduced, because I only remember one of your names, and that wouldn't be fair to the other.
Sir Herbert Beerbohm Tree (1853-1917)
British actor-manager

Cocktails
That faint but sensitive enteric expectancy that suggests the desirability of a cocktail.
Christopher Morley (1890-1957)
American novelist, journalist

I must get out of these wet clothes and into a dry Martini.
Alexander Woollcott (1887-1943)
American columnist, critic

Coffee
The morning cup of coffee has an exhilaration about it which the cheering influence of the afternoon or evening cup of tea cannot be expected to reproduce.
Dr Oliver Wendell Holmes (1809-1894)
American writer, physician

Black as hell, strong as death, sweet as love.
Turkish proverb

Coffee in England is just toasted milk.
Christopher Fry (b. 1907)
British playwright

Coffee, which makes the politician wise,
And see through all things with his
half-shut eyes.
Alexander Pope (1688-1744)

Coincidence
It is only in literature that coincidences seem unnatural.
Robert Lynd (1879-1949)
Anglo-Irish essayist, journalist

Although we talk so much about coincidence we do not really believe in it. In our heart of hearts we think better of the universe, we are secretly convinced that it is not such a slipshod, haphazard affair, that everything in it has meaning.
J. B. Priestley (1894-1984)

Colour
Verde que te quiero verde,
Verde viento. Verde ramas.
Green how I love you green.
Green wind. Green branches.
Federico García Lorca (1899-1936)

I've been forty years discovering that the queen of all colours is black.
Auguste Renoir (1841-1919)

Artists can color the sky red because they know it's blue. Those of us who aren't artists must color things the way they really are or people might think we're stupid.
Jules Feiffer (b. 1929)
American cartoonist

Comedy
Life is a tragedy when seen in close-up, but a comedy in long-shot.
Charlie Chaplin (1889-1977)

Chaplin's genius was in comedy. He had no sense of humour.

Lita Grey
Chaplin's ex-wife

This fellow's wise enough to play the fool.

Viola, *Twelfth Night*
William Shakespeare (1564-1616)

The test of a real comedian is whether you laugh at him before he opens his mouth.

George Jean Nathan (1882-1958)
American critic

The first thing any comedian does on getting an unscheduled laugh is to verify the state of his buttons; the second is to look around to see if a cat has walked out on the stage.

W. C. Fields (1879-1946)

Everything is funny as long as it is happening to somebody else.

Will Rogers (1879-1935)
American humorist

Though it makes the unskilful laugh, cannot but make the judicious grieve.

Hamlet, *Hamlet*
William Shakespeare (1564-1616)

The only rules comedy can tolerate are those of taste, and the only limitations those of libel.

James Thurber (1894-1961)
American humorist, illustrator

Comedy is an escape, not from truth but from despair; a narrow escape into faith.

Christopher Fry (b. 1907)
British playwright

I had rather have a fool to make me merry than experience to make me sad.

Rosalind, *As You Like It*
William Shakespeare (1564-1616)

Comedy, like sodomy, is an unnatural act.

Marty Feldman (1933-1982)
British comedian

Committees

The English way is a committee – we are born with a belief in a green cloth, clean pens and twelve men with grey hair.

Walter Bagehot (1826-1877)
English economist, critic

A committee is a *cul de sac* to which ideas are lured and then quietly strangled.

John A. Lincoln

The heaping together of paintings by Old Masters in museums is a catastrophe; likewise, a collection of a hundred Great Brains makes one big fathead.

Carl Jung (1875-1961)

The Commonplace

La generalidad de los hombres nadamos en el océano de la vulgaridad.
Most of us swim in the ocean of the commonplace.

Pio Baroja (1872-1956)
Spanish novelist, essayist

The characteristic of the hour is that the commonplace mind, knowing itself to be commonplace, has the assurance to proclaim the rights of the commonplace and impose them wherever it will.

José Ortega y Gasset (1883-1955)
Spanish essayist, philosopher

Little minds are interested in the extraordinary great minds in the commonplace.

Elbert Hubbard (1856-1915)
American author

Thou unassuming common-place
Of Nature, with that homely face.

William Wordsworth (1770-1850)

The Lord prefers common-looking people. That is the reason He makes so many of them.

Abraham Lincoln (1809-1865)

SEE Butler on BANALITY; Galbraith on BOREDOM; Stevenson on POETRY; Lynd on SINCERITY; Masefield on TRAGEDY

Communism

La propriété c'est le vol.
Property is theft.

Pierre-Joseph Proudhon (1809-1865)
French political theorist

What is a Communist? One who has yearnings
For equal division of unequal earnings.

Ebenezer Elliot (1781-1849)
English pamphleteer, poet

In communist society, where nobody has one exclusive sphere of activity but each can become accomplished in any branch he wishes, society regulates the general production and thus makes it possible for me ... to hunt in the morning, fish in the afternoon, rear cattle in the evening, criticise after dinner, just as I have a mind, without ever becoming hunter, fisherman, herdsman or critic.

Karl Marx (1818-1883)

Russian Communism is the illegitimate child of Karl Marx and Catherine the Great.

Clement Attlee (1883-1967)
British Labour politician, Prime Minister

Communism, being the lay form of Catholicism, and indeed meaning the same thing, has never had any lack of chaplains.

George Bernard Shaw (1856-1950)

Communists are people who fancied that they had an unhappy childhood.
Gertrude Stein (1874-1946)
American writer

Send your son to Moscow and he will return an anti-Communist; send him to the Sorbonne and he will return a Communist.
Félix Houphouët-Boigny (b. 1905)
President of the Ivory Coast

Communism has never come to power in a country that was not disrupted by war or corruption, or both.
John F. Kennedy (1917-1963)

Our fear that Communism might someday take over most of the world blinds us to the fact that anti-communism already has.
American analyst, 1967

The crusade against Communism was even more imaginary than the spectre of Communism.
A. J. P. Taylor (b. 1906)
British historian

I detest communism, because it is the negation of liberty ... I am not a communist because communism concentrates and absorbs all the powers of society into the state.
Mikhail Bakunin (1814-1876)
Russian political theorist

Communism is not love. Communism is a hammer which we use to crush the enemy.
Mao Ze dong (1893-1976)

So we, who are united in mind and soul, have no hesitation about sharing property. All is common among us – except our wives.
Tertullian (160-240)
Roman theologian

SEE MARXISM; Nixon on SCHOOL; SOCIALISM; Solzhenitsyn on The USSR

Commuters

A man who shaves and takes a train,
And then rides back to shave again.
E. B. White (1899-1985)
American author, editor

The doors are shut in the evening;
And they know no songs.
G. K. Chesterton (1874-1936)

Company

Company, villainous company, hath been the spoil of me.
Falstaff, *King Henry IV part I*
William Shakespeare (1564-1616)

Who sleepeth with dogs shall rise with fleas.*
John Florio (1553-1626)
English lexicographer, translator

Spanish version: Quien con perros se acuesta con pulgas se levanta.

You could read Kant by yourself, if you wanted; but you must share a joke with someone else.
Robert Louis Stevenson (1850-1894)

All who joy would win must share it –
Happiness was born a twin.
Lord Byron (1788-1824)

I had three chairs in my house: one for solitude, two for friendship, three for society.
H. D. Thoreau (1817-1862)

Fan the sinking flame of hilarity with the wing of friendship; and pass the rosy wine.
Charles Dickens (1812-1870)

SEE Swift on DINNER PARTIES; FRIENDS; FRIENDSHIP; Twain on HAPPINESS; SOLITUDE

Compatibility

Madam, I have been looking for a person who disliked gravy all my life; let us swear eternal friendship.
Sydney Smith (1771-1845)
English writer, clergyman

Competition

We throw all our attention on the utterly idle question whether A has done as well as B, when the only question is whether A has done as well as he could.
William Graham Sumner (1840-1900)
American sociologist

Thou shalt not covet; but tradition
Approves all forms of competition.
A. H. Clough (1819-1861)
English poet

So long as the system of competition in the production and exchange of the means of life goes on, the degradation of the arts will go on; and if that system is to last for ever, then art is doomed, and will surely die; that is to say, civilization will die.
William Morris (1834-1896)
English artist, writer, printer

SEE Ruskin on CRAFTSMANSHIP

Complacency

The singular completeness of limited men.
Thomas Carlyle (1795-1881)
Scottish author

The plain working truth is that it is not only good for people to be shocked occasionally, but absolutely necessary to the progress of society that they should be shocked pretty often.
George Bernard Shaw (1856-1950)

The greatest of faults is to be conscious of none.
Thomas Carlyle (1795-1881)
Scottish author

Complaint

The wheel that squeaks the loudest is the one that gets the grease.
> Josh Billings (1818-1885)
> American humorist

It is a general popular error to suppose the loudest complainers for the public to be the most anxious for its welfare.
> Edmund Burke (1729-1797)
> Irish philosopher, statesman

It is a folly of too many to mistake the echo of a London coffee-house for the voice of the kingdom.
> Jonathan Swift (1667-1745)

The trouble with this country is that there are too many people going about saying 'The trouble with this country is . . .'
> Sinclair Lewis (1885-1951)
> American novelist

Depend upon it that if a man talks of his misfortunes there is something in them that is not disagreeable to him.
> Dr Samuel Johnson (1709-1784)

Can anybody remember when the times were not hard, and money not scarce?
> R. W. Emerson (1803-1882)
> American essayist, poet,
> philosopher

When I meet a man whose name I can't remember, I give myself two minutes, then if it is a hopeless case I always say 'And how is the old complaint?'
> Benjamin Disraeli (1804-1881)

SEE Austen on PITY

Compliments

I can live for two months on a good compliment.
> Mark Twain (1835-1910)

Nothing is so silly as the expression of a man who is being complimented.
> André Gide (1869-1951)

Women are never disarmed by compliments. Men always are.
> Oscar Wilde (1854-1900)

Some people pay a compliment as if they expected a receipt.
> Kin (F. McKinney) Hubbard (1868-1930)
> American humorist, journalist

Whenever a man's friends begin to compliment him about looking young, he may be sure that they think he is growing old.
> Washington Irving (1783-1859)
> American author

SEE FLATTERY; Hinkson on IRELAND

Compromise

This world may be divided into those who take it or leave it and those who split the difference.
> Father Ronald Knox (1888-1957)
> British clergyman, writer

All government – indeed every human benefit and enjoyment, every virtue and every prudent act – is founded on compromise and barter.
> Edmund Burke (1729-1797)
> Irish philosopher, statesman

If one cannot catch a bird of paradise, better take a wet hen.
> Nikita Khruschchev (1894-1971)

A compromise is the art of dividing a cake in such a way that everyone believes that he has got the biggest piece.
> Dr Ludwig Erhard (1897-1977)
> East German politician

Conferences

A conference is a gathering of important people who singly can do nothing, but together can decide that nothing can be done.
> Fred Allen (1894-1957)
> American humorist

No grand idea was ever born in a conference, but a lot of foolish ideas have died there.
> F. Scott Fitzgerald (1896-1940)

Meetings are indispensable when you don't want to do anything.
> J. K. Galbraith (b. 1908)
> American economist

SEE COMMITTEES

Confessions

There is no refuge from confession but suicide, and suicide is confession.
> Daniel Webster (1782-1852)
> American lawyer, statesman

All the good writers of confessions, from Augustine onwards, are men who are still a little in love with their sins.
> Anatole France (1884-1924)
> French author

We only confess our little faults to persuade people that we have no big ones.
> François, Duc de La Rochefoucauld (1613-1680)
> French writer, moralist

Before confession, be perfectly sure that you do not wish to be forgiven.
> Katherine Mansfield (1888-1923)
> New Zealand-born writer

It is the confession, not the priest, that gives us absolution.
> Oscar Wilde (1854-1900)

A Protestant, if he wants aid or advice on any matter, can only go to his solicitor.
> Benjamin Disraeli (1804-1881)

SEE Menen on CATHOLICISM;

Fairbanks on GOSSIP; Chesterton, Sheen on PSYCHOANALYSIS; Gibran on SIN

Conformity

Where an opinion is general, it is usually correct.
Jane Austen (1775-1817)

Every generation laughs at the old fashions, but follows religiously the new.
H. D. Thoreau (1817-1862)

For not all have the gift of martyrdom.
John Dryden (1631-1700)

Once conform, once do what other people do because they do it, and a lethargy steals over all the finer nerves and faculties of the soul. She becomes all outer show and inward emptiness; dull, callous, and indifferent.
Virginia Woolf (1882-1941)

That so few now dare to be eccentric marks the chief danger of the time.
John Stuart Mill (1806-1873)

People have fallen into a foolish habit of speaking of orthodoxy as something heavy, humdrum and safe. There never was anything so perilous or so exciting as orthodoxy.
G. K. Chesterton (1874-1936)

I think it would be terrific if everybody was alike.
Andy Warhol (1930?-1987)

When all think alike, then no one is thinking.
Walter Lippman (1889-1974)
American journalist

The strongest bulwark of authority is uniformity; the least divergence from it is the greatest crime.
Emma Goldman (1869-1940)
American anarchist

SEE Russell on CONVENTION; Emerson on SOCIETY; Kronenberger on SUBURBS

Conscience

La conciencia es una enfermedad.
Conscience is a sickness.
Miguel de Unamuno (1864-1936)
Spanish philosopher, poet, novelist

Conscience: the inner voice which warns us that someone may be looking.
H. L. Mencken (1880-1956)
American journalist

Conscience is, in most men, an anticipation of the opinion of others.
Sir Henry Taylor (1800-1886)
English author

A man's conscience and his judgement is the same thing, and as the judgement, so also the conscience, may be erroneous.
Thomas Hobbes (1588-1679)

The Non-Conformist Conscience makes cowards of us all.
Sir Max Beerbohm (1872-1956)
British author

Conscience is thoroughly well-bred and soon leaves off talking to those who do not wish to hear it.
Samuel Butler (1835-1902)
English author

Conscience has no more to do with gallantry than it has with politics.
R. B. Sheridan (1751-1816)

At times, although one is perfectly in the right, one's legs tremble; at other times, although one is completely in the wrong, birds sing in one's soul.
V. V. Rozinov

SEE Newman on DELIBERATION; de Madariaga on the ENGLISH; Shakespeare on LOVE; Howells on PRINCIPLES; Smith on The SOUL

Consensus

It is not much matter which we say, but mind, we must all say the same.
Lord Melbourne (1779-1848)
English statesman, Prime Minister

We must indeed all hang together, or, most assuredly, we shall all hang separately.
Benjamin Franklin (1706-1790)

Consequences

There's no limit to how complicated things can get, on account of one thing always leading to another.
E. B. White (1899-1985)
American author, editor

Logical consequences are the scarecrows of fools and the beacons of wise men.
T. H. Huxley (1825-1895)
English biologist

Nothing is worth doing unless the consequences may be serious.
Hypatia, *Misalliance*
George Bernard Shaw (1856-1950)

That's the penalty we have to pay for our acts of foolishness – someone else always suffers for them.
Alfred Sutro (1863-1933)
British dramatist

SEE Ingersoll on NATURE

Conservatives

One of the greatest pains to human nature is the pain of a new idea.
Walter Bagehot (1826-1877)
English economist, critic

What is conservatism? Is it not adherence to the old and tried, against the new and untried?
Abraham Lincoln (1809-1865)

When it is not necessary to change, it is
necessary not to change.
Lord Falkland (1610-1643)
English statesman, patron

Conservative. A statesman who is enamored
of existing evils, as distinguished from a
Liberal, who wishes to replace them with
others.
Ambrose Bierce (1842-1914)
American author

A conservative is a man who is too cowardly
to fight and too fat to run.
Elbert Hubbard (1856-1915)
American author

Men are conservatives when they are least
vigorous, or when they are most luxurious.
They are conservatives after dinner.
R. W. Emerson (1803-1882)
American essayist, poet, philosopher

That man's the true Conservative
Who lops the moulder'd branch away.
Lord Tennyson (1809-1892)

The English never abolish anything. They put
it in cold storage.
A. N. Whitehead (1861-1947)
British philosopher

When a nation's young men are conservative,
its funeral bell is already rung.
H. W. Beecher (1813-1887)
American clergyman, editor, writer

Sir, we must beware of needless innovation,
especially when guided by logic.
Sir Winston Churchill (1874-1965)

Some fellows get credit for being conservative
when they are only stupid.
Kin (F. McKinney) Hubbard (1868-1930)
American humorist, journalist

SEE Strindberg on DOUBT; Amis,
Disraeli on POLITICAL PARTIES;
TRADITION

Consistency
Consistency is the last refuge of the unimag-
inative.
Oscar Wilde (1854-1900)

A foolish consistency is the hobgoblin of little
minds, adored by little statesmen and philosophers and divines.
R. W. Emerson (1803-1882)
American essayist, poet, philosopher

Consistency is contrary to nature, contrary to
life. The only completely consistent people are
the dead.
Aldous Huxley (1894-1963)

The Constitution
A Constitution should be short and obscure.
Napoleon Bonaparte (1769-1821)

Our constitution is in actual operation; everything appears to promise that it will last; but
in this world nothing is certain but death and
taxes.
Benjamin Franklin (1706-1790)

In questions of power, let no more be heard of
confidence in man, but bind him down from
mischief by the chains of the constitution.
Thomas Jefferson (1743-1826)

SEE Hardy on INCONSISTENCY

The Consumer Society
Conspicuous consumption of valuable goods
is a means of reputability to the gentleman of
leisure.
Thorstein Veblen (1857-1929)
American social scientist

The power of consumer goods . . . has been
engendered by the so-called liberal and progressive demands of freedom, and, by appro-
priating them, has emptied them of their
meaning, and changed their nature.
Pier Paolo Pasolini (1922-1975)
Italian film director, essayist

. . . Everything from toy guns that spark
To flesh-coloured Christs that glow in
the dark
It's easy to see without looking too far
That not much is really sacred.
Bob Dylan (b. 1941)

With the supermarket as our temple and the
singing commercial as our litany, are we likely
to fire the world with an irresistable vision of
America's exalted purposes and inspiring way
of life?
Adlai Stevenson (1900-1965)
American Democratic politician

Nowadays people know the price of everything and the value of nothing.
Oscar Wilde (1854-1900)

SEE Lerner on PROPERTY

Contemporaries
To have been alive with him was to have
dined at the table of history.
Cassandra (Sir William Connor) (1909-1967)
British journalist
of Sir Winston Churchill

Contentment
That blessed mood
In which the burthen of the mystery,
In which the heavy and the weary
weight
Of all this unintelligible world
Is lightened.
William Wordsworth (1770-1850)

Tomorrow, do thy worst, for I have
lived today.
John Dryden (1631-1700)

Y mientras miserablemente
se están los otros abrasando
en sed insaciable
del no durable mando,
tendido yo a la sombra esté cantando.
And so, while others miserably pledge themselves the insatiable pursuit of ambition and brief power, I will be stretched out in the shade, singing.
> Fray Luís de León (c. 1527-1591)
> Spanish poet

I have a most peaceable disposition. My desires are for a modest hut, a thatched roof, but a good bed, good food, very fresh milk and butter, flowers in front of my window and a few pretty trees by my door. And should the good Lord wish to make me really happy, he will allow me the pleasure of seeing about six or seven of my enemies hanged upon those trees.
> Heinrich Heine (1797-1856)
> German poet, journalist

SEE HAPPINESS

Controversy

Abuse is often of service. There is nothing so dangerous to an author as silence. His name, like the shuttlecock, must be beat backward and forward, or it falls to the ground.
> Dr Samuel Johnson (1709-1784)

When a thing ceases to be a subject of controversy, it ceases to be a subject of interest.
> William Hazlitt (1778-1830)
> English essayist

Impartial. Unable to perceive any promise of personal advantage from espousing either side of a controversy.
> Ambrose Bierce (1842-1914)
> American author

SEE Newman on ABUSE

Convention

Nobody can live in society without conventions. The reason why sensible people are as conventional as they can bear to be is that conventionality saves so much time and thought and trouble and social friction of one sort or another that it leaves them much more leisure for freedom than unconventionality does.
> George Bernard Shaw (1856-1950)

Conventional people are roused to fury by departure from convention, largely because they regard such departure as a criticism of themselves.
> Bertrand Russell (1872-1970)

There is nothing more conventional than the convention of unconventionality.
> R. H. Benson (1871-1914)
> British novelist

Conversation

With thee conversing I forget all time.
> John Milton (1608-1674)

Talk to every woman as if you loved her, and to every man as if he bored you, and at the end of your first season you will have the reputation of possessing the most perfect social tact.
> Oscar Wilde (1854-1900)

Great talkers are so constituted that they do not know their own thoughts until, on the tide of their particular gift, they hear them issuing from their mouths.
> Thornton Wilder (1897-1975)
> American author

Say nothing good of yourself, you will be distrusted; say nothing bad of yourself, you will be taken at your word.
> Joseph Roux (1834-1886)
> French priest and writer

Inquisitive people are merely funnels of conversation. They do not take in anything for their own use, but merely to pass it on to others.
> Sir Richard Steele (1672-1729)
> English dramatist, essayist, editor

No man would listen to you talk if he didn't know it was his turn next.
> Ed (E. W.) Howe (1853-1937)
> American journalist, novelist

I find we are growing serious, and then we are in great danger of being dull.
> William Congreve (1670-1729)
> English dramatist

Sir, you have but two topics, yourself and me. I am sick of both.
> Dr Samuel Johnson (1709-1784)

We often forgive those who bore us, but we cannot forgive those whom we bore.
> François, Duc de
> La Rochefoucauld (1613-1680)
> French writer, moralist

Your ignorance cramps my conversation.
> Anthony Hope Hawkins (1863-1933)
> British novelist

Silence is the unbearable repartee.
> G. K. Chesterton (1874-1936)

He speaks to Me as if I was a public meeting.
> Queen Victoria (1819-1901)
> *of Mr Gladstone*

When we talk in company we lose our unique tone of voice, and this leads us to make statements which in no way correspond to our real thoughts.
> Friedrich Nietzsche (1844-1900)

Ideally I'd like to spend two evenings a week

talking to Proust and another conversing with the Holy Ghost.

Edna O'Brien (b. 1936)
Irish author

And when you stick on conversation's burrs,
Don't strew your pathway with those dreadful urs.

Dr Oliver Wendell Holmes (1809-1894)
American writer, physician

SEE Barrie, Chesterton, Hitchcock on DINNER PARTIES; English Proverb on GENTLEMEN; Thrale on Dr JOHNSON; Cory on NOSTALGIA; Smith on SILENCE; Molière on SPEECHES; Hazlitt on WIT

Cookery

We may live without poetry, music and art;
We may live without conscience, and live without heart;
We may live without friends; we may live without books;
But civilised man cannot live without cooks.

Owen Meredith (Edward R. Bulwer, Earl of Lytton) (1831-1891)
English poet, diplomat

'Tis an ill cook that cannot lick his own fingers.

Servant, *Romeo and Juliet*
William Shakespeare (1564-1616)

Be content to remember that those who can make omlettes properly can do nothing else.

Hilaire Belloc (1870-1953)
British author

SEE Gauguin on ARTISTS; Jerrold on HUMANITY; Duke of Edinburgh on ROYALTY; Frost, Meredith on WIVES; Wolfe on WOMEN

Correspondence

As cold waters to a thirsty soul, so is good news from a far country.

Bible, Proverbs

An intention to write never turns into a letter. A letter must happen to one like a surprise, and one may not know where in the day there was room for it to come into being.

Rainer Maria Rilke (1875-1926)
German poet

Letters give us great lives at their most characteristic, their most glorious, and their most terrible moments. Here history and biography meet.

W. Lincoln Schuster

His letters teach the morals of a whore, and the manners of a dancing master.

Dr Samuel Johnson (1709-1784)
of Lord Chesterfield

SEE Waugh on COURTESY; Acton on HISTORY

Corruption

God is merciful and men are bribable, and that's how his will is done on earth as it is in Heaven. Corruption is our only hope. As long as there's corruption, there'll be merciful judges and even the innocent may get off.

Bertolt Brecht (1898-1956)
trans. Eric Bentley

The jingling of the guinea helps the hurt that honour feels.

Lord Tennyson (1809-1892)

When I want to buy up any politician I always find the anti-monopolists the most purchasable – they don't come so high.

William Vanderbilt (1821-1885)
American industrialist

Don't take a nickel, just hand them your business card.

Richard M. Daley (1902-1975)
American politician

An upright minister asks what recommends a man; a corrupt minister, who.

C. C. Colton (1780-1832)
English author, clergyman

I am against government by crony.

Harold L. Ickes (1874-1952)
American politician
resignation speech

Corruption . . . the most infallible symptom of constitutional liberty.

Edward Gibbon (1737-1794)

I have often noticed that a bribe . . . has that effect – it changes a relation. The man who offers a bribe gives away a little of his own importance; the bribe once accepted, he becomes the inferior, like a man who has paid for a woman.

Graham Greene (b. 1904)

The sun shineth upon the dunghill, and is not corrupted.

John Lyly (1554-1606)
English author

SEE Kennedy on ELECTIONS; Wolfe on JOURNALISM; Wilson on SECRETS; Book of Common Prayer on TRADITION; Chesterton on WEALTH

The Cosmos

The cosmos is about the smallest hole that a man can hide his head in.

G. K. Chesterton (1874-1936)

Nothing puzzles me more than time and space; and yet nothing troubles me less, as I never think about them.

Charles Lamb (1775-1834)
English essayist, critic

I don't pretend to understand the universe, it is a great deal bigger than I am.
Thomas Carlyle (1795-1881)
Scottish author

The universe is one of God's thoughts.
Friedrich von Schiller (1759-1805)

Law rules throughout the universe, a Law which is not intelligent but Intelligence.
R. W. Emerson (1803-1882)
American essayist, poet,
philosopher

Thou canst not stir a flower
Without troubling of a star.
Francis Thompson (1859-1907)
English poet

I rather feel that deep in the soul of mankind there is a reflection as on the surface of a mirror, of a mirror-calm lake, of the beauty and harmony of the universe.
Prince of Wales (b. 1948)

The cosmos is a gigantic fly-wheel making ten thousand revolutions a minute. Man is a sick fly taking a dizzy ride on it. Religion is the theory that the wheel was designed and set spinning to give him the ride.
H. L. Mencken (1880-1956)
American journalist

'Tis very puzzling on the brink
Of what is called Eternity to stare,
And know more of what is *here*,
than *there*.
Lord Byron (1788-1824)

SEE Huxley on CHESS; Priestley on
COINCIDENCE

Country Life
I live not in myself, but I become
Portion of that around me; and to me
High mountains are a feeling, but
the hum
Of human cities torture.
Lord Byron (1788-1824)

Our present city populations are so savage that they drive even the most public-spirited country people to put up barbed wire all over the place. They are no more to be trusted with trees and animals than a baby can be trusted with a butterfly.
George Bernard Shaw (1856-1950)

I have no relish for the country; it is a kind of healthy grave.
Sydney Smith (1771-1845)
English writer, clergyman

Anybody can be good in the country; there are no temptations there.
Oscar Wilde (1854-1900)

The lowest and vilest alleys of London do not present a more dreadful record of sin than does the smiling and beautiful countryside.
Sir Arthur Conan Doyle (1859-1930)

There is nothing good to be had in the country, or, if there is, they will not let you have it.
William Hazlitt (1778-1830)
English essayist

I nauseate walking; 'tis a country diversion; I loathe the country.
William Congreve (1670-1729)
English dramatist

Separate from the pleasure of your company, I don't much care if I never see another mountain in my life.
Charles Lamb (1775-1834)
English essayist, critic
to Wordsworth

Oh lord! I don't know which is the worst of the country, the walking or the sitting at home with nothing to do.
Mrs Warren, *Mrs Warren's Profession*
George Bernard Shaw (1856-1950)

It is quiet here and restful and the air is delicious. There are gardens everywhere, nightingales sing in the gardens and police spies lie in the bushes.
Maxim Gorky (1868-1936)

SEE Colton, Cowley on CITY LIFE

Country Music
I have long harboured a suspicion that most country songwriters moonlight as speech-writers for President Reagan or scriptwriters for 'Dallas', since they share a desire to reduce all life to the dimensions of a B-movie.
Paul Lashmar
Observer, 1986

Courage
Courage is almost a contradiction in terms. It means a strong desire to live taking the form of a readiness to die.
G. K. Chesterton (1874-1936)

There is no such thing as bravery; only degrees of fear.
John Wainwright (b. 1921)
British author

A great part of courage is the courage of having done the thing before.
R. W. Emerson (1803-1882)
American essayist, poet, philosopher

Perfect courage is to do without witnesses what one would be capable of doing with the world looking on.
François, Duc de La Rochefoucauld (1613-1680)
French writer, moralist

Courage is a quality so necessary for maintaining virtue that it is always respected, even when it is associated with vice.
Dr Samuel Johnson (1709-1784)

Fortunately for themselves and the world, nearly all men are cowards and dare not act on what they believe. Nearly all our disasters come of a few fools having the 'courage of their convictions'.

Coventry Patmore (1823-1896)
English poet

'I'm very brave generally', he went on in a low voice: 'only today I happen to have a headache'.

Lewis Carroll (1832-1898)

Until the day of his death, no man can be sure of his courage.

Jean Anouilh (b. 1910)
French dramatist

Courtesy

We cannot always oblige, but we can always speak obligingly.

Voltaire (1694-1778)

Politeness is good nature regulated by good sense.

Sydney Smith (1771-1845)
English writer, clergyman

Politeness is the art of choosing among one's real thoughts.

Abel Stevens (1815-1897)
American clergyman, editor

There can be no defence like elaborate courtesy.

E. V. Lucas (1868-1938)
British journalist, essayist

The civilities of the great are never thrown away.

Dr Samuel Johnson (1709-1784)

It is true there are many very polite men, but none that I ever heard of who were not either fascinating women or obeying them.

G. K. Chesterton (1874-1936)

It is wise to apply the oil of refined politeness to the mechanism of friendship.

Colette (1873-1954)

The English are polite by telling lies. The Americans are polite by telling the truth.

Malcolm Bradbury (b. 1932)
British author

His courtesy was somewhat extravagant. He would write and thank people who wrote to thank him for wedding presents and when he encountered anyone as punctilious as himself the correspondence ended only with death.

Evelyn Waugh (1903-1966)

SEE MANNERS

Cowardice

A cowardly act! What do I care about that? You may be sure that I should never fear to commit one if it were to my advantage.

Napoleon Bonaparte (1769-1821)

For all men would be cowards if they durst.

John Wilmot, Earl of Rochester (1647-1680)
English courtier, poet

Cowardice, as distinguished from panic, is almost always simply a lack of ability to suspend the functioning of the imagination.

Ernest Hemingway (1899-1961)

I'm a hero with coward's legs.

Spike Milligan (b. 1918)
British comedian, humorous writer

The last thing a woman will consent to discover in a man whom she loves or on whom she simply depends, is want of courage.

Joseph Conrad (1857-1924)

If you can't stand the heat, get out of the kitchen.

Harry S. Truman (1884-1972)

SEE Shaw on HEROES; Shaw on HUMILITY; Twain on TEMPTATION

Craftsmanship

Nothing should be made by man's labour which is not worth making, or which must be made by labour degrading to the makers.

William Morris (1834-1896)
English artist, writer, printer

There is hardly anything in the world that some man cannot make a little worse and sell a little cheaper.

John Ruskin (1819-1900)
English critic

A man cannot make a pair of shoes rightly unless he do it in a devout manner.

Thomas Carlyle (1795-1881)
Scottish author

Mastery is not something that strikes in an instant, like a thunderbolt, but a gathering power that moves steadily through time, like weather.

John Gardner (1933-1982)
American author

No man who is occupied in doing a very difficult thing, and doing it very well, ever loses his self-respect.

George Bernard Shaw (1856-1950)

SEE Hippocrates on DOCTORS

Creation

God's first creature, which was light.

Francis Bacon (1561-1626)

And the Lord God formed man of the dust of the ground, and breathed into his nostrils the breath of life; and man became a living soul.

Bible, Genesis

God created Adam lord of all living creatures, but Eve spoiled it all.
> Martin Luther (1483-1546)

El mundo està mal hecho.
The world is a botched job.
> Gabriel García Márquez (b. 1928)
> Colombian writer

Man was created a little lower than the angels, and has been getting a little lower ever since.
> Josh Billings (1818-1875)
> American humorist

God made man merely to hear some praise
Of what he'd done on those Five Days.
> Christopher Morley (1890-1957)
> American novelist, journalist

Se Dios no hubiera descansado el domingo, habría tenido tiempo de terminar el mundo.
If God hadn't rested on Sunday, he might have had time to finish off the world.
> Gabriel García Márquez (b.1928)
> Colombian writer

Thou didst create the night, but I made the lamp.
Thou didst create clay, but I made the cup.
Thou didst create the deserts, mountains and forests,
I produced the orchards, gardens and groves.
It is I who made the glass out of stone,
And it is I who turn a poison into an antidote.
> Urdu poet (unknown)

Everyone is as God made him, and often a great deal worse.
> Miguel de Cervantes (1547-1616)

I sometimes think that God in creating man somewhat overestimated his ability.
> Oscar Wilde (1854-1900)

We have no reason to suppose that we are the Creator's last word.
> George Bernard Shaw (1856-1950)

Creeds
I believe in one God and no more, and I hope for happiness beyond this life. I believe in the equality of man; and I believe that religious duties consist in doing justice, loving mercy, and endeavouring to make our fellow-creatures happy.
> Thomas Paine (1737-1809)

We hold these truths to be self-evident: that all men are created equal; that they are endowed by their Creator with certain unalienable rights; that among these are life, liberty, and the pursuit of happiness.
> Thomas Jefferson (1743-1826)

A man must not swallow more beliefs than he can digest.
> Havelock Ellis (1859-1939)
> British psychologist, author

I believe in Michelangelo, Velasquez, and Rembrandt; in the might of design, the mystery of colour, the redemption of all things by Beauty everlasting; and the message of Art that has made these hands blessed. Amen. Amen.
> Dubedat, *The Doctor's Dilemma*
> George Bernard Shaw (1856-1950)

I believe in the total depravity of inanimate things . . . the elusiveness of soap, the knottiness of strings, the transitory nature of buttons, the inclination of suspenders to twist and of hooks to forsake their lawful eyes and cleave only unto the hairs of their hapless owner's head.
> Katharine Ashley (1840-1916)

What a man believes may be ascertained, not from his creed, but from the assumptions on which he habitually acts.
> George Bernard Shaw (1856-1950)

When suave politeness, tempering bigot zeal,
Corrected 'I believe' to 'One does feel'.
> Father Ronald Knox (1888-1957)
> British clergyman, writer

SEE BELIEF; Huxley on SCIENCE

Cricket
Casting a ball at three straight sticks and defending the same with a fourth.
> Rudyard Kipling (1865-1936)

If Stalin had learned to play cricket the world might now be a better place to live in.
> Dr R. Downey (1881-1953)
> Archbishop of Liverpool

SEE Stoppard on SPORT

Crime
Money is the fruit of evil as often as the root of it.
> Henry Fielding (1707-1754)

Crimes, like virtues, are their own rewards.
> George Farquhar (1678-1707)
> Irish dramatist

There are crimes which become innocent and even glorious through their splendour, number, and excess.
> François, Duc de La Rochefoucauld (1613-1680)
> French writer, satirist

Successful crimes alone are justified.
> John Dryden (1631-1700)

He threatens many that hath injured one.
> Ben Jonson (1573-1637)

Abscond. To 'move' in a mysterious way, commonly with the property of another.
Ambrose Bierce (1842-1914)
American author

The thief. Once committed beyond a certain point he should not worry himself too much about not being a thief any more. Thieving is God's message to him. Let him try and be a good thief.
Samuel Butler (1835-1902)
English author

A thief believes everybody steals.
Ed (E. W.) Howe (1853-1937)
American journalist, novelist

A burglar who respects his art always takes his time before taking anything else.
O. Henry (1862-1910)
American short story writer

Crimine ab uno disce omnis.
From a single crime know the nation.
Virgil (70-19 BC)

Crimes of which a people is ashamed constitute its real history. The same is true of man.
Jean Genet (1910-1986)

Far more university graduates are becoming criminals every year than are becoming policemen.
Philip Goodhart (b. 1925)
British Conservative politician

When rich villains have need of poor villains, poor ones may make what price they will.
Borachio, *Much Ado About Nothing*
William Shakespeare (1564-1616)

If weakness may excuse, what murderer, what traitor, parricide, incestuous, sacrilegious, but may plead it? All wickedness is weakness.
John Milton (1608-1674)

SEE Shenstone on HONESTY; Mencken on POVERTY; Chesterton on PROPERTY; Fletcher on SIN; Emerson on VILLAINS

Crises

The time is out of joint. O cursed spite,
That ever I was born to set it right!
Hamlet, *Hamlet*
William Shakespeare (1564-1616)

There can't be a crisis next week. My schedule is already full.
Henry Kissinger (b. 1923)

The situation in Germany is serious but not hopeless; the situation in Austria is hopeless but not serious.
Austrian proverb
collected by
Franklin Pierce Adams (1881-1960)

When written in Chinese the word crisis is composed of two characters. One represents danger and the other represents opportunity.
John F. Kennedy (1917-1963)

Criticism

Criticism is the endeavour to find, to know, to love, to recommend, not only the best, but all the good, that has been known and thought and written in the world.
George Saintsbury (1845-1933)
British literary critic

Of all the cants which are canted in this canting world, – though the cant of hypocrites may be the worst, – the cant of criticism is the most tormenting!
Laurence Sterne (1713-1768)
English author

It is the nature of the artist to mind excessively what is said about him. Literature is strewn with the wreckage of men who have minded beyond reason the opinions of others.
Virginia Woolf (1882-1941)

A blind man will not thank you for a looking-glass.
18th century English proverb

You should not say it is not good. You should say you do not like it; and then, you know, you're perfectly safe.
J. M. Whistler (1834-1903)
American artist

On an occasion of this kind it becomes more than a moral duty to speak one's mind. It becomes a pleasure.
Oscar Wilde (1854-1900)

I like criticism, but it must be my way.
Mark Twain (1835-1910)

Do not use a hatchet to remove a fly from your friend's forehead.
Chinese proverb

To many people dramatic criticism must seem like an attempt to tattoo soap bubbles.
John Mason Brown (1900-1969)
American essayist

I find that when I dislike what I see on the stage I can be vastly amusing, but when I write about something I like I find that I am appallingly dull.
Sir Max Beerbohm (1872-1956)
British author

Your manuscript is both good and original; but the part that is good is not original, and the part that is original is not good.
Dr Samuel Johnson (1709-1784)

As a work of art it has the same status as a long conversation between two not very bright drunks.

> Clive James (b. 1939)
> *Australian writer, critic*
> *of Princess Daisy by Judith Krantz*

Join it.

> Oscar Wilde (1854-1900)
> *advice to a writer who*
> *complained of a conspiracy of silence about his books*

SEE Welles on ACTORS; Cocteau on ARTISTS; Browne on CENSORSHIP; Swift on FAME; Vorster on SOUTH AFRICA

Critics

Reviewers, with some rare exceptions, are a most stupid and malignant race. As a bankrupt thief turns thief-taker in despair, so an unsuccessful author turns critic.

> P. B. Shelley (1792-1822)

Nature, when she invented, manufactured, and patented her authors, contrived to make critics of the chips that were left.

> Dr Oliver Wendell Holmes (1809-1894)
> *American writer, physician*

A louse in the locks of literature.

> Lord Tennyson (1809-1892)
> *of J. Churton Collins*

A critic is a bundle of biases held loosely together by a sense of taste.

> Whitney Balliet (b. 1926)
> *American writer*

It is impossible to think of a man of any actual force and originality . . . who spent his whole life appraising and describing the work of other men.

> H. L. Mencken (1880-1956)
> *American journalist*

Asking a working writer what he thinks about critics is like asking a lamp-post what it feels about dogs.

> Christopher Hampton (b. 1946)
> *British playwright*

As long as there are readers to be delighted with calumny, there will be found reviewers to calumniate.

> S. T. Coleridge (1772-1834)

I would rather be attacked than unnoticed. For the worst thing you can do to an author is to be silent as to his works.

> Dr Samuel Johnson (1709-1784)

> Though by whim, envy, or resentment led,
> They damn those authors whom they never read.

> Charles Churchill (1731-1764)
> *English clergyman, poet*

I never read a book before reviewing it; it prejudices one so.

> Sydney Smith (1771-1845)
> *English writer, clergyman*

There are two kinds of dramatic critics: destructive and constructive. I am a destructive. There are two kinds of guns: Krupp and pop.

> George Jean Nathan (1882-1958)
> *American critic*

A good drama critic is one who perceives what is happening in the theatre of his time. A great drama critic also perceives what is not happening.

> Kenneth Tynan (1927-1980)
> *British critic*

Never trust the artist. Trust the tale. The proper function of the critic is to save the tale from the artist who created it.

> D. H. Lawrence (1885-1930)

What we ask of him is that he should find out for us more than we can find out for ourselves.

> Arthur Symons (1865-1945)
> *English poet, critic*

> A man must serve his time to every trade
> Save censure — critics all are ready made.

> Lord Byron (1788-1824)

SEE Bovee on WRITERS

Cruelty

The impulse to cruelty is, in many people, almost as violent as the impulse to sexual love — almost as violent and much more mischievous.

> Aldous Huxley (1894-1963)

The infliction of cruelty with a good conscience is a delight to moralists.

> Bertrand Russell (1872-1970)

Weak men are apt to be cruel.

> George Savile, Lord Halifax (1633-1695)
> *English statesman, author*

Crying

I wept not, so to stone within I grew.

> Dante Alighieri (1265-1321)

> I have full cause of weeping; but this heart
> Shall break into a hundred thousand flaws,
> Or ere I'll weep.

> Lear, *King Lear*
> William Shakespeare (1564-1616)

It is only to the happy that tears are a luxury.

> Thomas Moore (1779-1852)
> *Irish poet*

There are people who laugh to show their fine teeth; and there are those who cry to show their good hearts.

> Joseph Roux (1834-1886)
> *French priest and writer*

Women's weapons, water-drops.
> William Shakespeare (1564-1616)

Oh! too convincing – dangerously dear –
In woman's eye the unanswerable tear!
> Lord Byron (1788-1824)

Crying is the refuge of plain women, but the ruin of pretty ones.
> Oscar Wilde (1854-1900)

'It opens the lungs, washes the countenance, exercises the eyes, and softens down the temper', said Mr Bumble. 'So cry away'.
> *Oliver Twist*
> Charles Dickens (1812-1870)

Whatever tears one may shed, in the end one always blows one's nose.
> Heinrich Heine (1797-1856)
> German poet, journalist

Cults
What is a cult? It just means not enough people to make a minority.
> Robert Altman (b. 1922)
> American film director

A cult is a religion with no political power.
> Tom Wolfe (b. 1931)
> American journalist, author

Culture
Culture, the acquainting ourselves with the best that has been known and said in the world, and thus with the history of the human spirit.
> Matthew Arnold (1822-1888)
> English poet, critic

Instead of dirt and poison, we have rather chosen to fill our hives with honey and wax; thus furnishing mankind with the two noblest of things, which are sweetness and light.
> Jonathan Swift (1667-1745)

Culture is the bed-rock, the final wall, against which one leans one's back in a god-forsaken chaos.
> John Cowper Powys (1872-1963)
> British author, poet

One ought, every day at least, to hear a little song, read a good poem, see a fine picture, and, if it were possible, to speak a few reasonable words.
> Johann Wolfgang von Goethe (1749-1832)

The poor have no business with culture and should beware of it. They cannot eat it; they cannot sell it; they can only pass it on to others and that is why the world is full of hungry people ready to teach us anything under the sun.
> Aubrey Menen (b. 1912)
> British novelist, essayist

Culture is an instrument wielded by professors to manufacture professors, who, when their turn comes, will manufacture professors.
> Simone Weil (1909-1943)
> French mystic, philosopher

Mrs Ballinger is one of the ladies who pursue Culture in bands, as though it were dangerous to meet it alone.
> Edith Wharton (1862-1937)
> American novelist

One of the surest signs of the Philistine is his reverence for the superior tastes of those who put him down.
> Pauline Kael (b. 1919)
> American critic

SEE McCarthy on STATUS

Cunning
'Frank and explicit' – that is the right line to take when you wish to conceal your own mind and to confuse the minds of others.
> Benjamin Disraeli (1804-1881)

With foxes we must play the fox.
> Thomas Fuller (1654-1734)
> English physician

The greatest cunning is to have none at all.
> Carl Sandburg (1878-1967)
> American poet

And all your future lies beneath your hat.
> John Oldham (1653-1683)
> English poet

SEE DISCRETION

Curiosity
Curiosity is one of the most permanent and certain characteristics of a vigorous intellect.
> Dr Samuel Johnson (1709-1784)

Disinterested intellectual curiosity is the life blood of real civilization.
> G. M. Trevelyan (1876-1962)
> British historian

We never stop investigating. We are never satisfied that we know enough to get by. Every question we answer leads on to another question. This has become the greatest survival trick of our species.
> Desmond Morris (b. 1928)
> British anthropologist

The thirst to know and understand,
A large and liberal discontent.
> Sir William Watson (1858-1935)
> British poet

Be not curious in unnecessary matters: for more things are shewed unto thee than men understand.
> Apocrypha, Ecclesiasticus

He that breaks a thing to find out what it is has left the path of wisdom.
> J. R. R. Tolkien (1892-1973)

Cynics

What is the use of straining after an amiable view of things, when a cynical view is most likely to be the true one?

George Bernard Shaw (1956-1950)

Cynicism is intellectual dandyism.

George Meredith (1828-1909)
English author

A cynic is just a man who found out when he was about ten that there wasn't any Santa Claus, and he's still upset.

James Gould Cozzens (1903-1978)
American author

A cynic is not merely one who reads bitter lessons from the past, he is one who is prematurely disappointed in the future.

Sydney J. Harris (b. 1917)
American journalist

It takes a clever man to turn cynic, and a wise man to be clever enough not to.

Fannie Hurst (1889-1968)
American novelist, playwright

What is a cynic? A man who knows the price of everything and the value of nothing.

Oscar Wilde (1854-1900)

Cynics are only happy in making the world as barren for others as they have made it for themselves.

George Meredith (1828-1909)
English author

Cynic. A blackguard whose faulty vision sees things as they are, not as they ought to be.

Ambrose Bierce (1842-1914)
American author

SEE Berkeley on HONESTY

D

Dancing

Dancing with abandon, turning a tango into a fertility rite.
>
> Marshall Pugh (b. 1925)
> British journalist, author

I just put my feet in the air and move them around.
>
> Fred Astaire (1899-1987)

Custom has made dancing sometimes necessary for a young man; therefore mind it while you learn it that you may learn to do it well, and not be ridiculous, though in a ridiculous act.
>
> Lord Chesterfield (1694-1773)
> English statesman and man of letters
> to his son

Dancing is a wonderful training for girls, it's the first way you learn to guess what a man is going to do before he does it.
>
> Christopher Morley (1890-1957)
> American novelist, journalist

These sort of boobies think that people come to balls to do nothing but dance; whereas everyone knows that the real business of balls is either to look out for a wife, to look after a wife, or to look after somebody else's wife.
>
> R. S. Surtees (1803-1864)
> English novelist

How inimitably graceful children are in general – before they learn to dance.
>
> S. T. Coleridge (1772-1834)

Neminem saltare sobrius, nisi forte insanit.
No sober man dances, unless he happens to be mad.
>
> Cicero (106-43 BC)

The greater the fool the better the dancer.
>
> Theodore Hook (1788-1841)
> English novelist and wit

The body never lies.
>
> Martha Graham (b. 1894)
> American dancer, choreographer

Ballet is the ectoplasm of music.
>
> Russell Green

SEE Wilde on CAPITAL PUNISHMENT

The Dead

He has out-soared the shadow of our night;
Envy and calumny, and hate and pain,
And that unrest which men miscall delight,
Can touch him not, and torture not again;
From the contagion of the world's slow stain,
He is secure.
>
> P. B. Shelley (1792-1822)
> *of John Keats, died aged 25*

On doit des égards aux vivants; on ne doit aux morts que la vérité.
To the living we owe respect, but to the dead we owe only the truth.
>
> Voltaire (1694-1778)

The living are the dead on holiday.
>
> Maurice de Maeterlinck (1862-1949)
> Belgian author

Each in his narrow cell for ever laid,
The rude forefathers of the hamlet sleep.
>
> Thomas Gray (1716-1771)

The graveyards are full of people the world could not do without.
>
> Elbert Hubbard (1856-1915)
> American author

No motion has she now, no force,
She neither hears nor sees;
Rolled around in earth's diurnal course,
With rocks and stones, and trees.
>
> William Wordsworth (1770-1850)

Be the green grass above me
With showers and dewdrops wet;
And if thou wilt, remember,
And if thou wilt, forget.
>
> Christina Rossetti (1830-1894)
> English poet, lyricist

After life's fitful fever, he sleeps well;
Treason has done his worst: nor steel, nor poison,
Malice domestic, foreign levy, nothing
Can touch him further.
>
> Macbeth, *Macbeth*
> William Shakespeare (1564-1616)

An orphan's curse would drag to hell
  A spirit from on high;
But oh! more horrible than that
  Is the curse in a dead man's eye.
                    S. T. Coleridge (1772-1834)

I do not make war against the dead.
                    Homer (8th century BC)

Abiit ad plures.
He has gone over to the majority.
                    Petronius (1st century AD)
                    Roman satirist

Either he's dead or my watch has stopped.
                    Groucho Marx (1895-1977)

We therefore commit his body to the ground;
earth to earth, ashes to ashes, dust to dust.
                    The Book of Common Prayer

Death

The last enemy that shall be destroyed is
death.
                    Saint Paul (3-67)

All men think all men mortal, but themselves.
                    Edward Young (1683-1765)
                    English poet, playwright

We die before we have learned to live.
                    Stephen Winsten (*fl.* 1946-1951)

Teach me to live that I may dread
The grave as little as my bed.
                    Thomas Ken (1637-1711)
                    English churchman, hymn-writer

Christianity has made of death a terror which
was unknown to the gay calmness of the
Pagan.
                    Ouida (Marie Louise de la Ramée) (1839-1908)
                    English novelist

It is impossible that anything so natural, so
necessary, and so universal as death should
ever have been designed by Providence as an
evil to mankind.
                    Jonathan Swift (1667-1745)

It is as natural to die as to be born; and to a
little infant, perhaps, the one is as painful as
the other.
                    Francis Bacon (1561-1626)

We all labour against our own cure, for death
is the cure of all diseases.
                    Sir Thomas Browne (1605-1682)
                    English doctor, author

But I will be a bridegroom in my
  death
And run into't as to a lover's
  bed.
                    Antony, *Antony and Cleopatra*
                    William Shakespeare (1564-1616)

How gladly would I meet
Mortality, my sentence, and be earth

Insensible! how glad would lay me
  down,
As in my mother's lap! There I
  should rest
And sleep secure.
                    John Milton (1608-1674)

How often are we to die before we go right off
this stage? In every friend we lose a part of
ourselves, and the best part.
                    Alexander Pope (1688-1744)

Whoever has lived long enough to find out
what life is, knows how deep a debt of
gratitude we owe to Adam, the first great
benefactor of our race. He brought death into
the world.
                    Mark Twain (1835-1910)

Death is the veil which those who
  live call life:
They sleep, and it is lifted.
                    P. B. Shelley (1792-1822)

Winter is on my head, but eternal spring is in
my heart. The nearer I approach the end the
plainer I hear around me the immortal
symphonies of the worlds which invite me.
                    Victor Hugo (1802-1885)

The grave's a fine and private place,
But none, I think, do there embrace.
                    Andrew Marvell (1621-1678)

Though lovers be lost love shall not;
And death shall have no dominion.
                    Dylan Thomas (1914-1953)

Man is a noble animal, splendid in ashes, and
pompous in the grave.
                    Sir Thomas Browne (1605-1682)
                    English doctor, author

I am a temporary enclosure for a temporary
purpose; that served, my skull and teeth, my
idiosyncrasy and desire, will disperse, I
believe, like the timbers of a booth after the
fair.
                    H. G. Wells (1866-1946)

Death, which ends the feuds of unimportant
persons, lets loose the tongue over the characters of the great. Kings are especially sufferers.
                    J. A. Froude (1818-1894)
                    English author

I come to bury Caesar, not to praise
  him.
The evil that men do lives after them,
The good is oft interred with their
  bones.
                    Mark Antony, *Julius Caesar*
                    William Shakespeare (1564-1616)

Death hath a thousand doors to let
  out life;
I shall find one.
                    Philip Massinger (1583-1640)
                    English playwright

Like figures on an ancient clock,
Warrior, or saint, or clown
(All's one to the machine), that wake
When each stale hour is done,
And with preliminary whirr
Play their allotted role,
Stiffly advance, engage, retire
Trembling a little still,
So blandly nodding Death and I
Nearer and nearer march,
At the click of night and the click of
day
— Click-clack! We approach, we
approach!
> C. D. Andrews (b. 1913)
> British poet, scholar

Men must endure
Their going hence, even as their
coming hither:
Ripeness is all.
> Edgar, *King Lear*
> William Shakespeare (1564-1616)

Yet nightly pitch my moving tent
A day's march nearer home.
> James Montgomery (1771-1854)
> English poet

I have a rendez-vous with Death
At some disputed barricade.
> Alan Seeger (1888-1916)
> British soldier, poet

O death, where is thy sting? O grave, where is
thy victory?
> Saint Paul (3-67)

The hour of departure has arrived, and we go
our ways — I to die and you to live. Which is
the better, only God knows.
> Socrates (469-399 BC)

La mort ne surprend point le sage,
Il est toujours prêt à partir.
Death never takes the wise man by surprise, he
is always ready to go.
> Jean de la Fontaine (1621-1695)
> French poet, fabulist

Life does not cease to be funny when people
die any more than it ceases to be serious when
people laugh.
> Ridgeon, *The Doctor's Dilemma*
> George Bernard Shaw (1856-1950)

I have fought a good fight, I have finished my
course, I have kept the faith.
> Saint Paul (3-67)

And I saw, and behold, a pale horse: and he
that sat upon him, his name was Death.
> John the Divine (1st century AD)

Cheerio, see you soon.
> *epitaph on gravestone*

Death: Dying

It is not death, but dying, which is terrible.
> Henry Fielding (1707-1754)

I do not believe that any man fears to be dead,
but only the stroke of death.
> Francis Bacon (1561-1626)

It's not that I'm afraid to die. I just don't want
to be there when it happens.
> Woody Allen (b. 1935)

It is certain that to most men the preparation
for death has been a greater torment than the
suffering of it.
> Michel de Montaigne (1533-1592)
> French essayist

To die is to leave off dying and do the thing
once for all.
> Samuel Butler (1835-1902)
> English author

I warmed both hands before the fire
of life;
It sinks and I am ready to depart.
> Walter Savage Landor (1775-1864)
> English author

I am prepared to meet my Maker. Whether my
Maker is prepared for the great ordeal of
meeting me is another matter.
> Sir Winston Churchill (1874-1965)
> *on the eve of his 75th birthday*

Do not go gentle into that good
night,
Old age should burn and rage at
close of day;
Rage, rage, against the dying of
the light.
> Dylan Thomas (1914-1953)

I will be conquered; I will not capitulate.
> Dr Samuel Johnson (1709-1784)
> *in his last illness*

I die hard. But I am not afraid to go.
> George Washington (1732-1799)

Truth sits upon the lips of dying men.
> Matthew Arnold (1822-1888)
> English poet, critic

A certain amount of research on Last Dis-
patches from the edge of the tomb has been
made, but I feel that there has always been a
tendency on the part of the imminent mourner
to tart the script up a bit.
> Cassandra (Sir William Connor) (1909-1967)
> British journalist

Nothing in his life
Became him like the leaving it; he
died
As one that had been studied in his
death
To throw away the dearest thing he
owed,

As 'twere a careless trifle.
Malcolm, *Macbeth*
William Shakespeare (1564-1616)

So that he seemed not to relinquish life, but to leave one home for another.
Cornelius Nepos (1st century BC)
Roman historian, biographer

Many men on the point of an edifying death would be furious if they were suddenly restored to health.
Cesare Pavese (1908-1950)
Italian novelist

It matters not how a man dies, but how he lives. The act of dying is not of importance, it lasts so short a time.
Dr Samuel Johnson (1709-1784)

He had been, he said, an unconscionable time dying; but he hoped that they would excuse it.
King Charles II of Great Britain (1630-1685)

Authority forgets a dying king.
Lord Tennyson (1809-1892)

We all of us waited for him to die. The family sent him a cheque every month, and hoped he'd get on with it quietly, without too much vulgar fuss.
Jimmy, *Look Back in Anger*
John Osborne (b. 1929)
British playwright

As virtuous men pass mildly away,
And whisper to their souls to go,
Whilst some of their sad friends do say
The breath goes now, and some say no.
John Donne (c. 1571-1631)

I feel no pain dear mother now
But oh, I am so dry!
O take me to a brewery
And leave me there to die.
anonymous, 19th century

We often congratulate ourselves at the moment of waking from a troubled dream; it may be so at the moment of death.
Nathaniel Hawthorne (1804-1864)
American novelist

Die, my dear doctor! That's the last thing I shall do!
Lord Palmerston (1784-1865)
English politician, Prime Minister

He that dies pays all debts.
Stephano, *The Tempest*
William Shakespeare (1564-1616)

SEE Allen on The AFTERLIFE; Stalin on GENOCIDE; Maurois on LIFE; Bridges on LOVERS; St Anselm on PHILOSOPHY; Shaw on SCIENCE; Bright on WAR

Debauchery

It is the hour to be drunken! to escape being the martyred slaves of time, be ceaselessly drunk. On wine, on poetry, or on virtue, as you wish.
Charles Baudelaire (1821-1867)

My main problem is reconciling my gross habits with my net income.
Errol Flynn (1909-1959)

An improper mind is a perpetual feast.
Logan Pearsall Smith (1865-1946)
American essayist

His face was filled with broken commandments.
John Masefield (1878-1967)
English poet, playwright

Not joy, but joylessness, is the mother of debauchery.
Friedrich Nietzsche (1844-1900)

SEE ORGIES; Shaw on PUNISHMENT

Debts

In the midst of life we are in debt.
Ethel Watts Mumford (1878-1940)
American novelist, humorous writer

Small debts are like small shot; they are rattling on every side, and can scarcely be escaped without a wound; great debts are like cannon, of loud noise but little danger.
Dr Samuel Johnson (1709-1784)

Some people use one half their ingenuity to get into debt, and the other half to avoid paying it.
George D. Prentice (1802-1870)
American poet, journalist

Everybody in Vanity Fair must have remarked how well those live who are comfortably and thoroughly in debt; how they deny themselves nothing; how jolly and easy they are in their minds.
W. M. Thackeray (1811-1863)
English author

Creditor. One of a tribe of savages dwelling beyond the Financial Straits and dreaded for their desolating incursions.
Ambrose Bierce (1842-1914)
American author

A creditor is worse than a slave-owner; for the master owns only your person, but a creditor owns your dignity, and can command it.
Victor Hugo (1802-1885)

They hired the money, didn't they?
Calvin Coolidge (1872-1933)
American Republican politician, President
of the European allies, 1925,
in difficulty over repaying
war debts

Creditors have better memories than debtors.
Benjamin Franklin (1706-1790)

Forgetfulness. A gift of God bestowed upon debtors in compensation for their destitution of conscience.
Ambrose Bierce (1842-1914)
American author

No man's credit is as good as his money.
Ed (E. W.) Howe (1853-1937)
American journalist, novelist

There are but two ways of paying debt — increase of industry in raising income, increase of thrift in laying it out.
Thomas Carlyle (1795-1881)
Scottish author

To John I ow'd great obligation;
But John, unhappily, thought fit
To publish it to all the nation:
Sure John and I are more than quit.
Matthew Prior (1664-1721)
English poet, diplomat

Speak not of my debts unless you mean to pay them.
17th century English proverb

SEE Shakespeare on DEATH: Dying

Decisions

It is always thus, impelled by a state of mind which is destined not to last, that we make our irrevocable decisions.
Marcel Proust (1871-1922)

Some of his decisions were accurate. A stopped watch is right twice a day.
anonymous

Decide promptly, but never give any reasons. Your decisions may be right, but your reasons are sure to be wrong.
Lord Mansfield (1705-1793)
Scottish judge

The wrong way always seems the more reasonable.
George Moore (1852-1933)
Irish author

Decisiveness is often the art of timely cruelty.
Henri Becque (1837-1899)
French playwright

SEE Galbraith on CONFERENCES;
Franklin on DINNER PARTIES;
INDECISION

Decline

Statesmen and beauties are very rarely sensible of the gradations of their decay.
Lord Chesterfield (1694-1773)
English statesman and man of letters

As favour and riches forsake a man, we discover in him the foolishness they concealed,

and which no one perceived before.
Jean de la Bruyère (1645-1696)
French writer, moralist

Like our shadows,
Our wishes lengthen as the sun declines.
Edward Young (1683-1765)
English poet

SEE Addison on STARDOM

Decolonisation

Many politicians lay it down as a self-evident proposition that no people ought to be free until they are fit to use their freedom. The maxim is worthy of the fool in the old story who resolved not to go into the water until he had learned to swim.
Lord Macaulay (1800-1859)
English historian

To subtract from your own sovereignty in favour of a friend is much wiser than losing it all to an enemy.
Sir Robert Menzies (1894-1978)
Australian politician, Prime Minister

The wind of change is blowing through the continent. Whether we like it or not, this growth of national consciousness is a political fact.
Harold Macmillan, Lord Stockton (1894-1986)
British Conservative politician, Prime Minister
of Africa

It is ... nauseating to see Mr Gandhi, a seditious Middle Temple lawyer now posing as a fakir of a type well known in the East, striding half-naked up the steps of the Vice-regal Palace, while he is still organising and conducting a defiant campaign of civil disobedience, to parley on equal terms with the representative of the King Emperor.
Sir Winston Churchill (1874-1965)

SEE Nehru on EMPIRE

Defecation

Where there is a stink of shit there is a smell of being.
Antonin Artaud (1896-1948)
French theatre producer, actor, theorist

Defiance

Though I sit down now, the time will come when you will hear me.
Benjamin Disraeli (1804-1881)

Deliberation

Deliberation. The act of examining one's bread to determine which side it is buttered on.
Ambrose Bierce (1842-1914)
American author

If you think before you speak, the other fellow gets in his joke first.
Ed (E. W.) Howe (1853-1937)
American journalist, novelist

It is often said that second thoughts are best. So they are in matters of judgement, but not in matters of conscience.
> Cardinal John Newman (1801-1890)
> English churchman, theologian

Delinquency

He that seeks trouble never misses.
> 17th century English proverb

You go to other people's grounds, you run 'em, it's just enjoyment all the time... Like a tennis player gets all geared up to play, we get geared up to fight... Tribal, innit? Football is one tribe onto another... We fight 'cos we like fighting. If they banned drink we'd still fight.
> English football fan, 1985

I would there were no age between sixteen and three-and-twenty, or that youth would sleep out the rest; for there is nothing in the between but getting wenches with child, wronging the ancientry, stealing, fighting.
> Shepherd, *The Winter's Tale*
> William Shakespeare (1564-1616)

It would surely be far better for them and for the community at large if they all stayed at home and read a little light pornography.
> Sir Ian Gilmour (b. 1926)
> British Conservative politician

Every normal man must be tempted, at times, to spit on his hands, hoist the black flag, and begin slitting throats.
> H. L. Mencken (1880-1956)
> American journalist

Gentleman-rankers out on the spree,
Damned from here to Eternity.
> Rudyard Kipling (1865-1936)

Certain lewd fellows of the baser sort.
> Bible, Acts

There is a public mischief in your mirth.
> William Cowper (1731-1800)
> English poet

SEE Burke on STYLE

Demagogues

There have been many great men that have flattered the people, who ne'er loved them.
> William Shakespeare (1564-1616)

A demagogue is a person with whom we disagree as to which gang should mismanage the country.
> Don Marquis (1878-1937)
> American humorist, journalist

The secret of the demagogue is to make himself as stupid as his audience so that they believe they are as clever as he.
> Karl Kraus (1874-1936)
> Austrian poet, journalist

Democracy

An institution in which the whole is equal to the scum of the parts.
> Keith Preston (1884-1927)
> American poet, humorist

Democracy is the recurrent suspicion that more than half of the people are right more than half of the time.
> E. B. White (1899-1985)
> American author, editor

The most dangerous foe to truth and freedom in our midst is the compact majority, yes, the damned, compact, liberal majority.
> Henrik Ibsen (1828-1906)

I do not believe in the collective wisdom of individual ignorance.
> Thomas Carlyle (1795-1881)
> Scottish writer

Nor is the people's judgement always true;
The most may err as grossly as the few.
> John Dryden (1631-1700)

Democracy is the power of equal votes for unequal minds.
> *attributed to* Charles I of England (1600-1649)

Democracy is only an experiment in government, and it has the obvious disadvantage of merely counting votes instead of weighing them.
> W. R. Inge (1860-1954)
> Dean of St Paul's, London

It's not the voting that's democracy, it's the counting.
> Tom Stoppard (b. 1937)
> British playwright

When great changes occur in history, when great principles are involved, as a rule the majority are wrong.
> Eugene Debs (1855-1926)
> American trade unionist, co-founder of the Socialist Party of the United States

The majority never has the right on its side. Never I say! That is one of the social lies that a free, thinking man is bound to rebel against. Who makes up the majority in any given country? Is it the wise men or the fools? I think we must agree that the fools are in a terrible overwhelming majority, all the wide world over.
> Henrik Ibsen (1828-1906)

No man is good enough to govern another man without that other's consent.
> Abraham Lincoln (1809-1865)

As I would not be a *slave*, so I would not be a *master*. This expresses my idea of democracy.
> Abraham Lincoln (1809-1865)

Two cheers for democracy: one because it admits variety and two because it permits criticism.

> E. M. Forster (1879-1970)

Man's capacity for justice makes democracy possible, but man's inclination to injustice makes democracy necessary.

> Reinhold Niebuhr (1892-1971)
> American theologian, historian

The freeman, casting with unpurchased hand
The vote that shakes the turrets of the land.

> Dr Oliver Wendell Holmes (1809-1894)
> American writer, physician

The ballot is stronger than the bullet.

> Abraham Lincoln (1809-1865)

A fanatical belief in democracy makes democratic institutions impossible.

> Bertrand Russell (1872-1970)

There is a limit to the application of democratic methods. You can inquire of all the passengers as to what type of car they like to ride in, but it is impossible to question them as to whether to apply the brakes when the train is at full speed and accident threatens.

> Leon Trotsky (1879-1940)

Whatever democracy may be theoretically, one is sometimes tempted to define it practically as standardized and commercialized melodrama.

> Irving Babbit (1865-1933)
> American author, critic

Democracy substitutes election by the incompetent many for appointment by the corrupt few.

> George Bernard Shaw (1856-1950)

La democracia es un abuso de las estadisticas.
Democracy is an abuse of statistics.

> Jorge Luis Borges (1899-1986)

Democracy which began by liberating man politically has developed a dangerous tendency to enslave him through the tyranny of majorities and the deadly power of their opinion.

> Ludwig Lewisohn (1882-1956)
> American author, critic

Democracy becomes a government of bullies tempered by editors.

> R. W. Emerson (1803-1882)
> American essayist, poet, philosopher

Democracy means simply the bludgeoning of the people by the people for the people.

> Oscar Wilde (1854-1900)

Democracy: in which you say what you like and do what you're told.

> Gerald Barry (1898-1968)
> British journalist

Let the people think they govern and they will be governed.

> William Penn (1644-1718)
> religious leader, founder of Pennsylvania

I confess I enjoy democracy immensely. It is incomparably idiotic, and hence incomparably amusing.

> H. L. Mencken (1880-1956)
> American journalist

SEE ELECTIONS

Despair

I am in that temper that if I were under water I would scarcely kick to come to the top.

> John Keats (1795-1821)

There is no vulture like despair.

> Lord Lansdowne (1667-1735)
> English poet, dramatist

Melancholy, indeed, should be diverted by every means but drinking.

> Dr Samuel Johnson (1709-1784)

I want to be forgotten even by God.

> Robert Browning (1812-1889)

Despotism

When you take a benevolent man and make him a despot, his despotism survives but his benevolence rather fades away.

> Bertrand Russell (1872-1970)

The sin and sorrow of despotism is not that it does not love men, but that it loves them too much and trusts them too little.

> G. K. Chesterton (1874-1936)

Those in possession of absolute power can not only prophesy and make their prophecies come true, but they can also lie and make their lies come true.

> Eric Hoffer (1902-1983)
> American philosopher

A despot doesn't fear eloquent writers preaching freedom – he fears a drunken poet who may crack a joke that will take hold.

> E. B. White (1899-1985)
> American author, editor

Dictators ride to and fro upon tigers which they dare not dismount. And the tigers are getting hungry.

> Sir Winston Churchill (1874-1965)
> *in 1936*

SEE Chamfort on HISTORY; TYRANNY

Destiny

We are no more free agents than the queen of clubs when she takes the knave of hearts.

> Lady Mary Wortley Montagu (1689-1762)
> English society figure, letter writer

Destiny. A tyrant's authority for crime and a fool's excuse for failure.

> Ambrose Bierce (1842-1914)
> American author

We are not permitted to choose the frame of our destiny. But what we put into it is ours.
> Dag Hammarskjöld (1905-1961)
> Swedish statesman, Secretary-General of UN

He that is born to be hanged shall never be drowned.
> English proverb

Ça ira.
> Benjamin Franklin (1706-1790)
> on the American Revolution

SEE Priestley on COINCIDENCE; Khayyám on LIFE; Hubbard on MANAGEMENT; Reagan on Ronald REAGAN

The Devil

Better to reign in Hell, than to serve in Heaven.
> John Milton (1608-1674)

We may not pay Satan reverence, for that would be indiscreet, but we can at least respect his talents.
> Mark Twain (1835-1910)

An apology for the Devil — it must be remembered that we have only heard one side of the case. God has written all the books.
> Samuel Butler (1835-1902)
> English author

The Prince of Darkness is a gentleman.
> Edgar, King Lear
> William Shakespeare (1564-1616)

It is so stupid of modern civilization to have given up believing in the devil when he is the only explanation of it.
> Father Ronald Knox (1888-1957)
> British clergyman, writer

And Satan trembles when he sees
The weakest saint upon his knees.
> William Cowper (1731-1800)
> English poet

Diaries

'The horror of that moment', the King went on, 'I shall never, never forget!' 'You will, though', the Queen said, 'if you don't make a memorandum of it'.
> Lewis Carroll (1832-1898)

I always say, keep a diary and someday it'll keep you.
> Mae West (1892-1980)

It's the good girls who keep the diaries; the bad girls never have the time.
> Tallulah Bankhead (1902-1968)
> American actress

Dilettantes

A smattering of everything and a knowledge of nothing.
> Charles Dickens (1812-1870)

A man must love a thing very much if he not only practises it without any hope of fame and money, but even ... without any hope of doing it well.
> G. K. Chesterton (1874-1936)

Dilettante: a philanderer who seduces the several arts and deserts each in turn for another.
> Oliver Herford (1863-1935)
> American poet, illustrator

Dinner Parties

Men that can have communication in nothing else can sympathetically eat together, can still rise into some glow of brotherhood over food and wine.
> Thomas Carlyle (1795-1881)
> Scottish writer

He showed me his bill of fare to tempt me to dine with him; said I, I value not your bill of fare, give me your bill of company.
> Jonathan Swift (1667-1745)

To every man alive, one must hope, it has in some manner happened that he has talked with his more fascinating friends round a table on some night when all the numerous personalities unfolded themselves like great tropical flowers.
> G. K. Chesterton (1874-1936)

Where the guests at a gathering are well-acquainted, they eat twenty per cent more than they otherwise would.
> Ed (E. W.) Howe (1853-1937)
> American journalist, novelist

A dinner lubricates business.
> Lord Stowell (William Scott) (1745-1836)
> English lawyer

Take counsel in wine, but resolve afterwards in water.
> Benjamin Franklin (1706-1790)

The best number for a dinner party is two — myself and a dam' good head waiter.
> Nubar Gulbenkian (1897-1972)
> oil millionaire

I had rather munch a crust of brown bread and an onion in a corner, without ado or ceremony, than feed upon a turkey at another man's table, where I am forced to chew slowly, drink little, wipe my mouth every minute, and cannot sneeze or cough, or do other things that are the privileges of liberty and solitude.
> Miguel de Cervantes (1547-1616)

The object of a dinner is not to eat and drink, but to join in merrymaking and make a lot of noise. For that reason, he who drinks half drinks best.
> Lin Yutang (1895-1976)
> Chinese writer

It isn't so much what's on the table that matters as what's on the chairs.
W. S. Gilbert (1836-1911)
English librettist

In dinner talk it is perhaps allowable to fling any faggot rather than let the fire go out.
J. M. Barrie (1860-1937)
British playwright

If you want to shine as a diner-out, the best way is to know something which others do not know, and not to know many things which everybody knows. This takes much less reading, and ... makes you a really good listener.
Coventry Patmore (1823-1896)
English poet

Don't talk about yourself, it will be done when you leave.
Addison Mizner (1872-1933)
American architect, writer

Conversation is the enemy of good wine and food.
Alfred Hitchcock (1899-1980)

A host is like a general: calamities often reveal his genius.
Horace (65-8 BC)

When her guests were awash with
  champagne and with gin
She was recklessly sober, as sharp
  as a pin.
William Plomer (1903-1973)
British writer

This was a good enough dinner, to be sure; but it was not a dinner to *ask* a man to.
Dr Samuel Johnson (1709-1784)

After a good dinner, one can forgive anybody, even one's own relations.
Oscar Wilde (1854-1900)

When at length they rose to go to bed, it struck each and as he followed his neighbour upstairs that the one before him walked very crookedly.
R. S. Surtees (1803-1864)
English novelist

It's what the guests say as they swing out of the drive that counts.
anonymous
New York Times

Long meals make short lives.
Sir John Lubbock, Lord Avebury (1834-1915)
British banker, scientist, author

Forsan et haec olim meminisse iuvabit.
Perhaps one day this too will be pleasant to remember.
Virgil (70-19 BC)

SEE Thoreau on GOVERNMENT;

Nietzsche on GUESTS; Shaw on REVOLUTIONARIES

Diplomacy

Diplomacy is to do and say
The nastiest things in the
  nicest way.
Isaac Goldberg (1887-1938)
American critic

A diplomat is a man who always remembers a woman's birthday but never remembers her age.
Robert Frost (1875-1963)
American poet

A really good diplomat does not go in for victories, even when he wins them.
Walter Lippman (1889-1974)
American journalist

Let us never negotiate out of fear, but let us never fear to negotiate.
John F. Kennedy (1917-1963)

A man-of-war is the best ambassador.
Oliver Cromwell (1599-1658)

A diplomat these days is nothing but a head-waiter who's allowed to sit down occasionally.
Peter Ustinov (b. 1921)
British actor, wit

If you are to stand up for your Government you must be able to stand up to your Government.
Sir Harold, later Lord, Caccia (b. 1905)
while British ambassador at Washington

I have discovered the art of fooling diplomats; I speak the truth and they never believe me.
Camillo di Cavour (1810-1861)
Italian statesman

Diplomacy: lying in state.
Oliver Herford (1863-1935)
American poet, illustrator

Babies in silk hats playing with dynamite.
Alexander Woollcott (1887-1943)
American columnist, critic

SEE TACT

Disappointment

There are two tragedies in life. One is to lose your heart's desire. The other is to gain it.
Mendoza, *Man and Superman*
George Bernard Shaw (1856-1950)

The world hath failed to impart
The joy our youth forebodes,
Failed to fill up the void which
  in our breasts we bear.
Matthew Arnold (1822-1888)
English poet, critic

Él que espera lo mucho espera lo poco.
He who expects much can expect little.
Gabriel García Márquez (b. 1928)
Colombian writer

'Blessed is the man who expects nothing, for he shall never be disappointed' was the ninth beatitude.
Alexander Pope (1688-1744)

Disasters

Our sympathy is cold to the relation of distant misery.
Edward Gibbon (1737-1794)

Man's extremity is God's opportunity.
John Flavel (1630-1691)
English evangelist, author

Calamities are of two kinds: misfortune to ourselves, and good fortune to others.
Ambrose Bierce (1842-1914)
American author

Oh, dry the starting tear, for they were heavily insured.
W. S. Gilbert (1836-1911)
English librettist

The collapsed slag heap looks weirdly, wickedly voluptuous as you see it from a distance, for it sprawls into the village like a reclining female monster, a wanton Negress shifting awkwardly on her smelly hams. The sense of outrage and impotent disgust seems to coil itself in the very walk of those who approach the defilement, their gumboots slipslopping in the slime.
Dennis Potter (b. 1935)
British playwright
of the Aberfan disaster, 1966

SEE Benson on FANATICS; Attlee on
The PRESS

Disc Jockeys

This particularly rapid, unintelligible
patter
Isn't generally heard, and if it is it
doesn't matter!
W. S. Gilbert (1836-1911)
English librettist

Radio news is bearable. This is due to the fact that while the news is being broadcast the disc jockey is not allowed to talk.
Fran Lebowitz (b. 1951)
American journalist

SEE WILDE on UNDERSTANDING

Discretion

Nothing is more dangerous than a friend without discretion; even a prudent enemy is preferable.
Jean de la Fontaine (1621-1695)
French poet, fabulist

As a jewel of gold in a swine's snout, so is a fair woman which is without discretion.
Bible, Psalms

Una bocca chiusa non prende mosche.
A closed mouth catches no flies.
Italian proverb

Give thy thoughts no tongue,
Nor any unproportioned thought his
act.
Be thou familiar, but by no means
vulgar.
Those friends thou hast, and their
adoption tried,
Grapple them to thy soul with hoops
of steel.
Polonius, Hamlet
William Shakespeare (1564-1616)

What is called discretion in men is called cunning in animals.
Jean de la Fontaine (1621-1695)
French poet, fabulist

A wise man sees as much as he ought, not as much as he can.
Michel de Montaigne (1533-1592)
French essayist

Be wiser than other people, if you can, but do not tell them so.
Lord Chesterfield (1694-1773)
English statesman and man of letters

He that has a secret should not only hide it, but hide that he has it to hide.
Thomas Carlyle (1795-1881)
Scottish author

When the strong command, obedience is best.
Sir Henry Newbolt (1862-1938)
British poet

Not right out, but stealthily, like a parson's damn.
Thomas Hardy (1840-1928)

SEE CUNNING

Disgrace

Oh! no! we never mention her,
Her name is never heard;
My lips are now forbid to speak
That once familiar word.
Thomas H. Bayly (1797-1839)
English writer, poet

Dissatisfaction

The idiot who praises with
enthusiastic tone
All centuries but this and every
country but his own.
W. S. Gilbert (1836-1911)
English librettist

As long as I have a want, I have a reason for living. Satisfaction is death.
Gregory, Overruled
George Bernard Shaw (1856-1950)

With me, its just a genetic dissatisfaction with everything.
Woody Allen (b. 1935)

Dissent

In a world of fugitives
The person taking the opposite
direction
Will appear to run away.
T. S. Eliot (1888-1965)

It is dangerous to be right in matters on which the established authorities are wrong.
Voltaire (1694-1778)

Discussion in America means dissent.
James Thurber (1894-1961)
American humorist, illustrator

In a democracy dissent is an act of faith. Like medicine, the test of its value is not in its taste, but its effects.
J. W. Fulbright (b. 1905)
American Democratic politician

Divorce

The only solid and lasting peace between a man and his wife is doubtless a separation.
Lord Chesterfield (1694-1773)
English statesman and man of letters

Divorce is probably of nearly the same date as marriage. I believe, however, that marriage is some weeks the more ancient.
Voltaire (1694-1778)

It is he who has broken the bond of marriage – not I. I only break its bondage.
Oscar Wilde (1854-1900)

A Roman divorced from his wife, being highly blamed by his friends, who demanded, 'Was she not chaste? Was she not fair? Was she not fruitful?' holding out his shoe, asked them whether it was not new and well made. 'Yet', added he, 'none of you can tell where it pinches me'.
Plutarch (46-120)

Judges, as a class, display, in the matter of arranging alimony, that reckless generosity which is found only in men who are giving away someone else's cash.
P. G. Wodehouse (1881-1975)

You never realize how short a month is until you pay alimony.
John Barrymore (1882-1942)
American author

SEE Fosdick, Storr on MARRIAGE

Doctors

I wasn't driven into medicine by a social conscience but by rampant curiosity.
Jonathan Miller (b. 1936)
British writer, doctor

God heals, and the doctor takes the fee.
Benjamin Franklin (1706-1790)

The art of medicine consists of amusing the patient while Nature cures the disease.
Voltaire (1694-1778)

The best doctors in the world are Doctor Diet, Doctor Quiet and Doctor Merryman.
Jonathan Swift (1667-1745)

A skilful leech is better far
Than half a hundred men of war.
Samuel Butler (1612-1680)
English poet

One finger in the throat and one in the rectum make a good diagnostician.
Sir William Osler (1849-1919)
Canadian physician

Doctors think a lot of patients are cured who have simply quit in disgust.
Don Herold (b. 1889)
American humorous writer, artist

While others meanly asked whole
months to slay
I oft dispatched the patient in a
day.
Sir Samuel Garth (1661-1719)
English physician, poet

He wastes no time with patients: and when you have to die, he will finish the business quicker than anybody else.
Molière (1622-1673)

What I call a good patient is one who, having found a good physician, sticks to him till he dies.
Dr Oliver Wendell Holmes (1809-1894)
American writer, physician

Cured yesterday of my disease,
I died last night of my physician.
Matthew Prior (1664-1721)
English poet, diplomat

While the doctors consult, the patient dies.
English proverb

The doctor found, when she was dead,
Her last disorder mortal.
Oliver Goldsmith (1728-1774)

My doctor gave me six months to live but when I couldn't pay the bill he gave me six months more.
Walter Matthau (b. 1920)

There are worse occupations in the world than feeling a woman's pulse.
Laurence Sterne (1713-1768)
English author

Taking a lady's hand gives her confidence in her physician.
Sir William Osler (1849-1919)
Canadian physician

Life is short and the art is long.
Hippocrates (c. 460-c. 370 BC)
Greek physician
of the art of healing

SEE Piozzi on LIFE; Hubbard on
POVERTY

Doctrine

Punch is very much like the Church of
England. It is doctrinally inexplicable, but it
goes on.
Malcolm Muggeridge (b. 1903)
British journalist

There are men who would even be afraid to
commit themselves on the doctrine that castor
oil is a laxative.
Camille Flammarion (1842-1925)
French astronomer, clergyman

Example moves the world more than doctrine.
Henry Miller (1891-1980)

Doctrine is nothing but the skin of truth set up
and stuffed.
H. W. Beecher (1813-1887)
American clergyman, editor, writer

SEE Defoe on TEACHERS

Dogmatism

The greater the ignorance the greater the
dogmatism.
Sir William Osler (1849-1919)
Canadian physician

Dogmas are fences round the mystery.
Saint Augustine (354-430)

Dogmatism does not mean the absence of
thought, but the end of thought.
G. K. Chesterton (1874-1936)

Any stigma will do to beat a dogma.
Philip Guedalla (1889-1944)
British author

Dogmatism is puppyism come to its full
growth.
Douglas Jerrold (1803-1857)
English playwright, humorist

SEE Butler, Newman on RELIGION

Dogs

To his dog, every man is Napoleon; hence the
constant popularity of dogs.
Aldous Huxley (1894-1963)

The great pleasure of a dog is that you may
make a fool of yourself with him and not only
will he not scold you, but he will make a fool
of himself too.
Samuel Butler (1835-1902)
English author

If your home burns down, rescue the dogs. At
least they'll be faithful to you.
Lee Marvin (b. 1924)

A dog teaches a boy fidelity, perseverance, and
to turn around three times before lying down.
Robert Benchley (1889-1945)
American humorous writer

Well-washed and well-combed domestic pets
grow dull; they miss the stimulus of fleas.
Francis Galton (1822-1911)
British scientist

Near this spot are deposited the remains of
one who possessed Beauty without Vanity,
Strength without Insolence, Courage without
Ferocity, and all the Virtues of Man, without
his Vices. This Praise, which would be unmean
Flattery if inscribed over human ashes, is but a
just tribute to the Memory of Boatswain, a
Dog.
Lord Byron (1788-1824)

Dog. A kind of additional or subsidiary Deity
designed to catch the overflow and surplus of
the world's worship.
Ambrose Bierce (1842-1914)
American author

If you pick up a starving dog and make him
prosperous, he will not bite you; that is the
principal difference between a dog and a man.
Mark Twain (1835-1910)

SEE Shaw on CLASS; Kraus, Pope on
LOYALTY

Doubt

Between the conception and the creation
Between the emotion and the response,
Falls the Shadow.
T. S. Eliot (1888-1965)

When we are not sure, we are alive.
Graham Greene (b. 1904)

There is a vulgar incredulity, which in historical matters, as well as in those of religion,
finds it easier to doubt than to examine.
Sir Walter Scott (1771-1832)

The first step towards philosophy is incred-
ulity.
Denis Diderot (1713-1784)
French philosopher, *encyclopédiste*

Why do men hate and despise the doubter?
Because doubt is evolution, and society hates
evolution because it disturbs the peace.
J. A. Strindberg (1849-1912)

I beseech you, in the bowels of Christ, think it
possible you may be mistaken.
Oliver Cromwell (1599-1658)

Half the failures of this world arise from
pulling in one's horse as he is leaping.
Julius Hare (1795-1855) and
Augustus Hare (1792-1834)
English clerics, writers

SEE Unamuno on FAITH;
Bible on INDECISION

Dreaming

We never stop seeing, perhaps this is why we dream.
> Johann Wolfgang von Goethe (1749-1832)

In bed my real love has always been the sleep that rescued me by allowing me to dream.
> Luigi Pirandello (1867-1936)
> Italian author, playwright

One of the characteristics of the dream is that nothing surprises us in it. With no regret, we agree to live in it with strangers, completely cut off from our habits and friends.
> Jean Cocteau (1889-1963)
> French writer, film director

How many of our daydreams would darken into nightmares, were there any danger of their becoming true.
> Logan Pearsall Smith (1865-1946)
> American essayist

In the drowsy dark cave of the mind
dreams build their nest with fragments
dropped from day's caravan.
> Rabindranath Tagore (1861-1941)
> Indian author, philosopher

When we can't dream any longer we die.
> Emma Goldman (1869-1940)
> American anarchist

SEE Williams on PSYCHOANALYSIS;
Shaw on VISIONARIES

Dress

She looked as though she had been poured into her clothes and had forgotten to say 'when'.
> P. G. Wodehouse (1881-1975)
> British novelist

A fine woman shews her charms to most advantage when she seems most to conceal them. The finest bosom in nature is not so fine as imagination forms.
> Dr Gregory (18th century)
> from A Father's Legacy to His Daughters

I have heard with admiring submission the experience of the lady who declared that the sense of being well-dressed gives a feeling of inward tranquillity which religion is powerless to bestow.
> R. W. Emerson (1803-1882)
> American essayist, poet, philosopher

The prettiest dresses are worn to be taken off.
> Jean Cocteau (1891-1963)
> French writer, film director

The trouble about most Englishwomen is that they will dress as if they had been a mouse in a previous incarnation, or hope to be one in the next.
> Dame Edith Sitwell (1887-1964)
> British writer, poet

Englishwomen's shoes look as if they had been made by someone who had often heard shoes described, but had never seen any.
> Margaret Halsey (b. 1910)
> American author

There is not so variable a thing in nature as a lady's head-dress.
> Joseph Addison (1672-1719)
> English essayist

Taking off my stays at the end of the day makes me happier than anything I know.
> Joyce Grenfell (1910-1980)
> British actress

All women's dresses are merely variations on the eternal struggle between the admitted desire to dress and the unadmitted desire to undress.
> Lin Yutang (1895-1976)
> Chinese writer

Silk was invented so that women could go naked in clothes.
> Muhammad (570-632)

Where's the man could ease a heart
Like a satin gown?
> Dorothy Parker (1893-1967)
> American humorous writer

When men wish to be safely impressive, as judges, priests or kings, they ... wear skirts. ... The whole world is under petticoat government.
> G. K. Chesterton (1874-1936)

It is an interesting question how far men would retain their relative rank if they were divested of their clothes.
> H. D. Thoreau (1817-1862)

Great men are seldom over-scrupulous in the arrangement of their attire.
> Charles Dickens (1812-1870)

I hold that gentleman to be the best-dressed whose dress no one observes.
> Anthony Trollope (1815-1882)
> English novelist

You look rather rash my dear your colors don't quite match your face.
> Daisy Ashford (1881-1972)
> British writer of The
> Young Visiters, aged 9

SEE Berger on NUDITY

Drink

O God! that men should put an enemy in their mouths to steal away their brains.
> Cassio, Othello
> William Shakespeare (1564-1616)

Drink! for you know not whence you
    came nor why:
Drink! for you know not why you
    go, nor where.
> from *The Rubáiyát of Omar Khayyám*
> trans. Edward Fitzgerald (1809-1883)

Malt does more than Milton can
    To justify God's ways to man.
> A. E. Housman (1859-1936)
> British poet, classical scholar

The sway of alcohol over mankind is unques-
tionably due to its power to stimulate the
mystical faculties of human nature.
> William James (1842-1910)
> American psychologist, philosopher

The heart which grief hath cankered
Hath one unfailing remedy – the
    Tankard.
> C. S. Calverley (1831-1884)
> English poet

Ale, man, ale's the stuff to drink
For fellows whom it hurts to think.
> A. E. Housman (1859-1936)
> British poet, classical scholar

What two ideas are more inseparable than
beer and Britannia?
> Sydney Smith (1771-1845)
> English writer, clergyman

They who drink beer will think beer.
> Washington Irving (1783-1859)
> American author

Bring in the bottled lightning, a clean tumbler,
and a corkscrew.
> Charles Dickens (1812-1870)

A torchlight procession marching down your
throat.
> John O'Sullivan (1813-1895)
> American journalist
> *of whisky*

A sudden violent jolt of it has been known to
stop the victim's watch, snap his suspenders
and crack his glass eye right across.
> Irvin S. Cobb (1876-1944)
> American author
> *of moonshine corn liquor*

Fill it up. I take as large draughts of liquor as I
did of love. I hate a flincher in either.
> Mrs Trapes, *The Beggar's Opera*
> John Gay (1685-1732)

I can't say whether we had more wit amongst
us than usual, but I am certain we had more
laughing, which answered the end just as well.
> Oliver Goldsmith (1728-1774)

Drink not the third glass, which thou
    canst not tame,
When once it is within thee.
> George Herbert (1593-1633)
> English clergyman, poet

He smiled a kind of sickly smile, and
    curled up on the floor,
And the subsequent proceedings
    interested him no more.
> Francis Brett Harte (1836-1902)
> American author

A man who exposes himself when he is
intoxicated, has not the art of getting drunk.
> Dr Samuel Johnson (1709-1784)

Better belly burst than good liquor be lost.
> Jonathan Swift (1667-1745)

'I wonder what pleasure men can take in
making beasts of themselves!' 'I wonder,
madam, that you have not penetration enough
to see the strong inducement to this excess; for
he who makes a *beast* of himself gets rid of the
pain of being a man'.
> Dr Samuel Johnson (1709-1784)

Drunkenness is nothing but voluntary madness.
> Seneca (c. 5-65)
> Roman writer, philosopher, statesman

Drunkenness is temporary suicide.
> Bertrand Russell (1872-1970)

When I played drunks I had to remain sober
because I didn't know how to play them when
I was drunk.
> Richard Burton (1925-1984)

What soberness conceals, drunkenness reveals.
> Latin proverb

An honest man, that is not quite sober, has
nothing to fear.
> Joseph Addison (1672-1719)
> English essayist

It provokes the desire, but it takes away the
performance. Therefore much drink may be
said to be an equivocator with lechery.
> Porter, *Macbeth*
> William Shakespeare (1564-1616)

There are some sluggish men who are
improved by drinking, as there are fruits that
are not good until they are rotten.
> Dr Samuel Johnson (1709-1784)

Friendships are not always preserved in
alcohol.
> *wayside pulpit*

Alcohol is like love: the first kiss is magic, the
second is intimate, the third is routine. After
that you just take the girl's clothes off.
> Raymond Chandler (1888-1959)

There are two things that will be believed of
any man whatsoever, and one of them is that
he has taken to drink.
> Booth Tarkington (1869-1946)
> American author

The rapturous, wild, and ineffable
    pleasure

Of drinking at somebody else's
expense.
H. S. Leigh (1837-1883)
English author

I drink for the thirst to come.
François Rabelais (1492-1553)

Drink, and be mad, then; 'tis your
country bids!
Gloriously drunk, obey th'important
call!
William Cowper (1731-1800)
English poet

Drink: Abstinence Total abstinence is
easier to me than perfect moderation.
Saint Augustine (354-430)

I was T.T. until prohibition.
Groucho Marx (1895-1977)

I'm only a beer teetotaller, not a champagne
teetotaller.
Proserpine, *Candida*
George Bernard Shaw (1856-1950)

I'd hate to be a teetotaller. Imagine getting up
in the morning and knowing that's as good as
you're going to feel all day.
Dean Martin (b. 1917)

Water flowed like wine.
William M. Evarts (1818-1901)
American statesman

SEE Dryden on The ARMY; COCKTAILS;
Johnson on DESPAIR; Johnson on HEROES;
WINE; Wilde on WORK

Drugs

One man's poison is another man's drug.
Father Ronald Knox (1888-1957)
British clergyman, writer

Thou source of all my bliss and all
my woe,
That found'st me poor at first,
and keep'st me so.
Oliver Goldsmith (1728-1774)

Thou hast the keys of Paradise, oh just, subtle,
and mighty opium!
Thomas de Quincey (1785-1859)
English author

Everything one does in life, even love, occurs
in an express train racing towards death. To
smoke opium is to get out of the train while it
is still moving. It is to concern oneself with
something other than life, with death.
Jean Cocteau (1889-1963)
French writer, film director

It is not opium which enables me to work, but
its absence; and to feel its absence it must
from time to time pass through me.
Antonin Artaud (1896-1948)
French theatre producer, actor, theorist

Opiate. An unlocked door in the prison of
Identity. It leads into the jail yard.
Ambrose Bierce (1842-1914)
American author

*Ce n'est plus une ardeur dans mes veines
cachée:
C'est Vénus tout entière à sa proie
attachée.*
It's no longer a warmth hidden in my veins:
it's Venus entire and whole fastening on her
prey.
Jean Racine (1639-1699)

They shoulda called me Little Cocaine, I was
sniffing so much of the stuff! My nose got big
enough to back a diesel truck in, unload it,
and drive it right out again.
Little Richard (b. 1932)

Cocaine isn't habit-forming. I should know –
I've been using it for years.
Tallulah Bankhead (1902-1968)
American actress

The only reason that cocaine is such a rage
today is that people are too dumb and lazy to
get themselves together to roll a joint.
Jack Nicholson (b. 1937)

Is marijuana addictive? Yes, in the sense that
most of the really pleasant things in life are
worth endlessly repeating.
Richard Neville (b. 1941)
Australian journalist

I'll die young, but it's like kissing God.
Lenny Bruce (1923-1966)

SEE ADDICT; Nietzsche on
CHRISTIANITY; Artaud on SUFFERING

Dullness

The midwife laid her hand on his
Thick Skull,
With this Prophetick blessing –
Be Thou Dull.
John Dryden (1631-1700)

Sir, he was dull in company, dull in his closet,
dull everywhere. He was dull in a new way,
and that made people think him great.
Dr Samuel Johnson (1709-1784)
of Thomas Gray

He is not only dull in himself, but the cause of
dullness in others.
Samuel Foote (1720-1777)
English dramatist

Prudent Dulness marked him for a mayor.
Charles Churchill (1731-1764)
English clergyman, poet

It is to be noted that when any of this paper
appears dull, there is a design in it.
Sir Richard Steele (1672-1729)
English dramatist, essayist, editor

There are no uninteresting things, there are only uninterested people.

G. K. Chesterton (1874-1936)

SEE BORES; Mencken on CERTAINTY

Duty

God is inconceivable, immortality is unbelievable, but duty is peremptory and absolute.

George Eliot (1819-1880)

The consciousness of a duty performed gives us music at midnight.

George Herbert (1593-1633)
English clergyman, poet

I sighed as a lover, I obeyed as a son.

Edward Gibbon (1737-1794)

When a stupid man is doing something he is ashamed of, he always declares that it is his duty.

Apollodorus, *Caesar and Cleopatra*
George Bernard Shaw (1856-1950)

Duty. That which sternly impels us in the direction of profit, along the line of desire.

Ambrose Bierce (1842-1914)
American author

SEE Shaw on POLITICIANS

E

Eccentricity

We might define an eccentric as a man who is a law unto himself, and a crank as one who, having determined what the law is, insists on laying it down to others.
Louis Kronenberger (1904-1980)
American critic, author, editor

So long as a man rides his hobby-horse peaceably and quietly along the King's highway, and neither compels you or me to get up behind him, – pray, Sir, what have either you or I to do with it?
Laurence Sterne (1713-1768)
English author

SEE Mill on CONFORMITY

Ecology

The nation that destroys its soil destroys itself.
Franklin D. Roosevelt (1882-1945)

We abuse land because we regard it as a commodity belonging to us. When we see land as a community to which we belong, we may begin to use it with love and respect.
Aldo Leopold (1886-1948)
American forester

The sun, the moon and the stars would have disappeared long ago, had they happened to be within reach of predatory human hands.
Havelock Ellis (1859-1939)
British psychologist

SEE Durrell on NATURE; POLLUTION

Economics

Only one fellow in ten thousand understands the currency question, and we meet him every day.
Kin (F. McKinney) Hubbard (1868-1930)
American humorist, journalist

I learned more about economics from one South Dakota dust storm than I did in all my years in college.
Hubert Humphrey (1911-1978)
American Democratic politician

If all economists were laid end to end, they would not reach a conclusion.
George Bernard Shaw (1856-1950)

In the usual (though certainly not in every) public decision on economic policy, the choice is between courses that are almost equally good or equally bad. It is the narrowest decisions that are most ardently debated. If the world is lucky enough to enjoy peace, it may even one day make the discovery, to the horror of doctrinaire free-enterprisers and doctrinaire planners alike, that what is called capitalism and what is called socialism are both capable of working quite well.
J. K. Galbraith (b. 1908)
American economist

Call a thing immoral or ugly . . . a peril to the peace of the world or to the well-being of future generations: as long as you have not shown it to be 'uneconomic' you have not really questioned its right to exist, grow and prosper.
E. F. Schumacher (1911-1977)
American author

Economising

Live within your income. Always have something saved at the end of the year. Let your imports be more than your exports, and you'll never go far wrong.
Dr Samuel Johnson (1709-1784)

How easy it is for a man to die rich, if he will but be contented to live miserable.
Henry Fielding (1707-1754)

The timid man calls himself cautious, the sordid man thrifty.
Publilius Syrus (1st century BC)
Roman writer of mimes

Frugality is a handsome income.
Erasmus (1466-1536)

There is no profit in going to bed early if the result is twins.
country saying

SEE MEANNESS

The Economy

Everyone is always in favour of general economy and particular expenditure.
Sir Anthony Eden (1897-1977)
British Conservative politician, Prime Minister

If you want to raise a certain cheer in the House of Commons, make a general panegyric

on economy; if you want to invite a sure defeat, propose a particular saving.
financier quoted by Walter Bagehot

Every bright spot the White House finds in the economy is like the policeman bending over the body in the alley and saying cheerfully 'Two wounds are fatal. The other one is not so bad'.
John F. Kennedy (1917-1963)
when Senator

The notion dies hard that in some sort of way exports are patriotic but imports are immoral.
Lord Harlech (1918-1985)
British ambassador at Washington

We might come closer to balancing the budget if all of us lived closer to the Commandments and the Golden Rule.
Ronald Reagan (b. 1911)

SEE Weil on WAR

Editing

Si j'écris quatre mots, j'en effacerai trois.
Of every four words I write, I strike out three.
Nicolas Boileau (1636-1711)
French poet, critic

Read your own compositions, and when you meet with a passage which you think is particularly fine, strike it out.
Dr Samuel Johnson (1709-1784)

Art should simplify . . . finding what convention of form and what detail one can do without and yet preserve the spirit of the whole – so that all that one has suppressed and cut away is there to the reader's consciousness as much as if it were in type on the page.
Willa Cather (1876-1947)
American author

What I have crossed out I didn't like. What I haven't crossed out I'm dissatisfied with.
Cecil B. de Mille (1881-1959)
attributed, attached to script

God sends meat and the devil sends cooks.
Thomas Deloney (c. 1550-1600)
English balladist, writer

Je n'ai fait celle-ci plus longue que parce que je n'ai pas eu le loisir de la faire plus courte.
I have only made this [letter] longer because I have not had the time to make it shorter.
Blaise Pascal (1623-1662)

SEE Quiller-Couch, Smith on WRITING

Editors

Editor: a person employed on a newspaper, whose business it is to separate the wheat from the chaff, and to see that the chaff gets printed.
Elbert Hubbard (1856-1915)
American author

Rides in the whirlwind and directs the storm.
Joseph Addison (1672-1719)
English essayist

SEE Emerson on DEMOCRACY

Education

There's a new tribunal now, higher
    than God's –
The educated man's!
Robert Browning (1812-1889)

What sculpture is to a block of marble, education is to the soul.
Joseph Addison (1672-1719)
English essayist

Educate men without religion and you make them but clever devils.
Duke of Wellington (1769-1852)

Why should we subsidize intellectual curiosity?
Ronald Reagan (b. 1911)

Education is the ability to listen to almost anything without losing your temper or your self-confidence.
Robert Frost (1874-1963)
American poet

The first thing education teaches you to do is to walk alone.
Alfred Aloysius Horn (1861-1931)

The first idea that the child must acquire in order to be actively disciplined is that of the difference between good and evil; and the task of the educator lies in seeing that the child does not confound good with immobility, and evil with activity.
Maria Montessori (1870-1952)
Italian educator

Education is what remains when we have forgotten all that we have been taught.
George Savile, Lord Halifax (1633-1695)
English statesman, author

Education is an admirable thing, but it is well to remember from time to time that nothing that is worth knowing can be taught.
Oscar Wilde (1854-1900)

Education does not mean teaching people to know what they do not know; it means teaching them to behave as they do not behave.
John Ruskin (1819-1900)
English critic

The primary purpose of a liberal education is to make one's mind a pleasant place in which to spend one's time.
Sydney J. Harris (b. 1917)
American journalist

No man who worships education has got the best out of education. . . Without a gentle contempt for education no man's education is complete.
G. K. Chesterton (1874-1936)

British parents are very ready to call for a system of education which offers equal opportunity to all children except their own.
Lord Eccles (b. 1904)
British Conservative politician

True education makes for inequality; the inequality of individuality, the inequality of success, the glorious inequality of talent, of genius.
Felix E. Schelling (1858-1945)
American educator

Workers of England be wise, and then you *must* be free, for you will be *fit* to be free.
Charles Kingsley (1819-1875)
English author, clergyman

Education makes a people easy to lead, but difficult to drive; easy to govern but impossible to enslave.
Lord Brougham (1778-1868)
Scottish Whig politician

It is not the insurrections of ignorance that are dangerous, but the revolts of intelligence.
J. R. Lowell (1819-1891)
American poet

Human history becomes more and more a race between education and catastrophe.
H. G. Wells (1866-1946)

When a man's education is finished, he is finished.
E. A. Filene (1860-1937)
American businessman, financier

SEE Shaw on CLASS; Chesterton on FOREIGNERS; Hughes on PLAY; PRIVATE EDUCATION; Trevelyan on READING; SCHOOL; STUDENTS; TEACHERS; UNIVERSITY

Egoism

Man can be defined as the animal that can say 'I', that can be aware of himself as a separate entity.
Erich Fromm (1900-1980)
American psychologist

The great act of faith is when a man decides that he is not God.
Justice Oliver Wendell Holmes (1841-1935)
American jurist

Egotist. A person of low taste, more interested in himself than me.
Ambrose Bierce (1842-1914)
American author

Talk to a man about himself and he will listen for hours.
Benjamin Disraeli (1804-1881)

A self-made man; who worships his creator.
John Bright (1811-1889)
English Radical politician
of Benjamin Disraeli

The idea that egotism is the basis of the general welfare is the principle on which competitive society has been built.
Erich Fromm (1900-1980)
American psychologist

An inflated consciousness is always egocentric and conscious of nothing but its own existence. It is incapable of learning from the past, incapable of understanding contemporary events, and incapable of drawing right conclusions about the future. It is hypnotized by itself and therefore cannot be argued with. It inevitably dooms itself to calamities that must strike it dead.
Carl Jung (1875-1961)

Edith was a little country bounded on the north, south, east and west by Edith.
Martha Ostenso (1900-1963)
American author

SEE Wilding on ACTORS; Fuller on BORES; Webb on GENIUS; SELF

Elections

There's small choice in rotten apples.
Hortensia, *The Taming of the Shrew*
William Shakespeare (1564-1616)

Vote for the man who promises least. He'll be the least disappointing.
Bernard Baruch (1870-1965)
American financier

I never vote for anyone. I always vote against.
W. C. Fields (1879-1946)

It doesn't matter who you vote for, the government always gets in.
graffito in London, 1970s

Bad officials are elected by good citizens who do not vote.
George Jean Nathan (1882-1958)
American critic

I just received the following wire from my generous Daddy: 'Dear Jack, Don't buy a single vote more than necessary. I'll be damned if I'm going to pay for a landslide'.
John F. Kennedy (1917-1963)

The Republicans have a 'me too' candidate running on a 'yes but' platform, advised by a 'has been' staff.
Adlai Stevenson (1900-1965)
American Democratic politician

Indeed, you won the elections, but I won the count.
Anastasio Somoza (1896-1956)
dictator of Nicaragua
to an opponent accusing him
of rigging the election

SEE Pope on GOVERNMENT

Eloquence

Ah, si je pouvais pisser comme il parle!
> Georges Clemenceau (1841-1929)
> French politician, Prime Minister
> *of David Lloyd George*

The finest eloquence is that which gets things done; the worst is that which delays them.
> David Lloyd George (1863-1945)·
> Welsh Liberal politician, Prime Minister

Genuinely good remarks surprise their author as well as his audience.
> Joseph Joubert (1754-1824)
> French essayist, moralist

In the midwives' phrase, a perfect conception with an easy delivery.
> Alexander Pope (1688-1744)

L'art de la parenthèse est un des grands secrets de l'éloquence dans la Société.
The art of the parenthesis is one of the great secrets of eloquence in Society.
> Nicolas-Sébastien Chamfort (1741-1794)
> French writer, wit

To say that he was not at a loss for a word is one of the great understatements of all time. He was not at a loss for 500,000 words and we heard 'em, every one.
> Cassandra (Sir William Connor) (1909-1967)
> British journalist

He talked on for ever; and you wished him to talk on for ever.
> William Hazlitt (1778-1830)
> English essayist
> *of Coleridge*

When a man gets talking about himself, he seldom fails to be eloquent and often reaches the sublime.
> Josh Billings (1818-1885)
> American humorist

SEE Inge, Junius on PERSUASION;
Molière on SPEECHES

Embarrassment

Man is the only animal that blushes. Or needs to.
> Mark Twain (1835-1910)

We never forgive those who make us blush.
> Jean-François de La Harpe (1739-1803)
> French poet, playwright

Emotion

Half our mistakes in life arise from feeling where we ought to think, and thinking where we ought to feel.
> J. Churton Collins (1848-1908)
> English author, critic, scholar

The advantage of the emotions is that they lead us astray.
> Oscar Wilde (1854-1900)

'There are strings', said Mr Tappertit, '. . . in the human heart that had better not be wibrated'.
> Barnaby Rudge
> Charles Dickens (1812-1870)

The young man who has not wept is a savage, and the old man who will not laugh is a fool.
> George Santayana (1863-1952)
> American philosopher, poet

He is not affected by the reality of distress touching his heart, but by the showy resemblance of it striking his imagination. He pities the plumage, but forgets the dying bird.
> Thomas Paine (1737-1809)
> pamphleteer, revolutionary
> *of Edmund Burke*

SEE Arnold on RELIGION

Empire

Not once or twice in our rough
 island-story
The path of booty was the way
 to glory.
> anonymous

We seem, as it were, to have conquered and peopled half the world in a fit of absence of mind.
> Sir J. R. Seeley (1834-1895)
> English classicist, historian

If Germany is to become a colonising power, all I say is, 'God speed her!'. She becomes our ally and partner in the execution of the great purposes of Providence for the advantage of mankind.
> W. E. Gladstone (1809-1898)
> *in 1885*

With a hero at head, and a nation
Well gagged and well drilled and
 well cowed,
And a gospel of war and damnation,
Has not Empire a right to be proud?
> A. C. Swinburne (1837-1909)

To plunder, to slaughter, to steal, these things they misname empire; and where they make a wilderness, they call it peace.
> Tacitus (c. 55-c. 120)
> Roman historian
> *of the Romans*

The reluctant obedience of distant provinces generally costs more than it [the territory] is worth.
> Lord Macaulay (1800-1859)
> English historian

The conquest of the earth, which mostly means the taking it away from those who have a different complexion or slightly flatter noses than ourselves, is not a pretty thing when you look into it.
> Joseph Conrad (1857-1924)

The British Government in India is like a tooth that is decaying but is still strongly embedded. It is painful, but it cannot be easily pulled out.
Jawaharlal Nehru (1889-1964)
in 1935

All empires die of indigestion.
Napoleon Bonaparte (1769-1821)

And the end of the fight is a tombstone white
with the name of the late deceased,
And the epitaph drear: 'A Fool lies here
who tried to hustle the East'.
Rudyard Kipling (1865-1936)

How is the Empire?
King George V of Great Britain (1865-1936)
last words

SEE DECOLONISATION; Hitler on NATIONALISM

Encyclopedias
The man consulting it finds the thing he wants; he also finds how many thousand things there are that he does not want.
G. K. Chesterton (1874-1936)

Enemies
Enemies are so stimulating.
Katharine Hepburn (b. 1907)

To have a good enemy, choose a friend: he knows where to strike.
Diane de Poitiers (1499-1566)
mistress of Henri II of France, patron

I choose my friends for their good looks, my acquaintances for their good characters, and my enemies for their intellects. A man cannot be too careful in the choice of his enemies.
Oscar Wilde (1854-1900)

I'm lonesome. They are all dying. I have hardly a warm personal enemy left.
J. M. Whistler (1834-1903)
American artist

For my enemy is dead, a man as divine as myself is dead.
Walt Whitman (1819-1892)

Treating your adversary with respect is giving him an advantage to which he is not entitled.
Dr Samuel Johnson (1709-1784)

Despise the enemy strategically, but take him seriously tactically.
Mao Ze dong (1893-1976)

There are men whose enmity is a compliment.
J. A. Froude (1818-1894)
British author

Speak well of your enemies, sir, you made them.
Oren Arnold (*fl.* 1963)

You must embrace the man you hate, if you

cannot be justified in knocking him down.
Lord Chesterfield (1694-1773)
English statesman and man of letters

Am I not destroying my enemies when I make friends of them?
Abraham Lincoln (1809-1865)

Take heed of enemies reconciled, and of meat twice boiled.
Spanish proverb

Nothing ever perplexes an adversary so much as an appeal to his honour.
Benjamin Disraeli (1804-1881)

She is as implacable an adversary as a wife suing for alimony.
William Wycherley (1640-1716)
English dramatist

If you would injure your neighbour, better not do it by halves.
George Bernard Shaw (1856-1950)

I do not approve the extermination of the enemy; the policy of exterminating or, as it is barbarously said, liquidating enemies, is one of the most alarming developments of modern war and peace, from the point of view of those who desire the survival of culture. One needs the enemy.
T. S. Eliot (1888-1965)

You have many enemies, that know not why they are so, but, like to village-curs, bark when their fellows do.
King Henry, *King Henry VIII*
William Shakespeare (1564-1616)

I have only ever made one prayer to God, a very short one: 'O Lord, make my enemies ridiculous'. And God granted it.
Voltaire (1694-1778)

Oh, I am heartily tired of hearing what Lee is going to do. Try to think what we are going to do ourselves.
Ulysses S. Grant (1822-1885)

SEE Heine, Wilde on FORGIVENESS; Canning on FRIENDS; Napoleon on GENERALS; Browne on HUMAN NATURE; Sterne on JOKERS; Hitler on LEADERSHIP; Barrie on MOTIVES; Cassandra on PUBLIC LIFE; Schopenhauer on SUCCESS; Wellington on WINNING

England
This blessed plot, this earth, this realm, this England.
Gaunt, *King Richard II*
William Shakespeare (1564-1616)

I am sure my bones would not rest in an English grave, or my clay mix with the earth of that country. I believe the thought would drive me mad on my death-bed could I suppose that any of my friends would be base enough to convey my carcase back to her soil. I would not even feed her worms if I could help it.

> Lord Byron (1788-1824)

England, surely, is the paradise of little men, and the purgatory of great ones.

> Cardinal John Newman (1801-1890)
> English churchman, theologian

What a pity it is that we have no amusements in England but vice and religion!

> Sydney Smith (1771-1845)
> English writer, clergyman

In England there are sixty different religions, and only one sauce.

> Francesco Caraccioli (1752-1799)
> Neapolitan naval commander

The expression 'as right as rain' must have been invented by an Englishman.

> W. Lyon Phelps (1865-1943)
> American educator, author

The English winter – ending in July,
To recommence in August.

> Lord Byron (1788-1824)

Summer has set in with its usual severity.

> S. T. Coleridge (1772-1834)

The best sun we have is made of Newcastle coal.

> Horace Walpole (1717-1797)
> English writer

I shall continue to praise the English climate till I die, even if I die of the English climate.

> G. K. Chesterton (1874-1936)

I am living in the Midlands
That are sodden and unkind.

> Hilaire Belloc (1870-1953)
> British author

One has no great hopes from Birmingham. I always say there is something direful in the sound.

> Jane Austen (1775-1817)

The shortest way out of Manchester is notoriously a bottle of Gordon's gin.

> William Bolitho (1890-1930)
> British author

A Yorkshireman, like a dragoon, is nothing without his horse.

> R. S. Surtees (1803-1864)
> English novelist

For Cambridge people rarely smile,
Being urban, squat, and packed
   with guile.

> Rupert Brooke (1887-1915)
> British poet

An acre in Middlesex is better than a principality in Utopia.

> Lord Macaulay (1800-1859)
> English historian

Kent, sir – everybody knows Kent – apples, cherries, hops, and women.

> Jingle, *The Pickwick Papers*
> Charles Dickens (1812-1870)

The rolling English drunkard made the rolling English road.

> G. K. Chesterton (1874-1936)

SEE Wells on REFORM; Whitehorn on The WEATHER

The English

Stands the church clock at ten to three?
And is there honey still for tea?

> Rupert Brooke (1887-1915)
> British poet

English life, while very pleasant, is rather bland. I expected kindness and gentility and I found it, but there is such a thing as too much couth.

> S. J. Perelman (1904-1979)
> American humorist

The English (it must be owned) are rather a foul-mouthed nation.

> William Hazlitt (1778-1830)
> English essayist

The English are probably the most tolerant, least religious people on earth.

> Rabbi David Goldberg (b. 1939)
> Minister of the Liberal Jewish Synagogue, London

I should like my country well enough if it were not for my countrymen.

> Horace Walpole (1717-1797)
> English writer

To be an Englishman is to belong to the most exclusive class there is.

> Ogden Nash (1902-1971)
> American poet

He was inordinately proud of England and he abused her incessantly.

> H. G. Wells (1866-1946)

We do not covet anything from any nation except their respect.

> Sir Winston Churchill (1874-1965)

They are like their own beer: froth on the top, dregs at the bottom, the middle excellent.

> Voltaire (1694-1778)

One has often wondered whether . . . there is anything so unintelligent, so unapt to perceive how the world is really going, as an ordinary young Englishman of our upper class.

> Matthew Arnold (1822-1888)
> English poet, critic

It is to the middle-class we must look for the safety of England.

> W. M. Thackeray (1811-1863)
> English author

L'Angleterre est une nation de boutiquiers.
          Napoleon Bonaparte (1769-1821)

You never find an Englishman among the under-dogs – except in England, of course.
          Evelyn Waugh (1903-1966)

The English have all the material requisites for the revolution. What they lack is the spirit of generalisation and revolutionary ardour.
          Karl Marx (1818-1883)

Whenever he met a great man he grovelled before him and mylorded as only a free-born Englishman can do.
          W. M. Thackeray (1811-1863)
          English author

Englishmen never will be slaves; they are free to do whatever the Government and public opinion allow them to do.
          The Devil, *Man and Superman*
          George Bernard Shaw (1856-1950)

You can get the English to do anything if you put it to them the right way. The trouble with the English is they try all the wrong ways first.
          John Masefield (1878-1967)
          British poet, playwright

Now I understand how it is that they form a great nation. It is merely because they stand and let you thump them until you are tired, and then they proceed to do what they intended to do from the first.
          H. Seton Merriman (1862-1903)
          English novelist

The Anglo-Saxon conscience does not prevent the Anglo-Saxon from sinning; it merely prevents him from enjoying his sin.
          Salvador de Madariaga (1886-1978)
          Spanish writer, critic, diplomat

How hard it is to make an Englishman acknowledge that he is happy.
          W. M. Thackeray (1811-1863)
          English author

The people of England are never so happy as when you tell them they are ruined.
          Arthur Murphy (1727-1805)
          Irish dramatist

The Englishman never enjoys himself except for a noble purpose.
          A. P. Herbert (1890-1971)
          British author, politician

You will never find an Englishman in the wrong. He does everything on principle. He fights you on patriotic principles; he robs you on business principles; he enslaves you on imperial principles; he bullies you on manly principles; he supports his king on loyal principles; and cuts off his king's head on republican principles.
          Napoleon, *The Man of Destiny*
          George Bernard Shaw (1856-1950)

Le sombre Anglais, même dans ses amours,
Veut raisonner toujours.
The gloomy Englishman always wants to reason things out, even in his love affairs.
          Voltaire (1694-1778)

As soon as sex comes up we collectively say 'Er . . .' instead of 'Aha!'
          Wayland Young (b. 1923)
          British politician, writer

Continental people have sex lives; the English have hot-water bottles.
          George Mikes (b. 1912)
          Czech humorist

Cool, and quite English, imperturbable.
          Lord Byron (1788-1824)

The English have an extraordinary ability for flying into a great calm.
          Alexander Woollcott (1887-1943)
          American columnist, critic

The Englishman has all the qualities of a poker except its occasional warmth.
          Daniel O'Connell (1775-1847)
          Irish nationalist politician

It is not that the Englishman can't feel – it is that he is afraid to feel. He has been taught at his public school that feeling is bad form. He must not express great joy or sorrow, or even open his mouth too wide when he talks – his pipe might fall out if he did.
          E. M. Forster (1879-1970)

Stoicism, the sublimest kind of stupidity. Modesty, the proudest kind of grovelling.
          Gustave Flaubert (1821-1880)

Even crushed against his brother in the Tube the average Englishman pretends desperately that he is alone.
          Germaine Greer (b. 1939)
          Australian feminist writer

Not only England, but every Englishman is an island.
          Novalis (Friedrich von Hardenberg) (1772-1801)
          German poet

. . . A scene that is all English and stiff upper lip. Nothing is said that can be regretted. Nothing is said that can even be remembered.
          Caroline A. Lejeune (1897-1973)
          British film critic

Silence – a conversation with an Englishman.
          Heinrich Heine (1797-1856)
          German poet, journalist

But Lord! to see the absurd nature of Englishmen, that cannot forbear laughing and jeering at everything that looks strange.
          Samuel Pepys (1633-1703)

We do not regard Englishmen as foreigners.

We look on them only as rather mad Norwegians.

Halvard Lange
Norwegian Prime Minister, 1958

SEE The BRITISH; Whitehead on CONSERVATIVES; Bradbury on COURTESY; Halsey, Sitwell on DRESS; Mikes on FOOD; Smith on IRELAND; Shaw on MORALITY; Beecham on MUSIC; Barrie, Wilson on The SCOTS; Muggeridge on SEX; Shaw on VICE

Ennui

Life is as tedious as a twice-told tale,
Vexing the dull ear of a drowsy man.

Lewis, *King John*
William Shakespeare (1564-1616)

She, while her lover pants upon her breast,
Can mark the carvings in an Indian chest.

Alexander Pope (1688-1744)

La chair est triste, hélas! et j'ai lu tous les livres.
The flesh is weary, alas, and I've read all the books.

Stéphane Mallarmé (1842-1898)
French Symbolist poet

They remind me of a very tired rich man who said to his chauffeur 'Drive off that cliff, James, I want to commit suicide'.

Adlai Stevenson (1900-1965)
American Democratic politician

Ah! que la vie est quotidienne.
What a day-to-day affair life is.

Jules Laforgue (1860-1887)
French Symbolist poet

SEE BOREDOM

Enthusiasm

In things pertaining to enthusiasm, no man is sane who does not know how to be insane on proper occasions.

H. W. Beecher (1813-1887)
American clergyman, editor, writer

Daniel Webster struck me much like a steam-engine in trousers.

Sydney Smith (1771-1845)
English writer, clergyman

. . . talk about God as though nobody had ever heard of Him before.

Russell Lynes (b. 1910)
American editor, critic

It is unfortunate, considering that enthusiasm moves the world, that so few enthusiasts can be trusted to speak the truth.

A. J. Balfour (1848-1930)
British Conservative politician, Prime Minister

Enthusiam. A distemper of youth, curable by small doses of repentance in connection with outward applications of experience.

Ambrose Bierce (1842-1914)
American author

Envy

Some folks rail against other folks, because other folks have what some folks would be glad of.

Henry Fielding (1707-1754)

Envy is a kind of praise.

John Gay (1685-1732)
English playwright

Envy among other ingredients has a mixture of the love of justice in it. We are more angry at undeserved that at deserved good fortune.

William Hazlitt (1778-1830)
English essayist

Envy is capable of serving the valuable social function of making the rich moderate their habits for fear of arousing it.

Sir Keith Joseph (b. 1918)
British Conservative politician

Glamour cannot exist without personal social envy being a common and widespread emotion.

John Berger (b. 1926)
British critic

His scorn of the great is repeated too often to be real; no man thinks much of that which he despises.

Dr Samuel Johnson (1709-1784)

SEE Beerbohm on GENIUS

Epigrams

If with the literate, I am
Impelled to try an epigram,
I never seek to take the credit;
We all assume that Oscar said it.

Dorothy Parker (1893-1967)
American humorous writer

Paradox with him was only truth standing on its head to attract attention.

Richard Le Gallienne (1866-1947)
British poet
of Oscar Wilde

An epigram is only a wisecrack that's played at Carnegie Hall.

Oscar Levant (1906-1972)
American pianist, composer

Is this true or only clever?

Augustine Birrell (1850-1933)
British Liberal politician

Epigrams succeed where epics fail.

Persian proverb

SEE Wilde on PLATITUDES

Epitaphs

In lapidary inscriptions a man is not upon oath.

> Dr Samuel Johnson (1709-1784)

Epitaph: A belated advertisement for a line of goods that has been discontinued.

> Irvin S. Cobb (1876-1944)
> American author

Reading the epitaphs, our only salvation lies in resurrecting the dead and burying the living.

> Paul Eldridge (b. 1888)
> American author

Posterity will ne'er survey
A nobler grave than this:
Here lie the bones of Castlereagh:
Stop, traveller, and piss.

> Lord Byron (1788-1824)

Equality

The social process requires the standardisation of man, and this standardisation is called equality.

> Erich Fromm (1900-1980)
> American psychologist

The defect of equality is that we only desire it with our superiors.

> Henri Becque (1837-1899)
> French playwright

Subordination tends greatly to human happiness. Were we all upon an equality, we should have no other enjoyment than mere animal pleasure.

> Dr Samuel Johnson (1709-1784)

There is nothing that so strikes men with fear as the saying that they are all the sons of God.

> G. K. Chesterton (1874-1936)

If there is a human being who is freer than I, then I shall necessarily become his slave. If I am freer than another, then he will become my slave. Therefore, equality is the absolutely necessary condition for freedom ... freedom outside of equality can create only privilege.

> Mikhail Bakunin (1814-1876)
> Russian political theorist

SEE Nietzsche on EXERCISE; Foote on GAMBLING; France on The LAW

Eternity

Our theories of the eternal are as valuable as are those which a chick which has not broken its way through its shell might form of the outside world.

> Gautama the Buddha
> (c. 560-c. 480 BC)

Eternity is a terrible thought. I mean, where's it going to end?

> Tom Stoppard (b. 1937)
> British playwright

SEE Shaw on IMMORTALITY

Europe

Can we never extract the tapeworm of Europe from the brain of our countrymen?

> R. W. Emerson (1803-1882)
> American essayist, poet, philosopher

There are a whole group of people in Europe who are constantly anti-American, who have never forgiven us for the Marshall Plan.

> General Vernon Walters (b. 1917)
> American ambassador to the UN

Europe has what we do not have yet, a sense of the mysterious and inexorable limits of life, a sense, in a word, of tragedy. And we have what they sorely need: a sense of life's possibilities.

> James Baldwin (b. 1924)
> American author

Their Europeanism is nothing but imperialism with an inferiority complex.

> Denis Healey (b. 1917)
> British Labour politician
> *of the Conservative Party*

SEE Fisher on RACE

Euthanasia

O, let him pass! He hates him
That would upon the rack of this
   tough world
Stretch him out longer.

> Kent, *King Lear*
> William Shakespeare (1564-1616)

Evil

All men are evil and will declare themselves to be so when occasion is offered.

> Sir Walter Raleigh (1552-1618)

It is a sin to believe evil of others, but it is seldom a mistake.

> H. L. Mencken (1880-1956)
> American journalist

The belief in a supernatural source of evil is not necessary; men alone are quite capable of every wickedness.

> Joseph Conrad (1857-1924)

So far as we are human, what we do must be either evil or good: so far as we do evil or good, we are human: and it is better, in a paradoxical way, to do evil than to do nothing: at least we exist.

> T. S. Eliot (1888-1965)

When choosing between two evils, I always like to try the one I've never tried before.

> Mae West (1892-1980)

But evil is wrought by want of Thought
As well as want of Heart!

> Thomas Hood (1799-1845)
> English poet

SEE Hardy on TEMPTATION;
WICKEDNESS; Chrysostom, Tertullian on
WOMEN

Evolution

While Darwinian Man, though
well-behaved.
At best is only a monkey shaved!

W. S. Gilbert (1836-1911)
English librettist

I repudiate with indignation and abhorrence
those new-fangled theories.

Benjamin Disraeli (1804-1881)
of Darwinism

The question is this – Is man an ape or an
angel? My Lord, I am on the side of the
angels.

Benjamin Disraeli (1804-1881)

SEE Strindberg on DOUBT; Shaw on
HERESY; Shaw on RELIGION

Examinations

Examinations are formidable even to the best
prepared, for the greatest fool may ask more
than the wisest man can answer.

C. C. Colton (1780-1832)
English author, clergyman

Examinations, sir, are pure humbug from
beginning to end. If a man is a gentleman he
knows quite enough, and if he is not a
gentleman whatever he knows is bad for him.

Oscar Wilde (1854-1900)

Do not on any account attempt to write on
both sides of the paper at once.

W. C. Sellar (1898-1951) and
R. J. Yeatman (1897-1968)
British authors

I was thrown out of college for cheating on
the metaphysics exam: I looked into the soul
of another boy.

Woody Allen (b. 1935)

Exasperation

Lord Ronald said nothing; he flung himself
from the room, flung himself upon his horse
and rode madly off in all directions.

Stephen Leacock (1869-1944)
Canadian humorist and economist

Your damned nonsense can I stand twice or
once, but sometimes always, by God, never.

Hans Richter (1843-1916)
German conductor
to the second flute in the
Covent Garden orchestra

Inanimate objects are classified scientifically
into three major categories – those that don't
work, those that break down and those that
get lost.

Russell Baker (b. 1925)
American humorist

Sir, you have tasted two whole worms; you
have hissed all my mystery lectures and have
been caught fighting a liar in the quad; you

will leave by the next town drain.

attributed to Rev. W. A. Spooner (1844-1930)
Warden of New College, Oxford

Excellence

Le mieux est l'ennemi du bien.
The best is the enemy of the good.

Voltaire (1694-1778)

Few things are harder to put up with than the
annoyance of a good example.

Mark Twain (1835-1910)

One shining quality lends a lustre to another,
or hides some glaring defect.

William Hazlitt (1778-1830)
English essayist

Excess

Moderation is a fatal thing. Nothing succeeds
like excess.

Oscar Wilde (1854-1900)

The road of excess leads to the palace of
wisdom.

William Blake (1757-1827)

Man's chief difference from the brutes lies in
the exuberant excess of his subjective propen-
sities. Prune his extravagance, sober him, and
you undo him.

William James (1842-1910)
American psychologist, philosopher

Macaulay is well for a while, but one wouldn't
live under Niagara.

Thomas Carlyle (1795-1881)
Scottish author

Excuses

A person who is going to commit an inhuman
act invariably excuses himself by saying, 'I'm
only human, after all'.

Sydney J. Harris (b. 1917)
American journalist

And oftentimes excusing of a fault
Doth make the fault the worse by
the excuse.

Pembroke, King John
William Shakespeare (1564-1616)

Two wrongs don't make a right, but they
make a good excuse.

Thomas Szasz (b. 1920)
American psychiatrist

There is hardly any man so strict as not to
vary a little from truth when he is to make an
excuse.

George Savile, Lord Halifax (1633-1695)
English statesman, author

SEE Addison on LYING

Exercise

A few hours of mountain climbing turn a
rascal and a saint into two pretty similar
creatures. Fatigue is the shortest way to

Equality and Fraternity – and, in the end, Liberty will surrender to Sleep.
Friedrich Nietzsche (1844-1900)

That's not exercise, it's flagellation.
Noël Coward (1899-1973)
of squash

Exercise is bunk. If you are healthy you don't need it, if you are sick you shouldn't take it.
Henry Ford (1863-1947)

The only athletic sport I ever mastered was backgammon.
Douglas Jerrold (1803-1857)
English playwright, humorist

Whenever I feel like exercise I lie down until the feeling passes.
Robert M. Hutchins (1899-1977)
American educator, writer

I like long walks, especially when they are taken by people who annoy me.
Fred Allen (1894-1957)
American comic

Another good reducing exercise consists in placing both hands against the table edge and pushing back.
Robert Quillen (1887-1948)
American journalist

I get my exercise acting as a pallbearer to my friends who exercise.
Chauncey Depew (1834-1928)
American Republican politician

SEE Wilde on BLOODSPORTS; SPORT

Exertion
There's no taking trout with dry breeches.
Miguel de Cervantes (1547-1616)

I wish to preach, not the doctrine of ignoble ease, but the doctrine of the strenuous life.
Theodore Roosevelt (1858-1919)

Existence
A man said to the universe: 'Sir, I exist!' 'However', replied the universe, 'that fact has not created in me a sense of obligation'.
Stephen Crane (1871-1900)
American author, journalist

Man is the only animal for whom his own existence is a problem which he has to solve.
Erich Fromm (1900-1980)
American psychologist

Common sense tells us that our existence is but a brief crack of light between two eternities of darkness.
Vladimir Nabokov (1899-1977)

The individual who has to justify his existence by his own efforts is in eternal bondage to himself.
Eric Hoffer (1902-1983)
American philosopher

Being is the great explainer.
H. D. Thoreau (1817-1862)

SEE Prince of Wales on ROYALTY

Experience
Experience is the name everyone gives to their mistakes.
Oscar Wilde (1854-1900)

Experience. The wisdom that enables us to recognise in an undesirable old acquaintance the folly that we have already embraced.
Ambrose Bierce (1842-1914)
American author

We learn from experience that men never learn anything from experience.
George Bernard Shaw (1856-1950)

Experience comprises illusions lost, rather than wisdom gained.
Joseph Roux (1834-1886)
French priest and writer

If a man deceives me once, shame on him; if he deceives me twice, shame on me.
Italian proverb

Experience is a comb which nature gives to men when they are bald.
Eastern proverb

What a man knows at fifty which he didn't know at twenty is, for the most part, incommunicable.
Adlai Stevenson (1900-1965)
American Democratic politician

Experience is a good teacher, but her fees are very high.
W. R. Inge (1860-1954)
Dean of St Paul's, London

And the wild regrets, and the bloody sweats,
None knew so well as I:
For he who lives more lives than one
More deaths than one must die.
Oscar Wilde (1854-1900)

Men may rise on stepping-stones
Of their dead selves to higher things.
Lord Tennyson (1809-1892)

Experience is not what happens to a man. It is what a man does with what happens to him.
Aldous Huxley (1894-1963)

SEE Howe on ADVICE; Estienne, Grattan on AGE; Shakespeare on COMEDY; Blake on EXCESS; Cyprian on TRAINING; Ascham on WISDOM

Experts
An expert is one who knows more and more about less and less.
Nicholas Murray Butler (1862-1948)
President of Columbia University

Never forget that if you leave your law to judges and your religion to bishops you will presently find yourself without either law or religion.

> George Bernard Shaw (1856-1950)

Everyone should learn to do one thing supremely well because he likes it, and one thing supremely well because he detests it.

> B. W. M. Young (b. 1922)
> British administrator

This world is run by people who know how to do things. They know how things work. They are *equipped*. Up there, there's a layer of people who run everything. But we – we're just peasants. We don't understand what's going on, and we can't do anything.

> Doris Lessing (b. 1919)
> British author

How could I have been so far off base? All my life I've known better than to depend on the experts. How could I have been so stupid, to let them go ahead?

> John F. Kennedy (1917-1963)
> *after the Bay of Pigs fiasco*

An expert is a man who has made all the mistakes which can be made in a very narrow field.

> Niels Bohr (1885-1962)
> Danish physicist

SEE Butler, Chesterton on JURIES

Extravagance

I am dying beyond my means.

> Oscar Wilde (1854-1900)

I'm living so far beyond my income that we may almost be said to be living apart.

> Saki (H. H. Munro) (1870-1916)
> Scottish author

My candle burns at both ends;
It will not last the night;
But ah, my foes, and oh, my friends –
It gives a lovely light!

> Edna St Vincent Millay (1892-1950)
> American poet

Let us all be happy, and live within our means, even if we have to borrow the money to do it with.

> Artemus Ward (1834-1867)
> American journalist

Extremism

So over violent or over civil
That every man with him
was God or Devil.

> John Dryden (1631-1700)

I would remind you that extremism in the defence of liberty is no vice. And let me remind you also that moderation in the pursuit of justice is no virtue.

> Barry Goldwater (b. 1909)
> American Republican politician

What is objectionable, what is dangerous about extremists is not that they are extreme, but that they are intolerant. The evil is not what they say about their cause, but what they say about their opponents.

> Robert Kennedy (1925-1968)

SEE St Augustine on DRINK: Abstinence

F

Faces

I have always considered my face a convenience rather than an ornament.
Dr Oliver Wendell Holmes (1809-1894)
American writer, physician

The tartness of his face sours ripe grapes.
Menenius, *Coriolanus*
William Shakespeare (1564-1616)

He had a face like a benediction.
Miguel de Cervantes (1547-1616)

My face looks like a wedding cake that has been left out in the rain.
W. H. Auden (1907-1973)

I have eyes like those of a dead pig.
Marlon Brando (b. 1924)

I guess I look like a rock quarry that someone has dynamited.
Charles Bronson (b. 1922)

As a beauty I'm not a great star.
Others are handsomer far;
But my face – I don't mind it
Because I'm behind it;
It's the folks out in front that I jar.
A. H. Euwer (b. 1877-?)
American author

Once seen, that antique-mapped face is never forgotten – a bloodhound with a head cold, a man who is simultaneously biting on a bad lobster and caught by the neck in lift-doors, a mad scientist's amalgam of Wallace Beery and Yogi Bear.
Alan Brien (b. 1925)
British novelist, journalist
of Walter Matthau

At fifty everyone has the face he deserves.
George Orwell (1903-1950)
last entry in his notebook

Was this the face that launch'd a
  thousand ships,
And burnt the topless towers of
  Ilium?
Christopher Marlowe (1564-1593)

'What is your fortune, my pretty maid?'
'My face is my fortune, Sir', she said.
nursery rhyme

SEE Twain on APPEARANCES;
BEARDS; Masefield on
DEBAUCHERY; NOSES

Facts

Facts are stubborn things.
Tobias Smollett (1721-1771)
Scottish novelist, surgeon

Nobuddy kin talk as interestin' as th'feller that's not hampered by facts or information.
Kin (F. McKinney) Hubbard (1868-1930)
American humorist, journalist

Reporting facts is the refuge of those who have no imagination.
Luc, Marquis de Vauvenargues (1715-1747)
French moralist

It is the spirit of the age to believe that any fact, however suspect, is superior to any imaginative exercise, no matter how true.
Gore Vidal (b. 1925)

Oh, don't tell me of facts – I never believe facts: you know Canning said nothing was so fallacious as facts, except figures.
Sydney Smith (1771-1845)
English writer, clergyman

He wasn't exactly hostile to facts but he was apathetic about them.
Wolcott Gibbs (1902-1958)
American critic

SEE Scott on NEWSPAPERS;
Twain on PROPAGANDA;
Russell on RELIGION

Failure

There is not a fiercer hell than the failure in a great object.
John Keats (1795-1821)

We are all of us failures – at least, the best of us are.
J. M. Barrie (1860-1937)
British playwright

Our business in this world is not to succeed, but to continue to fail, in good spirits.
Robert Louis Stevenson (1850-1894)

In the lexicon of youth, which Fate reserves

For a bright manhood, there is no
  such word
As — fail!
> Edward Bulwer-Lytton (1803-1873)
> English novelist, playwright

I cannot give you the formula for success, but
I can give you the formula for failure — which
is: Try to please everybody.
> Herbert B. Swope (1882-1958)
> American journalist

There are two kinds of men who never
amount to much: those who cannot do what
they are told, and those who can do nothing
else.
> Cyrus H. Curtis (1850-1933)
> American newspaper publisher

There is something distinguished about even
his failures; they sink not trivially but with a
certain air of majesty; like a great ship, its
flags flying, full of holes.
> George Jean Nathan (1882-1958)
> American critic
> of Eugene O'Neill

He was a self-made man who owed his lack of
success to nobody.
> Joseph Heller (b. 1923)
> American novelist

It is mighty presumptuous on your part to
suppose your small failures of so much
consequence that you must talk about them.
> Dr Oliver Wendell Holmes (1809-1894)
> American writer, physician

A man's life manifests itself as a failure; what
he has attempted he will not achieve. He will
not even succeed in thinking what he wants to
think or in feeling what he wants to feel.
> Jean-Paul Sartre (1905-1980)

Everyone is born a king, and most people die
in exile.
> Oscar Wilde (1854-1900)

Everyone pushes a falling fence.
> Chinese proverb

SEE Hare on DOUBT; Maugham on
SUCCESS

Faith

It was the schoolboy who said, 'Faith is
believing what you know ain't so'.
> Mark Twain (1835-1910)

Faith is often the boast of the man who is too
lazy to investigate.
> F. M. Knowles (b. 1877)
> American journalist, playwright

'Faith' means not *wanting* to know what is
true.
> Friedrich Nietzsche (1844-1900)

What is faith but a kind of betting or
speculation after all? It should be, 'I bet that
my Redeemer liveth'.
> Samuel Butler (1835-1902)
> English author

Faith. Belief without evidence in what is told
by one who speaks without knowledge, of
things without parallel.
> Ambrose Bierce (1842-1914)
> American author

Faith is the substance of things hoped for, the
evidence of things not seen.
> Bible, Hebrews

Faith declares what the senses do not see, but
not the contrary of what they see.
> Blaise Pascal (1623-1662)

Faith begins as an experiment and ends as an
experience.
> W. R. Inge (1860-1954)
> Dean of St Paul's, London

To believe only possibilities is not Faith, but
mere Philosophy.
> Sir Thomas Browne (1603-1682)
> English physician, author

Philosophic argument, especially that drawn
from the vastness of the universe, in com-
parison with the apparent insignificance of this
globe, has sometimes shaken my reason for
the faith that is in me; but my heart has
always assured and reassured me that the
gospel of Jesus Christ must be Divine Reality.
The Sermon on the Mount cannot be a mere
human production. This belief enters into the
very depth of my conscience. The whole
history of man proves it.
> Daniel Webster (1782-1852)
> American lawyer, statesman
> spoken on the eve of his death
> and carved as his epitaph

The faith that stands on authority is not faith.
> R. W. Emerson (1803-1882)
> American essayist, poet, philosopher

It is the heart which experiences God, and not
the reason. This, then, is faith: God felt by the
heart, not by the reason.
> Blaise Pascal (1623-1662)

Reason is our soul's left hand, Faith
  her right,
By these we reach divinity.
> John Donne (c. 1571-1631)

Faith may be defined briefly as an illogical
belief in the occurrence of the improbable.
> H. L. Mencken (1880-1956)
> American journalist

It is as absurd to argue men, as to torture
them, into believing.
> Cardinal John Newman (1801-1890)
> English churchman, theologian

'You say you *believe*', said Count de X., an extreme Catholic, to the good Protestant minister. 'You people believe, but we *know*'.
André Gide (1869-1951)

I admire the serene assurance of those who have religious faith. It is wonderful to observe the calm confidence of a Christian with four aces.
Mark Twain (1835-1910)

Fe que no duda es fe muerta.
Faith which does not doubt is dead faith.
Miguel de Unamuno (1864-1937)
Spanish writer, philosopher

How many things we held yesterday as articles of faith which today we tell as fables.
Michel de Montaigne (1533-1592)
French essayist

SEE Johnson on The AFTERLIFE

Fallibility
The fellow that says, 'I may be wrong, but –' does not believe there can be any such possibility.
Kin (F. McKinney) Hubbard (1868-1930)
American humorist, journalist

To be positive. To be mistaken at the top of one's voice.
Ambrose Bierce (1842-1914)
American author

The first faults are theirs that commit them, the second theirs that permit them.
18th century English proverb

A man should never be ashamed to own he has been in the wrong, which is but saying, in other words, that he is wiser to-day than he was yesterday.
Jonathan Swift (1667-1745)

Mistakes are, after all, the foundations of truth, and if a man does not know what a thing *is*, it is at least an increase in knowledge if he knows what it is *not*.
Carl Jung (1875-1961)

Even the youngest of us may be wrong sometimes.
George Bernard Shaw (1856-1950)

SEE Goethe on LYING; Szasz on MATURITY; Eliot on PROPHECY

Fame
America has a genius for the encouragement of fame.
G. K. Chesterton (1874-1936)

Happy is the man who hath never known what it is to taste of fame – to have it is a purgatory, to want it is a Hell!
Edward Bulwer-Lytton (1803-1873)
English novelist, playwright

Fame is proof that the people are gullible.
R. W. Emerson (1803-1882)
American essayist, poet, philosopher

A celebrity is one who is known to many persons he is glad he doesn't know.
H. L. Mencken (1880-1956)
American journalist

After a fellow gets famous it doesn't take long for someone to bob up that used to sit by him at school.
Kin (F. McKinney) Hubbard (1868-1930)
American humorist, journalist

Not to know me argues yourself unknown.
John Milton (1608-1674)

What you are thunders so loud that I cannot hear what you say.
R. W. Emerson (1803-1882)
American essayist, poet, philosopher

The fame of a great man ought always to be estimated by the means used to acquire it.
François, Duc de La Rochefoucauld (1613-1680)
French writer, moralist

I had not achieved a success; but I had provoked an uproar; and the sensation was so agreeable that I resolved to try again.
George Bernard Shaw (1856-1950)

It is a mark of many famous people that they cannot part with their brightest hour.
Lillian Hellman (1907-1984)
American playwright

A friend recently said, 'Just imagine *not* being famous – what would happen?' And all of a sudden I saw the face of a passer-by on the street and the oddest feeling came over me.
Gloria Swanson (1897-1983)
American actress

Publicity in women is detestable. Anonymity runs in their blood. The desire to be veiled still possesses them. They are not even now as concerned about the health of their fame as men are, and, speaking generally, will pass a tombstone or a signpost without feeling an irresistible desire to cut their names on it.
Virginia Woolf (1882-1941)

Being a celebrity is like rape.
John McEnroe (b. 1959)

It's either vilification or sanctification, and both piss me off.
Bob Geldof (b. 1954)

Censure is the tax a man pays to the public for being eminent.
Jonathan Swift (1667-1745)

I would much rather have men ask why I have no statue than why I have one.
Cato the Elder (234-149 BC)
Roman statesman

The strongest poison ever known
Came from Caesar's laurel crown.
William Blake (1757-1827)

If fame will fall to me only after death, I am in no hurry for it.
Martial (43-104)

SEE Franklin on BOOKS; de Montandré on GREATNESS; Schopenhauer on HONOUR; Cassandra on POLITICIANS

Family

The family . . . home of all social vices, where children are taught to tell their first lie; the charitable institution for all lazy women.
J. A. Strindberg (1849-1912)

The family is the place where the most ridiculous and least respectable things in the world go on.
Ugo Betti (1892-1953)
Italian playwright

No matter how many communes anybody invents, the family always creeps back.
Margaret Mead (1901-1978)
American anthropologist

He that hath wife and children have given hostages to fortune; for they are impediments to great enterprises, either of virtue or mischief.
Francis Bacon (1561-1626)

Man is the head of the family, woman the neck that turns the head.
Chinese aphorism

If Absolute Sovereignty be not necessary in a State, how comes it to be so in a family?
Mary Astell (1666-1731)
English feminist writer

[He] didn't dare to, because his father had a weak heart and habitually threatened to drop dead if anybody hurt his feelings. You may have noticed that people with weak hearts are the tyrants of English married life.
The Bishop of Chelsea, *Getting Married*
George Bernard Shaw (1856-1950)

Be kind to your mother-in-law, and if necessary pay for her board at some good hotel.
Josh Billings (1818-1885)
American humorist

The awe and dread with which the untutored savage contemplates his mother-in-law are amongst the most familiar facts of anthropology.
James G. Frazer (1854-1941)
Scottish classicist, anthropologist

If you want to know how old a woman is, ask her sister-in-law.
Ed (E. W.) Howe (1853-1937)
American journalist, novelist

For there is no friend like a sister
In calm or stormy weather;
To cheer one on the tedious way,
To fetch one if one goes astray,
To lift one if one totters down,
To strengthen whilst one stands.
Christina Rossetti (1830-1894)
English poet, lyricist

Big sisters are the crab grass in the lawn of life.
Charles Schulz (b. 1922)
American cartoonist

Relations are simply a tedious pack of people who haven't got the remotest knowledge of how to live nor the smallest instinct about when to die.
Oscar Wilde (1854-1900)

I advise thee to visit thy relations and friends; but I advise thee not to live too near to them.
Thomas Fuller (1654-1734)
English physician

When our relatives are at home, we have to think of all their good points or it would be impossible to endure them. But when they are away, we console ourselves for their absence by dwelling on their vices.
The Captain, *Heartbreak House*
George Bernard Shaw (1856-1950)

I can't help detesting my relations. I suppose it comes from the fact that none of us can stand other people having the same faults as ourselves.
Oscar Wilde (1854-1900)

God gives us our relatives; thank God we can choose our friends.
Ethel Watts Mumford (1878-1940)
American novelist, humorous writer

A poor relation – is the most irrelevant thing in nature.
Charles Lamb (1775-1834)
English essayist, critic

Accidents will occur in the best-regulated families.
Mr Micawber, *David Copperfield*
Charles Dickens (1812-1870)

SEE Wilde on DINNER PARTIES; FATHER; Dickens on GREATNESS; MOTHER; PARENTS

Fanatics

A fanatic is a man that does what he thinks the Lord would do if he knew the facts of the case.
Finley Peter Dunne (1867-1936)
American journalist, humorist

Defined in psychological terms, a fanatic is a man who consciously overcompensates a secret doubt.
Aldous Huxley (1894-1963)

A fanatic is one who can't change his mind and won't change the subject.
Sir Winston Churchill (1874-1965)

Fanaticism consists in redoubling your effort when you have forgotten your aim.
George Santayana (1863-1952)
American philosopher, poet

Without fanaticism we cannot accomplish anything.
Eva Perón (1919-1952)

There are few catastrophes so great and irremediable as those that follow an excess of zeal.
R. H. Benson (1871-1914)
British novelist

The worst of madmen is a saint run mad.
Alexander Pope (1688-1744)

Fanatics are men with strong tastes for drink trying hard to keep sober.
Elbert Hubbard (1856-1915)
American author

Mere human beings cannot afford to be fanatical about anything. Not even about justice or loyalty. The fanatic for justice ends by murdering a million helpless people to clear a space for his law courts. If we are to survive on this planet there must be compromises.
Storm Jameson (1891-1986)
British novelist

SEE Junius on PERSUASION; Keats on SECTS

Farewells
Laughter is not at all a bad beginning for a friendship, and it is far the best ending for one.
Oscar Wilde (1854-1900)

Let's have one other gaudy night.
Antony, Antony and Cleopatra
William Shakespeare (1564-1616)

Let us eat and drink; for tomorrow we shall die.
Bible, Isaiah

Partir, c'est mourir un peu.
French proverb

When I died last, and, Dear, I die
As often as from thee I go.
John Donne (c. 1571-1631)

Every parting gives a foretaste of death, every reunion a hint of the resurrection.
Arthur Schopenhauer (1788-1860)
German philosopher

It is amazing how nice people are to you when they know you are going away.
Michael Arlen (1895-1956)
British novelist

It is never any good dwelling on goodbyes. It is not the being together that it prolongs, it is the parting.
Elizabeth Bibesco (1897-1945)
British author

All farewells should be sudden.
Lord Byron (1788-1824)

Farmers
Our Farmers round, well pleased with constant gain,
Like other farmers, flourish and complain.
George Crabbe (1754-1832)
English poet, clergyman

A good farmer is nothing more nor less than a handy man with a sense of humus.
E. B. White (1899-1985)
American author, editor

The master's eye is the best fertilizer.
Pliny the Elder (c. 23-79)
Roman scholar

How can he get wisdom ... whose talk is of bullocks?
Apocrypha, Ecclesiasticus

Fascism
The destiny of history has united you [Hitler] with myself and the Duce in an indissoluble way.
General Franco (1892-1975)

Fascism is a European inquietude. It is a way of knowing everything – history, the state, the achievement of the proletarianisation of public life, a new way of knowing the phenomena of our epoch.
J. A. Primo de Rivera (1903-1936)
Spanish Falangist politician

We enter parliament in order to supply ourselves, in the arsenal of democracy, with its own weapons... If democracy is so stupid as to give us free tickets and salaries for this bear's work, that is its affair... We do not come as friends, nor even as neutrals. We come as enemies. As the wolf bursts into the flock, so we come.
Joseph Goebbels (1897-1945)
in 1928

Fascism, the more it considers and observes the future and the development of humanity, quite apart from political considerations of the moment, believes neither in the possibility nor the utility of perpetual peace.
Benito Mussolini (1883-1945)

Fascism is Capitalism plus Murder.
Upton Sinclair (1878-1968)
American writer, Socialist politician

Because Fascism is a lie, it is condemned to literary sterility. And when it is past, it will

have no history, except the bloody history of murder.
Ernest Hemingway (1899-1961)

Fascism is not in itself a new order of society. It is the future refusing to be born.
Aneurin Bevan (1897-1960)
British Labour politician

Fascism was a counter-revolution against a revolution that never took place.
Ignazio Silone (1900-1978)
Italian writer, Socialist politician

Fashion

Fashion is gentility running away from vulgarity, and afraid of being overtaken.
William Hazlitt (1778-1830)
English essayist

Fashion is that by which the fantastic becomes for a moment the universal.
Oscar Wilde (1854-1900)

In olden days a glimpse of stocking
Was looked on as something shocking
But now, God knows,
Anything goes.
Cole Porter (1893-1964)

A fashionable woman is always in love – with herself.
François, Duc de La Rochefoucauld (1613-1680)
French writer, moralist

I cannot and will not cut my conscience to fit this year's fashions.
Lillian Hellman (1907-1984)
American playwright
in letter to Chairman of the
House Committee on un-American
Activities

You don't have to signal a social conscience by looking like a frump. Lace knickers won't hasten the holocaust, you can ban the bomb in a feather boa just as well as without, and a mild interest in the length of hemlines doesn't necessarily disqualify you from reading *Das Kapital* and agreeing with every word.
Jill Tweedie (b. 1936)
British journalist

One had as good be out of the world, as out of the fashion.
Colley Cibber (1671-1757)
English actor-manager, playwright

Fashion is made to become unfashionable.
Coco Chanel (1883-1971)
French *couturière*

After all, what is fashion? From the artistic point of view, it is usually a form of ugliness so intolerable that we have to alter it every six months.
Oscar Wilde (1854-1900)

Father

As fathers commonly go, it is seldom a misfortune to be fatherless; and considering the general run of sons, as seldom a misfortune to be childless.
Lord Chesterfield (1694-1773)
English statesman and man of letters

No man is responsible for his father. That is entirely his mother's affair.
Margaret Turnbull (1890-1942)
American writer, politician

The worst misfortune that can happen to an ordinary man is to have an extraordinary father.
Austin O'Malley (1858-1932)
American oculist, writer

To be a successful father there's one absolute rule: when you have a kid, don't look at it for the first two years.
Ernest Hemingway (1899-1961)

What harsh judges fathers are to all young men!
Terence (c. 190-159 BC)
Roman dramatist

The fundamental defect of fathers is that they want their children to be a credit to them.
Bertrand Russell (1872-1970)

An unforgiving eye, and a damned disinheriting countenance.
R. B. Sheridan (1751-1816)

One father is more than a hundred schoolmasters.
17th century English proverb

Leontine: An only son, sir, might expect more indulgence.
Croaker: An only father, sir, might expect more obedience.
The Good-Natur'd Man
Oliver Goldsmith (1728-1774)

Diogenes struck the father when the son swore.
Robert Burton (1577-1640)
English clergyman, author

Sir Walter, being strangely surprised and put out of his countenance at so great a table, gives his son a damned blow over the face. His son, as rude as he was, would not strike his father, but strikes over the face the gentleman that sat next to him and said 'Box about: 'twill come to my father anon'.
John Aubrey (1626-1697)
English antiquary

When I was a boy of fourteen, my father was so ignorant I could hardly stand to have the old man around. But when I got to be twenty-one, I was astonished at how much he had learned in seven years.
Mark Twain (1835-1910)

We think our fathers fools, so wise
we grow;
Our wiser sons, no doubt will
think us so.
>> Alexander Pope (1688-1744)

The father's thankless position in the family is to be everybody's breadwinner, everybody's enemy.
>> J. A. Strindberg (1849-1912)

His father watched him across the gulf of years and pathos which always must divide a father from his son.
>> J. P. Marquand (1893-1960)
>> American novelist

In peace the sons bury their fathers, but in war the fathers bury their sons.
>> Croesus (d. c. 560 BC)
>> Lydian king

You're a kind of father figure to me, Dad.
>> Alan Coren (b. 1938)
>> British editor, humorist

>> SEE PARENTS

Fault-finding

If we had no faults we should not take so much pleasure in noticing them in others.
>> François, Duc de La Rochefoucauld (1613-1680)
>> French writer, moralist

To find out a girl's faults, praise her to her girl friends.
>> Benjamin Franklin (1706-1790)

Always mistrust a subordinate who never finds fault with his superior.
>> J. Churton Collins (1848-1908)
>> English author, critic, scholar

There are persons who always find a hair in their plate of soup for the simple reason that, when they sit down before it, they shake their heads until one falls in.
>> Friedrich Hebbel (1813-1863)
>> German dramatist

Clean your finger before you point at my spots.
>> Benjamin Franklin (1706-1790)

Favours

He that has once done you a kindness will be more ready to do you another than he whom you yourself have obliged.
>> Benjamin Franklin (1706-1790)

The pleasure we derive from doing favours is partly in the feeling it gives us that we are not altogether worthless.
>> Eric Hoffer (1902-1983)
>> American philosopher

Too great a hurry to discharge an obligation is a kind of ingratitude.
>> François, Duc de La Rochefoucauld (1613-1680)
>> French writer, moralist

When some men discharge an obligation, you can hear the report for miles around.
>> Mark Twain (1835-1910)

>> SEE La Rouchefoucauld on GRATITUDE

Fear

If hopes were dupes, fears may be liars.
>> A. H. Clough (1819-1861)
>> English poet

Let me assert my firm belief that the only thing we have to fear is fear itself.
>> Franklin D. Roosevelt (1882-1945)

No passion so effectually robs the mind of all its powers of acting and reasoning as fear.
>> Edmund Burke (1729-1797)
>> Irish philosopher, statesman

There is no terror in a bang, only in the anticipation of it.
>> Alfred Hitchcock (1899-1980)

I am not afraid of anything. If you fear God you do not fear anything else.
>> Colonel Muhammar Qaddafi (b. 1938)

Those who love to be feared, fear to be loved. Some fear them, but they fear everyone.
>> Jean Pierre Camus (1582-1652)

>> SEE St John on LOVE

Feminism

The Queen is most anxious to enlist everyone who can speak or write to join in checking this mad, wicked folly of 'Woman's Rights' with all its attendant horrors on which her poor, feeble sex is bent, forgetting every sense of womanly feeling and propriety.
>> Queen Victoria (1819-1901)

A society in which women are taught anything but the management of a family, the care of men, and the creation of the future generation is a society which is on the way out.
>> L. Ron Hubbard (1911-1986)
>> founder of scientology

Movements born in hatred very quickly take on the characteristics of the thing they oppose.
>> J. S. Habgood (b. 1927)
>> Archbishop of York
>> of ultra-feminists, in 1986

If men will not do us justice, they shall do us violence.
>> Emmeline Pankhurst (1857-1928)
>> British suffragette

The history of men's opposition to women's emancipation is more interesting perhaps than the story of that emancipation itself.
>> Virginia Woolf (1882-1941)

If the abstract rights of man will bear discussion and explanation, those of women, by a parity of reasoning, will not shrink from the same test; though a different opinion prevails in this country.

Mary Wollstonecraft (1759-1797)
English feminist writer

The true Republic: men, their rights and nothing more; women, their rights and nothing less.

Susan Anthony (1820-1906)
American suffragette

Anyone who knows anything of history knows that great social changes are impossible without the feminine upheaval. Social progress can be measured exactly by the social position of the fair sex; the ugly ones included.

Karl Marx (1818-1883)

Women's liberation, if it abolishes the patriarchal family, will abolish a necessary substructure of the authoritarian state, and once that withers away Marx will have come true willy-nilly, so let's get on with it.

Germaine Greer (b. 1939)
Australian feminist writer

I owe nothing to Women's Lib.

Margaret Thatcher (b. 1925)

Women get more unhappy the more they try to liberate themselves.

Brigitte Bardot (b. 1933)

The people I'm furious with are the women's liberationists. They keep getting up on soapboxes and proclaiming women are brighter than men. That's true, but it should be kept quiet or it ruins the whole racket.

Anita Loos (1893-1981)
American screenwriter

The suffering of either sex – of the male who is unable, because of the way in which he was reared, to take the strong initiating or patriarchal role that is still demanded of him, or of the female who has been given too much freedom of movement as a child to stay placidly within the house as an adult – this suffering, this discrepancy, this sense of failure in an enjoined role, is the point of leverage for social change.

Margaret Mead (1901-1978)
American anthropologist

There must be a world revolution which puts an end to all materialistic conditions hindering woman from performing her natural role in life and driving her to carry out man's duties in order to be equal in rights.

Colonel Muhammar Qaddafi (b. 1938)

People call me feminist whenever I express sentiments that differentiate me from a doormat or a prostitute.

Rebecca West (1892-1983)
British author

A woman without a man is like a fish without a bicycle.

Gloria Steinem (b. 1934)
American feminist writer

SEE Mathews on PROTEST;
Oppenheim on REVOLUTIONARIES

Fertility

Earth is here so kind, that just tickle her with a hoe and she laughs with a harvest.

Douglas Jerrold (1803-1857)
English playwright, humorist

The disruptive powers of excessive national fecundity may have played a greater part in bursting the bonds of convention than either the power of ideas or the errors of autocracy.

John Maynard Keynes (1883-1946)

The management of fertility is one of the most important functions of adulthood.

Germaine Greer (b. 1939)
Australian feminist writer

I'm hurt, hurt and humiliated beyond endurance. . . Seeing the wheat ripening, the fountains never ceasing to give water, the sheep bearing hundreds of lambs, the she-dogs . . . until it seems the whole country rises to show me its tender sleeping young while I feel two hammer-blows here instead of the mouth of my child.

Yerma, *Yerma*
Federico García Lorca (1898-1936)

SEE Greer on PROCREATION

Fiction

Fiction is Truth's elder sister.

Rudyard Kipling (1865-1936)

For if the proper study of mankind is man, it is evidently more sensible to occupy yourself with the coherent, substantial and significant creatures of fiction than with the irrational and shadowy figures of real life.

W. Somerset Maugham (1874-1965)

The novel, if it be anything, is contemporary history, an exact and complete reproduction of social surroundings of the age we live in.

George Moore (1852-1933)
Irish author

If you write fiction you are, in a sense, corrupted. There's a tremendous corruptibility for the fiction writer because you're dealing mainly with sex and violence. These remain the basic themes, they're the basic themes of Shakespeare whether you like it or not.

Anthony Burgess (b. 1917)
British author

In the true novel, as opposed to reportage and chronicle, the main action takes place inside the characters' skull and ribs.

Arthur Koestler (1905-1983)
British author

Generally speaking people are plagued with problems that they are unable to solve. To escape them they pick up a detective story, become completely absorbed, help bring the investigation to a successful conclusion, switch off the light and go to sleep.

Erle Stanley Gardner (1899-1970)

The thriller is an extension of the fairy tale. It is melodrama so embellished as to create the illusion that the story being told, however unlikely, could be true.

Raymond Chandler (1888-1959)

The best part of the fiction in many novels is the notice that the characters are purely imaginary.

Franklin Pierce Adams (1881-1960)
American journalist, humorist

When the characters are really alive before their author, the latter does nothing but follow them in their action, in their words, in the situations which they suggest to him.

Luigi Pirandello (1867-1936)
Italian playwright

Novels so often provide an anodyne and not an antidote, glide one into torpid slumbers instead of rousing one with a burning brand.

Virginia Woolf (1882-1941)

The principle of procrastinated rape is said to be the ruling one in all the great bestsellers.

V. S. Pritchett (b. 1900)
British writer, critic

The good ended happily, and the bad unhappily. That is what Fiction means.

Oscar Wilde (1854-1900)

SEE Hemingway on LITERATURE, Wilde on WRITERS

Fidelity

Fidelity. A virtue peculiar to those who are about to be betrayed.

Ambrose Bierce (1842-1914)
American author

Young men want to be faithful and are not; old men want to be faithless and cannot.

Oscar Wilde (1854-1900)

The cruellest revenge of a woman is to remain faithful to a man.

Jacques Bossuet (1627-1704)
French churchman

No man worth having is true to his wife, or can be true to his wife, or ever was, or ever will be so.

Sir John Vanbrugh (1664-1726)
English playwright, architect

Those who are faithful know only the trivial side of love: it is the faithless who know love's tragedies.

Oscar Wilde (1854-1900)

SEE LOYALTY; Shaw on VIRTUE

Fire

Man is the animal that has made friends with the fire.

Henry Van Dyke (1852-1933)
American clergyman, author

No spectacle is nobler than a blaze.

Dr Samuel Johnson (1709-1784)

Flattery

Madam, before you flatter a man so grossly to his face, you should consider whether or not your flattery is worth his having.

Dr Samuel Johnson (1709-1784)

Blarney is flattery laid on so thin you love it; baloney is flattery laid on so thick you hate it.

Fulton Sheen (1895-1979)
American clergyman, author

La lisonja hace amigos, y la verdad enemigos. Flattery makes friends and truth makes enemies.

Spanish proverb

The art of pleasing consists in being pleased.

William Hazlitt (1778-1830)
English essayist

Just praise is only a debt, but flattery is a present.

Dr Samuel Johnson (1709-1784)

Very ugly or very beautiful women should be flattered on their understanding, mediocre ones on their beauty.

Lord Chesterfield (1694-1773)
English statesman and man of letters

What really flatters a man is that you think him worth flattering.

Broadbent, John Bull's Other Island
George Bernard Shaw (1856-1950)

Praise undeserv'd is satire in disguise.

anonymous, 18th century

I should have praised you more had you praised me less.

King Louis XIV of France (1638-1715)
to Bossuet

SEE La Rochefoucauld on ADMIRATION; COMPLIMENTS; Chinese Proverb on HUMILITY; Chesterfield on INGRATIATION; Shakespeare on POLITICIANS; Moore on POWER; Smith on PRAISE; Disraeli on ROYALTY

Flirting

No matter how happily a woman may be married, it always pleases her to discover that there is a nice man who wishes that she were not.

H. L. Mencken (1880-1956)
American journalist

Flirtation, attention without intention.

Max O'Rell (Paul Blouet) (1848-1903)
French journalist, lecturer, critic

When she raises her eyelids it's as if she were taking off all her clothes.
Colette (1873-1954)

Ah, beautiful passionate body
That has never ached with a heart!
A. C. Swinburne (1837-1909)

What attracts us in a woman rarely binds us to her.
J. Churton Collins (1848-1908)
British author, critic, scholar

So much alarm'd that she is quite
    alarming,
All Giggle, Blush — half Pertness,
    and half Pout.
Lord Byron (1788-1824)

Whoever loves above all the approach of love will never know the joy of attaining it.
Antoine de Saint-Exupéry (1900-1944)
French aviator, writer

Men do make passes at girls who wear glasses — but it all depends on their frames.
optician, 1964

SEE Wilde on MARRIAGE; Talleyrand on
SEDUCTION; Johnson on
SELF-IMAGE

Food

To eat is human, to digest divine.
Charles Copeland (1860-1952)
American educator

A man seldom thinks with more earnestness of anything than he does of his dinner.
Dr Samuel Johnson (1709-1784)

He was a bold man who first swallowed an oyster.
King James I of England (1566-1625)

On the continent people have good food; in England people have good table manners.
George Mikes (b. 1912)
Czech humorist

'Dish or no dish', rejoined the Caledonian, 'there's a deal o' fine confused feedin' about it, let me tell you'.
John Brown (1810-1882)
Scottish essayist, physician
of haggis

Part of the secret of success in life is to eat what you like and let the food fight it out inside.
Mark Twain (1835-1910)

The right diet directs sexual energy into the parts that matter.
Barbara Cartland (b. 1901)
British author

Everything you see, I owe to spaghetti.
Sophia Loren (b.1934)

No man is lonely while eating spaghetti; it requires so much attention.
Christopher Morley (1890-1957)
American novelist, journalist

There is no love sincerer than the love of food.
Tanner, *Man and Superman*
George Bernard Shaw (1856-1950)

Il faut manger pour vivre et non pas vivre pour manger.
One should eat to live, not live to eat.
Molière (1622-1673)

Seeing is deceiving. It's eating that's believing.
James Thurber (1894-1964)
American humorist, illustrator

SEE Brecht on MORALITY

Fools

They never open their mouths without subtracting from the sum of human knowledge.
Thomas B. Reed (1839-1902)
American lawyer, politician

A fellow who is always declaring he's no fool usually has his suspicions.
Wilson Mizner (1876-1933)
American dramatist, wit

He was born stupid, and greatly increased his birthright.
Samuel Butler (1835-1902)
English author

Ordinarily he was insane, but he had lucid moments when he was merely stupid.
Heinrich Heine (1797-1856)
German poet, journalist

However big the fool, there is always a bigger fool to admire him.
Nicolas Boileau (1636-1711)
French poet and critic

Limbus fatuorum is the name given by the old schoolmen to the intermediate region between heaven and hell, where dwelt what Dante calls 'the praiseless and the blameless dead', or, in other words, fools, idiots and lunatics.
John Milton (1608-1674)

Whenever a man does a thoroughly stupid thing, it is always from the noblest motives.
Oscar Wilde (1854-1900)

As a dog returneth to his vomit, so a fool returneth to his folly.
Bible, Proverbs

There are two kinds of fools: one says, 'This is old, therefore it is good'; the other says, 'This is new, therefore it is better'.
W. R. Inge (1860-1954)
Dean of St Paul's, London

A fool and his words are soon parted.
William Shenstone (1714-1763)
English poet

It has been said that there is no fool like an old fool, except a young fool. But the young fool has first to grow up to be an old fool to realise what a damn fool he was when he was a young fool.

Harold Macmillan, Lord Stockton (1894-1986)
British Conservative politician, Prime Minister

The ultimate result of shielding men from the effects of folly, is to fill the world with fools.

Herbert Spencer (1820-1903)
English philosopher

Qui vit sans folie n'est pas si sage qu'il croit. He who lives without folly isn't so wise as he thinks.

François, Duc de La Rochefoucauld (1613-1680)
French writer, moralist

I always treat fools and coxcombs with great ceremony; true good breeding not being a sufficient barrier against them.

G. K. Chesterton (1874-1936)

There are more fools than knaves in the world, else the knaves would not have enough to live upon.

Samuel Butler (1612-1680)
English poet

The dulness of the fool is the whetstone of the wits.

Celia, *As You Like It*
William Shakespeare (1564-1616)

If it were not for the company of fools, a witty man would often be greatly at a loss.

François, Duc de La Rochefoucauld (1613-1680)
French writer, moralist

The most difficult character in comedy is the fool, and he must be no fool who plays that part.

Miguel de Cervantes (1547-1616)

In the vain laughter of folly wisdom hears half its applause.

George Eliot (1819-1880)

Let us be thankful for the fools. But for them the rest of us could not succeed.

Mark Twain (1835-1910)

Suffer fools gladly; they may be right.

Holbrook Jackson (1874-1948)
British author

SEE Tree on IMITATION; Byron, Johnson on LAUGHTER; Fielding on MARRIAGE; Billings on PERSUASION

Force

I have with me two gods, Persuasion and Compulsion.

Themistocles (c. 514-c. 449 BC)
Athenian statesman

The use of force alone is but temporary. It may subdue for a moment; but does not remove the necessity of subduing again: and a nation is not governed, which is perpetually to be conquered.

Edmund Burke (1729-1797)
Irish philosopher, statesman

Some people draw a comforting distinction between 'force' and 'violence' ... I refuse to cloud the issue by such word-play ... the power which establishes a state is violence; the power which maintains it is violence; the power which eventually overthrows it is violence... Call an elephant a rabbit only if it gives you comfort to feel that you are about to be trampled to death by a rabbit.

Kenneth Kaunda (b. 1924)
Zambian statesman, President

I think that the sacredness of human life is a purely municipal ideal of no validity outside the jurisdiction. I believe that force, mitigated as far as may be by good manners, is the *ultima ratio*, and between two groups of men that want to make inconsistent kinds of world I see no remedy except force... It seems to me that every society rests on the death of men.

Justice Oliver Wendell Holmes (1841-1935)
American jurist

Foreigners

Who's 'im, Bill? A stranger! 'Eave 'arf a brick at 'im.

Punch 1854

They spell it Vinci and pronounce it Vinchy; foreigners always spell better than they pronounce.

Mark Twain (1835-1910)

Modern man ... is educated to understand foreign languages and misunderstand foreigners.

G. K. Chesterton (1874-1936)

Don't imagine I regard foreigners as inferior – they fascinate me.

Harold Wilson (b. 1916)
British Labour politician, Prime Minister

I've always had a weakness for foreign affairs.

Mae West (1892-1980)

Forgiveness

Forgiveness is the key to action and freedom.

Hannah Arendt (1906-1975)
American political philosopher

Always forgive your enemies; nothing annoys them so much.

Oscar Wilde (1854-1900)

Forgive! How many will say, 'forgive',
   and find
A sort of absolution in the sound
To hate a little longer!

Lord Tennyson (1809-1892)

One should forgive one's enemies, but not before they are hanged.
Heinrich Heine (1797-1856)
German poet, journalist

Nobody ever forgets where he buried a hatchet.
Kin (F. McKinney) Hubbard (1868-1930)
American humorist, journalist

Many promising reconciliations have broken down because, while both parties came prepared to forgive, neither party came prepared to be forgiven.
Charles Williams (1886-1945)
British author

'*Tout comprendre, c'est tout pardonner*' is an error, the fact being that the secret of forgiving everything is to understand nothing.
George Bernard Shaw (1856-1950)

How shall I lose the sin, yet keep the sense,
And love the offender, yet detest the offence?
Alexander Pope (1688-1744)

The stupid neither forgive nor forget; the naïve forgive and forget; the wise forgive but do not forget.
Thomas Szasz (b. 1920)
American psychiatrist

'I can forgive, but I cannot forget', is only another way of saying, 'I cannot forgive'.
H. W. Beecher (1813-1887)
American clergyman, editor, writer

I have looked on a lot of women with lust. I've committed adultery in my heart many times. God recognises I will do this and forgives me.
Jimmy Carter (b. 1924)
during Presidential campaign, 1976

God will forgive me; that is His business.
Heinrich Heine (1797-1856)
German poet, journalist

We never ask God to forgive anybody except where we haven't.
Elbert Hubbard (1856-1915)
American author

SEE Le Rochefoucauld on CONVERSATION; Wilde on DINNER PARTIES; Heine on GOD; Russian Proverb on GUILT; Lavater on The PUBLIC

Foul Play
He could not see a belt without hitting below it.
Margot Asquith (1864-1945)
socialite, wife of Prime Minister Herbert Asquith
of Lloyd George

Quit fouling like a wimp. If you're gonna foul, knock the crap outta him.
Norm Stewart, Missouri Tigers' basketball coach
to 6ft 9in Dan Bingenheimer

For nothing can seem foul to those that win.
King Henry, *King Henry IV part I*
William Shakespeare (1564-1616)

France
France, famed in all great arts, in none supreme.
Matthew Arnold (1822-1888)
English poet, critic

How can anyone govern a nation that has two hundred and forty different kinds of cheese?
Charles de Gaulle (1890-1970)

France is the only place where you can make love in the afternoon without people hammering on your door.
Barbara Cartland (b. 1901)
British author

Liberté! Fraternité! Sexualité!
graffito in Paris Métro

Everything ends this way in France – everything. Weddings, christenings, duels, burials, swindlings, diplomatic affairs – everything is a pretext for a good dinner.
Jean Anouilh (b. 1910)
French playwright

. . . So damn your food and damn your wines,
Your twisted loaves and twisting vines,
Your *table d'hôte*, your *à la carte*,
Your land, your history, your art.
From now on you can keep the lot.
Take every single thing you've got,
Your land, your wealth, your men, your dames,
Your dream of independent power,
And dear old Konrad Adenauer,
And stick them up your Eiffel Tower.
Anthony Jay (b. 1930)
British writer, journalist
extract from verse on France's rejection of Britain's entry into EEC, 1963

The French are a logical people, which is one reason the English dislike them so intensely. The other is that they own France, a country which we have always judged to be much too good for them.
Robert Morley (b. 1908)
British actor, wit

France is a country where the money falls apart in your hands and you can't tear the toilet paper.
Billy Wilder (b. 1906)
American film director

SEE PARIS

Fraternity

I have a dream that one day on the red hills of Georgia the sons of former slaves and the sons of former slave owners will be able to sit down together at the table of brotherhood.

Martin Luther King (1929-1968)

I believe in the brotherhood of all men, but I don't believe in wasting brotherhood on anyone who doesn't want to practise it with me. Brotherhood is a two-way street.

Malcolm X (1924-1965)
American radical leader

SEE Gill on WAR

Freedom

L'homme est né libre, et partout il est dans les fers.
Man was born free, and everywhere he is in chains.

Jean-Jacques Rousseau (1712-1778)

All that makes existence valuable to anyone depends on the enforcement of restraints upon the actions of other people.

John Stuart Mill (1806-1873)

Freedom is always freedom for the one who thinks differently.

Rosa Luxemburg (1870-1919)
German revolutionary

None who have always been free can understand the terrible fascinating power of the hope of freedom to those who are not free.

Pearl Buck (1892-1973)
American novelist

Freedom is never voluntarily given by the oppressor; it must be demanded by the oppressed.

Martin Luther King (1929-1968)

Freedom is not worth having if it does not connote freedom to err.

M. K. Gandhi (1869-1948)

The great trouble with the young people today is their freedom; they can no longer disobey.

Jean Cocteau (1889-1963)
French writer, film director

The free way of life proposes ends, but it does not prescribe means.

Robert Kennedy (1925-1968)

We got a free country here in this island, only none of us is free, but even so we is unfree equally.

Wolf Mankowitz (b. 1924)
British author

Only very slowly and late have men come to realise that unless freedom is universal it is only extended privilege.

Christopher Hill (b. 1912)
British historian

No human being, however great, or powerful, was ever so free as a fish.

John Ruskin (1819-1900)
English critic

The basic test of freedom is perhaps less in what we are free to do than in what we are free not to do.

Eric Hoffer (1902-1983)
American philosopher

I gave my life for freedom – this I know:
For those who bade me fight had told me so.

W. N. Ewer (1885-1976)

Freedom does not always win. This is one of the bitterest lessons of history.

A. J. P. Taylor (b. 1906)
British historian

SEE Bakunin on EQUALITY; FREEDOM OF SPEECH; LIBERTY; Engels on NECESSITY; Shaw on SACRIFICE; Lenin on The STATE

Freedom of Speech

Give me the liberty to know, to utter, and to argue freely according to conscience, above all liberties.

John Milton (1608-1674)

Every man has a right to utter what he thinks truth, and every man has a right to knock him down for it.

Dr Samuel Johnson (1709-1784)

People hardly ever make use of the freedom they have, for example, freedom of thought; instead they demand freedom of speech as a compensation.

Sören Kierkegaard (1813-1855)
Danish philosopher

Liberty of thought means liberty to communicate one's thought.

Salvador de Madariaga (1886-1978)
Spanish diplomat, writer, critic

The sound of tireless voices is the price we pay for the right to hear the music of our own opinions.

Adlai Stevenson (1900-1965)
American Democratic politician

It is now virtually impossible for the media in Britain to expose official wrongdoing without technically breaking the law.

Donald Trelford (b. 1937)
British newspaper editor
in 1986

Freedom of speech does not give a person the right to shout 'Fire!' in a crowded theatre.

Justice Oliver Wendell Holmes (1841-1935)
American jurist '

I disapprove of what you say, but I will defend to the death your right to say it.
epitome of Voltaire (1694-1778)

SEE FREEDOM; LIBERTY

Friendlessness

Friendless. Having no favors to bestow. Destitute of fortune. Addicted to utterance of truth and common sense.
Ambrose Bierce (1842-1914)
American author

No one can have a higher opinion of him than I have – and I think he is a dirty little beast.
W. S. Gilbert (1836-1911)
English librettist

SEE Shelley on LEADERSHIP

Friendliness

The social, friendly, honest man,
　Whate'er he be,
'Tis he fulfils great Nature's plan,
　And none but he!
Robert Burns (1759-1796)

A friend to all is a friend to none.
Greek proverb

The American has dwindled into an Odd Fellow – one who may be known by the development of his organ of gregariousness.
H. D. Thoreau (1817-1862)

SEE Waugh on AMERICA

Friends

What is a friend? A single soul dwelling in two bodies.
Aristotle (384-322 BC)

So long as we are loved by others I should say that we are almost indispensable; and no man is useless while he has a friend.
Robert Louis Stevenson (1850-1894)

Il est plus honteux de se défier de ses amis que d'en être trompé.
It is more shameful to distrust one's friends than to be deceived by them.
François, Duc de La Rochefoucauld (1613-1680)
French writer, moralist

It is in the thirties that we want friends. In the forties we know that they won't save us any more than love did.
F. Scott Fitzgerald (1896-1940)

If you would have friends, first learn to do without them.
Elbert Hubbard (1856-1915)
American author

It's the friends you can call up at 4 am that matter.
Marlene Dietrich (b. 1901)

I do then with my friends, as I do with my books. I would have them where I can find

them, but I seldom use them.
R. W. Emerson (1803-1882)
American essayist, poet, philosopher

We cherish our friends not for their ability to amuse us, but for ours to amuse them.
Evelyn Waugh (1903-1966)

I do not believe that friends are necessarily the people you like best, they are merely the people who got there first.
Peter Ustinov (b. 1921)
British actor, wit

Friends are like fiddle strings, they must not be screwed too tight.
English proverb

Most people enjoy the inferiority of their best friends.
Lord Chesterfield (1694-1773)
English statesman and man of letters

Dans l'adversité de nos meilleurs amis, nous trouvons toujours quelque chose qui ne nous déplaît pas.
In the misfortunes of our best friends we always find something not altogether displeasing to us.
François, Duc de La Rochefoucauld (1613-1680)
French writer, moralist

Give me the avowed, the erect, the
　manly foe,
Bold I can meet – perhaps may
　turn his blow;
But of all plagues, good Heaven,
　thy wrath can send,
Save, save, oh save me from the
　Candid Friend.
George Canning (1770-1827)
English statesman, Prime Minister

Instead of loving your enemies, treat your friends a little better.
Ed (E. W.) Howe (1853-1937)
American journalist, novelist

SEE ACQUAINTANCE; Talleyrand on ALTRUISM; Auden on ARGUMENT; La Fontaine on DISCRETION; de Poitiers on ENEMIES; Mumford on FAMILY; Horace on GREATNESS; Welles on HARD TIMES; Gay on HYPOCRISY; Bennet on JUDGEMENTS; Milligan on MONEY; Sargent on PORTRAITS

Friendship

A sudden thought strikes me; – let us swear an eternal friendship.
John Hookham Frere (1769-1846)
British diplomat, author

Be courteous to all, but intimate with few, and let those few be well tried before you give them your confidence. True friendship is a plant of slow growth, and must undergo and withstand the shocks of adversity before it is

entitled to the appellation.
George Washington (1732-1799)

Si on me presse de dire pourquoi je l'aimais, je sens que cela ne se peut s'exprimer, qu'en répondant: 'Parce que c'était lui; parce que c'était moi'.
If I am pressed to say why I loved him, I feel it could only be explained by answering: 'Because it was him; because it was me'.
Michel de Montaigne (1533-1592)
French essayist

Men seem to kick friendship around like a football, but it doesn't seem to crack. Women treat it as glass and it goes to pieces.
Anne Morrow Lindbergh (b. 1906)
American poet, essayist (wife of
Charles Lindbergh)

Oh, the pious friendships of the female sex!
William Congreve (1670-1729)
English dramatist

The endearing elegance of female friendship.
Dr Samuel Johnson (1709-1784)

If a man does not make new acquaintance as he advances through life, he will soon find himself alone. A man, Sir, should keep his friendship in constant repair.
Dr Samuel Johnson (1709-1784)

Friendship is Love, without his wings!
Lord Byron (1788-1824)

Love is only chatter,
Friends are all that matter.
Gelett Burgess (1866-1951)
American humorist

Friendship is a disinterested commerce between equals; love, an abject intercourse between tyrants and slaves.
Oliver Goldsmith (1728-1774)

Friendship may, and often does, grow into love, but love never subsides into friendship.
Lord Byron (1788-1824)

That's what friendship means: sharing the prejudice of experience.
Charles Bukowski (b.1920)
American author

L'amour est aveugle; l'amitié ferme les yeux.
Love is blind; friendship closes its eyes.
anonymous

Friendship creates only the illusion of not being alone.
Orson Welles (1915-1985)

SEE ACQUAINTANCE; Smith on AGE: Old Age; Talleyrand on ALTRUISM; Colette on COURTESY; Pope on DEATH; Wayside Pulpit on DRINK; Rossetti on FAMILY; Stevenson on MARRIAGE; Moore on POWER

Fun

Most of the time I don't have much fun. The rest of the time I don't have any fun at all.
Woody Allen (b. 1935)

All the animals except man know that the principal business of life is to enjoy it.
Samuel Butler (1835-1902)
English author

For present joys are more to flesh and
  blood
Than a dull prospect of a distant
  good.
John Dryden (1631-1700)

Fun is a good thing but only when it spoils nothing better.
George Santayana (1863-1952)
American philosopher, poet

People must not do things for fun. We are not here for fun. There is no reference to fun in any Act of Parliament.
A. P. Herbert (1890-1971)
British author, politician

Function

The question of common sense is always 'What is it good for?' – a question which would abolish the rose and be answered triumphantly by the cabbage.
J. R. Lowell (1819-1891)
American poet, editor

Utility is the great idol of the age, to which all powers must do service and all talents swear allegiance.
Friedrich von Schiller (1759-1805)

Funerals

Our respect for the dead, when they are just dead, is something wonderful.
John Ruskin (1819-1900)
English critic

When we attend the funerals of our friends we grieve for them, but when we go to those of other people it is chiefly our own deaths that we mourn for.
Gerald Brenan (b. 1894)
British writer

As grand
And griefless as a rich man's funeral.
Sidney Thompson Dobell (1824-1874)
English poet

Funeral pomp is more for the vanity of the living than for the honour of the dead.
François, Duc de La Rochefoucauld (1613-1680)
French writer, moralist

I did not attend his funeral; but I wrote a nice letter saying I approved of it.
Mark Twain (1835-1910)

The only reason I might go to the funeral is to make absolutely sure that he's dead.

> 'an eminent editor', of Lord
> Beaverbrook, quoted by
> Anthony Sampson, Anatomy of
> Britain Today, 1965

Futility

I have measured out my life with coffee spoons.

> T. S. Eliot (1888-1965)

A constant smirk upon the face, and a whiffling activity of the body, are strong indications of futility.

> Lord Chesterfield (1694-1773)
> English statesman and man of letters

As futile as a clock in an empty house.

> James Thurber (1894-1961)
> American humorist, illustrator

The Future

Tomorrow is the most important thing in life. Comes into us at midnight very clean. It's perfect when it arrives and it puts itself in our hands. It hopes we've learned something from yesterday.

> John Wayne (1907-1979)

The future is called 'perhaps,' which is the only possible thing to call the future. And the important thing is not to allow that to scare you.

> Tennessee Williams (1914-1983)

Future. That period of time in which our affairs prosper, our friends are true and our happiness is assured.

> Ambrose Bierce (1842-1914)
> American author

We should all be concerned about the future because we will have to spend the rest of our lives there.

> C. F. Kettering (1876-1958)
> American engineer, industrialist

I have a Vision of the Future, chum.
The workers' flats in fields of soya beans
Tower up like silver pencils.

> John Betjeman (1906-1984)
> British poet

Gambling

Il y a deux grand plaisirs dans le jeu, celui de gagner et celui de perdre.
There are two great pleasures in gambling: that of winning and that of losing.
French proverb

Gambling promises the poor what property performs for the rich – something for nothing.
George Bernard Shaw (1856-1950)

It is the child of avarice, the brother of iniquity, and the father of mischief.
George Washington (1732-1799)

No wife can endure a gambling husband unless he is a steady winner.
Lord Dewar (1864-1930)
British writer, politician, businessman

The only man who makes money following the races is one who does it with a broom and shovel.
Elbert Hubbard (1865-1915)
American author

Time spent in a casino is time given to death, a foretaste of the hour when one's flesh will be diverted to the purposes of the worm and not the will.
Rebecca West (1892-1983)
British author

Death and dice level all distinctions.
Samuel Foote (1720-1777)
English dramatist

SEE Butler on FAITH

Gardens

God Almighty first planted a garden. And indeed it is the purest of human pleasures.
Francis Bacon (1561-1626)

Annihilating all that's made
To a green thought in a green shade.
Andrew Marvell (1621-1678)

Chaque fleur est une âme à la Nature éclose.
Every flower is a soul blossoming out to nature.
Gérard de Nerval (1808-1855)
French writer, translator

*Éstas, que fueron pompa y alegria,
Dispertando al albor de la mañana,*
*A la tarde serán lástima vana,
Durmiendo en brazos de la noche fría.*
These flowers, which were splendid and sprightly,
Waking in the dawn of the morning,
In the evening will be a pitiful frivolity,
Sleeping in the night's cold arms.
Pedro Calderón de la Barca (1600-1681)
Spanish playwright

What is a weed? A plant whose virtues have not yet been discovered.
R. W. Emerson (1803-1882)
American essayist, poet, philosopher

Training is everything. The peach was once a bitter almond; cauliflower is nothing but cabbage with a college education.
Mark Twain (1835-1910)

What a man needs in gardening is a cast-iron back, with a hinge in it.
Charles D. Warner (1829-1900)
American essayist, novelist

Gays

This sort of thing may be tolerated by the French – but we are British, thank God.
Viscount Montgomery (1887-1976)
British soldier

Homosexuality is a sickness, just as are baby-rape or wanting to become head of General Motors.
Eldridge Cleaver (b. 1935)
American black leader, writer

There is probably no sensitive heterosexual alive who is not preoccupied with his latent homosexuality.
Norman Mailer (b. 1923)

This is a celebration of individual freedom, not of homosexuality. No government has the right to tell its citizens when or whom to love. The only queer people are those who don't love anybody.
Rita Mae Brown (b. 1944)
American feminist writer
of the Gay Olympics, 1982

The only way we'll have real pride is when we demand recognition of a culture that isn't just sexual. It's all there – all through history we've been there; but we have to claim it, and identify who was in it, and articulate what's in our minds and hearts and all our creative contributions to this earth. And until we do that, and until we organise ourselves block by neighbourhood by city by state into a united visible community that fights back, we're doomed.

> Ned, *The Normal Heart*
> Larry Kramer (b. 1935)
> American playwright, novelist

SEE Kramer on AIDS

Generals

I made all my generals out of mud.

> Napoleon Bonaparte (1769-1821)

One murder made a villain, millions a hero.

> Beilby Porteous (1731-1808)
> English clergyman, writer

All through history it's the nations that have given most to the generals and the least to the people that have been the first to fall.

> Harry S. Truman (1884-1972)

Humility must always be the portion of any man who receives acclaim earned in the blood of his followers and the sacrifices of his friends.

> Dwight D. Eisenhower (1890-1969)

Soldiers win battles and generals get the credit.

> Napoleon Bonaparte (1769-1821)

The best generals I have known were stupid or absent-minded men. . . Not only does a good army commander not need any special qualities, on the contrary he needs the absence of the highest and best human attributes – love, poetry, tenderness, and philosophic inquiring doubt. He should be limited, firmly convinced that what he is doing is very important (otherwise he will not have sufficient patience), and only then will he be a brave leader. God forbid that he should be humane, should love, or pity, or think of what is just and unjust.

> Leo Tolstoy (1828-1910)
> from *War and Peace*
> *trans.* Louise and Aylmer Maude

It is better to have a lion at the head of an army of sheep than a sheep at the head of an army of lions.

> Daniel Defoe (1661-1731)

My centre is giving way, my right is in retreat; situation excellent. I shall attack.

> Ferdinand Foch (1851-1929)
> French general

Put your trust in God, my boys, and keep your powder dry.

> Valentine Blacker (1778-1823)
> British soldier, historian
> *of Oliver Cromwell*

You must not fight too often with one enemy, or you will teach him all your art of war.

> Napoleon Bonaparte (1769-1821)

War is too important a matter to be left to the generals.

> Georges Clemenceau (1841-1929)
> French statesman

SEE The ARMY; Montgomery on POLITICIANS

The Generation Gap

Every generation is a secret society and has incommunicable enthusiasms, tastes and interests which are a mystery both to its predecessors and to posterity.

> Arthur Chapman (1873-1935)
> American poet, author

Our tastes greatly alter. The lad does not care for the child's rattle, and the old man does not care for the young man's whore.

> Dr Samuel Johnson (1709-1784)

The old know what they want; the young are sad and bewildered.

> Logan Pearsall Smith (1865-1946)
> American essayist

We have to hate our immediate predecessors to get free of their authority.

> D. H. Lawrence (1885-1930)

The denunciation of the young is a necessary part of the hygiene of older people, and greatly assists the circulation of their blood.

> Logan Pearsall Smith (1865-1946)
> American essayist

It is all that the young can do for the old, to shock them and keep them up to date.

> George Bernard Shaw (1856-1950)

One of these days there will be a terrible revolt of the old against the young.

> St John Ervine (1888-1971)
> British dramatist, novelist

SEE AGE; Burke, Harris on ARROGANCE

Generosity

Give all thou canst; high Heaven rejects the lore
Of nicely-calculated less or more.

> William Wordsworth (1770-1850)

Liberality consists less in giving a great deal than in gifts well-timed.

> Jean de la Bruyère (1645-1696)
> French writer, moralist

What is called generosity is usually only the vanity of giving; we enjoy the vanity more than the thing given.

> François, Duc de La Rochefoucauld (1613-1680)
> French writer, moralist

We must be aware of the dangers which lie in our most generous wishes. Some paradox of

our nature leads us, when once we have made our fellow men the objects of our enlightened interest, to go on to make them the objects of our pity, then of our wisdom, ultimately of our coercion.
Lionel Trilling (1905-1975)
American critic

As for the largest-hearted of us, what is the word we write most often in our cheque-books? – 'Self'.
Eden Philpotts (1862-1960)
British author

Don't be selfish. If you have something you do not want, and know someone who has no use for it, give. In this way you can be generous without expenditure of self-denial and also help another to be the same.
Elbert Hubbard (1856-1915)
American author

It is always so pleasant to be generous, though very vexatious to pay debts.
R. W. Emerson (1803-1882)
American essayist, poet, philosopher

It's better to give than to lend, and it costs about the same.
Sir Philip Gibbs (1877-1962)
British author, journalist

SEE Lever on GOVERNMENT

Genius

The divine egoism that is genius.
Mary Webb (1881-1927)
British author

Genius is an infinite capacity for taking life by the scruff of the neck.
Christopher Quill

The dullard's envy of brilliant men is always assuaged by the suspicion that they will come to a bad end.
Sir Max Beerbohm (1872-1956)
British author

To mediocrity genius is unforgivable.
Elbert Hubbard (1856-1915)
American author

Doing easily what others find difficult is talent; doing what is impossible for talent is genius.
Henri Amiel (1821-1881)
Swiss philosopher, poet

Mediocrity knows nothing higher than itself, but talent instantly recognises genius.
Sir Arthur Conan Doyle (1859-1930)

Every man of genius is considerably helped by being dead.
Robert Lynd (1879-1949)
Anglo-Irish essayist, journalist

The measure of a master is his success in

bringing all men round to his opinion twenty years later.
R. W. Emerson (1803-1882)
American essayist, poet, philosopher

Masterpieces are not single and solitary births; they are the outcome of many years of thinking in common, of thinking by the body of the people, so that the experience of the mass is behind the single voice.
Virginia Woolf (1882-1941)

If we are to have genius we must put up with the inconvenience of genius, and that the world will never do; it wants geniuses, but would like them just like other people.
George Moore (1852-1933)
Irish author

Since when was genius found respectable?
Elizabeth Barrett Browning (1806-1861)

Great wits are sure to madness near allied.
John Dryden (1631-1700)

The most effective way of shutting our minds against a great man's ideas is to take them for granted and admit he was great and have done with him.
George Bernard Shaw (1856-1950)

Everybody denies I am a genius – but nobody ever called me one!
Orson Welles (1915-1985)

Good God! What a genius I had when I wrote that book.
Jonathan Swift (1667-1745)
of The Tale of a Tub

A man who is a genius and doesn't know it probably isn't.
Stanislaus J. Lec (b. 1909)
Polish poet

Milton, Madam, was a genius that could cut a Colossus from a rock; but he could not carve heads upon cherry-stones.
Dr Samuel Johnson (1709-1784)

Man can climb to the highest summits, but he cannot dwell there long.
Morell, Candida
George Bernard Shaw (1856-1950)

The genius of Einstein leads to Hiroshima.
Pablo Picasso (1881-1973)

SEE Disraeli on INNOVATION; Wilde on SELF-IMAGE; Hazlitt, Jonson on SHAKESPEARE; Reynolds on WORK; Heine, Lowell on WRITERS

Genocide

A single death is a tragedy, a million deaths is a statistic.
Josef Stalin (1879-1953)

After all there is but one race – humanity.
George Moore (1852-1933)
Irish author

Gentlemen

I can make a lord, but only God almighty can make a gentleman.
King James I of England (1566-1625)

Education begins a gentleman, conversation completes him.
18th century English proverb

He was the product of an English public school and university ... no scholar, but essentially a gentleman.
H. Seton Merriman (1862-1903)
English novelist

A gentleman is one who never hurts anyone's feelings unintentionally.
Oscar Wilde (1854-1900)

Almost an Emperor and not quite a gentleman.
Lord Ancaster (1867-1951)
British politician, administrator
of Hugh, 5th earl of Lonsdale

He is every other inch a gentleman.
Rebecca West (1892-1983)
British author

I am parshial to ladies if they are nice. I suppose it is my nature. I am not quite a gentleman but you would hardly notice it.
Daisy Ashford (1881-1972)
British writer of The
Young Visiters, aged 9

It is at unimportant moments that a man is a gentleman. At important moments he ought to be something better.
G. K. Chesterton (1874-1936)

Anyone can be heroic from time to time, but a gentleman is something you have to be all the time.
Luigi Pirandello (1867-1936)
Italian playwright, author

I do not know the American gentleman, God forgive me for putting two such words together.
Charles Dickens (1812-1870)

The only infallible rule we know is, that the man who is always talking about being a gentleman never is one.
R. S. Surtees (1803-1864)
English novelist

SEE Cromwell on The ARMY; Johnson on BLOODSPORTS; Wilde on EXAMINATIONS; Macaulay on The NAVY; Congreve on UNIVERSITY

Germany

We Germans will never produce another Goethe, but we may produce another Caesar.
Oswald Spengler (1880-1936)
German philosopher, historian
in 1925

They are a fine people but quick to catch the disease of anti-humanity. I think it's because of their poor elimination. Germany is a headquarters for constipation.
George Grosz (1893-1959)
German artist

Everything ponderous, viscous, and solemnly clumsy, all long-winded and boring types of style are developed in profuse variety among Germans.
Friedrich Nietzsche (1844-1900)

Whenever the literary German dives into a sentence, that is the last you are going to see of him till he emerges on the other side of his Atlantic with his verb in his mouth.
Mark Twain (1835-1910)

Getting On

Getting on is the opium of the middle classes.
Walter James (b. 1912)
British journalist

There are only two ways of getting on in the world: by one's own industry, or by the stupidity of others.
Jean de la Bruyère (1645-1696)
French writer, moralist

No one rises so high as he who knows not whither he is going.
Oliver Cromwell (1599-1658)

When you are getting kicked from the rear it means you're in front.
Fulton Sheen (1895-1979)
American author, clergyman

You have to be a bastard to make it, and that's a fact. And the Beatles are the biggest bastards on Earth.
John Lennon (1940-1980)

The path of social advancement is, and must be, strewn with broken friendships.
H. G. Wells (1866-1946)

To establish oneself in the world, one does all one can to seem established there already.
François, Duc de La Rochefoucauld (1613-1680)
French writer, moralist

The trouble with the rat-race is that even if you win, you're still a rat.
Lily Tomlin (b. 1939)
American comedy actress

SEE AMBITION; PROMOTION; Barrie on The SCOTS; SUCCESS; WINNING

Give and Take

Do unto the other feller the way he's like to do unto you an' do it fust.
Edward Noyes Westcott (1847-1898)
American novelist

Do not do unto others as you would that they should do unto you. Their tastes may not be the same.
George Bernard Shaw (1856-1950)

It is explained that all relationships require a little give and take. This is untrue. Any partnership demands that we give and give and give and at the last, as we flop into our graves exhausted, we are told that we didn't give enough.
Quentin Crisp (b. 1908)
British author

Glory

Avoid shame but do not seek glory – nothing so expensive as glory.
Sydney Smith (1771-1845)
English writer, clergyman

The paths of glory lead but to the grave.
Thomas Gray (1716-1771)

Military glory – the attractive rainbow that rises in showers of blood.
Abraham Lincoln (1809-1865)

Is it not passing brave to be a King,
And ride in triumph through Persepolis?
Christopher Marlowe (1564-1593)

I have touch'd the highest point of all
my greatness,
And from that full meridian of my
glory
I haste now to my setting.
Wolsey, King Henry VIII
William Shakespeare (1564-1616)

The final event to himself has been, that as he rose like a rocket, he fell like the stick.
Thomas Paine (1737-1809)
pamphleteer, revolutionary
of Edmund Burke

What is glory? It is to have a lot of nonsense talked about you.
Gustave Flaubert (1821-1880)

SEE Hugo on POPULARITY

God

Of course there's no such thing as a totally objective person, except Almighty God, if she exists.
Antonia Fraser (b. 1932)
British historian

God is an unutterable sigh, planted in the depths of the soul.
Jean Paul Richter (1763-1825)
German author

The most beautiful of all emblems is that of God, whom Timaeus of Locris describes under the image of 'A circle whose centre is everywhere and circumference nowhere'.
Voltaire (1694-1778)

God, that dumping ground of our dreams.
Jean Rostand (1894-1977)
French biologist, writer

The only excuse for God is that he doesn't exist.
Stendhal (1783-1842)

I believe in the incomprehensibility of God.
Honoré de Balzac (1799-1850)

A comprehended God is no God.
John Chrysostom (345-407)
Greek ecclesiast and hermit

Every conjecture we can form with regard to the works of God has as little probability as the conjectures of a child with regard to the works of a man.
Thomas Reid (1710-1796)
Scottish philosopher

No statement about God is simply, literally true. God is far more than can be measured, described, defined in ordinary language, or pinned down to any particular happening.
David Jenkins (b. 1925)
theologian, bishop of Durham

If God made us in His image we have certainly returned the compliment.
Voltaire (1694-1778)

If the triangles made a god, they would give him three sides.
Charles de Montesquieu (1689-1755)
French philosopher, lawyer

Somewhere in the bible it say Jesus' hair was like lamb's wool, I say. Well, say Shug, if he came to any of these churches we talking bout he'd have to have it conked before anybody paid him any attention. The last thing niggers want to think about they God is that his hair kinky.
Alice Walker (b. 1944)
American author, critic

And almost every one when age,
Disease, or sorrows strike him,
Inclines to think there is a God,
Or something very like Him.
A. H. Clough (1819-1861)
English poet

God is for men and religion for women.
Joseph Conrad (1857-1924)

But if God had wanted us to think with our wombs, why did He give us a brain?
Clare Boothe Luce (b. 1903)
American diplomat, writer

God uses lust to impel men to marry, ambition to office, avarice to earning, and fear to faith. God led me like an old blind goat.
Martin Luther (1483-1546)

A man with God is always in the majority.
John Knox (1505-1572)
Scottish Presbyterian leader

One, with God, is always a majority, but

many a martyr has been burned at the stake while the votes were being counted.
Thomas B. Reed (1839-1902)
American lawyer, politician

Comme vous savez, Dieu est d'ordinaire pour les gros escadrons contre les petits.
As you know, God is generally on the side of the big squadrons against the small ones.
Comte de Bussy-Rabutin (1618-1693)
French soldier, writer

Dieu n'est pas pour les gros bataillons, mais pour ceux qui tirent le mieux.
God is not on the side of the big battalions, but on the side of those who shoot best.
Voltaire (1694-1778)

To believe in God for me is to feel that there is a God, not a dead one, or a stuffed one, but a living one, who with irresistible force urges us towards more loving.
Vincent Van Gogh (1853-1890)

In the faces of men and women I see God,
and in my own face in the glass,
I find letters from God dropt in the street,
and every one is sign'd by God's name.
And I leave them where they are,
for I know that wheresoe'er I go,
Others will punctually come for ever and ever.
Walt Whitman (1819-1892)

No man hates God without first hating himself.
Fulton Sheen (1895-1979)
American clergyman, author

Throw away thy rod,
Throw away thy wrath;
O my God,
Take the gentle path.
George Herbert (1593-1633)
English clergyman, poet

God will forgive me the foolish remarks I have made about Him just as I will forgive my opponents the foolish things they have written about me, even though they are spiritually as inferior to me as I to thee, O God!
Heinrich Heine (1797-1856)
German poet, journalist

God will provide – ah, if only He would till He does!
Yiddish proverb

By the year 2000 we will, I hope, raise our children to believe in human potential, not God.
Gloria Steinem (b. 1934)
American feminist writer

If God wants us to do a thing, He should make his wishes sufficiently clear. Sensible people will wait till He has done this before paying much attention to Him.
Samuel Butler (1835-1902)
English author

God is a verb, not a noun.
R. Buckminster Fuller (1895-1983)
American architect, engineer

We were deceived by the wisdom of the serpent, but we are freed by the foolishness of God.
Saint Augustine (354-430)

An act of God was defined as *something which no reasonable man could have expected.*
A. P. Herbert (1890-1971)
British author, politician

I have never understood why it should be considered derogatory to the Creator to suppose that he has a sense of humour.
W. R. Inge (1860-1954)
Dean of St Paul's, London

Why is it when we talk to God, we're said to be praying – but when God talks to us, we're schizophrenic?
Lily Tomlin (b. 1939)
American comedy actress

Gawd knows, an' 'E won't split on a pal.
Rudyard Kipling (1865-1936)

SEE Merton on ART; Shaw on The BRITISH; CREATION; Pascal on FAITH; Heine on FORGIVING; France, Greek Proverb on LUCK; Cary on MIRACLES; Day on PRAYER; St Peter on PRIVILEGE; St Paul on The STATUS QUO

Goddesses

A woman clothed with the sun, and the moon under her feet, and upon her head a crown of twelve stars.
John the Divine (1st century AD)

And some to Mecca turn to pray, and I toward thy bed, Yasmin.
James Elroy Flecker (1884-1915)
British poet

What, when drunk, one sees in other women, one sees in Garbo sober.
Kenneth Tynan (1927-1980)
British critic

Golf

A day spent in a round of strenuous idleness.
William Wordsworth (1770-1850)

It is almost impossible to remember how tragic a place the world is when one is playing golf.
Robert Lynd (1879-1949)
Anglo-Irish essayist, journalist

Golf is a good walk spoiled.
Mark Twain (1835-1910)

A golf course outside a big town serves an excellent purpose in that it segregates, as though in a concentration camp, all the idle and idiot well-to-do.
Sir Osbert Sitwell (1892-1969)
British writer, poet

Golf is a game whose aim is to hit a very small ball into an even smaller hole, with weapons singularly ill-designed for the purpose.
Sir Winston Churchill (1874-1965)

Good Deeds

The luxury of doing good surpasses every other personal enjoyment.
John Gay (1685-1732)
English playwright

It is the mark of a good action that it appears inevitable in retrospect.
Robert Louis Stevenson (1850-1894)

That best portion of a good man's life,
His little, nameless, unremembered acts
Of kindness and of love.
William Wordsworth (1770-1850)

The greatest pleasure I know is to do a good action by stealth, and to have it found out by accident.
Charles Lamb (1775-1834)
English essayist, critic

Verily the kindness that gazes upon itself in a mirror turns to stone,
And a good deed that calls itself by tender names becomes the parent to a curse.
Kahlil Gibran (1883-1931)
Syrian poet, mystic

Die Tat ist alles, nichts der Ruhm.
The deed is all, not the glory.
Johann Wolfgang von Goethe (1749-1832)

Every good deed is more than three parts pride.
Gustave Flaubert (1821-1880)

The last temptation is the greatest treason:
To do the right deed for the wrong reason.
T.S. Eliot (1888-1965)

SEE ALTRUISM; BENEFACTORS; CHARITY; Shaw on INTENTIONS; La Rochefoucauld on MOTIVES; Burke on STYLE

Goodness

People cannot remain good unless good is expected of them.
Bertolt Brecht (1898-1956)

To be good, according to the vulgar standard of goodness, is obviously quite easy. It merely requires a certain amount of sordid terror, a certain lack of imaginative thought, and a certain low passion for middle-class respectability.
Oscar Wilde (1854-1900)

When I'm good, I'm very good, but when I'm bad I'm better.
Mae West (1892-1980)

SEE KINDNESS

Gossip

And all who told it added something new,
And all who heard it made enlargements too.
Alexander Pope (1688-1744)

If it is abuse – why one is always sure to hear of it from one damned good-natured friend or other!
R. B. Sheridan (1751-1816)

It takes your enemy and your friend, working together, to hurt you to the heart: the one to slander you and the other to get the news to you.
Mark Twain (1835-1910)

Alas! they had been friends in youth;
But whispering tongues can poison truth.
S. T. Coleridge (1772-1834)

Il y a un démon qui met des ailes à certaines nouvelles et qui les lâche comme des aigles dans l'espace.
There is a demon that puts wings on certain tales and launches them like eagles into space.
Alexandre Dumas (1802-1870)

Gossip is the art of saying nothing in a way that leaves practically nothing unsaid.
Walter Winchell (1897-1972)
American columnist

Gossip: sociologists on a mean and petty scale.
Woodrow Wilson (1856-1924)

Nobody's interested in sweetness and light.
Hedda Hopper (1890-1966)
Hollywood actress, gossip columnist

Show me someone who never gossips, and I'll show you someone who isn't interested in people.
Barbara Walters (b. 1931)
American television personality

Gossip is vice enjoyed vicariously.
Elbert Hubbard (1856-1915)
American author

At every word a reputation dies.
Alexander Pope (1688-1744)

Confidante. One entrusted by A with the secrets of B confided to herself by C.
Ambrose Bierce (1842-1914)
American author

If all men knew what others say of them, there would not be four friends in the world.
Blaise Pascal (1623-1662)

How awful to reflect that what people say of us is true.
Logan Pearsall Smith (1865-1946)
American essayist

The sewing-circle – the Protestant confessional where each one confesses, not her own sins, but the sins of her neighbors.
Charles B. Fairbanks (1827-1859)

They come together like the coroner's inquest, to sit upon the murdered reputations of the week.
William Congreve (1670-1729)
English dramatist

None are so fond of secrets as those who do not mean to keep them.
C. C. Colton (1780-1832)
English author

In scandal as in robbery, the receiver is always thought as bad as the thief.
Lord Chesterfield (1694-1773)
English statesman and man of letters

Backbite. To 'speak of a man as you find him' when he can't find you.
Ambrose Bierce (1842-1914)
American author

Tattlers also and busybodies, speaking things which they ought not.
Saint Paul (3-67)

She poured a little social sewage into his ears.
George Meredith (1828-1909)
English author

Ah, well, the truth is always one thing, but in a way it's the other thing, the gossip, that counts. It shows where people's hearts lie.
Paul Scott (1920-1978)
British author

SEE Creighton on HISTORY; Howe on REPUTATION; Wilde on SCANDAL; Wilde on SLANDER; Connolly on SUICIDE

Government

The Athenians govern the Greeks; I govern the Athenians; you, my wife, govern me; your son governs you.
Themistocles (c. 528-c. 462 BC)
Athenian statesman

The punishment which the wise suffer who refuse to take part in the government, is to live under the government of worse men.
Plato (428-347 BC)

Men are not governed by justice, but by law or persuasion. When they refuse to be governed by law or persuasion, they have to be governed by force or fraud, or both.
Lord Summerhayes, *Misalliance*
George Bernard Shaw (1856-1950)

Il faut, dans le gouvernement, des bergers et des bouchers.
Governments need to have both shepherds and butchers.
Voltaire (1694-1778)

Government is like a baby. An alimentary canal with a big appetite at one end and no sense of responsibility at the other.
Ronald Reagan (b. 1911)

Government is emphatically a machine: to the discontented a 'taxing machine', to the contented a 'machine for securing property'.
Thomas Carlyle (1795-1881)
Scottish author

Government has no other end than the preservation of property.
John Locke (1632-1704)

The hatred Americans have for their own government is pathological . . . at one level it is simply thwarted greed: since our religion is making a buck, giving a part of that buck to any government is an act against nature.
Gore Vidal (b. 1925)

The business of Government is to see that no other organisation is as strong as itself.
Woodrow Wilson (1856-1924)

The marvel of all history is the patience with which men and women submit to burdens unnecessarily laid upon them by their governments.
William E. Borah (1865-1940)
American politician

To be governed is to be watched, inspected, spied upon, directed, lawridden, regulated, penned up, indoctrinated, preached at, checked, appraised, seized, censured, commanded by beings who have neither title, knowledge nor virtue.
Pierre-Joseph Proudhon (1809-1865)
French social theorist

Nothing is so galling to a people not broken in from the birth as a paternal, or in other words a meddling government, a government which tells them what to read and say and eat and drink and wear.
Lord Macaulay (1800-1859)
English historian

We mustn't be stiff and stand-off, you know. We must be thoroughly democratic, and patronize everybody without distinction of class.
Broadbent, *John Bull's Other Island*
George Bernard Shaw (1856-1950)

The government of the world I live in was not framed, like that of Britain, in after-dinner conversations over the wine.
H. D. Thoreau (1817-1862)

At the very heart of British government there is a luxuriant and voluntary exclusion of talent.
Brian Chapman (b. 1923)
British academic

It is the duty of Her Majesty's Government neither to flap nor to falter.
Harold Macmillan, Lord Stockton (1894-1986)
British Conservative politician, Prime Minister

The authorities were at their wit's end, nor had it taken them long to get there.
Desmond MacCarthy (1877-1952)
British critic

Generosity is a part of my character, and I therefore hasten to assure this Government that I will never make an allegation of dishonesty against it wherever a simple explanation of stupidity will suffice.
Leslie (Baron) Lever (1905-1977)
British solicitor, Labour politician

The art of government is the organization of idolatry.
George Bernard Shaw (1856-1950)

The object of government in peace and in war is not the glory of rulers or of races, but the happiness of the common man.
William Beveridge (1879-1963)
British economist

For forms of government let fools contest,
Whate'er is best administered is best.
Alexander Pope (1688-1744)

Mankind, when left to themselves, are unfit for their own government.
George Washington (1732-1799)

Let us treat men and women well; treat them as if they were real; perhaps they are.
R. W. Emerson (1803-1882)
American essayist, poet, philosopher

SEE Colton, Ickes on CORRUPTION; Graffito on ELECTIONS; Rogers on JOKERS; Phillips on NEWSPAPERS; Disraeli on OPPOSITION; Jefferson on The PRESS; Russell, Shaw on RELIGION; Bentham on SECRETS; Shaw, Voltaire on TAXATION

Graffiti

There was so much handwriting on the wall that even the wall fell down.
Christopher Morley (1890-1957)
American novelist, journalist

Gratitude

Maybe the only thing worse than having to give gratitude constantly ... is having to accept it.
William Faulkner (1897-1962)

La reconnaissance de la plupart des hommes n'est qu'une secrète envie de recevoir de plus grands bienfaits.
In most of mankind gratitude is merely a secret hope of further favours.
François, Duc de La Rochefoucauld (1613-1680)
French writer, moralist

Gratitude is a sickness suffered by dogs.
Josef Stalin (1879-1953)

There are minds so impatient of inferiority that their gratitude is a species of revenge, and they return benefits, not because recompense is a pleasure but because obligation is a pain.
Dr Samuel Johnson (1709-1784)

We seldom find people ungrateful so long as we are in a condition to render them service.
François, Duc de La Rochefoucauld (1613-1680)
French writer, moralist

He receives comfort like cold porridge.
Sebastian, *The Tempest*
William Shakespeare (1564-1616)

Is it not possible to eat me without insisting that I sing the praises of my devourer?
Feodor Dostoievski (1821-1881)

Greatness

Some are born great, some achieve greatness, and some have greatness thrust upon'em.
Malvolio, quoting letter, *Twelfth Night*
William Shakespeare (1564-1616)

Great men hallow a whole people, and lift up all who live in their time.
Sydney Smith (1771-1845)
English writer, clergyman

The great are only great because we carry them on our shoulders.
Claude Dubosc de Montandré (17th century)
French writer, pamphleteer

Great men are rarely isolated mountain-peaks; they are summits of ranges.
T. W. Higginson (1823-1911)
American clergyman, writer

Everybody comes along at the right time. . . Leonardo was lucky because he came along at the right time. Oscar Wilde was lucky because he came at the right time – if he hadn't gone to court and been martyred he wouldn't be such a cult hero now. Or Jesus Christ – if he came back now he would really be up the shit because there's no capital punishment.
David Bailey (b. 1938)
British photographer

Nothing great will ever be achieved without

great men, and men are great only if they are determined to be so.
Charles de Gaulle (1890-1970)

Power tends to corrupt, and absolute power corrupts absolutely. Great men are almost always bad men.
Lord Acton (1834-1902)
English historian

What millions died that Caesar might be great!
Thomas Campbell (1777-1844)
Scottish poet

No great man lives in vain. The history of the world is but the biography of great men.
Thomas Carlyle (1795-1881)
Scottish writer

The world, will, in the end, follow only those who have despised as well as served it.
Samuel Butler (1835-1902)
English author

It is a melancholy truth that even great men have their poor relations.
Charles Dickens (1812-1870)

We are both great men, but I have succeeded better in keeping it a profound secret than he has.
Bill (E. W.) Nye (1850-1896)
American journalist, humorous writer

To have a great man for a friend seems pleasant to those who have never tried it; those who have, fear it.
Horace (65-8 BC)

To be great is to be misunderstood.
R. W. Emerson (1803-1882)
American essayist, poet, philosopher

SEE Froude on DEATH; Shakespeare on GLORY; Chesterton on HEROES; Burke on MOTIVES; La Bruyère on PUBLIC LIFE; Holmes on SCHOLARSHIP

Greed

Avarice, sphincter of the heart.
Matthew Green (1696-1737)
English poet

Avarice, the spur of industry.
David Hume (1711-1776)

The love of money is the root of all evil.
Saint Paul (3-67)

Greed, like the love of comfort, is a kind of fear.
Cyril Connolly (1903-1974)
British critic

Avarice is generally the last passion of those lives of which the first part has been squandered in pleasure, and the second devoted to ambition.
Dr Samuel Johnson (1709-1784)

So for a good old-gentlemanly vice, I think I must take up with avarice.
Lord Byron (1788-1824)

There is enough for the needy but not for the greedy.
M. K. Gandhi (1869-1948)

SEE Swift on DRINK

Grief

Grief fills the room up of my absent child,
Lies in his bed, walks up and down with me,
Puts on his pretty looks, repeats his words.
Constance, King John
William Shakespeare (1564-1616)

Grief is the agony of an instant: the indulgence of grief the blunder of a life.
Benjamin Disraeli (1804-1881)

What we call mourning for our dead is perhaps not so much grief at not being able to call them back as it is grief at not being able to want to do so.
Thomas Mann (1875-1955)

The display of grief makes more demands than grief itself. How few men are sad in their own company.
Seneca (c. 5-65)
Roman writer, philosopher, statesman

We often console ourselves for being unhappy by a certain pleasure in appearing so.
François, Duc de La Rochefoucauld (1613-1680)
French writer, moralist

Pain hardens, and great pain hardens greatly, whatever the comforters say, and suffering does not ennoble, though it may occasionally lend a certain rigid dignity of manner to the suffering frame.
A. S. Byatt (b. 1936)
British author

In all the silent manliness of grief.
Oliver Goldsmith (1728-1774)

Sorrow, the great idealizer.
J. R. Lowell (1819-1891)
American poet, editor

People in distress never think that you feel enough.
Dr Samuel Johnson (1709-1784)

Nothing becomes so offensive so quickly as grief. When fresh it finds some one to console it, but when it becomes chronic, it is ridiculed, and rightly.
Seneca (c. 5-65)
Roman writer, philosopher, statesman

Weeping may endure for a night, but joy cometh in the morning.
Bible, Psalms

SEE Calverley on DRINK; Smith on MONEY; UNHAPPINESS; Fuller on WIDOWHOOD

The Grotesque

She resembles the Venus de Milo: she is very old, has no teeth, and has white spots on her yellow skin.

Heinrich Heine (1797-1856)
German poet, journalist

Her skin was white as leprosy.

S. T. Coleridge (1772-1834)

Grudges

I was angry with my friend.
I told my wrath, my wrath did end.
I was angry with my foe:
I told it not, my wrath did grow.

William Blake (1757-1827)

Kindnesses are easily forgotten; but injuries? – what worthy man does not keep those in mind?

W. M. Thackeray (1811-1863)
English author

To have a grievance is to have a purpose in life.

Eric Hoffer (1902-1983)
American philosopher

SEE Bible on PREJUDICE

Guerrilla Warfare

Insurrection – by means of guerrilla bands – is the true method of warfare for all nations desirous of emancipating themselves from a foreign yoke. . . It is invincible, indestructible.

Giuseppe Mazzini (1805-1872)
Italian nationalist leader

It is necessary to turn political crisis into armed crisis by performing violent actions that will force those in power to transform the military situation into a political situation. That will alienate the masses, who, from then on, will revolt against the army and the police and blame them for this state of things.

Carlos Marighella (d. 1969)
Brazilian guerrilla leader
from his Minimanual of the Urban Guerrilla

The conventional army loses if it does not win. The guerrilla wins if he does not lose.

Henry Kissinger (b. 1923)

Guests

Mankind is divisible into two great classes: hosts and guests.

Sir Max Beerbohm (1872-1956)
British author

The first day a man is a guest, the second a burden, the third a pest.

Edouard Laboulaye (1811-1883)
French writer, satirist

Some people can stay longer in an hour than others can in a week.

W. D. Howells (1837-1920)
American author

Fish and visitors smell in three days.

Benjamin Franklin (1706-1790)

If you'd lose a troublesome visitor, lend him money.

Benjamin Franklin (1706-1790)

Frank Harris is invited to all the great houses in England – once.

Oscar Wilde (1854-1900)

When a man has been highly honoured and has eaten a little he is most benevolent.

Friedrich Nietzsche (1844-1900)

SEE DINNER PARTIES; HOSPITALITY

Guilt

Guilt has very quick ears to an accusation.

Henry Fielding (1707-1754)

I had most need of blessing, and 'Amen'
Stuck in my throat.

Macbeth, *Macbeth*
William Shakespeare (1564-1616)

The offender never forgives.

Russian proverb

True guilt is guilt at the obligation one owes to oneself to be oneself.

R. D. Laing (b. 1927)
British psychiatrist

H

Habit

Custom, then, is the great guide of human life.
David Hume (1711-1776)

Habit with him was all the test of truth,
'It must be right: I've done it from my youth.'
George Crabbe (1754-1832)
English clergyman, poet

The chains of habit are too weak to be felt until they are too strong to be broken.
Dr Samuel Johnson (1709-1784)

The second half of a man's life is made up of nothing but the habits he has acquired during the first half.
Feodor Dostoievski (1821-1881)

Choose the best life, habit will make it pleasant.
Epictetus (c. 55–c. 135)
Stoic philosopher

To fall into a habit is to begin to cease to be.
Miguel de Unamuno (1864-1936)
Spanish writer, philosopher

SEE Book of Common Prayer, Mill on TRADITION

Hair

Fair tresses man's imperial race ensnare,
And beauty draws us with a single hair.
Alexander Pope (1688-1744)

The hair in the head is worth two in the brush.
Oliver Herford (1863-1935)
American poet, illustrator

The only thing that can stop hair falling is the floor.
Will Rogers (1879-1935)
American humorist

Hair, in fact, is probably the bane of most women's lives.
Joan Collins (b. 1933)

The lovely hair that Galla wears
Is hers – who could have thought it?
She swears 'tis hers; and true she swears,
For I know where she bought it!
Martial (c. 40-c. 104)

SEE BALDNESS; BEARDS

Handshakes

There is a hand that has no heart in it, there is a claw or paw, a flipper or fin, a bit of wet cloth to take hold of, a piece of unbaked dough on the cook's trencher, a cold clammy thing we recoil from.
C. A. Bartol (1813-1900)
American clergyman

His handshake ought not to be used except as a tourniquet.
Margaret Halsey (b. 1910)
American author

I hate the giving of the hand unless the whole man accompanies it.
R. W. Emerson (1803-1882)
American essayist, poet, philosopher

Never extend your hand further than you can withdraw it.
Seumas MacManus (1869-1960)
Irish author

Happiness

We all want to be happy, and we're all going to die... You might say those are the only two unchallengeably true facts that apply to every human being on this planet.
William Boyd (b. 1952)
British novelist

We are never happy: we can only remember that we were so once.
Alexander Smith (1830-1867)
Scottish poet

On n'est jamais si malheureux qu'on croit, ni si heureux qu'on espère.
One is never as unhappy as one thinks, nor as happy as one had hoped to be.
François, Duc de La Rochefoucauld (1613-1680)
French writer, moralist

Ask yourself whether you are happy, and you cease to be so.
John Stuart Mill (1806-1873)

Happiness is a mystery, like religion, and should never be rationalised.
G. K. Chesterton (1874-1936)

Give a man health and a course to steer, and

he'll never stop to trouble about whether he's happy or not.
Brassbound, *Captain Brassbound's Conversion*
George Bernard Shaw (1856-1950)

The search for happiness is one of the chief sources of unhappiness.
Eric Hoffer (1902-1983)
American philosopher

Happiness is an imaginary condition formerly often attributed by the living to the dead, now usually attributed by adults to children, and by children to adults.
Thomas Szasz (b. 1920)
American psychiatrist

Sotto
Ogni clima, ogni ciel, si chiama indarno
Felicità, vive tristezza e regna.
Under all skies, all weathers, man's happiness lies always elsewhere; sorrow lives and reigns.
Giacomo Leopardi (1798-1837)
Italian poet

If we only wanted to be happy it would be easy; but we want to be happier than other people, which is almost always difficult, since we think them happier than they are.
Charles de Montesquieu (1689-1755)
French political theorist

I can sympathise with people's pains, but not with their pleasures. There is something curiously boring about somebody else's happiness.
Aldous Huxley (1894-1963)

Oh! how bitter a thing it is to look into happiness through another man's eyes.
Orlando, *As You Like It*
William Shakespeare (1564-1616)

Grief can take care of itself, but to get the full value from joy you must have somebody to divide it with.
Mark Twain (1835-1910)

We have no more right to consume happiness without producing it than to consume wealth without producing it.
Morell, *Candida*
George Bernard Shaw (1856-1950)

Love kills happiness, happiness kills love.
Miguel de Unamuno (1864-1936)
Spanish philosopher, poet, novelist

The happiest time in any man's life is when he is in red-hot pursuit of a dollar with a reasonable prospect of overtaking it.
Josh Billings (1818-1885)
American humorist

The greatest happiness of the greatest number is the foundation of morals and legislation.
Jeremy Bentham (1748-1832)
English philosopher, political theorist, jurist

Happiness is no laughing matter.
Richard Whately (1787-1863)
Archbishop of Dublin

Here's a new day. O Pendulum move slowly!
Harold Munro (1879-1932)
British poet, critic

SEE Byron on COMPANY; CONTENTMENT; Smith on HOME; Wilde on MEN: and Women; Shaw on SACRIFICE; Shaw on UNHAPPINESS

Hard Times

When you are down and out something always turns up – and it is usually the noses of your friends.
Orson Welles (1915-1985)

There were times my pants were so thin I could sit on a dime and tell if it was heads or tails.
Spencer Tracy (1900-1967)

Life isn't meant to be easy. It's hard to take being on the top – or on the bottom. I guess I'm something of a fatalist. You have to have a sense of history, I think, to survive some of these things. . . Life is one crisis after another.
Richard Nixon (b. 1913)

Thy fate is the common fate of all;
Into each life some rain must fall.
H. W. Longfellow (1807-1882)

SEE ADVERSITY

Haste

A nation rushing hastily too and fro, busily employed in idleness.
Phaedrus (1st century AD)
Roman fabulist

He sows hurry and reaps indigestion.
Robert Louis Stevenson (1850-1894)

No-wher so bisy a man as he ther nas,
And yet he semed bisier than he was.
Geoffrey Chaucer (1340-1400)

Whoever is in a hurry, shows that the thing he is about is too big for him.
Lord Chesterfield (1694-1773)
English statesman and man of letters

No man who is in a hurry is quite civilised.
Will Durant (1885-1981)
American historian

What is the use of running when you are on the wrong road?
proverb

SEE Browning on AGE; Carroll on MODERN TIMES

Hate

Men hate more steadily than they love.
Dr Samuel Johnson (1709-1784)

Now hatred is by far the longest pleasure;

Men love in haste, but they detest
at leisure.
Lord Byron (1788-1824)

What we need is hatred. From it our ideas are
born.
Jean Genet (1910-1986)

We hold our hate too choice a thing
For light and careless lavishing.
Sir William Watson (1858-1935)
British poet

Impotent hatred is the most horrible of all
emotions; one should hate nobody whom one
cannot destroy.
Johann Wolfgang von Goethe (1749-1832)

*Proprium humani ingenii est odisse quem
laeseris.*
It is human nature to hate the man whom you
have hurt.
Tacitus (c. 55-c. 120)
Roman historian

Always remember others may hate you but
those who hate you don't win unless you hate
them. And then you destroy yourself.
Richard Nixon (b. 1913)

I never hated a man enough to give him his
diamonds back.
Zsa Zsa Gabor (b. 1920)

SEE Hazlitt on ANTIPATHY;
La Rochefoucauld, Strindberg on LOVE

Health

He had had much experience of physicians,
and said 'the only way to keep your health is
to eat what you don't want, drink what you
don't like, and do what you druther not'.
Mark Twain (1835-1910)

Attention to health is the greatest hindrance to
life.
Plato (428-347 BC)

Cheerfulness, sir, is the principal ingredient in
the composition of health.
Arthur Murphy (1727-1805)
Irish dramatist

The preservation of health is a *duty*. Few seem
conscious that there is such a thing as physical
morality.
Herbert Spencer (1820-1903)
English philosopher

SEE Haldane on ANXIETY

Heartbreak

Had we never loved sae kindly,
Had we never loved sae blindly,
Never met – or never parted –
We had ne'er been broken-hearted.
Robert Burns (1759-1796)

When your heart is broken, your boats are
burned: nothing matters any more. It is the

end of happiness and the beginning of peace.
Ellie, *Heartbreak House*
George Bernard Shaw (1856-1950)

How else but through a broken heart
May Lord Christ enter in?
Oscar Wilde (1854-1900)

Heaven

Heaven is the place where the donkey at last
catches up with the carrot.
anonymous

It is a curious thing that every creed promises
a paradise which will be absolutely uninhabit-
able for anyone of civilised taste.
Evelyn Waugh (1903-1966)

What they do in heaven we are ignorant of;
what they do not do we are told expressly.
Jonathan Swift (1667-1745)

Hell is paved with good intentions, but heaven
goes in for something more dependable. Solid
gold.
Joyce Cary (1888-1957)
British author

Our remedies oft in ourselves do lie,
Which we ascribe to heaven.
Helena, *All's Well That Ends Well*
William Shakespeare (1564-1616)

SEE Nietzsche on PARADISE

Hell

Lasciate ogni speranza voi ch'entrate!
Abandon all hope, you who enter here!
Dante (1265-1321)

The most frightening idea that has ever
corroded human nature – the idea of eternal
punishment.
John, Lord Morley (1838-1923)
British writer, Liberal politician

Hell is paved with priests' skulls.
John Chrysostom (345-407)
Greek ecclesiast and hermit

They order things so damnably in hell.
Hilaire Belloc (1870-1953)
British author

Here there is no hope, and consequently no
duty, no work, nothing to be gained by
praying, nothing to be lost by doing what you
like. Hell, in short, is a place where you have
nothing to do but amuse yourself.
The Statue, *Man and Superman*
George Bernard Shaw (1856-1950)

A fool's paradise is a wise man's hell.
Thomas Fuller (1608-1661)
English cleric

Hell is oneself; Hell is alone, the other figures
in it merely projections. There is nothing to
escape from and nothing to escape to. One is
always alone.
George Eliot (1819-1880)

L'Enfer, c'est les autres.
Hell is other people.
Jean-Paul Sartre (1905-1980)

Hell hath no limits, nor is circum-
scribed
In one self place; for where we are
is hell,
And where hell is, must we ever be.
Christopher Marlowe (1564-1593)

If there were only some shorter and more
direct route to the devil, it would save an
awful lot of sorrow and anxiety in this world.
Kin (F. McKinney) Hubbard (1868-1930)
American humorist, journalist

I hold it to be the inalienable right of anybody
to go to hell in his own way.
Robert Frost (1874-1963)
American poet

I verily think that a man buyeth hell here with
so much pain that he might have heaven with
less than the one-half.
Sir Thomas More (1478-1535)

SEE Shaw on IMMORTALITY; Shaw on
INTENTIONS; Shaw on LEISURE;
Shelley on LONDON; Shaw on MUSIC

Heresy

All evolution in thought and conduct must at
first appear as heresy and misconduct.
George Bernard Shaw (1856-1950)

Heresy is only another word for freedom of
thought.
Graham Greene (b. 1904)

A heresy can spring only from a system that is
in full vigour.
Eric Hoffer (1902-1983)
American philosopher

A man may be a heretic in the truth; and if he
believe things only because his pastor says so,
or the assembly so determines, without knowing other reason, though his belief be true, yet
the very truth he holds becomes his heresy.
John Milton (1608-1674)

Every heresy has been an effort to narrow the
Church.
G. K. Chesterton (1874-1936)

The appellation of heretics has always been
applied to the less numerous party.
Edward Gibbon (1737-1794)

His hand will be against every man, and every
man's hand against him.
Bible, Genesis

That is the whole problem with being a
heretic. One usually must think out everything
for oneself.
Aubrey Menen (b. 1912)
British novelist, essayist

What forests of laurel we bring, and the tears
of mankind, to those who stood firm against
the opinion of their contemporaries!
R. W. Emerson (1803-1882)
American essayist, poet, philosopher

For my name and memory I leave to men's
charitable speeches, and to foreign nations and
the next ages.
Francis Bacon (1561-1626)

You pronounce sentence upon me with greater
fear than I receive it.
Giordano Bruno (1548-1600)
Italian philosopher
*to the inquisitors who had
condemned him to death*

SEE DISSENT

Hermits

The hunchback in the park
A solitary mister
Propped between trees and water.
Dylan Thomas (1914-1953)

The life of a solitary man will be certainly
miserable, but not certainly devout.
Dr Samuel Johnson (1709-1784)

To fly from, need not be to hate, mankind.
Lord Byron (1788-1824)

He travels fastest who travels alone.
Rudyard Kipling (1865-1936)

Like two doomed ships that pass in
storm
We had crossed each other's way:
But we made no sign, we said no
word,
We had no word to say.
Oscar Wilde (1854-1900)

The world forgetting, by the world forgot.
Alexander Pope (1688-1744)

Wandering stars, to whom is reserved the
blackness of darkness forever.
Bible, Jude

The true ascetic counts nothing his own save
his harp.
Joachim of Flora (c. 1130-c. 1202)
Italian mystic, theologian

And meanwhile we have gone on living,
Living and partly living,
Picking together the pieces,
Gathering faggots at nightfall,
Building a partial shelter,
For sleeping and eating and drinking
and laughter.
T. S. Eliot (1888-1965)

SEE SOLITUDE

Heroes

How can man die better
Than facing fearful odds,

For the ashes of his fathers
And the temples of his Gods?
Lord Macaulay (1800-1859)
English historian

A hero is no braver than an ordinary man, but he is brave five minutes longer.
R. W. Emerson (1803-1882)
American essayist, poet, philosopher

How prudently we proud men compete for nameless graves, while now and then some starveling of Fate forgets himself into immortality.
Wendell Phillips (1811-1884)
American abolitionist, orator

Heroes are created by popular demand, sometimes out of the scantiest materials.
Gerald W. Johnson (b. 1890)
American author

If we are marked to die, we are enow
To do our country loss; and to live,
The fewer men, the greater share of honour.
King Henry, *King Henry V*
William Shakespeare (1564-1616)

Let us therefore brace ourselves to our duties, and so bear ourselves that, if the British Empire and its Commonwealth last for a thousand years, men will still say, 'This was their finest hour'.
Sir Winston Churchill (1874-1965)

Unhappy the land that is in need of heroes.
Bertolt Brecht (1898-1956)

No pain, no palm; no thorns, no throne; no gall, no glory; no cross, no crown.
William Penn (1644-1718)
religious leader, founder of Pennsylvania

Had we lived I should have had a tale to tell of the hardihood, endurance and courage of my companions which would have stirred the heart of every Englishman. These rough notes and our dead bodies must tell the tale.
Captain R. F. Scott (1868-1912)
British antarctic explorer
last message

Having seen what my injuries were, I knew it was not necessary to die.
Lieut.-Gen. Sir Steuart Pringle (b. 1928)
Royal Marines
following bomb attempt on his life

One who never turned his back but
marched breast forward,
Never doubted clouds would break,
Never dreamed, though right were
worsted, wrong would triumph.
Held we fall to rise, are baffled
to fight better,
Sleep to wake.
Robert Browning (1812-1889)

What is our task? To make Britain a fit country for heroes to live in.
David Lloyd George (1863-1945)
Welsh Liberal politician,
Prime Minister

I am convinced that a light supper, a good night's sleep, and a fine morning, have sometimes made a hero of the same man, who, by an indigestion, a restless night, and rainy morning, would have proved a coward.
Lord Chesterfield (1694-1773)
English statesman
and man of letters

Claret is the liquor for boys; port for men; but he who aspires to be a hero must drink brandy.
Dr Samuel Johnson (1709-1784)

The more characteristic American hero in the earlier day, and the more beloved type at all times, was not the hustler but the whittler.
Mark Sullivan (1874-1952)
American journalist

The really great man is the man who makes every man feel great.
G. K. Chesterton (1874-1936)

Now stiff on a pillar with phallic air
Nelson's stylite in Trafalgar Square
Reminds the British what once they were.
Lawrence Durrell (b. 1914)
British author

Ultimately a hero is a man who would argue with the Gods, and awakens devils to contest his vision.
Norman Mailer (b. 1923)

Show me a hero and I will write you a tragedy.
F. Scott Fitzgerald (1896-1940)

The greatest obstacle to being heroic is the doubt whether one may not be going to prove one's self a fool.
Nathaniel Hawthorne (1804-1864)
American novelist

You cannot be a hero without being a coward.
George Bernard Shaw (1856-1950)

Seldom any splendid story is wholly true.
Dr Samuel Johnson (1709-1784)

Every hero becomes a bore at last.
R. W. Emerson (1803-1882)
American essayist, poet, philosopher

SEE Porteous on GENERALS; Geldof on SAINTHOOD; Moore on SELF-IMAGE

Hero-Worship
I do honour the very flea of his dog.
Ben Jonson (1573-1637)

Sir, you are making a monarchy of what should be a republic.

Oliver Goldsmith (1728-1774)
reproving Boswell's idolisation of Johnson's work

Hero-worship is strongest where there is least regard for human freedom.

Herbert Spencer (1820-1903)
English philosopher

Historians

Events in the past may be roughly divided into those which probably never happened and those which do not matter. That is what makes the trade of historian so attractive.

W. R. Inge (1860-1954)
Dean of St Paul's, London

Very few things happen at the right time, and the rest do not happen at all; the conscientious historian will correct these defects.

Herodotus (484-425 BC)

History repeats itself; historians repeat each other.

Philip Guedalla (1889-1944)
British author

Historians are like deaf people who go on answering questions that no one has asked them.

Leo Tolstoy (1828-1910)

God cannot alter the past; that is why he is obliged to connive at the existence of historians.

Samuel Butler (1835-1902)
English author

A historian is a prophet in reverse.

Friedrich von Schlegel (1772-1829)
German historian, literary critic

Historian: an unsuccessful novelist.

H. L. Mencken (1880-1956)
American journalist

The first duty of an historian is to be on his guard against his own sympathies.

J. A. Froude (1818-1894)
British author

The middle sort of historians (of which the most part are) spoil all; they will chew our meat for us.

Michel de Montaigne (1533-1592)
French essayist

To give an accurate and exhaustive account of that period would need a far less brilliant pen than mine.

Sir Max Beerbohm (1872-1956)
British author

Another damned, thick, square book! Always scribble, scribble, scribble! Eh! Mr Gibbon?

William Henry, Duke of Gloucester (1743-1805)
brother of George III

Sapping a solemn creed with solemn sneer.

Lord Byron (1788-1824)
of Gibbon

In analysing history do not be too profound, for often the causes are quite superficial.

R. W. Emerson (1803-1882)
American essayist, poet, philosopher

History

The principal office of history I take to be this: to prevent virtuous actions from being forgotten, and that evil words and deeds should fear an infamous reputation with posterity.

Tacitus (c. 55-c. 120)
Roman historian

Those who cannot remember the past are condemned to repeat it.

George Santayana (1863-1952)
American philosopher, poet

History repeats itself, first as tragedy, second as farce.

Karl Marx (1818-1883)

Every time history repeats itself the price goes up.

anonymous

History is Philosophy teaching by examples.

Henry St John (Viscount Bolingbroke) (1678-1751)
English politician, intriguer

But what experience and history teach is this – that peoples and governments have never learned anything from history, or acted on the principles deduced from it.

Georg Hegel (1770-1831)

History is bunk.

Henry Ford (1863-1947)

There is nothing new in the world except the history you do not know.

Harry S. Truman (1884-1972)

Only the history of free peoples is worth our attention; the history of men under a despotism is merely a collection of anecdotes.

Nicolas-Sébastien Chamfort (1741-1794)
French writer, wit

The essential matter of history is not what happened but what people thought or said about it.

Frederic W. Maitland (1850-1906)
English writer on law

History, a distillation of Rumour.

Thomas Carlyle (1795-1881)
Scottish author

Ancient histories are but fables that have been agreed upon.

Voltaire (1694-1778)

History is the crystallisation of popular beliefs.

Donn Piatt (1819-1891)
American journalist

Gossip is none the less gossip because it comes from venerable antiquity.
Mandell Creighton (1843-1901)
English prelate, historian

If a man could say nothing against a character but what he can prove, history could not be written.
Dr Samuel Johnson (1709-1784)

History is better written from letters. . . No public character has ever stood the revelation of private utterance and correspondence.
Lord Acton (1834-1902)
English historian

The so-called lessons of history are for the most part the rationalisation of the victors. History is written by the survivors.
Max Lerner (b. 1902)
American academic

History. An account, mostly false, of events, mostly unimportant, which are brought about by rulers, mostly knaves, and soldiers, mostly fools.
Ambrose Bierce (1842-1914)
American author

History, which is, indeed, little more than the register of the crimes, follies, and misfortunes of mankind.
Edward Gibbon (1737-1794)

The history of the world is the record of a man in quest of his daily bread and butter.
Hendrik Van Loon (1882-1944)
American journalist, historian

Who has fully realised that history is not contained in thick books but lives in our very blood?
Carl Jung (1875-1961)

English history is all about men liking their fathers, and American history is all about men hating their fathers and trying to burn down everything they ever did.
Malcolm Bradbury (b. 1932)
British author

That great dust-heap called 'history'.
Augustine Birrell (1850-1933)
British Liberal politician

SEE Emerson on MINORITIES; Eliot on WOMEN

Holland
Where the broad ocean leans against the land.
Oliver Goldsmith (1728-1774)

Apart from cheese and tulips, the main product of the country is advocaat, a drink made from lawyers.
Alan Coren (b. 1938)
British editor, humorist

Hollywood
Strip away the phony tinsel of Hollywood and you find the real tinsel underneath.
Oscar Levant (1906-1972)
American pianist, composer

Hollywood is a place where people from Iowa mistake each other for a star.
Fred Allen (1894-1957)
American comic

How much talent, initiative, genius and creative ability have been destroyed by the film industry in its ruthlessly efficient sausage machine?
Ingmar Bergman (b. 1918)
Swedish film and theatre director

You can't call Hollywood 'The Industry' any more. Today we have a chance to put our personal fantasies on film.
John Frankenheimer (b. 1930)
American director

In a mere half-century, films have gone from silent to unspeakable.
Doug Larson

Hollywood is like being nowhere and talking to nobody about nothing.
Michelangelo Antonioni (b. 1912)
Italian film director

To survive there, you need the ambition of a Latin-American revolutionary, the ego of a grand opera tenor, and the physical stamina of a cow pony.
Billie Burke (1885-1970)
American actress

In Europe an actor is an artist. In Hollywood, if he isn't working, he's a bum.
Anthony Quinn (b. 1915)

To be an Englishman in the film business is to know what it's like to be colonialised.
Tony Garnett (b. 1936)
British film producer

You can seduce a man's wife there, attack his daughter and wipe your hands on his canary, but if you don't like his movie you're dead.
Joseph von Sternberg (1894-1969)
American director

Working for Warner Brothers is like fucking a porcupine. It's a hundred pricks against one.
Wilson Mizner (1876-1933)
American dramatist, wit

An associate producer is the only guy in Hollywood who will associate with a producer.
Fred Allen (1894-1957)
American comic

Hollywood's a place where they'll pay you a

thousand dollars for a kiss, and fifty cents for your soul.
Marilyn Monroe (1926-1962)

Hollywood is the only place in the world where an amicable divorce means each one gets fifty per cent of the publicity.
Lauren Bacall (b. 1924)

The way things are going I'd be more interested in seeing Cleopatra play the life of Elizabeth Taylor.
Earl Wilson (b. 1907)
American author

I've been around so long I can remember Doris Day before she was a virgin.
Groucho Marx (1890-1977)

I want a movie that starts with an earthquake and works up to a climax.
Samuel Goldwyn (1882-1974)

'Too caustic?' To hell with the cost, we'll make the picture anyway.
Samuel Goldwyn (1882-1974)

You can fool all the people all the time if the advertising is right and the budget is big enough.
Joseph E. Levine (b. 1905)
American film producer, executive

Hollywood's trade, which is dreams at so many dollars per thousand feet, is managed by businessmen pretending to be artists and by artists pretending to be businessmen. In this queer world nobody stays as he was; the artist begins to lose his art, and the businessman becomes temperamental and overbalanced.
J. B. Priestley (1894-1984)

If we have to kiss Hollywood goodbye, it may be with one of those tender, old-fashioned, seven-second kisses as exchanged between two people of the opposite sex with all their clothes on.
Anita Loos (1893-1981)
American screenwriter

SEE CINEMA

Home

A comfortable house is a great source of happiness. It ranks immediately after health and a good conscience.
Sydney Smith (1771-1845)
English writer, clergyman

Home is the place where, when you
have to go there,
They have to take you in.
Robert Frost (1875-1963)
American poet

Never weather-beaten sail more willing bent to shore.
Thomas Campion (1567-1620)
English poet

Home is where the heart is.
Pliny the Elder (23-79)
Roman scholar

Every man likes the smell of his own farts.
Icelandic proverb
collected by W. H. Auden and
Louis Kronenberger

A man's home may seem to be his castle on the outside; inside, it is more often his nursery.
Clare Boothe Luce (b. 1903)
American diplomat, writer

Many a man who thinks to found a home discovers that he has merely opened a tavern for his friends.
Norman Douglas (1868-1952)
British author

Charity begins at home, and justice begins next door.
Charles Dickens (1812-1870)

I hate housework! You make the beds, you do the dishes — and six months later you have to start all over again.
Joan Rivers (b. 1935)
American comedienne

Everybody's always talking about people breaking into houses ... but there are more people in the world who want to break out of houses.
Thornton Wilder (1897-1975)
American author

Houses are built to live in, and not to look on: therefore let use be preferred before uniformity.
Francis Bacon (1561-1626)

Have nothing in your home that you do not know to be useful or believe to be beautiful.
William Morris (1834-1896)
English artist, writer, printer

I want a house that has got over all its troubles; I don't want to spend the rest of my life bringing up a young and inexperienced house.
Jerome K. Jerome (1859-1927)
British author

Une maison est une machine-à-habiter.
A house is a machine for living in.
Le Corbusier (1887-1965)

SEE Saki on POVERTY

Honesty

A few honest men are better than numbers.
Oliver Cromwell (1599-1658)

Honest men are the soft easy cushions on which knaves repose and fatten.
Thomas Otway (1652-1685)
English dramatist

It should seem that indolence itself would incline a person to be honest; as it requires

infinitely greater pains and contrivance to be a knave.
> William Shenstone (1714-1763)
> British poet

It would be ingratitude in some men to turn honest when they owe all they have to their knavery.
> George Savile, Lord Halifax (1633-1695)
> English statesman, author

Though I am not naturally honest, I am so sometimes by chance.
> Autolycus, *The Winter's Tale*
> William Shakespeare (1564-1616)

There's one way to find out if a man is honest – ask him. If he says 'yes', you know he is crooked.
> Groucho Marx (1895-1977)

He who says there is no such thing as an honest man, you may be sure is himself a knave.
> Bishop George Berkeley (1685-1753)
> Irish philosopher

Nothing astonishes men so much as common sense and plain dealing.
> R. W. Emerson (1803-1882)
> American essayist, poet, philosopher

Always be ready to speak your mind, and a base man will avoid you.
> William Blake (1757-1827)

Don't be ashamed to say what you are not ashamed to think.
> Michel de Montaigne (1533-1592)
> French essayist

I am afraid we must make the world honest before we can honestly say to our children that honesty is the best policy.
> George Bernard Shaw (1856-1950)

It is kindness to refuse immediately what you intend to deny.
> Publilius Syrus (1st century BC)
> Roman writer of mimes

SEE Canning on FRIENDS; Sargent on PORTRAITS; Shaw on SINCERITY

Honour

Fame is something which must be won; honour is something which must not be lost.
> Arthur Schopenhauer (1788-1860)
> German philosopher

Sans l'argent l'honneur n'est qu'une maladie.
Without money honour is merely a disease.
> Jean Racine (1639-1699)

The louder he talked of his honour, the faster we counted our spoons.
> R. W. Emerson (1803-1882)
> American essayist, poet, philosopher

As to honour – you know – it's a very fine

medieval inheritance, which women never got hold of. It wasn't theirs.
> Joseph Conrad (1857-1924)

SEE Saurin on The LAW

Hope

Hope, the patient medicine
For disease, disaster, sin.
> Wallace Rice (1859-1939)
> American poet, editor

Take hope from the heart of man and you make him a beast of prey.
> Ouida (Marie Louise de la Ramée) (1839-1908)
> English novelist

Hope in every sphere of life is a privilege that attaches to action. No action, no hope.
> Peter Levi (b. 1931)
> British Professor of Poetry

Still bent to make some port he
knows not where,
Still standing for some false
impossible shore.
> Matthew Arnold (1822-1888)
> English poet, critic

He that lives upon hope will die fasting.
> Benjamin Franklin (1706-1790)

The miserable have no other medicine
But only hope.
> Claudio, *Measure for Measure*
> William Shakespeare (1564-1616)

Vows begin when hope dies.
> Leonardo da Vinci (1425-1519)

Hope is the universal liar.
> R. G. Ingersoll (1833-1899)
> American lawyer

SEE Chesterton on MIDDLE AGE

Horses

The horse, the horse! The symbol of surging potency and power of movement, of action, in man.
> D. H. Lawrence (1885-1930)

Nothing does as much for the insides of a man than the outsides of a horse.
> Ronald Reagan (b. 1911)

They say princes learn no art truly, but the art of horsemanship. The reason is, the brave beast is no flatterer. He will throw a prince as soon as his groom.
> Ben Jonson (1573-1637)

Go anywhere in England where there are natural, wholesome, contented, and really nice English people; and what do you always find? That the stables are the real centre of the household.
> Lady Utterwood, *Heartbreak House*
> George Bernard Shaw (1856-1950)

A horse is dangerous at both ends and uncomfortable in the middle.
Ian Fleming (1908-1964)
British author

SEE Salinger on CARS

Hospitality

Hospitality consists in a little fire, a little food, and an immense quiet.
R. W. Emerson (1803-1882)
American essayist, poet, philosopher

We'll teach you to drink deep ere you depart.
Hamlet, *Hamlet*
William Shakespeare (1564-1616)

Be not forgetful to entertain strangers: for thereby some have entertained angels unawares.
Bible, Hebrews

We shall always keep a spare corner in our heads to give passing hospitality to our friends' opinions.
Joseph Joubert (1754-1824)
French essayist, moralist

SEE GUESTS; Douglas on HOME

Hotels

It used to be a good hotel, but that proves nothing – I used to be a good boy.
Mark Twain (1835-1910)

Why do they put the Gideon Bibles only in the bedrooms, where it's usually too late?
Christopher Morley (1890-1957)
American novelist, journalist

The House of Lords

The dust and silence of the upper shelf.
Lord Macaulay (1800-1859)
English historian

Five hundred men, ordinary men, chosen accidentally from among the unemployed.
David Lloyd George (1863-1945)
Welsh Liberal politician, Prime Minister

Twenty thousand thieves landed at Hastings. These founders of the House of Lords were greedy and ferocious dragoons, sons of greedy and ferocious pirates.
R. W. Emerson (1803-1882)
American essayist, poet, philosopher

Where might is, the right is:
Long purses make strong swords.
Let weakness learn meekness:
God save the House of Lords!
A. C. Swinburne (1837-1909)

The typical backwoods peer had three qualities. He knew how to kill a fox, how to get rid of a bad tenant, and how to discard an unwanted mistress. A man with those three qualities would certainly have something to

contribute to the work of the House of Lords.
Lord Winster (1885-1961)
British Labour politician

My Lord Bath, you and I are now two as insignificant men as any in England.
Sir Robert Walpole (1676-1745)
English statesman
on his elevation to the House of Lords

The cure for admiring the House of Lords is to go and look at it.
Walter Bagehot (1826-1877)
English economist, critic

Lives the man that can figure a naked Duke of Windlestraw addressing a naked House of Lords?
Thomas Carlyle (1795-1881)
Scottish author

When I'm sitting on the Woolsack in the House of Lords I amuse myself by saying 'Bollocks' *sotto voce* to the bishops.
Lord Hailsham (b. 1907)
British Conservative politician

Human Nature

At his present best many of his [Man's] ways are so unpleasant that they are unmentionable in polite society, and so painful that he is compelled to pretend that pain is often a good.
George Bernard Shaw (1856-1950)

It is easier to denature plutonium than to denature the evil spirit of man.
Albert Einstein (1879-1955)

Men are so made that they can resist sound argument, and yet yield to a glance.
Honoré de Balzac (1799-1850)

Only this distinguishes us from the other animals: we drink when we are not thirsty and we make love on the spur of any moment.
Pierre de Beaumarchais (1732-1799)
French dramatist

I have found men more kind than I expected, and less just.
Dr Samuel Johnson (1709-1784)

Even a tax-gatherer must find his feelings rather worked upon at times.
Charles Dickens (1812-1870)

Not one is altogether noble nor altogether trustworthy nor altogether consistent; and not one is altogether vile. Not a single one but has at some time wept.
H. G. Wells (1866-1946)

Yet is every man his own greatest enemy, and as it were his own executioner.
Sir Thomas Browne (1605-1682)
English physician, author

SEE Twain on KILLING

Humanism

Progressivist optimism modified by fashionable despair.
Bernard Williams (b. 1929)
British philosopher, author

The splendour of human life, I feel sure, is greater to those who are not dazzled by the divine radiance.
Bertrand Russell (1872-1970)

Humanity

We are all more simply human than otherwise.
Harry Stack Sullivan (1892-1949)
American psychiatrist

What a piece of work is man! How noble in reason! How infinite in faculty! in form and moving, how express and admirable! in action, how like an angel! in apprehension, how like a god! the beauty of the world! the paragon of animals!
Hamlet, *Hamlet*
William Shakespeare (1564-1616)

Man is a little soul carrying around a corpse.
Epictetus (c. 55-c. 135)
Stoic philosopher

Man is a tool-making animal.
Benjamin Franklin (1706-1790)

The greatest animal in creation, the animal who cooks.
Douglas Jerrold (1803-1857)
English playwright and humorist

Man is the only animal that can remain on friendly terms with the victims he intends to eat until he eats them.
Samuel Butler (1835-1902)
English author

Self-preservation, nature's first great law,
All the creatures, except man, doth awe.
Andrew Marvell (1621-1678)

Man is the only animal that laughs and weeps; for he is the only animal that is struck with the difference between what things are and what they might have been.
William Hazlitt (1778-1830)
English essayist

Man is an exception, whatever else he is. If it is not true that a divine being fell, then we can only say that one of the animals went entirely off its head.
G. K. Chesterton (1874-1936)

One definition of man is 'an intelligence served by organs'.
R. W. Emerson (1803-1882)
American essayist, poet, philosopher

A being darkly wise, and rudely great.
Alexander Pope (1688-1744)

Ye shall be as gods, knowing good and evil.
Bible, Genesis

I'm always acutely conscious of the Force Behind — (Fate, God, our biological past creating our present, whatever one calls it — Mystery certainly) — and of the eternal tragedy of man in his glorious, self-destructive struggle to make the force express him instead of being, as an animal is, an infinitesimal incident in its expression.
Eugene O'Neill (1888-1953)

Human affairs are not serious, but they have to be taken seriously.
Iris Murdoch (b. 1919)
Irish author

He's not the finest character that ever lived. But he's a human being, and a terrible thing is happening to him. So attention must be paid.
Arthur Miller (b. 1915)

Humanity I love you because
when you're hard up you pawn your
intelligence to buy a drink.
e.e.cummings (1894-1962)

Were it not for the presence of the unwashed and the half-educated, the formless, queer and incomplete, the unreasonable and absurd, the infinite shapes of the delightful human tadpole, the horizon would not wear so wide a grin.
F. M. Colby (1865-1925)
American editor, essayist

We are, to put it mildly, in a mess, and there is a strong chance that we shall have exterminated ourselves by the end of the century. Our only consolation will have to be that, as a species, we have had an exciting term of office.
Desmond Morris (b. 1928)
British anthropologist

Such is the human race. Often it does seem such a pity that Noah . . . didn't miss the boat.
Mark Twain (1835-1910)

SEE Knox on ABSURDITY; Pascal on ADMIRATION; Smith on BUSINESS; CREATION; Twain on EMBARRASSMENT; Gilbert on EVOLUTION; James on EXCESS; Butler on FUN; Ouida on HOPE; Johnson on IDLENESS; Addison on LAUGHTER; Moore on LOVE; Huxley on MORALITY; Whitehead on NATURE; Shaw on PARASITES; Boethius on SELF-KNOWLEDGE; Gay on SOCIABILITY

Humiliation

One can reach a point of humiliation where violence is the only outlet.
Arthur Koestler (1905-1983)
British author

The one thing to do is to do nothing. Wait. . .
You will find that you survive humiliation and
that's an experience of incalculable value.

T. S. Eliot (1888-1965)

Humility

It is always the secure who are humble.

G. K. Chesterton (1874-1936)

Turning the other cheek is a kind of moral ju-
jitsu.

Gerald Stanley Lee (1862-1944)
American academic

Don't be humble, you're not that great.

Golda Meir (1898-1978)

At home I am a nice guy: but I don't want the
world to know. Humble people, I've found,
don't get very far.

Muhammad Ali (b. 1942)

Those men are most apt to be obsequious and
conciliating abroad who are under the discipline of shrews at home.

Washington Irving (1783-1859)
American author

The old humility made a man doubtful about
his efforts, which might make him work
harder. But the new humility makes a man
doubtful about his aims, which will make him
stop working altogether.

G. K. Chesterton (1874-1936)

Hugo, like a priest, always has his head bowed
– bowed so low that he can see nothing but
his own navel.

Charles Baudelaire (1821-1867)

If you bow at all bow low.

Chinese proverb

Leave it to the coward to make a religion of
his cowardice by preaching humility.

George Bernard Shaw (1856-1950)

SEE Kissinger on APPLAUSE;
Coleridge on PRIDE

Humour

Humor is emotional chaos remembered in
tranquillity.

James Thurber (1894-1961)
American humorist, illustrator

A difference of taste in jokes is a great strain
on the affections.

George Eliot (1819-1880)

SEE Lewis on INSULTS; JOKERS;
SENSE OF HUMOUR; Woolf on
TRANSLATION; Coleridge on WIT

Hunger

Hunger is insolent, and will be fed.

Alexander Pope (1688-1744)

No one can worship God or love his neighbour on an empty stomach.

Woodrow Wilson (1856-1924)

You cannot reason with a hungry belly; it has
no ears.

Greek proverb

A buena hambre no hay mal pan.
There is no such thing as bad bread when you
have a good appetite.

Gabriel García Márquez (b. 1928)
Colombian writer

La mejor salsa del mundo es el hambre.
Hunger is the best sauce in the world.

Miguel de Cervantes (1547-1616)

SEE Brecht on MORALITY; Howell
on REBELLION

Husbands

I began as a passion and ended as a habit, like
all husbands.

George Bernard Shaw (1856-1950)

A husband is what is left of the lover after the
nerve has been extracted.

Helen Rowland (1875-1950)
American journalist

I know many married men, I even know a few
happily-married men, but I don't know one
who wouldn't fall down the first open coal-
hole running after the first pretty girl who
gave him a wink.

George Jean Nathan (1882-1958)
American critic

He is dreadfully married. He's the most
married man I ever saw in my life.

Artemus Ward (1834-1867)
American journalist

Being a husband is a whole-time job. That is
why so many husbands fail. They cannot give
their entire attention to it.

Arnold Bennett (1867-1931)
British novelist

The majority of husbands remind me of an
orang-utan trying to play the violin.

Honoré de Balzac (1799-1850)

If there were no husbands, who would look
after our mistresses?

George Moore (1852-1933)
Irish author

A little in drink, but at all times your faithful
husband.

Sir Richard Steele (1672-1729)
English essayist, dramatist, editor
midnight letter to his wife

Can you support the expense of a husband,
hussy, in gaming, drinking and whoring? Have
you money enough to carry on the daily
quarrels of man and wife about who shall
squander most?

Peachum, *The Beggar's Opera*
John Gay (1685-1732)

Husbands, love your wives, and be not bitter against them.
Saint Paul (3-67)

A good husband makes a good wife.
Robert Burton (1577-1640)
English clergyman, author

Husbands never become good. They merely become proficient.
H. L. Mencken (1880-1956)
American journalist

I revere the memory of Mr F. as an estimable man and most indulgent husband, only necessary to mention Asparagus and it appeared or to hint at any little delicate thing to drink and it came like magic in a pint bottle; it was not ecstasy but it was comfort.
Flora Finching, Little Dorrit
Charles Dickens (1812-1870)

Nothing flatters a man as much as the happiness of his wife; he is always proud of himself as the source of it.
Dr Samuel Johnson (1709-1784)

There you are you see, quite simply, if you cannot have your dear husband for a comfort and a delight, for a breadwinner and a crosspatch, for a sofa, a chair or a hotwater bottle, one can use him as a Cross to be borne.
Stevie Smith (1902-1971)
British poet

... a moody, broody Oriental. He was twenty years older than me but it might as well have been a hundred. He was really three hundred years behind me.
Zsa Zsa Gabor (b. 1919)
of her first husband, Burham Belge

Every man who is high up likes to think he has done it all himself, and the wife smiles and lets it go at that.
J. M. Barrie (1860-1937)
British playwright

He knows little who will tell his wife all he knows.
Thomas Fuller (1608-1661)
English cleric

An archaeologist is the best husband any woman can have: the older she gets, the more interested he is in her.
Agatha Christie (1891-1976)

It is ridiculous to think you can spend your entire life with just one person. Three is about the right number. Yes, I imagine three husbands would do it.
Clare Boothe Luce (b. 1903)
American diplomat, writer

Husbands are chiefly good lovers when they are betraying their wives.
Marilyn Monroe (1926-1962)

SEE Voltaire on ADULTERY; Irving on HUMILITY; MARRIAGE; Gay on VILLAINS; WIVES

Hygiene
Bath twice a day to be really clean, once a day to be passably clean, once a week to avoid being a public nuisance.
Anthony Burgess (b. 1917)
British author

I've never had a great many baths and ... it does not make a great difference to health. .. As for appearance, most of that is underneath and nobody sees it.
Hugh Gaitskell (1906-1963)
British Labour politician
proposing an economy drive, 1947

Henry IV's feet and armpits enjoyed an international reputation.
Aldous Huxley (1894-1963)

SEE Miller on SMELLS

Hypocrisy
The smyler with the knife under the cloke.
Geoffrey Chaucer (1340-1400)

Hypocrisy, the only evil that walks invisible.
John Milton (1608-1674)

An open foe may prove a curse,
But a pretended friend is worse.
John Gay (1685-1732)
English playwright

A fav'rite has no friend.
Thomas Gray (1716-1771)

The two maxims of any great man at court are always to keep his countenance and never to keep his word.
Jonathan Swift (1667-1745)

With affection beaming in one eye and calculation out of the other.
Charles Dickens (1812-1870)

A hypocrite combines the smooth appearance of virtue with the solid satisfaction of vice.
C. E. M. Joad (1891-1953)
British author, academic

L'hypocrisie est un hommage que le vice rend à la vertu.
Hypocrisy is a tribute that vice pays to virtue.
François, Duc de La Rochefoucauld (1613-1680)
French writer, moralist

No man is a hypocrite in his pleasures.
Dr Samuel Johnson (1709-1784)

Hypocrisy in anything whatever may deceive the cleverest and most penetrating man, but the least wide-awake of children recognizes it, and is revolted by it, however ingeniously it may be disguised.
Leo Tolstoy (1828-1910)

SEE Huxley on PATRONAGE

Idealism

When they come downstairs from their ivory towers, idealists are apt to walk straight into the gutter.

Logan Pearsall Smith (1865-1946)
American essayist

We are all in the gutter, but some of us are looking at the stars.

Oscar Wilde (1854-1900)

A man gazing at the stars is proverbially at the mercy of the puddles in the road.

Alexander Smith (1830-1867)
Scottish poet

The idealist is incorrigible: if he is thrown out of his heaven he makes an ideal of his hell.

Friedrich Nietzsche (1844-1900)

He was one of those men who think that the world can be saved by writing a pamphlet.

Benjamin Disraeli (1804-1881)

It is useless for the sheep to pass resolutions in favour of vegetarianism while the wolf remains of a different opinion.

W. R. Inge (1860-1954)
Dean of St Paul's, London

One should never put on one's best trousers when going out to battle for freedom and truth.

Henrik Ibsen (1828-1906)

Saddle your dreams afore you ride 'em.

Mary Webb (1881-1927)
British author

An idealist is a person who helps other people to be prosperous.

Henry Ford (1863-1947)

An idealist is a man who looks at a rose, and thinks, because it smells sweet, it will make better soup than a cabbage.

H. L. Mencken (1880-1956)
American journalist

Idealism increases in direct proportion to one's distance from the problem.

John Galsworthy (1867-1933)

Idealism is the despot of thought, just as politics is the despot of will.

Mikhail Bakunin (1814-1876)
Russian political theorist

The idealist walks on tiptoe, the materialist on his heels.

Malcolm de Chazal (b. 1902)
French writer

We for a certainty are not the first
Have sat in taverns while the
    tempest hurled
Their hopeful plans to emptiness,
    and cursed
Whatever brute and blackguard
    made the world.

A. E. Housman (1859-1936)
British poet, classical scholar

SEE Wilkie, Wilson on AMERICA; Chesterton on AMERICANS; Pearse on IRELAND; Burke on MOTIVES

Ideas

Such as take lodgings in a head that's to be let unfurnished.

Samuel Butler (1612-1680)
English poet

Daring ideas are like chessmen moved forward; they may be beaten, but they may start a winning game.

Johann Wolfgang von Goethe (1749-1832)

If anyone has a new idea in this country, there are twice as many people who advocate putting a man with a red flag in front of it.

Duke of Edinburgh (b. 1921)

Uneducated clever women, who have seen much of the world, are in middle life so much the most cultured part of the community. They have been saved from this horrible burden of inert ideas.

A. N. Whitehead (1861-1947)
British philosopher

An Idea isn't responsible for the people who believe in it.

Don Marquis (1878-1937)
American humorist, journalist

SEE Lec on IDEOLOGY

Ideology

In a war of ideas it is people who get killed.
> Slanislaus J. Lec (b. 1909)
> Polish poet

Always recognise that human individuals are ends, and do not use them as means to your end.
> Immanuel Kant (1724-1804)

Our blight is ideologies – they are the long-expected Antichrist!
> Carl Jung (1875-1961)

SEE Galbraith on ECONOMICS

Idleness

The insupportable labour of doing nothing.
> Sir Richard Steele (1672-1729)
> English essayist, dramatist, editor

Idleness is an appendix to nobility.
> Robert Burton (1577-1640)
> English clergyman, author

Idleness is only a coarse name for my infinite capacity for living in the present.
> Cyril Connolly (1903-1974)
> British critic

'Tis the voice of the sluggard; I heard him complain,
'You have wak'd me too soon, I must slumber again'.
> Isaac Watts (1674-1748)
> English hymn-writer

I look upon indolence as a sort of suicide; for the man is effectually destroyed, though the appetites of the brute may survive.
> Lord Chesterfield (1694-1773)
> English statesman and man of letters

Laziness. Unwarranted repose of manner in a person of low degree.
> Ambrose Bierce (1842-1914)
> American author

Perhaps man is the only being that can properly be called idle.
> Dr Samuel Johnson (1709-1784)

You must have been warned against letting the golden hours slip by. Yes, but some of them are golden only because we let them slip.
> J. M. Barrie (1860-1937)
> British playwright

What is this life if, full of care,
We have no time to stand and stare?
> W. H. Davies (1871-1940)
> British poet

It is better to have loafed and lost than never to have loafed at all.
> James Thurber (1894-1961)
> American humorist, illustrator

A loafer always has the correct time.
> Kin (F. McKinney) Hubbard (1868-1930)
> American humorist, journalist

Life is too short to do anything for oneself that one can pay others to do for one.
> W. Somerset Maugham (1874-1965)

To do great work a man must be very idle as well as very industrious.
> Samuel Butler (1835-1902)
> English author

It is impossible to enjoy idling thoroughly unless one has plenty of work to do.
> Jerome K. Jerome (1859-1927)
> British author

Life is mostly froth and bubble.
Two things stand like stone:
Dodging duty at the double,
Leaving work alone.
> anonymous

Convent. A place of retirement for women who wish for leisure to meditate upon the sin of idleness.
> Ambrose Bierce (1842-1914)
> American author

SEE Tolstoy on The ARMY; Hutchins on EXERCISE; Wordsworth on GOLF; Phaedrus on HASTE; Scott on INERTIA; Cresswell on POETS; Shaw on REASON; Colette on SMOKING; Johnson on UNEMPLOYMENT

Ignorance

Ignorance is the mother of devotion.
> Dean Henry Cole (1500-1580)
> English prelate

Where ignorance is bliss,
'Tis folly to be wise.
> Thomas Gray (1716-1771)

Ignorance is not innocence, but sin.
> Robert Browning (1812-1889)

Nothing in the world is more dangerous than sincere ignorance and conscientious stupidity.
> Martin Luther King (1929-1968)

Better be ignorant of a matter than half know it.
> Publilius Syrus (1st century BC)
> Roman writer of mimes

What you don't know would make a great book.
> Sydney Smith (1771-1845)
> English writer, clergyman

Everybody is ignorant, only on different subjects.
> Will Rogers (1879-1935)
> American humorist

SEE Inge, Newman on KNOWLEDGE;

Marlowe on RELIGION; Gray on
THINKING; Montagu on YOUTH

Illness

If prolonged it cannot be severe, and if severe, it cannot be prolonged.

Seneca (c. 5-65)
Roman writer, philosopher, statesman

Long illness is the real vampirism: think of living a year or two after one is dead, by sucking the life-blood out of a frail young creature at one's bedside!

Dr Oliver Wendell Holmes (1809-1894)
American writer, physician

We are so fond of one another, because our ailments are the same.

Jonathan Swift (1667-1745)

All interest in disease and death is only another expression of interest in life.

Thomas Mann (1875-1955)

Illness is the doctor to whom we pay most heed; to kindness, to knowledge, we make promise only; pain we obey.

Marcel Proust (1871-1922)

I have Bright's disease and he has mine.

S. J. Perelman (1904-1979)
American humorist

Illusions

An era can be said to end when its basic illusions are exhausted.

Arthur Miller (b. 1915)

It is respectable to have no illusions – and safe – and profitable, and dull.

Joseph Conrad (1857-1924)

There are three things which every man thinks he can do – namely, drive a gig, edit a newspaper, and farm a small property.

Sydney Smith (1771-1845)
English writer, clergyman

We must select the illusion which appeals to our temperament, and embrace it with passion if we want to be happy.

Cyril Connolly (1903-1974)
British critic

Illusions: of Grandeur

I recoil, overcome with the glory of my rosy hue and the knowledge that I, a mere cock, have made the sun rise.

Edmond Rostand (1868-1918)
French poet, playwright

Some people think that Davis has a God complex, but this is absurd. On the seventh day, *he* works.

Dick Schaap (b. 1934)
American journalist
of Sammy Davis Jr.

He never wrote a letter or a message wherein he did not speak of God as if the Creator was waiting to see him in the lobby.

Elbert Hubbard (1856-1915)
American author
of Kaiser Wilhelm II

Imagination

Heard melodies are sweet, but those unheard
Are sweeter.

John Keats (1795-1821)

Imagination is the eye of the soul.

Joseph Joubert (1754-1824)
French essayist, moralist

One's real life is so often the life that one does not lead.

Oscar Wilde (1854-1900)

[Man] does not see the real world. The real world is hidden from him by the wall of imagination.

George Gurdjieff (1874-1949)
Russian mystic, author

You can't depend on your judgement when your imagination is out of focus.

John F. Kennedy (1917-1963)

SEE de Vauvenargues on FACTS
Macaulay on POETS

Imitation

A man never knows what a fool he is until he hears himself imitated by one.

Sir Herbert Beerbohm Tree (1853-1917)
British actor-manager

The only good copies are those which make us see the absurdity of bad originals.

François, Duc de La Rochefoucauld (1613-1680)
French writer, moralist

When people are free to do as they please, they usually imitate each other.

Eric Hoffer (1902-1983)
American philosopher

Almost all absurdity of conduct arises from the imitation of those whom we cannot resemble.

Dr Samuel Johnson (1709-1784)

To do exactly the opposite is also a form of imitation.

G. C. Lichtenberg (1742-1799)
German physicist, writer

Immortality

He had decided to live for ever or die in the attempt.

Joseph Heller (b. 1923)
American author

The average man, who does not know what to do with this life, wants another one which shall last forever.

Anatole France (1844-1924)
French author

What man is capable of the insane self-conceit of believing that an eternity of himself would be tolerable even to himself?

George Bernard Shaw (1856-1950)

The idea of immortality . . . will continue . . . as long as love kisses the lips of death. It is the rainbow – Hope, shining upon the tears of grief.

R. G. Ingersoll (1833-1899)
American lawyer

Il importe à toute la vie de sçavoir si l'âme est mortelle ou immortelle.
Our very life depends on our knowing whether the soul is mortal or immortal.

Blaise Pascal (1623-1662)

I don't want to achieve immortality through my work. . . I want to achieve it through not dying.

Woody Allen (b. 1935)

To himself everyone is an immortal; he may know that he is going to die, but he can never know that he is dead.

Samuel Butler (1835-1902)
English author

If you wish to live forever you must be wicked enough to be irretrievably damned; in hell alone do people retain their sinful nature: that is too say, their individuality.

George Bernard Shaw (1856-1950)

SEE Woolwich on The CHURCH; St Paul on DEATH; Ertz on SUNDAYS

Impotence

Thou treacherous, base deserter of my flame,
False to my passion, fatal to my fame,
Through what mistaken magic dost thou prove
So true to lewdness, so untrue to love?

John Wilmot, Earl of Rochester (1647-1680)
English courtier, poet

SEE Grant on SEDUCTION

Inconsistency

Do I contradict myself?
Very well then I contradict myself,
(I am large, I contain multitudes).

Walt Whitman (1819-1892)

Like the British Constitution; she owes her success in practice to her inconsistencies in principle.

Thomas Hardy (1840-1928)

People who honestly mean to be true really contradict themselves much more rarely than those who try to be 'consistent'.

Dr Oliver Wendell Holmes (1809-1894)
American writer, physician

SEE Alther on OPINION

Indecision

How long halt ye between two opinions?

Bible, Kings

Neither have they hearts to stay,
Nor wit enough to run away.

Samuel Butler (1612-1680)
English poet

We know what happens to people who stay in the middle of the road. They get run over.

Aneurin Bevan (1897-1960)
British Labour politician

There is no more miserable human being than one in whom nothing is habitual but indecision.

William James (1842-1910)
American psychologist, philosopher

He who hesitates is sometimes saved.

James Thurber (1894-1961)
American humorist, illustrator

Independence

Independence I have long considered the grand blessing of life, the basis of every virtue – and independence I will ever secure by contracting my wants, though I were to live on a barren heath.

Mary Wollstonecraft (1759-1797)
English feminist writer

It is very easy for rich people to preach the virtues of self-reliance to the poor. It is also very foolish, because, as a matter of fact, the wealthy, so far from being self-reliant, are dependent on the constant attention of scores, and sometimes even hundreds, of persons who are employed in waiting on them and ministering to their wants.

Sir Winston Churchill (1874-1965)

The man who goes alone can start today; but he who travels with another must wait till that other is ready.

H. D. Thoreau (1817-1862)

It's the man who dares to take, who is independent, not he who gives.

D. H. Lawrence (1885-1930)

SEE Cobbett on POVERTY

Indifference

I regard you with an indifference closely bordering on aversion.

Robert Louis Stevenson (1850-1894)

The worst sin towards our fellow creatures is not to hate them, but to be indifferent to them; that's the essence of inhumanity.

Anderson, *The Devil's Disciple*
George Bernard Shaw (1856-1950)

Nothing is more conducive to peace of mind than not having any opinion at all.

G. C. Lichtenberg (1742-1799)
German physicist, writer

Lukewarmness I account a sin as great in love as in religion.

Abraham Cowley (1618-1667)
English author

SEE APATHY

Individuality

Comrades! We must abolish the cult of the individual decisively, once and for all.

Nikita Khrushchev (1894-1971)

Why runners make lousy communists. In a word, *individuality.* It's the one characteristic all runners, as different as they are, seem to share... Stick with it. Push yourself. Keep running. And you'll never lose that wonderful sense of individuality you now enjoy. Right, comrade?

advertisement for running
shoes at the 1984 Olympic
Games in Los Angeles

No member of a crew is praised for the rugged individuality of his rowing.

R. W. Emerson (1803-1882)
American essayist, poet, philosopher

When God decides to destroy a man in the struggle of life He first cultivates his individuality.

Henrik Ibsen (1828-1906)

Resistance to the organized mass can be effected only by the man who is as well organized in his individuality as the mass itself.

Carl Jung (1875-1961)

SEE Shaw on IMMORTALITY

Inequality

When Adam delved and Eve span,
Who was then the gentleman?

John Ball (hanged 1381)
English priest and agitator

I never could believe that Providence had sent a few men into the world, ready booted and spurred to ride, and millions ready saddled and bridled to be ridden.

Richard Rumbold (1622-1685)
English soldier, conspirator

The rich man in his castle,
The poor man at his gate,
God made them, high or lowly,
And order'd their estate.

Cecil F. Alexander (1818-1895)
English poetess

If human equality is to be forever averted – if the High, as we have called them, are to keep their places permanently – then the prevailing mental condition must be controlled insanity.

George Orwell (1903-1950)

The true pleasure of life is to live with your inferiors.

W. M. Thackeray (1811-1863)
English author

There is always inequality in life. Some men are killed in a war and some men are wounded and some men never leave the country. Life is unfair.

John F. Kennedy (1917-1963)

Don linajes sólos hay en el mundo, como decía una abuela mía, que son el tenir y el non tenir.
There are only two families in the world, as a grandmother of mine used to say, the haves and the have-nots.

Miguel de Cervantes (1547-1616)

We need inequality in order to eliminate poverty.

Sir Keith Joseph (b. 1918)
British Conservative politician

SEE CLASS; Schelling on EDUCATION;
Woolf on SELF-CONFIDENCE

Inertia

Fixed like a plant on his peculiar spot,
To draw nutrition, propagate, and rot.

Alexander Pope (1688-1744)

When a man hasn't a good reason for doing a thing, he has a good reason for letting it alone.

Sir Walter Scott (1771-1832)

Nothing happens, nobody comes, nobody goes, it's awful.

Samuel Beckett (b. 1906)

Infallibility

I may have my faults, but being wrong ain't one of them.

Jimmy Hoffa (1913-1983)
American trade unionist

Even the youngest among us is not infallible.

Benjamin Jowett (1817-1893)
English scholar, essayist

The famous Dogma of Papal Infallibility is by far the most modest pretension of the kind in existence. Compared with our infallible democracies, our infallible medical councils, our infallible astronomers, and our infallible judges, and our infallible parliaments the Pope is on his knees in the dust confessing his ignorance before the throne of God, asking only that as to certain historical matters on which he has clearly more sources of information open to him than anyone else his decision shall be taken as final.

George Bernard Shaw (1856-1950)

SEE Shaw on the CHURCH; Steele on
The CHURCH OF ENGLAND;
Carlyle on COMPLACENCY

Inflation

The best way to destroy the capitalist system is to debauch the currency. By a continuing process of inflation governments can confiscate, secretly and unobserved, an important part of the wealth of their citizens.
John Maynard Keynes (1883-1946)

One of the principal troubles about inflation is that the public likes it.
Lord Woolton (1883-1964)
British Conservative politician

A double Scotch is about the size of a small Scotch before the war, and a single Scotch is nothing more than a dirty glass.
Lord Dundee (b. 1902)

I haven't heard of anybody who wants to stop living on account of the cost.
Kin (F. McKinney) Hubbard (1868-1930)
American humorist, journalist

SEE Thatcher on RECESSION

Ingratiation

He makes people pleased with him by making them first pleased with themselves.
Lord Chesterfield (1694-1773)
English statesman and man of letters

The art of pleasing consists in being pleased.
William Hazlitt (1778-1830)
English essayist

Take here the grand secret – if not of pleasing all, yet of displeasing none – court medocrity, avoid originality, and sacrifice to fashion.
Johann Kaspar Lavater (1741-1801)
Swiss divine, poet

You might as well fall flat on your face as lean over too far backwards.
James Thurber (1894-1961)
American humorist, illustrator

SEE Swope on FAILURE, Johnson on INSULTS

Inheritance

My sword I give to him that shall succeed me in my pilgrimage, and my courage and skill to him that can get it.
John Bunyan (1628-1688)

It's going to be fun to watch and see how long the meek can keep the earth after they inherit it.
Kin (F. McKinney) Hubbard (1868-1930)
American humorist, journalist

He's a fool that makes his doctor his heir.
Benjamin Franklin (1706-1790)

The weeping of an heir is laughter in disguise.
Michel de Montaigne (1533-1592)
French essayist

Never say you know a man until you have divided an inheritance with him.
Johann Kaspar Lavater (1741-1801)
Swiss divine, poet

All heiresses are beautiful.
John Dryden (1631-1700)

Innocence

Every harlot was a virgin once.
William Blake (1757-1827)

I used to be Snow White – but I drifted.
Mae West (1892-1980)

Innocence ends when one is stripped of the delusion that one likes oneself.
Joan Didion (b. 1934)
American writer

Innocence is like a dumb leper who has lost his bell, wandering the world, meaning no harm.
Graham Greene (b. 1904)

Only the old are innocent. That is what the Victorians understood, and the Christians. Original sin is the property of the young. The old grow beyond corruption very quickly.
Malcolm Bradbury (b. 1932)
British author

Men do not suspect faults which they do not commit.
Dr Samuel Johnson (1709-1784)

He was a simple soul who had not been introduced to his own subconscious.
Warwick Deeping (1877-1950)
British author

Look for me in the nurseries of heaven.
Francis Thompson (1859-1907)
English poet

Innovation

He who anticipates his century is generally persecuted when living, and always pilfered when dead.
Benjamin Disraeli (1804-1881)

A 'new thinker', when studied closely, is merely a man who does not know what other people have thought.
F. M. Colby (1865-1925)
American editor, essayist

New and stirring ideas are belittled, because if they are not belittled the humiliating question arises, 'Why then are you not taking part in them?'
H. G. Wells (1866-1946)

The new always carries with it the sense of violation, of sacrilege. What is dead is sacred; what is new, that is, *different*, is evil, dangerous, or subversive.
Henry Miller (1891-1980)

SEE Twain on ORIGINALITY

Insignificance

We are merely the stars' tennis-balls,
struck and bandied
Which way please them.
> John Webster (1580-1625)
> English dramatist

No! I am not Prince Hamlet, nor was
meant to be:
Am an attendant lord, one that will
do
To swell a progress, start a scene or
two, advise the prince.
> T. S. Eliot (1888-1965)

It needs more skill than I can tell
To play the second fiddle well.
> C. H. Spurgeon (1834-1892)
> English preacher

My own idear is that these things are as piffle
before the wind.
> Daisy Ashford (1881-1972)
> British writer of The
> Young Visiters, aged 9

There is nothing insignificant.
> S. T. Coleridge (1772-1834)

SEE Shakespeare on LIFE

Inspiration

Stung by the splendour of a sudden thought.
> Robert Browning (1812-1889)

The inspirations of today are the shams of
tomorrow – the purpose has departed.
> Elbert Hubbard (1856-1915)
> American author

You beat your pate, and fancy wit
will come;
Knock as you please, there's
nobody at home.
> Alexander Pope (1688-1744)

My sole inspiration is a telephone call from a
director.
> Cole Porter (1893-1964)

SEE Emerson on PASSION

Instinct

Be a good animal, true to your animal
instincts.
> D. H. Lawrence (1885-1930)

The natural man has only two primal passions
– to get and to beget.
> Sir William Osler (1849-1919)
> Canadian physician

Instinct. When the house burns one forgets
even lunch. Yes, but one eats it later in the
ashes.
> Friedrich Nietzsche (1844-1900)

Mistrust first impulses, they are always good.
> Charles, Count Talleyrand (1754-1838)
> French statesman

SEE Bradley on PHILOSOPHY

Institutions

Wherever a man goes, men will pursue him
and paw him with their dirty institutions, and,
if they can, constrain him to belong to their
desperate oddfellow society.
> H. D. Thoreau (1817-1862)

The whole history of civilization is strewn
with creeds and institutions which were invaluable at first and deadly afterwards.
> Walter Bagehot (1826-1877)
> English economist, critic

An institution is the lengthened shadow of one
man.
> R. W. Emerson (1803-1882)
> American essayist, poet, philosopher

The more rational an institution is the less it
suffers by making concessions to others.
> George Santayana (1863-1952)
> American philosopher, poet

All establishments die of dignity. They are too
proud to think themselves ill, and to take a
little physic.
> Sydney Smith (1771-1845)
> English writer, clergyman

Every institution not only carries within it the
seeds of its own dissolution, but prepares the
way for its most hated rival.
> W. R. Inge (1860-1954)
> Dean of St Paul's, London

Insults

An injury is much sooner forgotten than an
insult.
> Lord Chesterfield (1694-1773)
> English statesman and man of letters

If I have said something to hurt a man once, I
shall not get the better of this by saying many
things to please him.
> Dr Samuel Johnson (1709-1784)

There are two insults which no human will
endure: the assertion that he hasn't a sense of
humor, and the doubly impertinent assertion
that he has never known trouble.
> Sinclair Lewis (1885-1951)
> American novelist

No one can be as calculatedly rude as the
British, which amazes Americans, who do not
understand studied insult and can only offer
abuse as a substitute.
> Paul Gallico (1897-1976)
> American novelist

SEE ABUSE; Addison on AGE: Old Age

Insurance

What can't be cured must be insured.
> Oliver Herford (1863-1935)
> American poet, illustrator

Insurance. An ingenious modern game of chance in which the player is permitted to enjoy the comfortable conviction that he is beating the man who keeps the table.
Ambrose Bierce (1842-1914)
American author

SEE Gilbert on DISASTERS

Integrity
A man should be upright, not be kept upright.
Marcus Aurelius (121-180)
Roman emperor, philosopher

Few men have virtue to withstand the highest bidder.
George Washington (1732-1799)

Integrity without knowledge is weak and useless, and knowledge without integrity is dangerous and dreadful.
Dr Samuel Johnson (1709-1784)

Intellectuals
The noble temptation to see too much in everything.
G. K. Chesterton (1874-1936)

We should take care not to make the intellect our god; it has, of course, powerful muscles, but no personality.
Albert Einstein (1879-1955)

And still they gaz'd, and still the
  wonder grew,
That one small head could carry
  all he knew.
Oliver Goldsmith (1728-1774)

Nothing mattered except states of mind, chiefly our own.
John Maynard Keynes (1883-1946)
British economist

An intellectual is someone whose mind watches itself. I am happy to be both halves, the watcher and the watched.
Albert Camus (1913-1960)

Swollen in head, weak in legs, sharp in tongue but empty in belly.
Mao Ze dong (1893-1976)
on intellectuals

To the man-in-the-street, who, I'm
  sorry to say,
Is a keen observer of life,
The word 'Intellectual' suggests
  straight away
A man who's untrue to his
  wife.
W. H. Auden (1907-1973)

An intellectual is a man who doesn't know how to park a bike.
Spiro Agnew (b. 1918)
American Republican politician

A highbrow is a person educated beyond his intelligence.
J. Brander Matthews (1852-1929)
American essayist, critic

Intellectuals can tell themselves anything, sell themselves any bill of goods, which is why they are so often patsies for the ruling classes in nineteenth-century France and England, or twentieth-century Russia and America.
Lillian Hellman (1907-1984)
American playwright

Una palabra nueva, terminada en ismo, que no la conociera nadie, era para él un regalo de los dioses.
A new word ending in 'ism' that no one else knew was for him a gift of the gods.
Pio Baroja (1872-1956)
Spanish novelist, essayist

The good are so harsh to the clever,
The clever so rude to the good!
Elizabeth Wordsworth (1840-1932)
British educator

Intellectuals are the most intolerant of all people.
Paul Durcan (b. 1944)
Irish poet

For all your answers are great and excellent; and which a man can hardly understand.
Apocrypha

SEE Shakespeare on OBESITY

Intelligence
There is nobody so irritating as somebody with less intelligence and more sense than we have.
Don Herold (b. 1889)
American humorous writer, artist

The successful man will see just so much more than his neighbours as they will be able to see, too, when it is shown them, but not enough to puzzle them.
Samuel Butler (1835-1902)
English author

C'est une grande habileté que de savoir cacher son habileté.
The height of cleverness is being able to conceal it.
François, Duc de La Rochefoucauld (1613-1680)
French writer, moralist

The third-rate mind is only happy when it is thinking with the majority. The second-rate mind is only happy when it is thinking with the minority. The first-rate mind is only happy when it is thinking.
A. A. Milne (1882-1956)
British author

There are three types of intelligent person: the first so intelligent that being called very

intelligent must seem natural and obvious; the second sufficiently intelligent to see that he is being flattered, not described; the third so little intelligent that he will believe anything.
John Fowles (b. 1926)
British author

This intelligence-testing business reminds me of the way they used to weigh hogs in Texas. They would get a long plank, put it over a cross-bar, and somehow tie the hog on one end of the plank. They'd search all around till they found a stone that would balance the weight of the hog and they'd put that on the other end of the plank. Then they'd guess the weight of the stone.
John Dewey (1859-1952)
American teacher, philosopher, reformer

Here is a startling alternative which to the English, alone among great nations, has not been startling but a matter of course. Here is a casual assumption that a choice must be made between goodness and intelligence; that stupidity is first cousin to moral conduct, and cleverness the first step into mischief; that reason and God are not on good terms with each other.
John Erskine (1879-1951)
American author

There may be an optimum level of intelligence and perhaps we have already exceeded it. Our brains may be too big – dooming us as Triceratops was doomed by his armour.
Arthur C. Clarke (b. 1917)
British author

As far as I can remember, there is not one word in the Gospels in praise of intelligence.
Bertrand Russell (1872-1970)

I have finally come to the conclusion that a good reliable set of bowels is worth more to a man than any quantity of brains.
Josh Billings (1818-1885)
American humorist

SEE Emerson on HUMANITY; Alther on OPINION; La Rochefoucauld on SELF-DECEPTION

Intentions

'Let me get my arms about you', says the bear. 'I have not the smallest intention of squeezing you'.
Sydney Smith (1771-1845)
English writer, clergyman

No one would remember the Good Samaritan if he'd only had good intentions – he had money too.
Margaret Thatcher (b. 1925)

The world is ruled by deeds, not by good intentions, and one efficient sinner is worth ten futile saints and martyrs.
George Bernard Shaw (1856-1950)

'He means well' is useless unless he does well.
Plautus (254-184 BC)
Roman playwright

With malice towards none; with charity for all; with firmness in the right, as God gives us to see the right – let us strive on to finish the work we are in.
Abraham Lincoln (1809-1865)

Moral of the Work. In war: resolution. In defeat: defiance. In victory: magnanimity. In peace: goodwill.
Sir Winston Churchill (1874-1965)

Hell is paved with good intentions, not bad ones. All men mean well.
George Bernard Shaw (1856-1950)

Most mistaken people mean well, and all mistaken people mean something.
G. K. Chesterton (1874-1936)

His designs were strictly honourable, as the phrase is, that is to rob a lady of her fortune by way of marriage.
Henry Fielding (1707-1754)

Man has his will, – but woman has her way.
Dr Oliver Wendell Holmes (1809-1894)
American writer, physician

SEE Morley on DANCING; Eliot on GOOD DEEDS; Shaw on MOTIVES

Internationalism

My country is the world, and my religion is to do good.
Thomas Paine (1737-1809)
pamphleteer, revolutionary

A steady patriot of the World alone,
The friend of every country but his own.
George Canning (1770-1827)
English statesman, Prime Minister

Interest does not tie nations together; it sometimes separates them. But sympathy and understanding does unite them.
Woodrow Wilson (1856-1924)

We deny your internationalism, because it is a luxury which only the upper classes can afford; the working people are hopelessly bound to their native shores.
Benito Mussolini (1883-1945)
addressed to the Socialists

Intervention

The full potentialities of human fury cannot be reached until a friend of both parties tactfully intervenes.
G. K. Chesterton (1874-1936)

Those who in quarrels interpose,
Must often wipe a bloody nose.
John Gay (1685-1732)
English playwright

'If everybody minded their own business', the

Duchess said in a hoarse growl, 'the world would go round a deal faster than it does'.
Lewis Carroll (1832-1898)

SEE Howe on PRAYER

Interviews

I cried, 'Come tell me how you live!' And thumped him on the head.
Lewis Carroll (1832-1898)

It is not every question that deserves an answer.
Publilius Syrus (1st century BC)
Roman writer of mimes

I'm notorious for giving a bad interview. I'm an actor and I can't help but feel I'm boring when I'm on as myself.
Rock Hudson (1925-1985)

If I possessed the power of conveying unlimited sexual attraction through the potency of my voice, I would not be reduced to accepting a miserable pittance from the BBC for interviewing a faded female in a damp basement.
Gilbert Harding (1907-1960)
British broadcaster
on being asked to sound more
sexy when interviewing Mae West

It is hardly ever any use to go and interview people. If they are at all nice to meet they will not want to meet you.
Evelyn Waugh (1903-1966)

SEE McDonald on POLITICIANS;
Signoret on The PRESS

Intimacy

You don't hold any mystery for me, darling, do you mind? There isn't a particle of you that I don't know, remember, and want.
Elyot, Private Lives
Noël Coward (1899-1973)

Intimacies between women often go backwards, beginning in revelation and ending up in small talk without loss of esteem.
Elizabeth Bowen (1899-1973)
Anglo-Irish writer

If ever a man and his wife, or a man and his mistress, who pass nights as well as days together, absolutely lay aside all good breeding, their intimacy will soon degenerate into a coarse familiarity.
Lord Chesterfield (1694-1773)
English statesman and man of letters

To really know someone is to have loved and hated him in turn.
Marcel Jouhandeau (1888-1979)
French writer

Introspection

The terrible fluidity of self-revelation.
Henry James (1843-1916)

When a man is wrapped up in himself he makes a pretty small package.
John Ruskin (1819-1900)
English critic

Investment

'Tis money that begets money.
Thomas Fuller (1654-1734)
English physician

We cannot eat the fruit while the tree is in blossom.
Benjamin Disraeli (1804-1881)

There is no finer investment for any community than putting milk into babies.
Sir Winston Churchill (1874-1965)

There are two times in a man's live when he should not speculate: when he can't afford it, and when he can.
Mark Twain (1835-1910)

Involvement

None of us liveth to himself, and no man dieth to himself.
Saint Paul (3-67)

No man is an island entire of itself; every man is a part of the main... Any man's death diminishes me because I am involved in mankind, and therefore never send to know for whom the bell tolls; it tolls for thee.
John Donne (c. 1571-1631)

I postpone death by living, by suffering, by error, by risking, by giving, by losing.
Anaïs Nin (1914-1977)
French novelist

To say yes, you have to sweat and roll up your sleeves and plunge both hands into life up to the elbows. It is easy to say no, even if saying no means death.
Jean Anouilh (b. 1910)
French playwright

SEE Debs on PROTEST

Ireland

Ireland is the old sow that eats her farrow.
James Joyce (1882-1941)

Fightin' like divils for conciliation, an' hatin' each other for the love of God.
Charles James Lever (1809-1872)
Irish novelist

Put an Irishman on the spit, and you can always get another Irishman to turn him.
George Bernard Shaw (1856-1950)

The Irish are a fair people; they never speak well of one another.
Dr Samuel Johnson (1709-1784)

The moment the very name of Ireland is mentioned, the English seem to ... act with the barbarity of tyrants and the fatuity of idiots.

Sydney Smith (1771-1845)
English writer, clergyman

Like all Irishmen I suffer from agrophobia — fear of agriculture. In England farming is a hobby or an affectation. In Ireland it's a tragic existence.

Brendan Behan (1923-1964)
Irish playwright

In Ireland there is so little sense of compromise that a girl has to choose between perpetual adoration and perpetual pregnancy.

George Moore (1852-1933)
Irish author

There is an Irish way of paying compliments as though they were irresistible truths which makes what would otherwise be an impertinence delightful.

Katharine Tynan Hinkson (1861-1931)
Irish poet, novelist

The Gael is not like other men; the spade, and the loom, and the sword are not for him. But a destiny more glorious than that of Rome, more glorious than that of Britain, awaits him: to become the saviour of idealism in modern intellectual and social life.

Patrick Pearse (1879-1916)
Irish nationalist, educator

My one claim to originality among Irishmen is that I have never made a speech.

George Moore (1852-1933)
Irish author

Ireland: Northern Ireland Anyone who isn't confused here doesn't really understand what is going on.

man in Belfast

Irony

Jésus a pleuré, Voltaire a souri; c'est de cette larme divine et de ce sourire humain qu'est faite la douceur de la civilisation actuelle.
Jesus wept; Voltaire smiled. From that divine tear and from that human smile is derived the grace of present civilisation.

Victor Hugo (1802-1885)

The free mind must have one policeman. Irony.

Elbert Hubbard (1856-1915)
American author

Isolation

We're all of us sentenced to solitary confinement inside our own skins, for life.

Tennessee Williams (1911-1983)

Im übrigen ist es zuletzt die grösste Kunst, sich zu beschränken und zu isolieren.
The last and greatest art is to limit and isolate oneself.

Johann Wolfgang von Goethe (1749-1832)

SEE Proust on VICE

Israel

In Israel, in order to be a realist you must believe in miracles.

David Ben Gurion (1886-1973)
Israeli statesman

Israel itself was nothing more than one of the consequences of imperialism.

Gamal Abdul Nasser (1918-1970)

The greatest security for Israel is to create new Egypts.

Ronald Reagan (b. 1911)

My generation, dear Ron, swore on the Altar of God that whoever proclaims the intent of destroying the Jewish state or the Jewish people, or both, seals his fate.

Menachem Begin (b. 1913)
Israeli politician, Prime Minister
letter to Reagan

We Jews have a secret weapon in our struggle with the Arabs — we have no place to go.

Golda Meir (1898-1978)

Italy

Midnight, and love, and youth, and Italy!

Edward Bulwer-Lytton (1803-1873)
English novelist, playwright

A man who has not been in Italy, is always conscious of an inferiority.

Dr Samuel Johnson (1709-1784)

Everyone soon or late comes round by Rome.

Robert Browning (1812-1889)

Venice is like eating an entire box of chocolate liqueurs in one go.

Truman Capote (b. 1924)

Italia! oh Italia! thou who hast
The fatal gift of beauty.

Lord Byron (1788-1824)

Italy is a poor country full of rich people.

Richard Gardner (b. 1927)
American diplomat, former US ambassador
in Rome

Italien ist ein geographischer Begriff.
Italy is a geographical expression.

Prince Metternich (1773-1859)
Austrian statesman

Thou Paradise of exiles, Italy!

P. B. Shelley (1792-1822)

Travelling is the ruin of all happiness! There's no looking at a building here after seeing Italy.

Fanny Burney (1752-1840)
English author

I love the language, that soft bastard
    Latin,
Which melts like kisses from a
    female mouth,

And sounds as if it should be writ
on satin
With syllables which breathe of the
sweet South.

Lord Byron (1788-1824)

Lump the whole thing! say that the Creator
made Italy from designs by Michael Angelo!

Mark Twain (1835-1910)

Open my heart and you will see,
Graved inside of it, 'Italy'.

Robert Browning (1812-1889)

J

Jazz

Jazz is the big brother of the blues. If a guy's playing blues like we play, he's in high school. When he starts playing jazz it's like going on to college, to a school of higher learning.

B. B. King (b. 1925)
blues guitarist

Jazz is the only music in which the same note can be played night after night but differently each time.

Ornette Coleman (b. 1930)
jazz musician

Playing 'bop' is like playing Scrabble with all the vowels missing.

Duke Ellington (1899-1974)

I'll play it first and tell you what it is later.

Miles Davis (b. 1926)

SEE Holiday on SONG

Jealousy

Love is as strong as death; jealousy is cruel as the grave.

Bible, Song of Solomon

I had rather be a toad,
And live upon the vapour of a dungeon,
Than keep a corner of the thing I love
For others' uses.

Othello, *Othello*
William Shakespeare (1564-1616)

Jealousy, that dragon which slays love under the pretence of keeping it alive.

Havelock Ellis (1859-1939)
British psychologist

What does a strict guard avail, as a lewd wife cannot be watched and a chaste one does not have to be?

John of Salisbury (1115-1180)
English scholar, philosopher

To jealousy, nothing is more frightful than laughter.

Françoise Sagan (b. 1935)

I had been happy, if the general camp,
Pioneers and all, had tasted her sweet body,
So I had nothing known.

Othello, *Othello*
William Shakespeare (1564-1616)

SEE Wells on MORAL INDIGNATION

The Jews

The world is divided into two groups of nations – those which want to expel the Jews and those which do not want to receive them.

Chaim Weizmann (1874-1952)
Jewish statesman

The Jews are among the aristocracy of every land; if a literature is called rich in the possession of a few classic tragedies, what shall we say to a national tragedy lasting for fifteen hundred years, in which the poets and actors were also the heroes.

George Eliot (1819-1880)

I determine who is a Jew.

Hermann Goering (1893-1946)

I don't like 'Ebrews. They work harder; they're more sober; they're honest, and they're everywhere.

John Galsworthy (1867-1933)

The Jews generally give value. They make you pay; but they deliver the goods. In my experience the men who want something for nothing are invariably Christians.

The Nobleman, *Saint Joan*
George Bernard Shaw (1856-1950)

The Jews are a frightened people. Nineteen centuries of Christian love have broken their nerves.

Israel Zangwill (1864-1926)
British author

From the beginning, the Christian was the theorizing Jew; consequently the Jew is the practical Christian.

Karl Marx (1818-1883)

The pursuit of knowledge for its own sake, an almost fanatical love of justice and the desire for personal independence – these are the features of the Jewish tradition which make me thank my stars that I belong to it.

Albert Einstein (1879-1955)

With Judaism we have a relationship which we do not have with any other religion. You are our dearly beloved brothers and, in a certain way, it could be said that you are our elder brothers.

Pope John Paul II (b. 1920)

A Jewish man with parents alive is a fifteen-year-old boy, and will remain a fifteen-year-old boy until they die.
Philip Roth (b. 1933)
American author

Pessimism is a luxury that a Jew can never allow himself.
Golda Meir (1898-1978)
SEE ISRAEL

Dr Johnson

I hate mankind, for I think myself one of the best of them, and I know how bad I am.
Dr Samuel Johnson (1709-1784)

Johnson's conversation was by much too strong for a person accustomed to obsequious-ness and flattery; it was mustard in a young child's mouth.
Hester Piozzi (Mrs Thrale) (1739-1821)
English writer

Now that the old lion is dead every ass thinks he may kick at him.
Samuel Parr (1747-1825)
English schoolteacher

Dr Johnson can be thankful that God invented Boswell before science invented the pocket tape recorder.
reviewer in The Guardian, 1986
SEE Boswell on SOCIABILITY;
Goldsmith on WRITERS

Jokers

Alas, poor Yorick! I knew him, Horatio: a fellow of infinite jest, of most excellent fancy.
Hamlet, Hamlet
William Shakespeare (1564-1616)

I remain just one thing, and one thing only — and that is a clown. It places me on a far higher plane than any politician.
Charlie Chaplin (1889-1977)

All human race would fain be wits,
And millions miss for one that hits.
Alexander Pope (1688-1744)

I don't know jokes; I just watch the govern-ment and report the facts.
Will Rogers (1879-1935)
American humorist

The difficulty with humorists is that they will mix what they believe with what they don't; whichever seems likelier to win an effect.
John Updike (b. 1932)

The teller of a mirthful tale has latitude allowed him. We are content with less than absolute truth.
Charles Lamb (1775-1834)
English essayist, critic

Motley's the only wear.
Jacques, As You Like It
William Shakespeare (1564-1616)

Who makes a pun will pick a pocket.
English proverb

The marvellous thing about a joke with a double meaning is that it can only mean one thing.
Ronnie Barker (b. 1929)
British comedian

Sir, to be facetious it is not necessary to be indecent.
J. E. T. Rogers (1823-1890)
British political economist

For every ten jokes thou hast got an hundred enemies.
Laurence Sterne (1713-1768)
English author

He jests at scars that never felt a wound.
Romeo, Romeo and Juliet
William Shakespeare (1564-1616)
SEE Grey on COMEDY; Goldsmith on
The RICH

Journalism

It was long ago in my life as a simple reporter that I decided that facts must never get in the way of truth.
James Cameron (1911-1985)
British journalist

Doctors bury their mistakes. Lawyers hang them. But journalists put theirs on the front page.
anonymous

There is much to be said in favour of modern journalism. By giving us the opinions of the uneducated it keeps us in touch with the ignorance of the community. By carefully chronicling the current events of contempor-ary life it shows us of what very little importance such events really are. By invari-ably discussing the unnecessary it makes us understand what things are requisite for culture, and what are not.
Oscar Wilde (1854-1900)

The man must have a rare recipe for melan-choly, who can be dull in Fleet Street.
Charles Lamb (1775-1834)
English essayist, critic

A certain squalid knot of alleys where the town's bad blood once slept corruptly.
Robert Browning (1812-1889)
of Fleet Street

What a squalid and irresponsible little profes-sion it is at the moment. Nothing prepares you for how bad Fleet Street really is until it craps on you from a great height.
Ken Livingstone (b. 1945)
British Labour politician

You cannot hope to bribe or twist
(Thank God) the British journalist.

But seeing what the man will do
Unbribed, there's no occasion to.
Humbert Wolfe (1885-1940)
British poet, author

Give someone half a page in a newspaper and they think they own the world.
Jeffrey Bernard
British journalist

I guess I'll have to gain 60lb, start smoking a cigar and wear clothes that don't match.
Garth lorg
Toronto Blue Jays baseball player
on starting a newspaper column

There is but one way for a newspaperman to look at a politician, and that is down.
Frank H. Simonds (1878-1936)
American journalist, author

Most rock journalism is people who can't write interviewing people who can't talk for people who can't read.
Frank Zappa (b. 1940)
American rock musician

Journalism is still an under-developed profession and, accordingly, newspapermen are quite often regarded as were surgeons and musicians a century ago, as having the rank, roughly speaking, of barbers and riding masters.
Walter Lippman (1889-1974)
American journalist

Journalism will kill you, but it will keep you alive while you're at it.
Horace Greeley (1811-1872)
American newspaper editor, politician

SEE NEWSPAPERS; The PRESS;
WAR CORRESPONDENTS

Judgement Day

And I saw the dead, small and great, stand before God; and the books were opened.
John the Divine (1st century AD)

Thou art weighed in the balances, and found wanting.
Bible, Daniel

Judgements

I have lived in this world just long enough to look carefully the second time into things that I am the most certain of the first time.
Josh Billings (1818-1885)
American humorist

Pour juger les choses grandes et hautes, il faut une âme de même, autrement nous leur attribuons le vice qui est le nôtre.
To make judgements on things that are great and high, a soul of the same stature is needed, otherwise we ascribe to them the vices which belong to us.
Michel de Montaigne (1533-1592)
French essayist

It is well, when one is judging a friend, to remember that he is judging you with the same godlike and superior impartiality.
Arnold Bennett (1867-1931)
British novelist

We are all inclined to judge ourselves by our ideals; others by their acts.
Harold Nicolson (1886-1968)
British diplomat, writer

Speak of me as I am; nothing extenuate,
Nor set down aught in malice.
Othello, *Othello*
William Shakespeare (1564-1616)

Judges

A judge is not supposed to know anything about the facts of life until they have been presented in evidence and explained to him at least three times.
Lord Chief Justice Parker (1900-1972)
British judge

A justice and his clerk is now little more than a blind man and his dog.
William Shenstone (1714-1763)
English poet

And summed up so well that it came to far more than the witnesses had ever said.
Lewis Carroll (1832-1898)

SEE Wodehouse on DIVORCE; Pope on
TRIALS

Juries

Our civilization has decided . . . that determining the guilt or innocence of men is a thing too important to be trusted to trained men. . . When it wants a library catalogued, or the solar system discovered, or any trifle of that kind, it uses up its specialists. But when it wishes anything done which is really serious, it collects twelve of the ordinary men standing round. The same thing was done, if I remember right, by the Founder of Christianity.
G. K. Chesterton (1874-1936)

A jury consists of twelve persons chosen to decide who has the better lawyer.
Robert Frost (1875-1963)
American poet

The public do not know enough to be experts, yet know enough to decide between them.
Samuel Butler (1835-1902)
English author

The jury, passing on the prisoner's life,
May have in the sworn twelve a thief
or two
Guiltier than him they try.
Angleo, *Measure for Measure*
William Shakespeare (1564-1616)

'Write that down,' the King said to the jury,
and the jury eagerly wrote down all three

dates on their slates, and then added them up, and reduced the answer to shillings and pence.
Lewis Carroll (1832-1898)

SEE Pope on TRIALS

Justice

Let justice be done, though the world perish.
Holy Roman Emperor Ferdinand I (1503-1564)

Justice is my being allowed to do whatever I like. Injustice is whatever prevents my doing so.
Samuel Butler (1835-1902)
English author

Injustice is relatively easy to bear: what stings is justice.
H. L. Mencken (1880-1956)
American journalist

Justice is too good for some people and not good enough for the rest.
Norman Douglas (1868-1952)
British author

The love of justice is, in most men, nothing more than the fear of suffering injustice.
François, Duc de La Rochefoucauld (1613-1680)
French writer, moralist

It is better that ten guilty persons escape than one innocent suffer.
Sir William Blackstone (1723-1780)
English jurist

A rape! a rape!... Yes, you have ravish'd justice; forced her to do your pleasure.
John Webster (1590-1625)
English dramatist

A good parson once said that where mystery begins religion ends. Cannot I say, as truly at least, of human laws, that where mystery begins justice ends?
Edmund Burke (1729-1797)
Irish philosopher, statesman

Justice consists in doing no injury to men; decency in giving them no offence.
Cicero (106-43 BC)

Justice must tame, whom mercy cannot win.
Sir George Savile, Lord Halifax (1633-1695)
English statesman, author

When justice has spoken, humanity must have its turn.
Pierre Vergniaud (1753-1793)
French revolutionary leader

A God all mercy is a God unjust.
Edward Young (1683-1765)
English poet

Justice is a concept. Muscle is the reality.
Linda Blandford
correspondent, The Guardian

Only a socially just country has the right to exist.
Pope John Paul II (b. 1920)

Life *is* unfair.
Milton Friedman (b. 1912)
American economist

SEE McIlvanney on The LAW; Bennett on The PRESS

K

Killing

Kill one man and you are a murderer. Kill millions and you are a conqueror. Kill all and you are a God.

Jean Rostand (1894-1977)
French biologist, writer

All creatures kill – there seems to be no exception. But of the whole list man is the only one that kills for fun; he is the only one that kills in malice, the only one that kills for revenge.

Mark Twain (1835-1910)

To live without killing is a thought which could electrify the world, if men were only capable of staying awake long enough to let the thought soak in.

Henry Miller (1891-1980)

SEE ASSASSINATION; Clark on BLOODSPORTS; MURDER

Killjoys

Dost thou think, because thou art virtuous, there shall be no more cakes and ale?

Sir Toby Belch, Twelfth Night
William Shakespeare (1564-1616)

We'll show you too some elders of the town,
Whose only joy is to put joy down.

A. P. Herbert (1890-1971)
British author, politician

Kindness

He was so benevolent, so merciful a man that, in his mistaken passion, he would have held an umbrella over a duck in a shower of rain.

Douglas Jerrold (1803-1857)
English playwright, humorist

If you're naturally kind you attract a lot of people you don't like.

William Feather (b. 1889)
American businessman

When kindness has left people, even for a few moments, we become afraid of them as if their reason has left them.

Willa Cather (1876-1947)
American author

Benevolent people are very apt to be one-sided and fussy, and not of the sweetest temper if others will not be good and happy in their way.

Sir Arthur Helps (1813-1875)
British author

True kindness presupposes the faculty of imagining as one's own the suffering and joy of others.

André Gide (1869-1951)

Do not ask me to be kind; just ask me to act as though I were.

Jules Renard (1864-1910)
French novelist, playwright

Kissing

The sound of a kiss is not so loud as that of a cannon, but its echo lasts a great deal longer.

Dr Oliver Wendell Holmes (1809-1894)
American writer, physician

He took the bride about the neck
And kiss'd her lips with such a clamorous smack
That at the parting all the church did echo.

Gremio (of Petruchio), The Taming of the Shrew
William Shakespeare (1564-1616)

But his kiss was so sweet,
And so closely he pressed,
That I languished and pined
Till I granted the rest.

John Gay (1685-1732)
English playwright

He kissed likewise the maid in the kitchen, and seemed upon the whole a most loving, kissing, kind-hearted gentleman.

William Cowper (1731-1800)
English poet

The kiss originated when the first male reptile licked the first female reptile, implying in a subtle, complimentary way that she was as succulent as the small reptile he had for dinner the night before.

F. Scott Fitzgerald (1896-1940)

When women kiss, it always reminds me of prize-fighters shaking hands.

H. L. Mencken (1880-1956)
American journalist

What lies lurk in kisses.
> Heinrich Heine (1797-1856)
> German poet, journalist

A kiss can be a comma, a question mark or an exclamation point. That's basic spelling that every woman ought to know.
> Mistinguett (1873-1956)
> French dancer, singer

Knowledge

The fruit of the tree of knowledge always drives man from some paradise or other.
> W. R. Inge (1860-1954)
> Dean of St Paul's, London

For lust of knowing what should not
be known,
We take the Golden Road to
Samarkand.
> James Elroy Flecker (1844-1915)
> British poet

Woman first discovered that the fruit of knowledge was good to look upon, good to eat, and fairly digestible; and for the example of eating, sensible men are all grateful.
> Elbert Hubbard (1856-1915)
> American author

Children with Hyacinth's temperament don't know better as they grow older; they merely know more.
> Saki (H. H. Munro) (1870-1916)
> Scottish author

The important thing is not to know more than all men, but to know more at each moment than any particular man.
> Johann Wolfgang von Goethe (1749-1832)

The struggling for knowledge has a pleasure in it like that of wrestling with a fine woman.
> George Savile, Lord Halifax (1633-1695)
> English statesman, author

Les gens de qualité savent tout sans avoir jamais rien appris.
People of quality know everything without ever having learned anything.
> Molière (1622-1673)

We must make up our minds to be ignorant of much, if we would know anything.
> Cardinal John Newman (1801-1890)
> English churchman, theologian

The longer the island of knowledge, the longer the shoreline of wonder.
> Ralph W. Sockman (1889-1970)
> American clergyman

It gets harder the more you know. Because the more you find out the uglier everything seems.
> Frank Zappa (b. 1940)
> American rock musician

To know all is not to forgive all. It is to despise everybody.
> Quentin Crisp (b. 1908)
> British author

Knowledge is power, if you know it about the right person.
> Ethel Watts Mumford (1878-1940)
> American, novelist, humorous writer

If ye had not ploughed with my heifer, ye had not found out my riddle.
> Bible, Judges

SEE Chesterfield, Emerson on LEARNING;
Spencer on SCIENCE

L

Ladies

A lady is a woman who makes a man behave like a gentleman.

Russell Lynes (b. 1910)
American editor, critic

To behold her is an immediate check to loose behaviour; to love her is a liberal education.

Sir Richard Steele (1672-1729)
English essayist, dramatist, editor

Ermined and minked and Persian-
lambed,
Be-puffed (be-painted, too,
alas!)
Be-decked, be-diamonded –
be-damned!
The Women of the Better
Class.

Oliver Herford (1863-1935)
American poet, illustrator

It was not a bosom to repose upon, but it was a capital bosom to hang jewels upon.

Charles Dickens (1812-1870)

A lady is one who never shows her underwear unintentionally.

Lillian Day (b. 1893)
American writer

. . . A lady is nothing very specific. One man's lady is another man's woman; sometimes, one man's lady is another man's wife. Definitions overlap but they almost never coincide.

Russell Lynes (b. 1910)
American editor, critic

Landlords

With one hand he put a penny in the urn of poverty, and with the other took a shilling out.

Rev. Robert Pollok (1798-1827)
Scottish poet

They have given us into the hands of the new unhappy lords,
Lords without anger and honour, who dare not carry their swords.
They fight by shuffling papers; they have bright dead alien eyes;
They look at our labour and laughter as a tired man looks at flies.

G. K. Chesterton (1874-1936)

Language

Nothing is more common than for men to think that because they are familiar with words they understand the ideas they stand for.

Cardinal John Newman (1801-1890)
English churchman, theologian

One of the difficulties in the language is that all our words from loose using have lost their edge.

Ernest Hemingway (1899-1961)

If thought corrupts language, language can also corrupt thought.

George Orwell (1903-1950)

In the end we shall make thoughtcrime literally impossible, because there will be no words in which to express it.

George Orwell (1903-1950)

Language is a uniquely human characteristic. Each person has programmed into his genes a faculty called universal grammar.

Noam Chomsky (b. 1928)
American philosopher

Broadly speaking, the short words are the best, and the old words best of all.

Sir Winston Churchill (1874-1965)

Je parle espagnol à Dieu, italien aux femmes, français aux hommes et allemand à mon cheval.
I speak Spanish to God, Italian to women, French to men and German to my horse.

attributed to
Holy Roman Emperor Charles V (1500-1558)

The more one thinks about Latin the easier it is to see why the Roman Empire fell.

Lord Derby (b. 1918)
British administrator

SEE Jonson on SPEECH

Laughter

If we may believe our logicians, man is distinguished from all other creatures by the faculty of laughter.

Joseph Addison (1672-1719)
English essayist

In my mind, there is nothing so illiberal and so

ill-bred, as audible laughter.
Lord Chesterfield (1694-1773)
English statesman, man of letters

Je me presse de rire de tout, de peur d'être obligé d'en pleurer.
I hasten to laugh at everything for fear of being obliged to weep at it.
Pierre de Beaumarchais (1732-1799)
French dramatist

What provokes you to risibility, Sir? Have I said anything that you understand? Then I ask pardon of the rest of the company.
Dr Samuel Johnson (1709-1784)

Nothing can confound a wise man more than laughter from a dunce.
Lord Byron (1788-1824)

I believe they talked of me, for they laughed consumedly.
George Farquhar (1678-1707)
Irish dramatist

The vulgar often laugh, but never smile, whereas well-bred people often smile, but seldom laugh.
Lord Chesterfield (1694-1773)
English statesman, man of letters

A thing derided is a thing dead; a laughing man is stronger than a suffering man.
Gustave Flaubert (1821-1880)

SEE Wilde on FAREWELLS; Eliot on FOOLS; Sagan on JEALOUSY; Franklin on TEETH; Chesterfield on WIT

The Law

Who thinks the Law has anything to do with Justice? It's what we have because we can't have Justice.
William McIlvanney (b. 1936)
British novelist

One of the greatest delusions in the world is the hope that the evils of this world can be cured by legislation.
Thomas B. Reed (1839-1902)
American lawyer, politician

An unpaid legislature and an unpaid magistracy are institutions essentially aristocratic — contrivances for keeping legislature and judicature exclusively in the hands of those who can afford to serve without pay.
John Stuart Mill (1806-1873)
English philosopher, political economist, Liberal MP

La majestueuse égalité des lois, qui interdit au riche comme au pauvre de coucher sous les ponts, de mendier dans les rues et de voler du pain.
The law, in its majestic equality, forbids rich and poor alike to sleep under bridges, beg in the streets or steal bread.
Anatole France (1844-1924)

Law grinds the poor, and rich men rule the law.
Oliver Goldsmith (1728-1774)

Without law no little souls fresh from God would be branded illegitimate as soon as they reach earth.
Elbert Hubbard (1856-1915)
American author

The law is sort of hocus-pocus science, that smiles in yer face while it picks yer pocket.
Charles Macklin (1697-1797)
Irish actor, dramatist

Laws like houses, lean on one another.
Edmund Burke (1729-1797)
Irish philosopher, statesman

If you have ten thousand regulations you destroy all respect for the law.
Sir Winston Churchill (1874-1965)

I know no method to secure the repeal of bad or obnoxious laws so effective as their stringent execution.
Ulysses S. Grant (1822-1885)

I've been told that since the beginning of civilization, millions and millions of laws have not improved on the Ten Commandments one bit.
Ronald Reagan (b. 1911)

Laws are dumb in times of war.
Cicero (106-43 BC)

The law often allows what honour forbids.
William Saurin (1757-1839)
Irish politician

Courts of law, and all the paraphernalia and folly of law ... cannot be found in a rational state of society.
Robert Owen (1771-1858)
Welsh social reformer

Salus populi suprema est lex.
The good of the people is the greatest law.
Cicero (106-43 BC)

SEE Young on BUSINESS

Lawyers

The only road to the highest stations in this country is that of the law.
Sir William Jones (1746-1794)
English orientalist, jurist

Lawyers know life practically. A bookish man should always have them to converse with.
Dr Samuel Johnson (1709-1784)

A lawyer without history or literature is a mechanic, a mere working mason; if he possesses some knowledge of these, he may venture to call himself an architect.
Sir Walter Scott (1771-1832)

Whenever you wish to do anything against the

Leadership

law, Cicely, always consult a good solicitor first.
> Sir Howard, *Captain Brassbound's Conversion*
> George Bernard Shaw (1856-1950)

I once heard you say that it took you twenty years to recover from your legal training – from the habit of mind that is bent on making out a case rather than on seeing the large facts of a situation in their proportion.
> W. H. Page (1855-1918)
> American diplomat, publisher
> to *Woodrow Wilson*

A solicitor is a man who calls in a person he doesn't know to sign a contract he hasn't seen to buy property he doesn't want with money he hasn't got.
> Sir Dingwall Bateson (1898-1967)
> President of the Law Society, 1952-1953

A society of men bred up from their youth in the art of proving by words multiplied for the purpose that white is black and black is white according as they are paid.
> Jonathan Swift (1667-1745)

There is the prostitute, one who lets out her body for hire. A dreadful thing, but are we ourselves so innocent? Do not lawyers, for instance, let out their brains for hire?
> Lord Brabazon (1884-1964)
> British motorist, aviator, politician

Woe unto you, lawyers! For ye have taken away the key of knowledge: ye entered not in yourselves, and them that were entering in ye hindered.
> Jesus (4 BC-29 AD)

Bluster, sputter, question, cavil; but be sure your argument is intricate enough to confound the court.
> William Wycherley (1640-1716)
> English dramatist

Lawyers' are like lovers' quarrels.
> Lord Campbell (1779-1861)
> English jurist

There are few grave legal questions involved in a poor estate.
> Ed (E. W.) Howe (1853-1937)
> American journalist, novelist

I think we may class the lawyer in the natural history of monsters.
> John Keats (1795-1821)

I really went to the Bar because I thought it would be easier to go on the stage after failing at the Bar than to go to the Bar after failing on the stage.
> Lord Gardiner (b. 1900)
> former Lord Chancellor of Great Britain

If there were no bad people there would be no good lawyers.
> Charles Dickens (1812-1870)

Leadership

It is a fine thing to command, even if it be only a herd of cattle.
> Miguel de Cervantes (1547-1616)

To be
Omnipotent but friendless is to reign.
> P. B. Shelley (1792-1822)

To be a leader of men one must turn one's back on men.
> Havelock Ellis (1859-1939)
> British psychologist

Charlatanism of some degree is indispensable to effective leadership.
> Eric Hoffer (1902-1983)
> American philosopher

Only he can command who has the courage and initiative to disobey.
> William McDougall (1871-1938)
> British psychologist

We were not born to sue, but to command.
> King Richard, *King Richard II*
> William Shakespeare (1564-1616)

It is always a great mistake to command when you are not sure you will be obeyed.
> Honoré, Comte de Mirabeau (1749-1791)
> French statesman

Keep your fears to yourself, but share your courage with others.
> Robert Louis Stevenson (1850-1894)

Follow me if I advance! Kill me if I retreat! Revenge me if I die!
> Ngo Dinh Diem (d. 1963)
> *on becoming President of*
> *Vietnam, 1954*

The efficiency of the truly national leader consists primarily in preventing the division of the attention of a people, and always in concentrating it on a single enemy.
> Adolf Hitler (1889-1945)

For if the trumpet give an uncertain sound, who shall prepare himself to the battle?
> Saint Paul (3-67)

The wise man who is not heeded is counted a fool, and the fool who proclaims the general folly first and loudest passes for a prophet and Führer, and sometimes it is luckily the other way round as well, or else mankind would long since have perished of stupidity.
> Carl Jung (1875-1961)

I am a lone monk walking the world with a leaky umbrella.
> Mao Ze dong (1893-1976)

What is the throne? A bit of wood, gilt and draped. I am the state. Here it is I alone who represent the people. Even if I had done wrong you should not have accused me publicly.

People wash their dirty linen at home. France has more need of me than I of France.
Napoleon Bonaparte (1769-1821)
to the French Senate in 1814

In Poland everyone is a leader.
Lech Walesa (b. 1943)

We want a few mad people now. See where the sane ones have landed us!
Poulengey, *Saint Joan*
George Bernard Shaw (1856-1950)

Omnium consensu capax imperii nisi imperasset.
No one would have doubted his ability to reign had he never been emperor.
Tacitus (c. 55-c. 120)
Roman historian
of Emperor Galba

So long as the people of any country place their hopes of political salvation *in leadership of any description*, so long will disappointment attend them.
William Lovett (1800-1877)
English Chartist leader

SEE Defoe on GENERALS; Ledru-Rollin on MOBS; Halifax on OBEDIENCE; Rogers on POLITICAL PARTIES

Learning

A little learning is a dangerous thing;
Drink deep, or taste not the Pierian spring:
There shallow draughts intoxicate the brain,
And drinking largely sobers us again.
Alexander Pope (1688-1744)

A learned fool is one who has read everything, and simply remembered it.
Josh Billings (1818-1885)
American humorist

His knowledge of books had in some degree diminished his knowledge of the world.
William Shenstone (1714-1763)
English poet

Learning. The kind of ignorance distinguishing the studious.
Ambrose Bierce (1842-1914)
American author

No person ever knew so much that was so little of purpose.
R. W. Emerson (1803-1882)
American essayist, poet, philosopher
of Macaulay

He not only overflowed with learning, but stood in the slop.
Sydney Smith (1771-1845)
English writer, clergyman
of Macaulay as conversationalist

All other men are specialists, but his specialism is omniscience.
Sir Arthur Conan Doyle (1859-1930)
of Mycroft Holmes

A learned blockhead is a greater blockhead than an ignorant one.
Benjamin Franklin (1706-1790)

Wear your learning, like your watch, in a private pocket: and do not merely pull it out and strike it; merely to show that you have one.
Lord Chesterfield (1694-1773)
English statesman and man of letters

Pedantry is the dotage of knowledge.
Holbrook Jackson (1874-1948)
British author

Erudition. Dust shaken out of a book into an empty skull.
Ambrose Bierce (1842-1914)
American author

Some people will never learn anything; for this reason, because they understand everything too soon.
Alexander Pope (1688-1744)

The man who is too old to learn was probably always too old to learn.
Henry S. Haskins (b. 1875)
American author

With just enough of learning to misquote.
Lord Byron (1788-1824)

SEE Young on QUOTATIONS; Penn on READING; SCHOLARSHIP; Hazlitt on SHAKESPEARE

Lebanon

Here, even the law of the jungle has broken down.
Walid Jumblatt (b. 1949)
Leader of the Lebanese Druze

The Left

Leftwingers are incapable of conspiring because they are all egomaniacs.
Norman Mailer (b. 1923)

SEE COMMUNISM; MARXISM; SOCIALISM

Leisure

A perpetual holiday is a good working definition of hell.
George Bernard Shaw (1856-1950)

More free time means more time to waste. The worker who used to have only a little time in which to get drunk and beat his wife now has time to get drunk, beat his wife – and watch TV.
Robert M. Hutchins (b. 1899)
American educator, writer

Liberals

Leisure is the mother of philosophy.
Thomas Hobbes (1588-1679)

The basis on which good repute in any highly organized industrial community ultimately rests is pecuniary strength; and the means of showing pecuniary strength, and so of gaining or retaining a good name, are leisure and a conspicuous consumption of goods.
Thorstein Veblen (1857-1929)
American social scientist

To be able to fill leisure intelligently is the last product of civilisation.
Bertrand Russell (1872-1970)

Liberals

Cosmopolitan critics, men who are the friends of every country save their own.
Benjamin Disraeli (1804-1881)

They act as if they supposed that to be very sanguine about the general improvement of mankind is a virtue that relieves them from taking trouble about any improvement in particular.
John, Lord Morley (1838-1923)
British writer, Liberal politician

The liberals have not softened their view of actuality to make themselves live closer to the dream, but instead sharpen their perceptions and fight to make the dream actuality or give up the battle in despair.
Margaret Mead (1901-1978)
American anthropologist

Liberalism . . . is the supreme form of generosity; it is the right which the majority concedes to minorities and hence it is *the noblest cry* that has ever resounded in this planet.
José Ortega y Gasset (1883-1955)
Spanish essayist, philosopher

We who are liberal and progressive know that the poor are our equals in every sense except that of being equal to us.
Lionel Trilling (1905-1975)
American critic

I sit on a man's back, choking him and making him carry me, and yet assure myself and others that I am very sorry for him and wish to ease his lot by all possible means – except by getting off his back.
Leo Tolstoy (1828-1910)

The Liberal State is a mask behind which there is no face; it is a scaffolding behind which there is no building.
Benito Mussolini (1883-1945)

The worst enemy of the new radicals are the old liberals.
Vladimir Ilyich Lenin (1870-1924)

Liberation

We sure liberated the hell out of this place.
American soldier in ruined French village
quoted by Max Miller

Liberty

I know not what course others may take; but as for me, give me liberty or give me death.
Patrick Henry (1736-1799)
American statesman

Liberty means responsibility. That is why most men dread it.
George Bernard Shaw (1856-1950)

He that would make his own liberty secure must guard even his enemy from oppression.
Thomas Paine (1737-1809)
pamphleteer, revolutionary

Liberty has never come from the government. Liberty has always come from the subjects of it. The history of liberty is a history of resistance.
Woodrow Wilson (1856-1924)

A regard for liberty, though a laudable passion, ought commonly to be subordinate to a reverence for established government.
David Hume (1711-1776)

It is true that liberty is precious – so precious that it must be rationed.
attributed to Vladimir Ilyich Lenin (1870-1924)

It will be found an unjust and unwise jealousy to deprive a man of his natural liberty upon a supposition that he may abuse it.
Oliver Cromwell (1599-1658)

Of what use is political liberty to those who have no bread? It is of value only to ambitious theorists and politicians.
Jean-Paul Marat (1743-1793)
French revolutionary

The condition upon which God hath given liberty to man is eternal vigilance.
John Philpot Curran (1750-1817)
Irish lawyer, politician

I see that you, too, put up monuments to your great dead.
anonymous Frenchman
arriving by sea in New York during Prohibition

SEE Gibbon on CORRUPTION; FREEDOM; Jefferson, Paine on PATRIOTISM; Wilkie on REPRESSION; Halifax on REVOLUTION

Libraries

Knowledge is of two kinds. We know a subject ourselves, or we know where we can find information upon it.
Dr Samuel Johnson (1709-1784)

A man should keep his little brain attic stocked with all the furniture that he is likely to use, and the rest he can put away in the lumber room of his library, where he can get it if he wants it.

Sir Arthur Conan Doyle (1859-1930)

The true University of these days is a collection of books.

Thomas Carlyle (1795-1881)
Scottish author

Every library should try to be complete on something, if it were only the history of pinheads.

Dr Oliver Wendell Holmes (1809-1894)
American writer, physician

My library was dukedom large enough.

Prospero, *The Tempest*
William Shakespeare (1564-1616)

Meek young men grow up in libraries.

R. W. Emerson (1803-1882)
American essayist, poet, philosopher

Life

Life. A spiritual pickle preserving the body from decay.

Ambrose Bierce (1842-1914)
American author

Life is a *mauvais quart d'heure* made up of exquisite moments.

Oscar Wilde (1854-1900)

The dreamcrossed twilight between birth and dying.

T. S. Eliot (1888-1965)

Life is an offensive, directed against the repetitious mechanisms of the universe.

A. N. Whitehead (1861-1947)
British philosopher

Life is the art of drawing sufficient conclusions from insufficient premises.

Samuel Butler (1835-1902)
English author

Life consists of what a man is thinking of all day.

R. W. Emerson (1803-1882)
American essayist, poet, philosopher

Mon métier et mon art c'est vivre.
Living is my profession and my art.

Michel de Montaigne (1533-1592)
French essayist

Either the soul is immortal and we shall not die, or it perishes with the flesh, and we shall not know then that we are dead. Live, then, as if you were eternal.

André Maurois (1885-1967)
French author

May you live all the days of your life.

Jonathan Swift (1667-1745)

There's night and day, brother, both sweet things; sun, moon, and stars, brother, all sweet things; there's likewise a wind on the heath. Life is very sweet, brother; who would wish to die?

George Borrow (1803-1881)
English author

Life is like playing a violin solo in public and learning the instrument as one goes on.

Samuel Butler (1835-1902)
English author

Life can only be understood backwards; but it must be lived forwards.

Sören Kierkegaard (1813-1855)
Danish philosopher

'Tis all a Chequer-board of Nights and
Days
Where Destiny with Men for Pieces
plays:
Hither and thither moves, and
mates and slays,
And one by one back in the Closest
lays.

from the *Rubáiyát of Omar Khayyám*
trans. Edward Fitzgerald (1809-1883)

As flies to wanton boys, are
we to the gods;
They kill us for their sport.

Gloucester, *King Lear*
William Shakespeare (1564-1616)

Life is a zoo in a jungle.

Peter de Vries (b. 1910)
American author

The meaning of life is that it stops.

Franz Kafka (1883-1924)

But there is good news yet to hear and
fine things to be seen
Before we go to Paradise by way of
Kensal Green.

G. K. Chesterton (1874-1936)

It is a tale
Told by an idiot, full of sound and fury;
Signifying nothing.

Macbeth, *Macbeth*
William Shakespeare (1564-1616)

Man that is born of woman hath but a short time to live, and is full of misery. He cometh up, and is cut down, like a flower; he fleeth as it were a shadow, and never continueth in one stay.

Book of Common Prayer

A useless life is an early death.

Johann Wolfgang von Goethe (1749-1832)

We should kick and struggle and determine to live as long as we can. For however long we live, we shall feel at the last that we have not got half the things into life that we ought to have done.

Benjamin Jowett (1817-1893)
English scholar, essayist

The force that through the green fuse
  drives the flower
Drives my green age; that blasts the
  roots of trees
Is my destroyer.

Dylan Thomas (1914-1953)

A physician can sometimes parry the scythe of death, but has no power over the sand in the hourglass.

Hester Piozzi (Mrs Thrale) (1741-1821)
English writer

The days of our years are threescore years and ten; and if by reason of strength they be fourscore years, yet is their strength labour and sorrow; for it is soon cut off, and we fly away.

Bible, Psalms

Droll thing life is – that mysterious arrangement of merciless logic for a futile purpose. The most you can hope from it is some knowledge of yourself – that comes too late – a crop of unextinguishable regrets.

Joseph Conrad (1857-1924)

Vivre est une maladie dont le sommeil nous soulage toutes les seize heures. C'est un palliatif. La mort est le remède.
Living is a sickness from which sleep provides relief every sixteen hours. It's a palliative. The remedy is death.

Nicolas-Sébastien Chamfort (1741-1794)
French writer, wit

When I hear somebody sigh that 'Life is hard', I am always tempted to ask, 'Compared to what?'

Sydney J. Harris (b. 1917)
American journalist

I should have no objection to a repetition of the same life from its beginning, only asking the advantages authors have in a second edition to correct some faults of the first.

Benjamin Franklin (1706-1790)

Is life worth living? This is a question for an embryo, not for a man.

Samuel Butler (1835-1902)
English author

Life is an end in itself, and the only question as to whether it is worth living is whether you have had enough of it.

Dr Oliver Wendell Holmes (1809-1894)
American writer, physician

SEE Chaplin on COMEDY;
Laforgue on ENNUI

Literature

Literature – the most seductive, the most deceiving, the most dangerous of professions.

John, Lord Morley (1838-1923)
English writer, Liberal politician

Literature is the effort of man to indemnify himself from the wrongs of his condition.

R. W. Emerson (1803-1882)
American essayist, poet, philosopher

Literature flourishes best when it is half a trade and half an art.

W. R. Inge (1860-1954)
Dean of St Paul's, London

Literature is the orchestration of platitudes.

Thornton Wilder (1897-1975)
American author

Great literature is simply language charged with meaning to the utmost possible degree.

Ezra Pound (1885-1972)

The cultivation of literary pursuits forms the basis of all sciences, and in their perfection consist the reputation and prosperity of kingdoms.

Marquês de Pombal (1699-1782)
Portuguese statesman

Literature is always a good card to play for Honours. It makes people think that Cabinet ministers are educated.

Arnold Bennett (1867-1931)

Our American professors like their literature clear and cold and pure and very dead.

Sinclair Lewis (1885-1951)
American novelist

All that is literature seeks to communicate power: all that is not literature, to communicate knowledge.

Thomas de Quincey (1785-1859)
English author

Literature . . . is the union of suffering with the instinct for form.

Thomas Mann (1875-1955)

All good books are alike in that they are truer than if they had really happened.

Ernest Hemingway (1899-1961).

Great literature must spring from an upheaval in the author's soul. If that upheaval is not present then it must come from the works of any other author which happens to be handy and easily adapted.

Robert Benchley (1889-1945)
American humorous writer

A classic is something that everybody wants to have read and nobody wants to read.

Mark Twain (1835-1910)

Speak of the moderns without contempt, and of the ancients without idolatry.
Lord Chesterfield (1694-1773)
English statesman and man of letters

SEE Goldsmith on HERO-WORSHIP; WRITERS; WRITING

Litigation

Come, agree, the law's costly.
Jonathan Swift (1667-1745)

To go to law and not be out of one's mind is scarcely granted to the saints.
St Francis de Sales (1567-1622)
French churchman, devotional writer
(patron saint of journalists)

I was never ruined but twice: once when I lost a lawsuit, and once when I won one.
Voltaire (1694-1778)

Keep out of Chancery... It's being ground to bits in a slow mill; it's being roasted at a slow fire; it's being stung to death by single bees; it's being drowned by drops; it's going mad by grains.
Tom Jarndyce, *Bleak House*
Charles Dickens (1812-1870)

Litigant. A person about to give up his skin for the hope of retaining his bones.
Ambrose Bierce (1842-1914)
American author

For certain people, after fifty, litigation takes the place of sex.
Gore Vidal (b.1925)

SEE TRIALS

Living Together

Do you think your mother and I should have lived comfortably so long together if ever we had been married? Baggage!
Peachum, *The Beggar's Opera*
John Gay (1685-1732)

Selfishness is not living as one wishes to live, it is asking others to live as one wishes to live.
Oscar Wilde (1854-1900)

It is better to dwell in a corner of the house-top than with a brawling woman in a wide house.
Bible, Proverbs

Logic

Walter Shandy attributed most of his son's misfortunes to the fact that at a highly critical moment his wife had asked him if he had wound the clock, a question so irrelevant that he despaired of the child's ever being able to pursue a logical train of thought.
Laurence Sterne (1713-1768)
English author

London

Dear damned distracting town.
Alexander Pope (1688-1744)

Behold now this vast city; a city of refuge, the mansion-house of liberty, encompassed and surrounded with His protection.
John Milton (1608-1674)

London, that great sea, whose ebb and flow
At once is deaf and loud.
P. B. Shelley (1792-1822)

That monstrous tuberosity of civilised life, the capital of England.
Thomas Carlyle (1795-1881)
Scottish author

Here falling houses thunder on your head,
And here a female atheist talks you dead.
Dr Samuel Johnson (1709-1784)

The worst place in the world for a good woman to grow better in.
Sir John Vanbrugh (1664-1726)
English playwright,
architect

London is a modern Babylon.
Benjamin Disraeli (1804-1881)

Hell is a city much like London –
A populous and a smoky city;
There are all sorts of people undone,
And there is little or no fun done;
Small justice shown, and still less pity.
P. B. Shelley (1792-1822)

London is a roost for every bird.
Benjamin Disraeli (1804-1881)

I have passed all my days in London, until I have formed as many and intense local attachments as any of you mountaineers can have done with dead nature. The lighted shops of the Strand and Fleet Street, the innumerable trades, tradesmen, and customers, coaches, waggons, playhouses, all the bustle and wickedness round about Covent Garden, the very women of the town, the watchmen, drunken scenes, rattles... I often shed tears in the motley Strand from fullness of joy at so much life.
Charles Lamb (1775-1834)
English essayist,
critic

Was für Plunder!
What rubbish!
Marshal Gebhard Blücher (1742-1819)
Prussian general
on first view of London

You find no man, at all intellectual, who is willing to leave London. No, Sir, when a man is tired of London, he is tired of life; for there is in London all that life can afford.
Dr Samuel Johnson (1709-1784)

A broken heart is a very pleasant complaint

for a man in London if he has a comfortable income.
> Ann, *Man and Superman*
> George Bernard Shaw (1856-1950)

It is strange with how little notice, good, bad or indifferent, a man may live and die in London.
> Charles Dickens (1812-1870)

Enfin, dans un amas de choses, sombre, immense,
Un peuple noir, vivant et mourant en silence.
Finally, within a huge and sombre mass of things, a blackened people, living and dying in silence.
> Henri Auguste Barbier (1805-1882)
> French poet

SEE CITY LIFE

Loneliness

Only in a house where one has learnt to be lonely does one have this solicitude for *things*. One's relation to them, the daily seeing or touching, begins to become love, and to lay one open to pain.
> Elizabeth Bowen (1899-1973)
> Anglo-Irish novelist

Loneliness is to endure the presence of one who does not understand.
> Elbert Hubbard (1856-1915)
> American author

Who knows what true loneliness is — not the conventional word but the naked terror? To the lonely themselves it wears a mask.
> Joseph Conrad (1857-1924)

Man's loneliness is but his fear of life.
> Eugene O'Neill (1888-1953)

SEE Thoreau on CITY LIFE;
Garland, Joplin on STARDOM;
Eliot on SUSPICION

Loquacity

They never taste who always drink;
They always talk who never think.
> Matthew Prior (1664-1721)
> English poet, diplomat

To talk without thinking is to shoot without aiming.
> 18th century English proverb

The habit of common and continuous speech is a symptom of mental deficiency. It proceeds from not knowing what is going on in other people's minds.
> Walter Bagehot (1826-1877)
> English economist, critic

The round-faced man in black entered, and dissipated all doubts on the subject, by beginning to talk. He did not cease while he stayed; nor has he since, that I know of.
> William Hazlitt (1778-1830)
> English essayist
> *of Coleridge*

He can compress the most words into the smallest ideas, of any man I ever met.
> Abraham Lincoln (1809-1865)

Half the world is composed of people who have something to say and can't, and the other half who have nothing to say and keep on saying it.
> Robert Frost (1874-1963)
> American poet

There are few wild beasts more to be dreaded than a talking man having nothing to say.
> Jonathan Swift (1667-1745)

I prefer tongue-tied knowledge to ignorant loquacity.
> Cicero (106-54 BC)

The only way to entertain some folks is to listen to them.
> Kin (F. McKinney) Hubbard (1868-1930)
> American humorist, journalist

SEE La Rochefoucauld on ANECDOTES;
Jonson on AGE: Old Age; Stevenson on
POLITICIANS; Smith on SILENCE

Losing

We are not interested in the possibilities of defeat.
> Queen Victoria (1819-1901)

Victory has a hundred fathers but defeat is an orphan.
> Galeazzo Ciano (1903-1944)
> Italian Fascist leader

We have resolved to endure the unendurable and suffer what is unsufferable.
> Emperor Hirohito of Japan (b. 1901)
> *following the dropping of the*
> *atomic bomb on Hiroshima*

One of the first businesses of a sensible man is to know when he is beaten, and to leave off fighting at once.
> Samuel Butler (1835-1902)
> English author

What makes us so bitter against people who outwit us is that they think themselves cleverer than we are.
> François, Duc de La Rochefoucauld (1613-1680)
> French writer, moralist

Show me a good loser and I will show you a loser.
> Paul Newman (b. 1925)

Love

O lyric Love, half angel and half bird
And all a wonder and a wild desire.
> Robert Browning (1812-1889)

What a recreation it is to be in love! It sets the heart aching so delicately, there's no taking a wink of sleep for the pleasure of the pain.
George Colman the Younger (1762-1836)
English dramatist

All the little emptiness of love!
Rupert Brooke (1887-1915)
British poet

True love is like ghosts, which everyone talks about and few have seen.
François, Duc de La Rochefoucauld (1613-1680)
French writer, moralist

Whoso loves believes the impossible.
Elizabeth Barrett Browning (1806-1861)

When one is in love one begins to deceive oneself.
And one ends by deceiving others.
Oscar Wilde (1854-1900)

Love is too young to know what conscience is.
William Shakespeare (1564-1616)

There is no fear in love; but perfect love casteth out fear.
Saint John (1st century AD)

Many people when they fall in love look for a little haven of refuge from the world, where they can be sure of being admired when they are not admirable, and praised when they are not praiseworthy.
Bertrand Russell (1872-1970)

Love is a gross exaggeration of the difference between one person and everybody else.
George Bernard Shaw (1856-1950)

Love is the wisdom of the fool and the folly of the wise.
Dr Samuel Johnson (1709-1784)

People who are not in love fail to understand how an intelligent man can suffer because of a very ordinary woman. This is like being surprised that anyone should be stricken with cholera because of a creature so insignificant as the comma bacillus.
Marcel Proust (1871-1922)

Love is a disease which fills you with a desire to be desired.
Henri, Comte de Toulouse-Lautrec (1864-1901)

Love's like the measles – all the worse when it comes late in life.
Douglas Jerrold (1803-1857)
English playwright, humorist

Stay me with flagons, comfort me with apples, for I am sick of love.
Bible, Song of Solomon

How sad and bad and mad it was –
But then, how it was sweet!
Robert Browning (1812-1889)

It is best to love wisely, no doubt; but to love foolishly is better than not to be able to love at all.
W. M. Thackeray (1811-1863)
English author

To say the truth, reason and love keep little company together now-a-days.
Bottom, A Midsummer Night's Dream
William Shakespeare (1564-1616)

Love is not really blind – the bandage is never so tight but that it can peep.
Elbert Hubbard (1856-1915)
American author

Love is not blind; that is the last thing it is. Love is bound; and the more it is bound the less it is blind.
G. K. Chesterton (1874-1936)

Take me to you, imprison me. For I,
Except you enthrall me, never shall be free,
Nor ever chaste, except you ravish me.
John Donne (c. 1571-1631)

Love seeks not to possess, but to be possessed.
R. H. Benson (1871-1914)
British novelist

If there's delight in love, 'tis when I see
That heart, which others bleed for, bleed for me.
William Congreve (1670-1729)
English dramatist

Do you want to enjoy her love, or do you want to dominate it?
John Drinkwater (1882-1937)
British author

Love doesn't grow on the trees like apples in Eden – it's something you have to make. And you must use your imagination to make it too, just like anything else. It's all work, work.
Joyce Cary (1888-1957)
British novelist

Much more genius is needed to make love than to command armies.
Ninon de Lenclos (1620-1705)
French society lady and wit

When first we met we did not guess
That Love would prove so hard a master.
Robert Bridges (1844-1930)
British poet

The course of true love never did run smooth.
Lysander, A Midsummer Night's Dream
William Shakespeare (1564-1616)

Never the time and the place and the loved one all together!
Robert Browning (1812-1889)

A thick head can do as much damage as a hard heart.

> H. W. Dodds (1889-1980)
> President, Princeton University

Every theory of love, from Plato down, teaches that each individual loves in the other sex what he lacks in himself.

> G. Stanley Hall (1844-1924)
> American psychologist, philosopher, educator

En amour il y a toujours quelqu'un qui embrasse et quelqu'un qui offre sa joue.
In love, there is always one who kisses and one who offers the cheek.

> French proverb

We are nearer loving those who hate us than those who love us more than we wish.

> François, Duc de La Rochefoucauld (1613-1680)
> French writer, moralist

The fickleness of the women I love is only equalled by the infernal constancy of the women who love me.

> Charteris, *The Philanderer*
> George Bernard Shaw (1856-1950)

I love her and she loves me, and we hate each other with a wild hatred born of love.

> J. A. Strindberg (1849-1912)

The more one loves a mistress, the more one is ready to hate her.

> François, Duc de La Rochefoucauld (1613-1680)
> French writer, moralist

> If she herself will not love,
> Nothing can make her:
> The devil take her!
> > Sir John Suckling (1609-1642)
> > English poet

> And I shall find some girl perhaps,
> And a better one than you,
> With eyes as wise, but kindlier,
> And lips as soft, but true,
> And I daresay she will do.
> > Rupert Brooke (1887-1915)
> > British poet

Men have died from time to time, and worms have eaten them, but not for love.

> Rosalind, *As You Like It*
> William Shakespeare (1564-1616)

When love grows diseas'd, the best thing we can do is to put it to a violent death; I cannot endure the torture of a ling'ring and consumptive passion.

> Sir George Etherege (1635-1691)
> English dramatist, diplomat

Love never dies of starvation, but often of indigestion.

> Ninon de Lenclos (1620-1705)
> French society lady and wit

Love is like linen, often changed, the sweeter.

> Phineas Fletcher (1582-1650)
> English poet

It is better to love two too many than one too few.

> Sir John Harington (1561-1612)
> English writer, courtier

One can find women who have never had one love affair, but it is rare indeed to find any who have had only one.

> François, Duc de La Rochefoucauld (1613-1680)
> French writer, moralist

Women fall in love through their ears and men through their eyes.

> Woodrow Wyatt (b. 1918)
> British journalist, Labour politician

In women pity begets love, in men love begets pity.

> J. Churton Collins (1848-1908)
> British author, critic, scholar

Love is the history of a woman's life; it is an episode in man's.

> Madame de Staël (1766-1817)
> French writer, wit

Falling in love is a matter of intermittent propinquity; the cure for it, propinquity.

> Elbert Hubbard (1856-1915)
> American author

Familiar acts are beautiful through love.

> P. B. Shelley (1792-1822)

Love does not consist in gazing at each other but in looking together in the same direction.

> Antoine de Saint-Exupéry (1900-1944)
> French aviator, writer

One of the glories of society is to have created woman where Nature made a female, to have created a continuity of desire where Nature only thought of perpetuating the species; *in fine*, to have invented love.

> George Moore (1852-1933)
> Irish author

A new commandment I give unto you, that ye love one another.

> Jesus (4 BC-AD 29)

Love: First Love First love is only a little foolishness and a lot of curiosity.

> Broadbent, *John Bull's Other Island*
> George Bernard Shaw (1856-1950)

The magic of first love is our ignorance that it can ever end.

> Benjamin Disraeli (1804-1881)

We always believe our first love is our last, and our last love our first.

> George Whyte-Melville (1821-1878)
> Scottish author

In her first passion woman loves her
lover,
In all the others all she loves is
love.
Lord Byron (1788-1824)

Love: At First Sight
I did but see her passing by
And yet I love her till I die.
Thomas Ford (1580-1648)
English composer

Where both deliberate, the love is slight:
Who ever lov'd, that lov'd not at first
sight?
Christopher Marlowe (1564-1593)

The only true love is love at first sight; second
sight dispels it.
Israel Zangwill (1864-1926)
British author

SEE Marvell on DEATH; Wilde on
FIDELITY; Shaw on FOOD; Unamuno
on HAPPINESS; HEARTBREAK; Bible
on JEALOUSY; LOVERS; Baudelaire,
Coleridge, Collins, Maupassant,
Russell, Swift, Wycherley on MARRIAGE;
Goldsmith on PASSION; Etherege on
PROMISES; Pascal on REASON; France on
RELIGION; Antiphanes on SECRETS;
Donne, Gauguin, Perelman on SEX; Walsh on
SUICIDE

Lovers
And the lovers lie abed with all their griefs in
their arms.
Dylan Thomas (1914-1953)

Imparadised in one another's arms.
John Milton (1608-1674)

Busy old fool, unruly Sun,
Why dost thou thus,
Through windows and through curtains
call on us?
Must to thy motions lovers' seasons
run?
John Donne (c. 1571-1631)

We that are true lovers run into strange
capers.
Touchstone, As You Like It
William Shakespeare (1564-1616)

A lover is someone who gives as much
consideration to your warts as you do, and
continues to admire you as you do. Many love
affairs are simply servings of self-pity for two.
Alan Brien (b. 1925)
British novelist, journalist

Every man wants a woman to appeal to his
better side, his nobler instincts and his higher
nature – and another woman to help him
forget them.
Helen Rowland (1875-1950)
American journalist

A mistress should be like a little country
retreat near the town; not to dwell in
constantly, but only for a night and away.
William Wycherley (1640-1716)
English dramatist

One can be a soldier without dying, and a
lover without sighing.
Edwin Arnold (1832-1904)
British poet

I would not miss your face, your neck, your
hands, your limbs, your bosom and certain
other of your charms. Indeed, not to become
boring by naming them all, I could do without
you, Chloe, altogether.
Martial (43-104)

Nay but you, who do not love her,
Is she not pure gold, my mistress?
Robert Browning (1812-1889)

Age cannot wither her, not custom stale
Her infinite variety. Other women cloy
The appetites they feed, but she makes
hungry
Where most she satisfies.
Enobarbus, Antony and Cleopatra
William Shakespeare (1564-1616)

When Death to either shall come,
– I pray it be first to me.
Robert Bridges (1844-1930)
British poet

Love ceases to be a pleasure when it ceases to
be a secret.
Aphra Behn (1640-1689)
English playwright, poet

A lover without indiscretion is no lover at all.
Thomas Hardy (1840-1928)

Amantium irae amoris integratio est.
Lovers' quarrels are the renewal of love.
Terence (c. 190-159 BC)
Roman dramatist

The difference is wide that the sheets will not
decide.
Proverb

At the beginning of love and at its end, lovers
are embarrassed if left alone.
Jean de la Bruyère (1656-1696)
French writer, moralist

There are few people who are not ashamed of
their love affairs when the infatuation is over.
François, Duc de La Rochefoucauld (1613-1680)
French writer, moralist

Scratch a lover and find a foe.
Dorothy Parker (1893-1967)
American humorous writer

Queen Guinevere, for whom I make here a
little mention, that while she lived she was a
true lover, and therefore she had a good end.
Sir Thomas Malory (c. 1430-1471)

SEE Moore on HUSBANDS; Catullus on PROMISES

Loyalty

If you are not too long, I will wait for you all my life.

Oscar Wilde (1854-1900)

Intreat me not to leave thee, or to return from following after thee: for whither thou goest, I will go; and where thou lodgest, I will lodge: thy people shall be my people, and thy God my God.

Bible, Ruth

Histories are more full of examples of the fidelity of dogs than of friends.

Alexander Pope (1688-1744)

To be sure, the dog is loyal. But why, on that account, should we take him as an example? He is loyal to men, not to other dogs.

Karl Kraus (1874-1936)
Austrian poet, journalist

There are two kinds of fidelity, that of dogs and that of cats: you, gentlemen, have the fidelity of cats, who never leave the house.

Napoleon Bonaparte (1769-1821)
speaking after he had escaped from Elba, to French courtiers who had not followed him there

We are all the President's men.

Henry Kissinger (b. 1923)
after invasion of Cambodia, 1970

No man can serve two masters.

Jesus (4 BC-AD 29)

SEE FIDELITY; Queen Elizabeth I on ROYALTY

Luck

now and then
there is a person born
who is so unlucky
. that he runs into accidents
which started out to happen
to somebody else.

Don Marquis (1878-1937)
American humorist, journalist

La Fortune a toujours tort.
Luck's always to blame.

Jean de la Fontaine (1621-1695)
French poet, fabulist

It often amuses me to hear men impute all their misfortunes to fate, luck, or destiny, whilst their successes or good fortune they ascribe to their own sagacity, cleverness or penetration.

S. T. Coleridge (1772-1834)

Chance is a word that does not make sense. Nothing happens without a cause.

Voltaire (1694-1778)

Chance is perhaps the pseudonym of God when he does not wish to sign his work.

Anatole France (1844-1924)
French author

When God throws the dice are loaded.

Greek proverb

Fortune's a right whore: If she give ought, she deals it in small parcels, that she may take away all at one swoop.

John Webster (1580-1625)
English dramatist

If at first you do succeed, don't take any more chances.

Kin (F. McKinney) Hubbard (1868-1930)
American humorist, journalist

Watch out when you're getting all you want; fattening frogs ain't in luck.

Joel Chandler Harris (1848-1908)
American author

There is death in the pot.

Bible, Kings

Lust

Abstinence sows sand all over
The ruddy limbs and flaming hair,
But desire gratified
Plants fruits of life and beauty there.

William Blake (1757-1827)

The trouble with life is that there are so many beautiful women and so little time.

John Barrymore (1882-1942)
American actor

This is the monstruosity in love, lady, that the will is infinite and the execution confined; that the desire is boundless, and the act a slave to limit.

Troilus, *Troilus and Cressida*
William Shakespeare (1564-1616)

He is every woman's man and every man's woman.

Gaius Scribonius Curio (d. 53 BC)
Roman consul
of Julius Caesar

What most men desire is a virgin who is a whore.

Edward Dahlberg (b. 1900)
American author

People will insist ... on treating the *mons Veneris* as though it were Mount Everest.

Aldous Huxley (1894-1963)

Down, wanton, down! Have you no shame
That at the whisper of Love's name,
Or Beauty's, presto! up you raise
Your angry head and stand and gaze?

Robert Graves (1895-1985)
British poet, novelist

We have two tyrannous physical passions;
concupiscence and chastity. We become mad
in pursuit of sex: we become equally mad in
the persecution of that pursuit.
George Bernard Shaw (1856-1950)

Luxury

Give us the luxuries of life, and we will
dispense with its necessities.
J. L. Motley (1814-1877)
American historian

The lust for comfort, that stealthy thing that
enters the house a guest, and then becomes a
host, and then a master.
Kahlil Gibran (1883-1931)
Syrian mystic, poet

The saddest thing I can imagine is to get used
to luxury.
Charlie Chaplin (1889-1977)

Living in the lap of luxury isn't bad, except
you never know when luxury is going to stand
up.
Orson Welles (1915-1985)

Lying

A little inaccuracy sometimes saves tons of
explanation.
Saki (H.H. Munro) (1870-1916)
Scottish author

And, after all, what is a lie? 'Tis but
The truth in masquerade.
Lord Byron (1788-1824)

Oh what a tangled web we weave
When first we practise to deceive!
Sir Walter Scott (1771-1832)

Most lies are quite successful, and human
society would be impossible without a great
deal of good-natured lying.
George Bernard Shaw (1856-1950)

The silent colossal National Lie that is the
support and confederate of all the tyrannies
and shams and inequalities and unfairnesses
that afflict the peoples – that is the one to
throw bricks and sermons at.
Mark Twain (1835-1910)

The great mass of people . . . will more easily
fall victim to a big lie than to a small one.
Adolf Hitler (1889-1945)

No man spreads a lie with so good a grace as
he that believes it.
John Arbuthnot (1667-1735)
Scottish writer, physician

No man lies so boldly as the man who is
indignant.
Friedrich Nietzsche (1844-1900)

Women lie about their age; men about their
income.
William Feather (b. 1889)
American businessman

When I make a mistake every one can see it,
but not when I lie.
Johann Wolfgang von Goethe (1749-1832)

Husband a lie, and trump it up in some
extraordinary emergency.
Joseph Addison (1672-1719)
English essayist

Good lies need a leavening of truth to make
them palatable.
William McIlvanney (b. 1936)
British novelist

The best liar is he who makes the smallest
amount of lying go the longest way.
Samuel Butler (1835-1902)
English author

He did not stand shivering upon the brink, he
was a thorough-paced liar, and plunged at
once into the depths of your credulity.
Charles Lamb (1775-1834)
English essayist, critic

I do not mind lying, but I hate inaccuracy.
Samuel Butler (1835-1902)
English author

The cruellest lies are often told in silence.
Robert Louis Stevenson (1850-1894)

If you are going to lie, you go to jail for the lie
rather than the crime. So believe me, don't
ever lie.
Richard Nixon (b. 1913)
to John Dean III, due to testify
before Watergate Committee, April 1973

A lie will easily get you out of a scrape, and
yet, strangely and beautifully, rapture possesses
you when you have taken the scrape and left
out the lie.
C. E. Montague (1867-1928)
British author, journalist

He will lie even when it is inconvenient, the
sign of the true artist.
Gore Vidal (b. 1925)

It is hard to believe that a man is telling the
truth when you know that you would lie if
you were in his place.
H. L. Mencken (1880-1956)
American journalist

The liar's punishment is not in the least that
he is not believed, but that he cannot believe
anyone else.
George Bernard Shaw (1856-1950)

SEE Shakespeare on AGE: Old Age;
Halifax on EXCUSES; Gay on
MEN AND WOMEN; Byron on POETS;
Carlyle on POLITICIANS; Lichtenberg
on PROPAGANDA; Hoffer on
SELF-DECEPTION; Disraeli on
STATISTICS; Blake on TRUTH;
Nietzsche on VISIONARIES; Hubbard on WIVES

Machinery

From coupler-flange to spindle-guide I
see Thy Hand, O God –
Predestination in the stride o' yon
connectin'-rod.
Rudyard Kipling (1865-1936)

The machine does not isolate man from the
great problems of nature but plunges him
more deeply into them.
Antoine de Saint-Exupéry (1900-1944)
French aviator, writer

Machines are worshipped because they are
beautiful and valued because they confer
power; they are hated because they are
hideous and loathed because they impose
slavery.
Bertrand Russell (1872-1970)

Ever since our love for machines replaced the
love we used to have for our fellow men,
catastrophes proceed to increase.
Man Ray (1890-1976)
French photographer

Men have become the tools of their tools.
H. D. Thoreau (1817-1862)

SEE TECHNOLOGY

Madness

Babylon in all its desolation is a sight not so
awful as that of the human mind in ruins.
Scrope Berdmore Davies (1783-1852)

The mind is its own place, and in itself
Can make a Heaven of Hell, a Hell of
Heaven.
John Milton (1608-1674)

Insanity is often the logic of an accurate mind
overtaxed.
Dr Oliver Wendell Holmes (1809-1894)
American writer, physician

It is his reasonable conversation which mostly
frightens us in a madman.
Anatole France (1844-1924)
French author

We must remember that every 'mental' symptom is a veiled cry of anguish. Against what?
Against oppression, or what the patient exper-

iences as oppression. The oppressed speak a
million tongues. . . .
Thomas Szasz (b. 1920)
American psychiatrist

Schizophrenic behaviour is a special strategy
that a person invents in order to live in an
unlivable situation.
R. D. Laing (b. 1927)
British psychiatrist

Schizophrenia is the name for a condition that
most psychiatrists ascribe to patients they call
schizophrenic.
R. D. Laing (b. 1927)
British psychiatrist

In the past, men created witches: now they
create mental patients.
Thomas Szasz (b. 1920)
American psychiatrist

If a patient is poor he is committed to a public
hospital as a 'psychotic'. If he can afford a
sanatorium, the diagnosis is 'neurasthenia'. If
he is wealthy enough to be in his own home
under the constant watch of nurses and physicians, he is simply 'an indisposed eccentric'.
Pierre Janet (1859-1947)
French physician, psychologist

SEE Shakespeare on POWER; Bagehot on
ROYALTY

Make-up

God hath given you one face, and you make
yourselves another.
Hamlet, Hamlet
William Shakespeare (1564-1616)

Most women are not so young as they are
painted.
Sir Max Beerbohm (1872-1956)
British author

I always wear boot polish on my eyelashes,
because I am a very emotional person and it
doesn't run when I cry.
Barbara Cartland (b. 1901)
British novelist

[Be it resolved] that all women, of whatever
age, rank, profession, or degree; whether

virgin maids or widows; that shall after the passing of this Act, impose upon and betray into matrimony any of His Majesty's male subjects, by scents, paints, cosmetics, washes, artificial teeth, false hair, Spanish wool, iron stays, hoops, high-heeled shoes, or bolstered hips, shall incur the penalty of the laws now in force against witchcraft, sorcery, and such like misdemeanours, and that the marriage, upon conviction, shall stand null and void.
Act of Parliament, 1670

SEE Holmes on FACES

Management

A man is known by the company he organizes.
Ambrose Bierce (1842-1914)
American author

The ability to deal with people is as purchasable a commodity as sugar or coffee. And I pay more for that ability than for any other under the sun.
John D. Rockefeller (1839-1937)
American industrialist,
philanthropist

The trouble with senior management to an outsider is that there are too many one-ulcer men holding down two-ulcer men's jobs.
Duke of Edinburgh (b. 1921)

The great requisite for the prosperous management of ordinary business is the want of imagination.
William Hazlitt (1778-1830)
English essayist

The eye of a master will do more work than both his hands.
Benjamin Franklin (1706-1790)

The good governor should have a broken leg and keep at home.
Miguel de Cervantes (1547-1616)

I always suspect a director who says he can afford to be away from the office only for a week at a time. This generally means either that he is a frightened man or else he is thoroughly inefficient and incapable of delegation.
Sir Robert Powell (b. 1909)
British businessman, civil servant

Executive ability is deciding quickly and getting somebody else to do the work.
J. G. Pollock (1871-1937)

I won't keep a dog and bark myself.
Jonathan Swift (1667-1745)

Let us have patience with our inferiors. They are ourselves of yesterday.
Isaac Goldberg (1887-1938)
American critic

There is something rarer than ability. It is the ability to recognise ability.
Elbert Hubbard (1856-1915)
American author

Lots of folks confuse bad management with destiny.
Kin (F. McKinney) Hubbard (1868-1930)
American humorist, journalist

I am a young executive.
No cuffs than mine are cleaner;
I have a Slimline brief-case
and I use the firm's Cortina.
John Betjeman (1906-1984)
British poet

SEE BUSINESS; Frost, Russell on WORK; Giraudoux on The WORKING CLASS

Mañana

Procrastination is the art of keeping up with yesterday.
Don Marquis (1878-1937)
American humorist, journalist

Procrastination is the thief of time.
Edward Young (1683-1765)
English poet

Don't put off till tomorrow what can be enjoyed today.
Josh Billings (1818-1885)
American humorist

SEE Wells on REFORM

Manners

I don't recall your name but your manners are familiar.
Oliver Herford (1863-1935)
American poet, illustrator

Good manners are made up of petty sacrifices.
R. W. Emerson (1803-1882)
American essayist, poet,
philosopher

Unruly manners or ill-timed applause
Wrong the best speaker or the justest cause.
Alexander Pope (1688-1744)

Good breeding consists in concealing how much we think of ourselves and how little we think of the other person.
Mark Twain (1835-1910)

The society of women is the foundation of good manners.
Johann Wolfgang von Goethe (1749-1832)

Manhood is melted into courtesies, valour into compliment, and men are only turned into tongue.
Beatrice, Much Ado About Nothing
William Shakespeare (1564-1616)

If a person has no delicacy, he has you in his power.
> William Hazlitt (1778-1830)
> English essayist

I have always been of the mind that in a democracy manners are the only effective weapons against the bowie-knife.
> J. R. Lowell (1819-1891)
> American poet, editor

The highest perfection of politeness is only a beautiful edifice, built, from the base to the dome, of ungraceful and gilded forms of charitable and unselfish lying.
> Mark Twain (1835-1910)

SEE James on ARISTOCRACY; COURTESY; Perelman on The ENGLISH; Chesterfield on INTIMACY; TACT

Marketing

You can automate the production of cars but you cannot automate the production of customers.
> Walter Reuther (1907-1970)
> American trade union leader

Marriage

For this cause shall a man leave his father and mother, and shall be joined unto his wife, and they two shall be one flesh.
> Saint Paul (3-67)

The marriage state, with and without the affection suitable to it, is the completest image of Heaven and Hell we are capable of receiving in this life.
> Sir Richard Steele (1672-1729)
> English essayist, dramatist, editor

By all means marry: if you get a good wife you'll become happy; if you get a bad one, you'll become a philosopher.
> Socrates (469-399 BC)

One was never married, and that's his hell; another is, and that's his plague.
> Robert Burton (1577-1640)
> English clergyman, author

It is like a cage; one sees the birds outside desperate to get in, and those inside equally desperate to get out.
> Michel de Montaigne (1533-1592)
> French essayist

There is, indeed, nothing that so much seduces reason from vigilance, as the thought of passing life with an amiable woman.
> Dr Samuel Johnson (1709-1784)

Marriage is a great institution, but I'm not ready for an institution yet.
> Mae West (1892-1980)

Marriage is popular because it combines the maximum of temptation with the maximum of opportunity.
> George Bernard Shaw (1856-1950)

Be not hasty to marry; it's better to have one plough going than two cradles; and more profit to have a barn filled than a bed.
> Thomas Fuller (1608-1661)
> English cleric

Marriage. The state or condition of a community consisting of a master, a mistress and two slaves, making in all, two.
> Ambrose Bierce (1842-1914)
> American author

I would rather be a beggar and single than a queen and married.
> Queen Elizabeth I of England (1533-1603)

I gravely doubt whether women ever were married by capture. I think they pretended to be; as they still do.
> G. K. Chesterton (1874-1936)

It is always incomprehensible to a man that a woman should ever refuse an offer of marriage.
> Jane Austen (1775-1817)

Alas, she married another. They frequently do. I hope she is happy – because I am.
> Artemus Ward (1834-1867)
> American journalist

Marriage is the only adventure open to the cowardly.
> Voltaire (1694-1778)

The greatest sacrifice in marriage is the sacrifice of the adventurous attitude towards life.
> George Bernard Shaw (1856-1950)

You, that are going to be married, think things can never be done too fast; but we, that are old, and know what we are about, must elope methodically, madam.
> Oliver Goldsmith (1728-1774)

I am not against hasty marriages, where a mutual flame is fanned by an adequate income.
> Wilkie Collins (1824-1889)
> English novelist

To church the parties went,
At once with carnal and devout intent.
> Alexander Pope (1688-1744)

Let us embrace, and from this very moment vow an eternal misery together.
> Thomas Otway (1652-1685)
> English dramatist

The world must be peopled. When I said I would die a bachelor, I did not think I should live till I were married.
> Benedick, *Much Ado About Nothing*
> William Shakespeare (1564-1616)

When a man marries, dies, or turns Hindoo, his best friends hear no more of him.
P. B. Shelley (1792-1822)

In marriage, a man becomes slack and selfish, and undergoes a fatty degeneration of his moral being.
Robert Louis Stevenson (1850-1894)

When a girl marries she exchanges the attentions of many men for the inattention of one.
Helen Rowland (1875-1950)
American journalist

Many a man in love with a dimple makes the mistake of marrying the whole girl.
Stephen Leacock (1869-1944)
Canadian humorist and economist

When the blind leads the blind, no wonder they both fall into matrimony.
George Farquhar (1678-1707)
Irish dramatist

The deep, deep bliss of the double bed after the hurly-burly of the chaise longue.
Mrs Patrick Campbell (1865-1940)
British actress

They flaunt their conjugal felicity in one's face, as if it were the most fascinating of sins.
Oscar Wilde (1854-1900)

Marriage is a ghastly public confession of a strictly private intention.
Ian Hay (1876-1952)
British author

Marriage is like a dull meal with the dessert at the beginning.
Henri, Comte de Toulouse-Lautrec (1864-1901)

'Tis safest in matrimony to begin with a little aversion.
R. B. Sheridan (1751-1816)

It doesn't much signify whom one marries, for one is sure to find next morning that it was someone else.
Samuel Rogers (1763-1855)
English poet

They dream in courtship, but in wedlock wake.
Alexander Pope (1688-1744)

Before marriage, a man will lie awake thinking about something you said; after marriage, he'll fall asleep before you finish saying it.
Helen Rowland (1875-1950)
American journalist

There is a lot to get used to in the first year of marriage. One wakes up in the morning and finds a pair of pigtails on the pillow that were not there before.
Martin Luther (1483-1546)

The critical period in matrimony is breakfast-time.
A. P. Herbert (1890-1971)
British author, politician

The most difficult year of marriage is the one you're in.
Franklin P. Jones

A man who marries a woman to educate her falls into the same fallacy as the woman who marries a man to reform him.
Elbert Hubbard (1856-1915)
American author

Marrying to increase love is like gaming to become rich; you only lose what little stock you had before.
William Wycherley (1640-1716)
English dramatist

Marriage is law, and love is instinct.
Guy de Maupassant (1850-1893)

Though women are angels, yet wedlock's the devil.
Lord Byron (1788-1824)

Venus, a beautiful, good-natured lady, was the goddess of love; Juno, a terrible shrew, the goddess of marriage: and they were always mortal enemies.
Jonathan Swift (1667-1745)

Being unable to abolish love, the Church has decided at least to disinfect it, and has invented marriage.
Charles Baudelaire (1821-1867)

Love as a relation between men and women was ruined by the desire to make sure of the legitimacy of children.
Bertrand Russell (1872-1970)

Marriage has no *natural* relation to love. Marriage belongs to society; it is a social contract.
S. T. Coleridge (1772-1834)

The chain of wedlock is so heavy that it takes two to carry it, sometimes three.
Alexandre Dumas (1803-1870)

There can only be one end to marriage without love, and that is love without marriage.
J. Churton Collins (1848-1908)
British author, critic, scholar

Keep your eyes wide open before marriage, and half-shut afterwards.
Benjamin Franklin (1706-1790)

Marriage always demands the greatest understanding of the art of insincerity possible between two human beings.
Vicki Baum (1888-1960)
American writer

Every time a woman makes herself laugh at

her husband's often-told jokes she betrays him. The man who looks at his woman and says 'What would I do without you?' is already destroyed.

Germaine Greer (b. 1939)
Australian feminist writer

The amount of women in London who flirt with their own husbands is perfectly scandalous. It looks so bad. It is simply washing one's clean linen in public.

Oscar Wilde (1854-1900)

Once you are married, there is nothing for you, not even suicide, but to be good.

Robert Louis Stevenson (1850-1894)

After a few years of marriage a man can look right at a woman without seeing her and a woman can see right through a man without looking at him.

Helen Rowland (1875-1950)
American journalist

Twenty years of romance make a woman look like a ruin, but twenty years of marriage make her something like a public building.

Oscar Wilde (1854-1900)

Without love, hatred, joy, or fear,
They led – a kind of – as it were:
Nor wish'd, nor car'd, nor laugh'd, nor cried:
And so they liv'd, and so they died.

Matthew Prior (1664-1721)
English poet, diplomat

In my conscience I believe the baggage loves me, for she never speaks well of me herself, nor suffers any body else to rail at me.

William Congreve (1670-1729)
English dramatist

A successful marriage is an edifice that must be rebuilt every day.

André Maurois (1885-1967)
French writer

A marriage is likely to be called happy if neither party ever expected to get much happiness out of it.

Bertrand Russell (1872-1970)

Whenever a husband and wife begin to discuss their marriage, they are giving evidence at an inquest.

H. L. Mencken (1880-1956)
American journalist

Marriage is one long conversation, chequered by disputes.

Robert Louis Stevenson (1850-1894)

A wise woman will always let her husband have her way.

R. B. Sheridan (1751-1816)

One fool at least in every married couple.

Henry Fielding (1707-1754)

Incompatibility. In matrimony a similarity of tastes, particularly the taste for domination.

Ambrose Bierce (1842-1914)
American author

The calmest husbands make the stormiest wives.

Isaac d'Israeli (1766-1848)
English man of letters,
father of Benjamin Disraeli

Marriages not infrequently break up because the more compliant partner eventually feels compelled to re-assert his or her lost, separate identity.

Anthony Storr (b. 1920)
British psychiatrist

It is not marriage that fails; it is the people that fail. All that marriage does is to show people up.

H. E. Fosdick (1878-1969)
American Baptist minister

A good marriage is at least 80 per cent good luck in finding the right person at the right time. The rest is trust.

Nanette Newman (b. 1934)
British actress

Only one marriage I regret. I remember after I got that marriage licence I went across from the marriage bureau to a bar for a drink. The bartender said, 'What will you have, sir?' And I said, 'A glass of hemlock'.

Ernest Hemingway (1899-1961)

I've been married once on the level, and twice in America.

Texas Guinan (188?-1934)
Canadian entertainer

The plural of spouse is spice.

Christopher Morley (1890-1957)
American novelist, journalist

Wen you're a married man, Samivel, you'll understand a good many things as you don't understand now; but vether it's worth goin' through so much, to learn so little, as the charity-boy said ven he got to the end of the alphabet, is a matter of taste.

Mr Weller, The Pickwick Papers
Charles Dickens (1812-1870)

Marriage has many pains, but celibacy has no pleasures.

Dr Samuel Johnson (1709-1784)

Even if we take matrimony at its lowest, even if we regard it as no more than a sort of friendship recognised by the police.

Robert Louis Stevenson (1850-1894)

Marriage develops a binocular view of life, both masculine and feminine.

Dr William Brown (1881-1962)

Marriage is an act of will that signifies and

involves a mutual gift, which unites the spouses and binds them to their eventual souls, with whom they make up a sole family – a domestic church.
Pope John Paul II (b. 1920)

The value of marriage is not that adults produce children, but that children produce adults.
Peter de Vries (b. 1910)
American writer

SEE Molière on BOOKS; DIVORCE; HUSBANDS; Goldsmith on PASSION; Shaw on VIRTUE; WIVES; Keats on WOMEN

Martyrdom

If a man hasn't discovered something that he will die for, he isn't fit to live.
Martin Luther King (1929-1968)

Man is ready to die for an idea, provided that idea is not quite clear to him.
Paul Eldridge (b. 1888)
American writer

It is the cause, not the death, that makes the martyr.
Napoleon Bonaparte (1769-1821)

A cause may be inconvenient, but it's magnificent. It's like champagne or high shoes, and one must be prepared to suffer for it.
Arnold Bennett (1867-1931)

What signify a few lives lost in a century or two? The tree of liberty must be refreshed from time to time with the blood of patriots and tyrants. It is its natural manure.
Thomas Jefferson (1743-1826)

I don't mind martyrdom for a policy in which I believe, but I object to being burnt for someone else's principles.
John Galsworthy (1867-1933)

There have been quite as many martyrs for bad causes as for good ones.
Hendrik Van Loon (1882-1944)
American journalist, historian

I am very fond of truth, but not at all of martyrdom.
Voltaire (1694-1778)

Martyrdom is an unnecessary complication to a first-rate mind.
Stephen Winsten (fl. 1946-1951)

The tyrant dies and his rule is over; the martyr dies and his rule begins.
Sören Kierkegaard (1813-1855)
Danish philosopher

It is well for his peace that the saint goes to his martyrdom. He is spared the sight of the horror of his harvest.
Oscar Wilde (1854-1900)

The torments of martyrdom are probably most keenly felt by the bystanders.
R. W. Emerson (1803-1882)
American essayist, poet, philosopher

Play the man, Master Ridley; we shall this day light such a candle, by God's grace, in England, as I trust shall never be put out.
Bishop Hugh Latimer (1485-1555)
English churchman, Protestant martyr
at his execution pyre

In a few minutes I am going out to shape all the singing tomorrows.
Gabriel Péri
French Communist leader
before his execution by the
Germans, 1942

But whether on the scaffold high,
Or in the battle's van;
The fittest place where man can die
Is where he dies for man.
Michael J. Barry (fl. 1845-1886)

Precious in the sight of the Lord is the death of his saints.
Bible, Psalms

A thing is not necessarily true because a man dies for it.
Oscar Wilde (1854-1900)

SEE Barker on The AFTER-LIFE; Dryden on CONFORMITY; Ewer on FREEDOM; Reed on GOD; Hubbard on PERSECUTION; Chesterton, Shaw on SELF-DENIAL; Eco on VISIONARIES

Marxism

The Marxist analysis has got nothing to do with what happened in Stalin's Russia: it's like blaming Jesus Christ for the Inquisition in Spain.
Tony Benn (b. 1925)
British Labour politician

Marxism is essentially a product of the bourgeois mind.
J. A. Schumpeter (1883-1950)
American economist, socialist

All I know is I'm not a Marxist.
Karl Marx (1818-1883)

SEE COMMUNISM; SOCIALISM

The Masses

I can't help feeling wary when I hear anything said about the masses. First you take their faces from 'em, calling them the masses, and then you accuse 'em of not having any faces.
J. B. Priestley (1894-1984)

The people are that part of the state which does not know what it wants.
Georg Hegel (1770-1831)
German philosopher

It's no go the Government grants, it's no
go the elections,
Sit on your arse for fifty years and hang
your hat on a pension.

Louis MacNeice (1907-1963)
British poet

The forgotten man at the bottom of the
economic pyramid.

Franklin D. Roosevelt (1882-1945)

The mind of the people is like mud, from
which arise strange and beautiful things.

W. J. Turner (1889-1946)
British poet

Masses are always breeding grounds of
psychic epidemics.

Carl Jung (1875-1961)

SEE Bacon on SINCERITY

Masturbation

Don't knock it, it's sex with someone you
love.

Woody Allen (b. 1935)

Masturbation: the primary sexual activity of
mankind. In the nineteenth century it was a
disease; in the twentieth, it's a cure.

Thomas Szasz (b. 1920)
American psychiatrist

Mathematics

The concept of number is the obvious distinction between the beast and man. Thanks to
number, the cry becomes song, noise acquires
rhythm, the spring is transformed into a
dance, force becomes dynamic, and outlines
figures.

Joseph Marie de Maistre (1753-1821)
French author

I admit that twice two makes four is an
excellent thing, but if we are to give everything
its due, twice two makes five is sometimes a
very charming thing too.

Feodor Dostoievski (1821-1881)

Mathematics is the only science where one
never knows what one is talking about nor
whether what is said is true.

Bertrand Russell (1872-1970)

As far as the laws of mathematics refer to
reality, they are not certain, and as far as they
are certain, they do not refer to reality.

Albert Einstein (1879-1955)

Stand firm in your refusal to remain conscious
during algebra. In real life, I assure you, there
is no such thing as algebra.

Fran Lebowitz (b. 1951)
American journalist

I have hardly ever known a mathematician
who was capable of reasoning.

Plato (427-347 BC)

Mathematics possesses not only truth, but
supreme beauty – a beauty cold and austere,
like that of sculpture.

Bertrand Russell (1872-1970)

I could never make out what those damned
dots meant.

Lord Randolph Churchill (1849-1894)
English statesman
of decimal points

SEE Debussy on MUSIC

Maturity

A child becomes an adult when he realizes that
he has a right not only to be right but also to
be wrong.

Thomas Szasz (b. 1920)
American psychiatrist

We have not passed that subtle line between
childhood and adulthood until we move from
the passive voice to the active voice – that is,
until we have stopped saying 'It got lost', and
say, 'I lost it'.

Sydney J. Harris (b. 1917)
American journalist

Your lordship, though not clean past your
youth, hath yet some smack of age in you,
some relish of the saltness of time.

Falstaff, King Henry IV part 2
William Shakespeare (1564-1616)

When people are old enough to know better
they are old enough to do worse.

Hesketh Pearson (1887-1964)
British biographer

One of the signs of passing youth is the birth
of a sense of fellowship with other human
beings as we take our place among them.

Virginia Woolf (1882-1941)

To be adult is to be alone.

Jean Rostand (1894-1977)
French biologist

SEE AGE: Old Age; MIDDLE AGE

Meanness

Meanness is more in half-doing than in
omitting acts of generosity.

Elbert Hubbard (1856-1915)
American author

Mere parsimony is not economy. . . Expense,
and great expense, may be an essential part of
true economy.

Edmund Burke (1729-1797)
Irish philosopher, statesman

It was said of old Sarah, Duchess of
Marlborough, that she never puts dots over
her i's, to save ink.

Horace Walpole (1717-1797)
English author

There are many things that we would throw

away, if we were not afraid that others might pick them up.

Oscar Wilde (1854-1900)

Man hoards himself when he has nothing to give away.

Edward Dahlberg (b. 1900)
American novelist, poet, critic

SEE ECONOMISING

Medicine

Some fell by laudanum, and some by steel,
And death in ambush lay in every pill.

Sir Samuel Garth (1661-1719)
English physician, poet

Medicine is a collection of uncertain prescriptions, the results of which, taken collectively, are more fatal than useful to mankind. Water, air, and cleanliness are the chief articles in my pharmacopoeia.

Napoleon Bonaparte (1769-1821)

The desire to take medicine is perhaps the greatest feature which distinguishes man from animals.

Sir William Osler (1849-1919)
Canadian physician

Vaccination is the medical sacrament corresponding to baptism.

Samuel Butler (1835-1902)
English author

Half the modern drugs could well be thrown out of the window, except that the birds might eat them.

Martin Henry Fischer (1879-?)

The whole imposing edifice of modern medicine is like the celebrated tower of Pisa – slightly off balance.

Prince of Wales (b. 1948)

SEE DOCTORS; Rice, Shakespeare on HOPE

Memory

A memory is what is left when something happens and does not completely unhappen.

Edward de Bono (b. 1933)
British author

Memory, the priestess,
kills the present
and offers its heart to the shrine of the dead past.

Rabindranath Tagore (1861-1941)
Indian author, philosopher

But the iniquity of oblivion blindly scattereth her poppy, and deals with the memory of men without distinction to merit of perpetuity.

Sir Thomas Browne (1605-1682)
English physician, author

Life is all memory, except for the one present moment that goes by you so quick you hardly catch it going.

Tennessee Williams (1914-1983)

Many a man fails to become a thinker for the sole reason that his memory is too good.

Friedrich Nietzsche (1844-1900)

But each day brings its petty dust
Our soon-chok'd souls to fill,
And we forget because we must,
And not because we will.

Matthew Arnold (1822-1888)
English poet, critic

SEE La Rochefoucauld on ANECDOTES; NOSTALGIA

Men

How can a Woman scruple entire Subjection, how can she forbear to admire the worth and excellency of a Superior Sex, if she at all considers it? Have not all the great Actions that have been performed in the World been done by Men? Have not they founded Empires and overturn'd them? Do not they make Laws and continually repeal and amend them? Their vast Minds lay Kingdoms Waste, no bounds or measures can be prescrib'd to their Desires. . . They make Worlds and ruin them, form Systems of universal nature and dispute eternally about them; their pen gives worth to the most trifling Controversy. . .

Mary Astell (1666-1737)
English feminist writer

One of the things being in politics has taught is that men are not a reasoned or reasonable sex.

Margaret Thatcher (b. 1925)

The male sex still constitute in many ways the most obstinate vested interest one can find.

Lord Longford (b. 1905)
British author, moralist

Women think of being a man as a gift. It is a duty. Even making love can be a duty. A man has always got to get it up, and love isn't always enough.

Norman Mailer (b. 1923)

A hard man's good to find – but you'll mostly find him asleep.

Mae West (1892-1980)

One hell of an outlay for a very small return with most of them.

Glenda Jackson (b. 1937)

I require only three things in a man. He must be handsome, ruthless, and stupid.

Dorothy Parker (1893-1967)
American humorous writer

Women want mediocre men, and men are

working hard to become as mediocre as possible.
Margaret Mead (1901-1978)
American anthropologist

There is a vast difference between the savage and the civilised man, but it is never apparent to their wives until after breakfast.
Helen Rowland (1875-1950)
American journalist

Men are those creatures with two legs and eight hands.
Jayne Mansfield (1932-1967)

Don't accept rides from strange men – and remember that all men are as strange as hell.
Robin Morgan (b. 1941)
American feminist

A hairy body, and arms stiff with bristles, gives promise of a manly soul.
Juvenal (40-125)

Macho does not prove mucho.
Zsa Zsa Gabor (b. 1919)

The more I see of men, the more I like dogs.
Madame de Staël (1766-1817)
French writer, wit

Men: and Women With men he can be rational and unaffected, but when he has ladies to please, every feature works.
Jane Austen (1775-1817)

I must have women – there is nothing unbends the mind like them.
Macheath, The Beggar's Opera
John Gay (1685-1732)
English playwright

The man who gets on best with women is the one who knows best how to get on without them.
Charles Baudelaire (1821-1867)

A man can be happy with any woman as long as he does not love her.
Oscar Wilde (1854-1900)

There are two things a real man likes – danger and play; and he likes woman because she is the most dangerous of playthings.
Friedrich Nietzsche (1844-1900)

All men are rapists and that's all they are. They rape us with their eyes, their laws, their codes.
Marilyn French (b. 1929)
American author

To be sure he's a 'Man', the male must see to it that the female be clearly a 'Woman', the opposite of a 'Man', that is, the female must act like a faggot.
Valerie Solanas (b. 1940)
American artist, writer

No men who think really deeply about women

retain a high opinion of them; men either despise women or they have never thought seriously about them.
Otto Weininger (1880-1903)
Viennese philosopher

Most men who run down women are only running down a certain woman.
Rémy de Gourmont (1858-1915)
French critic, novelist

Women love men for their defects; if men have enough of them women will forgive them everything, even their gigantic intellects.
Oscar Wilde (1854-1900)

Man is for woman a means; the end is always the child.
Friedrich Nietzsche (1844-1900)

Men know that women are an overmatch for them, and therefore they choose the weakest or the most ignorant. If they did not think so, they never could be afraid of women knowing as much as themselves.
Dr Samuel Johnson (1709-1784)

I feel sorry for men – they have more problems than women. In the first place they have to compete with women.
Françoise Sagan (b. 1935)

I do not think women understand how repelled a man feels when he sees a woman wholly absorbed in what she is thinking, unless it is her child, or her husband, or her lover. It gives one gooseflesh.
Rebecca West (1892-1983)
British writer

SEE MEN AND WOMEN; Coward on PROMISCUITY; WOMEN: and Men

Men and Women
More and more it appears that, biologically, men are designed for short, brutal lives and women for long miserable ones.
Estelle Ramey
Physiology Professor, Georgetown University 1985

Men have a much better time of it than women. For one thing, they marry later; for another thing, they die earlier.
H. L. Mencken (1880-1956)
American journalist

Woman submits to her fate; man makes his.
Émile Gaboriau (1835-1873)
French author

Men make Gods, and women worship them.
James G. Frazer (1854-1941)
Scottish classicist, anthropologist

'Tis strange what a man may do, and a woman yet think him an angel.
W. M. Thackeray (1811-1863)
English author

Sure men were born to lie, and women to believe them.

John Gay (1685-1732)
English playwright

What passes for woman's intuition is often nothing more than man's transparency.

George Jean Nathan (1882-1958)
American critic

Once a woman is made man's equal, she becomes his superior.

Margaret Thatcher (b. 1925)

You see an awful lot of smart guys with dumb women, but you hardly ever see a smart woman with a dumb guy.

Erica Jong (b. 1942)
American author

Women, when they have made a sheep of a man, always tell him that he is a lion with a will of iron.

Honoré de Balzac (1799-1850)

Men have as exaggerated an idea of their rights as women have of their wrongs.

Ed (E. W.) Howe (1853-1937)
American journalist, novelist

A man is as good as he has to be, and a woman as bad as she dares.

Elbert Hubbard (1856-1915)
American author

If men were as unselfish as women, women would very soon become more selfish than men.

J. Churton Collins (1848-1908)
English author, critic, scholar

When men and women agree, it is only in their conclusions; their reasons are always different.

George Santayana (1863-1952)
American philosopher, poet

To be happy with a man you must understand him a lot and love him a little. To be happy with a woman you must love her a lot and not try to understand her at all.

Helen Rowland (1875-1950)
American journalist

The little rift between the sexes is astonishingly widened by simply teaching one set of catchwords to the girls and another to the boys.

Robert Louis Stevenson (1850-1894)

What is most beautiful in virile men is something feminine; what is most beautiful in feminine women is something masculine.

Susan Sontag (b. 1933)
American essayist

The great renewal of the world will perhaps consist in this, that man and maid, freed from all false feeling and aversion, will seek each other not as opposites, but as brother and sister, as neighbours, and will come together as human beings.

Rainer Maria Rilke (1875-1926)
German poet

Men and women, women and men. It will never work.

Erica Jong (b. 1942)
American author

SEE Collins on AGE; Wilde on COMPLIMENTS; Lindbergh on FRIENDSHIP; Conrad on GOD; Collins, de Staël, Wyatt on LOVE; Howe on VIRTUE

Middle Age

Middle age is the time when a man is always thinking that in a week or two he will feel as good as ever.

Don Marquis (1878-1937)
American humorist, journalist

. . . youth is the period in which a man can be hopeless. The end of every episode is the end of the world. But the power of hoping through everything, the knowledge that the soul survives its adventures, that great inspiration comes to the middle-aged.

G. K. Chesterton (1874-1936)

From the middle of life onward, only he remains vitally alive who is ready to *die with life*.

Carl Jung (1875-1961)

My forties are the best time I have ever gone through.

Elizabeth Taylor (b. 1932)

All one's life as a young woman one is on show, a focus of attention, people notice you. You set yourself up to be noticed and admired. And then, not expecting it, you become middle-aged and anonymous. No one notices you. You achieve a wonderful freedom It is a positive thing. You can move about, unnoticed and invisible.

Doris Lessing (b. 1919)
British author

The really frightening thing about middle age is the knowledge that you'll grow out of it.

Doris Day (b. 1924)

SEE Grattan on AGE; Whitehead on IDEAS

Millionaires

I am not going to be quite as reclusive as I have been because it has apparently attracted so much attention that I have just got to live a somewhat modified life in order not to be an oddity.

Howard Hughes (1905-1976)
last public statement

It is impossible to think of Howard Hughes without seeing the apparently bottomless gulf between what we say we want and what we do want, between what we officially admire and secretly desire, between, in the largest sense, the people we marry and the people we love. In a nation which increasingly appears to prize social virtues, Howard Hughes remains not merely antisocial but grandly, brilliantly, surpassingly, asocial. He is the last private man, the dream we no longer admit.

Joan Didion (b. 1934)
American writer

No woman marries for money; they are all clever enough, before marrying a millionaire, to fall in love with him first.

Cesare Pavese (1908-1950)
Italian author

SEE The RICH

Minorities

No democracy can long survive which does not accept as fundamental to its very existence the recognition of the rights of minorities.

Franklin D. Roosevelt (1882-1945)

All history is a record of the power of minorities, and of minorities of one.

R. W. Emerson (1803-1882)
American essayist, poet, philosopher

It is always the minorities that hold the key to progress.

R. B. Fosdick (1883-1969)
American administrator, author

How a minority,
Reaching majority,
Seizing authority,
Hates a minority!

Leonard H. Robbins (1877-1947)
American author

SEE Altman on CULTS; Gibbon on HERESY

Miracles

For those who believe in God no explanation is needed; for those who do not believe in God no explanation is possible.

Father John Lafarge (b. 1880)
of the cures at Lourdes

A miracle may be accurately defined, a transgression of a law of nature by a particular volition of the Deity, or by the interposition of some invisible agent.

David Hume (1711-1776)

God is a character, a real and consistent being, or He is nothing. If God did a miracle He would deny His own nature and the universe would simply blow up, vanish, become nothing.

Joyce Cary (1888-1957)
British author

Miracles are the swaddling-clothes of infant churches.

Thomas Fuller (1608-1661)
English cleric

If a man is a fool for believing in a Creator, then he is a fool for believing in a miracle; but not otherwise.

G. K. Chesterton (1874-1936)

What sort of God are we portraying and believing in if we insist on what I will nickname 'the divine laser beam' type of miracle as the heart and basis of the Incarnation and the Resurrection?

David Jenkins, Bishop of Durham (b. 1925)

A miracle is an event which creates faith. That is the purpose and nature of miracles. Frauds deceive. An event which creates faith does not deceive; therefore it is not a fraud, but a miracle.

Archbishop, Saint Joan
George Bernard Shaw (1856-1950)

SEE Turgenev on PRAYER

Missionaries

Making the world safe for hypocrisy.

Thomas Wolfe (1900-1938)
American author

The Order of Jesuits is a sword whose hilt is at Rome and whose point is everywhere.

Abbé Guillaume Raynal (1713-1796)
French historian, philosopher

Let the heathen go to hell; help your neighbour.

Ed (E. W.) Howe (1853-1937)
American journalist, novelist

The Christian missionary may preach the gospel to the poor naked heathen, but the spiritual heathen who populate Europe have as yet heard nothing of Christianity.

Carl Jung (1875-1961)

A man found in the South Sea Islands a tribe of savages so meagre in intelligence that they could not lie. However, there were neighbouring islands where missionaries of several denominations had settled. And there the savages were not sunk quite so low.

Elbert Hubbard (1856-1915)
American author

Civilised men arrived in the Pacific armed with alcohol, syphilis, trousers, and the Bible.

Havelock Ellis (1859-1939)
British psychologist

Go practise if you please
With men and women: Leave a child
alone
For Christ's particular love's
sake!

Robert Browning (1812-1889)

SEE Macdonald on CHRISTIANITY

Mitigation

He reminds me of the man who murdered both his parents, and then, when sentence was about to be pronounced, pleaded for mercy on the grounds that he was an orphan.

Abraham Lincoln (1809-1865)

Friar Barnadine: Thou hast committed –
Barabas: Fornication? But that was in another country; and besides, the wench is dead.

Christopher Marlowe (1564-1593)

Mobs

That beast with many heads, the staggering multitude.

John Webster (1580-1625)
English playwright

The mob has many heads but no brains.

17th century English proverb

Each of you, individually, walks with the presence of a fox, but collectively you are geese.

Solon (c. 638-559 BC)
Athenian statesman

The tyranny of the multitude is a multiplied tyranny.

Edmund Burke (1729-1797)
Irish philosopher, statesman

Nouns of number, or multitude, such as *Mob, Parliament, Rabble, House of Commons, Regiment, Court of King's Bench, Den of Thieves*, and the like.

William Cobbett (1762-1835)
English essayist, politician, agriculturalist

Are we aware of our obligations to a mob? It is the mob that labour in your fields and serve in your houses – that man your navy, and recruit your army – that have enabled you to defy the world, and can also defy you when neglect and calamity have driven them to despair. You may call the people a mob; but do not forget that a mob too often speaks the sentiments of the people.

Lord Byron (1788-1824)
speech to the House of Lords
on the Luddites

There is an accumulative cruelty in a number of men, though none in particular are ill-natured.

George Savile, Lord Halifax (1633-1695)
English statesman, author

Eh! je suis leur chef, il fallait bien les suivre.
I'm their leader, I've got to follow them.

Alexandre Ledru-Rollin (1807-1874)
French politician, revolutionary
*among the Paris mob at the
barricades, 1848*

Moderation

Moderation is the silken string running through the pearl chain of all virtues.

Joseph Hall (1574-1656)
Bishop of Norwich

Moderation is a virtue only in those who are thought to have an alternative.

Henry Kissinger (b. 1923)

Tell a man whose house is on fire to give a moderate alarm; tell him to moderately rescue his wife from the hands of the ravisher; tell the mother to gradually extricate her babe from the fire into which it has fallen; but urge me not to use moderation in a case like the present.

W. L. Garrison (1805-1879)
American abolitionist
launching his newspaper The
Liberator *in his campaign
against slavery*

Any plan conceived in moderation must fail when the circumstances are set in extremes.

Prince Metternich (1773-1859)
Austrian statesman

La modération des personnes heureuses vient du calme que la bonne fortune donne a leur humeur.
Moderation in people who are contented comes from the calm that good fortune lends to their spirit.

François, Duc de La Rochefoucauld (1613-1680)
French writer, moralist

My God, Mr Chairman, at this moment I stand astonished at my own moderation.

Robert Clive (1725-1774)
British soldier, colonial administrator
*defending himself against
charges of embezzlement*

SEE St Augustine on DRINK: Abstinence;
Wilde on EXCESS; Shaw on SELF-DENIAL

Modern Times

It takes a kind of shabby arrogance to survive in our time, and a fairly romantic nature to want to.

Edgar Z. Friedenberg (b. 1921)
American sociologist

This strange disease of modern life,
With its sick hurry, its divided aims.

Matthew Arnold (1822-1888)
English poet, critic

No man lives without jostling and being jostled; in all ways he has to elbow himself through the world, giving and receiving offence.

Thomas Carlyle (1795-1881)
Scottish author

Now here, you see, it takes all the running you can do, to keep in the same place. If you want to get somewhere else, you must run at least twice as fast as that!

Lewis Carroll (1832-1898)

The horror of the Twentieth Century is the size of each event and the paucity of its reverberation.

Norman Mailer (b. 1923)

The atom bombs are piling up in the factories, the police are prowling through the cities, the lies are streaming from the loudspeakers, but the earth is still going round the sun.

George Orwell (1903-1950)

In these times you have to be an optimist to open your eyes when you wake in the morning.

Carl Sandburg (1878-1967)
American poet

Let nothing be called natural
In an age of bloody confusion,
Ordered disorder, planned caprice,
And dehumanised humanity, lest all things
Be held unalterable!

Bertolt Brecht (1898-1956)

The trouble with our age is that it is all signpost and no destination.

Louis Kronenberger (1904-1980)
American critic, editor, author

In the nineteenth century the problem was that God is dead; in the twentieth century the problem is that man is dead.

Erich Fromm (1900-1980)
American psychologist

SEE Phaedrus on HASTE

Modesty

Modesty: the gentle art of enhancing your charm by pretending not to be aware of it.

Oliver Herford (1863-1935)
American poet, illustrator

Modesty is the only sure bait when you angle for praise.

Lord Chesterfield (1694-1773)
English statesman and man of letters

He is a modest little man with much to be modest about.

Sir Winston Churchill (1874-1965)
of Clement Attlee

Blessed is the man who, having nothing to say, abstains from giving wordy evidence of the fact.

George Eliot (1819-1880)

The English instinctively admire any man who has no talent, and is modest about it.

James Agate (1877-1947)
British critic

I have often wished I had time to cultivate modesty. . . But I am too busy thinking about myself.

Dame Edith Sitwell (1887-1964)
British poet

Ah! Madam, . . . you know every thing in the world but your perfections, and you only know not those, because 'tis the top of perfection not to know them.

William Congreve (1670-1729)
English dramatist

SEE Flaubert on The ENGLISH; Gilbert on SELF-IMAGE

Money

There are few sorrows, however poignant, in which a good income is of no avail.

Logan Pearsall Smith (1865-1946)
American essayist

Ready money is Aladdin's lamp.

Lord Byron (1788-1824)

Money is the sinews of love, as of war.

George Farquhar (1678-1707)
Irish dramatist

Money is a singular thing. It ranks with love as man's greatest source of joy. And with death as his greatest source of anxiety. Money differs from an automobile, a mistress or cancer in being equally important to those who have it and those who do not.

J. K. Galbraith (b. 1908)
American economist

If you would like to know the value of money, go and try to borrow some.

Benjamin Franklin (1706-1790)

The value of money is that with it we can tell any man to go to the devil. It is the sixth sense which enables you to enjoy the other five.

W. Somerset Maugham (1874-1966)

They who are of the opinion that money will do everything, may very well be suspected to do everything for money.

George Savile, Lord Halifax (1633-1695)
English statesman, author

The want of money is the root of all evil.

Samuel Butler (1835-1902)
English author

We all need money, but there are degrees of desperation.

Anthony Burgess (b. 1917)
British author

Money is better than poverty, if only for financial reasons.

Woody Allen (b. 1935)

I don't like money, actually, but it quiets my nerves.

Joe Louis (1914-1981)
American boxer

Making money ain't nothing exciting to me. You might be able to buy a little better booze than the wino on the corner. But you get sick just like the next cat and when you die you're just as graveyard dead as he is.

Louis Armstrong (1900-1971)

Money doesn't talk, it swears.

Bob Dylan (b. 1941)

Money dignifies what is frivolous if unpaid for.

Virginia Woolf (1882-1941)

Money is like muck, not good except it be spread.

Francis Bacon (1561-1626)

One should look down on money but never lose sight of it.

André Prévot (fl. 1911)

There are few ways in which a man can be more innocently employed than in getting money.

Dr Samuel Johnson (1709-1784)

Men who make money rarely saunter; men who save money rarely swagger.

Edward Bulwer-Lytton (1803-1873)
English novelist, playwright

Money can't buy friends, but you can get a better class of enemy.

Spike Milligan (b. 1918)
British comedian, humorous writer

When I was young I used to think that money was the most important thing in life; now that I am old, I know it is.

Oscar Wilde (1854-1900)

When it is a question of money, everybody is of the same religion.

Voltaire (1694-1778)

SEE St Paul on GREED; Thatcher on INTENTIONS; Shaw on POVERTY

Monopolies
Monopolies are like babies: nobody likes them until they have got one of their own.

Lord Mancroft (b. 1914)
British Conservative politician

Marilyn Monroe
Can't act... Voice like a tight squeak... Utterly unsure of herself... Unable even to take refuge in her own insignificance.

Columbia Pictures comments

She was good at playing abstract confusion in the same way that a midget is good at being short.

Clive James (b. 1939)
Australian writer, critic

To put it bluntly, I seem to be a whole superstructure with no foundation. But I'm working on the foundation.

Marilyn Monroe (1926-1962)

Marilyn was mean. Terribly mean. The meanest woman I ever met around this town. I have never met anybody as mean as Marilyn Monroe or as utterly fabulous on the screen, and that includes Garbo.

Billy Wilder (b. 1906)
American writer and film director

Monte Carlo
That little state like Hampstead Heath in the South of France.

Lady Docker (b. 1900)

Moral Indignation
Compound for sins they are inclined to
By damning those they have no mind to.

Samuel Butler (1612-1680)
English poet

Moral indignation is jealousy with a halo.

H. G. Wells (1866-1946)

Moral indignation is in most cases two per cent moral, 48 per cent indignation and 50 per cent envy.

Vittorio de Sica (1901-1974)
Italian director

Morale
Morale is when your hands and feet keep on working when your head says it can't be done.

Admiral Ben Moreell (1892-1978)
American naval commander, businessman

Moralists
The same people who can deny others everything are famous for refusing themselves nothing.

Leigh Hunt (1784-1859)
English poet, critic, essayist

When we start deceiving ourselves into thinking not that we want something or need something, not that it is a pragmatic necessity for us to have it, but that it is a *moral imperative* that we have it, then is when we join the fashionable madmen, and then is when the thin whine of hysteria is heard in the land, and then is when we are in bad trouble.

Joan Didion (b. 1934)
American writer

We are told by moralists with the plainest faces that immorality will spoil our looks.

Logan Pearsall Smith (1865-1946)
American essayist

SEE PURITANS

Morality
Erst kommt das Fressen, dann kommt die Moral.
Grub first, then morality.

Bertolt Brecht (1898-1956)

Of moral purpose I see no trace in Nature. That is an article of exclusively human manufacture – and very much to our credit.
T. H. Huxley (1825-1895)
English biologist

Morality comes with the sad wisdom of age, when the sense of curiosity has withered.
Graham Greene (b. 1904)

Morality is the theory that every human act must be either right or wrong and that ninety-nine per cent of them are wrong.
H. L. Mencken (1880-1956)
American journalist

The nation's morals are like its teeth: the more decayed they are the more it hurts to touch them.
George Bernard Shaw (1856-1950)

We know no spectacle so ridiculous as the British public in one of its periodical fits of morality.
Lord Macaulay (1800-1859)
English historian

An Englishman thinks he is moral when he is only uncomfortable.
The Devil, Man and Superman
George Bernard Shaw (1856-1950)

If thy morals make thee dreary, depend upon it they are wrong.
Robert Louis Stevenson (1850-1894)

Morality is simply the attitude we adopt towards people we personally dislike.
Oscar Wilde (1854-1900)

Don't let us make imaginary evils, when you know we have so many real ones to encounter.
Oliver Goldsmith (1728-1774)

About morals, I know only that what is moral is what you feel good after and what is immoral is what you feel bad after.
Ernest Hemingway (1899-1961)

SEE Spencer on HEALTH; Johnson on PREACHING; Arnold, Shaw on RELIGION; Wilde on SCANDAL; Stevenson on TABOO

Mother

God could not be everywhere and therefore he made mothers.
Jewish proverb

With animals you don't see the male caring for the offspring. It's against nature. It is a woman's prerogative and duty, and a privilege.
Princess Grace of Monaco (1928-1982)

The commonest fallacy among women is that simply having children makes one a mother – which is as absurd as believing that having a piano makes one a musician.
Sydney J. Harris (b. 1917)
American journalist

Often women have babies because they can't think of anything better to do.
Lord Beaumont of Whitley (b. 1928)
British prelate, politician, journalist

If you bungle raising your children, I don't think whatever else you do well matters very much.
Jacqueline Kennedy Onassis (b. 1929)

A suburban mother's role is to deliver children obstetrically once, and by car for ever after.
Peter de Vries (b. 1910)
American author

He that would the daughter win
Must with the mother first begin.
17th century English proverb

Perhaps the greatest social service that can be rendered by anybody to the country and to mankind is to bring up a family. But here again, because there is nothing to sell, there is a very general disposition to regard a married woman's work as no work at all, and to take it as a matter of course that she should not be paid for it.
George Bernard Shaw (1856-1950)

There is no slave out of heaven like a loving woman; and, of all loving women, there is no such slave as a mother.
H. W. Beecher (1813-1887)
American clergyman, editor, writer

Since nothing was too much to do for him, she laid on him the intolerable burden of finding nothing too much to do for her.
James Gould Cozzens (1903-1978)
American author

There are times when parenthood seems nothing but feeding the mouth that bites you.
Peter de Vries (b. 1910)
American author

SEE PARENTS

Motives

We should often be ashamed of our finest actions if the world understood our motives.
François, Duc de La Rochefoucauld (1613-1680)
French writer, moralist

He never does a proper thing without giving an improper reason for it.
Lady Britomart, Major Barbara
George Bernard Shaw (1856-1950)

Great men will never do great mischief but for some great end.
Edmund Burke (1729-1797)
Irish philosopher, statesman

Men are not only bad from good motives, but also often good from bad motives.
G. K. Chesterton (1874-1936)

The motive for a deed usually changes during its performance: at least, after the deed has been done, it seems quite different.
Friedrich Hebbel (1813-1863)
German dramatist

No man does anything from a single motive.
S. T. Coleridge (1772-1834)

Never ascribe to an opponent motives meaner than your own.
J. M. Barrie (1860-1937)
British playwright

SEE Chesterton on HUMILITY; Blake on TRUTH

Murder
Yet who would have thought the old man to have had so much blood in him?
Lady Macbeth, *Macbeth*
William Shakespeare (1564-1616)

If once a man indulge himself in murder, very soon he comes to think little of robbing; and from robbing he next comes to drinking and Sabbath-breaking, and from that to incivility and procrastination.
Thomas de Quincey (1785-1859)
English author

Every murderer is probably somebody's old friend.
Agatha Christie (1891-1976)

SEE KILLING

Music
It is the only sensual pleasure without vice.
Dr Samuel Johnson (1709-1784)

Hearing often-times
The still, sad music of humanity.
William Wordsworth (1770-1850)

Is it not strange that sheep's guts should hale souls out of men's bodies?
Benedick, *Much Ado About Nothing*
William Shakespeare (1564-1616)

Hearing in the distance
Two mandolins like creatures in the dark
Creating the agony of ecstasy.
George Barker (b. 1913)
British author, poet

Swans sing before they die — 'twere no bad thing
Should certain persons die before they sing.
S. T. Coleridge (1772-1834)

Difficult do you call it, Sir? I wish it were impossible.
Dr Samuel Johnson (1709-1784)
of a violinist's playing

When music fails to agree to the ear, to soothe the ear and the heart and the senses, then it has missed its point.
Maria Callas (1923-1977)
Greek opera singer

Classical music is the kind that we keep hoping will turn into a tune.
Kin (F. McKinney) Hubbard (1868-1930)
American humorist, journalist

Music is the arithmetic of sounds as optics is the geometry of light.
Claude Debussy (1862-1918)

Good music resembles something. It resembles the composer.
Jean Cocteau (1889-1963)
French writer, film director

The good composer is slowly discovered, the bad composer is slowly found out.
Sir Ernest Newman (1868-1959)
British musicologist

I know only two tunes; one of them is 'Yankee Doodle', and the other isn't.
Ulysses S. Grant (1822-1885)

Canned music is like audible wallpaper.
Alistair Cooke (b. 1908)
British journalist, broadcaster

I do not see any good reason why the devil should have all the good tunes.
Rowland Hill (1744-1833)
English preacher, publisher of hymns

Hell is full of musical amateurs: music is the brandy of the damned.
Don Juan, *Man and Superman*
George Bernard Shaw (1856-1950)

The English may not like music — but they absolutely love the noise it makes.
Sir Thomas Beecham (1879-1961)
British conductor

There is something suspicous about music, gentlemen. I insist that she is, by her nature, equivocal. I shall not be going too far in saying at once that she is politically suspect.
Thomas Mann (1875-1955)

SEE Stravinsky on CINEMA;
Joachim on HERMITS; OPERA; POP;
ROCK AND ROLL; SONG

Myths
The great enemy of the truth is very often not the lie — deliberate, contrived and dishonest — but the myth — persistent, persuasive and unrealistic.
John F. Kennedy (1917-1963)

A myth is a fixed way of looking at the world which cannot be destroyed because, looked at through the myth, all evidence supports that myth.

Edward de Bono (b.1933)
British author

Contemporary man has rationalised the myths, but he has not been able to destroy them.

Octavio Paz (b. 1914)
Mexican poet

N

Nagging

Nagging is the repetition of unpalatable truths.

Edith, Lady Summerskill (1901-1980)
British Labour politician

Nationalism

Methinks I see in my mind a noble and puissant nation rousing herself like a strong man after sleep, and shaking her invincible locks. Methinks I see her as an eagle mewing her mighty youth, and kindling her undazzled eyes at the full midday beam.

John Milton (1608-1674)

No man has a right to fix the boundary of the march of a nation; no man has a right to say to his country – thus far shalt thou go and no further.

Charles Stewart Parnell (1846-1891)
Irish nationalist politician

Germany will either be a world power or will not be at all.

Adolf Hitler (1889-1945)
Mein Kampf

It is humiliating to remain with our hands folded while others write history. It matters little who wins. To make a people great it is necessary to send them to battle even if you have to kick their arses. That is what I shall do.

Benito Mussolini (1883-1945)
11 April 1940

Nations whose nationalism is destroyed are subject to ruin.

Colonel Muhammar Qaddafi (b. 1938)

After fifteen years of work I have achieved, as a common German soldier and merely with my fanatical will-power, the unity of the German nation, and have freed it from the death sentence of Versailles.

Adolf Hitler (1889-1945)
21 December 1941

The crazy combative patriotism that plainly threatens to destroy civilization is very largely begotten by the schoolmaster and the schoolmistress in their history lessons. They take the growing mind at a naturally barbaric phase and they inflame and fix its barbarism.

H. G. Wells (1866-1946)

SEE Aldington on PATRIOTISM

Nature

Anyone who has got any pleasure at all from nature should try to put something back. Life is like a superlative meal and the world is the maître d'hôtel. What I am doing is the equivalent of leaving a reasonable tip.

Gerald Durrell (b. 1925)
British conservationist and author

In nature there are neither rewards nor punishments – there are consequences.

R. G. Ingersoll (1833-1899)
American lawyer

However much you knock at nature's door, she will never answer you in comprehensible words.

Ivan Turgenev (1818-1883)

One impulse from a vernal wood
May teach you more of man,
Of moral evil and of good,
Than all the ages can.

William Wordsworth (1770-1850)

It is false dichotomy to think of nature *and* man. Mankind is that factor *in* nature which exhibits in its most intense form the plasticity of nature.

A. N. Whitehead (1861-1947)
British philosopher

All things are artificial, for nature is the art of God.

Sir Thomas Browne (1605-1682)
English physician, author

To be natural is to be obvious, and to be obvious is to be inartistic.

Oscar Wilde (1854-1900)

SEE Whistler on ART; Clark on BLOODSPORTS; Moore on LOVE; Huxley on MORALITY

The Navy

The royal navy of England hath ever been its greatest defence and ornament; it is its ancient and natural strength, the floating bulwark of our island.

Sir William Blackstone (1723-1780)
English jurist

Dans ce pays-ci il est bon de tuer de temps en temps un amiral pour encourager les autres.
In this country it's a good thing to shoot an admiral now and then to encourage the others.

Voltaire (1694-1778)
of England

Don't talk to me about naval tradition. It's nothing but rum, sodomy and the lash.

Sir Winston Churchill (1874-1965)

We sailors get money like horses, and spend it like asses.

Tobias Smollett (1721-1771)
Scottish novelist, surgeon

He was begotten in the galley and born under a gun. Every hair was a rope yarn, every finger a fish-hook, every tooth a marline-spike, and his blood right good Stockholm tar.

Naval epitaph

I must have the gentleman to haul and draw with the mariner, and the mariner with the gentleman... I would not know him, that would refuse to set his hand to a rope, but I know there is not any such here.

Sir Francis Drake (1540-1596)

There were gentlemen and there were seamen in the navy of Charles the Second. But the seamen were not gentlemen; and the gentlemen were not seamen.

Lord Macaulay (1800-1859)
English historian

A ship of war, a wooden world fabricated by the frail hand of man, the great bridge of the ocean, conveying to all habitable places death, pox and drunkenness.

Ned Ward (1667-1731)
English humorous writer

No man will be a sailor who has contrivance enough to get himself into a jail; for being in a ship is being in a jail, with the chance of being drowned... A man in a jail has more room, better food and commonly better company.

Dr Samuel Johnson (1709-1784)

The wonder is always new that any sane man can be a sailor.

R. W. Emerson (1803-1882)
American essayist, poet, philosopher

There is nothing – absolutely nothing – half so much worth doing as simply messing about in boats.

Kenneth Grahame (1859-1932)
British essayist, writer of children's books

We are as near to heaven by sea as by land.

Sir Humphrey Gilbert (1539-1583)
English navigator (*drowned at sea*)

Necessity

Necessity is the plea for every infringement of human freedom. It is the argument of tyrants; it is the creed of slaves.

William Pitt (1759-1806)
English politician, Prime Minister

Freedom is the recognition of necessity.

Friedrich Engels (1820-1895)

Whoever heard of a man of fortune in England talk of the necessaries of life? ... Whether we can afford it or no, we must have superfluities.

John Gay (1685-1732)
English playwright

We do what we must, and call it by the best names.

R. W. Emerson (1803-1882)
American essayist, poet, philosopher

Foul water will quench fire.

16th century English proverb

SEE Seneca on STATUS

Neighbours

We make our friends; we make our enemies; but God makes our next-door neighbour.

G. K. Chesterton (1874-1936)

Love your neighbour, yet pull not down your hedge.

George Herbert (1593-1633)
English clergyman, poet

Good fences make good neighbours.

Robert Frost (1874-1963)
American poet

For what do we live, but to make sport for our neighbours, and laugh at them in our turn?

Jane Austen (1775-1817)

SEE Shaw on PREACHING

Neurosis

Oh the nerves, the nerves; the mysteries of this machine called man! Oh the little that unhinges it: poor creatures that we are!

Charles Dickens (1812-1870)

As every man is hunted by his own daemon, vexed by his own disease, this checks all his activity.

R. W. Emerson (1803-1882)
American essayist, poet, philosopher

The psychotic person knows that two and two make five and is perfectly happy about it; the neurotic person knows that two and two make four, but is terribly worried about it.

radio doctor, 1954

Everything great in the world comes from neurotics. They alone have founded our religions and composed our masterpieces.

Marcel Proust (1871-1922)

The true believer is in a high degree protected

against the danger of certain neurotic afflictions; by accepting the universal neurosis he is spared the task of forming a personal neurosis.
Sigmund Freud (1856-1939)

Neurosis is always a substitute for legitimate suffering.
Carl Jung (1875-1961)

SEE ANXIETY

The New World

The pious ones of Plymouth who, reaching the Rock, first fell upon their own knees and then upon the aborigines.
William M. Evarts (1818-1901)
American statesman

The next Augustan age will dawn on the other side of the Atlantic. There will, perhaps, be a Thucydides at Boston, a Xenophon at New York, and, in time, a Virgil at Mexico, and a Newton at Peru. At last, some curious traveller from Lima will visit England and give a description of the ruins of St Pauls, like the editions of Balbec and Palmyra.
Horace Walpole (1717-1797)
English author

Europe and the UK are yesterday's world. Tomorrow is in the United States.
R. W. 'Tiny' Rowland (b. 1917)
British businessman

New York

New York, the nation's thyroid gland.
Christopher Morley (1890-1957)
American novelist, journalist

New York is a catastrophe – but a magnificent catastrophe.
Le Corbusier (1881-1965)
French architect

One belongs to New York instantly. One belongs to it as much in five minutes as in five years.
Thomas Wolfe (1900-1938)
American author

I miss the animal buoyancy of New York, the animal vitality. I did not mind that it had no meaning and no depth.
Anaïs Nin (b. 1914)
French novelist

If ever there was an aviary overstocked with jays it is that Yaptown-on-the-Hudson, called New York.
O. Henry (1862-1910)
American short story writer

I think that New York is not the cultural centre of America, but the business and administrative centre of American culture.
Saul Bellow (b. 1915)

[New York] is the place where all the aspirations of the Western World meet to form one vast master aspiration, as powerful as the suction of a steam dredge. It is the icing on the pie called Christian civilization.
H. L. Mencken (1880-1956)
American journalist

Living in New York is like coming all the time.
Gene Simmons
American rock musician

It is often said that New York is a city for only the very rich and the very poor. It is less often said that New York is also, at least for those of us who came there from somewhere else, a city for only the very young.
Joan Didion (b. 1934)
American writer

Newspapers

They are so filthy and bestial that no honest man would admit one into his house for a water-closet doormat.
Charles Dickens (1812-1870)

If words were invented to conceal thought, newspapers are a great improvement on a bad invention.
H. D. Thoreau (1817-1862)

All successful newspapers are ceaselessly querulous and bellicose. They never defend anyone or anything if they can help it; if the job is forced upon them, they tackle it by denouncing someone or something else.
H. L. Mencken (1880-1956)
American journalist

Possible? Is anything possible? Read the newspapers.
Duke of Wellington (1769-1852)

It is always the unreadable that occurs.
Oscar Wilde (1854-1900)

We welcome almost any break in the monotony of things, and a man has only to murder a series of wives in a new way to become known to millions of people who have never heard of Homer.
Robert Lynd (1879-1949)
Anglo-Irish essayist, journalist

Newspapers always excite curiosity. No one ever lays one down without a feeling of disappointment.
Charles Lamb (1775-1834)
English essayist, critic

The mission of a modern newspaper is to comfort the afflicted and afflict the comfortable.
anonymous

It is part of the social mission of every great newspaper to provide a refuge and a home for the largest possible number of salaried eccentrics.
Lord Thomson of Fleet (1894-1976)
Canadian newspaper publisher

By office boys for office boys.
Marquis of Salisbury (1830-1903)
English Conservative politician, Prime Minister
of the Daily Mail

Headlines twice the size of the events.
John Galsworthy (1867-1933)

Journalism consists largely in saying 'Lord Jones Dead' to people who never knew that Lord Jones was alive.
G. K. Chesterton (1874-1936)

Half the world does not know how the other half lives, but is trying to find out.
Ed (E. W.) Howe (1853-1937)
American journalist, novelist

Whenever people are well-informed they can be trusted with their own government.
Thomas Jefferson (1743-1826)

We live under a government of men and morning newspapers.
Wendell Phillips (1811-1884)
American abolitionist, orator

Neither in what it gives, nor in what it does not give, nor in the mode of presentation, must the unclouded face of truth suffer wrong. Comment is free but facts are sacred.
C. P. Scott (1846-1932)
British author, journalist

In the case of news, we should always wait for the sacrament of confirmation.
Voltaire (1694-1778)

Reading someone else's newspaper is like sleeping with someone else's wife. Nothing seems to be precisely in the right place, and when you find what you are looking for, it is not clear then how to respond to it.
Malcolm Bradbury (b. 1932)
British author

SEE EDITORS; JOURNALISM; The PRESS

Nicaragua
We are not going to tolerate these attacks from outlaw states run by the strangest collection of misfits, looney tunes and squalid criminals since the Third Reich.
Ronald Reagan (b. 1911)

SEE Somoza on ELECTIONS

Night
And the night shall be filled with music
And the cares, that infest the day,
Shall fold their tents, like the Arabs,
And as silently steal away.
H. W. Longfellow (1807-1882)

When man reassembles his fragmentary self and grows with the calm of a tree.
Antoine de Saint-Exupéry (1900-1944)
French aviator, writer

For the night
Shows stars and women in a better light.
Lord Byron (1788-1824)

In a real dark night of the soul it is always three o'clock in the morning.
F. Scott Fitzgerald (1896-1940)

SEE Johnson on BED; Herrick on SEX

Non-violence
It is my hope that as the Negro plunges deeper into the quest for freedom and justice he will plunge even deeper into the philosophy of non-violence. The Negro all over the South must come to the point that he can say to his white brother: 'We will match your capacity to inflict suffering with our capacity to endure suffering. We will meet your physical force with soul force. We will not hate you, but we will not obey your evil laws. We will soon wear you down by pure capacity to suffer.
Martin Luther King (1929-1968)

It is better to be violent, if there is violence in our hearts, than to put on the cloak of non-violence to cover impotence.
M. K. Gandhi (1869-1948)

The only thing that's been a worse flop than the organization of non-violence has been the organization of violence.
Joan Baez (b. 1941)

Passive resistance is an all-sided sword; it can be used anyhow; it blesses him who uses it and him against whom it is used without drawing a drop of blood; it produces far-reaching results. It never rusts and cannot be stolen. Competition between passive resisters does not exhaust them. The sword of passive resistance does not require a scabbard and one cannot be forcibly dispossessed of it.
M. K. Gandhi (1869-1948)

Noses
A big nose is the mark of a man affable, good, courteous, witty, liberal, brave, such as I am.
Edmond Rostand (1868-1918)
French poet, playwright

Give me a man with a good allowance of nose... When I want any good headwork done, I always choose a man, if suitable otherwise, with a long nose.
Napoleon Bonaparte (1769-1821)

Thy nose is as the tower of Lebanon which looketh towards Damascus.
Bible, Song of Solomon

Nostalgia
God gave us our memories so that we might have roses in December.
J. M. Barrie (1860-1937)
British playwright

I wept as I remembered how often you
and I
Had tired the sun with talking and
sent him down the sky.
> William J. Cory (1823-1892)
> English poet

Reminiscence makes one feel so deliciously
aged and sad.
> George Bernard Shaw (1856-1950)

A feeling of sadness and longing
That is not akin to pain,
And resembles sorrow only
As the mist resembles the rain.
> H. W. Longfellow (1807-1882)

The 'good old times' – all times,
When old, are good.
> Lord Byron (1788-1824)

Oh! the good times when we were so
unhappy.
> Alexandre Dumas (1803-1870)

Living in the past has one thing in its favour –
it's cheaper.
> anonymous

That is the land of lost content,
I see it shining plain,
The happy highways where I went
And cannot come again.
> A. E. Housman (1859-1936)
> British poet, classical scholar

SEE Smith on HAPPINESS

Novelty

Anything that calls itself new is doomed to a
short life.
> Tom Wolfe (b. 1931)
> American author, journalist

It is only the modern that ever becomes old-
fashioned.
> Oscar Wilde (1854-1900)

SEE Miller, Wells on INNOVATION;
Twain on ORIGINALITY

The Nuclear Age

The atom bomb was no 'great decision'. . . It
was merely another powerful weapon in the
arsenal of righteousness.
> Harry S. Truman (1884-1972)

The release of atomic energy has changed
everything except our way of thinking and
thus we are being driven unarmed towards a
catastrophe.
> Albert Einstein (1879-1955)

The terror of the atom age is not the violence
of the new power but the speed of man's
adjustment to it – the speed of his acceptance.
> E. B. White (1899-1985)
> American author, editor

No country without an atomic bomb could
properly consider itself independent.
> Charles de Gaulle (1890-1970)
> in 1968

Hitherto man had to live with the idea of
death as an individual; from now onward
mankind will have to live with the idea of its
death as a species.
> Arthur Koestler (1905-1983)
> British author

SEE Forster, Mason, Wells on The
ARMS RACE; Raphael on WAR

Nudity

Naked came I out of my mother's womb, and
naked shall I return thither.
> Bible, Job

We shift and bedeck and bedrape us,
Thou art noble and nude and antique.
> A. C. Swinburne (1837-1909)

Every young sculptor seems to think that he
must give the world some specimen of
indecorous womanhood, and call it Eve,
Venus, a Nymph, or any name that may
apologise for a lack of decent clothing.
> Nathaniel Hawthorne (1804-1864)
> American novelist

Nakedness reveals itself. Nudity is placed on
display. . . The nude is condemned to never
being naked. Nudity is a form of dress.
> John Berger (b. 1926)
> British critic

I have seen three emperors in their nakedness,
and the sight was not inspiring.
> Prince Otto von Bismarck (1815-1898)
> Prussian statesman

There is an unseemly exposure of the mind, as
well as of the body.
> William Hazlitt (1778-1830)
> English essayist

Verte desnuda es recordar la Tierra.
To see you naked is to recall the Earth.
> Federico García Lorca (1899-1936)

SEE Muhammad, Thoreau on DRESS;
Carlyle on The HOUSE OF LORDS;
Bible on PARADISE

Obedience

When a gentleman hath learned to obey he will grow very much fitter to command; his own memory will advise him not to command too rigorous punishments.
George Savile, Lord Halifax (1633-1695)
English statesman, author

Those who know the least obey the best.
George Farquhar (1678-1707)
Irish dramatist

It is much safer to obey than to rule.
Thomas à Kempis (1380-1471)
SEE Newbolt on DISCRETION

Obesity

Thou seest I have more flesh than another man, and therefore more frailty.
Falstaff, *King Henry IV part I*
William Shakespeare (1564-1616)

A big man has no time really to do anything but just sit and be big.
F. Scott Fitzgerald (1896-1940)

Imprisoned in every fat man, a thin one is wildly signalling to be let out.
Cyril Connolly (1903-1974)
British critic

Outside every fat man there is an even fatter man trying to close in.
Kingsley Amis (b. 1922)
British author

He must have had a magnificent build before his stomach went in for a career of its own.
Margaret Halsey (b. 1910)
American writer

That dark day when a man decides he must wear his belt under instead of over his cascading paunch.
Peter de Vries (b. 1910)
American author

Let me have men about me that are fat;
Sleek-headed men and such as sleep o' nights;
Yond' Cassius has a lean and hungry look;
He thinks too much; such men are dangerous.
Caesar, *Julius Caesar*
William Shakespeare (1564-1616)

Obstinacy

The difference between perseverance and obstinacy is that perseverance means a strong will and obstinacy means a strong won't.
Lord Dundee (b. 1902)

Obstinacy in a bad cause is but constancy in a good.
Sir Thomas Browne (1605-1682)
English physician, author

They defend their errors as if they were defending their inheritance.
Edmund Burke (1729-1797)
Irish philosopher, statesman

For every why he had a wherefore.
Samuel Butler (1612-1680)
English poet

He has a first-rate mind until he makes it up.
Violet Bonham-Carter, Lady Asquith (1887-1969)
British Liberal politician
of Sir Stafford Cripps

Like all weak men he laid an exaggerated stress on not changing one's mind.
W. Somerset Maugham (1874-1966)

I am firm. You are obstinate. He is a pig-headed fool.
Katharine Whitehorn
British journalist

None so deaf as those who won't hear.
16th century English proverb

SEE Shaw on CHANGE; Blake on OPINION

The Office

A molehill man is a pseudo-busy executive who comes to work at 9 am and finds a molehill on his desk. He has until 5 pm to make this molehill into a mountain. An accomplished molehill man will often have his mountain finished before lunch.
Fred Allen (1894-1957)
American comic

You can run an office without a boss, but you can't run an office without secretaries.
Jane Fonda (b. 1937)

He [Robert Benchley] and I had an office so

tiny that an inch smaller and it would have been adultery.
Dorothy Parker (1893-1967)
American humorous writer

SEE Wilde on STARDOM

Opera

Nothing is capable of being well set to music that is not nonsense.
Joseph Addison (1672-1719)
English essayist

Opera in English is, in the main, just about as sensible as baseball in Italian.
H. L. Mencken (1880-1956)
American journalist

Opinion

Opinion is holding something to be provisionally true which you do not know to be false.
Saint Bernard (1090-1153)

The man who never alters his opinion is like standing water, and breeds reptiles of the mind.
William Blake (1757-1827)

The public buys its opinions as it buys its meat, or takes in its milk, on the principle that it is cheaper to do this than to keep a cow. So it is, but the milk is more likely to be watered.
Samuel Butler (1835-1902)
English author

It's dull (as well as draughty) to keep an open mind.
Philip Guedalla (1889-1944)
British author

He never chooses an opinion; he just wears whatever happens to be in style.
Leo Tolstoy (1828-1910)

He thinks by infection, catching an opinion like a cold.
John Ruskin (1819-1900)
English critic

It's not that I don't have opinions, rather that I'm paid not to think aloud.
Yitzhak Navon (b. 1921)
Israeli politician, former President

I never offered an opinion till I was sixty, and then it was one which had been in our family for a century.
Benjamin Disraeli (1804-1881)

If you must tell me your opinions, tell me what you believe in. I have plenty of doubts of my own.
Johann Wolfgang von Goethe (1749-1832)

Opinions have vested interests just as men have.
Samuel Butler (1835-1902)
English author

New opinions are always suspected, and usually opposed, without any other reason but because they are not already common.
John Locke (1632-1704)

There is nothing a woman so dislikes as to have her old opinions quoted to her, especially when they confute new ones.
Katharine Tynan Hinkson (1861-1931)
Irish poet, novelist

I've always felt that a person's intelligence is directly reflected by the number of conflicting points of view he can entertain simultaneously on the same topic.
Lisa Alther (b. 1944)
American novelist

It is clear that thought is not free if the profession of certain opinions makes it impossible to earn a living.
Bertrand Russell (1872-1970)

SEE Joubert on HOSPITALITY; Lichtenberg on INDIFFERENCE; Twain on PSYCHIATRIC WARDS

Opportunity

How oft the sight of means to do ill deeds makes deeds ill done!
King John, *King John*
William Shakespeare (1564-1616)

Opportunity is the great bawd.
Benjamin Franklin (1706-1790)

Next to knowing when to seize an opportunity, the most important thing in life is to know when to forego an advantage.
Benjamin Disraeli (1804-1881)

I despise making the most of one's time. Half of the pleasures of life consist of the opportunities one has neglected.
Justice Oliver Wendell Holmes (1841-1935)
American jurist

SEE Dryden on TEMPTATION

Opposites

Without Contraries is no progression. Attraction and Repulsion, Reason and Energy, Love and Hate, are necessary to Human existence.
William Blake (1757-1827)

Opposition

Do not choose to be wrong for the sake of being different.
Lord Samuel (1870-1963)
British statesman

No Government can long be secure without a formidable Opposition.
Benjamin Disraeli (1804-1881)

Since we cannot match it let us take our revenge by abusing it.
Michel de Montaigne (1533-1592)
French essayist

SEE Kennedy on PROTEST

Oppression

You can't hold a man down without staying down with him.
Booker T. Washington (1856-1915)
American educator, reformer

The most potent weapon in the hands of the oppressor is the mind of the oppressed.
Steve Biko (1946-1977)

This is the negation of God erected into a system of Government.
W. E. Gladstone (1809-1898)

SEE DESPOTISM; Tolstoy on LIBERALS; Cromwell, Welensky on LIBERTY; Cromwell on LIBERTY; Szasz on MADNESS; Penn on PERSECUTION; REPRESSION

Optimism

In the midst of winter, I finally learned that there was in me an invincible summer.
Albert Camus (1913-1960)

A cheerful resignation is always heroic, but no phase of life is so pathetic as a forced optimism.
Elbert Hubbard (1856-1915)
American author

An optimist is a fellow who believes what's going to be will be postponed.
Kin (F. McKinney) Hubbard (1868-1930)
American humorist, journalist

An optimist is a guy who has never had much experience.
Don Marquis (1878-1937)
American humorist, journalist

These are not dark days; these are great days – the greatest days our country has ever lived.
Sir Winston Churchill (1874-1965)

Oh, yet we trust that somehow good
Shall be the final goal of ill!
Lord Tennyson (1809-1892)

Optimism is a kind of heart stimulant – the digitalis of failure.
Elbert Hubbard (1856-1915)
American author

Optimism: the world is the best of all possible worlds, and everything in it is a necessary evil.
F. H. Bradley (1846-1924)
British philosopher

The optimist proclaims that we live in the best of all possible worlds; and the pessimist fears this is true.
James Branch Cabell (1879-1958)
American novelist, essayist

Pessimism of the intellect; optimism of the will.
Antonio Gramsci (1891-1937)
Italian political theorist

Optimism. The doctrine or belief that every-thing is beautiful, including what is ugly.
Ambrose Bierce (1842-1914)
American author

Ah, well, there is just this world and then the next, and then all our troubles will be over.
old lady
quoted by L. O. Asquith

SEE Kennedy on The GOVERNMENT; Marquis on MIDDLE AGE; Sandburg on MODERN LIFE; Hubbard on PESSIMISM; Cassandra on PROPAGANDA

Orgasm

I may not be a great actress but I've become the greatest at screen orgasms. Ten seconds of heavy breathing, roll your head from side to side, simulate a slight asthma attack and die a little.
Candice Bergen (b. 1946)
American actress

When the ecstatic body grips
Its heaven, with little sobbing cries.
E. R. Dodds (1893-1979)
British classical scholar

SEE Shaw on GENIUS

Orgies

If God had meant us to have group sex, I guess he'd have given us all more organs.
Malcolm Bradbury (b. 1932)
British author

Originality

As soon as you can say what you think, and not what some other person has thought for you, you are on the way to being a remarkable man.
J. M. Barrie (1860-1937)
British playwright

Originality consists in thinking for yourself, and not in thinking unlike other people.
J. Fitzjames Stephen (1829-1894)
English jurist, writer

The more intelligent a man is, the more originality he discovers in men. Ordinary people see no difference between men.
Blaise Pascal (1623-1662)

A man with a new idea is a crank until the idea succeeds.
Mark Twain (1835-1910)

Originality is a thing we constantly clamour for, and constantly quarrel with.
Thomas Carlyle (1795-1881)
Scottish author

Originality is undetected plagiarism.
W. R. Inge (1860-1954)
Dean of St Paul's, London

Why can't somebody give us a list of things

that everybody thinks and nobody says, and another list of things that everybody says and nobody thinks.

Dr Oliver Wendell Holmes (1809-1894)
American writer, physician

Pereant qui ante nos nostra dixerunt.
Damn those who said our good things before us.

Aelius Donatus (4th century)
Roman grammarian

Tout est dit et l'on vient trop tard depuis plus de sept mille ans qu'il y a des hommes et qui pensent.
Everything has been said and we come more than seven thousand years of human thought too late.

Jean de la Bruyère (1645-1696)
French writer, moralist

A thought is often original, though you have uttered it a hundred times.

Dr Oliver Wendell Holmes (1809-1894)
American writer, physician

SEE Colby on INNOVATION

Oxford

Home of lost causes, and forsaken beliefs, and unpopular names, and impossible loyalties!

Matthew Arnold (1822-1888)
English poet, critic

The ancient seat of pedantry, where they manufacture prigs as fast as butchers in Chicago handle hogs.

R. B. Cunningham-Grahame (1852-1936)
British author

And when night
Darkens the streets, then wander forth
the sons
Of Belial, flown with insolence and
wine.

John Milton (1608-1674)

I was a modest, good-humoured boy. It is Oxford that has made me insufferable.

Sir Max Beerbohm (1872-1956)
British author

I had always imagined that Cliché was a suburb of Paris, until I discovered it to be a street in Oxford.

Philip Guedalla (1889-1944)
British author

Oxford and Cambridge

The King to Oxford sent a troop of
horse,
For Tories own no argument but force:
With equal skill to Cambridge books he
sent,
For Whigs admit no force but argument.

Sir William Browne (1692-1774)
English doctor

P

Pain

For we are born in other's pain,
And perish in our own.

Francis Thompson (1859-1907)
English poet

Pain with the thousand teeth.

Sir William Watson (1858-1935)
British poet

Paradise

And they were both naked, the man and his
wife, and were not ashamed.

Bible, Genesis

Here with a Loaf of Bread beneath
the Bough,
A Flask of Wine, a Book of Verse –
and Thou
Beside me singing in the
Wilderness –
And Wilderness is Paradise enow.

from *The Rubáiyát of Omar Khayyám*
trans. Edward Fitzgerald (1809-1883)

We, who have already borne on the road to
Paradise the lives of the best among us, want a
difficult, erect, implacable Paradise; a Paradise
where one can never rest and which has,
beside the threshold of the gates, angels with
swords.

J. A. Primo de Rivera (1903-1936)
Spanish Falangist politician

Everyone who has ever built anywhere a 'new
heaven' first found the power thereto in his
own hell.

Friedrich Nietzsche (1844-1900)

Paranoia

Depart from your enemies, yea, and beware of
your friends.

Apocrypha, Ecclesiasticus

Even a paranoid can have enemies.

Henry Kissinger (b. 1923)

A paranoid is a man who knows a little of
what's going on.

William S. Burroughs (b. 1914)
American author

SEE ANXIETY; Farquhar on LAUGHTER;
Hubbard on SENSITIVITY

Parasites

Man is the only animal that esteems itself rich
in proportion to the number and voracity of
its parasites.

George Bernard Shaw (1856-1950)

Fool that I was! upon my eagle wings
I bore this wren, till I was tired of
soaring
And now he mounts above me.

John Dryden (1631-1700)

Great fleas have little fleas upon their
backs to bite 'em,
And little fleas have lesser fleas, and
so ad infinitum.

Augustus De Morgan (1806-1871)
English mathematician

Parents

Parents are people who bear children, bore
teenagers, and board newlyweds.

anonymous

They fuck you up, your Mum and Dad.
They may not mean to, but they do.
And give you all the faults they had
And add some extra, just for you.

Philip Larkin (1922-1986)
British poet

Children begin by loving their parents. After a
time they judge them. Rarely, if ever, do they
forgive them.

Oscar Wilde (1854-1900)

If you must hold yourself up to your children
as an object lesson (which is not necessary),
hold yourself up as a warning and not as an
example.

George Bernard Shaw (1856-1950)

Go directly – see what she's doing, and tell her
she mustn't.

Punch, 1872

The suspicious parent makes an artful child.

Thomas G. Halliburton

Reasoning with a child is fine, if you can reach
the child's reason without destroying your
own.

John Mason Brown (1900-1969)
American essayist

I wish either my father or my mother, or indeed both of them, as they were in duty both equally bound to it, had minded what they were about when they begot me.
Laurence Sterne (1713-1768)
English author

How can I teach, how can I save,
This child whose features are my own,
Whose feet run down the ways where I have walked?
Michael Roberts (1902-1948)
British author

Respect the child. Be not too much his parent. Trespass not on his solitude.
R. W. Emerson (1803-1882)
American essayist, poet, philosopher

How selfhood begins with a walking away,
And love is proved in the letting go.
C. Day-Lewis (1904-1972)
British poet

SEE Billings, Confucius on CHILDREN; FATHER; MOTHER

Paris
The café of Europe.
Ferdinando Galiani (1728-1787)
Italian economist

When Paris sneezes, Europe catches cold.
Prince Metternich (1773-1859)
Austrian statesman

The French woman says, 'I am a woman and a Parisienne, and nothing foreign to me appears altogether human'.
R. W. Emerson (1803-1882)
American essayist, poet, philosopher

As an artist, a man has no home in Europe save Paris.
Friedrich Nietzsche (1844-1900)

Trade is art, and art's philosophy,
In Paris.
Elizabeth Barrett Browning (1806-1861)

If you are lucky enough to have lived in Paris as a young man, then wherever you go for the rest of your life, it stays with you, for Paris is a moveable feast.
Ernest Hemingway (1899-1961)

In Paris they simply stared when I spoke to them in French; I never did succeed in making those idiots understand their own language.
Mark Twain (1835-1910)

When good Americans die they go to Paris.
Oscar Wilde (1854-1900)

SEE Allen on TOURISM

Parliament
To anyone with politics in his blood, this place is like a pub to a drunkard.
David Lloyd George (1863-1945)
Welsh Liberal politician, Prime Minister of the House of Commons

You behold a range of exhausted volcanoes.
Benjamin Disraeli (1804-1881)
of the Front Bench

The Commons, faithful to their system, remained in a wise and masterly inactivity.
Sir James Mackintosh (1765-1832)
Scottish philosopher

Parliament is not a *congress* of ambassadors from different and hostile interests; which interests each must maintain, as an agent and advocate, against other agents and advocates; but parliament is a *deliberative* assembly of *one* nation, with *one* interest, that of the whole; where, not local purposes, not local prejudices ought to guide, but the general good, resulting from the general reason of the whole. You choose a member indeed; but when you have chosen him, he is not a member of Bristol, but he is a member of *parliament*.
Edmund Burke (1729-1797)
Irish philosopher, statesman

This place is the longest running farce in the West End.
Cyril Smith (b. 1928)
British Liberal politician

SEE The HOUSE OF LORDS

Partnership
And so we plough along, as the fly said to the ox.
H. W. Longfellow (1807-1882)

Mr Morgan buys his partners; I grow my own.
Andrew Carnegie (1835-1918)
American industrialist, philanthropist

When two men in a business always agree one of them is unnecessary.
William Wrigley Jr (1861-1932)
American businessman

Every sin is the result of a collaboration.
Stephen Crane (1871-1900)
American novelist, journalist

Passion
Some people lose control of their sluice gates of passion.
Worker's Daily, Beijing 1981

If we resist our passions, it is more because of their weakness than because of our strength.
François, Duc de La Rochefoucauld (1613-1680)
French writer, moralist

Passion, though a bad regulator, is a powerful spring.
R. W. Emerson (1803-1882)
American essayist, poet, philosopher

The passions are the only orators which always persuade.
François, Duc de La Rochefoucauld (1613-1680)
French writer, moralist

It seemed to me pretty plain, that they had more of love than matrimony in them.
Oliver Goldsmith (1728-1774)

The Past
The past is a foreign country; they do things differently there.
L. P. Hartley (1895-1972)
British author

Each has his past shut in him like the leaves of a book known to him by heart and his friends can only read the title.
Virginia Woolf (1882-1941)

We are well advised to keep on nodding terms with the people we used to be, whether we find them attractive company or not. . . We forget all too soon the things we thought we could never forget.
Joan Didion (b. 1934)
American writer

The only thing I regret about my past is the length of it. If I had to live my life again, I'd make the same mistakes, only sooner.
Tallulah Bankhead (1902-1968)
American actress

SEE Wilder on REGRET

Paternity
There was a young man in Rome that was very like Augustus Caesar; Augustus took knowledge of it and sent for the man, and asked him 'Was your mother never at Rome?' He answered 'No Sir; but my father was'.
Francis Bacon (1561-1626)

Maternity is a matter of fact; paternity is a matter of opinion.
anonymous

He that bulls the cow must keep the calf.
16th century proverb

SEE FATHER; PARENTS

Patience
With close-lipp'd Patience for our only friend,
Sad Patience, too near neighbour to Despair.
Matthew Arnold (1822-1888)
English poet, critic

Patience, the beggar's virtue.
Philip Massinger (1583-1640)
English dramatist

Patience, that blending of moral courage with physical timidity.
Thomas Hardy (1840-1928)

Patience is the virtue of an ass, that trots beneath his burden, and is quiet.
Lord Lansdowne (1667-1735)
English poet, dramatist

I'm extraordinarily patient provided I get my own way in the end.
Margaret Thatcher (b. 1925)

Beware the fury of a patient man.
John Dryden (1631-1700)

Never cut what you can untie.
Joseph Joubert (1754-1824)
French essayist, moralist

That which in mean men we entitle patience
Is pale cold cowardice in noble breasts.
Duchess of Gloucester, King Richard III
William Shakespeare (1564-1616)

Patriotism
Patriotism is your conviction that this country is superior to all others because you were born in it.
George Bernard Shaw (1856-1950)

My fellow Americans, ask not what your country can do for you – ask what you can do for your country.
John F. Kennedy (1917-1963)

I only regret that I have but one life to lose for my country.
Nathan Hale (1755-1776)
speech before being executed
as spy by the British

The summer soldier and the sunshine patriot will, in this crisis, shrink from the service of their country; but he that stands it NOW deserves the love and thanks of man and woman.
Thomas Paine (1737-1809)
pamphleteer, revolutionary

A man who is good enough to shed his blood for his country is good enough to be given a square deal afterwards.
Theodore Roosevelt (1858-1919)

Our country right or wrong. When right, to be kept right; when wrong, to be put right.
Carl Schurz (1829-1906)
German orator, later American
general and senator

'My country, right or wrong' is a thing that no patriot would think of saying except in a desperate case. It is like saying 'My mother, drunk or sober'.
G. K. Chesterton (1874-1936)

Patriotism has become a mere national self-assertion, a sentimentality of flag-cheering with no constructive duties.
H. G. Wells (1866-1946)

Patriotism is a lively sense of collective responsibility. Nationalism is a silly cock crowing on its own dunghill.
Richard Aldington (1892-1962)
British author

Never was patriot yet, but was a fool.
John Dryden (1631-1700)

To me, it seems a dreadful indignity to have a soul controlled by geography.
George Santayana (1863-1952)
American philosopher, poet

Where liberty dwells there is my country.
attributed to Thomas Jefferson (1743-1826)
and Thomas Paine (1737-1809)

Our country is wherever we are well off.
John Milton (1608-1674)

Whenever you hear a man speak of his love for his country, it is a sign that he expects to be paid for it.
H. L. Mencken (1880-1956)
American journalist

Patriotism is the last refuge of a scoundrel.
Dr Samuel Johnson (1709-1784)

In Dr Johnson's famous dictionary patriotism is defined as the last resort of a scoundrel. With all due respect to an enlightened but inferior lexicographer I beg to submit that it is the first.
Ambrose Bierce (1842-1914)
American author

True patriots we; for be it understood. We left our country for our country's good.
George Barrington (1755-1810)
celebrated pickpocket,
transported to Botany Bay

The proper means of increasing the love we bear our native country is to reside some time in a foreign one.
William Shenstone (1714-1763)
English poet

It has never happened to me that I've had to choose between betraying a friend and betraying my country, but if it ever does so happen I hope I have the guts to betray my country.
E. M. Forster (1879-1970)

I love my country better than my family, but I love human nature better than my country.
François Fénelon (1651-1715)
French prelate, writer

God has given you your country as cradle, and humanity as mother; you cannot rightly love your brethren of the cradle if you love not the common mother.
Giuseppe Mazzini (1805-1872)
Italian nationalist leader

I realise that patriotism is not enough. I must have no hatred or bitterness towards anyone.
Edith Cavell (1865-1915)
British nurse

SEE Walpole on The ENGLISH;
Canning on INTERNATIONALISM

Patronage

Patron — Commonly a wretch who supports with insolence, and is paid with flattery.
Dr Samuel Johnson (1709-1784)

If it were not for the intellectual snobs who pay — in solid cash — the tribute which philistinism owes to culture, the arts would perish with their starving practitioners. Let us thank heaven for hypocrisy.
Aldous Huxley (1894-1963)

Is not a patron, my lord, one who looks with unconcern on a man struggling for life in the water, and when he has reached ground, encumbers him with help?
Dr Samuel Johnson (1709-1784)

Toutes les fois que je donne une place vacante, je fais cent mécontents et un ingrat.
Every time I bestow a vacant office I make a hundred discontented persons and one ingrate.
Louis XIV of France (1638-1715)

The notice which you have been pleased to take of my labours, had it been early, had been kind; but it has been delayed till I am indifferent, and cannot enjoy it; till I am solitary, and cannot impart it; till I am known, and do not want it.
Dr Samuel Johnson (1709-1784)
to Lord Chesterfield

Payment

Give the labourer his wage before his perspiration be dry.
Muhammad (c. 570-632)

Cash nexus is not the sole nexus of man with man.
William Morris (1834-1896)
English artist, writer, printer

SEE Byron on BILLS

Peace

Since wars begin in the minds of men, it is in the minds of men that the defences of peace must be constructed.
UNESCO constitution

If you would preserve peace, then prepare for peace.
Barthélemy Enfantin (1776-1864)
French economist, industrialist

Peace hath her victories, no less renowned than War.
John Milton (1608-1674)

You may either win your peace or buy it: win it, by resistance to evil; buy it, by compromise with evil.
John Ruskin (1819-1900)
English critic

As I have counselled you to be slow in taking on a war, so advise I you to be slow in peace-making. Before ye agree look that the ground of your wars be satisfied in your peace, and that ye see a good surety for you and your people: otherways, an honourable and just war is more tolerable than a dishonourable and disadvantageous peace.
King James I of England (1566-1625)

Peace and tranquillity! I should think so! Every bird of prey wants it to consume its booty in comfort.
Johann Wolfgang von Goethe (1749-1832)

Solitudinem faciunt pacem appellant.
They make a wilderness and call it peace.
Tacitus (c. 55-c. 120)
Roman historian

You discharge your olive-branch as if from a catapult.
Cardinal John Newman (1801-1890)
English churchman, theologian

When we say 'War is over if you want it', we mean that if everyone demanded peace instead of another TV set, we'd have peace.
John Lennon (1940-1980)

Mankind has grown strong in eternal struggles and it will only perish through eternal peace.
Adolf Hitler (1889-1945)

The United States can declare peace upon the world, and win it.
Ely Culbertson (1891-1955)
American bridge champion

They shall beat their swords into plowshares, and their spears into pruninghooks: nation shall not lift up sword against nation, neither shall they learn war any more.
Bible, Isaiah

SEE APPEASEMENT; Vegetius on The ARMS RACE; Mussolini on FASCISM; St Augustine, Franklin on WAR

Perfection

Faultily faultless, icily regular, splendidly null,
Dead perfection, no more.
Lord Tennyson (1809-1872)

So much perfection argues rottenness somewhere.
Beatrice Webb (1858-1943)
British Fabian Socialist
of Sir Oswald Mosley

He has not a single redeeming defect.
Benjamin Disraeli (1804-1881)

The indefatigable pursuit of an unattainable Perfection even though it consist in nothing more than in the pounding of an old piano, is what alone gives a meaning to our lives on this unavailing star.
Logan Pearsall Smith (1865-1946)
American essayist

Striving to better, oft we mar what's well.
Albany, *King Lear*
William Shakespeare (1564-1616)

No barber shaves so close but another finds his work.
English proverb

SEE Congreve on MODESTY; Ayer on SCEPTICISM

Persecution

Martyrs and persecutors are the same type of man. As to which is the persecutor and which the martyr, this is only a question of transient power.
Elbert Hubbard (1856-1915)
American author

Whoever is right, the persecutor must be wrong.
William Penn (1644-1718)
religious leader, founder of Pennsylvania

The way of this world is to praise dead saints and persecute living ones.
Nathaniel Howe (1764-1837)
American clergyman

If they come for me in the morning, they will come for you at night.
Angela Davis (b. 1944)
American radical

Perseverance

The mass of men lead lives of quiet desperation.
H. D. Thoreau (1817-1862)

Under the bludgeonings of chance
My head is bloody, but unbowed.
W. E. Henley (1849-1903)
English author

God Almighty hates a quitter.
Samuel Fessenden (1847-1908)
American lawyer, politician

The troubles of our proud and angry dust
Are from eternity, and shall not fail.
Bear them we can, and if we can we must.
Shoulder the sky, my lad, and drink your ale.
A. E. Housman (1859-1936)
British poet, classical scholar

An arch never sleeps.
                                        Indian saying

Neither evil tongues,
Rash judgements, nor the sneers of
   selfish men,
Nor greetings where no kindness is,
   nor all
The dreary intercourse of daily life,
Shall e'er prevail against us.
                    William Wordsworth (1770-1850)

SEE OBSTINACY

Persuasion
He that winna be ruled by the rudder maun be
ruled by the rock.
                                        Scottish proverb

We are not won by arguments that we can
analyse but by tone and temper, by the
manner which is the man himself.
                        Samuel Butler (1835-1902)
                                        English author

The best way to convince a fool that he is
wrong is to let him have his own way.
                            Josh Billings (1818-1885)
                                        American humorist

There are two levers for moving men – interest
and fear.
                    Napoleon Bonaparte (1769-1821)

It was said that Mr Gladstone could persuade
most people of most things, and himself of
anything.
                                W. R. Inge (1860-1954)
                            Dean of St Paul's, London

There is a holy, mistaken zeal in politics, as
well as religion. By persuading others we
convince ourselves.
                            Junius (18th century)
                pseudonym of a writer never identified

SEE Newman on FAITH; La Rochefoucauld
on PASSION; Macaulay on SPEECHES

Perversion
Commit
The oldest sins the newest kind of ways.
                    King Henry, King Henry IV part 2
                    William Shakespeare (1564-1616)

The human knee is a joint and not an
entertainment.
                        Percy Hammond (1873-1936)
                                        American critic

SEE de Gourmont on CHASTITY

Pessimism
One has to have the courage of one's pessimism.
                            Ian McEwan (b. 1938)
                                        British author

It is wisdom in prosperity, when all is as thou
wouldst have it, to fear and suspect the worst.
                            Erasmus (c. 1466-1536)

She not only expects the worst, but makes the
worst of it when it happens.
                        Michael Arlen (1895-1956)
                                        British novelist

My pessimism goes to the point of suspecting
the sincerity of the pessimists.
                        Jean Rostand (1894-1977)
                            French biologist and writer

Do you know what a pessimist is? A man who
thinks everybody as nasty as himself, and
hates them for it.
                    George Bernard Shaw (1856-1950)

A pessimist is one who has been intimately
acquainted with an optimist.
                        Elbert Hubbard (1856-1915)
                                        American author

SEE Cabell, Gramsci on OPTIMISM

Philanthropy
To fish for honour with a silver hook.
                        Nicholas Breton (1545-1626)
                                        English poet

To enjoy a good reputation, give publicly, and
steal privately.
                            Josh Billings (1818-1885)
                                        American humorist

Philanthropist. A rich (and usually bald) old
gentleman who has trained himself to grin
while his conscience is picking his pocket.
                        Ambrose Bierce (1842-1914)
                                        American author

Philanthropy is the refuge of people who wish
to annoy their fellow creatures.
                            Oscar Wilde (1854-1900)

Philosophy
Unintelligible answers to insoluble problems.
                        Henry B. Adams (1838-1918)
                                        American historian

When he who hears doesn't know what he
who speaks means, and when he who speaks
doesn't know what he himself means – that is
philosophy.
                                Voltaire (1694-1778)

It's easy to answer the ultimate questions – it
saves you bothering with the immediate ones.
                    George, Epitaph for George Dillon
                                John Osborne (b. 1929)
                                        British playwright

I shall gladly obey His call; yet I would also
feel grateful if He would grant me a little
longer time with you, and if I could be
permitted to solve a question on the origin of
the soul.
                        Saint Anselm (1034-1109)
                        Italian churchman, theologian

Metaphysics is the finding of bad reasons for what we believe upon instinct; but to find these reasons is no less an instinct.

F. H. Bradley (1846-1924)
British philosopher

Metaphysics I detested. The science appeared to me an elaborate, diabolical invention for mystifying what was clear, and confounding what was intelligible.

W. E. Aytoun (1813-1865)
Scottish poet

Philosophy consists largely of one philosopher arguing that all others are jackasses. He usually proves it, and I should add that he also usually proves that he is one himself.

H. L. Mencken (1880-1956)
American journalist

There is only one thing that a philosopher can be relied on to do, and that is, to contradict other philosophers.

William James (1842-1910)
American psychologist, philosopher

As for the philosophers, they make imaginary laws for imaginary commonwealths.

Francis Bacon (1561-1626)

A blind man in a dark room looking for a black hat which is not there.

anonymous

All are lunatics, but he who can analyze his delusions is called a philosopher.

Ambrose Bierce (1842-1914)
American author

There is nothing so absurd but some philosopher has said it.

Cicero (106-43 BC)

I have tried too in my time to be a philosopher but, I don't know how, cheerfulness was always breaking in.

Oliver Edwards (1711-1791)
English lawyer

Bishop Berkeley destroyed this world in one volume octavo; and nothing remained, after his time, but mind; which experienced a similar fate from the hand of Mr Hume in 1737.

Sydney Smith (1771-1845)
English writer, clergyman

Any philosophy that can be put 'in a nutshell' belongs there.

Sydney J. Harris (b. 1917)
American journalist

Philosophies are devices for making it possible to do, coolly, continuously, and with a good conscience, things which otherwise one could do only in the heat of passion, spasmodically, and under the threat of subsequent remorse.

Aldous Huxley (1894-1963)

Philosophy stands in the same relation to the study of the actual world as masturbation to sexual love.

Karl Marx (1818-1883)

The flour is the important thing, not the mill; the fruits of philosophy, not the philosophy itself. When we ask what time it is we don't want to know how watches are constructed.

G. C. Lichtenberg (1742-1799)
German physicist, writer

For there was never yet philosopher
That could endure the toothache
patiently.

Leonato, Much Ado About Nothing
William Shakespeare (1564-1616)

SEE Diderot on DOUBT; Browne on FAITH; St John on HISTORY; Hobbes on LEISURE; Coleridge on POETS; Marx on REVOLUTION

Photography

A photograph is a secret about a secret. The more it tells you the less you know.

Diane Arbus (1923-1971)
American photographer

The magic of photography is metaphysical. What you see in the photograph isn't what you saw at the time. The real skill of photography is organised visual lying.

Terence Donovan (b. 1936)
British photographer

It takes a lot of imagination to be a good photographer. You need less imagination to be a painter, because you can invent things. But in photography everything is so ordinary; it takes a lot of looking before you learn to see the ordinary.

David Bailey (b. 1938)
British photographer

The virtue of the camera is not the power it has to transform the photographer into an artist, but the impulse it gives him to keep on looking.

Brooks Atkinson (b. 1894)
American critic, essayist

While there is perhaps a province in which the photograph can tell us nothing more than what we see with our own eyes, there is another in which it proves to us how little our eyes permit us to see.

Dorothea Lange (1895-1965)
American photographer

SEE Newman on The PRESS

Piety

Nothing is more repulsive than a furtively prurient spirituality; it is just as unsavoury as gross sensuality.

Carl Jung (1875-1961)

Their sighin', cantin', grace-proud faces,
Their three-mile prayers, and half-mile
graces.
Robert Burns (1759-1796)

A wicked fellow is the most pious when he
takes to it. He'll beat you all in piety.
Dr Samuel Johnson (1709-1784)

Piety is the tinfoil of pretense.
Elbert Hubbard (1856-1915)
American author

Bernard always had a few prayers in the hall
and some whiskey afterwards as he was rather
pious.
Daisy Ashford (1881-1972)
British writer of *The Young
Visiters*, aged 9

How holy people look when they are sea-sick!
Samuel Butler (1835-1902)
English author

Pity

When a man suffers himself, it is called
misery; when he suffers in the suffering of
another, it is called pity.
Saint Augustine (354-430)

Pity costs nothing, and ain't worth nothing.
Josh Billings (1818-1885)
American humorist

Pity is treason.
Maximilien Robespierre (1758-1794)
French revolutionary leader

If a madman were to come into this room with
a stick in his hand, no doubt we should pity
the state of his mind; but our primary
consideration would be to take care of ourselves. We should knock him down first, and
pity him afterwards.
Dr Samuel Johnson (1709-1784)

The wretched have no compassion.
Dr Samuel Johnson (1709-1784)

One cannot weep for the entire world, it is
beyond human strength. One must choose.
Jean Anouilh (b. 1910)
French dramatist

Those who do not complain are never pitied.
Jane Austen (1775-1817)

SEE Collins on LOVE; Brien on LOVERS

Plagiarism

Taking something from one man and making
it worse is plagiarism.
George Moore (1852-1933)
Irish author

It is a mean thief, or a successful author, that
plunders the dead.
Austin O'Malley (1858-1932)
American oculist, author

Most writers steal a good thing when they
can.
Bryan Waller Proctor (1787-1874)
English poet

He invades authors like a monarch, and what
would be theft in other poets is only victory in
him.
John Dryden (1631-1700)
of Ben Jonson

When you take stuff from one writer, it's
plagiarism; but when you take it from many
writers, it's research.
Wilson Mizner (1876-1933)

Whatever is well said by another, is mine.
Seneca (c. 5-65)
Roman writer, philosopher, statesman

It's a wise crack that knows its own father.
Raymond Clapper (1892-1944)
American journalist

SEE Inge on ORIGINALITY; France on
QUOTATIONS

Planning

When schemes are laid in advance, it is
surprising how often the circumstances fit in
with them.
Sir William Osler (1849-1919)
Canadian physician

It is a mistake to look too far ahead. Only one
link in the chain of destiny can be handled at a
time.
Sir Winston Churchill (1874-1965)

We are always getting ready to live, but never
living.
R. W. Emerson (1803-1882)
American essayist, poet, philosopher

Platitudes

In spite of his practical ability, some of his
experience had petrified into maxims and
quotations.
George Eliot (1819-1880)

In modern life nothing produces such an effect
as a good platitude. It makes the whole world
kin.
Oscar Wilde (1854-1900)

The Republicans stroke platitudes until they
purr like epigrams.
Adlai Stevenson (1900-1966)
American Democratic politician

A platitude is a truth we are tired of hearing.
Sir Godfrey Nicholson (b. 1901)
British businessman, Conservative politician

All generalisations are dangerous, even this
one.
Alexandre Dumas (1824-1895)

SEE Chesterton on BANALITY; Wilder
on LITERATURE; Huxley on PROVERBS

Play

Il faut noter, que les jeux d'enfants ne sont pas jeux: et les faut juger en eux, comme leurs plus sérieuses actions.
It should be noted that children's games are not merely games; one should regard them as their most serious activities.

> Michel de Montaigne (1533-1592)
> French essayist

Life isn't all beer and skittles; but beer and skittles, or something better of the same sort, must form a good part of every Englishman's education.

> Thomas Hughes (1822-1896)
> English author

If all the year were playing holidays,
To sport would be as tedious as to work.

> Prince Hal, *King Henry IV part I*
> William Shakespeare (1564-1616)

Men trifle with their business and their politics; but never trifle with their games. It brings truth home to them. They cannot pretend that they have won when they have lost, nor that they made a magnificent drive when they foozled it. The Englishman is at his best on the links, and at his worst in the Cabinet.

> George Bernard Shaw (1856-1950)

Public money is scarcely ever so well employed as in securing bits of waste ground and keeping them as open spaces.

> Sir Arthur Helps (1813-1875)
> English author

Amusement is the happiness of those who cannot think.

> Alexander Pope (1688-1744)

One half of the world cannot understand the pleasures of the other.

> Jane Austen (1775-1817)

> SEE CARDS; GAMBLING; GOLF; PLEASURE; SPORT

Pleasure

A man hath no better thing under the sun than to eat and to drink and to be merry.

> Bible, Ecclesiastes

Ah, make the most of what we yet may spend,
Before we too unto the Dust descend.

> from *The Rubáiyát of Omar Khayyám*
> trans. Edward Fitzgerald (1809-1883)

The truth is, I do indulge myself a little the more in pleasure, knowing that this is the proper age of my life to do it; and, out of my observation that most men that do thrive in the world do forget to take pleasure during the time that they are getting their estate, but reserve that till they have got one, and then it is too late for them to enjoy it.

> Samuel Pepys (1633-1703)
> *aged 33*

If I had no duties, and no reference to futurity, I would spend my life in driving briskly in a post-chaise with a pretty woman.

> Dr Samuel Johnson (1709-1784)

All the things I really like to do are either immoral, illegal, or fattening.

> Alexander Woollcott (1887-1943)
> American columnist, critic

Stolen waters are sweet, and bread eaten in secret is pleasant.

> Bible, Proverbs

Scratching is one of nature's sweetest gratifications, and the one nearest at hand.

> Michel de Montaigne (1533-1592)
> French essayist

> SEE Johnson on BLOODSPORTS;
> Johnson on HYPOCRISY; Austen,
> Shakespeare on PLAY

Poetry

Poetry is the spontaneous overflow of powerful feelings: it takes its origin from emotion recollected in tranquillity.

> William Wordsworth (1770-1850)

Poetry lifts the veil from the hidden beauty of the world, and makes familiar objects be as if they were not familiar.

> P. B. Shelley (1792-1822)

Poetry is what Milton saw when he went blind.

> Don Marquis (1878-1937)
> American humorist, journalist

That willing suspension of disbelief for the moment, which constitutes poetic faith.

> S. T. Coleridge (1772-1834)

Poetry is the supreme fiction, madame.

> Wallace Stevens (1879-1955)
> American poet

Poetry is truth in its Sunday clothes.

> Joseph Roux (1834-1886)
> French priest and writer

Poetry is man's rebellion against being what he is.

> James Branch Cabell (1879-1958)
> American novelist, essayist

Out of our quarrels with others we make rhetoric. Out of our quarrels with ourselves we make poetry.

> W. B. Yeats (1865-1939)

Poetry is what gets lost in translation.

> *attributed to* Robert Frost (1874-1963)

One merit of poetry few persons will deny: it says more and in fewer words than prose.

> Voltaire (1694-1778)

The world, we believe, is pretty well agreed in thinking that the shorter a prize poem is, the better.
Lord Macaulay (1800-1859)
English historian

Prose on certain occasions can bear a great deal of poetry; on the other hand, poetry sinks and swoons under a moderate weight of prose.
Walter Savage Landor (1775-1864)
English author

Writing free verse is like playing tennis with the net down.
Robert Frost (1875-1963)
American poet

Poetry should surprise by a fine excess and not by singularity – it should strike the Reader as a wording of his own highest thoughts, and appear almost a Remembrance.
John Keats (1795-1821)

Science is for those who learn; poetry, for those who know.
Joseph Roux (1834-1886)
French priest and writer

Knowledge of the subject is to the poet what durable materials are to the architect.
Dr Samuel Johnson (1709-1784)

The roaring of the wind is my wife and the stars through the window pane are my children. The mighty abstract idea I have of beauty in all things stifles the more divided and minute domestic happiness.
John Keats (1795-1821)

These poems, with all their crudities, doubts, and confusions, are written for the love of Man and in praise of God, and I'd be a damn' fool if they weren't.
Dylan Thomas (1914-1953)

After all, the commonplaces are the great poetic truths.
Robert Louis Stevenson (1850-1894)

Poetry is a mixture of common sense, which not all have, with an uncommon sense, which very few have.
John Masefield (1878-1967)
British poet, playwright

The mind that finds its way to wild places is the poet's; but the mind that never finds its way back is the lunatic's.
G. K. Chesterton (1874-1936)

Perhaps no person can be a poet, or can even enjoy poetry, without a certain unsoundness of mind.
Lord Macaulay (1800-1859)
English historian

Poetry is the language of a state of crisis.
Stéphane Mallarmé (1842-1898)
French Symbolist poet

Poetry is devil's wine.
Saint Augustine (354-430)

The poet's business is not to save the soul of man but to make it worth saving.
James Elroy Flecker (1884-1915)
British poet

Poetry is the language in which man explores his own amazement.
Christopher Fry (b. 1907)
British playwright

Poetry should be great and unobtrusive, a thing which enters into one's soul, and does not startle or amaze it with itself, but with its subject.
John Keats (1795-1821)

Publishing a volume of verse is like dropping a rose petal down the Grand Canyon and waiting for the echo.
Don Marquis (1878-1937)
American humorist, journalist

Poetry has never brought in enough to buy shoe-strings.
William Wordsworth (1770-1850)

There's no money in poetry, but then there's no poetry in money either.
Robert Graves (1895-1985)
British poet, novelist

A poem is not necessarily obscure because it does not aim to be popular. It is enough if a work be perspicuous to those for whom it is written.
S. T. Coleridge (1772-1834)

The one man who should never attempt an explanation of a poem is its author. If the poem can be improved by its author's explanations it never should have been published.
Archibald MacLeish (1892-1982)
American poet

Each venture
Is a new beginning, a raid on the
    inarticulate
With shabby equipment always
    deteriorating
In the general mess of imprecision
    of feeling.
T. S. Eliot (1888-1965)

When you are old and gray and full
    of sleep,
And nodding by the fire, take down
    this book.
W. B. Yeats (1865-1939)

Not marble nor the gilded monuments
Of princes shall outlive this powerful
    rhyme.
William Shakespeare (1564-1616)

Poets

I hate the whole race. . . There is no believing a word they say – your professional poets, I mean – there never existed a more worthless set than Byron and his friends for example.
Duke of Wellington (1769-1852)

Sir, I admit your general rule,
That every poet is a fool,
But you yourself may serve to show it,
That every fool is not a poet.
S. T. Coleridge (1772-1834)

Of course poets have morals and manners of their own.
Thomas Hardy (1840-1928)

Idleness, that is the curse of other men, is the nurse of poets.
Walter D'Arcy Cresswell (b. 1896)
British poet

The man who does not betake himself at once and desperately to sawing is called a loafer, though he may be knocking at the doors of heaven all the while.
H. D. Thoreau (1817-1862)

Could a man live by it, it were not unpleasant employment to be a poet.
Oliver Goldsmith (1728-1774)

To be a poet is a condition rather than a profession.
Robert Graves (1895-1985)
British poet, novelist

God's most candid critics are those of his children whom he has made poets.
Sir Walter Raleigh (1861-1922)
British academic

Poets are the unacknowledged legislators of the world.
P. B. Shelley (1792-1822)

Good artists exist simply in what they make, and consequently are perfectly uninteresting in what they are. A really great poet is the most unpoetical of all creatures. But inferior poets are absolutely fascinating. The worse their rhymes are, the more picturesque they look. The mere fact of having published a book of second-rate sonnets makes a man quite irresistible. He lives the poetry that he cannot write. The others write the poetry that they dare not realize.
Oscar Wilde (1854-1900)

Who shall measure the heat and violence of the poet's heart when caught and tangled in a woman's body?
Virginia Woolf (1882-1941)

As fire is kindled by fire, so is a poet's mind kindled by contact with a brother poet.
John Keble (1792-1866)
English clergyman, poet

I stood among them, but not of them;
in a shroud
Of thoughts which were not their thoughts.
Lord Byron (1788-1824)

That is what all poets do: they talk to themselves out loud; and the world overhears them. But it's horribly lonely not to hear someone else talk sometimes.
Marchbanks, *Candida*
George Bernard Shaw (1856-1950)

I am two fools, I know,
For loving, and for saying so
In whining poetry.
John Donne (c. 1571-1631)

Dr Donne's verses are like the peace of God: they pass all understanding.
King James I of England (1566-1625)

Poets utter great and wise things which they do not themselves understand.
Plato (427-347 BC)

Great poets are obscure for two opposite reasons; now, because they are talking about something too large for anyone to understand, and now again because they are talking about something too small for anyone to see.
G. K. Chesterton (1874-1936)

No man was ever yet a great poet without being at the same time a profound philosopher.
S. T. Coleridge (1772-1834)

Being a professor of poetry is rather like being a Kentucky colonel. It's not really a subject one can profess – unless one hires oneself out to write pieces for funerals or the marriages of dons.
W. H. Auden (1907-1973)

Nine-tenths of English poetic literature is the result either of vulgar careerism or of a poet trying to keep his hand in. Most poets are dead by their late twenties.
Robert Graves (1895-1985)
British poet, novelist

He lied with such a fervour of intention
There was no doubt he earned his
laureate pension.
Lord Byron (1788-1824)

A taste for drawing-rooms has spoiled more poets than ever did a taste for gutters.
Thomas Beer (1889-1940)
American essayist, novelist

But I, being poor, have only my dreams.
I have spread my dreams under your feet;
Tread softly, because you tread on my dreams.
W. B. Yeats (1865-1939)

If you want to write poetry you must earn a living some other way.
> T. S. Eliot (1888-1965)

The whole of my returns from the writing trade not amounting to seven score pounds.
> William Wordsworth (1770-1850)
> *aged 50*

In his youth, Wordsworth sympathised with the French Revolution, went to France, wrote good poetry, and had a natural daughter. At this period, he was a 'bad' man. Then he became 'good', abandoned his daughter, adopted correct principles, and wrote bad poetry.
> Bertrand Russell (1872-1970)

The reason Milton wrote in fetters when he wrote of Angels and God, and at liberty when of the Devils and Hell, is because he was a true poet, and of the Devil's party without knowing it.
> William Blake (1757-1827)

His imagination resembled the wings of an ostrich. It enabled him to run, though not to soar.
> Lord Macaulay (1800-1859)
> English historian
> *of Dryden*

Cibber! write all thy Verses upon Glasses,
The only way to save 'em from our Arses.
> Alexander Pope (1688-1744)
> *of Colley Cibber, Poet*
> *Laureate*

Careless thinking carefully versified.
> J. R. Lowell (1819-1891)
> American poet, editor
> *of Alexander Pope*

In poetry, no less than in life, he is 'a beautiful and ineffectual angel, beating in the void his luminous wings in vain'.
> Matthew Arnold (1822-1888)
> English poet, critic
> *of Shelley*

He found in stones the sermons he had already hidden there.
> Oscar Wilde (1854-1900)
> *of Wordsworth*

I listen to nature and mankind with astonishment, and I copy what they teach me without pedantry and without giving things meanings that I can't really be certain they have. Nobody, not even the poet, holds the secret of the world. But people's sufferings, the constant injustice that flows through the world, my own body and my own thoughts, prevent me from moving my house and dwelling among the stars.
> Frederico García Lorca (1898-1936)

Magnificently unprepared
For the long littleness of life.
> Frances Cornford (1886-1960)
> British poet
> *of Rupert Brooke*

Some rhyme a neebor's name to lash;
Some rhyme (vain thought!) for needfu' cash;
Some rhyme to court the country clash,
An' raise a din;
For me, an aim I never fash;
I rhyme for fun.
> Robert Burns (1759-1796)

SEE BYRON; Dryden on PLAGIARISM;
Horace on WINE

The Police

> *Con el alma de charol*
> *vienen por la carretera.*
> *Jorobados y nocturnos,*
> *por donde animan ordenan*
> *silencios de goma oscura*
> *y miedos de fina arena.*

With their souls of patent leather they come down the road. Hunched and nocturnal, where they breathe they impose silence of dark rubber and fear of fine sand.
> Federico García Lorca (1898-1936)

I'm not against the police; I'm just afraid of them.
> Alfred Hitchcock (1899-1980)

I have never seen a situation so dismal that a policeman couldn't make it worse.
> Brendan Behan (1923-1964)
> Irish playwright

You are thought here to be the most senseless and fit man for the constable of the watch.
> Dogberry, *Much Ado About Nothing*
> William Shakespeare (1564-1616)

Every society gets the kind of criminal it deserves. What is equally true is that every community gets the kind of law enforcement it insists on.
> Robert Kennedy (1925-1968)

SEE KILLJOYS

Political Parties

When great questions end, little parties begin.
> Walter Bagehot (1826-1877)
> English economist, critic

Party is the madness of many, for the gain of a few.
> Jonathan Swift (1667-1745)

A sect or a party is an elegant incognito devised to save a man from the vexation of thinking.
> R. W. Emerson (1803-1882)
> American essayist, poet, philosopher

The best party is but a kind of conspiracy against the rest of the nation.
> George Savile, Lord Halifax (1633-1695)
> English statesman, author

The party should agree to vent nothing but the truth for three months together, which will give them credit for six months' lying afterwards.
> John Arbuthnot (1667-1735)
> English writer, physician

The Democratic Party is like a mule – without pride of ancestry or hope of posterity.
> Ignatius Donnelly (1831-1901)
> American writer, politician

As usual the Liberals offer a mixture of sound and original ideas. Unfortunately none of the sound ideas is original and none of the original is sound.
> Harold Macmillan, Lord Stockton (1894-1986)
> British Conservative politician, Prime Minister

The Labour Party is a moral crusade or it is nothing.
> Harold Wilson (b. 1916)
> British Labour politician, Prime Minister

We have never yet had a Labour Government that knew what taking power really means; they always act like second-class citizens.
> Dora Russell (1894-1986)
> British author, campaigner

The lounge of the main hotel is full of jollity, with large comfortable men sitting in braces; the bar is packed with talkative intellectuals, full of witty disloyalties.
> Anthony Sampson (b. 1926)
> British journalist, author
> *at the Labour Party Conference*

What a genius the Labour Party has for cutting itself in half and letting the two parts writhe in public.
> Cassandra (Sir William Connor) (1909-1967)
> British journalist

Growing older, I have lost the need to be political, which means, in this country, the need to be left. I am driven into grudging toleration of the Conservative Party because it is the party of non-politics, of resistance to politics.
> Kingsley Amis (b. 1922)
> British author

In order to succeed in our party the back-bencher must be as wise as a dove and as innocent as a serpent. . . Not to be a monetarist in today's party is to suffer from a severe handicap; it is the political equivalent of being young, black, and unemployed.
> Julian Critchley (b. 1930)
> British Conservative politician
> *of the Conservative Party*

A Conservative government is an organised hypocrisy.
> Benjamin Disraeli (1804-1881)

No party is as bad as its leaders.
> Will Rogers (1879-1935)
> American humorist

Any party which takes credit for the rain must not be surprised if its opponents blame it for the drought.
> Dwight W. Morrow (1873-1931)
> American politician

All political parties die at last of swallowing their own lies.
> John Arbuthnot (1667-1735)
> English writer, physician

SEE ELECTIONS; Stevenson on PLATITUDES; Darling on POLITICIANS; Pope on PROPAGANDA; Thatcher on UNEMPLOYMENT

Politicians

Oh Lord, grant that we may not despise our rulers; and grant, oh Lord, that they may not act so we can't help it.
> Lyman Beecher (1775-1863)
> American preacher

There have been many great men that have flattered the people, who ne'er loved them.
> Second Officer, *Coriolanus*
> William Shakespeare (1564-1616)

Though it be a foul lie; set upon it a good face.
> Bishop John Bale (1495-1563)
> English ecclesiastic, dramatist

My choice early in life was either to be a piano-player in a whorehouse or a politician. And to tell the truth there's hardly any difference.
> Harry S. Truman (1884-1972)

He knows nothing; and he thinks he knows everything. That points clearly to a political career.
> Undershaft, *Major Barbara*
> George Bernard Shaw (1856-1950)

A politician is an arse upon which everyone has sat except a man.
> e.e.cummings (1894-1962)

Little other than a *red-tape* talking machine, and unhappy bag of parliamentary eloquence.
> Thomas Carlyle (1795-1881)
> Scottish author

A sophistical rhetorician, inebriated with the exuberance of his own verbosity.
> Benjamin Disraeli (1804-1881)
> *of Gladstone*

The most successful politician is he who says

what everybody is thinking most often and in the loudest voice.

Theodore Roosevelt (1858-1919)

Reader, suppose you were an idiot. And suppose you were a member of Congress. But I repeat myself.

Mark Twain (1835-1910)

A politician is a statesman who approaches every question with an open mouth.

Adlai Stevenson (1900-1965)
American Democratic politician

A statesman is a politician who is held upright by equal pressure from all directions.

Eric A. Johnston (1896-1963)
American entrepreneur

A politician thinks of the next election; a statesman, of the next generation.

James Freeman Clarke (1810-1888)
American theologian

A constitutional statesman is in general a man of common opinions and uncommon abilities.

Walter Bagehot (1826-1877)
English economist, critic

D'ye think that statesmen's kindnesses proceed from any principles but their own need?

Sir Robert Howard (1626-1698)
English dramatist

A politician will do anything to keep his job – even become a patriot.

William Randolph Hearst (1863-1951)
American newspaper magnate

The tragedy of one successful politician after another is the gradual substitution of narcissism for an interest in the community.

Bertrand Russell (1872-1970)

Your representative owes you, not his industry only, but his judgement; and he betrays instead of serving you if he sacrifices it to your opinion.

Edmund Burke (1729-1797)
Irish philosopher, statesman

Politicians are not people who seek power in order to implement policies they think necessary. They are people who seek policies in order to attain power.

Evelyn Waugh (1903-1966)

Our differences are policies, our agreements principles.

William McKinley (1843-1901)
American Republican politician,
President

To sacrifice one's honour to one's party is so unselfish an act that our most generous statesmen have not hesitated to do it.

Lord Darling (1849-1936)
British judge

We all know that Prime Ministers are wedded

to the truth, but like other wedded couples they sometimes live apart.

Saki (H. H. Munro) (1870-1916)
Scottish author

An honest politician is one who, when he is bought, will stay bought.

Simon Cameron (1799-1889)
American Republican politician

In fighting politicians you think you are winning and suddenly you find you have lost.

Viscount Montgomery (1887-1976)
British soldier

He was trying to save both his faces.

John Gunther (1901-1970)
American journalist

Whenever a man has cast a longing eye on offices, a rottenness begins in his conduct.

Thomas Jefferson (1743-1826)

There's just one rule for politicians all over the world: Don't say in Power what you say in Opposition; if you do, you only have to carry out what the other fellows have found impossible.

John Galsworthy (1867-1933)

There are hardly two creatures of a more differing species than the same man when pretending to a place and when in possession of it.

George Savile, Lord Halifax (1633-1695)
English statesman, author

To be out of place is not necessarily to be out of power.

Dr Samuel Johnson (1709-1784)

Resolv'd to ruin or to rule the state.

John Dryden (1631-1700)

The Right Honourable gentleman is indebted to his memory for his jests, and to his imagination for his facts.

R. B. Sheridan (1751-1816)

There is one statesman of the present day of whom I always say that he would have escaped making the blunders that he has made if he had only ridden more in omnibuses.

Sir Arthur Helps (1813-1875)
British author

He thinks like a Tory and talks like a Radical, and that's so important now-a-days.

Oscar Wilde (1854-1900)

He was a power politically for years, but he has never got prominent enough to have his speeches garbled.

Kin (F. McKinney) Hubbard (1868-1930)
American humorist, journalist

His watchword is always Duty; and he never forgets that the nation which lets its duty get on the opposite side to its interest is lost.

George Bernard Shaw (1856-1950)

In Pierre Elliot Trudeau Canada has at last produced a political leader worthy of assassination.

Irving Layton (b. 1912)
Canadian poet

You're not an MP, you're a gastronomic pimp.

Aneurin Bevan (1897-1960)
British Labour politician
to a colleague accused of attending too many public dinners

He has the lucidity which is the by-product of a fundamentally sterile mind.

Aneurin Bevan (1897-1960)
British Labour politician
of Neville Chamberlain, Prime Minister

He seems determined to make a trumpet sound like a tin whistle.

Aneurin Bevan (1897-1960)
British Labour politician
of Clement Attlee, Prime Minister

The Prime Minister has an absolute genius for putting flamboyant labels on empty luggage.

Aneurin Bevan (1897-1960)
British Labour politician
of Harold Macmillan

Such a gift horse to his opponents that it would be ungrateful for us to look him in the mouth.

Violet Bonham-Carter (Lady Asquith) (1887-1969)
British Liberal politician
of Aneurin Bevan

A lot of people misunderstand Barry. But actually, when you get to know him, he's quite reactionary.

Abu (b. 1924)
of Senator Goldwater

Women MPs have struck the bell of fame with a putty hammer.

Cassandra (Sir William Connor) (1909-1967)
British journalist

... notwithstanding all my violence in politicks and talking so much on that subject, I perfectly agree with you that no woman has any business to meddle with that or any other serious business, farther than giving her opinion (if she is ask'd).

Lady Bessborough (18th century)
letter to Lord Granville

I wouldn't want to mislead you by doing other than saying however easy it would be for me to answer the question you have asked, it is not fair for me to go further than I have. And I would not read too much into that.

Ian McDonald
Ministry of Defence spokesman
1982

As I interpret the President, we're now at the end of the beginning of the upturn of the downturn.

John F. Kennedy (1917-1963)
when Senator

There are two problems in my life. The political ones are insoluble and the economic ones are incomprehensible.

Sir Alec Douglas-Home (b. 1930)
British Conservative politician, Prime Minister

Exhortation to other people to *do something* is the last resort of politicians who are at a loss to know what to do themselves.

Sir Paul Chambers (1904-1981)
British industrialist

Get thee glass eyes,
And, like a scurvy politician, seem
To see the things thou dost not.

Lear, *King Lear*
William Shakespeare (1564-1616)

Can there be a more horrible object in existence than an eloquent man not speaking the truth?

Thomas Carlyle (1795-1881)
Scottish author

No man, I fear, can effect great benefits for his country without some sacrifice of the minor virtues.

Sydney Smith (1771-1845)
English writer, clergyman

SEE Kissinger on CRISES; Simonds on JOURNALISM; The PRESIDENT; Nixon on The PRESS; REAGAN; THATCHER; Chesterton on WEALTH

Politics

Man is by nature a political animal.

Aristotle (384-322 BC)

Politics is the science of how who gets what, when and why.

Sidney Hillman (1887-1946)
American trade unionist

He who gives food to the people will win.

Lech Walesa (b. 1943)

Magnanimity in politics is not seldom the truest wisdom; and a great empire and little minds go ill together.

Edmund Burke (1729-1797)
Irish philosopher, statesman

Politics is the diversion of trivial men who, when they succeed at it, become important in the eyes of more trivial men.

George Jean Nathan (1882-1958)
American critic

I claim not to have controlled events, but confess plainly that events have controlled me.

Abraham Lincoln (1809-1865)

Politics is not an exact science.
Prince Otto von Bismarck (1815-1898)
Prussian statesman

Practical politics consists in ignoring facts.
Henry B. Adams (1838-1918)
American historian

I am invariably of the politics of people at whose table I sit, or beneath whose roof I sleep.
George Borrow (1803-1881)
English writer

I could not be leading a religious life unless I identified myself with the whole of mankind, and that I could not do unless I took part in politics.
M. K. Gandhi (1869-1948)

Religion is organized to satisfy and guide the soul – politics does the same thing for the body.
Joyce Cary (1888-1957)
British author

I have never regarded politics as the arena of morals. It is the arena of interests.
Aneurin Bevan (1897-1960)
British Labour politician

In politics, what begins in fear usually ends in folly.
S. T. Coleridge (1772-1834)

Politics is not a bad profession. If you succeed there are many rewards, if you disgrace yourself you can always write a book.
Ronald Reagan (b. 1911)

SEE GOVERNMENT; PARLIAMENT;
Junius on PERSUASION

Polls
A straw vote only shows which way the hot air blows.
O. Henry (1862-1910)
American short story writer

Pollution
I durst not laugh, for fear of opening my lips and receiving the bad air.
Casca, *Julius Caesar*
William Shakespeare (1564-1616)

Pollution is nothing but the resources we are not harvesting. We allow them to disperse because we've been ignorant of their value.
R. Buckminster Fuller (1895-1983)
American architect, engineer

Eighty per cent of pollution is caused by plants and trees.
Ronald Reagan (b. 1911)

SEE ECOLOGY

Pop
Every popular song has at least one line or sentence that is perfectly clear – the line that fits the music.
Ezra Pound (1885-1972)

My reputation is a media creation.
John Lydon (formerly Johnny Rotten) (b. 1957)

The Pope
The Pope? How many divisions has *he* got?
Josef Stalin (1879-1953)
to Pierre Laval, French
foreign minister, in reply to
suggestion that the Soviet
Union should propitiate the
Pope

It is an error to believe that the Roman Pontiff can and ought to reconcile himself to, and agree with, progress, liberalism, and contemporary civilization.
Pope Pius IX (1792-1878)

SEE Ayscough on CATHOLICISM; Shaw
on INFALLIBILITY

Popularity
Popularity? It's glory's small change.
Victor Hugo (1802-1885)

I have never wished to cater to the crowd; for what I know they do not approve, and what they approve I do not know.
Epicurus (341-270 BC)

Popularity is a crime from the moment it is sought; it is only a virtue where man have it whether they will or no.
Lord Halifax (1796-1865)

He cast off his friends as a huntsman his pack,
For he knew when he pleas'd he could whistle them back.
Oliver Goldsmith (1728-1774)

Pornography
It's red hot, mate. I hate to think of this sort of book getting into the wrong hands. As soon as I've finished this, I shall recommend they ban it.
Tony Hancock (1924-1968)
British comedian
from script by Ray Galton and
Alan Simpson

A woman reading *Playboy* feels a little like a Jew reading a Nazi manual.
Gloria Steinem (b. 1934)
American feminist writer

I would like to see all people who read pornography or have anything to do with it put in a mental hospital for observation so we could find out what we have done to them.
Linda Lovelace (b. 1952)
American model, actress

Nine-tenths of the appeal of pornography is due to the indecent feelings concerning sex which moralists inculcate in the young; the other tenth is physiological, and will occur in one way or another whatever the state of the law may be.

Bertrand Russell (1872-1970)

Obscenity is such a tiny kingdom that a single tour covers it completely.

Heywood Broun (1888-1939)
American journalist, novelist

SEE Gilmour on DELINQUENCY

Portraits

Every time I paint a portrait I lose a friend.

John Sargent (1856-1925)
American artist

Every portrait that is painted with feeling is a portrait of the artist, not of the sitter.

Oscar Wilde (1854-1900)

There are only two styles of portrait painting; the serious and the smirk.

Charles Dickens (1812-1870)

When one starts from a portrait and seeks by successive eliminations to find pure form . . . one inevitably ends up with an egg. Similarly, by starting from an egg and following the opposite course, one can arrive at a portrait.

Pablo Picasso (1881-1973)

Most of our portrait painters are doomed to absolute oblivion. They never paint what they see. They paint what the public sees, and the public never sees anything.

Oscar Wilde (1854-1900)

Mr Lely, I desire you would use all your skill to paint my picture truly like me, and not flatter me at all; but remark all these rough-nesses, pimples, warts, and everything as you see me, otherwise I will never pay a farthing for it.

Oliver Cromwell (1599-1658)

Few persons who have ever sat for a portrait can have felt anything but inferior while the process is going on.

Anthony Powell (b. 1905)
British novelist

Posterity

When we are planning for posterity, we ought to remember that virtue is not heridatary.

Thomas Paine (1737-1809)
pamphleteer, revolutionary

Be careful of this – it is my *carte de visite* to posterity.

Jean-François Champollion (1790-1832)
French archaeologist
on his death-bed, giving his
printer the proofs of his
study deciphering the hieroglyphics
on the Rosetta stone

We are always doing something for Posterity, but I would fain see Posterity do something for us.

Joseph Addison (1672-1719)
English essayist

SEE Ade on WRITERS

Poverty

Oh, God! that bread should be so dear,
And flesh and blood so cheap.

Thomas Hood (1799-1845)
English poet

We all live in a state of ambitious poverty.

Juvenal (47-138)

Poverty does not mean the possession of little, but the lack of much.

Antipater of Macedonia (c. 397-c. 319 BC)
Macedonian general

Too poor for a bribe, and too proud
to importune,
He had not the method of making
a fortune.

Thomas Gray (1716-1771)
of his own character

This mournful truth is ev'rywhere
confessed,
Slow rises worth, by poverty depressed.

Dr Samuel Johnson (1709-1784)

The seven deadly sins. . . Food, clothing, firing, rent, taxes, respectability and children. Nothing can lift those seven millstones from man's neck but money; and the spirit cannot soar until the millstones are lifted.

Undershaft, *Major Barbara*
George Bernard Shaw (1856-1950)

The common argument that crime is caused by poverty is a kind of slander on the poor.

H. L. Mencken (1880-1956)
American journalist

Hark ye, Clinker, you are a most notorious offender. You stand convicted of sickness, hunger, wretchedness, and want.

Tobias Smollett (1721-1771)
Scottish novelist, surgeon

There's no scandal like rags, nor any crime so shameful as poverty.

George Farquhar (1678-1707)
Irish dramatist

Poverty is not a shame, but the being ashamed of it is.

Thomas Fuller (1608-1661)
English cleric

O world, how apt the poor are to be proud!

Olivia, *Twelfth Night*
William Shakespeare (1564-1616)

Poverty is no disgrace to a man, but it is confoundedly inconvenient.

Sydney Smith (1771-1845)
English clergyman, writer

The fundamental strength of Egypt's economy is its broad base of individual poverty.
Middle East correspondent, The Times,
London
February 1958

I think the advantages of self-dependent poverty for the purpose of developing moral fibre are greatly exaggerated.
J. K. Galbraith (b. 1908)
American economist
while US ambassador to India

There are 200 million poor in the world who would gladly take the vow of poverty if they could eat, dress and have a home like myself and many of those who profess the vow of poverty.
Fulton Sheen (1895-1979)
American clergyman, author

No man should commend poverty unless he is poor.
Saint Bernard (1091-1153)

My earliest emotions are bound to the earth and to the labours of the fields. I find in the land a profound suggestion of poverty and I love poverty above all other things; not sordid and famished poverty but poverty that is blessed – simple, humble, like brown bread.
Federico García Lorca (1898-1936)

Poverty keeps together more homes than it breaks up.
Saki (H. H. Munro) (1870-1916)
Scottish author

That's another advantage of being poor – a doctor will cure you faster.
Kin (F. McKinney) Hubbard (1868-1930)
American humorist, journalist

Resolve not to be poor: whatever you have, spend less. Poverty is a great enemy to human happiness; it certainly destroys liberty, and it makes some virtues impracticable, and others extremely difficult.
Dr Samuel Johnson (1709-1784)

To be poor and independent is very nearly an impossibility.
William Cobbett (1762-1835)
English journalist, essayist, politician

My father was second cousin to a baronet, and my mother the daughter of a country gentleman whose rule was, when in difficulties, mortgage. That was my sort of poverty.
George Bernard Shaw (1856-1950)

The prevalent fear of poverty among the educated classes is the worst moral disease from which our civilisation suffers.
William James (1842-1910)
American psychologist, philosopher

Poverty is an anomaly to rich people. It is very

difficult to make out why people who want dinner do not ring the bell.
Walter Bagehot (1826-1877)
English economist, critic

A good poor man is better than a good rich man because he has to resist more temptations.
Plato (428-347 BC)

The poorest He that is in England hath a life to live as the greatest He.
Thomas Raineborough (d. 1648)
Puritan soldier, politician

'No one has ever said it', observed Lady Caroline, 'but how painfully true it is that the poor have us always with them!'
Saki (H. H. Munro) (1870-1916)
Scottish author

Poverty has strange bedfellows.
Edward Bulwer-Lytton (1803-1873)
English novelist, playwright

I used to think I was poor. Then they told me I wasn't poor, I was needy. Then they told me it was self-defeating to think of myself as needy, I was deprived. Then they told me deprived was a bad image, I was underprivileged. Then they told me underprivileged was overused, I was disadvantaged. I still don't have a dime. But I sure have a great vocabulary.
Jules Feiffer (b. 1929)
American cartoonist

I hate the poor and look forward eagerly to their extermination.
George Bernard Shaw (1856-1950)

If you've ever really been poor, you remain poor at heart all your life.
Arnold Bennett (1867-1931)

Come away; poverty's catching.
Aphra Behn (1640-1689)
English playwright, poet

SEE Menen on CULTURE; Butler on MONEY; Johnson on UNEMPLOYMENT

Power

You cannot have power for good without having power for evil too. Even mother's milk nourishes murderers as well as heroes.
Cusins, Major Barbara
George Bernard Shaw (1856-1950)

Those who have been once intoxicated with power, and have derived any kind of emolument from it, even though but for one year, can never willingly abandon it.
Edmund Burke (1729-1797)
Irish philosopher, statesman

Power is the ultimate aphrodisiac.
Henry Kissinger (b. 1923)

A cock has great influence on his own dunghill.
Publilius Syrus (1st century BC)
Roman writer of mimes

Unused power slips imperceptibly into the hands of another.
Konrad Heiden (1901-1975)
German author

The purpose of getting power is to be able to give it away.
Aneurin Bevan (1897-1960)
British Labour politician

Power? It's like a Dead Sea fruit. When you achieve it, there is nothing there.
Harold Macmillan, Lord Stockton (1894-1986)
British Conservative politician, Prime Minister

Power admits no equal, and dismisses friendship for flattery.
Edward Moore (1712-1757)
English fabulist, dramatist

Madness in great ones must not unwatch'd go.
Claudius, Hamlet
William Shakespeare (1564-1616)

The good old rule
Sufficeth them, the simple plan,
That they should take, who have the power,
And they should keep who can.
William Wordsworth (1770-1850)

You only have power over people so long as you don't take *everything* away from them. But when you've robbed a man of everything he's no longer in your power – he's free again.
Alexander Solzhenitsyn (b. 1918)

They say power corrupts and perhaps it does. What I know, in myself, is quite a different thing. That power corrupts the people it is exercised over.
Raymond Williams (b. 1921)
British academic

Power, like a desolating pestilence,
Pollutes whate'er it touches.
P. B. Shelley (1792-1822)

Alexander at the head of the world never tasted the true pleasure that boys of his own age have enjoyed at the head of a school.
Horace Walpole (1717-1797)
English author

No man is good enough to be another man's master.
Undershaft, Major Barbara
George Bernard Shaw (1856-1950)

SEE Russell on DESPOTISM; Acton on GREATNESS; Adams on The PRESIDENT

Praise

Fondly we think we honour merit then,
When we but praise ourselves in other men.
Alexander Pope (1688-1744)

I will praise any man that will praise me.
Enobarbus, Antony and Cleopatra
William Shakespeare (1564-1616)

He who praises everybody praises nobody.
Dr Samuel Johnson (1709-1784)

I know of no manner of speaking so offensive as that of giving praise, and closing it with an exception.
Sir Richard Steele (1672-1729)
English essayist, dramatist, editor

Among the smaller duties of life I hardly know any one more important than that of not praising where praise is not due.
Sydney Smith (1771-1845)
English writer, clergyman

Praise yourself daringly, something always sticks.
Francis Bacon (1561-1626)

The advantage of doing one's praising for oneself is that one can lay it on so thick and exactly in the right places.
Samuel Butler (1835-1902)
English author

A continual feast of commendation is only to be attained by merit or by wealth.
Dr Samuel Johnson (1709-1784)

Eulogy. Praise of a person who has either the advantages of wealth and power, or the consideration to be dead.
Ambrose Bierce (1842-1914)
American author

The greatest mistake I made was not to die in office.
Dean Acheson (1893-1971)
American Democratic politician
on hearing eulogies to his successor as Secretary of State, John Foster Dulles, who died in office

SEE Johnson, Louis XIV on FLATTERY;
Chesterfield on MODESTY

Prayer

Bow, stubborn knees!
Claudius, Hamlet
William Shakespeare (1564-1616)

Pray. To ask the laws of the universe to be annulled on behalf of a single petitioner confessedly unworthy.
Ambrose Bierce (1842-1914)
American author

Whatever a man prays for, he prays for a miracle. Every prayer reduces itself to this: 'Great God, grant that twice two be not four'.
Ivan Turgenev (1818-1883)

Whatsoever we beg of God, let us also work for it.
Jeremy Taylor (1613-1667)
English churchman, writer

Serving God is doing good to man, but praying is thought an easier service and therefore more generally chosen.
Benjamin Franklin (1706-1790)

If you want to make a man very angry, get someone to pray for him.
Ed (E. W.) Howe (1853-1937)
American journalist, novelist

Prayer does not change God, but it changes him who prays.
Sören Kierkegaard (1813-1855)
Danish philosopher

The Lord's Prayer contains the sum total of religion and morals.
Duke of Wellington (1769-1852)

The man who says his prayers in the evening is a captain posting his sentries. After that, he can sleep.
Charles Baudelaire (1821-1867)

I throw myself down in my chamber, and I call in, and invite God, and his Angels thither, and when they are there, I neglect God and his Angels, for the noise of a fly, for the rattling of a coach, for the whining of a door.
John Donne (c. 1571-1631)

Prayer should be short, without giving God Almighty reasons why He should grant this or that. He knows best what is good for us.
John Selden (1584-1654)
English jurist, statesman

The best prayers have often more groans than words.
John Bunyan (1628-1688)

A short prayer enters heaven; a long drink empties the flagon.
Rabelais (1494-1553)

We often want one thing and pray for another, not telling the truth even to the gods.
Seneca (c. 5-65)
Roman writer, philosopher, statesman

He didn't actually accuse God of inefficiency, but when he prayed his tone was loud and angry, like that of a dissatisfied guest in a carelessly managed hotel.
Clarence Day (1874-1935)
American author

God is not a cosmic bell-boy for whom we can press a button to get things.
H. E. Fosdick (1878-1969)
American Baptist Minister

Prayer must never be answered: if it is, it ceases to be prayer and becomes correspondence.
Oscar Wilde (1854-1900)

I have lived to thank God that all my prayers have not been answered.
Jean Ingelow (1820-1897)
English poet

O Lord! thou knowest how busy I must be this day: if I forget thee, do not thou forget me.
Sir Jacob Astley (1579-1652)
English Royalist soldier

It is best to read the weather forecasts before we pray for rain.
Mark Twain (1835-1910)

SEE Voltaire on ENEMIES; Tomlin on GOD; Browne on SLEEP

Preaching

To be good is noble, but to teach others how to be good is nobler – and less trouble.
Mark Twain (1835-1910)

Preaching is heady wine. It is pleasant to tell people where they get off.
Arnold Lunn (1888-1974)
British author

Philosophy rests on the proposition that whatever is is right. Preaching begins by assuming that whatever is is wrong.
Elbert Hubbard (1856-1915)
American author

Go into the street, and give one man a lecture on morality, and another a shilling, and see which will respect you most.
Dr Samuel Johnson (1709-1784)

The best sermon is preached by the minister who has a sermon to preach and not by the man who has to preach a sermon.
William Feather (b. 1889)
American businessman

That we should practise what we preach is generally admitted; but anyone who preaches what he and his hearers practise must incur the gravest moral disapprobation.
Logan Pearsall Smith (1865-1946)
American essayist

Only the sinner has the right to preach.
Christopher Morley (1890-1957)
American novelist, journalist

The British churchgoer prefers a severe preacher because he thinks a few home truths will do his neighbours no harm.
George Bernard Shaw (1856-1950)

When I hear a man preach, I like to see him act as if he were fighting bees.
Abraham Lincoln (1809-1865)

I preached as never sure to preach again,
And as a dying man to dying men.
Richard Baxter (1615-1691)
English Nonconformist cleric

To preach long, loud, and Damnation, is the way to be cried up. We love a man that damns us, and we run after him again to save us.
John Selden (1584-1654)
English jurist, statesman

Nothing in the world delights a truly religious people so much as consigning them to eternal damnation.
James Hogg (1770-1835)
Scottish poet

An advantage itinerant preachers have over those who are stationary, the latter cannot well improve their delivery of a sermon by so many rehearsals.
Benjamin Franklin (1706-1790)

Not one clergyman in ten uses his own voice – he uses only an imitation.
Elbert Hubbard (1856-1915)
American author

The methodists love your big sinners, as proper subjects to work upon.
Horace Walpole (1717-1797)
English author

Few sinners are saved after the first twenty minutes of a sermon.
Mark Twain (1835-1910)

Even in the church, where boredom is prolific,
I hail thee first, Episcopalian bore:
Who else could serve as social soporific,
And without snoring teach the rest to snore.
Christopher Morley (1890-1957)
American novelist, journalist

The world runs after pulpit orators. They please the ear, and do not disturb the conscience. They move the emotions but do not change the will.
Cardinal Henry Manning (1808-1892)
English theologian

Prejudice

A great many people think they are thinking when they are merely rearranging their prejudices.
William James (1842-1910)
American psychologist, philosopher

A prejudice is a vagrant opinion without visible means of support.
Ambrose Bierce (1842-1914)
American author

Our prejudices are our mistresses; reason is at best our wife, very often needed, but seldom minded.
Lord Chesterfield (1694-1773)
English statesman and man of letters

One may no more live in the world without picking up the moral prejudices of the world than one will be able to go to hell without perspiring.
H. L. Mencken (1880-1956)
American journalist

The fathers have eaten a sour grape, and the children's teeth are set on edge.
Bible, Jeremiah

The President

I really don't think I'm worthy of the office, but I have to put the country before my own limitations.
Art Buchwald (b. 1925)
American humorist

When I was a boy I was told that anybody could become President; I'm beginning to believe it.
Clarence Darrow (1857-1938)
American lawyer, writer

Power is poison. Its effect on Presidents has always been tragic.
Henry B. Adams (1838-1918)
American historian

I have nothing to hide. The White House has nothing to hide.
Richard Nixon (b. 1913)

No man will ever carry out of the Presidency the reputation which carried him into it.
Thomas Jefferson (1743-1826)

Even the President of the United States sometimes must have to stand naked.
Bob Dylan (b. 1941)

As President Nixon says, presidents can do almost anything, and President Nixon has done many things that nobody would have thought of doing.
Golda Meir (1898-1978)

The (United States) presidential system just won't work any more. Anyone who gets in under it ought not to be allowed to serve.
Gore Vidal (b. 1925)

I sit here all day trying to persuade people to do the things they ought to have sense enough to do without my persuading them ... that's all the powers of the President amount to.
Harry S. Truman (1884-1972)

When you get to be President, there are all those things, the honors, the twenty-one gun salutes, all those things. You have to remember it isn't for you. It's for the Presidency.
Harry S. Truman (1884-1972)

Nothing would please the Kremlin more than to have the people of this country choose a second-rate President.
Richard Nixon (b. 1913)

I feel very proud, even though they didn't elect me, to be President of the Argentines.
General Galtieri (b. 1926)

In the Bob Hope Golf Classic the participation of President Gerald Ford was more than enough to remind you that the nuclear button was at one stage at the disposal of a man who might have either pressed it by mistake or else pressed it deliberately to obtain room service.
Clive James (b. 1939)
Australian writer, critic

We're an ideal political family, as accessible as Disneyland.
Maureen Reagan (b. 1941)
daughter of President Reagan

The buck stops here.
Harry S. Truman (1884-1972)

The Vice-President Once there were two brothers. One ran away to sea, the other was elected Vice-President, and nothing was ever heard of either of them again.
Thomas R. Marshall (1854-1925)
American lawyer, Vice-President

SEE Kissinger on LOYALTY; Kennedy on POLITICIANS; REAGAN

The Press

In old days men had the rack. Now they have the press.
Oscar Wilde (1854-1900)

The price of justice is eternal publicity.
Arnold Bennett (1867-1931)

No government ought to be without censors; and where the press is free none ever will.
Thomas Jefferson (1743-1826)

You know very well that whether you are on page one or page thirty depends on whether they fear you. It is just as simple as that.
Richard Nixon (b. 1913)
of the press

The freedom of the press works in such a way that there is not much freedom from it.
Princess Grace of Monaco (1928-1982)

The men with the muck-rake are often indispensable to the well-being of society, but only if they know when to stop raking the muck.
Theodore Roosevelt (1858-1919)

One gets the impression from the popular Press that rape has become the British national pastime.
Lord Wigoder (b. 1921)
British barrister, Liberal politician

Generally speaking, the Press lives on disaster.
Clement Attlee (1883-1967)
British Labour politician, Prime Minister

The Press can best be compared to haemorrhoids.
Gareth Davies
Welsh rugby captain

Photographers are the most loathsome inconvenience. They're merciless. They're the pits.
Paul Newman (b. 1925)

If you guys could get just one per cent of the stories right.
John McEnroe (b. 1959)
of the Press at Wimbledon, 1985

I'm sure if I have any plans, the Press will inform me.
Arthur Scargill (b. 1938)
British trade unionist

I got to know Ike's plumbing like the back of my hand. I could walk around his innards in the dark.
Cassandra (Sir William Connor) (1909-1967)
British journalist

The most important service rendered by the press and the magazines is that of educating people to approach printed matter with distrust.
Samuel Butler (1835-1902)
English author

Report me and my cause aright.
Hamlet, Hamlet
William Shakespeare (1564-1616)

Goodbye, and don't betray me too much.
Simone Signoret (1921-1985)
closing an interview

SEE JOURNALISM; NEWSPAPERS

Pride

My family pride is something inconceivable. I can't help it. I was born sneering.
W. S. Gilbert (1836-1911)
English librettist

I cannot dig; to beg I am ashamed.
Jesus (4 BC-29 AD)
in the parable of the unjust steward

And the Devil did grin, for his
darling sin
Is pride that apes humility.
S. T. Coleridge (1772-1834)

SEE Flaubert on GOOD DEEDS; Shakespeare on POVERTY

Primitive Life

No arts; no letters; no society; and which is worst of all continual fear and danger of violent death; and the life of man, solitary, poor, nasty, brutish, and short.
Thomas Hobbes (1588-1679)

So often among so-called 'primitives' one comes across spiritual personalities who immediately inspire respect, as though they were the fully matured products of an undisturbed fate.

Carl Jung (1875-1961)

Principles

When a fellow says, 'It ain't the money but the principle of the thing', it's the money.

Kin (F. McKinney) Hubbard (1868-1930)
American humorist, journalist

Principles have no real force except when one is well-fed.

Mark Twain (1835-1910)

The difficulty is to know conscience from self-interest.

W. D. Howells (1837-1920)
American author

It is easier to fight for one's principles than to live up to them.

Alfred Adler (1870-1937)
Austrian psychiatrist

SEE Shaw on The ENGLISH; Luther on RELIGION; Disraeli on TRADITION

Priorities

The three most important things a man has are, briefly, his private parts, his money, and his religious opinions.

Samuel Butler (1835-1902)
English author

The least pain in our little finger gives us more concern and uneasiness than the destruction of millions of our fellow-beings.

William Hazlitt (1778-1830)
English essayist

Prison

A Robin Redbreast in a cage
Puts all Heaven in a Rage.

William Blake (1757-1827)

The first prison I ever saw had inscribed on it 'Cease to do evil: learn to do well'; but as the inscription was on the outside, the prisoners could not read it.

George Bernard Shaw (1856-1950)

I know not whether Laws be right
Or whether Laws be wrong;
All that we know who live in gaol
Is that the wall is strong;
And that each day is like a year,
A year whose days are long.

from *Ballad of Reading Gaol*
Oscar Wilde (1854-1900)

In prison those things withheld from and denied the prisoner become precisely what he wants most of all.

Eldridge Cleaver (b. 1935)
American black leader, writer

Anyone who has been to an English public school will always feel comparatively at home in prison. It is the people brought up in the gay intimacy of the slums who find prison so soul-destroying.

Evelyn Waugh (1903-1966)

Stone walls do not a prison make
Nor iron bars a cage;
Minds innocent and quiet take
That for an hermitage.

Richard Lovelace (1618-1658)
English poet

The most anxious man in a prison is the governor.

George Bernard Shaw (1856-1950)

SEE Greer on ANXIETY

Private Education

A public school is a school which excludes all that could fit a man for standing behind a counter.

Charles Astor Bristed (1820-1874)

Public schools teach the young to argue without quarrelling, to quarrel without suspecting, and to suspect without slandering.

Dr Kurt Hahn (1886-1974)
German educationalist

First, religious and moral principles: secondly, gentlemanly conduct: thirdly, intellectual ability.

Thomas Arnold (1795-1842)
English educator, scholar

But, good gracious, you've got to educate him first. You can't expect a boy to be vicious till he's been to a good school.

Saki (H. H. Munro) (1870-1916)
Scottish author

Public schools are the nurseries of all vice and immorality.

Henry Fielding (1707-1754)

You can still buy five years' education at one of the best schools for less than half the cost of a Bentley.

Lord James of Rusholme (b. 1909)
British educator

SEE Waugh on PRISON

Private Interest

We must especially beware of that small group of selfish men who would clip the wings of the American Eagle in order to feather their own nests.

Franklin D. Roosevelt (1882-1945)

The little I know of it has not served to raise my opinion of what is vulgarly called the 'Monied Interest'; I mean, that blood-sucker, that muckworm, that calls itself 'the friend of government'.

William Pitt (1708-1778)
English politician, Prime Minister

Privilege

What men value in this world is not rights, but privileges.

H. L. Mencken (1880-1956)
American journalist

What men prize most is a privilege, even if it be that of a chief mourner at a funeral.

J. R. Lowell (1819-1891)
American poet

God is no respecter of persons.

Saint Peter (1st century AD)

Procreation

He plough'd her, and she cropp'd.

Agrippa, *Antony and Cleopatra*
William Shakespeare (1564-1616)

Common morality now treats childbearing as an aberration. There are practically no good reasons left for exercising one's fertility.

Germaine Greer (b. 1939)
Australian feminist writer

The purpose of population is not ultimately peopling earth. It is to fill heaven.

G. D. Leonard (b. 1921)
Bishop of London
1983

A hen is only an egg's way of making another egg.

Samuel Butler (1835-1902)
English author

SEE Keynes on FERTILITY; Browne,
Luther on SEX

Progress

The world is moving so fast these days that the man who says it can't be done is generally interrupted by someone doing it.

Elbert Hubbard (1856-1915)
American author

The longer I live the more keenly I feel that whatever was good enough for our fathers is not good enough for us.

Oscar Wilde (1854-1900)

The slogan of progress is changing from the full dinner pail to the full garage.

Herbert Hoover (1874-1964)
American Republican politician, President

All progress is based upon a universal innate desire on the part of every organism to live beyond its income.

Samuel Butler (1835-1902)
English author

The reasonable man adapts himself to the world; the unreasonable one persists in trying to adapt the world to himself. Therefore, all progress depends on the unreasonable man.

George Bernard Shaw (1856-1950)

There is a slow movement in history towards

the recognition of a man by his fellow man. When this happens all that has been done in the past will fall into place and find its true value.

Jean-Paul Sartre (1905-1980)
in his last interview

You can't say that civilisation don't advance, for in every war they kill you a new way.

Will Rogers (1879-1935)
American humorist

We have stopped believing in progress. What progress that is!

Jorge Luis Borges (1899-1986)

SEE Hooker, Shaw on CHANGE; Twain
on FATHER; Gladstone on REFORM

Promiscuity

Elyot: It doesn't suit women to be promiscuous.
Amanda: It doesn't suit men for women to be promiscuous.

Private lives
Noël Coward (1899-1973)

We still have these double standards where the emphasis is all on the male's sexual appetites – that it's OK for him to collect as many scalps as he can before he settles down and 'pays the price'. If a woman displays the same attitude, all the epithets that exist in the English language are laid at her door, and with extraordinary bitterness.

Glenda Jackson (b. 1937)

Europeans used to say Americans were puritanical. Then they discovered that we were not puritans. So now they say we are obsessed with sex.

Mary McCarthy (b. 1912)
American author

Permissiveness is simply removing the dust sheets from our follies.

Edna O'Brien (b. 1936)
Irish author

It is as absurd to say that a man can't love one woman all the time as it is to say that a violinist needs several violins to play the same piece of music.

Honoré de Balzac (1799-1850)

You were born with your legs apart. They'll send you to your grave in a Y-shaped coffin.

Joe Orton (1933-1967)
British playwright

The sexual freedom of today for most people is really only a convention, an obligation, a social duty, a social anxiety, a necessary feature of the consumer's way of life.

Pier Paolo Pasolini (1922-1975)
Italian film director, essayist

Like the bee its sting, the promiscuous leave

behind them in each encounter something of themselves by which they are made to suffer.
Cyril Connolly (1903-1974)
British critic

SEE Fletcher on LOVE

Promises

The man who promises everything is sure to fulfil nothing, and everyone who promises too much is in danger of using evil means in order to carry out his promises, and is already on the road to perdition.
Carl Jung (1875-1961)

Sed mulier cupido quod dicit amanti,
In vento et rapida scribere oportet aqua.
What a woman says to her avid lover should be written in wind and running water.
Catullus (87-54 BC)

Do not vow – our love is frail as is our life, and full as little in our power.
Sir George Etherege (1635-1691)
English dramatist, diplomat

Promises and pie-crust are made to be broken.
Jonathan Swift (1667-1745)

Half the promises people say were never kept, were never made.
Ed (E. W.) Howe (1853-1937)
American journalist, novelist

The rule is, jam tomorrow and jam yesterday – but never jam today.
Lewis Carroll (1832-1898)

It is not the oath that makes us believe the man, but the man the oath.
Aeschylus (525-456 BC)

SEE Leonardo on HOPE

Promotion

Comrades, you have lost a good captain to make him an ill general.
Michel de Montaigne (1533-1592)
French essayist

It is easier to appear worthy of a position one does not hold, than of the office which one fills.
François, Duc de La Rochefoucauld (1613-1680)
French writer, moralist

Every man who takes office in Washington either grows or swells, and when I give a man an office, I watch him carefully to see whether he is swelling or growing.
Woodrow Wilson (1856-1924)

SEE Carnegie on PARTNERSHIP; Frost on WORK

Propaganda

The three chief qualifications of a party writer are to stick at nothing, to delight in flinging dirt, and to slander in the dark by guess.
Alexander Pope (1688-1744)

Propaganda is that branch of the art of lying which consists in nearly deceiving your friends without quite deceiving your enemies.
F. M. Cornford (1874-1943)
British author

Nobody has ever succeeded in keeping nations at war except by lies.
Salvador de Madariaga (1886-1978)
Spanish diplomat, writer

As soon as by one's own propaganda even a glimpse of right on the other side is admitted, the cause for doubting one's own right is laid.
Adolf Hitler (1889-1945)

In our country the lie has become not just a moral category but a pillar of the State.
Alexander Solzhenitsyn (b. 1918)

He that has the worst cause makes the most noise.
proverb

Get your facts first, and then you can distort 'em as much as you please.
Mark Twain (1835-1910)

The most dangerous of all falsehoods is a slightly distorted truth.
G. C. Lichtenberg (1742-1799)
German physicist, writer

I have never seen pessimism in a Company prospectus.
Cassandra (Sir William Connor) (1909-1967)
British journalist

Why is propaganda so much more successful when it stirs up hatred than when it tries to stir up friendly feeling?
Bertrand Russell (1872-1970)

SEE Disraeli on IDEALISM

Property

Next to the right of liberty, the right of property is the most important individual right guaranteed by the Constitution and the one which, united with that of personal liberty, has contributed more to the growth of civilization than any other institution established by the human race.
William Taft (1857-1930)
American Republican politician, President

It is preoccupation with possession, more than anything else, that prevents men from living freely and nobly.
Bertrand Russell (1872-1970)

If property had simply pleasures, we could stand it; but its duties make it unbearable. In the interest of the rich we must get rid of it.
Oscar Wilde (1854-1900)

By abolishing private property one takes away the human love of aggression.
Sigmund Freud (1856-1939)

In our rich consumers' civilization we spin cocoons around ourselves and get possessed by our possessions.
Max Lerner (b. 1902)
American academic, journalist

If a man owns land, the land owns him.
R. W. Emerson (1803-1882)
American essayist, poet, philosopher

The law doth punish man or woman
That steals the goose from off the common,
But lets the greater felon loose,
That steals the common from the goose.
anonymous

Property is a god. This god already has its theology (called state politics and juridical right) and also its morality, the most adequate expression of which is summed up in the phrase: 'That man is worth so much!'
Mikhail Bakunin (1814-1876)
Russian political theorist

Thieves respect property. They merely wish the property to become their property that they may more perfectly respect it.
G. K. Chesterton (1874-1936)

SEE Proudhon on COMMUNISM;
Locke on GOVERNMENT; LANDLORDS;
Wells on SOCIALISM

Prophecy
Prophecy is the most gratuitous form of error.
George Eliot (1819-1880)

Prostitution
O unknown man,
Whose hunger on my hunger wrought,
Body shall give what body can,
Shall give you all – save what you sought.
E. R. Dodds (1893-1979)
British classical scholar

If a woman hasn't got a tiny streak of a harlot in her, she's a dry stick as a rule.
D. H. Lawrence (1855-1930)

If you want to buy my wares
Follow me and climb the stairs. . .
Love for sale.
Love for Sale
Cole Porter (1893-1964)

Prisons are built with stones of Law,
Brothels with bricks of Religion.
William Blake (1757-1827)

SEE Brabazon on LAWYERS;
Dahlberg on LUST

Protest
While there is a lower class, I am in it; while there is a criminal element, I am of it; and while there is a soul in prison, I am not free.
Eugene Debs (1855-1926)
American trade unionist

Lean, hungry, savage, anti-everythings.
Dr Oliver Wendell Holmes (1809-1894)
American writer, physician

One fifth of the people are against everything all the time.
Robert Kennedy (1925-1968)

Yippies, hippies, yahoos, Black Panthers, lions and tigers alike – I'd swap the whole damn zoo for the kind of young Americans I saw in Vietnam.
Spiro Agnew (b. 1918)
American Republican politician

It's the kind of gathering where one feels a need to apologise for never having been to prison.
Dame Vera Laughton Mathews (1888-1959)
British suffragette

If any demonstrator ever lays down in front of my car, it'll be the last car he'll ever lay down in front of.
George C. Wallace (b. 1919)
American Independent politician

I feel that I am a citizen of the American dream and that the revolutionary struggle of which I am a part is a struggle against the American nightmare.
Eldridge Cleaver (b. 1935)
American black leader, writer

America I'm putting my queer shoulder to the wheel.
Allen Ginsberg (b. 1926)

I pondered all these things and how men fight and lose the battle, and the thing that they fought for comes about in spite of their defeat, and, when it comes, turns out not to be what they meant, and other men have to fight for what they meant under another name.
William Morris (1834-1896)
English artist, writer, printer

Proverbs
A proverb is the wisdom of many and the wit of one.
Lord John Russell (1792-1878)
English statesman, Prime Minister

Proverbs are always platitudes until you have personally experienced the truth of them.
Aldous Huxley (1894-1963)

A country can be judged by the quality of its proverbs.
German proverb

Psychiatric Wards
The rule is perfect: in all matters of opinion our adversaries are insane.
Mark Twain (1835-1910)

Psychiatrists

A psychiatrist is a man who goes to the Folies-Bergère and looks at the audience.

Bishop Mervyn Stockwood (b. 1913)
British churchman, author

Psychiatrist: A man who asks you a lot of expensive questions your wife asks you for nothing.

Sam Bardell (b. 1915)

Institutional psychiatry is a continuation of the Inquisition. All that has changed really is the vocabulary and the social style. The vocabulary conforms to the intellectual expectations of our age: it is a pseudo-medical jargon that parodies the concepts of science. The social style conforms to the political expectations of our age: it is a pseudo-liberal social movement that parodies the ideals of freedom and rationality.

Thomas Szasz (b. 1920)
American psychiatrist

I have myself spent nine years in a lunatic asylum and have never suffered from the obsession of wanting to kill myself; but I know that each conversation with a psychiatrist in the morning, made me want to hang myself because I knew I could not strangle him.

Antonin Artaud (1896-1948)
French theatre producer, actor, theorist

Canst thou not minister to a mind
diseased;
Pluck from the misery a rooted
sorrow;
Raze out the written troubles of the
brain;
And, with some sweet oblivious
antidote
Cleanse the stuffed bosom of that
perilous stuff
Which weighs upon the heart?

Macbeth, *Macbeth*
William Shakespeare (1564-1616)

One should only see a psychiatrist out of boredom.

Muriel Spark (b. 1918)
British novelist

Psychoanalysis

Psychoanalysis is confession without absolution.

G. K. Chesterton (1874-1936)

Psychoanalysis is the probing of mind by mind; confession is the communion of conscience and God.

Fulton Sheen (1895-1979)
American clergyman, author

No doubt fate would find it easier than I do to relieve you of your illness. But you will be able to convince yourself that much will be gained

if we succeed in transforming your hysterical misery into common unhappiness.

Sigmund Freud (1856-1939)

'When dreams come true', the ballad
singer sang,
And loudly through the hall the
plaudits rang;
For some folk's time has been so
ill-employed
They've hardly glanced at either Jung
or Freud.

Iolo Aneurin Williams (1890-1962)
British author, journalist

Psychoanalysis cannot be considered a method of education if by education we mean the topiary art of clipping a tree into a beautiful artificial shape. But those who have a higher conception of education will prize most the method of cultivating a tree so that it fulfils to perfection its own natural conditions of growth.

Carl Jung (1875-1961)

Psychoanalysts believe that the only 'normal' people are those who cause no trouble either to themselves or anyone else.

A. J. P. Taylor (b. 1906)
British historian

Psycho-analysis pretends to investigate the Unconscious. The Unconscious by definition is what you are not conscious of. But the Analysts already know what's in it – they should, because they put it all in beforehand.

Saul Bellow (b. 1915)

Where *id* was, there shall *ego* be.

Sigmund Freud (1856-1939)

SEE Freud on SCIENCE

The Public

The public! How many fools does it take to make a public?

Nicolas-Sébastien Chamfort (1741-1794)
French writer, wit

If it has to choose who is to be crucified, the crowd will always save Barabbas.

Jean Cocteau (1889-1963)
French writer, film director

No one ever went broke underestimating the taste of the American public.

H. L. Mencken (1880-1956)
American journalist

Public opinion, a vulgar, impertinent, anonymous tyrant who deliberately makes life unpleasant for anyone who is not content to be the average man.

W. R. Inge (1860-1954)
Dean of St Paul's, London

Public Opinion, an attempt to organize the ignorance of the community and to elevate it

to the dignity of physical force.
Oscar Wilde (1854-1900)

When the people have no other tyrant, their own public opinion becomes one.
Edward Bulwer-Lytton (1803-1873)
English novelist, playwright

Il y a des siècles où l'opinion publique est la plus mauvaise des opinions.
There are times when public opinion is the worst of all opinions.
Nicolas-Sébastien Chamfort (1741-1794)
French writer, wit

If forty million people say a foolish thing it does not become a wise one, but the wise man is foolish to give them the lie.
W. Somerset Maugham (1874-1966)

The public, with its mob yearning to be instructed, edified and pulled by the nose, demands certainties; ... but there are no certainties.
H. L. Mencken (1880-1956)
American journalist

The public seldom forgive twice.
Johann Kaspar Lavater (1741-1801)
Swiss divine and poet

There is not a more mean, stupid, dastardly, pitiless, selfish, spiteful, envious, ungrateful animal than the public.
William Hazlitt (1778-1830)
English essayist

The Public is an old woman. Let her maunder and mumble.
Thomas Carlyle (1795-1881)
Scottish author

SEE The MASSES; Butler on OPINION; Wilde on PORTRAITS

Public Life
Public life is the paradise of voluble windbags.
George Bernard Shaw (1856-1950)

The General has dedicated himself so many times, he must feel like the cornerstone of a public building.
Adlai Stevenson (1900-1965)
American Democratic politician
of President Eisenhower

If you're there before it's over, you're on time.
Jimmy J. Walker (1881-1946)
American lawyer, Mayor of New York

The first lesson in public life is to make sure you have a strong corps of implacable enemies.
Cassandra (Sir William Connor) (1909-1967)
British journalist

Eminent posts make great men greater and little men less.
Jean de la Bruyère (1645-1696)
French writer, moralist

A man occupied with public or other important business cannot, and need not, attend to spelling.
Napoleon Bonaparte (1769-1821)

SEE Lavater on The PUBLIC

Publicity
Sir, if they should cease to talk of me I must starve.
Dr Samuel Johnson (1709-1784)

All publicity is good, except an obituary notice.
Brendan Behan (1923-1964)
Irish playwright

I have bought golden opinions from all sorts of people.
Macbeth, *Macbeth*
William Shakespeare (1564-1616)

A telescope will magnify a star a thousand times, but a good press agent can do even better.
Fred Allen (1894-1957)
American comic

To have news value is to have a tin can tied to one's tail.
T. E. Lawrence (1888-1935)
British soldier, scholar

I want it so that you can't wipe your ass on a piece of paper that hasn't got my picture on it.
Lyndon B. Johnson (1908-1973)
to his press agent

SEE Bennett on The PRESS

Pubs
There is no private house in which people can enjoy themselves so well as in a capital tavern.
Dr Samuel Johnson (1709-1784)

Where village statesmen talked with looks profound,
And news much older than their ale went round.
Oliver Goldsmith (1728-1774)

There is nothing which has yet been contrived by man, by which so much happiness is produced as by a good tavern or inn; a tavern chair is the throne of human felicity.
Dr Samuel Johnson (1709-1784)

Punctuality
He was always late on principle, his principle being that punctuality is the thief of time.
Oscar Wilde (1854-1900)

Punctuality is the virtue of the bored.
Evelyn Waugh (1903-1966)

I am a believer in punctuality though it makes me very lonely.
E. V. Lucas (1868-1938)
British author

L'exactitude est la politesse des rois.
Punctuality is the politeness of kings.
> Louis XVIII of France (1755-1824)
> SEE Walker on PUBLIC LIFE

Punishment

As a man chasteneth his son, so the Lord God chasteneth thee.
> Bible, Deuteronomy

The generality of men are naturally apt to be swayed by fear rather than reverence, and to refrain from evil rather because of the punishment that it brings than because of its own foulness.
> Aristotle (384-322 BC)

He deserves to be preached to death by wild curates.
> Sydney Smith (1771-1845)
> English clergyman, writer

Evil-doers are not to be allowed their way on the ground that they are unable to hurt our souls: the hurt may be in the cowardice or sloth that will not punish them.
> The Teaching of Epictetus
> T. W. Rolleston (1857-1920)
> Irish poet

Whenever the offence inspires less horror than the punishment, the rigour of penal law is obliged to give way to the common feelings of mankind.
> Edward Gibbon (1737-1794)

Thwackum was for doing justice, and leaving mercy to Heaven.
> Henry Fielding (1707-1754)

The first time a schoolmaster ordered me to take my trousers down I knew it was not from any doubt that he could punish me efficiently enough with them up.
> Sir Laurence Olivier (b. 1907)

He must have known me if he had seen me as he was wont to see me, for he was in the habit of flogging me constantly. Perhaps he did not recognise me by my face.
> Anthony Trollope (1815-1882)
> English novelist

The Bible warns very strongly that you are to obey your parents. The rod is considered old-fashioned in many homes. Psychiatrists say it will warp your personality. When I did something wrong as a boy, my mother warped part of me, but it wasn't my personality.
> Billy Graham (b. 1918)

Flogging is a form of debauchery.
> George Bernard Shaw (1856-1950)

I'm all for bringing back the birch, but only between consenting adults.
> Gore Vidal (b. 1925)

The only true way to make the mass of mankind see the beauty of justice is by showing to them in pretty plain terms the consequences of injustice.
> Sydney Smith (1771-1845)
> English clergyman, writer

And where the offence is, let the great axe fall.
> Claudius, *Hamlet*
> William Shakespeare (1564-1616)

Men are not hanged for stealing horses, but that horses may not be stolen.
> George Savile, Lord Halifax (1633-1695)
> English statesman, author

Distrust everyone in whom the impulse to punish is powerful.
> Friedrich Nietzsche (1844-1900)
> SEE CAPITAL PUNISHMENT; Morley on
> HELL; Young, Halifax on JUSTICE

Punk

Punks in their silly leather jackets are a cliché. I have never liked the term and have never discussed it. I just got on with it and got out of it when it became a competition.
> John Lydon (formerly Johnny Rotten) (b. 1957)

I can imagine him becoming a successful hairdresser, a singing Vidal Sassoon.
> Malcolm McLaren
> British rock impresario
> *of Johnny Rotten*

Puritans

Puritanism: The haunting fear that someone, somewhere, may be happy.
> H. L. Mencken (1880-1956)
> American journalist

The Puritan hated bearbaiting, not because it gave pain to the bear, but because it gave pleasure to the spectators.
> Lord Macaulay (1800-1859)
> English historian

A puritan is a person who pours righteous indignation into the wrong things.
> G. K. Chesterton (1874-1936)

The objection to Puritans is not that they try to make us think as they do, but that they try to make us do as they think.
> H. L. Mencken (1880-1956)
> American journalist

Intolerance is the besetting sin of moral fervour.
> A. N. Whitehead (1861-1947)
> British philosopher

The Puritan through Life's sweet garden goes
To pluck the thorn and cast away the rose.
> Kenneth Hare (1888-1962)
> British poet, author
> SEE Russell on RELIGION

Purity

To the pure all things are indecent.

Oscar Wilde (1854-1900)

Mud-pies gratify one of our first and best instincts. So long as we are dirty, we are pure.

Charles D. Warner (1829-1900)
American author

Quarrels

I find my wife hath something in her gizzard, that only waits an opportunity of being provoked to bring up; but I will not, for my content-sake, give it.
Samuel Pepys (1633-1703)

Next to the wound, what women make best is the bandage.
Barbey d'Aurevilly (1808-1889)
French novelist, poet, critic

The falling out of faithful friends, renewing is of love.
Richard Edwardes (1523-1566)
English poet

I strove with none; for none was worth my strife.
Walter Savage Landor (1775-1864)
English author

SEE Proverb, Terence on LOVERS;
Yeats on POETRY

Quotations

A book that furnishes no quotations is, *me judice*, no book – it is a plaything.
Thomas Love Peacock (1785-1866)
English author

The wisdom of the wise and the experience of the ages are perpetuated by quotations.
Benjamin Disraeli (1804-1881)

It is a good thing for an uneducated man to read books of quotations.
Sir Winston Churchill (1874-1965)

Some, for renown, on scraps of learning dote,
And think they grow immortal as they quote.
Edward Young (1683-1765)
English poet

One has to secrete a jelly in which to slip quotations down people's throats and one always secretes too much jelly.
Virginia Woolf (1882-1941)

We prefer to believe that the absence of inverted commas guarantees the originality of a thought, whereas it may be merely that the utterer has forgotten its source.
Clifton Fadiman (b. 1904)
American essayist

When a thing has been said and said well, have no scruple. Take it and copy it.
Anatole France (1844-1924)
French author

It is better to be quotable than to be honest.
Tom Stoppard (b. 1937)
British playwright

The surest way to make a monkey of a man is to quote him.
Robert Benchley (1889-1945)
American humorous writer

I often quote myself. It adds spice to my conversation.
George Bernard Shaw (1856-1950)

By necessity, by proclivity, and by delight, we all quote.
R. W. Emerson (1803-1882)
American essayist, poet, philosopher

Be sure you go to the author to get at HIS meaning, not to find yours.
John Ruskin (1819-1900)
English critic

SEE Byron on LEARNING; Mondale on REAGAN; Lynd on WEALTH

R

Race

It is a great shock at the age of five or six to find that in a world of Gary Coopers you are the Indian.
> James Baldwin (b. 1924)
> American author

I believe in white supremacy until the blacks are educated to a point of responsibility.
> John Wayne (1907-1979)

Segregation now, segregation tomorrow and segregation forever!
> George C. Wallace (b. 1919)
> American Independent politician

Segregation is the adultery of an illicit intercourse between injustice and immorality.
> Martin Luther King (1929-1968)

A racially integrated community is a chronological term timed from the entrance of the first black family to the exit of the last white family.
> Saul Alinsky (1909-1972)
> American radical

No one has been barred on account of his race from fighting or dying for America – there are no 'white' or 'colored' signs on the foxholes or graveyards of battle.
> John F. Kennedy (1917-1963)

I have no purpose to introduce political and social equality between the white and black races. There is a physical difference between the two, which, in my judgement, will probably for ever forbid their living together upon the footing of perfect equality; and inasmuch as it becomes a necessity that there must be a difference, I . . . am in favour of the race to which I belong having the superior position.
> Abraham Lincoln (1809-1865)

Whites must be made to realize that they are only human, not superior. Same with blacks. They must be made to realize that they are also human, not inferior.
> Steve Biko (1946-1977)

The trouble with our people is as soon as they got out of slavery they didn't want to give the white man nothing else. But the fact is, you got to give 'em something. Either your money, your land, your woman or your ass.
> Alice Walker (b. 1944)
> American author, critic

Every time I embrace a black woman I'm embracing slavery, and when I put my arms around a white woman, well I'm hugging freedom. The white man forbade me to have the white woman on pain of death. . . I will not be free until the day I can have a white woman in my bed.
> Eldridge Cleaver (b. 1935)
> American black leader, writer

The truth is that Mozart, Pascal, Boolean algebra, Shakespeare, parliamentary government, baroque churches, Newton, the emancipation of women, Kant, Marx, and Ballanchine ballets don't redeem what this particular civilization has wrought upon the world. The white race *is* the cancer of human history.
> Susan Sontag (b. 1933)
> American essayist

Purity of race does not exist. Europe is a continent of energetic mongrels.
> H. A. L. Fisher (1865-1940)
> British historian

Race prejudice is not only a shadow over the colored – it is a shadow over all of us, and the shadow is darkest over those who feel it least and allow its evil effects to go on.
> Pearl Buck (1892-1973)
> American novelist

Thank God I am black. White people will have a lot to answer for at the last judgement.
> Bishop Desmond Tutu (b. 1932)

SEE FRATERNITY; Galsworthy on The JEWS; Hammond on SLAVERY; Tutu on SOUTH AFRICA; Davis on STARDOM

Rain

Dark as the world of man, black as our loss –
Blind as the nineteen hundred and forty nails
Upon the Cross.
> Edith Sitwell (1887-1964)
> British writer, poet

The tanned appearance of many Londoners is not sunburn – it is rust.

London *Evening Standard*, 1961
*during Britain's wettest
winter on record*

Nature, like man, sometimes weeps for gladness.

Benjamin Disraeli (1804-1881)

SEE Phelps on ENGLAND; Ford on SCOTLAND; Watson on SEASONS; The WEATHER

Reactionaries

The march of the human mind is slow.

Edward Burke (1729-1797)
Irish philosopher, statesman

A reactionary is a somnambulist walking backwards.

Franklin D. Roosevelt (1882-1945)

He is a man walking backwards with his face to the future.

Aneurin Bevan (1897-1960)
British Labour politician
of Sir Walter Elliot

SEE Mill, Twain on TRADITION

Reading

Reading is to the mind what exercise is to the body.

Joseph Addison (1672-1719)
English essayist

There is a great deal of difference between the eager man who wants to read a book and the tired man who wants a book to read.

G. K. Chesterton (1874-1936)

Reading is sometimes an ingenious device for avoiding thought.

Sir Arthur Helps (1813-1875)
English writer

He has left off reading altogether, to the great improvement of his originality.

Charles Lamb (1775-1834)
English essayist, critic

Much reading is an oppression of the mind, and extinguishes the natural candle, which is the reason of so many senseless scholars in the world.

William Penn (1644-1718)
religious leader, founder of Pennsylvania

He had read much, but his contemplation was much more than his reading. He was wont to say that if he had read as much as other men he should have known no more than other men.

John Aubrey (1626-1697)
English antiquary, author
of Hobbes

A reading machine, always wound up and going,
He mastered whatever was not worth the knowing.

J. R. Lowell (1819-1891)
American poet, editor

'Tis the good reader that makes the good book.

R. W. Emerson (1803-1882)
American essayist, poet, philosopher

Reading a book is like re-writing it for yourself. . . You bring to a novel, anything you read, all your experience of the world. You bring your history and you read it in your own terms.

Angela Carter (b. 1940)
British author

Readers are of two sorts; one who carefully goes through a book, and the other who as carefully lets the book go through him.

Douglas Jerrold (1803-1857)
English playwright, humorist

Do not read, as children do, to amuse yourself, or, like the ambitious, for instruction. No, read in order to live.

Gustave Flaubert (1821-1880)

A man ought to read just as his inclination leads him; for what he reads as a task will do him little good.

Dr Samuel Johnson (1709-1784)

Education . . . has produced a vast population able to read but unable to distinguish what is worth reading.

G. M. Trevelyan (1876-1961)
British historian

As writers become more numerous, it is natural for readers to become more indolent.

Oliver Goldsmith (1728-1774)

I took a course in speed reading, learning to read straight down the middle of the page, and was able to read *War and Peace* in twenty minutes. It's about Russia.

Woody Allen (b. 1935)

To read between the lines was easier than to follow the text.

Henry James (1843-1916)

Choose an author as you choose a friend.

Wentworth Dillon, Earl of Roscommon
(c. 1633-1685)
Irish author

SEE Bacon, Kempis on BOOKS; Smith on CRITICS; Birrell on WRITING

Ronald Reagan

A triumph of the embalmer's art.

Gore Vidal (b. 1925)

People have an image of me that I might recklessly get us into a war.
Ronald Reagan (b. 1911)

Ronald Reagan has violated every principle for which America stands. He denies the jurisdiction of the World Court; he acts without consulting Congress and in opposition to the advice of US allies. Serving as judge, jury and executioner, he orders military strikes that kill civilians... The President has no legal power to order US forces to murder indiscriminately and to terrorise those he styles his enemies. Such acts constitute high crimes and misdemeanours. Reagan's subversion of the principles of truth and the rule of law is the greatest threat facing the American people and the world.
Ramsay Clark (b. 1927)
former US Attorney-General

As the age of television progresses the Reagans will be the rule, not the exception. To be perfect for television is all a President has to be these days.
Gore Vidal (b.1925)

You've got to be careful quoting Ronald Reagan, because when you quote him accurately it's called mud-slinging.
Walter F. Mondale (b.1928)
American Democratic politician

I've always believed there is a certain divine scheme of things. I'm not quite able to explain how my election happened or why I'm here, apart from believing it is part of God's plan for me.
Ronald Reagan (b. 1911)
on attaining governorship of California, 1966

Realism
You may be sure that when a man begins to call himself a 'realist', he is preparing to do something he is secretly ashamed of doing.
Sydney J. Harris (b. 1917)
American journalist

When you have got an elephant by the hind legs and he is trying to run away, it's best to let him run.
Abraham Lincoln (1809-1865)

It is folly to expect men to do all that they may reasonably be expected to do.
Richard Whately (1787-1863)
Archbishop of Dublin

Reality is something you rise above.
Liza Minnelli (b. 1946)

Reason
My own mind is my own church.
Thomas Paine (1737-1809)
pamphleteer, revolutionary

Sure, he, that made us with such large discourse,
Looking before and after, gave us not
That capability and godlike reason,
To fust in us unused.
Hamlet, *Hamlet*
William Shakespeare (1564-1616)

People are governed by the head; a kind heart is of little value in chess.
Nicolas-Sébastien Chamfort (1741-1794)
French writer, wit

Le coeur a ses raisons que la raison ne connaît point.
The heart has its reasons which reason does not know.
Blaise Pascal (1623-1662)

Reason is and ought to be the slave of the passions and can never pretend to any other office than to serve and obey them.
David Hume (1711-1776)

If you can engage people's pride, love, pity, ambition (or whatever is their prevailing passion), on your side, you need not fear what their reason can do against you.
Lord Chesterfield (1694-1773)
English statesman and man of letters

Irrationally held truths may be more harmful than reasoned errors.
T. H. Huxley (1825-1895)
English biologist

'It stands to reason' is a formula that gives its user the unfair advantage of at once invoking reason and refusing to listen to it.
H. W. Fowler (1858-1933)
British lexicographer

I'll not listen to reason... Reason always means what someone else has got to say.
Mrs E. C. Gaskell (1810-1865)
English novelist, biographer

I am sick of reasonable people: they see all the reasons for being lazy and doing nothing.
The Secretary, *Geneva*
George Bernard Shaw (1856-1950)

If the animals had reason, they would act just as ridiculous as we menfolks do.
Josh Billings (1818-1885)
American humorist

There is much to suggest that when human beings acquired the powers of conscious attention and rational thought they became so fascinated with these new tools that they forgot all else, like chickens hypnotized with their beaks to a chalk line.
A. E. Watts

SEE Greek proverb on HUNGER; Shakespeare on LOVE; Brown on PARENTS; Chesterfield on PREJUDICE

Rebellion

A hungry man is an angry man.
James Howell (1594-1666)
English diplomat, writer

A populace never rebels from passion for attack, but from impatience of suffering.
Edmund Burke (1729-1797)
Irish philosopher, statesman

I hold it that a little rebellion, now and then, is a good thing, and as necessary in the political world as storms in the physical.
Thomas Jefferson (1743-1826)

Rebellion to tyrants is obedience to god.
John Bradshaw (1602-1659)
English lawyer, regicide

No one can go on being a rebel too long without turning into an autocrat.
Lawrence Durrell (b. 1912)
British author

Insurrection. An unsuccessful revolution; disaffection's failure to substitute misrule for bad government.
Ambrose Bierce (1842-1914)
American author

SEE REVOLUTION

Recession

Most of us have stopped using silver every day.
Margaret Thatcher (b. 1925)

These dark days will be worth all they cost us if they teach us that our true destiny is not to be ministered unto but to minister to ourselves and to our fellow men.
Franklin D. Roosevelt (1882-1945)

SEE Truman on UNEMPLOYMENT

Recklessness

Always goes as if he had a spare neck in his pocket.
R. S. Surtees (1803-1864)
English novelist

We run carelessly to the precipice, after we have put something before us to prevent ourselves from seeing it.
Blaise Pascal (1623-1662)

Reform

Why, Sir, most schemes of political improvement are very laughable things.
Dr Samuel Johnson (1709-1784)

Every reform was once a private opinion.
R. W. Emerson (1803-1882)
American essayist, poet, philosopher

In England we have come to rely upon a comfortable time-lag of fifty years or a century intervening between the perception that something ought to be done and a serious attempt to do it.
H. G. Wells (1866-1946)

You cannot fight against the future. Time is on our side.
W. E. Gladstone (1809-1898)

Every reform is only a mask under cover of which a more terrible reform, which dares not yet name itself, advances.
R. W. Emerson (1803-1882)
American essayist, poet, philosopher

Moderate reformers always hate those who go beyond them.
J. A. Froude (1818-1894)
British author

All reformers are bachelors.
George Moore (1852-1933)
Irish author

SEE Hooker on CHANGE; Shaw on REVOLUTION

Regret

Nessun maggior dolore,
Che ricordarsi del tempo felice
Nella miseria.
There is no greater sorrow than to recall a happy time in the midst of wretchedness.
'Inferno', *Divina Commedia*
Dante (1265-1321)

It's no use asking people if they regret things. It would be like asking King Lear if he regretted dividing up his kingdom.
Malcolm Muggeridge (b. 1903)
British journalist

Regret is a woman's natural food, – she thrives upon it.
Sir Arthur Pinero (1855-1934)
British actor, playwright, essayist

My one regret in life is that I am not someone else.
Woody Allen (b. 1935)

Hindsight is always 20:20.
Billy Wilder (b. 1906)
American film director

Religion

Time consecrates; and what is grey with age becomes religion.
S. T. Coleridge (1772-1834)

If the stars should appear one night in a thousand years, how would men believe and adore!
R. W. Emerson (1803-1882)
American essayist, poet, philosopher

All religions begin with a revolt against morality, and perish when morality conquers them.
George Bernard Shaw (1856-1950)

The true meaning of religion is thus not simply morality but morality touched by emotion.
Matthew Arnold (1822-1888)
English poet, critic

From the age of fifteen, dogma has been the fundamental principle of my religion: I know no other religion; I cannot enter into the idea of any other sort of religion; religion, as a mere sentiment, is to me a dream and a mockery.
Cardinal John Newman (1801-1890)
English churchman, theologian

The truth of religion is in its ritual and the truth of dogma is in its poetry.
John Cowper Powys (1872-1963)
British author, poet

Men are not made religious by performing certain actions which are externally good, but they must first have righteous principles, and then they will not fail to perform virtuous actions.
Martin Luther (1484-1546)

Religion's in the heart, not in the knees.
Douglas Jerrold (1803-1857)
English playwright, humorist

I never sleep comfortably except when I am at sermon or when I pray to God.
François Rabelais (1494-1553)

If you are going to have religion at all, it is better to have it tough – blood and nails and vinegar.
Owen Chadwick (b. 1916)
British historian

Religion would not have any enemies if it were not an enemy to their vices.
Jean-Baptiste Massillon (1663-1742)
French preacher

Most men's anger against religion is as if two men should quarrel for a lady they neither of them care for.
George Savile, Lord Halifax (1633-1695)
English statesman, author

Irreligion. The principal one of the great faiths of the world.
Ambrose Bierce (1842-1914)
American author

We have just enough religion to make us hate, but not enough to make us love one another.
Jonathan Swift (1667-1745)

Men never do evil so completely and cheerfully as when they do it from religious conviction.
Blaise Pascal (1623-1662)

Men will wrangle for religion; write for it, fight for it; die for it; anything but live for it.
C. C. Colton (1780-1832)
English author, clergyman

I count religion but a childish toy,
And hold there is no sin but ignorance.
Christopher Marlowe (1564-1593)

Men despise religion; they hate it, and fear it is true.
Blaise Pascal (1623-1662)

People who feel themselves to be exiles in this world are mightily inclined to believe themselves citizens of another.
George Santayana (1863-1952)
American philosopher, poet

And lips say 'God be pitiful',
Who ne'er said 'God be praised'.
Elizabeth Barrett Browning (1806-1861)

What I mean by a religious person is one who conceives himself or herself to be the instrument of some purpose in the universe which is a high purpose, and is the motive power of evolution, that is of a continual ascent in organisation and power of life, and extension of life.
George Bernard Shaw (1856-1950)

After coming into contact with a religious man I always feel I must wash my hands.
Friedrich Nietzsche (1844-1900)

I have noticed all my life that many people think they have religion when they are troubled with dyspepsia.
R. G. Ingersoll (1833-1899)
American lawyer

Religion is the sigh of the oppressed creature, the heart of a heartless world, and the soul of soulless conditions. It is the *opium* of the people.
Karl Marx (1818-1883)

It is beyond our power to explain either the prosperity of the wicked or the afflictions of the righteous.
Talmud

Nobody can deny but religion is a comfort to the distressed, a cordial to the sick, and sometimes a restraint on the wicked; therefore, whoever would laugh or argue it out of the world, without giving some equivalent for it, ought to be treated as a common enemy.
Lady Mary Wortley Montagu (1689-1762)
English society figure, letter writer

It is necessary for men to be deceived in religion.
Marcus Terentius Varro (116-27 BC)
Roman writer

Religions die when they are proved to be true. Science is the record of dead religions.
Oscar Wilde (1854-1900)

Where it is a duty to worship the sun it is pretty sure to be a crime to examine the laws of heat.
John, Lord Morley (1838-1923)
English writer, Liberal politician

Religion has made an honest woman of the

supernatural, and we won't have it kicking over the traces again.
Christopher Fry (b. 1907)
British playwright

The various modes of worship which prevailed in the Roman world were all considered by the people as equally true; by the philosopher as equally false; and by the magistrate as equally useful.
Edward Gibbon (1737-1794)

Religion may in most of its forms be defined as the belief that the gods are on the side of the Government.
Bertrand Russell (1872-1970)

Government is impossible without a religion: that is, without a body of common assumptions. The open mind never acts.
George Bernard Shaw (1856-1950)

As nations improve, so do their gods.
G. C. Lichtenberg (1742-1799)
German physicist, writer

All religions are founded on the fear of the many and the cleverness of the few.
Stendhal (1783-1842)

Man is a being born to believe. And if no Church comes forward with its title-deeds of truth ... to guide him, he will find altars and idols in his own heart and his own imagination.
Benjamin Disraeli (1804-1881)

A maker of idols is never an idolater.
Chinese proverb

All the sweetness of religion is conveyed to the world by the hands of story-tellers and image-makers. Without their fictions the truths of religion would for the multitude be neither intelligible nor even apprehensible; and the prophets would prophesy and the teachers teach in vain.
George Bernard Shaw (1856-1950)

The more facts a religion takes account of, the greater is its victory, and that is why religions appeal to Puritan temperaments.
Bertrand Russell (1872-1970)

The fashion just now is a Roman Catholic frame of mind with an agnostic conscience: you get the medieval picturesqueness of the one with the modern conveniences of the other.
Saki (H. H. Munro) (1870-1916)
Scottish author

Impiety. Your irreverence toward my diety.
Ambrose Bierce (1842-1914)
American author

It matters little what profession, whether of religion or irreligion, a man may make,

provided only he follows it out with charitable inconsistency, and without insisting on it to the bitter end.
Samuel Butler (1835-1902)
English author

Religion has done love a great service by making it a sin.
Anatole France (1844-1924)
French author

Every religion of the beautiful ends in orgy.
Benjamin Disraeli (1804-1881)

Religion is by no means a proper subject of conversation in a mixed company.
Lord Chesterfield (1694-1773)
English statesman and man of letters

Religion is a way of walking, not a way of talking.
W. R. Inge (1860-1954)
Dean of St Paul's, London

The religion of one age is the literary entertainment of the next.
R. W. Emerson (1803-1882)
American essayist, poet, philosopher

Religion. A daughter of Hope and Fear, explaining to Ignorance the nature of the Unknowable.
Ambrose Bierce (1842-1914)
American author

SEE CHRISTIANITY; Twain on FAITH; Conrad on GOD; Barrie on SUCCESS; Burke on SUPERSTITION; Lunn on TOLERANCE

Repentance

Even in the shadow of death, two and two do not make six.
Leo Tolstoy (1828-1910)
on his deathbed, answering
pleas that he should return
to the Church

You cannot repent too soon, because you do not know how soon it may be too late.
Thomas Fuller (1608-1661)
English cleric

Most people repent of their sins by thanking God they ain't so wicked as their neighbors.
Josh Billings (1818-1885)
American humorist

Repentance is but want of power to sin.
John Dryden (1631-1700)

It is much easier to repent of sins that we have committed than to repent of those we intend to commit.
Josh Billings (1818-1885)
American humorist

Repression

Southern Rhodesia is only being turned into a police State in the sense that policemen are

being given greater authority to safeguard the fundamental liberties of the people.
Sir Roy Welensky (b. 1907)
Rhodesian politician, Prime Minister

We can never be sure that the opinion we are endeavouring to stifle is a false opinion; and even if we were sure, stifling it would be an evil still.
John Stuart Mill (1806-1873)

Whenever we take away the liberties of those whom we hate we are opening the way to loss of liberty for those we love.
Wendell L. Wilkie (1892-1944)
American lawyer, businessman, politician

SEE Cromwell on LIBERTY; Russell on OPINION; OPPRESSION

Reproach
They have a right to censure that have a heart to help.
William Penn (1644-1718)
religious leader, founder of Pennsylvania

There is luxury in self-reproach. When we blame ourselves we feel no one else has a right to blame us.
Oscar Wilde (1854-1900)

Reputation
What people say behind your back is your standing in the community.
Ed (E. W.) Howe (1853-1937)
American journalist, novelist

The great difficulty is first to win a reputation; the next to keep it while you live; and the next to preserve it after you die.
Benjamin Haydon (1786-1846)
British artist

Character is much easier kept than recovered.
Thomas Paine (1737-1809)
pamphleteer, revolutionary

Many a man's reputation would not know his character if they met on the street.
Elbert Hubbard (1856-1915)
American author

How many people live on the reputation of the reputation they might have made.
Dr Oliver Wendell Holmes (1809-1894)
American writer, physician

Many men and women enjoy popular esteem, not because they are known, but because they are unknown.
Nicolas-Sébastien Chamfort (1741-1794)
French writer, wit

Often women are virtuous because they value their reputation and prefer not to be disturbed.
François, Duc de La Rochefoucauld (1613-1680)
French writer, moralist

Reputation, reputation, reputation! O, I have lost my reputation! I have lost the immortal part of myself, and what remains is bestial.
Cassio, *Othello*
William Shakespeare (1564-1616)

SEE La Rochefoucauld on FAME; Congreve, Pascal, Pope, Smith on GOSSIP; Billings on PHILANTHROPY

Resignation
Mankind are more disposed to suffer, while evils are sufferable, than to right themselves by abolishing the forms to which they are accustomed.
Thomas Jefferson (1743-1826)

I can imagine no more comfortable frame of mind for the conduct of life than a humorous resignation.
W. Somerset Maugham (1874-1966)

A calm despair, without angry convulsions or reproaches directed at heaven, is the essence of wisdom.
Alfred de Vigny (1797-1863)
French poet, novelist, dramatist

What cannot be cured must be endured.
François Rabelais (1494-1553)

SEE Ferber on AGE: Old Age; Milton on BLINDNESS; Shakespeare on DEATH; Landor on DEATH: Dying; Hubbard on OPTIMISM

Resolve
What reinforcement we may gain from hope;
If not, what resolution from despair.
John Milton (1608-1674)

A person under the firm persuasion that he can command resources virtually has them.
Livy (59 BC-17 AD)

If I repeat 'My will be done', with the necessary degree of faith and persistency, the chances are that, sooner or later and somehow or other, I shall get what I want.
Aldous Huxley (1894-1963)

SEE Herford on WHIMSY

Respectability
The more things a man is ashamed of, the more respectable he is.
Tanner, *Man and Superman*
George Bernard Shaw (1856-1950)

Vanity is the cause of a great deal of virtue in man; the vainest are those who like to be thought respectable.
Sir Arthur Pinero (1855-1934)
British actor, playwright, essayist

Men have to do some awfully mean things to keep up their respectability.
George Bernard Shaw (1856-1950)

Virtue has never been as respectable as money.
Mark Twain (1835-1910)

SEE Wilde on GOODNESS; Chamfort on REPUTATION; Peacock on SNOBBERY

Retirement

Fear no more the heat o' the sun,
Nor the furious winter's rages;
Thou thy worldly task hast done,
Home art gone and ta'en thy wages.
William Shakespeare (1564-1616)

Have you ever been out for a late autumn walk in the closing part of the afternoon, and suddenly looked up to realize that the leaves have practically all gone? And the sun has set and the day gone before you knew it – and with that a cold wind blows across the landscape? That's retirement.
Stephen Leacock (1869-1944)
Canadian humorist and economist

Retirement is the ugliest word in the language.
Ernest Hemingway (1899-1961)

Few men of action have been able to make a graceful exit at the appropriate time.
Malcolm Muggeridge (b. 1903)
British journalist

Americans hardly ever retire from business: they are either carried out feet first or they jump from a window.
Professor A. L. Goodhart (1891-1978)
American lawyer

When a man retires and time is no longer a matter of urgent importance, his colleagues generally present him with a clock.
R. C. Sherriff (1896-1975)
British author

Eating's going to be a whole new ball game. I may even have to buy a new pair of trousers.
Lester Piggot (b. 1935)
British champion jockey
on his retirement

Retirement from the concert world is like giving up smoking. You have got to finish completely.
Beniamino Gigli (1890-1957)
Italian tenor

Lord Tyrawley and I have been dead these two years, but we don't choose to have it known.
Lord Chesterfield (1694-1773)
English statesman and man of letters

Revenge

If you prick us, do we not bleed? if you tickle us, do we not laugh? if you poison us, do we not die? and if you wrong us, shall we not revenge?
Shylock, *The Merchant of Venice*
William Shakespeare (1564-1616)

You slap my cheek and I'll turn it. But you slap my wife or my children, boy, and I'll *put you on the floor!*
Dr James Robison
American TV religious personality

Revenge is a kind of wild justice, which the more a man's nature runs to, the more ought law to weed it out.
Francis Bacon (1561-1626)

Revenge is often like biting a dog because the dog bit you.
Austin O'Malley (1858-1932)
American oculist, author

Nothing is more costly, nothing is more sterile, than vengeance.
Sir Winston Churchill (1874-1965)

And reassembling our afflicted
powers,
Consult how we may henceforth most
offend.
John Milton (1608-1674)

The devil himself has not yet created a suitable vengeance for the blood of a slain infant.
Menachem Begin (b. 1913)
Israeli politician, Prime Minister

A man that studieth revenge keeps his own wounds green.
Francis Bacon (1561-1626)

Revolution

The old order changeth, yielding place
to new,
And God fulfils himself in many ways.
Lord Tennyson (1809-1892)

A revolution is an opinion backed by bayonets.
Napoleon Bonaparte (1769-1821)

How much the greatest event it is that ever happened in the world! and how much the best!
Charles James Fox (1749-1806)
English Whig politician
of the fall of the Bastille

If there's no dancing, count me out.
Emma Goldman (1869-1940)
American anarchist
of the Russian Revolution

Inferiors revolt in order that they may be equal, and equals that they may be superior. Such is the state of mind which creates revolutions.
Aristotle (384-322 BC)

Revolutions have never lightened the burden of tyranny: they have only shifted it to another shoulder.
George Bernard Shaw (1856-1950)

When the people contend for their liberty they

seldom get anything by their victory but new masters.
George Savile, Lord Halifax (1633-1695)
English statesman, author

Every revolution evaporates and leaves behind only the slime of a new bureaucracy.
Franz Kafka (1883-1924)

The philosophers have only *interpreted* the world. The point, however, is to *change* it.
Karl Marx (1818-1883)

I wanted to change the world. But I have found that the only thing one can be sure of changing is oneself.
Aldous Huxley (1894-1963)

The only way to regenerate the world is to do the thing which lies nearest us, and not hunt after grand, far-fetched ones for ourselves.
Charles Kingsley (1819-1875)
English author, clergyman

He who would reform himself must first reform society.
George Bernard Shaw (1856-1950)

If we were to promise people nothing better than only revolution, they would scratch their heads and say: 'Is it not better to have good goulash?'
Nikita Khrushchev (1894-1971)

Revolution is not a dinner party, nor an essay, nor a painting, nor a piece of embroidery; it cannot be advanced softly, gradually, carefully, considerately, respectfully, politely, plainly and modestly.
Mao Ze dong (1893-1976)

I, John Brown, am now quite certain that the crimes of this guilty land will never be purged away but with Blood.
John Brown (1800-1859)
written on the day of his execution

The surest guide to the correctness of the path that women take is *joy in the struggle.* Revolution is the festival of the oppressed.
Germaine Greer (b. 1939)
Australian feminist writer

I have been ever of opinion that revolutions are not to be evaded.
Benjamin Disraeli (1804-1881)

SEE Ellis on CIVILIZATION; REBELLION; Hubbard on WOMEN

Revolutionaries

We are dead men on furlough.
Vladimir Ilyich Lenin (1870-1924)

I am thirty-three – the age of the good sans-culotte Jesus; an age fatal to revolutionists.
Camille Desmoulins (1760-1794)
French journalist, revolutionary,
to the Revolutionary Tribunal
on the eve of his execution

Es mejor morir de pie que vivir de rodillas.
It is better to die on your feet than to live on your knees.
Dolores Ibárruri, *La Pasionaria* (1895-1981)
Valencia, 1936

He that goeth about to persuade a multitude that they are not so well governed as they ought to be shall never want attentive and favourable hearers.
Richard Hooker (1554-1600)
English theologian

Revolutionary movements attract those who are not good enough for established institutions as well as those who are too good for them.
George Bernard Shaw (1856-1950)

The traditional figures of revolution, Rousseau, Karl Marx, Lenin and others, were no great emancipators of women and were themselves chauvinist. They left their wives slaving over a hot stove.
Sally Oppenheim (b. 1930)
British Conservative politician

Ceux qui parlent de révolution sans en référer explicitement à la vie quotidienne ont un cadavre dans la bouche.
Those who speak of revolution without making it real in their own daily lives talk with a corpse in their mouths.
Raoul Vaneigem (b. 1934)
Belgian political theorist

A man who has had his dinner is never a revolutionist: his politics are all talk.
George Bernard Shaw (1856-1950)

To be a revolutionary you have to be a human being. You must care about people who have no power.
Jane Fonda (b. 1937)

Revolutionaries do not make revolutions. The revolutionaries are those who know when power is lying in the street and then they can pick it up. Armed uprising by itself has never yet led to revolution.
Hannah Arendt (1906-1975)
American political philosopher

Every revolutionary ends up by becoming either an oppressor or a heretic.
Albert Camus (1913-1960)

SEE Molière on VOCATION

The Rich

He must have killed a lot of men to have made so much money.
Molière (1622-1673)

Anyone who makes a lot of money quickly must be pretty crooked – honest pushing away at the grindstone never made anyone a bomb.
Mandy Rice-Davies (b. 1944)
call-girl in British political scandal, 1963

He that maketh haste to be rich shall not be innocent.

Bible, Proverbs

If Heaven had looked upon riches to be a valuable thing, it would not have given them to such a scoundrel.

Jonathan Swift (1667-1745)

God shows his contempt for wealth by the kind of person he selects to receive it.

Austin O'Malley (1858-1932)
American oculist, author

O, what a world of vile,
ill-favoured faults,
Looks handsome in three hundred
pounds a year.

Anne, *The Merry Wives of Windsor*
William Shakespeare (1564-1616)

L'or, même à la laideur, donne un teint de beauté.
Gold lends a touch of beauty even to the ugly.

Nicolas Boileau (1636-1711)
French poet, critic

To suppose, as we all suppose, that we could be rich and not behave as the rich behave, is like supposing that we could drink all day and stay sober.

Logan Pearsall Smith (1865-1946)
American essayist

The rich never feel so good as when they are speaking of their possessions as responsibilities.

Robert Lynd (1879-1949)
Anglo-Irish essayist, journalist

Come, let us pity those who are better
off then we are.
Come, my friend, and remember that
the rich have butlers and no friends,
And we have friends and no butlers.

Ezra Pound (1885-1972)

The wretchedness of being rich is that you live with rich people.

Logan Pearsall Smith (1865-1946)
American essayist

The jests of the rich are ever successful.

Oliver Goldsmith (1728-1774)

Heiresses are never jilted.

George Meredith (1828-1909)
English author

The greatest luxury of riches is, that they enable you to escape so much good advice. The rich are always advising the poor, but the poor seldom venture to return the compliment.

Sir Arthur Helps (1813-1875)
British writer

I honestly wouldn't spend another winter in England, if I were you.

befurred lady to shivering beggar
Nicolas Bentley (1907-1978)
British artist, author, publisher

SEE Dobell on FUNERALS; Churchill
on INDEPENDENCE; France,
Goldsmith on The LAW;
MILLIONAIRES; Bagehot, Munro on
POVERTY; WEALTH

The Right

What we have to fear is the emergence from beneath, not from above, of some new energetic organisation which will say, 'Britain is a great country, kill the blacks and the Jews, replace this weak government with a strong one. Let's smarten ourselves up and wear a uniform'. For it will be Big Brother shouting these words. But, having read *Nineteen Eighty-Four*, he'll be too cunning to call himself Big Brother.

Anthony Burgess (b. 1917)
British author

McCarthyism is Americanism with its sleeves rolled.

Joseph McCarthy (1908-1957)
American Republican politician

They'll nail anyone who ever scratched his ass during the National Anthem.

Humphrey Bogart (1899-1957)
of the Un-American Activities Committee

Any time a politician tells you 'The Russians are coming', hang on to your wallet. It's just another raid on the treasury.

Gore Vidal (b. 1925)

I have a feeling that at any time about three million Americans can be had for any militant reaction against Law, decency, the Constitution, the Supreme Court, compassion and the rule of reason.

J. K. Galbraith (b. 1908)
American economist

Rock and Roll

Rock'n'roll is part of a pest to undermine the morals of the youth of our nation. It is sexualistic, unmoralistic and . . . brings people of both races together.

North Alabama White Citizens' Council *1950s*

Romance

Romance is a love affair in other than domestic surroundings.

Sir Walter Raleigh (1861-1922)
British academic

Is not this the true romantic feeling – not to desire to escape life, but to prevent life from escaping you?

Thomas Wolfe (1900-1938)
American author

Romance, like the rabbit at the dog track, is the elusive, fake, and never attained reward which, for the benefit and amusement of our masters, keeps us running and thinking in safe circles.
Beverly Jones (b. 1927)
American feminist writer

Nothing spoils a romance so much as a sense of humour in the woman.
Oscar Wilde (1854-1900)

SEE Bulwer-Lytton on ITALY;
Wilde on MARRIAGE

Royalty

Uneasy lies the head that wears a crown.
King Henry, *King Henry IV part 2*
William Shakespeare (1564-1616)

Royalty is a government in which the attention of the nation is concentrated on one person doing interesting actions.
Walter Bagehot (1826-1877)
English economist, critic

Kings are not born; they are made by universal hallucination.
George Bernard Shaw (1856-1950)

A king is a thing men have made for their own sakes, for quietness' sake. Just as if in a family one man is appointed to buy the meat.
John Selden (1584-1654)
English jurist, statesman

Royalty is but a feather in a man's cap; let children enjoy their rattle.
Oliver Cromwell (1599-1658)

And what, in a mean man, I should call folly, is in your majesty remarkable wisdom.
Philip Massinger (1583-1640)
English dramatist

Everyone likes flattery; and when you come to Royalty you should lay it on with a trowel.
Benjamin Disraeli (1804-1881)

Must! Is must a word to be addressed to princes? Little man, little man! thy father, if he had been alive, durst not have used that word.
Elizabeth I of England (1533-1603)
to Robert Cecil

I know the song ['There was an old man and he had an old sow'] and I can make all those noises at home but I cannot do them with a tiara on.
Queen Elizabeth II (b. 1926)

A careless song, with a little nonsense now and then, does not misbecome the monarch.
Horace Walpole (1717-1797)
English author

My only excuse for being so various is that I appear as 'chymist, fiddler, statesman and buffoon' entirely by request.
Duke of Edinburgh (b. 1921)

Vulgarity in a king flatters the majority of the nation.
George Bernard Shaw (1856-1950)

It has been said, not truly, but with a possible approximation to truth, that in 1802 every heriditary monarch was insane.
Walter Bagehot (1826-1877)
English economist, critic

Royalty is a neurosis.
Get well soon.
Adrian Mitchell (b. 1932)
British poet
*verse addressed to
the Prince of Wales*

All the time I feel I must justify my existence.
Prince of Wales (b. 1948)

Altogether the cost to the state of the monarchy is probably not less than two million pounds a year – as much as Omo and Daz spend on advertising.
Anthony Sampson (b. 1926)
British journalist, author
1965

The brood of that dutiful and pleasant gentlewoman Elizabeth II and her immediate connections is now distending the country with a brand-new and brazen aristocracy; a nouveau ancien régime.
New Statesman, 1986

The royal refugee our breed restores
With foreign courtiers and with
foreign whores,
And carefully repeopled us again
Throughout his lazy, long, lascivious
reign.
Daniel Defoe (1661-1731)
of Charles II of England

Though God hath raised me high, yet this I count the glory of my crown: that I have reigned with your loves.
Elizabeth I of England (1533-1603)

We live in what virtually amounts to a museum – which does not happen to a lot of people.
Duke of Edinburgh (b. 1921)

Oh, do turn it off, it is so embarrassing unless one is there – like hearing the Lord's Prayer when playing canasta.
Queen Elizabeth the Queen Mother (b. 1900)
*of the National Anthem played
at a televised Cup Final*

If you find you are to be presented to the Queen, do not rush up to her. She will eventually be brought around to you, like a dessert trolley at a good restaurant.
advice in the
Los Angeles Times, 1983

I never see any home cooking. All I get is fancy stuff.

Duke of Edinburgh (b. 1921)

I know I have the body of a weak and feeble woman, but I have the heart and stomach of a king, and of a king of England too.

Elizabeth I of England (1533-1603)

Don't forget your great guns, which are the most respectable arguments of the rights of kings.

Frederick the Great of Prussia (1712-1786)

Divine right of kings means the divine right of anyone who can get uppermost.

Herbert Spencer (1820-1903)
English philosopher

I cannot be indifferent to the assassination of a member of my profession. We should be obliged to shut up business if we, the Kings, were to consider the assassination of Kings as of no consequence at all.

Edward VII of Great Britain (1841-1910)
refusing to recognise the Karageorgevic régime in Serbia after the murder of King Alexander and the extermination of the Obrenovic dynasty, 1903

War is the trade of kings.

John Dryden (1631-1700)

My people and I have come to an agreement which satisfies us both. They are to say what they please, and I am to do what I please.

Frederick the Great of Prussia (1712-1786)

A king is not allowed the luxury of a good character. Our country has produced millions of blameless greengrocers, but not one blameless monarch.

King Magnus, *The Apple Cart*
George Bernard Shaw (1856-1950)

I do not oppose, it is my duty not to oppose; but observe that I warn.

Walter Bagehot (1826-1877)
English economist, critic
notional statement by a British constitutional sovereign

I am your anointed Queen. I will never be by violence constrained to do anything. I thank God I am endued with such qualities that if I were turned out of the Realm in my petticoat I were able to live in any place in Christome.

Elizabeth I of England (1533-1603)

There is not a single crowned head in Europe whose talents or merit would entitle him to be elected a vestryman by the people of any parish in America.

Thomas Jefferson (1743-1826)

I now quit altogether public affairs, and I lay down my burden.

Edward VIII of Great Britain (1894-1972)
abdication speech

Here lies our Sovereign Lord, the King
Whose word no man relies on:
He never says a foolish thing
Nor ever does a wise one.

John Wilmot, Earl of Rochester (1647-1680)
written on the door of Charles II's bedchamber

A prince who will not undergo the difficulty of understanding must undergo the danger of trusting.

George Savile, Lord Halifax (1633-1695)
English statesman, author

Put not your trust in princes.

Bible, Psalms

All my possessions for a moment of time.

Elizabeth I of England (1533-1603)
last words

SEE Tennyson on DEATH: Dying; Louis XIV on FLATTERY; Marlow on GLORY; Burke on TYRANNY

The Russians

They came to the court balls dropping pearls and vermin.

Lord Macaulay (1800-1859)
English historian

Let it be clearly understood that the Russian is a delightful person till he tucks in his shirt.

Rudyard Kipling (1865-1936)

I don't know a good Russian from a bad Russian. I can tell a good Frenchman from a bad Frenchman. I can tell a good Italian from a bad Italian. I know a good Greek when I see one. But I don't understand the Russians.

Franklin D. Roosevelt (1882-1945)

It's easier for a Russian to become an atheist than for anyone else in the world.

Feodor Dostoievski (1821-1881)

SEE Vidal on The RIGHT; The USSR

S

Sacrifice

The whole point of a sacrifice is that you give up something you never really wanted in the first place. People are doing it around you all the time. They give up their careers, say – or their beliefs – or sex.

> Jimmy, *Look Back in Anger*
> John Osborne (b. 1929)
> British playwright

The two things that worthless people sacrifice everything for are happiness and freedom, and their punishment is that they get both only to find that they have no capacity for the happiness and no use for the freedom.

> George Bernard Shaw (1856-1950)

Greater love hath no man than this, that he lay down his friends for his life.

> Jeremy Thorpe (b. 1929)
> British Liberal politician
> *following a Cabinet*
> *reorganisation by Prime Minister*
> *Harold Macmillan*

Sacrifice is a form of bargaining.

> Holbrook Jackson (1874-1948)
> British author

Too long a sacrifice
Can make a stone of the heart.

> W. B. Yeats (1865-1939)

SEE Lenin on CAPITALISM; Emerson on MANNERS; Chesterton on SELF-DENIAL; Maugham on WOMEN

Sainthood

Saint. A dead sinner revised and edited.

> Ambrose Bierce (1842-1914)
> American author

The only difference between the saint and the sinner is that every saint has a past and every sinner has a future.

> Oscar Wilde (1854-1900)

The fifty to eighty years required to see a candidate through to sainthood can exhaust the time and money of the sponsors.

> Cardinal Leon-Joseph Suenens (b. 1904)
> Belgian ecclesiastic

Being a saint, which I'm not, is a pain, to be honest.

> Bob Geldof (b. 1954)

Saints should always be judged guilty until they are proved innocent.

> George Orwell (1903-1950)

I have fought a good fight, I have finished my course, I have kept the faith.

> Saint Paul (3-67)

SEE Cowper on The DEVIL; Geldof on FAME; Bible, Wilde on MARTRYDOM; Howe on PERSECUTION

Salesmen

For a salesman there is no rock bottom to the life. He don't put a bolt to a nut, he don't tell you the law or give you medicine. He's a man way out there in the blue, riding on a smile and a shoeshine. And when they start not smiling back – that's an earthquake. And then you get yourself a couple of spots on your hat, and you're finished... A salesman is got to dream, boy. It comes with the territory.

> Arthur Miller (b. 1915)

Nothing is as irritating as the fellow that chats pleasantly while he's over-charging you.

> Kin (F. McKinney) Hubbard (1868-1930)
> American humorist, journalist

Bold knaves thrive without one grain of sense,
But good men starve for want of impudence.

> John Dryden (1631-1700)

Salvation

The salvation of the world depends on the men who will not take evil good-humouredly, and whose laughter destroys the fool instead of encouraging him.

> George Bernard Shaw (1856-1950)

No one can be redeemed by another. No God and no saint is able to shield a man from the consequence of his evil doings. Every one of us must become his own redeemer.

> Subhadra Bhikshu (d. 1917)
> author of *The Buddhist Way*

He who created us without our help will not save us without our consent.
Saint Augustine (354-430)

Human salvation lies in the hands of the creatively maladjusted.
Martin Luther King (1929-1968)

SEE Halifax on SELF-DEFENCE

Satire

Ridicule is the best test of truth.
Lord Chesterfield (1694-1773)
English statesman and man of letters

Satire is a sort of glass, wherein beholders do generally discover everybody's face but their own.
Jonathan Swift (1667-1745)

We audiences have tasted our own blood and liked it.
Alan Brien (b. 1925)
British novelist, journalist

Difficile est saturam non scribere.
It is difficult not to write satire.
Juvenal (c. 40-130)

Strange! that a Man who has wit enough to write a Satire should have folly enough to publish it.
Benjamin Franklin (1706-1790)

'My Lord – I must live' – once said a wretched author of satire to a minister who had reproached him for following so degrading a profession. 'I fail to see why', replied the Great Man coldly.
Jean-Jacques Rousseau (1712-1778)

The true end of satire is the amendment of vices by correction.
John Dryden (1631-1700)

Satire, though it may exaggerate the vice it lashes, is not justified in creating it in order that it may be lashed.
Anthony Trollope (1815-1882)
English novelist

Satire is the last flicker of originality in a passing epoch as it faces the onrush of staleness and boredom. Freshness has gone; bitterness remains.
A. N. Whitehead (1861-1947)
British philosopher

Scandal

An event has happened, upon which it is difficult to speak, and impossible to be silent.
Edmund Burke (1729-1797)
Irish philosopher, statesman

A stink is still worse for the stirring.
Miguel de Cervantes (1547-1616)

Many of the scandals that I have seen have begun from glossing over unpleasant facts.
Lord Chandos (1893-1972)
British industrialist, politician

History is made in the class struggle and not in bed.
Alex Mitchell
British left-wing journalist
following deposition of
leader of Workers' Revolutionary
Party amid sex scandal, 1985

Le scandale du monde est ce qui fait l'offense,
Et ce n'est pas pécher que pécher en silence.
It is the public scandal that offends; to sin in secret is no sin at all.
Molière (1622-1673)

Scandal is merely the compassionate allowance which the gay make to the humdrum. Think how many blameless lives are brightened by the blazing indiscretions of other people.
Saki (H. H. Munro) (1870-1916)
Scottish author

The malice of a good thing is the barb that makes it stick.
R. B. Sheridan (1751-1816)

Gossip is charming! History is merely gossip. But scandal is gossip made tedious by morality.
Oscar Wilde (1854-1900)

Nobody looks at the sun except at an eclipse.
Seneca (c. 5-65)
Roman writer, philosopher, statesman

SEE GOSSIP; Fielding on TEA

Scepticism

Scepticism is the chastity of the intellect.
George Santayana (1863-1952)
American philosopher, poet

It is by insisting on an impossible standard of perfection that the sceptic makes himself secure.
A. J. Ayer (b. 1910)
British philosopher

Truth, Sir, is a cow, which will yield sceptics no more milk; so they have gone to milk the bull.
Dr Samuel Johnson (1709-1784)

SEE DOUBT

Scholarship

The ink of the scholar is more sacred than the blood of the martyr.
Muhammad (c. 570-632)

Opposing one species of superstition to another, set them a quarrelling; while we ourselves, during their fury and contention, happily make our escape into the calm, though obscure, regions of philosophy.
David Hume (1711-1776)

The world's great men have not commonly been great scholars, nor great scholars great men.
> Dr Oliver Wendell Holmes (1809-1894)
> American writer, physician

He was a rake among scholars, and a scholar among rakes.
> Lord Macaulay (1800-1859)
> English historian
> *of Sir Richard Steele*

His studies were pursued but never effectually overtaken.
> H. G. Wells (1866-1946)

I cannot forgive a scholar his homeless despondency.
> R. W. Emerson (1803-1882)
> American essayist, poet, philosopher

There mark what ills the scholar's life assail:
Toil, envy, want, the patron, and the gaol.
> Dr Samuel Johnson (1709-1784)

Of making many books there is no end; and much study is a weariness of the flesh.
> Bible, Ecclesiastes

SEE LEARNING

School

The founding fathers in their wisdom decided that children were an unnatural strain on parents. So they provided jails called schools, equipped with tortures called education. School is where you go between when your parents can't take you and industry can't take you.
> John Updike (b. 1932)

Thou hast most traitorously corrupted the youth of the realm in erecting a grammar school.
> Jack Cade, *King Henry VI part 2*
> William Shakespeare (1564-1616)

What are schools for if not indoctrination against Communism?
> Richard Nixon (b. 1913)

I have never let my schooling interfere with my education.
> Mark Twain (1835-1910)

SEE EDUCATION; Walpole on POWER; PRIVATE EDUCATION; STUDENTS; TEACHERS; UNIVERSITY

Science

We vivisect the nightingale
To probe the secret of his note.
> T. B. Aldrich (1836-1907)
> American writer, editor

The universe is full of magical things, patiently waiting for our wits to grow sharper.
> Eden Phillpotts (1862-1960)
> British author

I seem to have been only a boy playing on the seashore, and diverting myself in now and then finding a smoother pebble or a prettier shell than ordinary, whilst the great ocean of truth lay all undiscovered before me.
> Sir Isaac Newton (1642-1727)

The marble index of a mind for ever
Voyaging through strange seas of
thought alone.
> William Wordsworth (1770-1850)
> *of a statue of Newton*

Nature and nature's laws lay hid in night;
God said 'Let Newton be!' and all was light.
> Alexander Pope (1688-1744)

It did not last: the Devil, howling 'Ho Let Einstein be!' restored the status quo.
> John Squire (1884-1958)
> British author

I am actually not at all a man of science, not an observer, not an experimenter, not a thinker. I am by temperament nothing but a conquistador – an adventurer.
> Sigmund Freud (1856-1939)

In everything that relates to science, I am a whole Encyclopaedia behind the rest of the world.
> Charles Lamb (1775-1834)
> English essayist, critic

When I am in the company of scientists I feel like a curate who has strayed into a drawing room full of dukes.
> W. H. Auden (1907-1973)

We are much beholden to Machiavel and others, that write what men do, and not what they ought to do.
> Francis Bacon (1561-1626)

Science commits suicide when it adopts a creed.
> T. H. Huxley (1825-1895)
> English biologist

Science knows only one commandment: contribute to science.
> Bertolt Brecht (1898-1956)

Creativity in science could be described as the act of putting two and two together to make five.
> Arthur Koestler (1905-1983)
> British author

We are much beholden to Machiavel and then it ought to be done. That if something has been invented, then we must use it. We don't stop to think of the possible consequences of its use.
> J. B. Priestley (1894-1984)

In the arts of life man invents nothing; but in
the arts of death he outdoes Nature herself,
and produces by chemistry and machinery all
the slaughter of plague, pestilence, and famine.
> The Devil, *Man and Superman*
> George Bernard Shaw (1856-1950)

*Il n'existe pas de sciences appliquées, mais
seulement des applications de la science.*
There are no such things as applied sciences,
only applications of science.
> Louis Pasteur (1822-1895)

Science is a collection of successful recipes.
> Paul Valéry (1871-1945)
> French poet, essayist

The true worth of a researcher lies in pursuing
what he did not seek in his experiment as well
as what he sought.
> Claude Bernard (1813-1878)
> French physiologist

Aristotle could have avoided the mistake of
thinking that women have fewer teeth than
men by the simple device of asking
Mrs Aristotle to open her mouth.
> Bertrand Russell (1872-1970)

The progress of science is strewn, like an
ancient desert trail, with the bleached skeleton
of discarded theories which once seemed to
possess eternal life.
> Arthur Koestler (1905-1983)
> British author

The great tragedy of science – the slaying of a
beautiful theory by an ugly fact.
> T. H. Huxley (1825-1895)
> English biologist

All science is dominated by the idea of
approximation.
> Bertrand Russell (1872-1970)

Science is organised knowledge.
> Herbert Spencer (1820-1903)
> English philosopher

The world, which took but six days to make,
is like to take us six thousand years to make
out.
> Sir Thomas Browne (1605-1682)
> English physician, author

The most incomprehensible thing about the
world is that it is comprehensible.
> Albert Einstein (1879-1955)

SEE Lamb on The COSMOS; Sockman
on KNOWLEDGE; Wilde on
RELIGION; TECHNOLOGY

Scotland

That garret of the earth – that knuckle-end of
England – that land of Calvin, oat-cakes, and
sulphur.
> Sydney Smith (1771-1845)
> English clergyman, writer

A land of meanness, sophistry and lust.
> Lord Byron (1788-1824)

The beauty of Scotland is that it is big enough
to be important in the UK and small enough
for everyone to know everyone else.
> George Younger (b. 1931)
> Conservative politician, Secretary of
> State for Scotland
> 1982

If the Scotch knew enough to go in when it
rained, they would never get any outdoor
exercise.
> Simeon Ford (fl. 1901-1903)

The noblest prospect that a Scotchman ever
sees is the high road, that leads him to
England.
> Dr Samuel Johnson (1709-1784)

In all my travels I never met with any one
Scotchman but what was a man of sense. I
believe everybody of that country that has
any, leaves it as fast as they can.
> Dr Francis Lockier (1667-1740)
> English prelate, man of letters

SEE Franklin on ARGUMENT

The Scots

There are few more impressive sights in the
world than a Scotsman on the make.
> J. M. Barrie (1860-1937)
> Scottish playwright

I have been trying all my life to like Scotch-
men, and am obliged to desist from the
experiment in despair.
> Charles Lamb (1775-1834)
> English essayist, critic

Much . . . may be made of a Scotchman, if he
be *caught* young.
> Dr Samuel Johnson (1709-1784)

As Dr Johnson never said, is there any
Scotsman without charm?
> J. M. Barrie (1860-1937)
> Scottish playwright

It requires a surgical operation to get a joke
well into a Scotch understanding. The only
idea of wit, or rather that inferior variety of
the electric talent which prevails occasionally
in the North, and which, under the name of
'Wut', is so infinitely distressing to people of
good taste, is laughing immoderately at stated
intervals.
> Sydney Smith (1771-1845)
> English clergyman, writer

Their learning is like bread in a besieged town:
every man gets a little, but no man gets a full
meal.
> Dr Samuel Johnson (1709-1784)

I've sometimes thought that the difference
between the Scotch and the English is that the

Scotch are hard in all other respects but soft with women, and the English are hard with women and soft in all other respects.
J. M. Barrie (1860-1937)
Scottish playwright

Minds like ours, my dear James, must always be above national prejudices, and in all companies it gives me true pleasure to declare that, as a people, the English are very little indeed inferior to the Scotch.
John Wilson (1785-1854)
Scottish philosopher

The Sea
They that go down to the sea in ships, that do business in great waters, these see the works of the Lord and his wonders in the deep.
Bible, Psalms

To me, the sea is like a person – like a child that I've known a long time. It sounds crazy, I know, but when I swim in the sea I talk to it. I never feel alone when I'm out there.
Gertrude Ederle (b. 1906)
30 years after becoming the first woman to swim the English Channel

for whatever we lose (like a you or a me)
it's always ourselves we find in the sea.
e.e.cummings (1894-1962)

The sea has never been friendly to man. At most it has been the accomplice of human restlessness.
Joseph Conrad (1857-1924)

The snotgreen sea. The scrotumtightening sea.
James Joyce (1882-1941)

SEE Butler on PIETY

Seasons
January grey is here,
Like a sexton by her grave;
February bears the bier,
March with grief doth howl and rave,
And April weeps – but, O ye hours!
Follow with May's fairest flowers.
Dirge for the Year
P. B. Shelley (1792-1822)

April, April,
Laugh thy girlish laughter;
Then, the moment after,
Weep thy girlish tears.
Sir William Watson (1858-1935)
British poet

Winter lingered so long in the lap of Spring that it occasioned a great deal of talk.
Bill (E. W.) Nye (1850-1896)
American journalist, humorous writer

Like a lovely woman late for her appointment
She's suddenly here, taking us unawares,
So beautifully annihilating expectation
That we applaud her punctual arrival.
Gerald Bullett (1893-1958)
British author, poet
of Spring

Summer set lip to earth's bosom bare
And left the flushed print in a poppy there.
Francis Thompson (1859-1907)
English poet

Autumn wins you best by this, it's mute
Appeal to sympathy for its decay.
Robert Browning (1812-1889)

Winter is icummen in,
Lhude sing Goddamm.
Raineth drop and staineth slop,
And how the wind doth ramm!
Sing: Goddamm.
Ezra Pound (1885-1972)

Secrets
Two things a man cannot hide: that he is drunk, and that he is in love.
Antiphanes (4th century BC)
Athenian playwright

Whoever wishes to keep a secret must hide the fact that he possesses one.
Johann Wolfgang von Goethe (1749-1832)

If you wish to preserve your secret, wrap it up in frankness.
Alexander Smith (1830-1867)
Scottish poet

How can we expect someone else to keep our secret if we have not been able to keep it ourselves?
François, Duc de La Rochefoucauld (1613-1680)
French writer, moralist

The vanity of being known to be trusted with a secret is generally one of the chief motives to disclose it.
Dr Samuel Johnson (1709-1784)

I have the most perfect confidence in your indiscretion.
Sydney Smith (1771-1845)
English writer, clergyman

There are some occasions when a man must tell half his secret, in order to conceal the rest.
Lord Chesterfield (1694-1773)
English statesman and man of letters

Everybody knows that corruption thrives in secret places ... and we believe it a fair presumption that secrecy means impropriety.
Woodrow Wilson (1856-1924)

Everything secret degenerates ... nothing is

safe that does not show how it can bear discussion and publicity.

Lord Acton (1834-1902)
English historian

Secrecy, being an instrument of conspiracy, ought never to be the system of a regular government.

Jeremy Bentham (1748-1832)
English philosopher, political theorist, jurist

The great, terrible, important powers of the world, like social caste and religious domination, always rest on secrets. A man is born on the wrong side of the street and can therefore never enter into certain drawing rooms, even though he be in every way superior to everyone in those drawing rooms. When you try to find out what the difference is between him and the rest, and why he is accursed, you find that the reason is a secret. It is a secret that a certain kind of straw hat is damnable. Little boys know these things about other little boys. The world is written over with mysterious tramp-languages and symbols of Masonic hieroglyphics.

Arthur Chapman (1873-1935)
American poet, author

There are no secrets better kept than the secrets that everybody guesses.

Crofts, *Mrs Warren's Profession*
George Bernard Shaw (1856-1950)

SEE Colton in GOSSIP; Behn on LOVERS;
Bible on PLEASURE

Sects

Fanatics have their dreams, wherewith
   they weave
A paradise for a sect.

John Keats (1795-1821)

'Tis a strange thing, Sam, that among us people can't agree the whole week because they go different ways upon Sundays.

George Farquhar (1678-1707)
Irish dramatist

Most people have some sort of religion. At least they know which church they're staying away from.

John Erskine (1879-1951)
American author

See how these Christians love one another.

Tertullian (c. 160–c. 230)
Roman theologian

It is becoming impossible for those who mix at all with their fellow-men to believe that the grace of God is distributed denominationally.

W. R. Inge (1860-1954)
Dean of St Paul's, London

And when religious sects ran mad,
He held, in spite of all their
   learning,

That if a man's belief is bad,
It will not be improved by burning.

Winthrop Mackworth Praed (1802-1839)
English poet

Every sect is a moral check on its neighbour. Competition is as wholesome in religion as in commerce.

Walter Savage Landor (1775-1864)
English author

All sects seem to me to be right in what they assert, and wrong in what they deny.

Johann Wolfgang von Goethe (1749-1832)

Seduction

The difference between rape and ecstasy is salesmanship.

Lord Thomson of Fleet (1894-1976)
Canadian publisher

A wise woman never yields by appointment. It should always be an unforeseen happiness.

Stendhal (1783-1842)

The resistance of a woman is not always proof of her virtue, but more often of her experience.

Ninon de Lenclos (1620-1705)
French society lady and wit

By keeping men off, you keep them on.

John Gay (1685-1732)
English playwright

Had we but world enough, and time,
This coyness, lady, were no crime.

Andrew Marvell (1621-1678)

In order to avoid being called a flirt, she always yielded easily.

Charles, Count Talleyrand (1754-1838)
French statesman

Men lose more conquests by their own awkwardness than by any virtue in the woman.

Ninon de Lenclos (1620-1705)
French society lady and wit.

If men knew all that women think, they'd be twenty times more daring.

Alphonse Karr (1808-1890)
French novelist, journalist

Men who do not make advances to women are apt to become victims to women who make advances to them.

Walter Bagehot (1826-1877)
English economist, critic

Older women are best because they always think they may be doing it for the last time.

Ian Fleming (1908-1964)
British author

The trouble with Ian is that he gets off with women because he can't get on with them.

Rosamund Lehmann (b. 1903)
British author
of Ian Fleming

To succeed with the opposite sex, tell her you're impotent. She can't wait to disprove it.

Cary Grant (1904-1986)

He in a few minutes ravished this fair creature, or at least would have ravished her, if she had not, by a timely compliance, prevented him.

Henry Fielding (1707-1754)

Weep not for little Leonie,
Abducted by a French Marquis!
Though loss of honour was a wrench,
Just think how it's improved her
French.

Harry Graham (1874-1936)
British author, rhymster

SEE Johnson on SELF-IMAGE

Self

We are all serving a life-sentence in the dungeon of self.

Cyril Connolly (1903-1974)
British critic

Man who man would be,
Must rule the empire of himself.

P. B. Shelley (1792-1822)

It is . . . amusing to find oneself thought to be very different from what one is, especially as one knows that one cannot really be at all like what one imagines oneself to be. It is a sort of trinity – three persons in one ass.

Robert Bridges (1844-1930)
British poet

Most human beings use their public life like a visiting card. They show it to others and say, This is me. The others take the card and think to themselves, If you say so. But most human beings have another life too, a grey one, lurking in the darkness, torturing us, a life we try to hide like an ugly sin.

Federico García Lorca (1898-1936)

SEE Huxley on APPEARANCES; EGOISM

Self-confidence

I have yet to encounter that common myth of weak men, an insurmountable barrier.

J. L. Allen (1849-1925)
American author

Those who believe that they are exclusively in the right are generally those who achieve something.

Aldous Huxley (1894-1963)

Self-confidence is the first requisite to great undertakings.

Dr Samuel Johnson (1709-1784)

I wish I was as cocksure of anything as Tom Macaulay is of everything.

Lord Melbourne (1779-1848)
English Whig politician, Prime Minister

Without self-confidence we are as babes in the cradle. And how can we generate this imponderable quality, which is yet so invaluable, most quickly? By thinking that other people are inferior to oneself. By feeling that one has some innate superiority – it may be wealth, or rank, a straight nose, or the portrait of a grandfather by Romney – for there is no end to the pathetic devices of the human imagination – over other people.

Virginia Woolf (1882-1941)

Self-control

When angry, count four; when very angry, swear.

Mark Twain (1835-1910)

He that would govern others, first should be the master of himself.

Philip Massinger (1583-1640)
English playwright

O! it is excellent
To have a giant's strength, but it is tyrannous
To use it like a giant.

Isabella, *Measure for Measure*
William Shakespeare (1564-1616)

Remember that there is always a limit to self-indulgence, but none to self-restraint.

M. K. Gandhi (1869-1948)

SEE Dickens on SELF-DENIAL;
Boileau on WRITERS

Self-deception

It is in the ability to deceive oneself that one shows the greatest talent.

Anatole France (1844-1924)
French author

We lie loudest when we lie to ourselves.

Eric Hoffer (1902-1983)
American philosopher

Nous aimons à être trompés.
We like to be deceived.

Blaise Pascal (1623-1662)

The surest way to be deceived is to consider oneself cleverer than others.

François, Duc de La Rochefoucauld (1613-1680)
French writer, moralist

We are never deceived; we deceive ourselves.

Johann Wolfgang von Goethe (1749-1832)

Most of our platitudes notwithstanding, self-deception remains the most difficult deception. The tricks that work on others count for nothing in that very well-lit back alley where one keeps assignations with oneself: no winning smiles will do here, no prettily drawn lists of good intentions.

Joan Didion (b. 1934)
American writer

SEE Wilde on LOVE; Pascal on RECKLESSNESS; Conrad on SELF-KNOWLEDGE; Demosthenes on SUCKERS

Self-defence

To the question, What shall we do to be saved in this World? there is no answer but this, Look to your Moat.
George Savile, Lord Halifax (1633-1695)
English statesman, author

Self-defence is nature's eldest law.
John Dryden (1631-1700)

These animals are so treacherous that they defend themselves against attackers!
anonymous, France

SEE Charles I on APOLOGIES; Lucas on COURTESY; Johnson on PITY

Self-denial

Subdue your appetites, my dears, and you've conquered human natur'.
Mr Squeers, Nicholas Nickleby
Charles Dickens (1812-1870)

Self-denial is not a virtue; it is only the effect of prudence on rascality.
George Bernard Shaw (1856-1950)

Self-denial is the shining sore on the leprous body of Christianity.
Frank Harris (1856-1931)
British journalist, novelist, biographer

Most of us have suffered from a certain sort of lady who by her perverse unselfishness gives more trouble than the selfish; who almost clamours for the unpopular dish and scrambles for the worst seat. Most of us have known parties or expeditions full of this seething fuss of self-effacement.
G. K. Chesterton (1874-1936)

Self-sacrifice enables us to sacrifice other people without blushing.
George Bernard Shaw (1856-1950)

Abstainer. A weak man who yields to the temptation of denying himself a pleasure.
Ambrose Bierce (1842-1914)
American author

SEE DRINK: Abstinence; Blake on LUST

Self-destructiveness

But I do nothing upon myself, and yet I am mine own Executioner.
John Donne (c. 1571-1631)

Self-doubt

The actor who took the role of King Lear played the king as though he expected someone to play the ace.
Eugene Field (1850-1895)
American author

He who undervalues himself is justly undervalued by others.
William Hazlitt (1778-1830)
English essayist

It is easy – terribly easy – to shake a man's faith in himself. To take advantage of that to break a man's spirit is devil's work.
Morell, Candida
George Bernard Shaw (1856-1950)

No man can make you feel inferior without your consent.
Eleanor Roosevelt (1884-1962)
American columnist, lecturer,
wife of F. D. Roosevelt

No, when the fight begins within himself,
A man's worth something.
Robert Browning (1812-1889)

SEE Hawthorne on HEROES; Hitler on PROPAGANDA

Self-image

I think it's one of the scars in our culture that we have too high an opinion of ourselves. We align ourselves with the angels instead of the higher primates.
Angela Carter (b. 1940)
British author

Monkeys are superior to men in this: when a monkey looks into a mirror, he sees a monkey.
Malcolm de Chazal (b. 1902)
French writer

The greatest magnifying glasses in the world are a man's own eyes when they look upon his own person.
Alexander Pope (1688-1744)

You've no idea what a poor opinion I have of myself – and how little I deserve it.
W. S. Gilbert (1836-1911)
English librettist

I have nothing to declare except my genius.
Oscar Wilde (1854-1900)
at the New York customs

The very purpose of existence is to reconcile the glowing opinion we have of ourselves with the appalling things that other people think about us.
Quentin Crisp (b. 1908)
British author

It is terrible to destroy a person's picture of himself in the interests of truth or some other abstraction.
Doris Lessing (b. 1919)
British writer

Nothing is more depressing than the conviction that one is not a hero.
George Moore (1852-1933)
Irish author

There are few things that we so unwillingly give up, even in advanced age, as the supposition that we still have the power of ingratiating ourselves with the fair sex.
Dr Samuel Johnson (1709-1784)

The ablest man I ever met is the man you think you are.
Franklin D. Roosevelt (1882-1945)

To love oneself is the beginning of a life-long romance.
Oscar Wilde (1854-1900)

He that falls in love with himself, will have no rivals.
Benjamin Franklin (1706-1790)

Self-love seems so often unrequited.
Anthony Powell (b. 1905)
British novelist

To have that sense of one's intrinsic worth which constitutes self-respect is potentially to have everything: the ability to discriminate, to love and to remain indifferent. To lack it is to be locked within oneself, paradoxically incapable of either love or indifference.
Joan Didion (b. 1934)
American writer

Self-respect – the secure feeling that no one, as yet, is suspicious.
H. L. Mencken (1880-1956)
American journalist

SEE Billings on ELOQUENCE; Swift on GENIUS; Didion on INNOCENCE; Hazlitt, Roosevelt on SELF-DOUBT; SELF-KNOWLEDGE

Self-knowledge
'Know thyself'? If I knew myself, I'd run away.
Johann Wolfgang von Goethe (1749-1832)

Il connaît l'univers et ne se connaît pas.
He knows the universe and does not know himself.
Jean de la Fontaine (1621-1695)
French poet, fabulist

No man ever understands quite his own artful dodges to escape from the grim shadow of self-knowledge.
Joseph Conrad (1857-1924)

In other living creatures the ignorance of themselves is nature, but in men it is a vice.
Boethius (480-525)
Roman philosopher

If people can be educated to see the lowly side of their own natures, it may he hoped that they will also learn to understand and to love their fellow men better. A little less hypocrisy and a little more tolerance towards oneself can only have good results in respect for our neighbour; for we are all too prone to transfer to our fellows the injustice and violence we inflict upon our own natures.
Carl Jung (1875-1961)

SEE James on INTROSPECTION; SELF-IMAGE

Self-pity
The dupe of friendship, and the fool of love; have I not reason to hate and to despise myself? Indeed I do; and chiefly for not having hated and despised the world enough.
William Hazlitt (1778-1830)
English essayist

God put self-pity by the side of despair like the cure by the side of the disease.
Albert Camus (1913-1960)

I never saw a wild thing
Sorry for itself.
A small bird will drop frozen dead
From a bough
Without ever having felt sorry for itself.
D. H. Lawrence (1885-1930)

Self-pity comes so naturally to all of us, that the most solid happiness can be shaken by the compassion of a fool.
André Maurois (1885-1967)
French author

Self-sufficiency
The proverb warns that, 'You should not bite the hand that feeds you'. But maybe you should, if it prevents you from feeding yourself.
Thomas Szasz (b. 1920)
American psychiatrist

Be thine own palace, or the world's thy jail.
John Donne (c. 1571-1631)

Sense of Humour
From the silence which prevails I conclude Lauderdale has been making a joke.
R. B. Sheridan (1751-1816)

Men will confess to treason, murder, arson, false teeth, or a wig. How many of them will own up to a lack of humour?
F. M. Colby (1865-1925)
American editor, essayist

A sense of humour keen enough to show a man his own absurdities will keep him from the commission of all sins, or nearly all, save those that are worth committing.
Samuel Butler (1835-1902)
English author

To appreciate nonsense requires a serious interest in life.
Gelett Burgess (1866-1951)
American humorist, illustrator

SEE Grey on COMEDY; Inge on GOD; LAUGHTER

Sensitivity

Some people are so sensitive that they feel snubbed if an epidemic overlooks them.
Kin (F. McKinney) Hubbard (1868-1930)
American humorist, journalist

Man is much more sensitive to the contempt of others than to contempt for himself.
Friedrich Nietzsche (1844-1900)

Exaggerated sensitiveness is an expression of the feeling of inferiority.
Alfred Adler (1870-1937)
Austrian psychiatrist

It is axiomatic that we should all think of ourselves as being more sensitive than other people because, when we are insensitive in our dealing with others, we cannot be aware of it at the time: conscious insensitivity is a self-contradiction.
W. H. Auden (1907-1973)

Sentimentality

Sentimentality is the emotional promiscuity of those who have no sentiment.
Norman Mailer (b. 1923)

Sentimentality is only sentiment that rubs you up the wrong way.
W. Somerset Maugham (1874-1965)

It is as healthy to enjoy sentiment as to enjoy jam.
G. K. Chesterton (1874-1936)

Sentimentality – that's what we call the sentiment we don't share.
Graham Greene (b. 1904)

A sentimentalist is simply one who desires to have the luxury of an emotion without paying for it.
Oscar Wilde (1854-1900)

Sentimentality is a superstructure covering brutality.
Carl Jung (1875-1961)

SEE Burroughs on UNHAPPINESS

Sex

And the world's shrunken to a heap
Of hot flesh straining on a bed.
E. R. Dodds (1893-1979)
British classical scholar

Love is not the dying moan of a distant violin – it's the triumphant twang of a bedspring.
S. J. Perelman (1904-1979)
American humorist

So must pure lovers' souls descend
T'affections and to faculties
Which sense may reach and apprehend;
Else a great prince in prison dies.
John Donne (c. 1571-1631)

For all the pseudo-sophistication of twentieth-century sex theory, it is still assumed that a man should make love as if his principal intention was to people the wilderness.
Germaine Greer (b. 1939)
Australian feminist writer

The reproduction of mankind is a great marvel and mystery. Had God consulted me in the matter, I should have advised him to continue the generation of the species by fashioning them of clay.
Martin Luther (1483-1546)

I could be content that we might procreate like trees, without conjunction, or that there were any way to perpetuate the world without this trivial and vulgar way of coition.
Sir Thomas Browne (1605-1682)
English physician, author

This sex attraction, though it is so useful for keeping the world peopled, has nothing to do with beauty: it blinds us to ugliness instead of opening our eyes to beauty.
George Bernard Shaw (1856-1950)

Making love? It's a communion with a woman. The bed is the holy table. There I find passion – and purification.
Omar Sharif (b. 1932)

Girls who put out are tramps. Girls who don't are ladies. This is, however, a rather archaic use of the word. Should one of you boys happen upon a girl who doesn't put out, do not jump to the conclusion that you have found a lady. What you have probably found is a lesbian.
Fran Lebowitz (b. 1951)
American journalist

Embraces are cominglings from the
Head to the Feet,
And not a pompous High Priest
entering by a Secret Place.
William Blake (1757-1827)

License my roving hands, and let
them go
Before, behind, between, above,
below.
John Donne (c. 1571-1631)

Sex, unlike justice, should not be seen to be done.
Evelyn Laye (b. 1900)
British actress, singer

Night makes no difference 'twixt the
Priest and Clerk:
Joan as my Lady is as good i'th'dark.
Robert Herrick (1591-1674)
English poet, critic

Enough if in the veins we know
Body's delirium, body's peace
– Ask not that ghost to ghost shall go,
Essence in essence merge and cease.
E. R. Dodds (1893-1979)
British classical scholar

In America sex is an obsession, in other parts of the world it is a fact.
Marlene Dietrich (b. 1901)

It has to be admitted that we English have sex on the brain, which is a very unsatisfactory place to have it.
Malcolm Muggeridge (b. 1903)
British journalist

I have long lost any capacity for surprise where sex is concerned.
Judge Geoffrey Howard (1889-1973)
British judge

There goes a saying, and 'twas shrewdly said,
Old fish at table, but young flesh in bed.
Alexander Pope (1688-1744)

Men always fall for frigid women because they put on the best show.
Fanny Brice (1891-1951)
American entertainer

All this fuss about sleeping together. For physical pleasure I'd sooner go to the dentist any day.
Evelyn Waugh (1903-1966)

Someone asked Sophocles: 'How do you stand in respect to the pleasures of sex? Are you still capable of intercourse?' 'Hush, sir', he said, 'It gives me the greatest joy to have escaped the clutches of that savage and fierce master'.
Plato (428-347 BC)
trans. A. D. Lindsay

When sexual indulgence has reduced a man to the shape of Lord Hailsham, sexual continence involves no more than a sense of the ridiculous.
Reginald Paget (b. 1908)
British Labour politician
during the Profumo debate, 1963

The more sex becomes a non-issue in people's lives, the happier they are.
Shirley Maclaine (b. 1934)

Sex is. There is nothing more to be done about it. Sex builds no roads, writes no novels and sex certainly gives no meaning to anything in life but itself.
Gore Vidal (b. 1925)

In Europe men and women have intercourse because they love each other. In the South Seas they love each other because they have had intercourse. Who is right?
Paul Gauguin (1848-1903)

Sex is an emotion in motion.
Mae West (1892-1980)

I think sex is dead anyway.
Elizabeth Taylor (b.1932)
in 1958

SEE Mikes, Young on The ENGLISH; Pope on ENNUI; MASTURBATION; ORGASM; ORGIES; PERVERSION; PROMISCUITY; Mtetwa on SPORT

Sex Appeal

'Tisn't beauty, so to speak, nor good talk necessarily. It's just IT. Some women'll stay in a man's memory if they once walked down a street.
Rudyard Kipling (1865-1936)

Being a sex symbol has to do with an attitude, not looks. Most men think it's looks, most women know otherwise.
Kathleen Turner (b. 1956)
American actress

Sex appeal is 50 per cent what you've got and 50 per cent what people think you've got.
Sophia Loren (b. 1934)

Being a sex symbol was rather like being a convict.
Raquel Welch (b. 1940)

Shakespeare

The remarkable thing about Shakespeare is that he is really very good – in spite of all the people who say he is very good.
Robert Graves (1895-1985)
British poet, author

He was not of an age, but for all time!
Ben Jonson (1573-1637)

He was the man who, of all modern, and perhaps ancient poets, had the largest and most comprehensive soul.
John Dryden (1631-1700)

A quibble is to Shakespeare what luminous vapours are to the traveller: he follows it at all adventures; it is sure to lead him out of his way and sure to engulf him in the mire.
Dr Samuel Johnson (1709-1784)

If we wish to know the force of human genius we should read Shakespeare. If we wish to see the insignificance of human learning we may study his commentators.
William Hazlitt (1778-1830)
English essayist

Shakespeare is the sexiest great writer in the language.
A. L. Rowse (b. 1903)
British academic

For I loved the man and do honour his memory, on this side idolatry, as much as any.
Ben Jonson (1573-1637)

I am more easily bored with Shakespeare and have suffered more ghastly evenings with Shakespeare than with any other dramatist I know.
Peter Brook (b. 1925)
British theatre director

It would positively be a relief to me to dig him up and throw stones at him.

George Bernard Shaw (1856-1950)

GOOD FREND FOR JESVS SAKE FORBEARE
TO DIGG THE DUST ENCLOASED HEARE
BLESE BE YE MAN YT SPARES THES STONES
AND CURST BE HE YT MOVES MY BONES

epitaph on Shakespeare's tomb at Stratford

Shame

We live in an atmosphere of shame. We are ashamed of everything that is real about us; ashamed of ourselves, of our relatives, of our income, of our accents, of our opinions, of our experience, just as we are ashamed of our naked skins.

Tanner, *Man and Superman*
George Bernard Shaw (1856-1950)

Shame is the feeling you have when you agree with the woman who loves you that you are the man she thinks you are.

Carl Sandburg (1878-1967)
American poet

Whoever blushes is already guilty; true innocence is not ashamed of anything.

Jean-Jacques Rousseau (1712-1778)

SEE La Rochefoucauld on LOVERS; Bible on PARADISE; Fuller on POVERTY; Shaw on RESPECTABILITY

George Bernard Shaw

Bernard Shaw is an excellent man; he has not an enemy in the world, and none of his friends like him.

Oscar Wilde (1854-1900)

The way Shaw believes in himself is very refreshing in these atheistic days when so many people believe in no God at all.

Israel Zangwill (1864-1926)
British author

Show Business

All my shows are great. Some of them are bad. But they are all great.

Lord Grade (b. 1906)
British film and TV entrepreneur

That's what show business is – sincere insincerity.

Benny Hill (b. 1925)
British comedian

SEE Levant on HOLLYWOOD

Significance

The tiniest hair casts a shadow.

Johann Wolfgang von Goethe (1749-1832)

SEE Priestley on COINCIDENCE

Silence

And when he had opened the seventh seal, there was silence in heaven about the space of half an hour.

John the Divine (1st century AD)

And Silence like a poultice comes
To heal the blows of sound.

Dr Oliver Wendell Holmes (1809-1894)
American writer, physician

I have been breaking silence these twenty-three years and have hardly made a rent in it.

H. D. Thoreau (1817-1862)

I have often repented speaking, but never of holding my tongue.

Xenocrates (396-315 BC)
Greek philosopher

Silence is the virtue of fools.

Francis Bacon (1561-1626)

Even a fool, when he holdeth his peace, is counted wise.

Bible, Proverbs

The most silent people are generally those who think most highly of themselves.

William Hazlitt (1778-1830)
English essayist

There may be other reasons for a man's not speaking in publick than want of resolution: he may have nothing to say.

Dr Samuel Johnson (1709-1784)

His enemies might have said before that he talked rather too much; but now he has occasional flashes of silence, that make his conversation perfectly delightful.

Sydney Smith (1771-1845)
English clergyman, writer
of Macaulay

That man's silence is wonderful to listen to.

Thomas Hardy (1840-1928)

SEE Emerson on APPLAUSE;
Chesterton on CONVERSATION;
Heine on The ENGLISH; Stevenson
on LYING; Eliot on MODESTY

Sin

One leak will sink a ship, and one sin will destroy a sinner.

John Bunyan (1628-1688)

That which we call sin in others, is experiment for us.

R. W. Emerson (1803-1882)
American essayist, poet, philosopher

A large part of mankind is angry not with the sins, but with the sinners.

Seneca (c. 5-65)
Roman writer, philosopher, statesman

Nothing makes one so vain as being told that one is a sinner.

Oscar Wilde (1854-1900)

Commit a sin twice and it will not seem a crime.

Rabbinical saying

To sin is in itself excusable; to be taken is a crime.
> John Fletcher (1579-1625)
> English dramatist

No matter how hard the times get, the wages of sin are always liberal and on the dot.
> Kin (F. McKinney) Hubbard (1868-1930)
> American humorist, journalist

There are only two sorts of men: the one the just, who believe themselves sinners; the other sinners, who believe themselves just.
> Blaise Pascal (1623-1662)

He that falls into sin is a man; that grieves at it, is a saint; that boasteth of it, is a devil.
> Thomas Fuller (1608-1661)
> English cleric

It makes a great difference whether a person is unwilling to sin, or does not know how.
> Seneca (c. 5-65)
> Roman writer, philosopher, statesman

To abstain from sin when a man cannot sin is to be forsaken by sin, not to forsake it.
> Saint Augustine (354-430)

Many are saved from sin by being so inept at it.
> Mignon McLaughlin
> American author

For God's sake, if you sin, take pleasure in it,
And do it for the pleasure. . .
> Gerald Gould (1885-1936)
> British poet

When we sin, we are all ashamed at the presence of our inferiors.
> John Chrysostom (345-407)
> Greek ecclesiast and hermit

Few love to hear the sins they love to act.
> Pericles, *Pericles*
> William Shakespeare (1564-1616)

Should we all confess our sins to one another we would all laugh at one another for our lack of originality.
> Kahlil Gibran (1883-1931)
> Syrian mystic, poet

A private sin is not so prejudicial in the world as a public indecency.
> Miguel de Cervantes (1547-1616)

When the righteous man turneth away from his righteousness that he hath committed and doeth that which is neither quite lawful nor quite right, he will generally be found to have gained in amiability what he has lost in holiness.
> Samuel Butler (1835-1902)
> English author

Christ died for our sins. Dare we make his

martyrdom meaningless by not committing them?
> Jules Feiffer (b. 1929)
> American cartoonist

Sin writes histories, goodness is silent.
> Johann Wolfgang von Goethe (1749-1832)

> SEE Wilson on The CHURCH OF ENGLAND; Milton on CRIME; de Madariaga on The ENGLISH; Marlowe on MITIGATION; Crane on PARTNERSHIPS; Twain on PREACHING; France, Marlowe on RELIGION; Billings, Dryden on REPENTANCE; Bierce, Wilde on SAINTHOOD; Molière on SCANDAL; Butler on SENSE OF HUMOUR

Sincerity

It is dangerous to be sincere unless you are also stupid.
> George Bernard Shaw (1856-1950)

Most remarks that are worth making are commonplace remarks. The thing that makes them worth saying is that we really mean them.
> Robert Lynd (1879-1949)
> Anglo-Irish essayist, journalist

I only desire sincere relations with the worthiest of my acquaintance, that they may give me an opportunity once in a year to speak the truth.
> H. D. Thoreau (1817-1862)

Do not wonder if the common people speak more truly than those of higher rank; for they speak with more safety.
> Francis Bacon (1561-1626)

> SEE La Rochefoucauld on SOCIABILITY

The Sixties

All that Swinging Sixties nonsense, we all thought it was passé at the time.
> David Bailey (b. 1938)
> British photographer

I was appalled when the San Francisco ethic didn't mushroom and envelope the whole world into this loving community of acid freaks. I was very naïve.
> Grace Slick (b. 1939)
> American rock singer

Slander

No character, however upright, is a match for constantly reiterated attacks, however false.
> Alexander Hamilton (1755-1804)
> American statesman

I will make a bargain with the Democrats. If they will stop telling lies about Republicans we will stop telling the truth about them.
> Chauncey Depew (1834-1928)
> American Republican politician

The slanders poured down like Niagara. If you take into consideration the setting – the war and the revolution – and the character of the accused – revolutionary leaders of millions who were conducting their party to the sovereign power – you can say without exaggeration that July 1917 was the month of the most gigantic slander in world history.
> Leon Trotsky (1879-1940)

Lie lustily, some filth will stick.
> Thomas Hall (1610-1665)
> English preacher, author

Our disputants put me in mind of the scuttlefish that, when he is unable to extricate himself, blackens the water about him till he becomes invisible.
> Joseph Addison (1672-1719)
> English essayist

Calumny differs from most other injuries in this dreadful circumstance: he who commits it can never repair it.
> Dr Samuel Johnson (1709-1784)

Slander-mongers and those who listen to slander, if I had my way, would all be strung up, the talkers by the tongue, the listeners by the ears.
> Plautus (254-184 BC)
> Roman playwright

It is perfectly monstrous the way people go about nowadays saying things against one, behind one's back, that are absolutely and entirely true.
> Oscar Wilde (1854-1900)

SEE GOSSIP; Franklin on SATIRE

Slang

Never was such a cracked tin whistle played on the splendid quarter-deck of the English spoken word.
> Cassandra (Sir William Connor) (1909-1967)
> British journalist

All slang is metaphor, and all metaphor is poetry.
> G. K. Chesterton (1874-1936)

Correct English is the slang of prigs who write history and essays. And the strongest slang of all is the slang of poets.
> George Eliot (1819-1880)

Slang is a language that rolls up its sleeves, spits on its hands and goes to work.
> Carl Sandburg (1878-1967)
> American poet

I know only two words of American slang, 'swell' and 'lousy'. I think 'swell' is lousy, but 'lousy' is swell.
> J. B. Priestley (1894-1984)

Slavery

In all social systems there must be a class to do the mean duties. . . It constitutes the very mudsills of society. . . Fortunately for the South, she found a race adapted to that purpose. . . We use them for that purpose and call them slaves.
> J. H. Hammond (1807-1864)
> American senator
> speech to the Senate, 1858

I tremble for my country when I reflect that God is just; that his justice cannot sleep forever.
> Thomas Jefferson (1743-1826)

Slavery is founded on the selfishness of man's nature – opposition to it on his love of justice. These principles are in eternal antagonism; and when brought into collision so fiercely as slavery extension brings them, shocks and throes and convulsions must ceaselessly follow.
> Abraham Lincoln (1809-1865)

Mister Ward, don't yur blud bile at the thawt that three million and a half of your culled brethren air a clanking their chains in the South? – Sez I, not a bile! Let 'em clank!
> Artemus Ward (1834-1867)
> American journalist

The distinguishing sign of slavery is to have a price, and to be bought for it.
> John Ruskin (1819-1900)
> English critic

SEE Emerson on WOMEN

Sleep

Sleep, dear Sleep, sweet harlot of the senses,
Delilah of the spirit.
> Christopher Morley (1890-1957)
> American novelist, journalist

All men whilst they are awake are in one common world: but each of them, when he is asleep, is in a world of his own.
> Plutarch (46-120)

We term sleep a death . . . by which we may be literally said to die daily; in fine, so like death, I dare not trust it without my prayers.
> Sir Thomas Browne (1605-1682)
> English physician, author

Sleep is when all the unsorted stuff comes flying out as from a dustbin upset in a high wind.
> William Golding (b. 1911)
> British author

Oh Sleep! it is a gentle thing,
Beloved from pole to pole,
To Mary Queen the praise be given!
She sent the gentle sleep from Heaven,
That slid into my soul.
> S. T. Coleridge (1772-1834)

Blessings on him that invented sleep! It covers
a man, thoughts and all, like a cloak; it is
meat for the hungry, drink for the thirsty, heat
for the cold, and cold for the hot. It is the
currency with which everything may be pur-
chased, and the balance that sets even king
and shepherd, simpleton and sage.
Miguel de Cervantes (1547-1616)

We are not hypocrites in our sleep.
William Hazlitt (1778-1830)
English essayist

Those   no-sooner-have-I-touched-the-pillow
people are past my comprehension. There is
something bovine about them.
J. B. Priestley (1894-1984)

Come Sleep! Oh Sleep, the certain knot
    of peace,
The baiting-place of wit, the balm of
    woe,
The poor man's wealth, the prisoner's
    release,
Th'indifferent judge between the high
    and low.
Sir Philip Sidney (1554-1586)

SEE DREAMING; Chamfort on LIFE;
Baudelaire on PRAYER; Rabelais on RELIGION

Sloanes
The wealthy curled darlings of our nation.
Brabantio, *Othello*
William Shakespeare (1564-1616)

A fine puss-gentleman that's all perfume.
William Cowper (1731-1800)
English poet

A clever, ugly man every now and then is
successful with the ladies, but a handsome fool
is irresistible.
W. M. Thackeray (1811-1863)
English author

Smells
I counted two and seventy stenches,
All well defined, and several stinks!
S. T. Coleridge (1772-1834)
of Cologne

The rankest compound of villainous smell that
ever offended nostril.
William Shakespeare (1564-1616)

Of nothing are you allowed to get the real
odour or savour. Everything is sterilized and
wrapped in cellophane. The only odour which
is recognised and admitted as an odour is
halitosis and of this all Americans live in
mortal dread.
Henry Miller (1891-1980)

The woman one loves always smells good.
Rémy de Gourmont (1858-1915)
French critic, novelist

SEE Artaud on DEFECATION

Smoking
A custom loathsome to the eye, hateful to the
nose, harmful to the brain, dangerous to the
lungs, and in the black, stinking fume thereof
nearest resembling the horrible Stygian smoke
of the pit that is bottomless.
King James I of England (1566-1625)

*Il n'est rien l'égal au tabac; c'est la passion des
honnêtes gens, et qui vit sans tabac, n'est pas
digne de vivre.*
There's nothing quite like tobacco; it's the
passion of decent folk, and whoever lives
without tobacco doesn't deserve to live.
Molière (1622-1673)

The pipe, with solemn interposing puff,
Makes half a sentence at a time enough;
The dozing sages drop the drowsy strain,
Then pause, and puff – and speak, and
    pause again.
William Cowper (1731-1800)
English poet

The believing we do something when we do
nothing is the first illusion of tobacco.
R. W. Emerson (1803-1882)
American essayist, poet, philosopher

Smokers, male and female, inject and excuse
idleness in their lives every time they light a
cigarette.
Colette (1873-1954)

O gioia la nube leggera!
What joy in that light cloud!
Ermanno Wolf-Ferrari (1876-1948)
Italo-German composer

But when I don't smoke I scarcely feel as if I'm
living. I don't feel as if I'm living unless I'm
killing myself.
Russell Hoban (b. 1925)
British author

I have every sympathy with the American who
was so horrified by what he had read of the
effects of smoking that he gave up reading.
Henry G. Strauss (later Lord Conesford) (b. 1892)

I kissed my first woman and smoked my first
cigarette on the same day; I have never had
time for tobacco since.
Arturo Toscanini (1867-1957)
Italian conductor

Tobacco is the tomb of love.
Benjamin Disraeli (1804-1881)

Smugness
I do not object to Gladstone's always having
the ace of trumps up his sleeve, but only to his
pretence that God had put it there.
Henry Labouchere (1831-1912)
English journalist, politician

Every man has a right to be conceited until he
is successful.
Benjamin Disraeli (1804-1881)

And then in the fulness of joy and hope,
Seemed washing his hands with invisible soap,
In imperceptible water.
Thomas Hood (1799-1845)
English poet

I seem to see looming between us that wincing, winsome face discharging, as though from some suppurating wound of the spirit, an unstaunchable ooze of sneers.
J. W. Lambert (b. 1917)
British author, journalist, broadcaster
of Malcolm Muggeridge

Of all the horrid, hideous notes of woe,
Sadder than owl-songs or the midnight blast,
Is that portentous phrase, 'I told you so'.
Lord Byron (1788-1824)

Snobbery
Snobbery – the 'pox Britannica'.
Anthony Sampson (b. 1926)
British journalist, author

It is impossible, in our condition of society, not to be sometimes a Snob.
W. M. Thackeray (1811-1863)
English author

Respectable means rich, and decent means poor. I should die if I heard my family called decent.
Thomas Love Peacock (1785-1866)
English author

Heaven grant him now some noble nook,
For, rest his soul! he'd rather be
Genteelly damn'd beside a Duke,
Then sav'd in vulgar company.
Thomas Moore (1779-1852)
Irish poet

Snobs talk as if they had begotten their own ancestors.
Herbert Agar (1897-1980)
American author, journalist

Philistine – a term of contempt applied by prigs to the rest of their species.
Sir Leslie Stephen (1832-1904)
British author, philosopher

Laughter would be bereaved if snobbery died.
Peter Ustinov (b. 1921)
British actor, wit

SEE Shaw on CLASS

Snubs
He was as irrepressibly good-humoured under ghastly snubs as a parliamentary candidate on the hustings.
Thomas Hardy (1840-1928)

Mrs Montagu has dropt me. Now, Sir, there are people whom one should like very well to drop, but would not wish to be dropt by.
Dr Samuel Johnson (1709-1784)

SEE Hubbard on SENSITIVITY

Sociability
On clean-shirt day he went abroad, and paid visits.
James Boswell (1740-1795)
Scottish biographer
of Dr Johnson

Of all animals of prey, man is the only sociable one. Every one of us preys upon his neighbour, and yet we herd together.
John Gay (1685-1732)
English playwright

What men call social virtue, good fellowship, is commonly but the virtue of pigs in a litter, which lie close together to keep each other warm.
H. D. Thoreau (1817-1862)

Scoundrels are always sociable.
Arthur Schopenhauer (1788-1860)
German philosopher

If you wish to appear agreeable in society you must consent to be taught many things which you already know.
Johann Kaspar Lavater (1741-1801)
Swiss divine, poet

Be really reserved with everybody, and seemingly reserved with nobody; for it is disagreeable to *seem* reserved, and dangerous *not* to be.
Lord Chesterfield (1694-1773)
English statesman and man of letters

He that will live in this world must be endowed with the three rare qualities of dissimulation, equivocation, and mental reservation.
Aphra Behn (1640-1689)
English playwright, poet

The most exhausting thing in life is being insincere. That is why so much social life is exhausting.
Anne Morrow Lindbergh (b. 1906)
American poet, essayist, wife of Charles Lindbergh

Nothing so much prevents our being natural as the desire to seem so.
François, Duc de La Rochefoucauld (1613-1680)
French writer, moralist

Once the realisation is accepted that even between the *closest* human beings infinite distances continue to exist, a wonderful living side by side can grow up, if they succeed in loving the distance between them which makes it possible for each to see the other whole against the sky.
Rainer Maria Rilke (1875-1926)
German poet
trans. Jane Barnard Green and
M. D. Herter Norton

Making a film with Garbo does not constitute an introduction.
Robert Montgomery (1904-1981)
American actor, director

SEE COMPANY; Carlyle, Chesterton, Patmore, Virgil on DINNER PARTIES; FRIENDLINESS

Socialism

For the right moment you must wait, as Fabius did most patiently, when warring against Hannibal, though many censured his delays; but when the time comes you must strike hard, as Fabius did, or your waiting will be in vain.
Frank Podmore (1855-1910)
English psychist and founder of the Fabian Society
from Fabian Society's first tract

El socialismo puede llegar sólo en bicicleta.
Socialism can only arrive by bicycle.
José Antonio Viera Gallo (b. 1943)
Chilean politician in Allende's government

We cannot outline socialism. What socialism will look like when it takes on its final form we do not know and cannot say.
Vladimir Ilyich Lenin (1870-1924)

In socialism there should always remain a trace of the anarchist and the libertarian, and not too much of the prig and the prude.
Anthony Crosland (1918-1977)
British Labour politician

Whether considered as a doctrine, or as an historical fact, or as a movement, socialism, if it really remains socialism, cannot be brought into harmony with the dogmas of the Catholic church... Religious socialism, Christian socialism, are expressions implying a contradiction in terms.
Pope Pius XI (1857-1939)

As with the Christian religion, the worst advertisement for Socialism is its adherents.
George Orwell (1903-1950)

Essentially Socialism is no more and no less than a criticism of the idea of property in the light of the public good.
H. G. Wells (1866-1946)

Socialism proposes no adequate substitute for the motive of enlightened selfishness that to-day is at the basis of all human labor and effort, enterprise and new activity.
William Taft (1857-1930)
American Republican politician, President

By concentrating on what is good in people, by appealing to their idealism and their sense of justice, and by asking them to put their faith in the future, socialists put themselves at a severe disadvantage.
Ian McEwan (b. 1948)
British author

Socialists make the mistake of confusing individual worth with success. They believe you cannot allow people to succeed in case those who fail feel worthless.
Kenneth Baker (b. 1934)
British Conservative politician

Socialism is simply the degenerate capitalism of bankrupt capitalists. Its one genuine object is to get more money for its professors.
H. L. Mencken (1880-1956)
American journalist

SEE Churchill on CAPITALISM; COMMUNISM; Galbraith on ECONOMICS; MARXISM; Shaw on TRADE UNIONS

Society

Society can only exist on the basis that there is some amount of polished lying and that no one says exactly what he thinks.
Lin Yutang (1895-1976)
Chinese writer

Society is a masked ball, where every one hides his real character, and reveals it in hiding.
R. W. Emerson (1803-1882)
American essayist, poet, philosopher

What are we going to get out of it, what's it all in aid of – is it really just for the sake of a gloved hand waving at you from a golden coach?
Jean, The Entertainer
John Osborne (b. 1929)
British playwright

Society everywhere is in conspiracy against the manhood of every one of its members... The virtue in most request is conformity. Self-reliance is its aversion. It loves not realities and creators, but names and customs.
R. W. Emerson (1803-1882)
American essayist, poet, philosopher

Never speak disrespectfully of Society, Algernon. Only people who can't get into it do that.
Oscar Wilde (1854-1900)

Solemnity

Never make people laugh. If you would succeed in life, you must be solemn, solemn as an ass. All the great monuments are built over solemn asses.
Thomas Corwin (1794-1865)
American politician

No one is exempt from talking nonsense: the misfortune is to do it solemnly.
Michel de Montaigne (1533-1592)
French essayist

No hay nada en el mundo que moleste más a un hombre que él que no se le tome en serio.

Nothing in the world annoys a man more than not being taken seriously.
> Palacio Valdés (1853-1938)
> Spanish novelist

Solemn people are generally humbugs.
> Bertrand Russell (1872-1970)

In the last analysis ability is commonly found to consist mainly in a high degree of solemnity.
> Ambrose Bierce (1842-1914)
> American author

SEE Lichtenberg on CEREMONY; Byron on HISTORIANS

Solitude

I never found the companion that was so companionable as solitude.
> H. D. Thoreau (1817-1862)

Whosoever is delighted in solitude is either a wild beast or a god.
> Francis Bacon (1561-1626)

There are some solitary wretches, who seem to have left the rest of mankind only as Eve left Adam, to meet the devil in private.
> Alexander Pope (1688-1744)

A solitude is the audience-chamber of God.
> Walter Savage Landor (1775-1864)
> English author

La chose plus grande du monde, c'est savoir être à soi.
The greatest thing in the world is to know how to be on your own.
> Michel de Montaigne (1533-1592)
> French essayist

In solitude, where we are LEAST alone.
> Lord Byron (1788-1824)

Solitude gives birth to the original in us, to beauty unfamiliar and perilous – to poetry. But also, it gives birth to the opposite: to the perverse, the illicit, the absurd.
> Thomas Mann (1875-1955)

Solitude is un-American.
> Erica Jong (b. 1942)
> American author

One can acquire everything in solitude except character.
> Stendhal (1783-1842)

Solitude is to the mind what fasting is to the body, fatal if it is too prolonged, and yet necessary.
> Luc, Marquis de Vauvenargues (1715-1747)
> French moralist

Solitude is dangerous to reason, without being favourable to virtue... Remember that the solitary mortal is certainly luxurious, probably superstitious, and possibly mad.
> Dr Samuel Johnson (1709-1784)

Solitude is the mother of anxieties.
> Publilius Syrus (1st century BC)
> Roman writer of mimes

Perhaps even one's feelings get tired, when one is alone with oneself.
> Ugo Betti (1892-1953)
> Italian playwright

Ships that pass in the night, and speak
  each other in passing,
Only a signal shown, and a distant
  voice in the darkness;
So on the ocean of life, we pass and
  speak one another,
Only a look and a voice, then
  darkness again and a silence.
> H. W. Longfellow (1807-1882)

Life without a friend is death without a witness.
> Spanish proverb

SEE Vaughan on AGE: Old Age; Osborne on ATHEISM; Eliot on HELL; HERMITS

Song

It is the best of all trades to make songs, and the second best to sing them.
> Hilaire Belloc (1870-1953)
> British author

Song: the licensed medium for bawling in public things too silly or sacred to be uttered in ordinary speech.
> Oliver Herford (1863-1935)
> American poet, illustrator

Aujourd'hui ce qui ne vaut pas la peine d'être dit, on le chante.
These days, what isn't worth saying is sung.
> Pierre de Beaumarchais (1732-1799)
> French dramatist

Odd life! must one swear to the truth of a song?
> Matthew Prior (1664-1721)
> English poet, diplomat

That's the wise thrush; he sings each
  song twice over,
Lest you should think he never could
  recapture
The first fine careless rapture!
> Robert Browning (1812-1889)

I can't stand to sing the same song the same way two nights in succession. If you can, then it ain't music, it's close order drill, or exercise or yodelling or something, not music.
> Billie Holliday (1915-1959)
> American blues singer

When Satan makes impure verses, Allah sends a divine tune to cleanse them.
> George Bernard Shaw (1856-1950)

I would rather be remembered by a song than by a victory.
Alexander Smith (1830-1867)
Scottish poet

SEE Hill on MUSIC

The Soul
The soul is a troublesome possession, and when man developed it he lost the Garden of Eden.
W. Somerset Maugham (1874-1965)

Most people sell their souls, and live with a good conscience on the proceeds.
Logan Pearsall Smith (1865-1946)
American essayist

Die schöne Seele hat kein anderes Verdienst, als dass sie ist.
A beautiful soul has no other merit than its existence.
Friedrich von Schiller (1759-1805)

The soul is the body and the body is the soul. They tell us they are different because they want to persuade us that we can keep our souls if we let them make slaves of our bodies.
Ellie, Heartbreak House
George Bernard Shaw (1856-1950)

The soul's a sort of sentimental wife,
That prays and whimpers of the
higher life.
Richard Le Gallienne (1866-1947)
British poet

Instead of being at the mercy of wild beasts, earthquakes, landslides, and inundations, modern man is battered by the elemental forces of his own psyche. This is the World Power that vastly exceeds all other powers on earth. The Age of Enlightenment, which stripped nature and human institutions of gods, overlooked the God of Terror who dwells in the human soul.
Carl Jung (1875-1961)

Toute âme est une melodie qu'il s'agit de renouer.
Every soul is a melody which needs renewing.
Stéphane Mallarmé (1842-1898)
French Symbolist poet

Why do you hasten to remove anything which hurts your eye, while if something affects your soul you postpone the cure until next year?
Horace (65-8 BC)

SEE Haldane on ANXIETY; Meredith on CERTAINTY; Woolf on CONFORMITY; Prince of Wales on The COSMOS; Pascal on IMMORTALITY; Fitzgerald on NIGHT; Carlyle on UNHAPPINESS

South Africa
I am fifty-two years of age. I am a bishop in the Anglican Church, and a few people might be constrained to say that I was reasonably responsible. In the land of my birth I cannot vote, whereas a young person of eighteen can vote. And why? Because he or she possesses that wonderful biological attribute – a white skin.
Bishop Desmond Tutu (b. 1932)

Is not our role to stand for the one thing which means our own salvation here but with which it will also be possible to save the world, and with which Europe will be able to save itself, namely the preservation of the white man and his state?
Hendrik Verwoerd (1901-1966)
South African politician, Prime Minister

Christ in this country would quite likely have been arrested under the Suppression of Communism Act.
Joost de Blank (1908-1968)
Archbishop of Cape Town (1957-1963)

As far as criticism is concerned, we don't resent that unless it is absolutely biased, as it is in most cases.
John Vorster (1915-1983)
South African politician, Prime Minister

The drama can only be brought to its climax in one of two ways – through the selective brutality of terrorism or the impartial horrors of war.
Kenneth Kaunda (b. 1924)
Zambian politician, President
of the situation in South
Africa, 1980

Together, hand in hand, with our matches and our necklaces, we shall liberate this country.
Winnie Mandela (b. 1934)

Space
Space is the stature of God.
Joseph Joubert (1754-1824)
French essayist, moralist

Le silence éternel de ces espaces infinis m'effraie.
The eternal silence of those infinite spaces terrifies me.
Blaise Pascal (1623-1662)

Space isn't remote at all. It's only an hour's drive away if your car could go straight upwards.
Sir Fred Hoyle (b. 1915)
British astronomer

Walking in space, man has never looked more puny or more significant.
Alexander Chase (b. 1926)
American journalist

Today we can no more predict what use mankind may make of the Moon than could

Columbus have imagined the future of the continent he had discovered.

Arthur C. Clarke (b. 1917)
British author

Space flights are merely an escape, a fleeing away from oneself, because it is easier to go to Mars or to the moon than it is to penetrate one's own being.

Carl Jung (1875-1961)

SEE Lamb, Schiller on The COSMOS

Speech

Language most shews a man: Speak, that I may see thee.

Ben Jonson (1573-1637)

Speech was given to man to disguise his thoughts.

Charles, Count Talleyrand (1754-1838)
French statesman

Let your speech be always with grace, seasoned with salt.

Saint Paul (3-67)

Many a man's tongue broke his nose.

Seumas MacManus (1869-1960)
Irish author

The stroke of the whip maketh marks in the flesh: but the stroke of the tongue breaketh the bones. Many have fallen by the edge of the sword: but not so many as have fallen by the tongue.

Apocrypha, Ecclesiasticus

Speak clearly, if you speak at all;
Carve every word before you let it fall.

Dr Oliver Wendell Holmes (1809-1894)
American writer, physician

If your face is not clean, wash it: don't cut your head off. If your diction is slipshod and impure, correct and purify it: don't throw it away and make shift for the rest of your life with a hideous affectation accent, false emphases, unmeaning pauses, aggravating slowness, ill-conditioned gravity, and perverse resolution to 'get it from the chest' and make it sound as if you got it from the cellar. Of course, if you are a professional humbug – a bishop or a judge, for instance – then the case is different; for the salary makes it seem worth your while to dehumanize yourself and pretend to belong to a different species.

George Bernard Shaw (1856-1950)

I don't want to talk grammar. I want to talk like a lady.

Liza, *Pygmalion*
George Bernard Shaw (1856-1950)

All speech, written or spoken, is a dead language, until it finds a willing and prepared hearer.

Robert Louis Stevenson (1850-1894)

SEE Wendell Holmes on CONVERSATION; WORDS

Speeches

Let thy speech be short, comprehending much in few words.

Aprocrypha, Ecclesiasticus

What orators lack in depth they make up to you in length.

Charles de Montesquieu (1689-1755)
French philosopher, writer, lawyer

Most people have ears, but few have judgement; tickle those ears, and, depend upon it, you will catch their judgements, such as they are.

Lord Chesterfield (1694-1773)
English statesman and man of letters

A good indignation makes an excellent speech.

R. W. Emerson (1803-1882)
American essayist, poet, philosopher

Strong men delight in forceful speech. Soldiers relish a speaker delivering himself a little unreservedly.

John Keble (1792-1866)
English cleric and poet

Begin low, speak slow; take fire, rise higher; when most impressed be self-possessed; at the end wax warm, and sit down in a storm.

anonymous

Adepts in the speaking trade
Keep a cough by them ready made.

Charles Churchill (1731-1764)
English clergyman, poet

He can best be described as one of those orators who, before they get up, do not know what they are going to say; when they are speaking, do not know what they are saying; and, when they have sat down, do not know what they have said.

Sir Winston Churchill (1874-1965)

He's a wonderful talker who has the art of telling you nothing in a great harangue.

Molière (1622-1673)

The object of oratory alone is not truth, but persuasion.

Lord Macaulay (1800-1859)
English historian

When a subject is highly controversial . . . one cannot hope to tell the truth. One can only show how one came to hold whatever opinion one does hold. One can only give one's audience the chance of drawing their own conclusions as they observe the limitations, the prejudices, the idiosyncrasies of the speaker.

Virginia Woolf (1882-1941)

She plunged into a sea of platitudes and with the powerful breast stroke of a Channel swimmer made her confident way towards the

white cliffs of the obvious.
W. Somerset Maugham (1874-1965)

He rose without a friend, and sat down
without an enemy.
Henry Grattan (1746-1820)
Irish politician
of a member of the Irish
Parliament

All you need to do to get a speech out of
Mr Choate is to open his mouth, drop in a
dinner, and up comes a speech.
Chauncey Depew (1834-1928)
American Republican politician
of Ambassador Joseph H. Choate

How many grave speeches which have surprised, shocked, and directed the nation, have
been made by Great Men too soon after a
noble dinner, words winged by the Press
without an accompanying and explanatory
wine list.
H. M. Tomlinson (1873-1958)
British novelist

It usually takes more than three weeks to
prepare a good impromptu speech.
Mark Twain (1835-1910)

Why doesn't the fellow who says, 'I'm no
speechmaker', let it go at that instead of giving
a demonstration.
Kin (F. McKinney) Hubbard (1868-1930)
American humorist, journalist

I do not object to people looking at their
watches when I am speaking. But I strongly
object when they start shaking them to make
certain they are still going.
Lord Birkett (1883-1962)
British lawyer, Liberal politician

You know very well that after a certain age a
man has only one speech.
George Bernard Shaw (1856-1950)

He hears
On all sides, from innumerable
tongues,
A dismal universal hiss, the sound
Of public scorn.
John Milton (1608-1674)

The great orator always shows a dash of
contempt for the opinions of his audience.
Elbert Hubbard (1856-1915)
American author

I never failed to convince an audience that the
best thing they could do was to go away.
Thomas Love Peacock (1785-1866)
English author

A speech is like a love affair: any fool can start
one but to end it requires considerable skill.
Lord Mancroft (b. 1914)
British Conservative politician

SEE Gaboriau on ACTION;
Nietzsche on GUESTS;
La Rochefoucauld on PASSION;
PREACHING; UNDERSTANDING

Spirituality

Zen does not confuse spirituality with think-
ing about God while one is peeling potatoes.
Zen spirituality is just to peel the potatoes.
Alan Watts (1915-1973)
American philosopher, author

Yoga in Mayfair or Fifth Avenue, or in any
other place which is on the telephone, is a
spiritual fake.
Carl Jung (1875-1961)

Spontaneity

The most decisive actions of our life – I mean
those that are most likely to decide the whole
course of our future – are, more often than
not, unconsidered.
André Gide (1869-1951)

SEE Twain on SPEECHES

Sport

Duas tantem res anxius optat,
Panem et Circenses.
Two things only the people anxiously desire,
bread and the Circus games.
Juvenal (40-125)

A ball player's got to be kept hungry to
become a big-leaguer. That's why no boy from
a rich family ever made the big leagues.
Joe DiMaggio (b. 1914)

Show me a good loser in professional sports
and I'll show you an idiot. Show me a good
sportsman and I'll show you a player I'm
looking to trade.
Leo Durocher (b. 1906)
American baseball manager

I don't like that Hubert H. Humphrey
Metrodome. It's a shame a great guy like
Humphrey had to be named after it.
Billy Martin
New York Yankees Manager
1985

I don't think I can be expected to take
seriously any game which takes less than three
days to reach its conclusion.
Tom Stoppard (b. 1937)
British playwright, cricket enthusiast
on baseball

It's like standing under a cold shower tearing
up five pound notes.
Edward Heath (b. 1916)
British Conservative politician, Prime Minister
of ocean-racing

All fighters are prostitutes and all promoters
are pimps.
Larry Holmes (b. 1949)
American boxing champion

New Yorkers love it when you spill your guts out there. Spill your guts at Wimbledon and they make you stop and clean it up.
Jimmy Connors (b. 1952)

If you're up against a girl with big boobs, bring her to the net and make her hit backhand volleys.
Billy Jean King (b. 1943)

A lot of beautiful girls may be made available to you before the game. Such traps are aimed at destabilising you. You are going to war, and must be on the lookout for all kinds of weapons.
King Mtetwa
Swaziland Home Affairs Minister, 1985
to Highlanders FC players
before match in Lesotho

Serious sport has nothing to do with fair play. It is bound up with hatred, jealousy, boastfulness, disregard of all rules and sadistic pleasure in witnessing violence: in other words it is war minus the shooting.
George Orwell (1903-1950)

Games are for people who can neither read nor think.
The Lady, On the Rocks
George Bernard Shaw (1856-1950)

SEE CRICKET; Coward on EXERCISE;
Stewart, Shakespeare on FOUL PLAY;
GOLF; Advertisement on
INDIVIDUALITY; Bowra on
UNIVERSITY; Mencken on WAR;
Mansell on WINNING

Stardom

Thy name is an ointment poured forth, therefore do the virgins love thee.
Bible, Song of Solomon

They are trying to make me into a fixed star. I am an irregular planet.
Martin Luther (1483-1546)

Being a star has made it possible for me to get insulted in places where the average Negro could never hope to get insulted.
Sammy Davis Jr (b. 1925)

You're not a star until they can spell your name in Karachi.
Humphrey Bogart (1899-1957)

I stopped believing in Santa Claus when I was six. Mother took me to see him in a department store and he asked for my autograph.
Shirley Temple (b. 1928)

God makes stars. I just produce them.
Sam Goldwyn (1882-1974)

In America I had two secretaries – one for autographs and the other for locks of hair. Within six months one had died of writer's

cramp, and the other was completely bald.
Oscar Wilde (1854-1900)

One thing about being successful is that I stopped being afraid of dying. Once you're a star you're dead already. You're embalmed.
Dustin Hoffman (b. 1937)

It's nice to be a part of history but people should get it right. I may not be perfect, but I'm bloody close.
John Lydon (formerly Johnny Rotten) (b. 1957)

There is not a more unhappy being than a superannuated idol.
Joseph Addison (1672-1719)
English essayist

If I'm such a legend, then why am I so lonely? If I'm such a legend, then why do I sit at home for hours staring at the damned telephone, hoping it's out of order, even calling the operator asking her if she's *sure* it's not out of order?
Judy Garland (1922-1969)

On stage I make love to 25,000 people; then I go home alone.
Janis Joplin (1943-1970)
American singer

SEE FAME

Staring

Oh! Death will find me long before
I tire
Of watching you.
Rupert Brooke (1887-1915)
British poet

I have known a vast quantity of nonsense talked about bad men not looking you in the face. Don't trust that conventional idea. Dishonesty will stare honesty out of countenance any day in the week if there is anything to be got by it.
Charles Dickens (1812-1870)

SEE Davies on IDLENESS

The State

The state includes the dead, the living, and the coming generations.
Edmund Burke (1729-1797)
Irish philosopher, statesman

The State is a collection of officials, different for different purposes, drawing comfortable incomes so long as the *status quo* is preserved. The only alteration they are likely to desire in the *status quo* is an increase of bureaucracy and of the power of bureaucrats.
Bertrand Russell (1872-1970)

A state without the means of some change is without the means of its own conservation.
Edmund Burke (1729-1797)
Irish philosopher, statesman

The State . . . is the most flagrant negation, the most cynical and complete negation of humanity.
> Mikhail Bakunin (1814-1876)
> Russian political theorist

The word *state* is identical with the word *war*.
> P. A. Kropotkin (1842-1921)
> Russian anarchist

The obligation of subjects to the sovereign is understood to last as long, and no longer, than the power lasteth by which he is able to protect them.
> Thomas Hobbes (1588-1679)

If the state is strong, it crushes us. If it is weak, we perish.
> Paul Valéry (1871-1945)
> French poet, essayist

While the state exists there is no freedom; when there is freedom there will be no state.
> Vladimir Ilyich Lenin (1870-1924)

The state is not abolished, it withers away.
> Friedrich Engels (1820-1895)

> SEE Kaunda on FORCE

Statistics
There are three kinds of lies: lies, damned lies, and statistics.
> Benjamin Disraeli (1804-1881)

Statistics are like alienists – they will testify for either side.
> Fiorello La Guardia (1882-1947)
> American politician, Mayor of New York

He uses statistics as a drunken man uses lampposts – for support rather than illumination.
> Andrew Lang (1844-1912)
> Scottish author

I could prove God statistically.
> George Gallup (1901-1984)
> American statistician, pollster

I always find that statistics are hard to swallow and impossible to digest. The only one I can ever remember is that if all the people who go to sleep in church were laid end to end they would be a lot more comfortable.
> Mrs Robert A. Taft

SEE Smith on FACTS; Stalin on GENOCIDE

Status
If we all wore crowns the kings would go bare-headed.
> R. H. Benson (1871-1914)
> British novelist

It is only middle-class people who, quite mistakenly, imagine that a lively pursuit of the latest in reading or painting will advance their status in the world.
> Mary McCarthy (b. 1912)
> American author

I don't know of anything better than a woman if you want to spend money where it'll show.
> Kin (F. McKinney) Hubbard (1868-1930)
> American humorist, journalist

It is the superfluous things for which men sweat.
> Seneca (c. 5-65)
> Roman writer, philosopher, statesman

> SEE Twain on AMERICA;
> Veblen on LEISURE

The Status Quo
The powers that be are ordained of God.
> Saint Paul (3-67)

> SEE Alexander, Orwell on
> INEQUALITY;
> Russell on The STATE

Strangers
I do desire we may be better strangers.
> Orlando, *As You Like It*
> William Shakespeare (1564-1616)

I have always depended on the kindness of strangers.
> Tennessee Williams (1914-1983)

Men always talk about the most important things to perfect strangers. In the perfect stranger we perceive man himself; the image of God is not disguised by resemblances to an uncle or doubts of the wisdom of a moustache.
> G. K. Chesterton (1874-1936)

Strength
My strength is as the strength of ten,
Because my heart is pure.
> Lord Tennyson (1809-1892)

What stronger breastplate than a heart untainted!
Thrice is he armed that hath his quarrel just,
And he but naked, though locked up in steel,
Whose conscience with injustice is corrupted.
> King Henry, *King Henry VI part 2*
> William Shakespeare (1564-1616)

Thrice is he armed that hath his quarrel just, but four times he who gets his blow in fust.
> Josh Billings (1818-1885)
> American humorist

There is only one right in the world and that right is one's own strength.
> Adolf Hitler (1889-1945)

Calmness and irony are the only weapons worthy of the strong.
> Émile Gaboriau (1835-1873)
> French author

The weak have one weapon: the errors of

those who think they are strong.
> Georges Bidault (1899-1983)
> French resistance leader, statesman

There may come a time when the lion and the lamb will lie down together, but I am still betting on the lion.
> Josh Billings (1818-1885)
> American humorist

SEE Wordsworth on POWER

Students

Disciples do owe their masters only a temporary belief, and a suspension of their own judgement till they be fully instructed; and not an absolute resignation nor perpetual captivity.
> Francis Bacon (1561-1626)

The average PhD thesis is nothing but a transference of bones from one graveyard to another.
> J. Frank Dobie (1888-1964)
> American author

Generally young men are regarded as radicals. This is a popular misconception. The most conservative persons I ever met are college undergraduates.
> Woodrow Wilson (1856-1924)

When I was a student at the Sorbonne in Paris I used to go out and riot occasionally. I can't remember now what side it was on.
> John Foster Dulles (1888-1959)
> American Republican politician

Study to be quiet, and to do your own business.
> Saint Paul (3-67)

Paul, thou art beside thyself; much learning doth make thee mad.
> Festus
> Bible, Acts of the Apostles

SEE EXAMINATIONS; Milton on OXFORD; SCHOOLS; UNIVERSITY

Style

I do not much dislike the matter, but The manner of his speech.
> Caesar, Antony and Cleopatra
> William Shakespeare (1564-1616)

She represents merely tone and technique without intelligence.
> Sir Ernest Newman (1868-1959)
> British musicologist

Properly understood style is not a seductive decoration added to a functional structure; it is of the essence of a work of art.
> Evelyn Waugh (1903-1966)

To me style is just the outside of content, and content the inside of style, like the outside and inside of the human body – both go together, they can't be separated.
> Jean-Luc Godard (b.1930)
> French writer, film director

Style consists in certain fashions, or certain eccentricities, or certain manners, of certain people, in certain situations, and possessed of a certain share of fashion or importance.
> Washington Irving (1783-1859)
> American author

In doing good, we are generally cold and languid and sluggish, but the works of malice and injustice are quite in another style. They are finished with a bold, masterly hand.
> Edmund Burke (1729-1797)
> Irish philosopher, statesman

Esau my brother is a hairy man, and I am a smooth man.
> Bible, Genesis

SEE FASHION; Pascal on WRITING

Subjectivity

The same battle in the clouds will be known to the deaf only as lightning and to the blind only as thunder.
> George Santayana (1863-1952)
> American philosopher, poet

He that is giddy thinks the world turns round.
> Widow, The Taming of the Shrew
> William Shakespeare (1564-1616)

We see things not as they are, but as we are.
> H. M. Tomlinson (1873-1958)
> British novelist

The fly sat upon the axel-tree of the chariot-wheel and said, What a dust do I raise!
> Francis Bacon (1561-1626)

The Suburbs

Heaven is not built of country seats
But little queer suburban streets.
> Christopher Morley (1890-1957)
> American novelist, journalist

Slums may well be breeding-grounds of crime, but middle-class suburbs are incubators of apathy and delirium.
> Cyril Connolly (1903-1974)
> British critic

Conformity may not always reign in the prosperous bourgeois suburb, but it ultimately always governs.
> Louis Kronenberger (1904-1980)
> American critic, author, editor

They were as fed horses in the morning: each one neighed after his neighbour's wife.
> Bible, Jeremiah

SEE Chesterton on COMMUTERS

Success

The moral flabbiness born of the exclusive worship of the bitch-goddess *success*. That – with the squalid cash interpretation put on the word success – is our national disease.
William James (1842-1910)
American psychologist, philosopher
letter to H. G. Wells

One's religion is whatever he is most interested in, and yours is Success.
J. M. Barrie (1860-1937)
British playwright

Everything yields to success, even grammar.
Victor Hugo (1802-1885)

The secret of success in life is known only to those who have not succeeded.
J. Churton Collins (1848-1908)
British author, critic, scholar

Whenever a friend succeeds a little something in me dies.
Gore Vidal (b. 1925)

We can come to look upon the deaths of our enemies with as much regret as we feel for those of our friends, namely, when we miss their existence as witnesses to our success.
Arthur Schopenhauer (1788-1860)
German philosopher

The road to success is filled with women pushing their husbands along.
Lord Dewar (1864-1930)
British writer,
politician, businessman

A successful man is one who makes more money than his wife can spend. A successful woman is one who can find such a man.
Lana Turner (b. 1920)
American actress

All you need in this life is ignorance and confidence, and then success is sure.
Mark Twain (1835-1910)

'Tis not in mortals to command success,
But we'll do more, Sempronius; we'll deserve it.
Joseph Addison (1672-1719)
English essayist

For a hundred that can bear adversity there is hardly one that can bear prosperity.
Thomas Carlyle (1795-1881)
Scottish author

The common idea that success spoils people by making them vain, egotistic, and self-complacent is erroneous; on the contrary, it makes them, for the most part, humble, tolerant, and kind. Failure makes people cruel and bitter.
W. Somerset Maugham (1874-1965)

The penalty of success is to be bored by the attentions of people who formerly snubbed you.
Mary W. Little (b. 1880)
American writer

Nothing recedes like success.
Walter Winchell (1897-1972)
American columnist

SEE Twain on FOOD; Twain on FOOLS; Butler on INTELLIGENCE; Coleridge on LUCK; Disraeli on SMUGNESS; Baker on SOCIALISM; Corwin on SOLEMNITY; Eldridge on WISDOM

Suckers

The most positive men are the most credulous.
Alexander Pope (1688-1744)

We are inclined to believe those whom we do not know, because they have never deceived us.
Dr Samuel Johnson (1709-1784)

A man is his own easiest dupe, for what he wishes to be true he generally believes to be true.
Demosthenes (c. 384-322 BC)
Greek politician

A certain portion of the human race has certainly a taste for being diddled.
Thomas Hood (1799-1845)
English poet

There's a sucker born every minute.
Phineas T. Barnum (1810-1891)
American showman

And remember, dearie, never give a sucker an even break.
W. C. Fields (1879-1946)

Suffering

God had one son on earth without sin, but never one without suffering.
Saint Augustine (354-430)

You are outside life, you are above life, you are afflicted with ills the ordinary person does not know, you transcend the normal level and that is what people hold against you, you poison their quietude, you corrode their stability. You feel repeated and fugitive pain, insoluble pain, pain outside thought, pain which is neither in the body, nor the mind, but which partakes of both. And I, who share your ills, I am asking: who should dare to restrict the means that bring us relief?
Antonin Artaud (1896-1948)
French theatre producer, actor, theorist
plea for free use of opium for sufferers including 'lucid madmen, tabetics, cancer patients and those afflicted with chronic meningitis'

It is not true that suffering ennobles the character; happiness does that sometimes, but

suffering for the most part, makes men petty and vindictive.
W. Somerset Maugham (1874-1965)

Few can believe that suffering, especially by others, is in vain. Anything that is disagreeable must surely have beneficial economic effects.
J. K. Galbraith (b. 1908)
American economist

There is one psychological peculiarity in the human being that always strikes one: to shun even the slightest signs of trouble on the outer edge of your existence at times of well-being . . . to try not to know about the sufferings of others and your own or one's own future sufferings, to yield in many situations, even important spiritual and central ones – as long as it prolongs one's well-being.
Alexander Solzhenitsyn (b. 1918)

One does not love a place less for having suffered in it.
Jane Austen (1775-1817)

How much atonement is enough? The bombing must be allowed as at least part-payment: those of our young people who are concerned about the moral problem posed by the Allied air offensive should at least consider the moral problem that would have been posed if the German civilian population had not suffered at all.
Clive James (b. 1939)
Australian critic, humorist

The only antidote to mental suffering is physical pain.
Karl Marx (1818-1883)

J'aime la majesté des souffrances humaines.
I love the majesty of human suffering.
Alfred de Vigny (1797-1863)
French poet, novelist, dramatist

SEE Byatt on GRIEF; Burke on REBELLION

Suicide

Je m'en vais enfin de ce monde, où il faut que le coeur se brise ou se bronze.
And so I leave this world, where the heart must either break or turn to lead.
Nicolas-Sébastien Chamfort (1741-1794)
French writer, wit
suicide note

The prevalence of suicide is a test of height in civilization; it means that the population is winding up its nervous and intellectual system to the utmost point of tension and that sometimes it snaps.
Havelock Ellis (1859-1939)
British psychologist

I take it that no man is educated who has

never dallied with the thought of suicide.
William James (1842-1910)
American psychologist, philosopher

It is always consoling to think of suicide: in that way one gets through many a bad night.
Friedrich Nietzsche (1844-1900)

If you are of the opinion that the contemplation of suicide is sufficient evidence of a poetic nature, do not forget that actions speak louder than words.
Fran Lebowitz (b. 1951)
American journalist

There are many who dare not kill themselves for fear of what the neighbours will say.
Cyril Connolly (1903-1974)
British critic

Razors pain you;
Rivers are damp;
Acids stain you
And drugs cause cramp;
Guns aren't lawful;
Nooses give;
Gas smells awful;
You might as well live.
Dorothy Parker (1893-1967)
American humorous writer

A lover forsaken a new love may get,
But a neck when once broken can never be set.
William Walsh (1663-1708)
English poet

However great a man's fear of life . . . suicide remains the courageous act, the clear-headed act of a mathematician. The suicide has judged by the laws of chance – so many odds against one, that to live will be more miserable than to die. His sense of mathematics is greater than his sense of survival.
Graham Greene (b. 1904)

It is the role of cowardice, not of courage, to crouch in a hole, under a massive tomb, to avoid the blows of fortune.
Michel de Montaigne (1533-1592)
French essayist

Just as I shall select my ship when I am about to go on a voyage, or my house when I propose to take a residence, so I shall choose my death when I am about to depart from life.
Seneca (c. 5-65)
Roman writer, philosopher, statesman

Dear World, I am leaving you because I am bored. I am leaving you with your worries. Good luck.
George Sanders (1906-1972)
British actor
suicide note

SEE Webster on CONFESSIONS;

Artaud on PSYCHIATRISTS;
Wertmuller on SUNDAYS

Sundays

Now once a weeke, upon our Sabbath
day,
It is enough to doo our small
devotion,
And then to follow any merrie
motion.
Edmund Spenser (1552-1599)

Sometimes there's nothing but Sundays for weeks on end. Why can't they move Sunday to the middle of the week so you could put it in the OUT tray on your desk.
Russell Hoban (b. 1925)
British author

Sabbath. A weekly festival having its origin in the fact that God made the world in six days and was arrested on the seventh.
Ambrose Bierce (1842-1914)
American author

Millions long for immortality who do not know what to do with themselves on a rainy Sunday afternoon.
Susan Ertz (1894-1985)
British novelist

Some rainy winter Sundays when there's a little boredom, you should always carry a gun. Not to shoot yourself, but to know exactly that you're always making a choice.
Lina Wertmuller (b. 1928)
Italian film director

It was a Sunday afternoon, wet and cheerless: and a duller spectacle this earth of ours has not to show than a rainy Sunday in London.
Thomas de Quincey (1785-1859)
English author

I spent a year in that town, one Sunday.
Warwick Deeping (1877-1950)
British author

Why do I do this every Sunday? Even the book reviews seem to be the same as last week's. Different books – same reviews.
Jimmy, Look Back in Anger
John Osborne (b. 1929)
British playwright

Superstition

Superstition is the religion of feeble minds.
Edmund Burke (1729-1797)
Irish philosopher, statesman

Superstition is godless religion.
Joseph Hall (1574-1656)
Bishop of Norwich

Supernaturalism is the mysticism of the materialist.
W. R. Inge (1860-1954)
Dean of St Paul's, London

Der Aberglaube ist die Poesie des Lebens.
Superstition is the poetry of life.
Johann Wolfgang von Goethe (1749-1832)

Survival

To survive it is often necessary to fight, and to fight you have to dirty yourself.
George Orwell (1903-1950)

To win your battle in this society, you've got to have your cave. Then food. Then some kind of mate. After that, everything's a luxury.
Rod Steiger (b. 1925)

If you live among wolves you have to act like a wolf.
Nikita Khrushchev (1894-1971)

Once one determines that he or she has a mission in life, that's it's not going to be accomplished without a great deal of pain, and that the rewards in the end may not outweigh the pain – if you recognise historically that always happens, then when it comes, you survive it.
Richard Nixon (b. 1913)

One can survive anything these days except death.
Oscar Wilde (1854-1900)

Before undergoing a surgical operation arrange your temporal affairs. You may live.
Ambrose Bierce (1842-1914)
American author

Nothing in life is so exhilirating as to be shot at without result.
Sir Winston Churchill (1874-1965)

I have never been so gloriously filled with life as I was at Auschwitz. It was . . . a triumph to do death down for just a few hours, for perhaps one more minute.
Nathan, aged eighteen
quoted by Charity Blackstock

J'ai vécu.
I survived.
Joseph, Comte Sieyès (1748-1836)
French revolutionary
*asked what he had done during
the Reign of Terror*

Suspicion

There is nothing makes a man suspect much, more than to know little.
Francis Bacon (1561-1626)

We are paid for our suspicions by finding what we suspected.
H. D. Thoreau (1817-1862)

We have to distrust each other. It is our only defence against betrayal.
Tennessee Williams (1914-1983)

What loneliness is more lonely than distrust?
George Eliot (1819-1880)

Swearing

Swearing

A whoreson jacknapes must take me up for swearing; as if I borrowed mine oaths of him and might not spend them at my pleasure. . . When a gentleman is disposed to swear, it is not for any standers-by to curtail his oaths, ha?

Cloten, *Cymbeline*
William Shakespeare (1564-1616)

The man who first abused his fellows with swear-words instead of bashing their brains out with a club should be counted among those who laid the foundations of civilization.

John Cohen (b. 1911)
British psychologist

Profanity furnishes a relief denied even to prayer.

Mark Twain (1835-1910)

Grant me some wild expressions, Heavens, or I shall burst.

George Farquhar (1678-1707)
Irish dramatist

Take not God's name in vain; select a time when it will have effect.

Ambrose Bierce (1842-1914)
American author

Swear me, Kate, like a lady as thou art, a good mouth-filling oath.

Hotspur, *King Henry IV part I*
William Shakespeare (1564-1616)

It comes to pass oft that a terrible oath, with a swaggering accent sharply twanged off, gives manhood more approbation than ever proof itself would have earned him.

Sir Toby Belch, *Twelfth Night*
William Shakespeare (1564-1616)

All were swearing steadily and quietly and all were using the same time-dishonoured Army oaths with such lavishness that made it necessary to split words open in the middle in order to cram all the obscenities in.

Cassandra (Sir William Connor) (1909-1967)
British journalist

A footman may swear but he cannot swear like a lord. He can swear as often, but can he swear with equal delicacy, propriety and judgement?

Jonathan Swift (1667-1745)

'Twas but my tongue, 'twas not my soul that swore.

Euripides (480-406 BC)

SEE Hardy on DISCRETION; Twain on SELF-CONTROL

Swindles

It was beautiful and simple as all truly great swindles are.

O. Henry (1862-1910)
American short story writer

I do not, more than another man, mind being cheated at cards; but I find it a little nauseating if my opponent then publicly ascribes his success to the partnership of the Most High.

F. E. Smith, Lord Birkenhead (1872-1930)
British Conservative politician, lawyer

Cheat me in the price, but not in the goods.

Thomas Fuller (1654-1734)
English physician

SEE Shakespeare on FOUL PLAY

Switzerland

I look upon Switzerland as an inferior sort of Scotland.

Sydney Smith (1771-1845)
English clergyman, writer

The Swiss . . . are not a people so much as a neat clean quite solvent business.

William Faulkner (1897-1962)

In Switzerland they had brotherly love, five hundred years of democracy and peace, and what did they produce? The cuckoo clock!

Orson Welles (1915-1985)
from the film *The Third Man*

T

Taboo

To make our idea of morality centre on forbidden acts is to defile the imagination and to introduce into our judgements of our fellow-men a secret element of gusto.
> Robert Louis Stevenson (1850-1894)

Perhaps the long ages during which pork had been prohibited had made it seem to the Jews as delicious as fornication.
> Bertrand Russell (1872-1970)

It's an odd thing, but now one *knows* it's profoundly moral and packed with deep spiritual significance a lot of the old charm seems to have gone.
> Osbert Lancaster (1908-1986)
> British cartoonist
> *Maudie Littlehampton on*
> Lady Chatterley's Lover

SEE DISGRACE

Tact

Tact consists in knowing how far we may go too far.
> Jean Cocteau (1889-1963)
> French writer, film director

Never claim as a right what you can ask as a favour.
> J. Churton Collins (1848-1908)
> British author, critic, scholar

Forbear to mention what thou canst not praise.
> Matthew Prior (1664-1721)
> English poet, diplomat

It's bad manners to begin courting a widow before she gets home from the funeral.
> Seumas MacManus (1869-1960)
> Irish author

'Tis not seasonable to call a man a traitor that has an army at his heels.
> John Selden (1584-1654)
> English jurist, statesman

Speak softly and carry a big stick.
> Theodore Roosevelt (1858-1919)

SEE Wilde on CONVERSATION

Talent

Whom the gods wish to destroy they first call promising.
> Cyril Connolly (1903-1974)
> British critic

A middling talent makes a more serene life.
> Iris Murdoch (b. 1919)
> Irish author

There's no shortage of talent. There's only a shortage of talent that can recognise talent.
> Jerry Wald (1911-1962)
> American writer-producer

If a man can write a better book, preach a better sermon, or make a better mouse-trap, than his neighbour, though he build his house in the woods, the world will make a beaten path to his door.
> attributed to R. W. Emerson (1803-1882)
> American essayist, poet, philosopher

Everyone has talent at twenty-five. The difficulty is to have it at fifty.
> Edgar Degas (1834-1917)
> French painter, sculptor

SEE Amiel, Conan Doyle on GENIUS;
Emerson on WRITERS

Taste

Ah, good taste! What a dreadful thing! Taste is the enemy of creativeness.
> Pablo Picasso (1881-1973)

People care more about being thought to have good taste than about being thought either good, clever or amiable.
> Samuel Butler (1835-1902)
> English author

A man of great common sense and good taste, – meaning thereby a man without originality or moral courage.
> George Bernard Shaw (1856-1950)

Entre le bon sens et le bon goût il y a la différence de la cause et son effet.
Between good sense and good taste there is the same difference as between cause and effect.
> Jean de la Bruyère (1645-1696)
> French writer, moralist

People who like this sort of thing will find this the sort of thing they like.
Abraham Lincoln (1809-1865)
of a book

What is exhilirating in bad taste is the aristocratic pleasure of giving offence.
Charles Baudelaire (1821-1867)

No taste is so acquired as that for someone else's quality of mind.
Cyril Connolly (1903-1974)
British critic

I wish you all sorts of prosperity, with a little more taste.
Alain-René Le Sage (1668-1747)
French playwright, novelist

SEE Connolly on VULGARITY

Taxation

In general, the art of government consists in taking as much money as possible from one party of the citizens to give to the other.
Voltaire (1694-1778)

A government which robs Peter to pay Paul can always depend on the support of Paul.
George Bernard Shaw (1856-1950)

The art of taxation consists in so plucking the goose as to obtain the largest amount of feathers with the least amount of hissing.
Jean Baptiste Colbert (1619-1683)
French statesman

They sing now. They will pay later.
Jules, Cardinal Mazarin (1602-1661)
French statesman
on the news that the people
of Paris greeted each of his
new taxes with a satirical
song

To tax and to please, no more than to love and to be wise, is not given to men.
Edmund Burke (1729-1797)
Irish philosopher, statesman

All money nowadays seems to be produced with a natural homing instinct for the Treasury.
Duke of Edinburgh (b. 1921)

We are looking for a wealth tax that will bring in sufficient revenue to justify having a wealth tax.
Dick Spring (b. 1950)
leader of Irish Labour Party, 1982

Taxes cause crime. When the tax rate reaches 25 per cent, there is an increase in lawlessness. America's tax system is inspired by Karl Marx.
Ronald Reagan (b. 1911)

The avoidance of taxes is the only pursuit that still carries any reward.
John Maynard Keynes (1883-1946)

To produce an income tax return that has any depth to it, any feeling, one must have Lived – and Suffered.
Frank Sullivan (1892-1976)
American humorist, journalist

SEE Franklin on CERTAINTY; Borah on GOVERNMENT; Dickens on TRUTH

Tea

What would the world do without tea? How did it exist?
Sydney Smith (1771-1845)
English writer, clergyman

Its proper use is to amuse the idle, relax the studious and dilute the full meals of those who cannot use exercise and will not use abstinence.
Dr Samuel Johnson (1709-1784)

If I had known there was no Latin word for tea I would have let the vulgar stuff alone.
Hilaire Belloc (1870-1953)
British author

Come oh come ye tea-thirsty restless ones – the kettle boils, bubbles and sings, musically.
Rabindranath Tagore (1861-1941)
Indian author, philosopher

Love and scandal are the best sweeteners of tea.
Henry Fielding (1707-1754)

While there's tea there's hope.
Sir Arthur Pinero (1855-1934)
British actor, playwright, essayist

SEE Holmes on COFFEE

Teachers

A teacher affects eternity.
Henry B. Adams (1838-1918)
American historian

It is the supreme art of the teacher to awaken joy in creative expression and knowledge.
Albert Einstein (1879-1955)

Arrogance, pedantry, and dogmatism are the occupational diseases of those who spend their lives directing the intellects of the young.
Henry S. Canby (1878-1961)
American author, editor

I owe a lot to my teachers and mean to pay them back some day.
Stephen Leacock (1869-1944)
Canadian humorist and economist

Why are we never quite at ease in the presence of a schoolmaster? Because we are conscious that he is not quite at his ease in ours. He is awkward, and out of place in the society of his equals. He comes like Gulliver from among his little people, and he cannot fit the stature of

his understanding to yours.
> Charles Lamb (1775-1834)
> English essayist, critic

Everybody who is incapable of learning has taken to teaching.
> Oscar Wilde (1854-1900)

He who can, does. He who cannot, teaches.
> George Bernard Shaw (1856-1950)

I am inclined to think that one's education has been in vain if one fails to learn that most schoolmasters are idiots.
> Hesketh Pearson (1887-1964)
> British biographer

The vanity of teaching often tempts a man to forget he is a blockhead.
> George Savile, Lord Halifax (1633-1695)
> English statesman, author

God forgive me for having thought it possible that a schoolmaster could be out and out a rational being.
> Sir Walter Scott (1771-1832)

The average schoolmaster is and always must be essentially an ass, for how can one imagine an intelligent man engaging in so puerile an avocation?
> H. L. Mencken (1880-1956)
> American journalist

He can receive no pleasure from a casual glimpse of Nature, but must catch at it as an object of instruction... He cannot relish a beggarman, or a gipsy, for thinking of the suitable improvement... A boy is at his board, and in his path, and in all his movements. He is boy-rid, sick of perpetual boy.
> Charles Lamb (1775-1834)
> English essayist, critic

A teacher is one who, in his youth, admired teachers.
> H. L. Mencken (1880-1956)
> American journalist

Slaves and schoolboys often love their masters.
> George Bernard Shaw (1856-1950)

One looks back with appreciation to the brilliant teachers, but with gratitude to those who touched our human feelings. The curriculum is so much necessary raw material, but warmth is the vital element for the growing plant and for the soul of the child.
> Carl Jung (1875-1961)

We loved the doctrine for the teacher's sake.
> Daniel Defoe (1661-1731)

A schoolmaster should have an atmosphere of awe, and walk wonderingly, as if he was amazed at being himself.
> Walter Bagehot (1826-1877)
> English economist, critic

A teacher should be sparing of his smile.
> William Cowper (1731-1800)
> English poet

We schoolmasters must temper discretion with deceit.
> Evelyn Waugh (1903-1966)

A pure pedantic schoolmaster, sweeping his living from the posteriors of little children.
> Ben Jonson (1572-1637)

> Well had the boding tremblers learned
> to trace
> The day's disasters in his morning
> face.
> Oliver Goldsmith (1728-1774)

A teacher should have maximal authority and minimal power.
> Thomas Szasz (b. 1920)
> American psychiatrist

The true teacher defends his pupils against his own personal influence.
> A. B. Alcott (1799-1888)
> American author, educator, mystic

No bubble is so irridescent or floats longer than that blown by the successful teacher.
> Sir William Osler (1849-1919)
> Canadian physician

It is when the gods hate a man with uncommon abhorrence that they drive him into the profession of a schoolmaster.
> Seneca (c. 5-65)
> Roman writer, philosopher, statesman

It were better to perish than to continue schoolmastering.
> Thomas Carlyle (1795-1881)
> Scottish author

The members of the most responsible, the least advertised, the worst paid, and the most richly rewarded profession in the world.
> Ian Hay (1876-1952)
> British author

Therefore for the love of God appoint teachers and schoolmasters, you that have the charge of youth; and give the teachers stipends worthy of their pains.
> Bishop Hugh Latimer (1485-1555)
> churchman, Protestant martyr, schoolmaster

SEE Wells on NATIONALISM; Olivier, Trollope on PUNISHMENT

Technology

Technology is the science of arranging life so that one need not experience it.
> anonymous

The drive toward complex technical achievement offers a clue to why the US is good at space gadgetry and bad at slum problems.
> J. K. Galbraith (b. 1908)
> American economist

Any sufficiently advanced technology is indistinguishable from magic.
Arthur C. Clarke (b. 1917)
British author

I claim that in losing the spinning wheel we lost our left lung. We are, therefore, suffering from galloping consumption. The restoration of the wheel arrests the progress of the fell disease.
M. K. Gandhi (1869-1948)

One machine can do the work of fifty ordinary men. No machine can do the work of one extraordinary man.
Elbert Hubbard (1856-1915)
American author

SEE MACHINERY; SCIENCE; Gallo on SOCIALISM

Teeth
She laughs at everything you say. Why? Because she has fine teeth.
Benjamin Franklin (1706-1790)

Smiling as if she had teeth of sugar that were always melting.
Rainer Maria Rilke (1875-1926)
German poet

The best of friends fall out, and so
His teeth had done some years ago.
Thomas Hood (1799-1845)
English poet

When examined by the Divisional Surgeon, defendant was very abusive, and when asked to clench his teeth he took them out, gave them to the doctor and said 'You clench them'.
Police report
Woking Herald and News

SEE Russell on SCIENCE

Television
Almost from the moment the horror occurred, television changed. It was no longer a small box containing entertainment, news, and sports; suddenly, it was a window opening onto violently unpredictable life in Washington and in Dallas, where a President had been assassinated.
Newsweek magazine, 1963
on coverage of Kennedy's assassination

Television is a whore. Any man who wants her full favours can have them in five minutes with a pistol.
anonymous

Television is the first truly democratic culture – the first culture available to everybody and entirely governed by what the people want. The most terrifying thing is what the people do want.
Clive Barnes (b. 1927)
British drama critic

Television is now so desperately hungry for material that they're scraping the top of the barrel.
Gore Vidal (b. 1925)

Let's face it, there are no plain women on television.
Anna Ford (b. 1943)
British television personality

TV has something in common with the world of racing: it is crowded with untrustworthy characters and bristles with opportunities to cheat.
Paul Johnson (b. 1928)
British journalist

You have debased [my] child... You have made him a laughing-stock of intelligence ... a stench in the nostrils of the gods of the ionosphere.
Dr Lee de Forest (1873-1961)
inventor of the audion tube
to National Association of
Broadcasters

Television is an invention that permits you to be entertained in your living room by people you wouldn't have in your home.
David Frost (b. 1939)

It is a medium of entertainment which permits millions of people to listen to the same joke at the same time, and yet remain lonesome.
T. S. Eliot (1888-1965)

They are simple and true and they compose one.
Pablo Casals (1876-1973)
on westerns

I find television very educational. Every time someone switches it on I go into another room and read a good book.
Groucho Marx (1890-1977)

I hate television. I hate it as much as peanuts. But I can't stop eating peanuts.
Orson Welles (1915-1985)

SEE James on CINEMA

Temper
We boil at different degrees.
R. W. Emerson (1803-1882)
American essayist, poet, philosopher

A lady of what is commonly called an uncertain temper – a phrase which being interpreted signifies a temper tolerably certain to make everybody more or less uncomfortable.
Charles Dickens (1812-1870)

A tart temper never mellows with age, and a sharp tongue is the only edged tool that grows keener with constant use.
Washington Irving (1783-1859)
American author

Temptation

Thou strong seducer, Opportunity.
John Dryden (1631-1700)

I am not over-fond of resisting temptation.
William Beckford (1759-1844)
English author

There are several good protections against temptation but the surest is cowardice.
Mark Twain (1835-1910)

Do you really think it is weakness that yields to temptation? I tell you that there are terrible temptations which it requires strength, strength and courage, to yield to.
Oscar Wilde (1854-1900)

'You oughtn't to yield to temptation.'
'Well, somebody must, or the thing becomes absurd.'
Anthony Hope Hawkins (1863-1933)
British novelist

Why resist temptation – there will always be more.
Don Herold (b. 1889)
American humorist writer, artist

The resolution to avoid an evil is seldom framed till the evil is so far advanced as to make avoidance impossible.
Thomas Hardy (1840-1928)

The only way to get rid of temptation is to yield to it.
Oscar Wilde (1854-1900)

The devil tempted Christ, but it was Christ who tempted the devil to tempt him.
Samuel Butler (1835-1902)
English author

Honest bread is very well – it's the butter that makes the temptation.
Douglas Jerrold (1803-1857)
English playwright, humorist

A little of what you fancy does you good.
Marie Lloyd (1870-1922)
British music hall entertainer

SEE Plato on POVERTY

Terrorism

A little group of wilful men reflecting no opinion but their own have rendered the great Government of the United States helpless and contemptible.
Woodrow Wilson (1856-1924)

After seeing *Rambo* last night I know what to do next time this happens.
Ronald Reagan (b. 1911)
following the hijack of an aeroplane carrying American passengers, 1985

They can run, but they can't hide.
Ronald Reagan (b. 1911)
following the interception of the plane carrying the hijackers of the Achille Lauro cruise-ship, 1985

No one can kill Americans and brag about it. No one.
Ronald Reagan (b. 1911)
after the attack on Libya, March 1986

Le plus grand danger de la bombe est dans l'explosion de bêtise qu'elle provoque.
The greatest danger of bombs is in the explosion of stupidity that they provoke.
Octave Mirabeau (1850-1917)
French writer, dramatist

SEE Marighella on GUERRILLA WARFARE

Texas

It is considerably smaller than Australia and British Somaliland put together. As things stand at present there is nothing much the Texans can do about this, and ... they are inclined to shy away from the subject in ordinary conversation, muttering defensively about the size of oranges.
Alex Atkinson
British humorous writer

If a man's from Texas, he'll tell you. If he's not, why embarrass him by asking?
John Gunther (1901-1970)
American journalist

Margaret Thatcher

She's the best man in England.
Ronald Reagan (b. 1911)

If I were married to her, I'd be sure to have dinner ready when she got home.
George Shultz (b. 1920)
American Republican politician, Secretary of State

This woman is headstrong, obstinate and dangerously self-opinionated.
report by Personnel Officer at ICI, rejecting her for a job in 1948

I'll stay until I'm tired of it. So long as Britain needs me, I shall never be tired of it.
Margaret Thatcher (b. 1925)

It was then that the iron entered my soul.
Margaret Thatcher (b. 1925)
on her time in Mr Heath's Cabinet

She has fought resolutely for the class she represents and there are some lessons we might learn from that.
Tony Benn (b. 1925)
British Labour politician

Theatre

Can this cockpit hold the vasty fields of France?
Chorus, *King Henry V*
William Shakespeare (1564-1616)

The theatre is the best way of showing the gap between what is said and what is seen to be done, and that is why, ragged and gap-toothed as it is, it has still a far healthier

potential than some poorer, abandoned arts.
David Hare (b. 1947)
British playwright

Every now and then, when you're on stage,
you hear the best sound a player can hear. It's
a sound you can't get in movies or in
television. It is the sound of a wonderful, deep
silence that means you've hit them where they
live.
Shelley Winters (b. 1922)

Long experience has taught me that in
England nobody goes to the theatre unless he
or she has bronchitis.
James Agate (1877-1947)
British critic

I open with a clock striking, to beget an awful
attention in the audience: it also marks the
time, which is four o'clock in the morning,
and saves a description of the rising sun, and a
great deal about gilding the eastern hemis-
phere.
R. B. Sheridan (1751-1816)

Drama is life with the dull bits cut out.
Alfred Hitchcock (1899-1980)

All tragedies are finish'd by death, all
comedies are ended by a marriage.
Lord Byron (1788-1824)

The drama's laws, the drama's patrons
give,
For we that live to please, must please
to live.
Dr Samuel Johnson (1709-1784)

A first night . . . notoriously distracting owing
to the large number of people who stand
about looking famous.
Denis Mackail (1892-1971)
British novelist

I have no time to read play-bills; one merely
comes to meet one's friends, and show that
one's alive.
Fanny Burney (1752-1840)
English author

It hath evermore been the notorious badge of
prostituted Strumpets and the lewdest Harlots,
to ramble abroad to Plays, to Playhouses;
whither no honest, chaste or sober Girls or
Women, but only branded Whores and
infamous Adulteresses, did usually resort in
ancient times.
William Prynne (1600-1669)
Puritan pamphleteer

To save the Theatre, the Theatre must be
destroyed, and actors and actresses all die of
the Plague . . . they make art impossible.
Eleanor Duse (1859-1924)
Italian actress

SEE Brown on CRITICISM; O'Neill
on TRAGEDY; Hall on WRITERS

Theology
Theology is the effort to explain the unknow-
able in terms of the not worth knowing.
H. L. Mencken (1880-1956)
American journalist

I have only a small flickering light to guide me
in the darkness of a thick forest. Up comes a
theologian and blows it out.
Denis Diderot (1713-1784)
French philosopher, encyclopédiste

In all systems of theology the devil figures as a
male person. Yet it is women who keep the
church going.
Don Marquis (1878-1937)
American humorist, journalist

It is an old habit with theologians to beat the
living with the bones of the dead.
R. G. Ingersoll (1833-1899)
American lawyer

My theology, briefly, is that the universe was
dictated but not signed.
Christopher Morley (1890-1957)
American novelist, journalist

Theories
It is a capital mistake to theorize before one
has data.
Sir Arthur Conan Doyle (1859-1930)

You know very well that unless you're a
scientist, it's much more important for a
theory to be shapely than for it to be true.
Christopher Hampton (b. 1946)
British playwright

No theory is good except on condition that
one uses it to go beyond.
André Gide (1869-1951)

A theory can be proved by experiment; but no
path leads from experiment to the birth of a
theory.
Albert Einstein (1879-1955)

SEE Engels on ACTION;
Rochester on CHILDREN; Huxley,
Koestler on SCIENCE

Therapy
They all sit around feeling very spiritual, with
their mental hands on each other's knees,
discussing sex as if it were the Art of Fugue.
Jimmy, Look Back in Anger
John Osborne (b. 1929)
British playwright

Thinking
An Englishman thinks seated; a Frenchman,
standing; an American, pacing; an Irishman,
afterward.
Austin O'Malley (1858-1932)
American oculist, author

It is difficult, if not impossible, for most
people to think otherwise than in the fashion

of their own period.
George Bernard Shaw (1856-1950)

Ils ne se servent de la pensée que pour autoriser leurs injustices, et n'emploient les paroles que pour déguiser leurs pensées.
[Men] use thought only to justify their injustices, and speech only to disguise their thoughts.
Voltaire (1694-1778)

There is no expedient to which man will not resort to avoid the real labour of thinking.
Sir Joshua Reynolds (1723-1792)
English painter

The extra calories needed for one hour of intense mental effort would be completely met by the eating of one oyster cracker or one half of a salted peanut.
Francis G. Benedict (1870-1957)
American chemist

Sixty minutes of thinking of any kind is bound to lead to confusion and unhappiness.
James Thurber (1894-1961)
American humorist, illustrator

Thought would destroy their paradise.
Thomas Gray (1716-1771)

The Third World

A nation's strength ultimately consists in what it can do on its own, and not in what it can borrow from others.
Indira Gandhi (1917-1984)

Our mistake was in the assumption that freedom – real freedom – would necessarily and with little trouble follow liberation from alien rule... Our countries are effectively being governed by people who have only the most marginal interest in our affairs.
Julius Nyerere (b. 1921)
African statesman,
President of Tanzania

The Third World is not a reality, but an ideology.
Hannah Arendt (1906-1975)
American political philosopher

Where there are two PhDs in a developing country, one is Head of State and the other is in exile.
Lord Samuel (1898-1978)
British administrator, author

Time

Time, the avenger!
Lord Byron (1788-1824)

Time, you old gipsy man,
Will you not stay,
Put up your caravan
Just for one day?
Ralph Hodgeson (1871-1962)
British poet

Time and I against any two.
Spanish proverb

Time: That which man is always trying to kill, but which ends in killing him.
Herbert Spencer (1820-1903)
English philosopher

As if you could kill time without injuring eternity.
H. D. Thoreau (1817-1862)

Time turns the old days to derision,
Our loves into corpses or wives;
And marriage and death and division
Make barren our lives.
A. C. Swinburne (1837-1909)

The surest poison is time.
R. W. Emerson (1803-1882)
American essayist, poet, philosopher

We must use time as a tool, not as a couch.
John F. Kennedy (1917-1963)

Time is very dangerous without a rigid routine. If you do the same thing every day at the same time for the same length of time, you'll save yourself from many a sink. Routine is a condition of survival.
Flannery O'Connor (1925-1964)
American author

It haunts me, the passage of time. I think time is a merciless thing. I think life is a process of burning oneself out and time is the fire that burns you. But I think the spirit of man is a good adversary.
Tennessee Williams (1914-1983)

O, call back yesterday, bid time return!
William Shakespeare (1564-1616)

O, for an engine to keep back all clocks!
Ben Jonson (1573-1637)

I recommend you to take care of the minutes: for hours will take care of themselves.
Lord Chesterfield (1694-1773)
English statesman and man of letters

Time is a great legalizer, even in the field of morals.
H. L. Mencken (1880-1956)
American journalist

Time *goes*, you say? Ah, no!
Alas, Time stays; *we* go.
Austin Dobson (1840-1921)
British author

Tout passe, tout casse, tout lasse.
Everything passes, everything perishes, everything palls.
anonymous

And thus the whirligig of time brings in his revenges.
Feste, *Twelfth Night*
William Shakespeare (1564-1616)

SEE Munro on HAPPINESS;
PUNCTUALITY

Tolerance

For ye suffer fools gladly, seeing ye yourselves
are wise.

Saint Paul (3-67)

Tout comprendre rend très indulgent.
To understand everything makes one very
indulgent.

Madame de Staël (1766-1817)
Frnch writer, wit

Broadmindedness is the result of flattening
highmindedness out.

George Saintsbury (1845-1933)
British literary critic

Toleration . . . is the greatest gift of the mind;
it requires the same effort of the brain that it
takes to balance oneself on a bicycle.

Helen Keller (1880-1968)

There is, however, a limit at which forbearance ceases to be a virtue.

Edmund Burke (1729-1797)
Irish philosopher, statesman

By being civilized we mean that there is a
certain list of things about which we permit a
man to have an opinion different from ours.
Usually they are things which we have ceased
to care about: for instance, the worship of
God.

Aubrey Menen (b. 1912)
British novelist, essayist

The modern theory that you should always
treat the religious convictions of other people
with profound respect finds no support in the
Gospels. Mutual tolerance of religious views is
the product not of faith, but of doubt.

Arnold Lunn (1888-1974)
British author

SEE Jackson on FOOLS

Torture

The healthy man does not torture others –
generally it is the tortured who turn into
torturers.

Carl Jung (1875-1961)

Pain forces even the innocent to lie.

Publilius Syrus (1st century BC)
Roman writer of mimes

There is only one thing that arouses animals
more than pleasure, and that is pain. Under
torture you are as if under the dominion of
those grasses that produce visions. Everything
you have heard told, everything you have read
returns to your mind, as if you were being
transported, not toward heaven, but toward
hell. Under torture you say not only what the
inquisitor wants, but also what you imagine
might please him, because a bond (this, truly,

diabolical) is established between you and
him.

Umberto Eco (b. 1932)
Italian scholar, novelist

Touch

O why do you walk through the fields in
gloves,
Missing so much and so much?
O fat white woman whom nobody loves,
Why do you walk through the fields in
gloves
When the grass is soft as the breast of
doves
And shivering sweet to the touch?

Frances Cornford (1886-1960)
British poet

Tourism

Sailing round the world in a dirty
gondola
Oh, to be back in the land of
Coca-Cola!

Bob Dylan (b. 1941)

The vagabond, when rich, is called a tourist.

Paul Richard (1874-1960)

C'est magnifique, mais ce n'est pas la gare.

anonymous taxi-passenger in
Paris, Riviera-bound,
delivered to St Lazare

The American arrives in Paris with a few
French phrases he has culled from a conversa-
tional guide or picked up from a friend who
owns a beret.

Fred Allen (1894-1957)
American comic

The time to enjoy a European trip is about
three weeks after unpacking.

George Ade (1866-1944)
American humorist, playwright

Well, I learned a lot. You'd be surprised.
They're all individual countries.

Ronald Reagan (b. 1911)
following tour of South
America, 1982

Worth seeing? Yes; but not worth going to
see.

Dr Samuel Johnson (1709-1784)
to Boswell's 'Is not the
Giant's Causeway worth
seeing?'

SEE Morley on The BRITISH; Burney
on ITALY; Twain on PARIS; TRAVEL

Trade Unions

The history of all countries shows that the
working class, exclusively by its own effort, is
able to develop only trade union consciousness.

Vladimir Ilyich Lenin (1870-1924)

Trade Unionism is not Socialism: it is the Capitalism of the Proletariat.
George Bernard Shaw (1856-1950)

Solidarity still exists inside us, even in those who deny it.
Lech Walesa (b. 1942)

It obviously hurt him to wear the dinner-jacket of respectability instead of the boiler suit of revolt.
Cassandra (Sir William Connor) (1909-1967)
British journalist
of Ted Hill, later Lord Hill,
leader of the Boilermakers'
Union

No king on earth is as safe in his job as a Trade Union official. There is only one thing that can get him sacked; and that is drink. Not even that, as long as he doesn't actually fall down.
Boanerges, The Apple Cart
George Bernard Shaw (1856-1950)

Unionism, seldom, if ever, uses such power as it has to insure better work; almost always it devotes a large part of that power to safe-guarding bad work.
H. L. Mencken (1880-1956)
American journalist

With all their faults, trade-unions have done more for humanity than any other organization of men that ever existed. They have done more for decency, for honesty, for education, for the betterment of the race, for the developing of character in man, than any other association of men.
Clarence Barrow (1857-1938)
American lawyer, writer

Tradition
A precedent embalms a principle.
Benjamin Disraeli (1804-1881)

Tradition means giving votes to the most obscure of all classes – our ancestors. It is the democracy of the dead. Tradition refuses to submit to the small and arrogant oligarchy of those who merely happen to be walking around.
G. K. Chesterton (1874-1936)

People will not look forward to posterity, who never look backward to their ancestors.
Edmund Burke (1729-1797)
Irish philosopher, statesman

Loyalty to petrified opinion never yet broke a chain or freed a human soul.
Mark Twain (1835-1910)

The despotism of custom is everywhere the standing hindrance to human advancement.
John Stuart Mill (1806-1873)

How long soever it hath continued, if it be against reason, it is of no force in law.
Sir Edward Coke (1552-1634)
English lawyer

There was never any thing by the wit of man so well devised, or so sure established, which in continuance of time hath not been corrupted.
Book of Common Prayer

Tragedy
Where the theatre is concerned, one must have a dream and the Greek dream in tragedy is the noblest ever.
Eugene O'Neill (1888-1953)

Commonplace people dislike tragedy because they dare not suffer and cannot exult.
John Masefield (1874-1967)
British poet, playwright

La tragédie sur la scène ne me suffit plus, je vais la transporter dans ma vie.
Tragedy on the stage is no longer enough for me, I shall bring it into my own life.
Antonin Artaud (1896-1948)
French theatre producer, actor, theorist

We begin to live when we have conceived life as a tragedy.
W. B. Yeats (1865-1939)

SEE Baldwin on EUROPE

Training
The helmsman is recognised in the tempest; the soldier is proven in warfare.
Saint Cyprian, Bishop of Carthage (210-258)

A man can seldom – very, very, seldom – fight a winning fight against his training: the odds are too heavy.
Mark Twain (1835-1910)

Tranquillisers
Threre's nought, no doubt, so much the spirit calms
As rum and true religion.
Lord Byron (1788-1824)

Translation
Traduttori, traditori.
Translators, traitors.
Italian proverb

A translator is to be like his author; it is not his business to excel him.
Dr Samuel Johnson (1709-1784)

Nor ought a genius less than his that writ
Attempt translation.
Sir John Denham (1615-1669)
English poet

Humour is the first of the gifts to perish in a foreign tongue.
Virginia Woolf (1882-1941)

SEE Frost on POETRY

Transport

What is this that roareth thus?
Can it be a Motor Bus?
Yes, the smell and hideous hum
Indicat Motorem Bum. . .
Domine, defende nos
Contra hos Motores Bos!
> Alfred D. Godley (1856-1925)
> British scholar

The tight compartment fills: our careful eyes
Go to explore each other's destinies.
> Harold Munro (1879-1932)
> British poet, critic

The coach jumbled us insensibly into some sort of familiarity.
> Sir Richard Steele (1672-1729)
> English essayist, dramatist, editor

Most people sulk in stage-coaches; I always talk.
> Sydney Smith (1771-1845)
> English writer, clergyman

Nothing helps scenery like ham and eggs.
> Mark Twain (1835-1910)

My experience of ships is that on them one makes an interesting discovery about the world. One finds one can do without it completely.
> Malcolm Bradbury (b. 1932)
> British author

I have done almost every human activity inside a taxi which does not require main drainage.
> Alan Brien (b. 1925)
> British novelist, journalist

Restore human legs as a means of travel. Pedestrians rely on food for fuel and need no special parking facilities.
> Lewis Mumford (b. 1895)
> American writer on environment

SEE CARS; Greer on The ENGLISH

Travel

But we have tasted wild fruit, listened to strange music;
And all shores of the earth are but as doors of an inn.
> Laurence Binyon (1869-1943)
> British poet

Navigare necesse est,
Vivere non est necesse.
Navigation is essential; life is not.
> Hanseatic proverb

When one realizes that his life is worthless he either commits suicide or travels.
> Edward Dahlberg (b. 1900)
> American novelist, poet, critic

The whole object of travel is not to set foot on foreign land; it is at last to set foot on one's own country as a foreign land.
> G. K. Chesterton (1874-1936)

To be really cosmopolitan a man must be at home even in his own country.
> T. W. Higginson (1823-1911)
> American clergyman, writer

I dislike feeling at home when I am abroad.
> George Bernard Shaw (1856-1950)

A man who leaves home to mend himself and others is a philosopher; but he who goes from country to country, guided by the blind impulse of curiosity, is a vagabond.
> Oliver Goldsmith (1728-1774)

All travelling becomes dull in exact proportion to its rapidity.
> John Ruskin (1819-1900)
> English critic

Extensive travelling induces a feeling of encapsulation, and travel, so broadening at first, contracts the mind.
> Paul Theroux (b. 1941)

In America there are two classes of travel — first-class and with children.
> Robert Benchley (1889-1945)
> American humorous writer

Like all great travellers, I have seen more than I remember, and remember more than I have seen.
> Benjamin Disraeli (1804-1881)

Travel is glamorous only in retrospect.
> Paul Theroux (b. 1941)

'If you wish to be thoroughly misinformed about a country, consult a man who has lived there for thirty years and speaks the language like a native'.
> George Bernard Shaw (1856-1950)
> *quoting Palmerston*

I travel light; as light, that is, as a man can travel who will still carry his body around because of its sentimental value.
> Christopher Fry (b. 1907)
> British playwright

Il faut être toujours botté et prêt à partir.
One should always have one's boots on and be ready to leave.
> Michel de Montaigne (1533-1592)
> French essayist

SEE Kipling on HERMITS; Thoreau on
INDEPENDENCE; TOURISM;
TRANSPORT

Treachery

Treason doth never prosper: what's the reason?
For if it prosper, none dare call it treason.
> Sir John Harington (1561-1612)
> English writer, courtier

Combinations of wickedness would overwhelm the world did not those who have long practised perfidy grow faithless to each other.
Dr Samuel Johnson (1709-1784)

Treason is loved of many, but the traitor hated of all.
Robert Greene (1558-1592)
English dramatist

All his usual formalities of perfidy were observed with scrupulous technique.
Sir Winston Churchill (1874-1965)
of Hitler's invasion of Russia

Trials

All trials are trials for one's life, just as all sentences are sentences of death.
Oscar Wilde (1854-1900)

Trial. A formal inquiry designed to prove and put upon record the blameless characters of judges, advocates and jurors.
Ambrose Bierce (1842-1914)
American author

Appeal. In law, to put the dice into the box for another throw.
Ambrose Bierce (1842-1914)
American author

The hungry judges soon the sentence sign,
And wretches hang that jurymen may dine.
Alexander Pope (1688-1744)

SEE LITIGATION

Trust

Trust everybody, but cut the cards.
Finley Peter Dunne (1867-1936)
American journalist, humorist

It is an equal failing to trust everybody, and to trust nobody.
18th century English proverb

I cannot give them my confidence; pardon me, gentlemen, confidence is a plant of slow growth in an aged bosom: youth is the season of credulity.
William Pitt (1708-1778)
English politician, Prime Minister

SEE Bible on ROYALTY; Johnson on SUCKERS; Aeschylus on TYRANNY; Wilde on WIVES

Truth

It is always the best policy to speak the truth, unless of course you are an exceptionally good liar.
Jerome K. Jerome (1859-1927)
British author

It takes two to speak the truth – one to speak, and another to hear.
H. D. Thoreau (1817-1862)

Telling the truth to people who misunderstand you is generally promoting falsehood.
Anthony Hope Hawkins (1863-1933)
British author

A truth that's told with bad intent
Beats all the lies you can invent.
William Blake (1757-1827)

To become properly acquainted with a truth we must first have disbelieved it, and disputed against it.
Prince Otto von Bismarck (1815-1898)
Prussian statesman

The terrible thing about the quest for truth is that you find it.
Rémy de Gourmont (1858-1915)
French critic, novelist

Men occasionally stumble over the truth, but most of them pick themselves up and hurry off as if nothing had happened.
Sir Winston Churchill (1874-1965)

In this world, truth can wait; she's used to it.
Douglas Jerrold (1803-1857)
English playwright, humorist

The truth would become more popular if it were not always stating ugly facts.
Henry S. Haskins (b. 1875)
American author

'It was as true', said Mr Barkis, 'as taxes is. And nothing's truer than them'.
David Copperfield
Charles Dickens (1812-1870)

It is the customary fate of new truths, to begin as heresies, and to end as superstitions.
T. H. Huxley (1825-1895)
English biologist

I am convinced that the desire to formulate truths is a virulent disease.
William James (1842-1910)
American psychologist, philosopher

There are no whole truths; all truths are half-truths. It is trying to treat them as whole truths that plays the devil.
A. N. Whitehead (1861-1947)
British philosopher

Perhaps the mission of those who love mankind is to make people laugh at the truth, *to make truth laugh*, because the only truth lies in learning to free ourselves from insane passion for the truth.
Umberto Eco (b. 1932)
Italian scholar, novelist

Truth . . . never comes into the world but like a bastard, to the ignominy of him that brought her forth.
John Milton (1608-1674)

God offers to every mind its choice between truth and repose. Take which you please; you can never have both.

> R. W. Emerson (1803-1883)
> American essayist, poet, philosopher

It is the calling of great men, not so much to preach new truths, as to rescue from oblivion those old truths which it is our wisdom to remember and our weakness to forget.

> Sydney Smith (1771-1845)
> English clergyman, writer

I tell the truth, not as much as I would but as much as I dare — and I dare more and more as I grow older.

> Michel de Montaigne (1533-1592)
> French essayist, moralist

An honest man speaks the truth, though it may give offence; a vain man, in order that it may.

> William Hazlitt (1778-1830)
> English essayist

Truth is the most valuable thing we have. Let us economize it.

> Mark Twain (1835-1910)

Truth is so important that it needs to be surrounded by a bodyguard of lies.

> George Shultz (b. 1920)
> American Republican politician, Secretary of
> State
> on the disinformation campaign against Libya,
> 1986

It is hard to believe that a man is telling the truth when you know that you would lie if you were in his place.

> H. L. Mencken (1880-1956)
> American journalist

It is better to remain silent than speak the truth ill-humouredly, and so spoil an excellent dish by covering it with bad sauce.

> Bishop Jean-Pierre Camus (1582-1652)

Truth that peeps
Over the glass's edge when dinner's done.

> Robert Browning (1812-1889)

Plato is dear to me, but dearer still is truth.

> Aristotle (384-322 BC)

The first wrote, wine is the strongest. The second wrote, the king is the strongest. The third wrote, women are strongest: but above all things truth beareth away the victory.

> Apocrypha, Esdras I

A man may be in as just possession of truth as of a city, and yet be forced to surrender.

> Sir Thomas Browne (1605-1682)
> English physician, author

When you have eliminated the impossible, whatever remains, however improbable, must be the truth.

> Sir Arthur Conan Doyle (1859-1930)

Let us begin by committing ourselves to the truth — to see it like it is, and tell it like it is — to find the truth, to speak the truth, and to live the truth.

> Richard Nixon (b. 1913)
> accepting Presidential
> nomination, 1968

What is truth? said jesting Pilate; and would not stay for an answer.

> Francis Bacon (1561-1626)

SEE Voltaire on The DEAD; Arnold on DEATH: Dying; Byron on LYING; Voltaire on MARTYRDOM; Scott on NEWSPAPERS; Seneca on PRAYER; Chesterfield on SATIRE; Johnson on WAR CORRESPONDENTS

Tyranny

I have sworn upon the altar of God eternal hostility against every form of tyranny over the mind of man.

> Thomas Jefferson (1743-1826)

It is far easier to act under conditions of tyranny than to think.

> Hannah Arendt (1906-1975)
> American political philosopher

The worst form of tyranny the world has ever known: the tyranny of the weak over the strong. It is the only tyranny that lasts.

> Oscar Wilde (1854-1900)

Kings will be tyrants from policy, when subjects are rebels from principle.

> Edmund Burke (1729-1797)
> Irish philosopher, statesman

In every tyrant's heart there springs in
    the end
This poison, that he cannot trust a
    friend.

> Aeschylus (525-456 BC)
> trans. Gilbert Murray

Like Cato, give his little senate laws,
And sit attentive to his own applause.

> Alexander Pope (1688-1744)

In the groves of their academy, at the end of every vista, you see nothing but the gallows.

> Edmund Burke (1729-1797)
> Irish philosopher, statesman

SEE DESPOTISM; Burke on MOBS; Bulwer-Lytton on The PUBLIC; Shaw on REVOLUTION

U

Understanding

Where I am not understood, it shall be concluded that something very useful and profound is couched underneath.

Jonathan Swift (1667-1745)

I have suffered from being misunderstood, but I would have suffered a hell of a lot more if I had been understood.

Clarence Darrow (1857-1938)
American lawyer, writer

Unless one is a genius, it is best to aim at being intelligible.

Anthony Hope Hawkins (1863-1933)
British author

Nowadays to be intelligible is to be found out.

Oscar Wilde (1854-1900)

If one does not understand a person, one tends to regard him as a fool.

Carl Jung (1875-1961)

A lot of words get spilled as the urge to be understood clashes with an aversion to being understood too well.

New York Times, 1985

I strive to be brief but I become obscure.

Horace (65-8 BC)

If you are sure you understand everything that is going on, you are hopelessly confused.

Walter F. Mondale (b. 1928)
American Democratic politician

Shallow understanding from people of good will is more frustrating than absolute misunderstanding from people of ill-will.

Martin Luther King (1929-1968)

SEE Apocrypha on INTELLECTUALS

Unemployment

You take my life when you take the means whereby I live.

Shylock, The Merchant of Venice
William Shakespeare (1564-1616)

A man willing to work, and unable to find work, is perhaps the saddest sight that fortune's inequality exhibits under this sun.

Thomas Carlyle (1795-1881)
Scottish author

To be idle and to be poor have always been reproaches, and therefore every man endeavours with his utmost care to hide his poverty from others, and his idleness from himself.

Dr Samuel Johnson (1709-1784)

It's a recession when your neighbour loses his job; it's a depression when you lose yours.

Harry S. Truman (1884-1972)

A man who has no office to go to – I don't care who he is – is a trial of which you can have no conception.

George Bernard Shaw (1856-1950)

The loss of one's job is a misfortune which should be borne with dignity and reticence.

Norman St John-Stevas (b. 1929)
British Conservative politician

He didn't riot. He got on his bike and looked for work.

Norman Tebbit (b. 1931)
British Conservative politician
of his unemployed father
during the Depression

Better wear out shoes than sheets.

17th century English proverb

Sometimes I've heard it said that Conservatives have been associated with unemployment. That's absolutely wrong. We'd have been drummed out of office if we'd had this level of unemployment.

Margaret Thatcher (b. 1925)
May 1977, when there were
1,269,000 out of work in the UK

O that we now had here
But one ten thousand of those men in England
That do no work today!

Westmoreland, King Henry V
William Shakespeare (1564-1616)

We believe that if men have the talent to invent new machines that put men out of work, they have the talent to put those men back to work.

John F. Kennedy (1917-1963)

SEE Smith on BUSINESS

Unhappiness

Unhappiness is not knowing what we want and killing ourselves to get it.
Don Herold (b. 1889)
American humorist, writer, artist

Man's unhappiness, as I construe, comes of his greatness; it is because there is an Infinite in him, which with all his cunning he cannot quite bury under the finite.
Thomas Carlyle (1795-1881)
Scottish writer

Unhappiness is best defined as the difference between our talents and our expectations.
Edward de Bono (b. 1933)
British writer

Let no one till his death be called unhappy. Measure not the work until the day's out and the labour done.
Elizabeth Barrett Browning (1806-1861)

In deep sadness there is no sentimentality.
William S. Burroughs (b. 1914)
American author

When sorrows come, they come not
  single spies.
But in battalions.
King, *Hamlet*
William Shakespeare (1564-1616)

He's simply got the instinct for being unhappy highly developed.
Saki (H. H. Munro) (1870-1916)
Scottish author

Men who are unhappy, like men who sleep badly, are always proud of the fact.
Bertrand Russell (1872-1970)

The world will never be long without some good reason to hate the unhappy.
Dr Samuel Johnson (1709-1784)

The secret of being miserable is to have leisure to bother about whether you are happy or not. The cure for it is occupation.
George Bernard Shaw (1856-1950)

SEE DESPAIR; GRIEF; Smith
on MONEY

Uniforms

This death's livery which walled its bearers from ordinary life was sign that they have sold their wills and bodies to the State: and contracted themselves into a service not the less abject for that its beginning was voluntary.
T. E. Lawrence (1888-1935)
British soldier, scholar

We know, Mr Weller – we, who are men of the world – that a good uniform must work its way with the women, sooner or later.
The Gentleman in Blue, *The Pickwick Papers*
Charles Dickens (1812-1870)

University

Europe crystallizes and slowly mummifies under the chains of its frontiers, its factories, its law courts, its universities. The frozen spirit cracks under the slabs of stone which press upon it. It's the fault of your mouldy systems, your logic of two and two makes four, it is your fault, University Chancellors, caught in the nets of your own syllogisms.
Antonin Artaud (1896-1948)
French theatre producer, actor, theorist

Universities incline wits to sophistry and affectation.
Francis Bacon (1561-1626)

Life at a university with its intellectual and inconclusive discussions at the postgraduate level is on the whole a bad training for the real world. Only men of very strong character surmount this handicap.
Sir Paul Chambers (1904-1981)
British industrialist

A university is an *alma mater*, knowing her children one by one, not a foundry, or a mint, or a treadmill.
Cardinal John Newman (1801-1890)
English churchman, theologian

A university should be a place of light, of liberty, and of learning.
Benjamin Disraeli (1804-1881)

With one or two exceptions, colleges expect their players of games to be reasonably literate.
Sir Maurice Bowra (1898-1971)
British classicist,
Warden of Wadham College, Oxford

'Tis well enough for a servant to be bred at university: but the education is a little too pedantic for a gentleman.
William Congreve (1670-1729)
English dramatist

They teach you anything in universities today. You can major in mud pies.
Orson Welles (1915-1985)

Socrates gave no diplomas or degrees, and would have subjected any disciple who demanded one to a disconcerting catechism on the nature of true knowledge.
G. M. Trevelyan (1876-1962)
British historian

Remote and ineffectual don.
Hilaire Belloc (1870-1953)
British author

A professor is one who talks in someone else's sleep.
W. H. Auden (1907-1973)

A man who has never gone to school may steal from a freight car; but if he has a university education, he may steal the whole railroad.

Theodore Roosevelt (1858-1919)

SEE EDUCATION; EXAMINATIONS; OXFORD; OXFORD AND CAMBRIDGE

The USSR

I cannot forecast to you the action of Russia. It is a riddle wrapped in a mystery inside an enigma.

Sir Winston Churchill (1874-1965)

In the Soviet Union everything happens slowly. Always remember that.

A. N. Shevchenko (b. 1930)
defecting Soviet diplomat

The Soviet Union will remain a one-party nation even if an opposition party were permitted – because everyone would join that party.

Ronald Reagan (b. 1911)

The Union of Soviet Socialist Republics is not just a country, but an empire – the largest and probably the last, in history.

Time magazine, 1980

No nation has ever devoured its heroes with such primordial zest.

Cassandra (Sir William Connor) (1909-1967)
British journalist

For us in Russia, communism is a dead dog, while, for many people in the West, it is still a living lion.

Alexander Solzhenitsyn (b. 1918)

I have been over into the future, and it works.

Lincoln Steffens (1866-1936)
American writer, editor
*to Bernard Baruch, on his
return from the Soviet Union
in 1919*

Our achievements leave class enemies breathless.

Leonid Brezhnev (1906-1982)

Give us time and we shall produce panties for your wives in colours which cannot be seen anywhere else.

Nikita Khrushchev (1894-1971)

They were right. The Soviet régime is not the embodiment of evil as you think in the West. They have laws and I broke them. I hate tea and they love tea. Who is wrong?

Alexander Zinoviev (b. 1922)
Soviet philosopher
*on his forced exile from the
Soviet Union*

SEE Thurber on APATHY; Attlee on COMMUNISM; Solzhenitsyn on PROPAGANDA; The RUSSIANS

Vanity

There was never yet fair woman but she made mouths in a glass.

Fool, *King Lear*
William Shakespeare (1564-1616)

The time he can spare from the adornment of his person he devotes to the neglect of his duties.

Dr Samuel Johnson (1709-1784)

Cure yourself of the condition of bothering about how you look to other people. Be concerned only ... with the idea God has of you.

Miguel de Unamuno (1864-1937)
Spanish philosopher, poet, novelist

We are so vain that we even care for the opinion of those we don't care for.

Marie von Ebner-Eschenbach (1830-1916)
Austrian author

SEE Pinero on RESPECTABILITY;
Johnson on SECRETS

Vegetarians

I have no doubt that it is a part of the destiny of the human race, in its gradual improvement, to leave off eating animals, as surely as the savage tribes have left off eating each other when they came in contact with the more civilized.

H. D. Thoreau (1817-1862)

Most vegetarians I ever see looked enough like their food to be classed as cannibals.

Finley Peter Dunne (1867-1936)
American journalist, humorist

A man of my spiritual intensity does not eat corpses.

George Bernard Shaw (1856-1950)

Vice

It seems impossible to root out of an Englishman's mind the notion that vice is delightful, and that abstention from it is privation.

George Bernard Shaw (1856-1950)

Vice is a creature of such hideous mien that the more you see it the better you like it.

Finley Peter Dunne (1867-1936)
American journalist, humorist

No exile at the South Pole or on the summit of Mont Blanc separates us more effectively from others than the practice of a hidden vice.

Marcel Proust (1871-1922)

How like herrings and onions our vices are in the morning after we have committed them.

S. T. Coleridge (1772-1834)

What maintains one vice would bring up two children.

Benjamin Franklin (1706-1790)

Le ciel défend, de vrai, certains contentements
Mais on trouve avec lui des accommodements.

It's true Heaven forbids some pleasures, but a compromise can usually be found.

Molière (1622-1673)

SEE Hubbard on GOSSIP; Joad, La Rochefoucauld on HYPOCRISY; Woollcott on PLEASURE; Massillon on RELIGION; Shaw on SELF-DENIAL; Lynd, Maurois on VIRTUE

Victims

I am a man more sinn'd against than sinning.

Lear, *King Lear*
William Shakespeare (1564-1616)

I hate victims who respect their executioners.

Jean-Paul Sartre (1905-1980)

Vietnam

Vietnam was what we had instead of happy childhoods.

Michael Herr (b.1940)
American journalist

This is not a jungle war, but a struggle for freedom on every front of human activity.

Lyndon B. Johnson (1908-1973)

North Vietnam cannot defeat or humiliate the United States. Only Americans can do that.

Richard Nixon (b. 1913)
November 1969

There is the guilt all soldiers feel for having broken the taboo against killing, a guilt as old as war itself. Add to this the soldier's sense of shame for having fought in actions that resulted, indirectly or directly, in the deaths of civilians. Then pile on top of that an attitude of social opprobrium, an attitude that made the fighting man feel personally morally responsible for the war, and you get your proverbial walking time bomb.

Philip Caputo
American author, Vietnam veteran
from his book A Rumor of War

Above all, Vietnam was a war that asked everything of a few and nothing of most in America.

Myra McPherson
American author
from Long Time Passing

I would like to ask a question. Would this sort of war or savage bombing which has taken place in Vietnam have been tolerated for so long had the people been European?

Indira Gandhi (1917-1984)

Villains

As there is a use in medicine for poison, so the world cannot move without rogues.

R. W. Emerson (1803-1882)
American essayist, poet, philosopher

In the old days villains had moustaches and kicked the dog. Audiences are smarter today. They don't want their villain to be thrown at them with green limelight on his face. They want an ordinary human being with failings.

Alfred Hitchcock (1899-1980)

As for an authentic villain, the real thing, the absolute, the artist, one rarely meets him even once in a lifetime. The ordinary bad hat is always in part a decent fellow.

Colette (1873-1954)

It takes a certain courage and a certain greatness even to be truly base.

Jean Anouilh (b. 1910)
French dramatist

Gamesters and highwaymen are generally very good to their whores, but they are the very devils to their wives.

Peachum, *The Beggar's Opera*
John Gay (1685-1732)

SEE Johnson on PIETY

Violence

In violence we forget who we are.

Mary McCarthy (b. 1912)
American author

If you strike a child, take care that you strike it in anger, even at the risk of maiming it for life. A blow in cold blood neither can nor should be forgiven.

George Bernard Shaw (1856-1950)

I write about violence as naturally as Jane Austen wrote about manners. Violence shapes and obsesses our society, and if we do not stop being violent we have no future.

Edward Bond (b. 1934)
British playwright

La violence, c'est bon pour ceux qui n'ont rien à perdre.
Violence suits those who have nothing to lose.

Jean-Paul Sartre (1905-1980)

SEE NON-VIOLENCE

Virtue

Be virtuous: not too much; just what's correct.
Excess in anything is a defect.

Jacques Monvel (1745-1812)
French actor, dramatist

Be virtuous and you will be eccentric.

Mark Twain (1835-1910)

What is virtue but the Trade Unionism of the married?

Don Juan, *Man and Superman*
George Bernard Shaw (1856-1950)

Men are virtuous because women are; women are virtuous from necessity.

Ed (E. W.) Howe (1873-1937)
American journalist, novelist

There are few good women who do not tire of their rôle.

François, Duc de La Rochefoucauld (1613-1680)
French writer, moralist

Feminine virtue is nothing but a convenient masculine invention.

Ninon de Lenclos (1620-1705)
French society lady and wit

Virtue has its own reward, but no sale at the box office.

Mae West (1892-1980)

The virtues of society are the vices of the saint.

R. W. Emerson (1803-1882)
American essayist, poet, philosopher

Virtue knows that it is quite impossible to get on without compromise, and tunes herself, as it were, a trifle sharp to allow for an inevitable fall in playing.

Samuel Butler (1835-1902)
English author

Fear God, and offend not the Prince nor his laws,
And keep thyself out of the magistrate's claws.

Thomas Tusser (c. 1520-c. 1580)
English writer on agriculture

That mixture of Christian sorrow and mundane relish which the virtuous employ in talking of the vicious.

André Maurois (1885-1967)
French author

By virtue we merely mean the avoidance of the vices that do not attract us.

Robert Lynd (1879-1949)
Anglo-Irish essayist, journalist

I cannot love anyone if I hate myself. That is the reason why we feel so extremely uncomfortable in the presence of people who are noted for their special virtuousness, for they radiate an atmosphere of the torture they inflict on themselves. That is not a virtue but a vice.

Carl Jung (1875-1961)

The chief assertion of religious morality is that white is a colour. Virtue is not the absence of vices or the avoidance of moral dangers; virtue is a vivid and separate thing, like pain or a particular smell.

G. K. Chesterton (1874-1936)

Men's evil manners live in brass, their virtues
We write in water.

Griffith, *King Henry VIII*
William Shakespeare (1564-1616)

La vertu refuse la facilité pour compagne . . . elle demande un chemin âpre et épineux.
Virtue shuns ease as a companion. It demands a rough and thorny path.

Michel de Montaigne (1533-1592)
French essayist

Assume a virtue, if you have it not.

Hamlet, *Hamlet*
William Shakespeare (1564-1616)

SEE Montaigne on CHASTITY; Twain on EXCELLENCE; Wordsworth on GOOD DEEDS; Joad, La Rochefoucauld on HYPOCRISY; Paine on POSTERITY; La Rochefoucauld on REPUTATION; Pinero, Twain on RESPECTABILITY

Visionaries

How beautiful upon the mountains are the feet of him that bringeth good tidings, that publisheth peace.

Bible, Isaiah

Sir, the pretending to extraordinary revelations and gifts of the Holy Ghost is a horrid thing, a very horrid thing.

Joseph Butler (1692-1752)
Bishop of Durham
to John Wesley

I just want to do God's will. And he's allowed me to go up to the mountain. And I've looked over, and I've seen the Promised Land.

Martin Luther King (1929-1968)

You see things; and say 'Why?' But I dream things that never were; and I say 'Why not?'

The Serpent, *Back to Methuselah*
George Bernard Shaw (1856-1950)

Fear prophets . . . and those prepared to die for the truth, for as a rule they make many others die with them, often before them, at times instead of them.

Umberto Eco (b. 1932)
Italian scholar, novelist

The visionary lies to himself, the liar only to others.

Friedrich Nietzsche (1844-1900)

Where there is no vision, the people perish.

Bible, Proverbs

'When the sun rises, do you not see a round disc of fire somewhat like a guinea?' 'O no, no, I see an innumerable company of the heavenly host crying, "Holy, Holy, Holy is the Lord God Almighty!" '

William Blake (1757-1827)

St Teresa of Avila described our life in this world as like a night at a second-class hotel.

Malcolm Muggeridge (b. 1903)
British journalist

SEE Ellis on CHRISTIANITY;
Shaw on LEADERSHIP

Vocation

Mönchlein, Mönchlein, du gehst einen schweren Gang.
Little monk, you are embarking on a difficult journey.

Martin Luther (1483-1546)
on the eve of his departure for Worms

The test of a vocation is the love of the drudgery it involves.

Logan Pearsall Smith (1865-1946)
American essayist

This is the true joy in life, the being used for a purpose recognised by yourself as a mighty one; the being thoroughly worn out before you are thrown on the scrap heap.

George Bernard Shaw (1856-1950)

*C'est une folie à nulle autre seconde,
De vouloir se mêler de corriger le monde.*
Of all follies there is none greater than wanting to put the world to rights.

Molière (1622-1673)

Vulgarity

It's worse than wicked, my dear, it's vulgar.

Punch, 19th century

Vulgarity is the garlic in the salad of taste.

Cyril Connolly (1903-1974)
British critic

A thing is not vulgar merely because it is common.

William Hazlitt (1778-1830)
English essayist

The higher a man stands, the more the word 'vulgar' becomes unintelligible to him.

John Ruskin (1819-1900)
English critic

Vulgarity is simply the conduct of other people.

Oscar Wilde (1854-1900)

SEE Wilde on WAR; Shaw on WRITING

Wales

With its wild names like peals of bells in the darkness.
> Dylan Thomas (1914-1953)

An impotent people, sick with inbreeding,
Worrying the carcase of an old song.
> R. S. Thomas (b. 1913)
> Welsh poet, clergyman

War

War's a brain-spattering, windpipe-splitting art.
> Lord Byron (1788-1824)

War is nothing more than the continuation of politics by other means.
> Karl von Clausewitz (1780-1831)
> Prussian soldier, strategist

War is only a cowardly escape from the problems of peace.
> Thomas Mann (1875-1955)

A long as there are sovereign nations possessing great power, war is inevitable.
> Albert Einstein (1879-1955)

What a country calls its vital economic interests are not the things which enable its citizens to live, but the things which enable it to make war. Petrol is more likely than wheat to be a cause of international conflict.
> Simone Weil (1909-1943)
> French philosopher, mystic

Roused by the lash of his own stubborn tail
Our lion now will foreign foes assail.
> John Dryden (1631-1700)

We go to gain a little patch of ground
That hath in it no profit but the name.
> Captain, Hamlet
> William Shakespeare (1564-1616)

The belief in the possibility of a short decisive war appears to be one of the most ancient and dangerous of human illusions.
> Robert Lynd (1879-1949)
> Anglo-Irish essayist, journalist

We are at a great disadvantage when we make war on people who have nothing to lose.
> Francesco Guicciardini (1483-1540)
> Italian historian, statesman

Oh, the brave Music of a distant Drum!
> from The Rubáiyát of Omar Khayyám
> trans. Edward Fitzgerald (1809-1883)

How good bad music and bad reasons sound when we march against an enemy.
> Friedrich Nietzsche (1844-1900)

The lamps are going out all over Europe; we shall not see them lit again in our lifetime.
> Lord Grey of Falloden (1862-1933)
> British statesman
> 3 August 1914

What passing-bells for these who die
  as cattle?
Only the monstrous anger of the guns.
> Wilfred Owen (1893-1918)
> British poet

The Angel of Death has been abroad throughout the land, you may almost hear the beating of his wings.
> John Bright (1811-1889)
> English radical politician

Lo! thy dread empire, Chaos! is restor'd;
Light dies before thy uncreating words:
Thy hand, great Anarch! lets the curtain
  fall,
And universal darkness buries all.
> Alexander Pope (1688-1744)

They have caused Egypt to stagger as a drunken man staggereth in his vomit.
> David Ben Gurion (1886-1973)
> Israeli statesman
> of the Israeli army in the 1956 Suez campaign

History shows that there are no invincible armies.
> Josef Stalin (1879-1953)

Here dead lie we because we did not
  choose
To live and shame the land from which
  we sprung.

Life, to be sure, is nothing much to lose;
But young men think it is, and we were young.
A. E. Housman (1859-1936)
British poet, classical scholar

The war has already almost destroyed that nation. . . I have seen, I guess, as much blood and disaster as any living man and it just turned my stomach the last time I was there. After I looked at that wreckage and those thousands of women and children and everything, I vomited.
General MacArthur (1880-1964)
of the Korean war

I have nothing to offer but blood, toil, tears and sweat.
Sir Winston Churchill (1874-1965)

. . . That strange feeling we had in the war. Have you found anything in your lives since to equal it in strength? A sort of splendid carelessness it was, holding us together.
Noël Coward (1899-1973)

War is elevating, because the individual disappears before the great conception of the state.
Heinrich von Treitschke (1834-1896)
German historian

The inevitableness, the idealism, and the blessing of war, as an indispensable and stimulating law of development, must be repeatedly emphasized.
Friedrich von Bernhardi (1849-1930)
German militarist
in Germany and the Next War

As long as war is regarded as wicked, it will always have its fascination. When it is looked upon as vulgar, it will cease to be popular.
Oscar Wilde (1854-1900)

What is it, after all, the people get?
Why! taxes, widows, wooden legs, and debt.
Francis Moore (1657-1715)
English astrologer, physician

What we have gained by the war is, in one word, all that we should have lost without it.
William Pitt (1759-1806)
English Prime Minister

And while I am talking to you mothers and fathers, I give you one more assurance. I have said this before, but I shall say it again and again and again: Your boys are not going to be sent into any foreign wars.
Franklin D. Roosevelt (1882-1945)
30 October 1940

War is the statesman's game, the priest's delight,

The lawyer's jest, the hired assassin's trade.
P. B. Shelley (1792-1822)

War is the only sport that is genuinely amusing. And it is the only sport that has any intelligible use.
H. L. Mencken (1880-1956)
American journalist

What war has always been is a puberty ceremony. It's a very rough one, but you went away a boy and came back a man, maybe with an eye missing or whatever but godammit you were a man and people had to call you a man thereafter.
Kurt Vonnegut (b. 1922)

For a war to be just three things are necessary – public authority, just cause, right motive.
Saint Thomas Aquinas (1225-1274)

Force and fraud are in war the two cardinal virtues.
Thomas Hobbes (1588-1679)

If both sides don't want war, how can war break out?
Menachem Begin (b. 1913)
Israeli politician, Prime Minister
in 1981

The purpose of all war is peace.
Saint Augustine (354-430)

More than an end to war, we want an end to the beginnings of all wars.
Franklin D. Roosevelt (1882-1945)

Of the four wars in my lifetime, none came about because the US was too strong.
Ronald Reagan (b. 1911)

My views with regard to war are well known. I grew up in a tradition where we consider all wars immoral.
Richard Nixon (b. 1913)

War has . . . become a luxury which only the small nations can afford.
Hannah Arendt (1906-1975)
American political philosopher

I'd like to see the government get out of war altogether and leave the whole feud to private industry.
Joseph Heller (b. 1923)
American novelist

At last, after innumerable glamorous and frightful years, mankind approaches a war which is *totally predictable from beginning to end.*
Frederic Raphael (b. 1931)
British author

Child of God, therefore children of God, therefore brothers. All wars are civil wars.
Eric Gill (1882-1940)
British sculptor

They talk about who won and who lost.
Human reason won. Mankind won.
> Nikita Khrushchev (1894-1971)
> *of the Cuban missile crisis, 1962*

There never was a good war or a bad peace.
> Benjamin Franklin (1706-1790)

SEE The ARMS RACE; Croesus on FATHER; Clemenceau, Napoleon on GENERALS; Lincoln on GLORY; GUERRILLA WARFARE; Cicero on The LAW; Mussolini on NATIONALISM; PEACE; Dryden on ROYALTY; VIETNAM; WAR CORRESPONDENTS; WAR CRIMES; Dryden on WINNING; Graves on YOUTH

War Correspondents

That front-line face, he never got anything on film that he didn't get on himself, after three years he'd turned into the thing he came to photograph.
> Michael Herr (b. 1940)
> American journalist

I will put in my poems that with you
is heroism upon land and sea,
And I will report all heroism from
an American point of view.
> Walt Whitman (1819-1892)

The first casualty when war comes is truth.
> Hiram Johnson (1866-1945)
> American Republican politician

The time to leave this place is when all white people begin to look alike.
> Paul Hoffman (b. 1929)
> American journalist
> *on leaving the Congo, 1961*

We all knew that if you stayed too long you became one of those poor bastards who had to have a war on all the time, and where was that?
> Michael Herr (b. 1940)
> American journalist

War Crimes

The worst atrocities are probably committed by those who are most afraid.
> Lord d'Abernon (1857-1941)
> British administrator, author

The next war criminals will come from the chemical and electronics industries.
> Alfred Krupp (1907-1967)
> German arms manufacturer
> *(imprisoned for war crimes, 1948-1951)*

Wealth

Ill fares the land, to hastening ills a prey,
Where wealth accumulates, and men decay.
> Oliver Goldsmith (1728-1774)

It is the interest of the commercial world that wealth should be found everywhere.
> Edmund Burke (1729-1797)
> Irish philosopher, statesman

Better see rightly on a pound a week than squint on a million.
> George Bernard Shaw (1856-1950)

Let us not be too particular; it is better to have old second-hand diamonds than none at all.
> Mark Twain (1835-1910)

Wealth is not without its advantages and the case to the contrary, although it has often been made, has never proved widely persuasive.
> J. K. Galbraith (b. 1908)
> American economist

There are few sorrows, however poignant, in which a good income is of no avail.
> Logan Pearsall Smith (1865-1946)
> American essayist

What I call loaded I'm not. What other people call loaded I am.
> Zsa Zsa Gabor (b. 1921)

If you can actually count your money then you are not really a rich man.
> J. Paul Getty (1892-1976)

I find all this money a considerable burden.
> John Paul Getty Jr
> 1985

What difference does it make how much you have? What you do not have amounts to much more.
> Seneca (c. 5-65)
> Roman writer, philosopher, statesman

The secret point of money and power in America is neither the things that money can buy nor power for power's sake ... but absolute personal freedom, mobility, privacy. It is the instinct which drove America to the Pacific, all through the nineteenth century, the desire to be able to find a restaurant open in case you want a sandwich, to be a free agent, live by one's own rules.
> Joan Didion (b. 1934)
> American writer

What is called a high standard of living consists in considerable measure in arrangements for avoiding muscular energy, increasing sensual pleasure, and enhancing caloric intake beyond any conceivable nutritional requirement. Nonetheless, the belief that increased production is a worthy social goal is very nearly absolute.
> J. K. Galbraith (b. 1908)
> American economist

Wealth, howsoever got, in England
makes
Lords of mechanics, gentlemen of
rakes;
Antiquity and birth are needless
here;
'Tis impudence and money makes
a peer.

Daniel Defoe (c. 1661-1731)

Wealth will be a protection against political corruption. The English statesman is bribed not to be bribed. He is born with a silver spoon in his mouth, so that he may never afterwards be found with the silver spoons in his pocket.

G. K. Chesterton (1874-1936)

But Satan now is wiser than of yore,
And tempts by making rich, not
making poor.

Alexander Pope (1688-1744)

If you look up a dictionary of quotations you will find few reasons for a sensible man to desire to become wealthy.

Robert Lynd (1879-1949)
Anglo-Irish journalist, essayist

SEE LUXURY; Twain on
RESPECTABILITY; The RICH;
George on The WORKING CLASS

The Weather

He maketh his sun to rise on the evil and on the good, and sendeth rain on the just and on the unjust.

Jesus (4 BC-29 AD)

It was so cold the other day, I almost got married.

Shelley Winters (b.1922)

Heat, ma'am! . . . it was so dreadful here that I found there was nothing left for it but to take off my flesh and sit in my bones.

Sydney Smith (1771-1845)
English writer, clergyman

Everybody talks about the weather, but nobody does anything about it.

Charles D. Warner (1829-1900)
American author

Don't knock the weather; nine-tenths of the people couldn't start a conversation if it didn't change once in a while.

Kin (F. McKinney) Hubbard (1868-1930)
American humorist, journalist

People get a bad impression of it [the English climate] by continually trying to treat it as if it was a bank clerk, who ought to be on time on Tuesday next, instead of philosophically seeing it as a painter, who may do anything so long as you don't try to predict what.

Katharine Whitehorn
British journalist

There is really no such thing as bad weather, only different kinds of good weather.

John Ruskin (1819-1900)
English critic

SEE Byron, Chesterton, Coleridge,
Phelps, Walpole on ENGLAND;
RAIN

Weddings

Of all actions of a man's life his marriage does least concern other people; yet of all actions of our life it is most meddled with by other people.

John Selden (1584-1654)
English jurist, statesman

If it were not for the presents, an elopement would be preferable.

George Ade (1866-1944)
American humorist, playwright

Strange to say what delight we married people have to see these poor fools decoyed into our condition.

Samuel Pepys (1633-1703)

That is ever the way. 'Tis all jealousy to the bride and good wishes to the corpse.

J. M. Barrie (1860-1937)
British playwright

A man looks pretty small at a wedding, George. All those good women standing shoulder to shoulder, making sure that the knot's tied in a mighty public way.

Thornton Wilder (1897-1975)
American author

The wedding march always reminds me of the music played when soldiers go into battle.

Heinrich Heine (1797-1856)
German poet, journalist

Welfare

'Tis not enough to help the feeble up, but to support him after.

Timon, *Timon of Athens*
William Shakespeare (1564-1616)

*E' benefizii si debbono fare a poco a poco,
acciò che si assaporino meglio.*
Benefits should be granted a little at a time, so that they may be the better enjoyed.

Niccolò Machiavelli (1469-1527)

Religion was nearly dead because there was no longer real belief in future life; but something was struggling to take its place – service – social service – the ants' creed, the bees' creed.

John Galsworthy (1867-1933)

We are faced with a choice between the work ethic that built this nation's character – and the new welfare ethic that could cause the American character to weaken.

Richard Nixon (b. 1913)

Whimsy

Unpredictability, too, can become monotonous.
Eric Hoffer (1902-1983)
American philosopher

She has a whim of iron.
Oliver Herford (1863-1935)
American poet, illustrator
of his wife

Wickedness

Wickedness is a myth invented by good people
to account for the curious attractiveness of
others.
Oscar Wilde (1854-1900)

Some wicked people would be less dangerous
had they no redeeming qualities.
François, Duc de La Rochefoucauld (1613-1680)
French writer, moralist

It is a fact that cannot be denied: the
wickedness of others becomes our own
wickedness because it kindles something evil
in our own hearts.
Carl Jung (1875-1961)

Wicked is not much worse than indiscreet.
John Donne (c. 1571-1631)

SEE Mencken on DELINQUENCY;
EVIL; Punch on VULGARITY;
Apocrypha on WOMEN

Widowhood

Take example by your father, my boy, and be
wery careful o' vidders all your life, specially if
they've kept a public house, Sammy.
Charles Dickens (1812-1870)

Sorrow for a husband is like a pain in the
elbow, sharp and short.
Thomas Fuller (1654-1734)
English physician

The comfortable estate of widowhood is the
only hope that keeps up a wife's spirits.
Peachum, *The Beggar's Opera*
John Gay (1685-1732)
English playwright

Of course I am shocked by his death, but not
nearly as shocked as when he walked out on
me.
Lady George-Brown
*of her husband, British
politician Lord George-Brown*

Widows are divided into two classes – the
bereaved and relieved.
anonymous

He first deceased; she for a little tried
To live without him, liked it not, and
died.
Sir Henry Wotton (1568-1639)
English diplomat, poet

Give unto them beauty for ashes, the oil of joy
for mourning.
Bible, Isaiah

SEE MacManus on TACT

Wills

Die, and endow a college, or a cat.
Alexander Pope (1688-1744)

He that defers his charity until he is dead is, if
a man weighs it rightly, rather liberal of
another man's goods than his own.
Francis Bacon (1561-1626)

The man who waits to make an entirely
reasonable will dies intestate.
George Bernard Shaw (1856-1950)

SEE Howe on LAWYERS

Wine

Nothing equals the joy of the drinker, except
the joy of the wine in being drunk.
French saying

You know, my Friends, with what a
brave Carouse
I made a Second Marriage in my house;
Divorced old barren Reason from my
Bed,
And took the Daughter of the Vine to
Spouse.
from *The Rubáiyát of Omar Khayyám*
trans. Edward Fitzgerald (1809-1883)

Drink no longer water, but use a little wine for
thy stomach's sake and thine often infirmities.
Saint Paul (3-67)

No poems can please for long or live that are
written by water-drinkers.
Horace (65-8 BC)

El agua, para los beyes; el vino, para los reyes.
Water for oxen, wine for kings.
Spanish proverb

A mind of the calibre of mine cannot derive its
nutriment from cows.
George Bernard Shaw (1856-1950)

The Grape that can with Logic absolute
The Two-and-Seventy jarring Sects confute.
from *The Rubáiyát of Omar Khayyám*
trans. Edward Fitzgerald (1809-1883)

One of the disadvantages of wine is that it
makes a man mistake words for thoughts.
Dr Samuel Johnson (1709-1784)

I may not here omit those two main plagues,
and common dotages of human kind, wine
and women, which have infatuated and
besotted myriads of people. They go commonly together.
Robert Burton (1577-1640)
English clergyman, author

The dipsomaniac and the abstainer are not only both mistaken, but they both make the same mistake. They both regard wine as a drug and not a drink.
> G. K. Chesterton (1874-1936)

Wine gives a man nothing. . . It only puts in motion what had been locked up in frost.
> Dr Samuel Johnson (1709-1784)

There is a devil in every berry of the grape.
> Qu'ran

I prefer the gout.
> Lord Derby (1865-1948)
> British administrator
> *on trying a South African
> port recommended for gout
> sufferers*

It's a Naïve Domestic Burgundy without Any Breeding, But I Think You'll be Amused by its Presumption.
> James Thurber (1894-1961)
> American humorist, illustrator
> *cartoon caption*

I often wonder what the Vintners buy
One-half so precious as the stuff
   they sell.
> from *The Rubáiyát of Omar Khayyám*
> trans. Edward Fitzgerald (1809-1883)

Ah! bouteille, ma mie,
Pourquoi vous videz-vous?
Ah, bottle, my friend, why do you empty yourself?
> Molière (1622-1673)

Wine makes a man better pleased with himself; I do not say that it makes him more pleasing to others.
> Dr Samuel Johnson (1709-1784)

SEE DRINK

Winning

Your first win is like making love and you enjoy it so much the first time that you want to do it again and again.
> Nigel Mansell (b. 1953)
> *on winning South African
> Grand Prix soon after his
> British victory, 1985*

I never thought myself beaten so long as I could present a front to the enemy. If I was beaten at one point I went to another, and in that way I won all my victories.
> Duke of Wellington (1769-1852)

We will get everything out of her [Germany] that you can squeeze out of a lemon and a bit more. . . I will squeeze her until you can hear the pips squeak.
> Sir Eric Geddes (1875-1937)
> Scottish Conservative politician
> *on war reparations after the
> First World War*

An intelligent victor will, whenever possible, present his demands to the vanquished in instalments.
> Adolf Hitler (1889-1945)
> *Mein Kampf*

Even victors are by victories undone.
> John Dryden (1631-1700)

Thrusting my nose firmly between his teeth, I threw him heavily to the ground on top of me.
> Mark Twain (1835-1910)

Une victoire racontée en détail, on ne sait plus ce qui la distingue d'une défaite.
A victory recounted in detail is hard to distinguish from a defeat.
> Jean-Paul Sartre (1905-1980)

That is the whole secret of successful fighting. Get your enemy at a disadvantage; and never, on any account, fight him on equal terms.
> Sergius, *Arms and the Man*
> George Bernard Shaw (1856-1950)

You may have to fight a battle more than once to win it.
> Margaret Thatcher (b. 1925)

Nothing except a battle lost can be half so melancholy as a battle won.
> Duke of Wellington (1769-1852)

When in doubt, win the trick.
> Edmond Hoyle (1672-1769)
> English writer on cards

SEE Shakespeare on FOUL PLAY;
Tomlin on GETTING ON; Khrushchev,
Pitt on WAR

Wisdom

Some folks are wise, and some are otherwise.
> Tobias Smollett (1721-1771)
> Scottish novelist, surgeon

There is somebody wiser than any of us, and that is everybody.
> Napoleon Bonaparte (1769-1821)

Every law which originated in ignorance and malice, and gratifies the passions from which it sprang, we call the wisdom of our ancestors.
> Sydney Smith (1771-1845)
> English clergyman, writer

The fear of the Lord is the beginning of wisdom.
> Bible, Psalms

Truth from his lips prevailed with
   double sway,
And fools, who came to scoff,
   remained to pray.
> Oliver Goldsmith (1728-1774)

It is the province of knowledge to speak, and it is the privilege of wisdom to listen.
> Dr Oliver Wendell Holmes (1809-1894)
> American writer, physician

To-morrow a stranger will say with masterly good sense precisely what we have thought and felt all the time.
R. W. Emerson (1803-1882)
American essayist, poet, philosopher

Clever people master life; the wise illuminate it and create fresh difficulties.
Emil Nolde (1867-1956)
German painter

History teaches us that men and nations behave wisely once they have exhausted all other alternatives.
Abba Eban (b. 1915)
Israeli politician

Many a crown of wisdom is but the golden chamberpot of success, worn with pompous dignity.
Paul Eldridge (b. 1888)
American writer

He who is only wise lives a sad life.
Voltaire (1694-1778)

C'est une grande folie de vouloir être sage tout seul.
It's the height of folly to want to be the only wise one.
François, Duc de La Rochefoucauld (1613-1680)
French writer, moralist

So wise so young, they say, do never live long.
Gloucester, *King Richard III*
William Shakespeare (1564-1616)

It is costly wisdom that is bought by experience.
Roger Ascham (1515-1568)
English writer, classical scholar

The cat, having sat upon a hot stove lid, will not sit upon a hot stove lid again. Nor upon a cold stove lid.
Mark Twain (1835-1910)

SEE Kingsley on EDUCATION; Birrell on EPIGRAMS; Blake on EXCESS; Gray on IGNORANCE; Massinger on ROYALTY; Chesterfield on YOUTH

Wit

Wit lies in recognising the resemblance among things which differ and the difference between things which are alike.
Madame de Staël (1766-1817)
French writer, wit

Wit is the clash and reconcilement of incongruities, the meeting of extremes round a corner.
Leigh Hunt (1784-1859)
English poet, critic, essayist

True wit is nature to advantage dressed, What oft was thought but ne'er so well expressed.
Alexander Pope (1688-1744)

Wit is a sword; it is meant to make people feel the point as well as see it.
G. K. Chesterton (1874-1936)

Surprise is so essential an ingredient of wit that no wit will bear repetition.
Sydney Smith (1771-1845)
English writer, clergyman

He's winding up the watch of his wit; by and by it will strike.
Sebastian, *The Tempest*
William Shakespeare (1564-1616)

A witty thing never excites laughter; it pleases only the mind and never distorts the countenance.
Lord Chesterfield (1694-1773)
English statesman and man of letters

There's a helluva distance between wisecracking and wit. Wit has truth in it; wisecracking is simply callisthenics with words.
Dorothy Parker (1893-1967)
American humorous writer

Wit and Humour – if any difference it is in duration – lightning and electric light. Same material, apparently; but one is vivid, and can do damage – the other fools along and enjoys elaboration.
Mark Twain (1835-1910)

Humour is consistent with pathos, whilst wit is not.
S. T. Coleridge (1772-1834)

Wit is the salt of conversation, not the food.
William Hazlitt (1778-1830)
English essayist

Brevity is the soul of wit.
Polonius, *Hamlet*
William Shakespeare (1564-1616)

SEE Moore on BYRON; La Rochefoucauld, Shakespeare on FOOLS; Smith on The SCOTS

Wives

Wives are young men's mistresses, companions for middle age, and old men's nurses.
Francis Bacon (1561-1626)

To suckle fools, and chronicle small beer.
William Shakespeare (1564-1616)

I chose my wife, as she did her wedding-gown, not for a fine glossy surface, but such qualities as would wear well.
Oliver Goldsmith (1728-1774)

He will hold thee, when his passion shall have spent its novel force,

Something better than his dog, a
little dearer than his horse.
Lord Tennyson (1809-1892)

In that second it dawned on me that I had
been living here for eight years with a strange
man and had borne him three children.
Henrik Ibsen (1828-1906)

Matrimonial devotion
Doesn't seem to suit her notion.
W. S. Gilbert (1836-1911)
English librettist

One can always recognise women who trust
their husbands; they look so thoroughly
unhappy.
Oscar Wilde (1854-1900)

The woman who cannot evolve a good lie in
defense of the man she loves is unworthy the
name of wife.
Elbert Hubbard (1856-1915)
American author

This comes of James teaching me to think for
myself, and never to hold back out of fear of
what other people may think of me. It works
beautifully as long as I think the same things
as he does.
Candida, *Candida*
George Bernard Shaw (1856-1950)

It's my old girl that advises. She has the head.
But I never own to it before her. Discipline
must be maintained.
Mr Bagnet, *Bleak House*
Charles Dickens (1812-1870)

Good wives and private soldiers should be
ignorant.
William Wycherley (1640-1716)
English dramatist

That's what a man wants in a wife, mostly; he
wants to make sure o' one fool as'll tell him
he's wise.
George Eliot (1819-1880)

A man likes his wife to be just clever enough
to comprehend his cleverness, and just stupid
enough to admire it.
Israel Zangwill (1864-1926)
British writer

If a woman has her PhD in physics, has
mastered in quantum theory, plays flawless
Chopin, was once a cheerleader, and is now
married to a man who plays baseball, she will
forever be 'former cheerleader married to star
athlete'.
Maryanne Ellison Simmons
wife of Milwaukee Brewers' catcher Ted Simmons

A man is in general better pleased when he has
a good dinner upon his table, than when his
wife talks Greek.
Dr Samuel Johnson (1709-1784)

Kissing don't last: cookery do!
George Meredith (1828-1909)
British author

There is one thing more exasperating than a
wife who can cook and won't, and that's the
wife who can't cook and will.
Robert Frost (1874-1963)
American poet

Accidents will occur in the best regulated
families, and in families not regulated by that
pervading influence which sanctifies while it
enhances the – a – I would say, in short, by
the influence of Woman, in the lofty character
of Wife, they may be expected with confidence
and must be borne with philosophy.
Mr Micawber, *David Copperfield*
Charles Dickens (1812-1870)

She'd have you spew up what you've drunk
when you were out.
Caecilius (2nd century BC)
Latin poet

Many men owe their success to their wives. I
owe my wife to my success.
anonymous millionaire

An ideal wife is any woman who has an ideal
husband.
Booth Tarkington (1869-1946)
American novelist, playwright

Those graceful acts, those thousand
decencies,
That daily flow from all her words
and actions.
John Milton (1608-1674)

SEE HUSBANDS; MARRIAGE; Dewar on
SUCCESS; WIDOWS

Women

Woman – a foe to friendship, an unescapable
punishment, a necessary evil.
John Chrysostom (345-407)
Greek ecclesiast and hermit

All wickedness is but little to the wickedness
of a woman.
Apocrypha, Ecclesiasticus

Women give themselves to God when the
Devil wants nothing more to do with them.
Sophie Arnould (1740-1802)
French operatic soprano

The judgement of God upon your sex endures
even today; and with it inevitably endures
your position of criminal at the bar of justice.
You are the gateway to the devil.
Tertullian (c. 160-c. 230)
Roman theologian

Woman's place is in the wrong.
James Thurber (1894-1961)
American humorist, illustrator

Women have a wonderful sense of right and wrong, but little sense of right and left.
> Don Herold (b. 1889)
> American humorous writer, artist

Give a woman an inch and she'll park a car on it.
> E. P. B. White (b. 1914)
> Chief Constable of Gloucestershire

In point of morals the average woman is, even for business, too crooked.
> Stephen Leacock (1869-1944)
> Canadian humorist and economist

A woman's appearance depends upon two things: the clothes she wears and the time she gives to her toilet... Against the first we bring the charge of ostentation, against the second of harlotry.
> Tertullian (c. 160-c. 230)
> Roman theologian

Aren't women prudes if they don't and prostitutes if they do?
> Kate Millet (b. 1934)
> American feminist writer

Taught from infancy that beauty is woman's sceptre, the mind shapes itself to the body, and roaming round its gilt cage, only seeks to adorn its prison.
> Mary Wollstonecraft (1759-1797)
> English feminist writer

Women are not much, but they are the best other sex we have.
> Don Herold (b. 1889)
> American humorous writer, artist

When children cease to be altogether desirable women cease to be altogether necessary.
> John Langdon-Davies (1897-1971)
> British author

A woman is like a teabag – only in hot water do you realise how strong she is.
> Nancy Reagan (b. 1923)

If women got a slap round the face more often, they'd be a bit more reasonable.
> Charlotte Rampling (b. 1945)
> British actress

Most women have no character at all.
> Alexander Pope (1688-1744)

The opinion I have of the generality of women – who appear to me as children to whom I would rather give a sugar plum than my time, forms a barrier against matrimony which I rejoice in.
> John Keats (1795-1821)

A woman might claim to retain some of the child's faculties, although very limited and defused, simply because she has not been encouraged to learn methods of thought and develop a disciplined mind. As long as educa-

tion remains largely induction ignorance will retain these advantages over learning and it is time that women impudently put them to work.
> Germaine Greer (b. 1939)
> Australian feminist writer

She was a gentlewoman, a scholar and a saint, and after having been three times married she took the vow of celibacy. What more could be expected of any woman?
> Elizabeth Wordsworth (1840-1932)
> English educator

As artists they're rot, but as providers they're oil wells; they gush. Norris said she never wrote a story unless it was fun to do. I understand Ferber whistles at her typewriter. And there was that poor sucker Flaubert rolling around on his floor for three days looking for the right word.
> Dorothy Parker (1893-1967)
> American humorous writer

A woman, especially, if she have the misfortune of knowing anything, should conceal it as well as she can.
> Jane Austen (1775-1817)

Thus women's secrets I've surveyed
And let them see how curiously they're made,
And that, tho' they of different sexes be,
Yet in the whole they are the same as we.
> from The Works of Aristotle
> in Four Parts, 1822, quoted
> by Germaine Greer

When a woman behaves like a man why doesn't she behave like a nice man?
> Dame Edith Evans (1888-1976)
> British actress

I am glad that I am not a man, as I should be obliged to marry a woman.
> Madame de Staël (1766-1817)
> French writer, wit

In the divorce court women complain of losing weight. Outside the divorce court they complain of putting it on.
> Sir Arthian Davies (1901-1979)
> British judge

A woman will always sacrifice herself if you give her the opportunity. It is her favourite form of self-indulgence.
> W. Somerset Maugham (1874-1965)

Good women always think it is their fault when someone else is being offensive. Bad women never take the blame for anything.
> Anita Brookner (b. 1938)
> British author

There is only one real tragedy in a woman's

life. The fact that her past is always her lover, and her future invariably her husband.

Oscar Wilde (1854-1900)

A woman's whole life is a history of the affections.

Washington Irving (1783-1859)
American author

The happiest women, like the happiest nations, have no history.

George Eliot (1819-1880)

There is no spectacle on earth more appealing than that of a beautiful woman in the act of cooking dinner for someone she loves.

Thomas Wolfe (1900-1938)
American author

If all men are born free, how is it that all women are born slaves?

Mary Astell (1666-1735)
English feminist writer

The slavery of women happened when the men were slaves of kings.

R. W. Emerson (1803-1882)
American essayist, poet, philosopher

Women live like Bats or Owls, labour like Beasts, and die like Worms.

Margaret Cavendish, Duchess of Newcastle
(1623-1673)
English writer

You can always rely on a society of equals taking it out on the women.

Alan Sillitoe (b. 1928)
British novelist

If ever there was a colonised race on this planet it's the female race, there's no question about that.

Shirley Maclaine (b. 1934)

Th' hand that rocks th' cradle is just as liable to rock the country.

Kin (F. McKinney) Hubbard (1868-1930)
American humorist, journalist

The great question that has never been answered, and which I have not yet been able to answer despite my thirty years of research into the feminine soul, is: What does a woman want?

Sigmund Freud (1856-1939)

For my part I distrust *all* generalizations about women, favourable and unfavourable, masculine and feminine, ancient and modern.

Bertrand Russell (1872-1970)

Being a woman is of special interest only to aspiring male transsexuals. To actual women it is merely a good excuse not to play football.

Fran Lebowitz (b. 1951)
American journalist

Women: and men   Women are told from their infancy and taught by the example of their mothers, that a little knowledge of human weakness, justly termed cunning, softness of temper, 'outward' obedience and a scrupulous attention to a puerile kind of propriety, will obtain for them the protection of man.

Mary Wollstonecraft (1759-1797)
English feminist writer

The only way for a woman to provide for herself decently is for her to be good to some man that can afford to be good to her.

Mrs Warren, *Mrs Warren's Profession*
George Bernard Shaw (1856-1950)

Brigands demand your money or your life; women demand both.

Samuel Butler (1835-1902)
English author

The way to fight a woman is with your hat — grab it and run.

John Barrymore (1882-1942)
American actor

Woman begins by resisting a man's advances and ends by blocking his retreat.

Oscar Wilde (1854-1900)

Here's to woman! Would that we could fall into her arms without falling into her hands.

Ambrose Bierce (1842-1914)
American author

She plucked from my lapel the invisible strand of lint (the universal act of woman to proclaim ownership).

O. Henry (1862-1910)
American short story writer

As much as women belong to us, we no longer belong to them.

Michel de Montaigne (1533-1592)
French essayist

Most women set out to try to change a man, and when they have changed him they do not like him.

Marlene Dietrich (b. 1904)

The only time a woman really succeeds in changing a man is when he's a baby.

Natalie Wood (1938-1981)

There is nothing women hate so much as to see men selfishly enjoying themselves without the solace of feminine society.

Katharine Tynan Hinkson (1861-1931)
Irish poet, novelist

A woman must choose: with a man liked by women, she is not sure; with a man disliked by women, she is not happy.

Anatole France (1844-1924)
French author

A woman may very well form a friendship

with a man, but for this to endure, it must be assisted by a little physical antipathy.
> Friedrich Nietzsche (1844-1900)

A man of sense only trifles with them, plays with them, humours and flatters them, as he does with a sprightly and forward child; but he neither consults them about, nor trusts them with, serious matters.
> Lord Chesterfield (1694-1773)
> English statesman and man of letters

Women have served all these centuries as looking-glasses possessing the magic and delicious power of reflecting the figure of man at twice its natural size.
> Virginia Woolf (1882-1941)

A man's women folk, whatever their outward show of respect for his merit and authority, always regard him secretly as an ass, and with something akin to pity. . . In this fact, perhaps, lies one of the best proofs of feminine intelligence or, as the common phrase makes it, feminine intuition.
> H. L. Mencken (1880-1956)
> American journalist

Perhaps women have always been in closer contact with reality than men: it would seem to be the just recompense for being deprived of idealism.
> Germaine Greer (b. 1939)
> Australian feminist writer

Women are not angels. They are as foolish as men in many ways; but they have had to devote themselves to life whilst men have had to devote themselves to death. . . Women have been forced to fear whilst men have been forced to dare: the heroism of a woman is to nurse and protect life, and of a man to destroy it and court death.
> George Bernard Shaw (1856-1950)

Being a woman is a terribly difficult trade, since it consists principally of dealing with men.
> Joseph Conrad (1857-1924)

I expect that Woman will be the last thing civilised by Man.
> George Meredith (1828-1909)
> British author

SEE Bierce, Engel, Lenclos, Mizner, de Poitiers on AGE; Coleridge on AGE: Old Age; Pugh on ANTIPATHY; Glasgow on ANXIETY; Collins on ARGUMENT; Surtees on BLOODSPORTS; Byron, Shakespeare, Wilde on CRYING; Bible on DISCRETION; Muhammad on DRESS; FEMINISM; Chesterfield on FLATTERY; Collins on FLIRTING; GODDESSES; Collins on HAIR; LADIES; Byron on LOVE: First Love;

Goethe on MANNERS; MEN: and Women; MEN AND WOMEN; Hinkson on OPINIONS; Cassandra on POLITICIANS; D'Aurevilly on QUARRELS; Pinero on REGRET; La Rochefoucauld on REPUTATION; Lenclos on SEDUCTION; Hubbard on STATUS; Burton on WINE; WIVES; Woolf on WRITERS

Words

Words are the clothes that thoughts wear – only the clothes.
> Samuel Butler (1835-1902)
> English author

Words, like eyeglasses, blur everything that they do not make clearer.
> Joseph Joubert (1754-1824)
> French essayist and moralist

Words ought to be a little wild for they are the assault of thoughts on the unthinking.
> John Maynard Keynes (1883-1946)

'When I use a word', Humpty Dumpty said in rather a scornful tone, 'it means just what I choose it to mean – neither more nor less'.
> Lewis Carroll (1832-1898)

Would you repeat that again, sir, for it soun's sae sonorous that the words droon the ideas?
> John Wilson (1785-1854)
> Scottish philosopher

One forgets words as one forgets names. One's vocabulary needs constant fertilisation or it will die.
> Evelyn Waugh (1903-1966)

Words are, of course, the most powerful drug used by mankind.
> Rudyard Kipling (1865-1936)

In fact, words are well adapted for description and arousing of emotions, but for many kinds of precise thought other symbols are much better.
> J. B. S. Haldane (1892-1964)
> British scientist

SEE LANGUAGE; SPEECH

Work

My father taught me to work; he did not teach me to love it.
> Abraham Lincoln (1809-1865)

I like work; it fascinates me. I can sit and look at it for hours. I love to keep it by me; the idea of getting rid of it nearly breaks my heart.
> Jerome K. Jerome (1859-1927)
> British author

Work with some men is as besetting a sin as idleness.
> Samuel Butler (1835-1902)
> English author

Work is the curse of the drinking classes.
Oscar Wilde (1854-1900)

Perpetual devotion to what a man calls his business is only to be sustained by perpetual neglect of many other things.
Robert Louis Stevenson (1850-1894)

Unchanging work at a uniform task kills the explosive flow of a man's animal spirits, which draw refreshing zest from a simple change of activity.
Karl Marx (1818-1883)

Clearly the most unfortunate people are those who must do the same thing over and over again, every minute, or perhaps twenty to the minute. They deserve the shortest hours and the highest pay.
J. K. Galbraith (b. 1908)
American economist

Work is of two kinds: first, altering the position of matter at or near the earth's surface relatively to other such matter; second, telling other people to do so. The first kind is unpleasant and ill-paid; the second is pleasant and highly paid.
Bertrand Russell (1872-1970)

Anyone can do any amount of work, provided it isn't the work he is *supposed* to be doing at that moment.
Robert Benchley (1889-1945)
American humorous writer

Nothing is really work unless you would rather be doing something else.
J. M. Barrie (1860-1937)
British playwright

If you have genius, industry will improve it; if you have none, industry will supply its place.
Sir Joshua Reynolds (1723-1792)
English painter

Il faut cultiver notre jardin. . . Quand l'homme fut mis dans le jardin d'Eden il y fut mis pour qu'il travaillât; ce qui prouve que l'homme n'est pas né pour le repos. . . Travaillons sans raisonner, c'est le seul moyen de rendre la vie supportable.
We must cultivate our own garden. When man was put in the garden of Eden he was put there so that he should work, which proves that man was not born to rest. Let us work without questioning, it is the only way to make life tolerable.
Voltaire (1694-1778)

We must hold a man amenable to reason for the choice of his daily craft or profession. It is not an excuse any longer for his deeds that they are the custom of his trade. What business has he with an evil trade?
R. W. Emerson (1803-1882)
American essayist, poet, philosopher

All professions are conspiracies against the laity.
Sir Patrick, *The Doctor's Dilemma*
George Bernard Shaw (1856-1950)

By working faithfully eight hours a day, you may eventually get to be a boss and work twelve hours a day.
Robert Frost (1874-1963)
American poet

When I was young I worked for a capitalist twelve hours a day and I was always tired. Now I work for myself twenty hours a day and I never get tired.
Nikita Khrushchev (1894-1971)

Work expands so as to fill the time available for its completion.
C. Northcote Parkinson (b. 1909)
British historian, author

The really efficient labourer will be found not to crowd his day with work, but will saunter to his task surrounded by a wide halo of ease and leisure.
H. D. Thoreau (1817-1862)

It is too difficult to think nobly when one thinks only of earning a living.
Jean-Jacques Rousseau (1712-1778)

Nothing dignifies human labour so much as the saving of it.
John Rodgers (b. 1906)
British administrator, politician

Work is the province of cattle.
Dorothy Parker (1893-1967)
American humorous writer

SEE Marx on COMMUNISM; Chesterton on HUMILITY; Schaap on ILLUSIONS: of Grandeur; The OFFICE; Ruskin on SLAVERY

The Working Class

The General Strike has taught the working class more in four days than years of talking could have done.
A. J. Balfour (1848-1930)
British Conservative politician, Prime Minister

The working-class is now issuing from its hiding-place to assert an Englishman's heaven-born privilege of doing as he likes, and is beginning to perplex us by marching where it likes, meeting where it likes, bawling what it likes, breaking what it likes.
Matthew Arnold (1822-1888)
English poet, critic

There are only three ways by which any individual can get wealth – by work, by gift, or by theft. And clearly, the reason why the workers get so little is that the beggars and

thieves get so much.
Henry George (1839-1897)
American economist

I tell you, sir, the only safeguard of order and discipline in the modern world is a standardized worker with interchangeable parts. That would solve the entire problem of management.
Jean Giraudoux (1882-1944)
French writer, diplomat

In every one of those little stucco boxes there's some poor bastard who's never free except when he's fast asleep and dreaming that he's got the boss down the bottom of a well and is bunging lumps of coal at him.
George Orwell (1903-1950)

I am a friend of the working-man, and I would rather be his friend than be one.
Clarence Darrow (1857-1938)
American lawyer, writer

SEE Mussolini on INTERNATIONALISM;
Lenin on TRADE UNIONS

Worldliness
I rather like the world. The flesh is pleasing and the Devil does not trouble me.
Elbert Hubbard (1856-1915)
American author

The world is a beautiful book, but of little use to him who cannot read it.
Carlo Goldoni (1707-1793)
Italian dramatist

I have been in love, and in debt, and in drink, this many and many a year.
Alexander Brome (1620-1666)
English poet

So many worlds, so much to do.
So little done, such things to be.
Lord Tennyson (1809-1892)

SEE La Fontaine on SELF-KNOWLEDGE

Worth
We never know the worth of water till the well is dry.
18th century English proverb

I have never believed in the superiority of the inferior.
H. G. Wells (1866-1946)

Nowadays people know the price of everything and the value of nothing.
Oscar Wilde (1854-1900)

SEE Baker on SOCIALISM

Writers
Give me a condor's quill! Give me Vesuvius' crater for an inkstand!
Herman Melville (1819-1891)

On the day when a young writer corrects his first proof sheets, he is as proud as a schoolboy who has just got his first dose of pox.
Charles Baudelaire (1821-1867)

Admitted into the company of paper blurrers.
Sir Philip Sidney (1554-1586)

Why did I write? whose sin to me
unknown
Dipt me in ink, my parents' or my
own?
Alexander Pope (1688-1744)

Why did I write? Because I found life unsatisfactory.
Tennessee Williams (1914-1983)

I know not, madam, that you have a right, upon moral principles, to make your readers suffer so much.
Dr Samuel Johnson (1709-1784)
to Mrs Sheridan

If you were to make little fishes talk, they would talk like whales.
Oliver Goldsmith (1728-1774)
to Dr Johnson

I portray men as they ought to be portrayed, but Euripides portrays them as they are.
Sophocles (c. 495-406 BC)
quoted by Aristotle

Without, or with, offence to friends
or foes,
I sketch your world exactly as it
goes.
Lord Byron (1788-1824)

If justice and truth take place, if he is rewarded according to his desert, his name will stink to all generations.
John Wesley (1703-1791)
of Lord Chesterfield

His style is chaos illumined by flashes of lightning. As a writer, he has mastered everything except language.
Oscar Wilde (1854-1900)
of George Meredith

He had a wonderful talent for packing thought close, and rendering it portable.
Lord Macaulay (1800-1859)
English historian
of Francis Bacon

Three-fifths of him genius, and two-fifths sheer fudge.
J. R. Lowell (1819-1891)
American poet, editor
of Edgar Allan Poe

He was worse than provincial – he was parochial.
Henry James (1843-1916)
of H. D. Thoreau

Henry James writes fiction as if it were a painful duty.
Oscar Wilde (1854-1900)

The work of Henry James has always seemed divisible by a simple dynastic arrangement into three reigns: James I, James II, and the Old Pretender.
Philip Guedalla (1889-1944)
British author

His writing is not about something. It is the thing itself.
Samuel Beckett (b. 1906)
of James Joyce

If the Christ were content with humble toilers for disciples, that wasn't good enough for our Bert. He wanted dukes' half sisters and belted earls wiping his feet with their hair; grand apotheosis of the snob, to humiliate the objects of his own awe by making them venerate him. In his brisk youth before he met Frieda and became a prophet, he was indeed a confidence man.
Angela Carter (b. 1940)
British author
of D. H. Lawrence

I don't regard Brecht as a man of iron-grey purpose and intellect, I think he is a theatrical whore of the first quality.
Peter Hall (b. 1930)
British theatre director

Writers are always selling somebody out.
Joan Didion (b. 1934)
American writer

I started out very quiet and I beat Mr Turgenev. Then I trained hard and I beat Mr de Maupassant. I've fought two draws with Mr Stendhal, and I think I had an edge in the last one. But nobody's going to get me in any ring with Mr Tolstoy unless I'm crazy or I keep getting better.
Ernest Hemingway (1899-1961)

The author who invents a title well
Will always find his covered
dulness sell.
Thomas Chatterton (1752-1770)
English poet

One man is as good as another until he has written a book.
Benjamin Jowett (1817-1893)
English scholar, essayist

How vain it is to sit down to write when you have not stood up to live.
H. D. Thoreau (1817-1862)

Talent alone cannot make a writer. There must be a man behind the book.
R. W. Emerson (1803-1882)
American essayist, poet, philosopher

For the sake of a few fine imaginative or domestic passages, are we to be bullied into a certain philosophy engendered in the whims of an egotist.
John Keats (1705-1821)

No one who cannot halt at self-imposed boundaries could ever write.
Nicolas Boileau (1636-1711)
French poet, critic

L'écrivain original n'est pas celui qui n'imite personne, mais celui que personne ne peut imiter.
An original writer is not one who imitates no one, but whom no one can imitate.
François-René de Chateaubriand (1768-1848)
French writer

Every great and original writer, in proportion as he is great and original, must himself create the taste by which he is to be relished.
William Wordsworth (1770-1850)

American writers want to be not good but great; and so are neither.
Gore Vidal (b. 1925)

The faults of great writers are generally excellencies carried to excess.
S. T. Coleridge (1772-1834)

Only a mediocre writer is always at his best.
W. Somerset Maugham (1874-1965)

No author is a man of genius to his publisher.
Heinrich Heine (1797-1856)
German poet, journalist

There is probably no hell for authors in the next world – they suffer so much from critics and publishers in this.
C. N. Bovee (1820-1904)
American editor, writer

After being turned down by numerous publishers, he decided to write for posterity.
George Ade (1866-1944)
American humorist, playwright

No man but a blockhead ever wrote except for money.
Dr Samuel Johnson (1709-1784)

The life of writing men has always been . . . a bitter business. It is notoriously accompanied, for those who wrote well, by poverty and contempt; or by fatuity and wealth for those who write ill.
Hilaire Belloc (1870-1953)
British author

Alas! a woman that attempts the pen,
Such a presumptuous creature is
esteemed,
The fault can by no virtue be
redeemed.
They tell us we mistake our sex and
way;

Good breeding, fashion, dancing,
dressing, play,
Are the accomplishments we should
desire;
To write, or read, or think, or to
enquire,
Would cloud our beauty, and exhaust
our time,
And interrupt the conquests of our
prime,
Whilst the dull manage of a servile
house
Is held by some our utmost art and
use.

Anne Finch, Lady Winchilsea (1660-1720)
English poet

The indifference of the world which Keats and Flaubert and other men of genius have found so hard to bear was in her case not indifference but hostility. The world did not say to her as it said to them, Write if you choose; it makes no difference to me. The world said with a guffaw, Write? What's the good of you writing?

Virginia Woolf (1882-1941)
on women writers

Writers don't need love. All they require is money.

John Osborne (b. 1929)
British playwright

Some day I hope to write a book where the royalties will pay for the copies I give away.

Clarence Darrow (1857-1938)
American lawyer, writer

If a writer has to rob his mother, he will not hesitate; the 'Ode on a Grecian Urn' is worth any number of old ladies.

William Faulkner (1897-1962)

A woman must have money and a room of her own if she is to write fiction.

Virginia Woolf (1882-1941)

A first edition of his work is a rarity, but a second is rarer still.

Franklin Pierce Adams (1881-1960)
American journalist, humorist

The man who is asked by an author what he thinks of his work is put to the torture and is not obliged to speak the truth.

Dr Samuel Johnson (1709-1784)

Any author who speaks about his own books is almost as bad as a mother who talks about her own children.

Benjamin Disraeli (1804-1881)

What no wife of a writer can ever understand is that a writer is working when he's staring out of the window.

Burton Rascoe (1892-1957)
American writer, editor

You must not suppose, because I am a man of letters, that I never tried to earn an honest living.

George Bernard Shaw (1856-1950)

SEE Joyce on ARTISTS; BYRON; Solzhenitsyn on CENSORSHIP; Johnson on CONTROVERSY; Johnson on CRITICS; Nathan on FAILURE; HISTORY; Dr JOHNSON; Chesterfield on LITERATURE; Dryden, O'Malley, Proctor on PLAGIARISM; SHAKESPEARE; Parker on WOMEN; WRITING

Writing

The insatiate itch of scribbling.

William Gifford (1756-1826)
English journalist

Writing is not a profession, but a vocation of unhappiness.

Georges Simenon (1904-1985)

The best way to become acquainted with a subject is to write a book about it.

Benjamin Disraeli (1804-1881)

The greatest part of a writer's time is spent in reading, in order to write; a man will turn over half a library to make one book.

Dr Samuel Johnson (1709-1784)

All books are either dreams or swords,
You can cut or you can drug with words.

Amy Lowell (1874-1925)
American poet, critic, biographer

I always write a good first line, but I have trouble in writing the others.

Molière (1622-1673)

'Fool!' said my muse to me, 'look in thy heart, and write'.

Sir Philip Sidney (1554-1586)

It is just when ideas are lacking that a phrase is most welcome.

Johann Wolfgang von Goethe (1749-1832)

I do most of my work sitting down; that's where I shine.

Robert Benchley (1889-1945)
American humorous writer

This morning I took out a comma and this afternoon I put it back again.

Oscar Wilde (1854-1900)

The paragraph is a great art form. I'm very interested in paragraphs and I write paragraphs very, very carefully.

Iris Murdoch (b. 1919)
Irish author

Composition is, for the most part, an effort of slow diligence and steady perseverance, to which the mind is dragged by necessity or resolution.

Dr Samuel Johnson (1709-1784)

I write when I'm inspired, and I see to it that I'm inspired at nine o'clock every morning.
Peter de Vries (b. 1910)
American author

Some collaboration has to take place in the mind between the woman and the man before the art of creation can be accomplished. Some marriage of opposites has to be consummated. The whole of the mind must lie wide open if we are to get the sense that the writer is communicating his experience with perfect fullness.
Virginia Woolf (1882-1941)

One becomes a writer, but one must be born a novelist. If a person has sensitivity, culture, and imagination, it is not difficult to become a writer. It is impossible to *become* a novelist, story-teller or fabler; either you have a natural gift for narrating, or you don't.
Alberto Moravia (b. 1907)
Italian novelist

Ultimately, literature is nothing but carpentry. With both you are working with reality, a material just as hard as wood.
Gabriel García Márquez (b. 1928)
Colombian author

True ease in writing comes from art,
not chance,
As those move easiest who have
learned to dance.
'Tis not enough no harshness gives
offence,
The sound must seem an echo to the
sense.
Alexander Pope (1688-1744)

C'est un métier que de faire un livre, comme de faire une pendule: il faut plus que de l'esprit pour être auteur.
Making books is a craft, like making clocks: it takes more than wit to be an author.
Jean de la Bruyère (1645-1696)
French writer, moralist

Writing, madam, 's a mechanic part of wit! A gentleman should never go beyond a song or a billet.
Sir George Etherege (1635-1691)
English dramatist, diplomat

I couldn't write the things they publish now, with no beginning and no end, and a little incest in the middle.
Irvin S. Cobb (1876-1944)
American writer

Good authors, too, who once knew
better words
Now only use four-letter words
Writing prose. . .
Anything goes.
Cole Porter (1893-1964)

Vulgarity is a necessary part of a complete author's equipment; and the clown is sometimes the best part of the circus.
George Bernard Shaw (1856-1950)

Style and structure are the essence of a book; great ideas are hogwash.
Vladimir Nabokov (1899-1977)

I'm always, always trying to interpret Life in terms of lives, never just lives in terms of characters.
Eugene O'Neill (1888-1953)

What I like in a good author is not what he says, but what he whispers.
Logan Pearsall Smith (1865-1946)
American essayist

How can I know what I think till I see what I say?
E. M. Forster (1879-1970)
riposte to maxim 'Never begin a sentence until you know how to end it'

The essence of prose is to perish — to be dissolved and replaced by the image it denotes.
Paul Valéry (1871-1945)
French poet, essayist

In literature the ambition of the novice is to acquire the literary language; the struggle of the adept is to get rid of it.
George Bernard Shaw (1856-1950)

When we see a natural style, we are astonished and delighted; for we expected to see an author, and we find a man.
Blaise Pascal (1623-1662)

My spelling is Wobbly. It's good spelling but it Wobbles, and letters get in the wrong places.
A. A. Milne (1882-1958)
British author

One should always aim at being interesting rather than exact.
Voltaire (1694-1778)

In all pointed sentences, some degree of accuracy must be sacrificed to conciseness.
Dr Samuel Johnson (1709-1784)

If you require a practical rule of me, I will present you with this: Whenever you feel an impulse to perpetrate a piece of exceptionally fine writing, obey it — wholeheartedly — and delete it before sending your manuscript to press. *Murder Your Darlings.*
Arthur Quiller-Couch (1863-1944)
British writer

In composing, as a general rule, run your pen through every other word you have written; you have no idea what vigour it will give your style.
Sydney Smith (1771-1845)
English clergyman, writer

Make'em laugh; make'em cry; make'em wait.
> Charles Reade (1814-1884)
> English novelist
> *advice to young author on
> writing novels*

Every drop of ink in my pen ran cold.
> Horace Walpole (1717-1797)
> English author

There are two literary maladies – writer's cramp and swelled head.
> Coulson Kernahan (1858-1943)
> British author

That's not writing, that's typing.
> Truman Capote (b. 1924)
> *of Jack Kerouac*

What is written without effort is in general read without pleasure.
> Dr Samuel Johnson (1709-1784)

Reading is not a duty, and has consequently no business to be made disagreeable.
> Augustine Birrell (1850-1933)
> English Liberal politician

There are three difficulties in authorship: to write anything worth the publishing, to find honest men to publish it, and to get sensible men to read it.
> C. C. Colton (1780-1832)
> English author, clergyman

The impulse to create beauty is rather rare in literary men. . . Far ahead of it comes the yearning to make money. And after the yearning to make money comes the yearning to make a noise.
> H. L. Mencken (1880-1956)
> American journalist

The only sensible ends of literature are, first, the pleasurable toil of writing; second, the gratification of one's family and friends; and, lastly, the solid cash.
> Nathaniel Hawthorne (1804-1864)
> American novelist

If you want to get rich from writing, write the sort of thing that's read by persons who move their lips when they're reading to themselves.
> Don Marquis (1878-1937)
> American humorist, journalist

Once in seven years I burn all my sermons; for it is a shame if I cannot write better sermons now than I did seven years ago.
> John Wesley (1703-1791)

Trivial personalities decomposing in the eternity of print.
> Virginia Woolf (1882-1941)

'Tis pleasant, sure, to see one's name in
  print;
A book's a book, although there's
  nothing in't.
> Lord Byron (1788-1824)

Camerado, this is no book,
Who touches this touches a man.
> Walt Whitman (1819-1892)

With sixty staring me in the face, I have developed inflammation of the sentence structure and definite hardening of the paragraphs.
> James Thurber (1894-1961)
> American humorist, illustrator

Of making many books there is no end; and much study is a weariness of the flesh.
> Bible, Ecclesiastes

The aim, if reached or not, makes great
  the life;
Try to be Shakespeare, leave the rest to
  fate.
> Robert Browning (1812-1889)

SEE AUTOBIOGRAPHY; BIOGRAPHY; EDITING; FICTION; Benchley, Emerson, Inge, Morley on LITERATURE; Mizner on PLAGIARISM; WRITERS

Youth

But thy eternal summer shall not fade.
William Shakespeare (1564-1616)

Those whom the gods love grow young.
Oscar Wilde (1854-1900)

I remember my youth and the feeling that will never come back any more – the feeling that I could last forever, outlast the sea, the earth, and all men.
Joseph Conrad (1857-1924)

He wears the rose of youth upon him.
Antony, *Antony and Cleopatra*
William Shakespeare (1564-1616)

Breathless, we flung us on the windy
hill,
Laughed in the sun, and kissed the
lovely grass.
Rupert Brooke (1887-1915)
British poet

There is nothing can pay one for that invaluable ignorance which is the companion of youth; those sanguine groundless hopes, and that lively vanity, which make all the happiness of life.
Lady Mary Wortley Montagu (1689-1762)
English society figure, letter writer

Towering in the confidence of twenty-one.
Dr Samuel Johnson (1709-1784)

A man loves the meat in his youth that he cannot endure in his age.
Benedick, *Much Ado About Nothing*
William Shakespeare (1564-1616)

O'er her warm cheek, and rising bosom,
move
The bloom of young Desire, and purple
light of Love.
Thomas Gray (1716-1771)

Bliss was it in that dawn to be alive,
But to be young was very heaven!
William Wordsworth (1770-1850)

Youth, large, lusty, loving – Youth, full
of grace, force, fascination,
Do you know that Old Age may come
after you, with equal grace, force,
fascination?
Walt Whitman (1819-1892)

Young men are apt to think themselves wise enough, as drunken men are apt to think themselves sober enough.
Lord Chesterfield (1694-1773)
English statesman and man of letters

I am not young enough to know everything.
J. M. Barrie (1860-1937)
British playwright

Youth is a period of missed opportunities.
Cyril Connolly (1903-1974)
British critic

Give me the young man who has brains enough to make a fool of himself!
Robert Louis Stevenson (1850-1894)

Don't let young people confide in you their aspirations; when they drop them, they will drop you.
Logan Pearsall Smith (1865-1946)
American essayist

The young always have the same problem – how to rebel and conform at the same time. They have now solved this by defying their parents and copying one another.
Quentin Crisp (b. 1908)
British author

What are these,
So withered, and so wild in their attire,
That look not like the inhabitants o'
the earth,
And yet are on't?
Banquo, *Macbeth*
William Shakespeare (1564-1616)

The wine of youth does not always clear with advancing years; sometimes it grows turbid.
Carl Jung (1875-1961)

The trouble with young people today is that emotionally and psychologically the West is due for another war and they can't have it – it's impossible.
Robert Graves (1895-1985)
British poet, author

Youth is a disease that must be borne with patiently! Time, indeed, will cure it.
R. H. Benson (1871-1914)
British novelist

What is more enchanting than the voices of young people when you can't hear what they say?

Logan Pearsall Smith (1865-1946)
American essayist

Only the young die good.

Oliver Herford (1863-1935)
American poet, illustrator

Whom the gods love die young no matter how long they live.

Elbert Hubbard (1856-1915)
American author

SEE ADOLESCENCE; CHILDHOOD; CHILDREN; Shakespeare on DELINQUENCY; Shaw on FALLIBILITY; Cocteau on FREEDOM; Ervine, Shaw, Smith on The GENERATION GAP

Z

Thou whoreson Zed! thou unnecessary letter!
Edgar, *King Lear*
William Shakespeare (1564-1616)

Index of sources

Index of subjects

(Entries in bold type refer to subject headings contained in the book and the pages where they occur. Other references are followed by the subject heading under which they are to be found.)

0 0 5 5 7 0 4

CONCISE COLUMBIA DICT
IONARY OF QUO

ANDREWS